IBPS Clerk

Prelims Exam

Latest Edition
Practice Kit

10 Tests
10 Mock Test

Based On Real Exam Pattern

✓ Thoroughly Revised and Updated

✓ Detailed Analysis of all MCQs

Title	: IBPS Clerk Prelims Exam
Author Name	: Mr. Rohit Manglik
Published By	: EduGorilla Community Pvt. Ltd.
Publishers Address	: 12/651, First Floor Opp. Arvindo Park, Near Jama Masjid, Indira Nagar, Lucknow, Uttar Pradesh-226016, India

Copyright EduGorilla

ISBN : 978-93-90332-00-7

Second Edition

Disclaimer EduGorilla

Compiled and created by EduGorilla Community Pvt. Ltd

Printed By EduGorilla Community Pvt. Ltd.

ROHIT MANGLIK
CEO, EduGorilla

Dear Applicants,

People say *"Success comes to those who work hard."* But I've seen people working hard for their exams day in and day out for marginal success. While others succeed in their examinations by putting in just half the work. So are they God Gifted? No! I believe that it's because they work *smart* and not just *hard*. Similarly, for your exams, you should strategize your preparation so as to increase the likelihood of success. Well with EduGorilla get ready to increase your *chances of selection* in your exam by *16x*.

EduGorilla helps you in not only working *hard* but also working in a *smart and strategic* manner. With EduGorilla's preparation package, you get a chance to make your exam preparation easy, and a fun learning path towards selection. Finding the right path to your preparations can be difficult if you don't know in which direction to head. Don't worry, we have you covered! EduGorilla will be your guide to success in your journey. With our Preparation Package, you can prepare strategically and beat the exam in just one attempt.

EduGorilla's Preparation Package includes-

• **Test Series**   • **Books**

Our preparation package is handcrafted as per the latest changes, expert opinions, and students' discretion. Thus, enabling you to get through each stage of the selection process for your exam.

Our Books are designed by the teachers and experts of the respective exam with a combined 150+ years of experience; to provide you with easy, efficient, and effective learning. Our books are smart, in the sense that not only do they give you the answers to the questions but also provide similar questions for practice.

EduGorilla's competent Test Series gives you real-time experience and confidence through which you can clear your offline or online exam in just one attempt. We currently host 83,000+ mock tests for 1,440+ competitive and academic exams.

Thus, EduGorilla misses no chance to assist you in your preparation and covers all stages of the exam, so that you don't have to look anywhere else.

We provide complete preparation packages for defense, banking, teaching, and other National & State-Level exams. Hence, it doesn't matter which exam you aspire to because you will reach your success.

ALL THE BEST !
Let EduGorilla be your Guide to Success.

Rohit Manglik,
Founder and CEO, EduGorilla

INTRODUCTION

EduGorilla focuses on guiding students to succeed in their examinations. With that in mind, our book, titled "IBPS Clerk : Prelims Exam", has been drafted through the collective efforts of our distinguished experts with 150+ years of combined experience. This book consists of questions that are created following the latest changes in the syllabus and exam pattern. We compiled the book on the basis of questions that are most likely to appear in the IBPS Clerk. Through EduGorilla's "IBPS Clerk : Prelims Exam" your chances of success will increase 16x.

EduGorilla does this through our Complete Preparation Package. This package consists of well-conceptualized and structured content in the form of questions that are tailor-made according to your needs and will help you practice for exams in a smart way by pinpointing all the necessary information. It also provides hints and solutions, along with a smart answer sheet for your self-evaluation. You can assess your shortcomings and work accordingly on areas that may require more of your attention.

EduGorilla promises to help you succeed in your examination and accomplish your dream goals. We believe in our aspirants and see them at the top of the merit list. And the first step towards the top is to start preparing with us. EduGorilla's "IBPS Clerk : Prelims Exam" includes the following attributes.

➤ Well-Researched Content

➤ Top-Notch Quality

➤ Detailed Answers and Analysis

➤ Smart Answer Sheet

➤ Exam Relevant Questions

Therefore, EduGorilla fortifies your preparation and makes it durable enough to help you stand tall and beat the examination.

IBPS Clerk

Scan QR code for Eligibility, Exam Pattern, Syllabus and more.

Book ID: 0508

TABLE OF CONTENTS

English Language

Ques (1-8):Directions: Read the passage carefully and select the best answer to each question out of the given five alternatives.

In a bid to ensure timely support to depositors of stressed banks, the government may bring amendment to DICGC Act in the monsoon session with the objective to provide account holders easy and time-bound access to funds to the extent of the deposit insurance cover. Last year, the government raised insurance cover on deposit five-folds to Rs 5 lakh with a view to provide support to depositors of **ailing** lenders like Punjab and Maharashtra Co-operative (PMC) Bank. Following the collapse of PMC Bank, Yes Bank and Lakshmi Vilas Bank NSE 4.79 % too came under stress leading to restructuring by the regulator and the government.

The amendment to the Deposit Insurance and Credit Guarantee Corporation (DICGC) Act, 1961 is the budget announcement made by the Finance Minister and the Bill is almost ready, sources said. It is expected that the Bill will be tabled in the upcoming monsoon session after being vetted by the Union Cabinet, sources added. Once the Bill becomes the law, it will provide immediate relief to thousands of depositors who had their money parked in stressed lenders such as PMC Bank and other small cooperative banks.

As per the current provisions, the deposit insurance of up to Rs 5 lakh comes into play when the licence of a bank is cancelled and liquidation process starts. DICGC, a wholly-owned subsidiary of the Reserve Bank of India, provides insurance cover on bank deposits. Finance Minister Nirmala Sitharaman in the Budget speech in February said the government had approved an increase in the Deposit Insurance cover from Rs 1 lakh to Rs 5 lakh for bank customers last year. It could not be presented in the Budget session due to **curtailment** of the last session following the spread of the second wave of COVID-19 pandemic.

It is to be noted that the enhanced deposit insurance cover of Rs 5 lakh is effective from February 4, 2020. The increase was done after a gap of 27 years as it was static since 1993. The cover is provided by the Deposit Insurance and Credit Guarantee Corporation (DICGC), a wholly-owned subsidiary of the RBI. With increased insurance cover, the banks are paying a higher premium of 12 paise against 10 paise per Rs 100 deposited without any additional burden on account holders. The deposit insurance scheme covers all banks operating in India, including private sector, cooperative, and even branches of foreign banks. There are some exemptions such as deposits of foreign governments, deposits of central and state governments, and inter-bank deposits.

It can be recalled that way back in 2009, the Raghuram Rajan committee on financial sector reforms had recommended strengthening the capacity of the DICGC, a more explicit system of prompt, corrective action, and making deposit insurance premia more risk-based.

Q.1 What is the main reason to make an amendment in the law?
A. to give the opportunity of easy access to the banking
B. to provide the useful services in any situation
C. to provide account holders easy and time-bound access
D. for the welfare of the customer experience
E. to put limits on the different frauds

Q.2 What changes will come after the bill has passed?
A. It will help the govt to gain the profits.
B. it will ease the banking conetivity.
C. The banks gain profit after it.
D. it will provide immediate relief to thousands of depositors.
E. It is important for the future of the banking system.

Q.3 Who can be benefitted from the deposit insurance scheme?
A. Only nationalized banks
B. All private banks with other foreign banks
C. mains branches of the banks
D. Rural banks
E. All private sector, cooperative and even branches of foreign banks.

Q.4 What can we infer from the passage?
A. The amendment is a good step to ease the burden of the depositors.
B. It can be harmful for the economy.
C. It will be a big gamble for the govt.
D. The insurance policy is just a mean of attraction for people.
E. This is a historic step in banking system.

Q.5 Consider the following statements and answer the question.
A. the government raised insurance cover on deposit five-folds to Rs. 5 lakh.
B. The amendment is brought by the suggestion of RBI.
C. The amendment is made to ease the burden of the depositors.
A. A is correct but B is wrong.
B. A and B are correct but C is wrong.
C. B and C are correct but A is wrong.
D. A and C are correct but B is wrong.
E. All are correct.

Q.6 Consider the following statements and choose the correct option.
A. the enhanced deposit insurance cover of Rs. 5 lakh.
B. The increase is never seen in Indian history.
C. DICGC is a subsidiary of the Indian govt.
A. B is correct but A and C are wrong.

B. A is correct but B and C are wrong.
C. All are right.
D. All are wrong.
E. C is correct but A and B are wrong.

Q.7 Which of the following is a synonym of the word curtailment?
A. Expansion
B. Abridgment
C. Dispersion
D. Dissipation
E. Scattering

Q.8 Which of the following is an antonym of the word 'ailing'?
A. Healthy
B. Invalid
C. Sickly
D. Weakly
E. Fragile

Ques (9-18):Direction: In the following passage some of the words have been left out. Read the passage carefully and select the correct answer for the given blank out of the given alternatives.

In an attempt to take on fake news, Google News has __(1)__ new measures. Google has updated its guidelines to prohibit sites that misrepresent or __(2)__ their country of origin or are __(3)__ at users in another country under false premises. "Sites included in Google News must not misrepresent, misstate, or conceal information about their ownership or primary purpose, or engage in coordinated activity to __(4)__ users," states the company guidelines. Google also allows publishers to file a spam report if they believe that another publisher has __(5)__ Google News inclusion guidelines. "While we may not take manual action in response to every report, spam reports are __(6)__ based on user impact, and in some cases may lead to complete __(7)__ of a spam site from Google News results," Google said. This move to keep dishonest sites from __(8)__ in Google News has been cheered by users worldwide. It comes in the wake of __(9)__ pressure on the Internet giant take initiative to stop the spread of fake news after allegations of Russian attempts to __(10)__ the 2016 US presidential election surfaced.

Q.9 Which of the following word fits the blank labelled as (1)?
A. Adored
B. Adorned
C. Adopted
D. Advised
E. Objected

Q.10 Which of the following word fits the blank labelled as (2)?
A. Conceal
B. Adjunct
C. Locate
D. Implant
E. Implicate

Q.11 Which of the following word fits the blank labelled as (3)?
A. Fed
B. Supplied
C. Thrown
D. Provided
E. Directed

Q.12 Which of the following word fits the blank labelled as (4)?
A. Engage
B. Mislead
C. Direct
D. Divert
E. Dilute

Q.13 Which of the following word fits the blank labelled as (5)?
A. Shaped
B. Manned
C. Shipped
D. Violated
E. Volatile

Q.14 Which of the following word fits the blank labelled as (6)?

A. Invaded
B. Prioritized
C. Shielded
D. Fielded
E. Boxed

Q.15 Which of the following word fits the blank labelled as (7)?
A. Banner
B. Winner
C. Representation
D. Refusal
E. Removal

Q.16 Which of the following word fits the blank labelled as (8)?
A. Appearing
B. Disappearing
C. Contacting
D. Vanishing
E. Whispering

Q.17 Which of the following word fits the blank labelled as (9)?
A. Roaring
B. Rotating
C. Mounting
D. Riveting
E. Hysterical

Q.18 Which of the following word fits the blank labelled as (10)?
A. Oust
B. Influence
C. Jest
D. Ban
E. Conflict

Ques (19-20):Direction: In the sentence given below, one/ more parts have errors and others are correct. Find out which part has an error and mark it as your answer. If there is no error, mark 'No error' as your answer.

Q.19 Don't forget checking out (A)/ our bulletin board where (B)/ you chat to and share your views with (C)/ fellow arctophiles from all corners of the globe.(D)
A. Only (A)
B. Only (B)
C. (A) and (B)
D. (C) and (D)
E. No error

Q.20 Many species also prefer to grow in moist places by streams,(A)/ lakes and the sea, though very few are normally(B)/ and probably none entirely, aquatic, being always(C)/ at certain seasons exposed for a longer or shorter period to the atmosphere(D)
A. Only (A)
B. (A) and (B)
C. Only (C)
D. (A) and (C)
E. No error

Ques (21-22):Direction: Read the sentence to find out whether there is any error in it or not. The error, if any, will be in one part of the sentence. The number of that part is the answer. If there is no error, the answer is (E). Ignore errors of punctuation, if any.

Q.21 After so many years, all the misunderstanding and disputes (A)/ are cleared between Ronaldo and I. We do share a very gruesome history,(B)/ even our family members loathe each other since the time of partition. (C)/ Years may have passed but feelings remained the same. (D)/ No error. (E)
A. (A)
B. (B)
C. (C)
D. (D)
E. (E)

Q.22 Everyone acknowledges her in the town but her (A)/ is very mischievous, stubborn, and arrogant. (B)/ She has been alone and all by herself her whole life (C)/ so that the reason everyone respects her and that's what made a survivor, a fighter and a living legend. (D)/ No error.

A. (A)　　　**B.** (B)　　　**C.** (C)　　　**D.** (D)
E. (E)

Q.23 Below a sentence is given which is divided into 4 segments. Identify the segment of the sentence which contains the grammatical error. If there is no error, mark 'No error' as your answer.

Research various subjects were made easy, as a variety of journals (A)/ on the subject were available in the (B)/ local markets of Mumbai. It was difficult to figure (C)/ out the defects that would serve as the basis of the dissertation. (D)

A. (B)　　　**B.** (C)　　　**C.** (A)　　　**D.** (D)
E. No error

Ques (24-25):Direction: The following question contains a sentence with one blank only. Below are given four words as answer choices. You have to choose an option with choices which can make the sentence complete.

Q.24 Rambabu is famous as generous politician because of his __________ humanitarian activities.

A. munificent

B. modality

C. ingenious

D. multifarious

A. A and B　　　**B.** C and D　　　**C.** B and C　　　**D.** A and D
E. A and C

Q.25 Neel's classmates are aware that he is __________ himself very often.

A. garrulous

B. aggrandizes

C. moot

D. predicament

A. A and B　　　**B.** B and D　　　**C.** D and C　　　**D.** A and D
E. B and C

Ques (26-30):Direction: In the question below, there is a word given in bold which is followed by five options. In each of the options, a pair of words is given which is either the pair of synonyms or antonyms or synonym & antonym of the word given in bold. Choose that pair as your answer.

Q.26 Boisterous

A. Rowdy: adversity

B. Calumny: Aspersion

C. Captivating: Desist

D. Clamorous: Placid

E. None of the above

Q.27 Contrary

A. Earthly: Fleshly

B. Blunt: Evasive

C. Dissimilar: Conflicting

D. Generic: Liberal

E. None of the above

Q.28 Decipher

A. Introvert: Intentional

B. Interpret: Distort

C. Mocking: Taunting

D. Rash: Sudden

E. None of the above

Q.29 Efface

A. Destroy: Obliterate　　　**B.** Undertake: Aspire

C. Conspire: Utilize　　　**D.** Secure: Plant

E. Construct: Demur

Q.30 Forsake

A. Desert: Renounce　　　**B.** Converge: Huddle

C. Hatred: Grudge　　　**D.** Retard: Prevent

E. None of the above

Numerical Ability

Q.31 Direction: What will come in place of question mark (?) in the following question?

13.33 + 33.31 + 331.13 = ?

A. 377.77　　　**B.** 354.77　　　**C.** 355.67　　　**D.** 301.67
E. 305.78

Q.32 Direction: What will come in the place of the question mark '?' in the following question?

14.28% of 490 – 71.43% of 63 = ?

A. 25　　　**B.** 49　　　**C.** 64　　　**D.** 81
E. 35

Q.33 Direction: What will come in the place of the question mark '?' in the following question?

42% of 250 + 115% of 480 = ?

A. 655　　　**B.** 657　　　**C.** 659　　　**D.** 653
E. 656

Q.34 Direction: What will come in the place of the question mark '?' in the following question?

450 ÷ 15 × 12 – 120 ÷ 4 × 12 + 1 = ?

A. -1　　　**B.** 0　　　**C.** 1　　　**D.** 2
E. -2

Q.35 Direction: What will come in the place of the question mark '?' in the following question?

$$\sqrt{\left[1331^{\left(\frac{1}{3}\right)} + 1728^{\left(\frac{1}{3}\right)} + 2\right]} = ?$$

A. 5　　　**B.** 6　　　**C.** 7　　　**D.** 8
E. 9

Q.36 Direction: What will come in the place of the question mark '?' in the following question?

66.66% of 480 + 37.5% of 832 = 120 + ?

A. 444　　　**B.** 512　　　**C.** 332　　　**D.** 412
E. 418

Q.37 Direction: What will come in the place of the question mark '?' in the following question?

$32^{0.16} \times 32^{0.4} \times 32^{0.5} = 128? \div 2$

A. 10   B. 1.1   C. 9   D. 0.9
E. 7

Q.38 Direction: What will come in the place of the question mark '?' in the following question?

$$\left(7\frac{5}{2} + 4\frac{7}{2}\right) \div 7\frac{3}{2} = 11\frac{5}{3} - \frac{2}{3} - ?$$

A. 15   B. 90   C. 25   D. 30
E. 10

Q.39 Direction: What should come in place of question mark '?' in the following question?

$$4\frac{2}{5} \div 1\frac{7}{15} + 5\frac{5}{3} \times 3\frac{3}{2} = ?$$

A. $22\frac{1}{3}$ B. $32\frac{2}{3}$
C. 33   D. 21
E. None of these

Q.40 Simplify $\dfrac{2\frac{3}{4}}{1\frac{5}{6}} \div \dfrac{7}{8} \times \left(\dfrac{1}{3} + \dfrac{1}{4}\right) + \dfrac{5}{7} \div \dfrac{3}{4} \times \dfrac{3}{4}$

A. $\frac{56}{77}$ B. $\frac{49}{80}$ C. $\frac{12}{7}$ D. $3\frac{2}{9}$
E. $\frac{37}{81}$

Q.41 Direction: In the given question, two equations numbered I and II are given. Solve both the equations and give the appropriate answer.

I. $x^2 - 15x + 54 = 0$

II. $y^2 - 13y + 36 = 0$

A.   x > y
B.   x < y
C.   x ≥ y
D.   x ≤ y
E.   Relation can't be established or x = y

Q.42 Direction: In the given question, two equations numbered I and II are given. Solve both the equations and mark the appropriate answer.

$x^2 - 13x + 40 = 0$

$y^2 - 11y + 24 = 0$

A.   x > y
B.   x < y
C.   x ≥ y
D.   x ≤ y
E.   Relation can't be established or x = y

Q.43 In a class there is 39 students, the average weight decreases by 4 kg, when a new student is joining the class. If the average weight of students is 64 kg. What is the weight of new student?

A. 90 kg   B. 96 kg   C. 110 kg   D. 85 kg
E. 80 kg

Q.44 A sum of Rs. 480480 is divided among A, B and C such that A receives 25% less than B and B receives 20% less than C. What is B's share?

A. 480480   B. 200200
C. 120120   D. 160160
E. None of these

Q.45 Direction: Find the wrong number in the given series:

3   9   23   99   479   2881   20159

A. 9   B. 23   C. 99   D. 479
E. 2881

Q.46 Direction: In each of the following number series, the wrong number is given, find out that number.

26, 39, 65, 91, 133, 169, 221

A. 26   B. 39   C. 133   D. 169
E. 221

Q.47 Direction: In the following number series, a wrong number is given. Find out the wrong number.

15, 17, 23, 34, 55

A.   15   B.   17
C.   34   D.   55
E.   None of these

Q.48 A Sum of money is invested in two parts in ratio of 3 : 5 both at simple interest. 1st part is invested at 16% and the 2nd part is at 12%. If the difference in simple interest is 1800, find the total sum of money invested. It is given that both parts are invested for 3 years.

A.   40,000   B.   50,000
C.   60,000   D.   20,000
E.   None of these

Q.49 Prity can do a piece of work in 34 days and Anant complete the same work in 51 days. So, find the time required to complete the same work if they work together.

A. $\frac{102}{5}$ B. $\frac{122}{5}$
C. $\frac{92}{5}$ D. $\frac{112}{5}$
E.   None of the above

Q.50 A milk vendor purchases 47.6 litres of milk containing milk and water in the ratio 9 : 4. He wants to make this a 11 : 5 mixture of milk and water and sell the entire quantity at the cost price. How much of water needs to be added?

A. 1.33 liter   B. 0.44 liter   C. 0.55 liter   D. 0.33 liter
E. 0.43 liter

Q.51 Abhay starts a business with Rs. 32,000. After a certain period, Suraj joined him, and invests Rs. 30,000. At the end of the year they divide the profit in the ratio of 8: 5. After how much time did Suraj join Abhay?

A.   1 month   B.   2 months
C.   3 months   D.   4 months
E.   None of these

Q.52 Direction: In the given question, two equations numbered I and II are given. You have to solve both the equations and mark the appropriate answer.

I. $x^2 - 7x + 10 = 0$

II. $y^2 - 11y + 24 = 0$

A.   If x > y
B.   If x ≥ y
C.   If x < y
D.   If x ≤ y

E. If x = y or the relationship cannot be established

Ques (53-57):Direction: The following table shows the sales of rice from a shop for 5 years. (The values are in kilogram)

Year	Basmati	Sonam	Silver	Golden
2000	300	500	400	100
2001	250	200	300	250
2002	320	400	200	100
2003	400	50	100	300
2004	50	700	900	800

Q.53 In the 2004 tsunami, if 50% of the net quantity of rice was spoilt and in that 50% of the rice varieties each were spoilt, then what percentage of golden rice is available out of the remaining for sale? (around of to nearest whole number)

A. 13%
B. 23%
C. 33%
D. 43%
E. None of these

Q.54 In 2003, if 20% of Silver which was left out after all the sales, were distributed among Ram, Shyam and Govind in the ratio 2 : 3 : 5. Find the quantity of Silver Govind got.

A. 20kg
B. 18kg
C. 15kg
D. 10 kg
E. None of these

Q.55 Over the given years, what is the ratio between maximum sales with minimum sales?

A. 12 : 23
B. 17 : 49
C. 23 : 12
D. 49 : 17
E. None of these

Q.56 What is the difference in the sale between 2002 and 2001?

A. 30 kg
B. 40 kg
C. 20 kg
D. 70 kg
E. None of these

Q.57 If cost of Basmati is Rs 70 per kg and it is sold for Rs 110, then find how much will be the revenue from Basmati in 2002 and 2004 together?

A. Rs 10,800
B. Rs 14,800
C. Rs 15,800
D. Rs 18,800
E. None of these

Q.58 Direction: What should come in place of the question mark (?) in the following number series.

8, 4.5 , 5.5 , 13 , 56 , ?

A. 254   **B.** 356   **C.** 456   **D.** 468
E. 396

Q.59 Direction: Find the missing number in series

5, 10, 16, 23, 31, 40, ?

A. 95   **B.** 100   **C.** 50   **D.** 105
E. 120

Q.60 A pit 4 m long, 6 m wide and 1100 cm deep is dug in a field. Find the volume of soil removed in cubic meters.

A. 112 m³   **B.** 167 m³   **C.** 264 m³   **D.** 117 m³

E. 217 m³

Q.61 The ratio of present age of P and Q is 7 : 5. Q's present age is 5/6 times of R's present age. If P is 5 years older than R, then find the ratio of age of P and R, 5 years from now.

A. 7 : 8   **B.** 8 : 9   **C.** 8 : 7   **D.** 9 : 8
E. 6 : 7

Q.62 Direction: In the given question, two equations numbered I and II are given. You have to solve both the equations and mark the appropriate answer.

I. 5x + 2y = 81
II. 3x + y = 15

A. x < y
B. x > y
C. x ≥ y
D. No relation in x and y or x = y
E. x ≤ y

Q.63 Direction: In the given question, two equations numbered I and II are given. Solve both the equations and mark the appropriate answer.

I. $2x^2 - 11x + 15 = 0$
II. $9y^2 - 12y + 4 = 0$

A. x > y
B. x < y
C. x ≥ y
D. x ≤ y
E. x = y or relation between x and y can not be established

Q.64 If $\tan\left(\frac{\alpha}{2}\right)$ and $\tan\left(\frac{\beta}{2}\right)$ are the roots of the equation $8x^2 - 26x + 15 = 0$, then the value of $\cos(\alpha + \beta)$ will be:

[UPSESSB TGT Mathematics, 2013]

A. 0   **B.** 1   **C.** −1   **D.** $-\frac{627}{725}$
E. −2

Q.65 A pack contains 4 blue, 2 red and 3 black pens. If 2 pens are drawn at random from the pack, not replaced and then another pen is drawn. What is the probability of drawing 2 blue and 1 black pens?

A. $\frac{2}{9}$ **B.** $\frac{1}{14}$ **C.** $\frac{2}{63}$ **D.** $\frac{2}{14}$
E. $\frac{1}{18}$

Reasoning Ability

Ques (66-67):Direction: Study the following information carefully and answer the question given below.

In a group of family, there are seven members A, B, C, D, E, F, and G. A and B are a married couple. A is being the male member. D is the only son of C, who is brother of A. E is the sister of D. B is the daughter-in-law of F, whose husband is G.

Q.66 Who is C to B?

A. Brother
B. Son-in-law
C. Nephew
D. Brother-in-law
E. None of these

Q.67 If P and C are the married couple, then how is P related to F?

A. Mother
B. Daughter-in-law
C. Mother-in-law
D. Sister-in-law
E. None of these

Ques (68-70):Direction: Study the following information carefully to answer the given question:

Six persons M, N, O, P, Q and R have different heights and weights. P is taller than only R. At least three persons are heavier than M. Number of persons taller than M is equal to number of persons shorter than O. R is heavier than Q but not than M. O is heavier than P but not the heaviest. No person has same position in both height and weight.

Q.68 Who among the following is the tallest?

A. N
B. Q
C. O
D. P
E. R

Q.69 How many persons are heavier than P?

A. Three
B. Four
C. Two
D. One
E. Five

Q.70 How many persons are shorter than M?

A. Four
B. Five
C. Two
D. Three
E. One

Q.71 Direction: Relationship between different elements is shown in the statements below. These statements are followed by 2 conclusions. Mark your answer on the basis of given statements and conclusions.

Statements: A < B ≤ C > D; C > E ≥ F; E > B

Conclusions:

(i) A < F

(ii) D < B

A. Only conclusion (i) follows
B. Only conclusion (ii) follows
C. Either conclusion (i) or conclusion (ii) follows
D. Both conclusions follow
E. None follows

Q.72 Direction: In the question, relationship between different elements is shown in the statements. These statements are followed by 2 conclusions. Mark answer as option given.

Statements: X = Y ≥ Z > V; V < P > Q; Q = T

Conclusions:

(I) X > V

(II) T ≤ Z

A. Only (I) follows
B. Only (II) follows
C. Both (I) & (II) follow
D. Neither (I) nor (II) follows
E. Either (I) or (II) follows

Q.73 Direction: In the following question assuming the given statements to be true, Find which conclusion among the given conclusions is/are definitely true and then give your answers accordingly.

Statements:

J < K ≥ L = Y > X; L < V ≥ D > I; D = R ≥ P

Conclusions:

I. P < K

II. X ≤ D

III. R > K

A. Only II is true
B. II and III are true
C. Only III is true
D. Only I is true
E. None is true

Q.74 Which of the following expression is definitely true if the given expression B < K and T < D are to be definitely true?

A. T < B ≤ G < D =K
B. B < T = G ≤ D > K
C. D < K > G = T ≥ B
D. B > D = G ≥ K ≥ T
E. None of these

Q.75 Direction: In the following question assuming the given statements to be True, find which of the conclusion among given conclusions is/are definitely true and then give your answers accordingly.

Statements: L < O = C ≥ A; X ≤ V < L = H

Conclusions:

I. C > H

II. X < O

A. Only II is True
B. Neither I nor II is True
C. Both I and II are True
D. Either I or II is True
E. Only I is True

Ques (76-80):Direction: Study the following information carefully to answer the questions that follow:

There are nine persons sitting around a circular table. Some are facing inside while some are facing outside the table. Only three persons are sitting between T and S, who is second to the right of U. R is fourth to the right of Q. T is not an immediate neighbour of U.V is second to the left of X and faces opposite direction of Q. W is not an immediate neighbour of U and sits third to the right of P. Q sits second to the right of the one who sits third to the left of U. W and P are facing same direction but opposite to R, S and X. Q does not face inside but in the middle of X and V.

Q.76 Who among the following sits immediate right of X?

A. P
B. R
C. T
D. Q
E. S

Q.77 What is the position of W with respect to V?

A. Fourth to the left
B. Fifth to the right
C. Third to the left
D. Fifth to the left
E. Both (A) & (B)

Q.78 How many persons are facing outside the table?

A. 4
B. 3
C. 6
D. 5
E. None of these

Q.79 Which of the following statement is true about R?

A.   R is immediate left of W
B.   R is second to the right of P
C.   R is fifth to the left of V
D.   R is immediate left of U
E.   All are correct

Q.80 If all the persons are arranged in English Alphabet series in anti-clockwise direction starting towards the right of P, how many persons will not change their positions after the rearrangement (excluding P)?

A. Three   **B.** Two   **C.** Four   **D.** One
E. Five

Ques (81-85):Direction: Study the following information carefully to answer the given question:

Y W @ 1 & C N 3 P L B 9 ↑ = D ◊ E 2 £ M V $ 7 # 4 F G 5

Q.81 How many such symbols are there in the above arrangement which are not immediately preceded by a number and also not immediately followed by a letter?

A. Nil   **B.** One
C. Two   **D.** Three
E. None of these

Q.82 C 1 3 W : 7 4 V G in the same way as N @ B = : ?

A. $ 4 2 D   **B.** V F 2 D   **C.** $ F 2 ◊   **D.** $ F £ D
E. $ F 2 D

Q.83 If the numbers immediately preceding the symbols are attached the value double their numerical value, then what will be sum of the value of all such numbers?

A. 22   **B.** 26
C. 36   **D.** 38
E. None of these

Q.84 Four of the following are alike in a certain way based on the above arrangement and hence form a group. Which one does not belong to the group?

A. ◊ V 2 M   **B.** ↑ 2 D E   **C.** L D B =   **D.** V F 7 4
E. & L N P

Q.85 If Y W @ 1 are written in the reverse order, & C N 3 are written in the reverse order and so on, then in the new arrangement which of the following will be exactly in the middle between 9 and $?

A. ↑   **B.** =
C. D   **D.** M
E. None of these

Ques (86-90):Direction: Read the given information carefully and answer the question asked below.

Five girls Aditi, Chaitrali, Deepa, Esha and Gauri are sitting in a row facing north in such a way that there is equal distance between adjacent girls (But not necessarily in the same order). Five boys Akash, Chetan, Deepak, Monu and Gaurav are facing south and sitting in such a way that each boy seated in a row faces another girl of the other row.

Gaurav sits at one of the extreme ends of the row. Only two boys sit between Gaurav and Akash. The one who faces Akash sits to the immediate left of Deepa. Only one girl sits between Deepa and Chaitrali. The one who faces Chaitrali sits to the immediate left of Chetan. Esha sits second to the right of Aditi. Neither Chaitrali nor Deepa faces Monu.

Q.86 Who among the following faces Deepa?
A. Akash   **B.** Gaurav   **C.** Deepak   **D.** Chetan
E. Monu

Q.87 How many boys sit between Deepak and Chetan?
A.   None
B.   One
C.   Two
D.   Three
E.   Cannot be determined

Q.88 Who among the following sit at extreme ends?
A. Akash, Esha   **B.** Gaurav, Deepa
C. Gaurav, Aditi   **D.** Monu, Chaitrali
E. Monu, Deepa

Q.89 Which of the following statement/statements is/are true about Deepak?
A.   Deepak sits opposite to Chaitrali
B.   Deepak sits in the middle of the row
C.   Deepak sits to the immediate right of Akash
D.   Either (B) or (C)
E.   Either (A) and (B)

Q.90 Four of the following five are alike in a certain way and hence form a group. Who among the following does not belong to that group?
A. Akash – Aditi   **B.** Chetan – Esha
C. Gaurav – Chaitrali   **D.** Monu – Gauri
E. Deepak – Chaitrali

Ques (91-95):Direction: In the question below are given three statements followed by three conclusions numbered I, II, and III. You have to take the given statements to be true even if they seem to be at variance with commonly known facts. Read all the conclusions and then decide which of the given conclusions logically follows from the given statements disregarding commonly known facts.

Q.91 Statements:
Some rich are poor.
Only a few kings are honest.
No honest is rich.
Conclusions:
I. All kings can be honest.
II. Some honest is not rich.
III. All poor is king.
A.   Only conclusion I follows
B.   Only conclusion II follows
C.   Conclusion I and III follow
D.   All conclusion follow
E.   None conclusion follows

Q.92 Statements:
No Facebook is WhatsApp.

No WhatsApp is App.

No App is Insta.

Conclusions:

I. Some Facebook is Insta.

II. Some App is WhatsApp.

III. Some Insta are WhatsApp.

A. Conclusion II and III follow

B. Only conclusion II follows

C. Conclusion I and III follow

D. Conclusion I and II follow

E. None follows

Q.93 Statements:

Only a few roads are royal.

Few roads are good.

Few royals are kings.

Conclusions:

I. All good can be roads.

II. All kings can be royal.

III. Some good is roads.

A. Only conclusion I follow

B. Only conclusion II follow

C. Conclusion I and III follow

D. All conclusion follows

E. None conclusion follows

Q.94 Statements:

All glass is mirror.

All mirror is virtual.

All virtual is real.

Conclusions:

I. Some real is glass.

II. All virtual is glass

III. All real is mirror

A. Only conclusion I follow

B. Only conclusion II follow

C. Conclusion I and III follow

D. All conclusion follows

E. None conclusion follows

Q.95 Statements:

All heart is stupid.

Only a few heart is strong.

Some fools are strong.

Conclusions:

I. All Strong is stupid.

II. Few fools are stupid.

III. All fools are stupid.

A. Only conclusion I follow

B. Only conclusion II follow

C. Conclusion I and III follow

D. All conclusion follows

E. None conclusion follows

Ques (96-100):Direction: Study the following information carefully and answer the question given below.

Seven friends Priya, Shreya, Julie, Neha, Pallavi, Asha, and Rekha, use a mobile phone of seven different brands viz. Samsung, Nokia, Oppo, Vivo, Apple, Realme, and Redmi, but not necessarily in the same order. Also, these seven people are registered on three different networks namely Airtel, Jio, and Idea. At least two persons are registered on one network.

Julie is registered on Airtel. Asha uses either Nokia or Vivo. Pallavi is registered on one of the networks only with the person who uses Nokia. Asha is registered on the same network as the Redmi user. Either Priya or Rekha uses Redmi. Priya and Julie are registered on the same network along with the Oppo user. Shreya is registered on Jio. The Apple user is not registered on Airtel. Priya does not use Samsung.

Q.96 Who uses Samsung mobile?

A. Asha **B.** Rekha **C.** Julie **D.** Priya

E. Shreya

Q.97 Which of the following is correctly matched?

A. Priya – Jio **B.** Asha – Airtel

C. Pallavi – Idea **D.** Neha – Airtel

E. Rekha – Jio

Q.98 Which among the following combination represents the people registered on Idea network?

A. Neha and Pallavi **B.** Priya and Asha

C. Neha and Rekha **D.** Asha and Rekha

E. Asha and Neha

Q.99 Pallavi uses which brand of phone?

A. Apple **B.** Redmi **C.** Samsung **D.** Realme

E. Oppo

Q.100 Who uses Oppo?

A. Priya **B.** Neha **C.** Asha **D.** Julie

E. Shreya

// Smart Answer Sheet //

Correct Percentage of students who answered correctly.   **Skipped** Percentage of students who skipped.

Q.	Ans.	Correct / Skipped	Q.	Ans.	Correct / Skipped	Q.	Ans.	Correct / Skipped	Q.	Ans.	Correct / Skipped	Q.	Ans.	Correct / Skipped
1	C	36.8 % / 37.3 %	17	C	15.47 % / 45.69 %	33	B	34.12 % / 57.86 %	49	A	13.1 % / 64.19 %	65	B	0.32 % / 92.12 %
2	D	42.2 % / 40.83 %	18	B	19.47 % / 45.69 %	34	C	31.17 % / 57.91 %	50	D	1.21 % / 64.82 %	66	D	27.26 % / 60.68 %
3	E	40.28 % / 41.75 %	19	A	15.37 % / 45.77 %	35	A	29.08 % / 57.99 %	51	D	6.98 % / 64.64 %	67	B	25.14 % / 61.91 %
4	A	34.92 % / 42.35 %	20	A	5.59 % / 46.49 %	36	B	17.99 % / 58.05 %	52	E	18.16 % / 65.54 %	68	B	8.85 % / 62.09 %
5	D	24.49 % / 42.49 %	21	B	18.07 % / 47.07 %	37	D	5.08 % / 58.29 %	53	C	3.37 % / 66.96 %	69	C	12.25 % / 63.58 %
6	B	26.41 % / 42.39 %	22	A	28.06 % / 47.28 %	38	E	19.81 % / 58.41 %	54	D	7.94 % / 68.99 %	70	D	9.44 % / 63.05 %
7	B	12.68 % / 42.83 %	23	C	21.61 % / 47.43 %	39	C	23.22 % / 58.62 %	55	D	5.44 % / 69.48 %	71	E	24.99 % / 62.23 %
8	A	21.04 % / 42.88 %	24	D	9.27 % / 48.04 %	40	C	16.91 % / 58.75 %	56	C	15.41 % / 70.03 %	72	A	28.91 % / 62.41 %
9	C	34.48 % / 43.57 %	25	A	8.36 % / 48.91 %	41	E	18.96 % / 59.07 %	57	B	5.67 % / 70.63 %	73	E	21.54 % / 62.44 %
10	A	19.22 % / 44.04 %	26	D	3.3 % / 79.43 %	42	E	18.24 % / 59.62 %	58	C	5.65 % / 71.3 %	74	A	24.63 % / 62.8 %
11	E	12.95 % / 44.17 %	27	B	1.86 % / 79.77 %	43	B	9.48 % / 59.85 %	59	C	19.05 % / 73.23 %	75	C	23.53 % / 62.73 %
12	B	25.35 % / 44.47 %	28	B	5.59 % / 79.85 %	44	D	12.61 % / 60.64 %	60	C	5.27 % / 74.1 %	76	C	2.01 % / 62.69 %
13	D	31.39 % / 44.76 %	29	A	3.28 % / 80.02 %	45	C	3.28 % / 61.27 %	61	C	5.42 % / 74.79 %	77	E	1.42 % / 68.74 %
14	B	24.38 % / 45.16 %	30	A	3.09 % / 80.06 %	46	C	10.88 % / 61.63 %	62	A	6.58 % / 75.85 %	78	D	1.69 % / 69.97 %
15	E	26.31 % / 45.48 %	31	A	39.81 % / 57.23 %	47	C	7.64 % / 62.58 %	63	A	10.05 % / 77.29 %	79	E	1.23 % / 69.78 %
16	A	22.24 % / 45.59 %	32	A	18.5 % / 57.61 %	48	A	3.13 % / 63.22 %	64	D	0.28 % / 91.83 %	80	B	1.74 % / 67.97 %

Q.	Ans.	Correct		Q.	Ans.	Correct		Q.	Ans.	Correct		Q.	Ans.	Correct		Q.	Ans.	Correct
		Skipped				Skipped				Skipped				Skipped				Skipped
81	C	15.58 %		85	A	3.15 %		89	B	9.21 %		93	D	12.19 %		97	D	1.42 %
		64.5 %				66.69 %				71.51 %				72.4 %				84.12 %
82	E	7.53 %		86	C	12.28 %		90	E	8.93 %		94	A	13.29 %		98	D	1.27 %
		64.87 %				66.81 %				71.13 %				74.33 %				85.59 %
83	D	6.37 %		87	A	11.56 %		91	B	11.51 %		95	E	8.78 %		99	A	1.27 %
		65.44 %				70.01 %				70.2 %				75.05 %				85.97 %
84	C	11.79 %		88	D	10.14 %		92	E	17.93 %		96	C	1.8 %		100	B	1.46 %
		66.11 %				70.81 %				71.64 %				76.0 %				85.38 %

//Hints and Solutions//

1. According to the first sentence of the first passage, the government may bring the amendment to DICGC Act in the monsoon session with **the objective to provide account holders easy and time-bound access to funds to the extent of the deposit insurance cover**.

Hence, the correct option is (C).

2. According to the last sentence of the second passage- it will provide immediate relief to thousands of depositors who had their money parked in stressed lenders such as PMC Bank and other small cooperative banks.

Hence, the correct option is (D).

3. According to the fourth sentence of the fourth passage, The deposit insurance scheme covers all banks operating in India, including private sector, cooperative and even branches of foreign banks.

Hence, the correct option is (E).

4. According to the line of the passage, Once the Bill becomes the law, it will provide immediate relief to thousands of depositors who had their money parked in stressed lenders such as PMC Bank and other small cooperative banks.

All the other options are irrelevant to the passage.

Hence, the correct option is (A).

5. According to the line of the passage, the government raised insurance cover on deposit five-folds to Rs 5 lakh with a view to provide support to depositors of ailing lenders like Punjab and Maharashtra Co-operative (PMC) Bank.

According to another line of the passage, the government may bring the amendment to DICGC Act in the monsoon session with the objective to provide account holders easy and time-bound access to funds to the extent of the deposit insurance cover.

Hence, the correct option is (D).

6. According to the line of the passage, It is to be noted that the enhanced deposit insurance cover of Rs. 5 lakh is effective from February 4, 2020. The increase was done after a gap of 27 years as it was static since 1993. The cover is provided by the Deposit Insurance and Credit Guarantee Corporation (DICGC), a wholly-owned subsidiary of the RBI.

Hence, the correct option is (B).

7. The meaning of the given word curtailment is the act of limiting something.

Let's see the meanings of the given options:

Abridgment- The process of making things shorter.

Expansion- when something increases in size, number or importance

Dispersion- The process by which things are spread

Dissipation- The process of disappearing

Scattering- a small number or amount of things in a particular area

By the meanings of the given words, we can say that abridgment is the right answer.

Hence, the correct option is (B).

8. The meaning of the word ailing is experiencing difficulty and problems.

Healthy means strong and well.

By the meanings of the given words, we can say that healthy is the right answer.

Hence, the correct option is (A).

9. Adoption is the act of taking something on as your own.

To adore is to love something.

To adorn is to decorate something.

To advise is to guide or counsel.

To object is to speak against a given point.

The sentence suggests that the blank must contain a verb that means 'to implement' or 'to take up'.

The only verb that reflects this meaning is 'adopted'.

Therefore, the correct answer is option (C).

Hence, the correct option is (C).

10. Conceal, a verb means to hide something/somebody; to prevent something/somebody from being seen or discovered.

Example- The editorial accused the government of concealing the truth.

- The sentence suggests that the blank must contain a verb that means 'to hide' the information about the websites.
- The only option that reflects this meaning is 'conceal'.

Hence, the correct option is (A).

11. The preposition used after the blank is 'at', which suggests that the blank must contain a verb that means 'aimed at' or 'projected at' the users.

The only verb from the given options that reflects this meaning is 'directed'.

None of the other options can be used along with the given preposition and form a meaningful sentence.

Hence, the correct option is (E).

12. Mislead (a verb) means to make somebody have the wrong idea or opinion about somebody/something.

Example- He then again said he really wanted to remain friends and he hadn't meant to mislead me.

- The passage talks about website malpractices, so the sentence must also be related to the context.

- The blank must contain a verb that means 'misdirect' or 'falsely guide' the users.
- The only option that reflects this meaning is 'mislead'.

Hence, the correct option is (B).

13. Violated means to break a rule, an agreement, etc; to not respect something; to spoil or damage something.

Example- She was attacked and violated by an unknown intruder.

- The sentence suggests that the blank must contain a verb that means 'did not agree with' or 'refused'.
- The only option that reflects this meaning is 'violated', which means abused.

Hence, the correct option is (D).

14. Prioritized means to treat something as being more important than other things.

Example- The organization was formed to prioritize the needs of older people.

- The sentence suggests that the spam reports are divided in a certain way.
- So, the blank must contain a verb that reflects the meaning 'divided'.
- Only 'prioritized' or divided according to priority is the apt solution here.

Hence, the correct option is (B).

15. Removal is the noun form of the verb to remove.

Removal means the action of taking somebody/something away.

The blank must contain a word that means completely being removed.

The only word that reflects the same meaning is 'removal'.

Hence, the correct option is (E).

16. Appearing means to seem (प्रतीत होना, लगना); to suddenly be seen; to come into sight (एकाएक दिखाई पड़ना; प्रकट होना)

Example- Cracks and fractures are appearing in the ancient wall.

- The sentence suggests that the dishonest sites can be removed from Google search results.
- This suggests that the blank must contain a verb that means 'showing up', which is only given by 'appearing'.

Hence, the correct option is (A).

17. Roaring means shouting strongly.

Rotating means moving in a circular motion.

Riveting means engrossing.

Hysterical means very anxious.

The blank must contain a word that means 'rising' or increasing pressure.

This is only given by the option (C), mounting.

Hence, the correct option is (C).

18. Influence means the power to affect, change or control somebody/something.

Example- She claims that her personal problems played no influence upon her decision to resign.

- The sentence suggests that the blank must contain a verb that means 'to tamper with' or to try to be associated with.
- The only option that reflects this meaning is 'influence'.

Hence, the correct option is (B).

19. The error is in the part (A) of the sentence.

'Don't forget to check' should be there in place of 'Don't forget checking'

When forget, regret and remember are followed by a gerund, the gerund refers to an action that happened earlier than the main verb.

When these verbs are followed by an infinitive, the infinitive refers to an action happening at the same time as the main verb, or later.

Example:

- Don't forget to meet him this morning. (You should meet him this morning.)
- I'll never forget meeting her for the first time. (I'll never forget when I met her for the first time)

Correct Sentence: 'Don't forget to check out our bulletin board where you chat to and share your views with fellow arctophiles from all corners of the globe.'

Hence, the correct option is (A).

20. The error is in the part (A) of the sentence; 'prefer growing' should be there in place of 'prefer to grow'

The verbs hate, love, like, & prefer are usually followed by a gerund when the meaning is general, and by the infinitive when they refer to a particular time or situation.

Example:

- I prefer walking to taking a bus. (I like walking better than taking the bus.)
- you prefer to walk, it will take you 30 minutes to school. (If you want to walk, it will take you 30 minutes to school.)

The correct sentence is: 'Many species also prefer growing in moist places by streams, lakes, and the sea, though very few are normally and probably none entirely, aquatic, being always at certain seasons exposed for a longer or shorter period to the atmosphere.'

Hence, the correct option is (A).

21. The error lies in the wrong usage of the pronoun 'I' in Part (B).

"I" will be replaced with "me", objective case of the pronoun.

Whenever any preposition is used in a sentence, we will always use objective case after it.

Also, the error lies in the wrong order of the pronouns 'Ronaldo and I' in Part (B).

The order of the personal pronouns 'Ronaldo and I' should be replaced by 'me and Ronaldo ' because in a sentence, when personal pronouns of different persons are used to convey a negative idea or confess any guilt or wrongdoings, then the order of the Personal Pronouns are- first comes the First Person Pronoun, second is the Second Person Pronoun and last comes the Third Person Pronoun.

For example- I, you and he are the reason for Stefan's unhappiness in life.

- The given sentence expresses a negative idea of misunderstanding and disputes, hence, the order of the personal pronouns should be changed.
- Therefore, 'me and Ronaldo' should be used instead of 'Ronaldo and I '.

Hence, the correct option is (B).

22. The error lies in the wrong usage of the pronoun 'her' in Part (A).

"her" will be replaced with "she", a subjective case of the pronoun.

But is used as a conjunction as well as a preposition.

But when used as conjunction gives the sense of connecting two sentences with reasoning.

But when used as a preposition gives the sense of except, excluding something.

In this sentence 'but' is used as a conjunction.

Whenever any conjunction is used in a sentence, we will always use a subjective case after it.

Correct Sentence: "Everyone acknowledges her in the town but she is very mischievous, stubborn and arrogant. She has been alone and all by herself her whole life so that the reason everyone respects her and that's what made a survivor, a fighter and a living legend."

Hence, the correct option is (A).

23. In the sentence 'Research various subjects were made easy, as a variety of journals were available in the local markets.' (Incorrect)

In such sentences 'various subjects' actually is one whole entity being considered, in such cases, we use 'was' instead of 'were' although both are past tense forms of the verb 'to be'.

'Researching various subjects was made easy, as a variety of journals on the subject were available in the local markets'. (correct)

Hence, the correct option is (C).

24. Modality means a particular mode in which (something) exists or is expressed or is experienced.

Ingenious means resourceful or clever or inventive or creative.

Munificent is an adjective which means (someone or something) being characterized by or displaying generosity.

Multifarious is also an adjective meaning (something) many oand of various types.

In the given context, these last two words fit well into the gap to make the sentence correct and complete.

Correct sentence: Rambabu is famous as generous politician because of his munificent and multifarious humanitarian activities.

Hence, the correct option is (D).

25. The word 'moot' which can be used as a verb, an adjective or even a noun. As a noun, the word 'moot' denotes some sort of gathering of people with a common interest.

Predicament signifies a dilemma or a difficulty or an 'unpleasant or embarrassing situation.

Garrulous is an adjective meaning (someone) excessive talkative, especially on trivial matters.

Aggrandize is a verb meaning to enhance the reputation of(someone) beyond what is justified by the facts.

In the given context, these last two words fit well into the gap to make the sentence correct and complete.

Correct sentence: Neel's classmates are aware that he is garrulous and aggrandizes himself very often.

Hence, the correct option is (A).

26. Boisterous: Noisy and mischievous

Synonyms: Clamorous, rowdy, raucous, rambunctious

Antonyms: Calm, placid, moderate, quiet, solemn

Hence we can see that clamorous and placid will give us the pair that provides us the combination of the synonym and the antonym of the given word. Adversity means some problem whereas aspersion refers to verbal exhibition of bad temper, captivating implies enthralling or entertaining. Desist means refrain from doing something.

This makes Option D the correct choice among the given options.

Hence, the correct option is (D).

27. Contrary: Antagonistic or opposite

Synonyms: Adverse, antithetical, conflicting, dissimilar

Antonyms: Similar, consistent, agreeable, friendly

Therefore we can see that dissimilar and conflicting both are similar in meaning to the word given in bold and that is why the pair with these two words will be our pick. Coming to the other given words, blunt means dull or insensitive whereas evasive implies deceitful or tricky. Earthly and fleshly both are similar in meaning and that mean carnal. Generic and liberal both mean catholic.

This makes Option C the correct choice among the given options.

Hence, the correct option is (B).

28. Decipher: Figure out or understand something

Synonyms: Interpret, decode, deduce, solve, translate

Antonyms: Misinterpret, distort, confuse, conceal

Therefore we can see that both interpret and distort are related to the word given in bold since the first one is similar in meaning whereas the second one is the opposite in meaning. Therefore we get our required pair of words with the synonym and the antonym. Introvert means reserved whereas intentional implies deliberate and mocking and taunting are synonyms to each other implying deriding or making fun of somebody or something. Rash and sudden can also be used as antonyms of the word deliberate.

This makes Option B the correct choice among the given options.

Hence, the correct option is (B).

29. Efface: Erase something or make one insignificant or inconspicuous

Synonyms: Destroy, obliterate, eliminate, exterminate, terminate

Antonyms: Retain, maintain, build, construct, produce, create

We can see that the pair of words that will come in handy in this case will be destroy and obliterate as both these words are similar in meaning to the given word in bold. Undertake and aspire both imply endeavour to do something whereas demur means disagree or hesitate.

This makes Option A the correct choice among the given options.

Hence, the correct option is (A).

30. Forsake: abandon or leave something or somebody

Synonyms: Desert, abandon, leave, renounce

Antonyms: Hold, maintain, Keep

Therefore both desert and renounce can be used as the synonyms of the given word and this is our required pair here. Coming to the other words, converge and huddle both imply gather around something. Hatred and grudge both are similar in meaning since they both imply aversion against something or somebody. Retard implies delay or hold back something and prevent also implies to stop something.

This makes Option A the correct choice among the given options.

Hence, the correct option is (A).

31. Given expression,

13.33 + 33.31 + 331.13 = ?

46.64 + 331.13 = ?

? = 377.77

Hence, the correct option is (A).

32. Given:

14.28% of 490 − 71.43% of 63 = ?

To solve this type of question, we can take use of conversion of percentage into fraction.

Also, follow the BODMAS rule according to the table given below:

B	Brackets in order (), {}, []	ब्रेकट (), {}, [] क्रम
O	Of	का
D	Division (÷)	विभाजन (÷)
M	Multiplication (×)	गुणा (×)
A	Addition (+)	जोड़ (+)
s	Subtraction (-)	घटाव (-)

Converting given percentages into fraction,

$$\Rightarrow 14.28\% = \frac{1}{7}$$

$$\Rightarrow 71.43\% = \frac{5}{7}$$

According to the given equation,

$$\Rightarrow \frac{1}{7} \times 490 - \frac{5}{7} \times 63 = ?$$

$$\Rightarrow 70 - 45 = ?$$

$$\Rightarrow 25 = ?$$

∴ The value of ? is 25.

Hence, the correct option is (A).

33. Given:

42% of 250 + 115% of 480 = ?

Follow the BODMAS rule according to the table given below:

B	Brackets in order (), {}, []	ब्रेकट (), {}, [] क्रम
O	Of	का
D	Division (÷)	विभाजन (÷)
M	Multiplication (×)	गुणा (×)
A	Addition (+)	जोड़ (+)
s	Subtraction (-)	घटाव (-)

42% of 250 + 115% of 480 = ?

$$\Rightarrow \left(\frac{42}{100}\right) \times 250 + \left(\frac{115}{100}\right) \times 480 = ?$$

$$\Rightarrow 105 + 552 = ?$$

$$\Rightarrow 657 = ?$$

∴ The value of ? is 657

Hence, the correct option is (B).

34. Given expression:

450 ÷ 15 × 12 − 120 ÷ 4 × 12 + 1 = ?

Follow BODMAS rule to solve this question,

450 ÷ 15 × 12 − 120 ÷ 4 × 12 + 1 = ?

$$\frac{450}{15} \times 12 - \frac{120}{4} \times 12 + 1 = ?$$

30 × 12 − 30 × 12 + 1 = ?

? = 1

∴ The value of '?' is 1.

Hence, the correct option is (C).

35. Follow BODMAS rule to solve this question, as per the order given below,

B	Brackets in order (), {}, []	ब्रेकट (), {}, [] क्रम
O	Of	का
D	Division (÷)	विभाजन (÷)
M	Multiplication (×)	गुणा (×)
A	Addition (+)	जोड़ (+)
s	Subtraction (-)	घटाव (-)

$$\sqrt{\left[1331^{\left(\frac{1}{3}\right)} + 1728^{\left(\frac{1}{3}\right)} + 2\right]} = ?$$

$$\sqrt{(11 + 12 + 2)}$$

$$= \sqrt{25} = 5$$

Hence, the correct option is (A).

36. Given:

66.66% of 480 + 37.5% of 832 = 120 + ?

Use the BODMAS rule to solve this question:

66.66% of 480 + 37.5% of 832 = 120 + ?

$$\Rightarrow \frac{2}{3} \times 480 + \frac{3}{8} \times 832 = 120 + ?$$

$$\Rightarrow 320 + 312 = 120 + ?$$

$$\Rightarrow ? = 512$$

∴ The value of ? is 512.

Hence, the correct option is (B).

37. Given:

$32^{0.16} \times 32^{0.4} \times 32^{0.5} = 128? \div 2$

Use the BODMAS rule to solve this question:

$$\Rightarrow 2^{5 \times 0.16} \times 2^{5 \times 0.4} \times 2^{5 \times 0.5} = 2^{7 \times ?} \div 2$$

On comparing powers of both sides, we get:

$$\Rightarrow 0.8 + 2 + 2.5 = 7 \times ? - 1$$

$$\Rightarrow 5.3 = 7 \times ? - 1$$

$$\Rightarrow 7 \times ? = 6.3$$

$$\Rightarrow ? = 0.9$$

Hence, the correct option is (D)

38. Follow BODMAS rule to solve this question, as per the order given below,

Step-1- Parts of an equation enclosed in 'Brackets' must be solved first, and in the bracket,

Step-2- Any mathematical 'Of' or 'Exponent' must be solved next,

Step-3- Next, the parts of the equation that contain 'Division' and 'Multiplication' are calculated,

Step-4- Last but not least, the parts of the equation that contain 'Addition' and 'Subtraction' should be calculated.

Given expression is,

$$\left(7\frac{5}{2} + 4\frac{7}{2}\right) \div 7\frac{3}{2} = 11\frac{5}{3} - \frac{2}{3} - ?$$

$$\Rightarrow \left(\frac{19}{2} + \frac{15}{2}\right) \div \frac{17}{2} = \frac{38}{3} - \frac{2}{3} - ?$$

$$\Rightarrow 17 \times \frac{2}{17} = \frac{38}{3} - \frac{2}{3} - ?$$

$$\Rightarrow 2 = \frac{(38 - 2)}{3} - ?$$

$$\Rightarrow 2 = 12 - ?$$

$$? = 10$$

Hence, the correct option is (E).

39. Use the BODMAS rule to solve this question:

Given:

$$4\frac{2}{5} \div 1\frac{7}{15} + 5\frac{5}{3} \times 3\frac{3}{2} = ?$$

$$\Rightarrow \frac{22}{5} \div \frac{22}{15} + \frac{20}{3} \times \frac{9}{2} = ?$$

$$\Rightarrow \frac{22}{5} \times \frac{15}{22} + 10 \times 3 = ?$$

$$\Rightarrow 3 + 30 = 33 = ?$$

∴ The value of '?' is 33.

Hence, the correct option is (C).

40. Given expression,

$$\Rightarrow ? = \frac{2\frac{3}{4}}{1\frac{5}{6}} \div \frac{7}{8} \times \left(\frac{1}{3} + \frac{1}{4}\right) + \frac{5}{7} \div \frac{3}{4} \times \frac{3}{4}$$

$$\Rightarrow ? = \frac{\frac{11}{4}}{\frac{11}{6}} \div \frac{7}{8} \times \left(\frac{1}{3} + \frac{1}{4}\right) + \frac{5}{7} \div \frac{3}{4} \times \frac{3}{4}$$

$$\Rightarrow ? = \frac{6}{4} \div \frac{7}{8} \times \left(\frac{7}{12}\right) + \frac{5}{7} \div \frac{3}{4} \times \frac{3}{4}$$

$$\Rightarrow ? = \frac{12}{7} \times \left(\frac{7}{12}\right) + \frac{20}{21} \times \frac{3}{4}$$

$$\Rightarrow ? = 1 + \frac{5}{7}$$

$$\Rightarrow ? = \frac{12}{7}$$

$$\therefore ? = \frac{12}{7}$$

Hence, the correct option is (C).

41. I. $x^2 - 15x + 54 = 0$

$$\Rightarrow x^2 - 6x - 9x + 54 = 0$$

$$\Rightarrow x(x - 6) - 9(x - 6) = 0$$

$$\Rightarrow (x - 6)(x - 9) = 0$$

$\Rightarrow x = 6$ or 9

II. $y^2 - 13y + 36 = 0$

$\Rightarrow y^2 - 9y - 4y + 36 = 0$

$\Rightarrow y(y - 9) - 4(y - 9) = 0$

$\Rightarrow (y - 9)(y - 4) = 0$

$\Rightarrow Y = 9$ or 4

x	sign	y
6	<	9
6	>	4
9	=	9
9	>	4

∴ Relation can't be established or x = y

Hence, the correct option is (E).

42. I. $x^2 - 13x + 40 = 0$

$\Rightarrow x^2 - 8x - 5x + 40 = 0$

$\Rightarrow x(x - 8) - 5(x - 8) = 0$

$\Rightarrow (x - 8)(x - 5) = 0$

$\Rightarrow x = 5$ or 8

II. $y^2 - 11y + 24 = 0$

$\Rightarrow y^2 - 3y - 8y + 24 = 0$

$\Rightarrow y(y - 3) - 8(y - 3) = 0$

$\Rightarrow (y - 3)(y - 8) = 0$

$\Rightarrow y = 3$ or 8

x	sign	y
5	>	3
5	<	8
8	>	3
8	=	8

∴ Relation can't be established or x = y

Hence, the correct option is (E).

43. Given:

A total number of students = 39.

The average weight of students is 64 kg.

The average weight decreases by 4 kg.

Total weight of class = 39 × 64 kg = 2496 kg

Total weight after new students joins = (39 + 1)(64 - 4) = 2400 kg

The weight of new student = Total weight of class - Total weight after new students joins.

$\Rightarrow$ 2496 kg - 2400 kg

$\Rightarrow$ 96 kg

∴ The weight of new student is 96 kg.

Hence, the correct option is (B).

44. Given:

Total money = Rs. 480480

A receives 25% less than B.

And B receives 20% less than C.

Let C's share be Rs. x

Then B's share = x of (100 - 20)%

$\Rightarrow x \times (80\%)$

$\Rightarrow x \times \left(\dfrac{80}{100}\right)$

$\Rightarrow x \times \left(\dfrac{4}{5}\right)$

$\Rightarrow \dfrac{4x}{5}$

And A's share = $\left(\dfrac{4x}{5}\right)$ of (100 - 25)%

$\Rightarrow \left(\dfrac{4x}{5}\right) \times (75\%)$

$\Rightarrow \left(\dfrac{4x}{5}\right) \times \left(\dfrac{75}{100}\right)$

$\Rightarrow \left(\dfrac{4x}{5}\right) \times \left(\dfrac{3}{4}\right)$

$\Rightarrow \dfrac{3x}{5}$

According to question,

$\left(\dfrac{3x}{5}\right) + \left(\dfrac{4x}{5}\right) + x = 480480$

$\Rightarrow \dfrac{(3x + 4x + 5x)}{5} = 480480$

$\Rightarrow \dfrac{12x}{5} = 480480$

$\Rightarrow 12x = 480480 \times 5$

$\Rightarrow x = \dfrac{(480480 \times 5)}{12}$

$\Rightarrow x = $ Rs. 200200

B's share = $\dfrac{4x}{5}$

$\Rightarrow \left(\dfrac{4}{5}\right) \times 200200$

$\Rightarrow$ Rs. 160160

∴ The share of B will be Rs. 160160.

Hence, the correct option is (D).

45. Given:

$3 \times 2 + 3 = 9$

$9 \times 3 - 4 = 23$

$23 \times 4 + 5 = 97$

$97 \times 5 - 6 = 479$

$479 \times 6 + 7 = 2881$

$2881 \times 7 - 8 = 20159$

∴ The wrong number is 99.

Hence, the correct option is (C).

46. Given:

26, 39, 65, 91, 133, 169, 221

Difference of these numbers on dividing them by 13,

$\Rightarrow \dfrac{26}{13} = 2$

$\Rightarrow \dfrac{39}{13} = 3$

$\Rightarrow \dfrac{65}{13} = 5$

$\Rightarrow \dfrac{91}{13} = 7$

$\Rightarrow \dfrac{143}{13} = 11$

$\Rightarrow \dfrac{169}{13} = 13$

$\Rightarrow \dfrac{221}{13} = 17$

∴ 143 will come in place of 133.

Hence, the correct option is (C).

47. Given:

15, 17, 23, 34, 55

Pattern of the given series can be explained as,

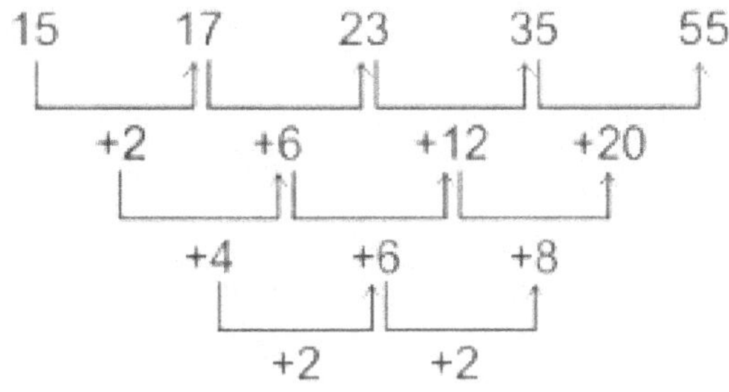

Since 35 will come in place of 34,

∴ The required wrong number will be 34.

Hence, the correct option is (C).

48. Given:

A Sum of money is invested in two parts in ratio of 3 : 5.

Difference of SI = 1800

1st part is invested at 16% and the 2nd part is at 12%.

$SI = \dfrac{PRT}{100}$

Let the sum for 1st part be 3x.

Let the sum for 2st part be 5x

Simple interest of 1st part = 3x × $\dfrac{16 \times 3}{100} = \dfrac{144x}{100}$

Similarly,

Simple interest of 2nd part = 5x × $\dfrac{12 \times 3}{100} = \dfrac{180x}{100}$

According to the question;

Difference of SI = 1800

$\Rightarrow \dfrac{180x}{100} - \dfrac{144x}{100} = 1800$

$\Rightarrow \dfrac{36x}{100} = 1800$

$\Rightarrow x = 5000$

Total Sum = 3x + 5x = 8x = 8 × 5000 = 40000

∴ The total sum invested in both the scheme is Rs. 40000.

Hence, the correct option is (A).

49. Given:

Prity can a work is 34 days, Anant can a work is 51 days.

Prity can do a piece of work in 34 days.

If a man can do a work in x days then he will do $\dfrac{1}{x}$ part of the work in 1 day.

work done by Prity in 1 day = $\dfrac{1}{34}$

Anant can do same work in 51 days.

work done by Anant in 1 day = $\dfrac{1}{51}$

work done by together – $\dfrac{1}{34} + \dfrac{1}{51}$

$\Rightarrow \dfrac{(3 + 2)}{102}$ (by taking LCM for 34 and 51 which is 102)

$\Rightarrow$ Total work done together is = $\dfrac{5}{102}$

Then total days are = $\dfrac{102}{5}$ days

∴ Total days is $\dfrac{102}{5}$ days

Hence, the correct option is (A).

50. The ratio of water in mixture 1 = $\dfrac{4}{13}$ (∵ The ratio of milk and water = 9 : 4)

The ratio of water in pure water = 1

Now these two are mixed to form our mixture 2 where the ratio is 11 : 5

∴ The ratio of water in mixture 2 = $\dfrac{5}{16}$

Let us apply the principle of the allegation.

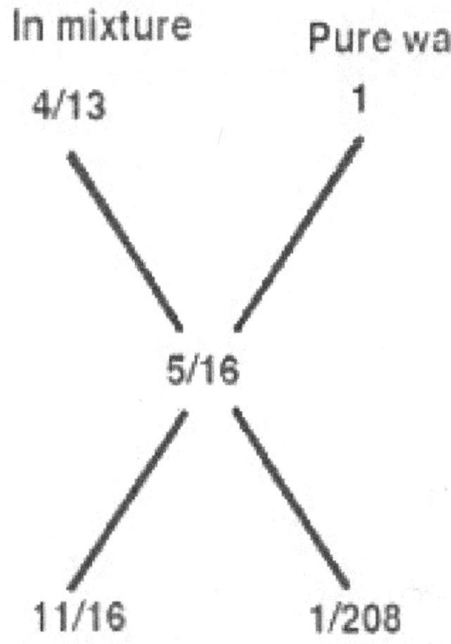

$\Rightarrow$ Mixture 1 : water = $\left(\dfrac{1-5}{16}\right) : \left(\dfrac{5}{16} - \dfrac{4}{13}\right) =$
$\dfrac{11}{16} : \dfrac{1}{208} = 143 : 1$

Given that Quantity of mixture 1 = 47.6 liter

$\Rightarrow$ 47.6 : ? = 143 : 1

$\Rightarrow$? = $\dfrac{47.6}{143}$ = 0.33 liter

$\therefore$ The amount of water needed to be added is 0.33 liter

Hence, the correct option is (D).

51. Given:

Capital amount by which Abhay started the business = Rs. 32000

Suraj invested in the business = Rs. 30000

Ratio of profit they divided at the end of year = 8 :5

Let Suraj invested for months = x months,

Ratio of profit = Capital of Abhay × Time: Capital of Suraj × Time

$\Rightarrow$ 8 : 5 = 32000 × 12: 30000 × x

$\Rightarrow$ x = $\dfrac{(32000 \times 12 \times 5)}{8}$ × 30000

$\Rightarrow$ x = 8 Months

$\therefore$ Suraj joined Abhay after 4 months.

Hence, the correct option is (D).

52. I. $x^2 - 7x + 10 = 0$

$\Rightarrow x^2 - 5x - 2x + 10 = 0$

$\Rightarrow x(x - 5) - 2(x - 5) = 0$

$\Rightarrow (x - 5) (x - 2) = 0$

$\Rightarrow$ x = 5 or x = 2

II. $y^2 - 11y + 24 = 0$

$\Rightarrow y^2 - 8y - 3y + 24 = 0$

$\Rightarrow y(y - 8) - 3(y - 8) = 0$

$\Rightarrow (y - 8) (y - 3) = 0$

$\Rightarrow$ y = 8 or y = 3

Value of x	Relation	Value of y
5	<	8
2	<	8
5	>	3
2	<	3

$\therefore$ The relationship cannot be established between x and y.

Hence, the correct option is (E).

53. Given:

Year	Basmati	Sonam	Silver	Golden
2000	300	500	400	100
2001	250	200	300	250
2002	320	400	200	100
2003	400	50	100	300
2004	50	700	900	800

Total quantity of rice in 2004 = 50 + 700 + 900 + 800 = 2450

Good quantity of rice available in 2004 = 50% × 2450 = 1225

Quantity od Golden available for sale = 50% × 800 = 400 kg

Percentage of golden in total quantity to be sold = $\dfrac{400}{1225}$ × 100
= 32.65% ≈ 33%

$\therefore$ Percentage of golden in total quantity to be sold is 33%.

Hence, the correct option is (C).

54. Given:

Year	Basmati	Sonam	Silver	Golden
2000	300	500	400	100
2001	250	200	300	250
2002	320	400	200	100
2003	400	50	100	300
2004	50	700	900	800

Quantity of Silver left out = 20% × 100 = 20 kg

Quantity of Silver Goviind will get = $\dfrac{5}{(2 + 3 + 5)}$ × 20 = 10 kg

$\therefore$ Quantity of Silver Goviind will get is 10 kg

Hence, the correct option is (D).

55. Given:

Sale of rice of 5 years,

Year	Basmati	Sonam	Silver	Golden	Total
2000	300	500	400	100	1300
2001	250	200	300	250	1000

2002	320	400	200	100	1020
2003	400	50	100	300	850
2004	50	700	900	800	2450

From the above data, we can say,

The maximum quantity of rice sold $= 2450$ kg

The minimum quantity of rice sold $= 850$ kg

Required ratio $= 2450 : 850 = 49 : 17$

Hence, the correct option is (D).

56. Given:

Year	Basmati	Sonam	Silver	Golden
2000	300	500	400	100
2001	250	200	300	250
2002	320	400	200	100
2003	400	50	100	300
2004	50	700	900	800

Difference = sale in 2002 - sale in 2001

From the above table,

Difference in sale = 1020 - 1000 = 20 kg

∴ The difference in sale is 20 kg

Hence, the correct option is (C).

57. Given:

sale of rice of 5 years

Year	Basmati	Sonam	Silver	Golden
2000	300	500	400	100
2001	250	200	300	250
2002	320	400	200	100
2003	400	50	100	300
2004	50	700	900	800

Total cost price of Basmati for 2002 and 2004 = 70 × (320 + 50) = Rs. 25900

Selling price of Basmati for 2002 and 2004 = 110 × (320 + 50) = Rs. 40700

Net revenue = 40700 - 25900 = Rs.14,800

Hence, the correct option is (B).

58. Given:

$\Rightarrow 8 \times 0.5 + 0.5 = 4.5$

$\Rightarrow 4.5 \times 1 + 1 = 5.5$

$\Rightarrow 5.5 \times 2 + 2 = 13$

$\Rightarrow 13 \times 4 + 4 = 56$

$\Rightarrow 56 \times 8 + 8 = 456$

∴ The required answer is 456.

Hence, the correct option is (C).

59. Given:

$\Rightarrow 5 + 5 = 10$

$\Rightarrow 10 + 6 = 16$

$\Rightarrow 16 + 7 = 23$

$\Rightarrow 23 + 8 = 31$

$\Rightarrow 31 + 9 = 40$

$\Rightarrow 40 + 10 = 50$

∴ The missing number is 50.

Hence, the correct option is (C).

60. Given:

Length of a pit = 4 m

Breadth of a pit = 6 m

Height of a pit = 1100 cm

Height = 1100 cm or 11 m

Volume of pit = length × breadth × height

Volume of soil = 4 × 6 × 11

$\Rightarrow 24 \times 11$

$\Rightarrow 264$ m³

∴ Volume of soil removed is 264 m³

Hence, the correct option is (C).

61. Let us consider the present age of P, Q and R as P years, Q years and S years respectively.

given, P $= \dfrac{7Q}{5}$

Also, R $= \dfrac{6Q}{5}$

And, P - R = 5

$\Rightarrow \dfrac{7Q}{5} - \dfrac{6Q}{5} = 5$

$\Rightarrow$ Q = 25 years

$\Rightarrow$ P = 35 years and R = 30 years

∴ the ratio of age of P and R, 5 years from now = 35 + 5 : 30 + 5 = 8 : 7

Hence, the correct option is (C).

62. According to the question,

3x + y = 15

$\Rightarrow$ y = 15 - 3x

$\Rightarrow$ 5x + 2(15 - 3x) = 81

$\Rightarrow$ 5x + 30 - 6x = 81

$\Rightarrow$ x = -51

y = 15 - 3x

$\Rightarrow$ y = 15 - 3(-51) = 168

Comparison between x and y (via Tabulation):

X	Y	Relation
-51	168	x < y

∴ x < y.

Hence, the correct option is (A).

63. Given:

I. $2x^2 - 11x + 15 = 0$

II. $9y^2 - 12y + 4 = 0$

From I,

$2x^2 - 11x + 15 = 0$

$\Rightarrow 2x^2 - 6x - 5x + 15 = 0$

$\Rightarrow 2x(x - 3) - 5(x - 3) = 0$

$\Rightarrow (x - 3)(2x - 5) = 0$

Taking,

$\Rightarrow (x - 3) = 0$ or $(2x - 5) = 0$

$\Rightarrow x = 3$ or $\left(\dfrac{5}{2}\right)$

From II,

$9y^2 - 12y + 4 = 0$

$\Rightarrow 9y^2 - 6y - 6y + 4 = 0$

$\Rightarrow 3y(3y - 2) - 2(3y - 2) = 0$

$\Rightarrow (3y - 2)(3y - 2) = 0$

Taking,

$\Rightarrow (3y - 2) = 0$

$\Rightarrow y = \dfrac{2}{3}$

Comparison between x and y (via Tabulation):

Value of x	Value of y	Relation
3	$\dfrac{2}{3}$	x > y
$\dfrac{5}{2}$	$\dfrac{2}{3}$	x > y

∴ x > y.

Hence, the correct option is (A).

64. Formula:

$$\tan(A + B) = \frac{\tan A + \tan B}{1 - \tan A \tan B}$$

$$\tan\left(\frac{\alpha}{2} + \frac{\beta}{2}\right) = \frac{\tan\frac{\alpha}{2} + \tan\frac{\beta}{2}}{1 - \tan\frac{\alpha}{2}\tan\frac{\beta}{2}}$$

The quadratic equations is $8x^2 - 26x + 15 = 0$.

$\Rightarrow 8x^2 - 20x - 6x + 15 = 0$

$\Rightarrow 4x(2x - 5) - 3(2x - 5) = 0$

$\Rightarrow (2x - 5)(4x - 3) = 0$

$\therefore x = \dfrac{5}{2} = \tan\dfrac{\alpha}{2}$ and $x = \dfrac{3}{4} = \tan\dfrac{\beta}{2}$

$$\tan\left(\frac{\alpha}{2} + \frac{\beta}{2}\right) = \frac{\frac{5}{2} + \frac{3}{4}}{1 - \frac{5}{2}\cdot\frac{3}{4}} = \frac{\frac{26}{8}}{1 - \frac{15}{8}} = \frac{-26}{7}$$

$$\therefore \cos(\alpha + \beta) = \frac{1 - \tan^2\left(\frac{\alpha+\beta}{2}\right)}{1 + \tan^2\left(\frac{\alpha+\beta}{2}\right)}$$

$$= \frac{1 - \left(\frac{6\pi 8}{40}\right)}{1 + \left(\frac{6\pi}{40}\right)} = \frac{-627}{725}$$

Hence, the correct option is (D).

65. Given,

Total Blue Pens: 4

Total Red Pens: 2

Total Black Pens: 3

Total Pens: $4 + 2 + 3 = 9$

Probability of drawing pens $= \dfrac{^4C_2}{^9C_2} = \dfrac{4\times3}{9\times8} = \dfrac{1}{6}$

After this, the pens are not replaced, which reduces the number of pens in the pack to 7

So, the probability of drawing 1 black pen from a pack of 7 pens would be $\dfrac{^2C_1}{^7C_1} = \dfrac{3}{7}$

Probability of drawing 2 blue pens and 1 black pen $= \dfrac{1}{6} \times \dfrac{3}{7} = \dfrac{1}{14}$

Hence, the correct option is (B).

Ques (66-67): From the given information,

Symbol in Diagram	Meaning
○	Female
□	Male
═══	Married Couple
───	Siblings
│	Difference of a Generation

1) A and B are a married couple.

2) A being the Male member.

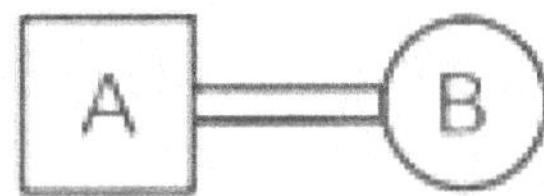

3) C is the brother of A.

4) D is the only son of C and E is the sister of D.

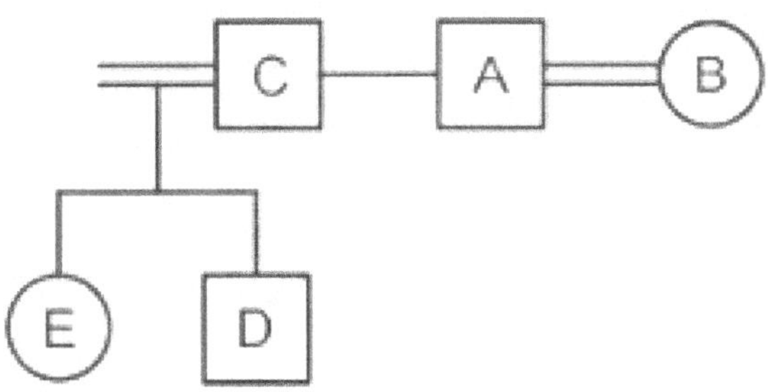

5) B is the daughter-in-law of F means F is the mother of A and C.

6) G is the husband of F.

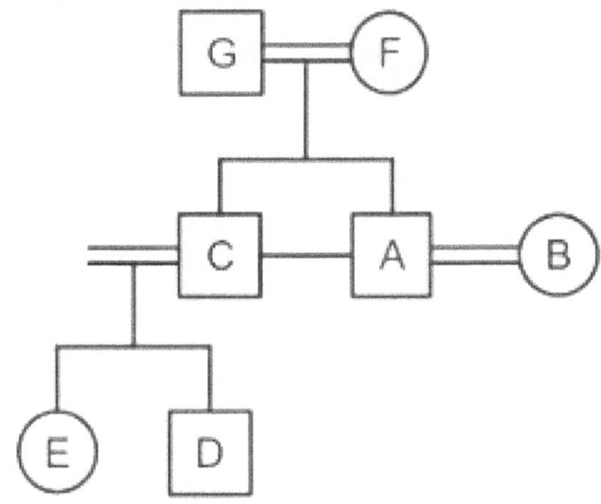

66. From the above relation, we got C as the brother of A and A is the husband of B.

So, C is the brother-in-law of B.

Hence, the correct option is (D).

67. From the above relation, We know that F is the mother of C.

If P and C are married couples, then P should be the wife of C as C is the male member.

So, P should be the Daughter-in-law of F.

Hence, the correct option is (B).

Ques (68-70):Persons: M, N, O, P, Q and R.

1) P is taller than only R.

Height: _ > _ > _ > _ > P > R

2) At least three persons are heavier than M.

3) R is heavier than Q but not than M.

Weight: _ > _ > _ > M > R > Q

4) Number of persons taller than M is equal to number of persons shorter than O.

Height: _ > _ > M/O > O/M > P > R

5) O is heavier than P but not the heaviest. So, N must be the heaviest.

Weight: N > O > P > M > R > Q

6) No person has same position in both height and weight. So, M must be taller than O. Also, Q must be taller than N.

Height: Q > N > M > O > P > R

Weight: N > O > P > M > R > Q

68. So, Q is the tallest.

Hence, the correct option is (B).

69. So, two persons are heavier than P.

Hence, the correct option is (C).

70. So, three persons are shorter than M.

Hence, the correct option is (D).

71. Given Statement: A < B ≤ C > D; C > E ≥ F; E > B

(i) A < F: False (A < B ≤ C > E ≥ F; There is no clear relation between A and F, hence can not conclude anything).

(ii) D < B: False (B ≤ C > D; There is no clear relation between B and D, hence can not conclude anything).

So, the correct answer is None follows.

Hence, the correct option is (E).

72. Given statements: X = Y ≥ Z > V; V < P > Q; Q = T

On combining: X = Y ≥ Z > V < P > Q = T

Conclusions:

(I) X > V - True (as per X = Y ≥ Z > V → X > V)

(II) T ≤ Z - False (X = Y ≥ Z > V < P > Q = T → thus clear relation between T and Z cannot be determined)

So, The correct answer is Only (I) Follows.

Hence, the correct option is (A).

73. Given statements:

J < K ≥ L = Y > X; L < V ≥ D > I; D = R ≥ P

Combining the given statements,

J < K ≥ L < V ≥ D > I and

J < K ≥ L < V ≥ D = R ≥ P

I. P < K → false (as K ≥ L < V ≥ D = R ≥ P = > clear relation between P and K cannot be determined)

II. X ≤ D → false (as X < Y = L < V ≥ D = > clear relation between X and D cannot be determined)

III. R > K → false (as K ≥ L < V ≥ D = R = > clear relation between R and K cannot be determined)

So, none of the given conclusions is true.

Hence, the correct option is (E).

74. (A) T < B ≤ G < D =K → True (as T < B ≤ G < D = K → B < K and T < B ≤ G < D → T < D)

(B) B < T = G ≤ D > K → False (as B < T = G ≤ D > K, opposite sign between B and k)

(C) D < K> G = T ≥ B → False (as D < K> G = T, opposite sign between T and D)

(D) B > D = G ≥ K ≥ T →False (as D = G ≥ K ≥ T → D ≥ T, ignore equal to (=) sign, both the signs are facing same direction and common sign (≥) towards D. But here we are getting extra equal (=) sign.

Hence, the correct option is (A).

75. Given statements: L < O = C ≥ A; X ≤ V < L = H

On combining: A ≤ C = O > L = H > V ≥ X

Conclusions:

I. C > H → True (as C = O > L = H → C > H)

II. X < O → True (as O > L = H > V ≥ X → O > X)

So, both I and II are True is the correct answer.

Hence, the correct option is (C).

Ques (76-80):Given that: There are nine persons sitting around a circular table. Some are facing inside while some are facing outside the table.

(As now we dont know who is facing inside or who is facing outside).

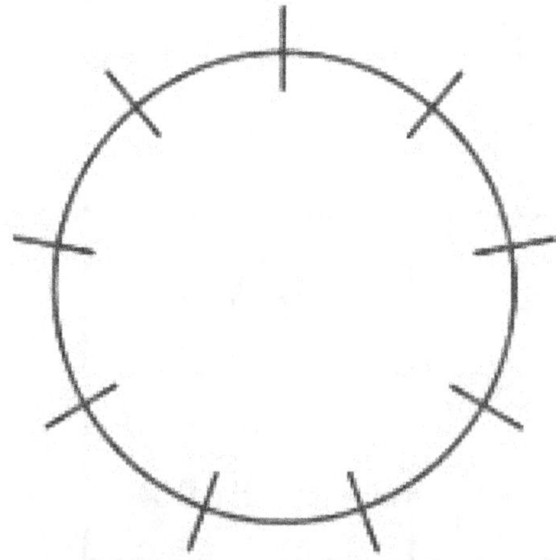

Q does not face inside → Means Q is facing outside.

R is fourth to the right of Q.

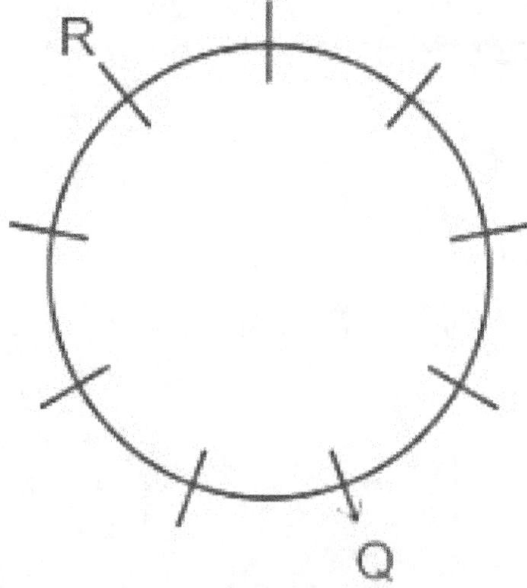

Q sits second to the right of the one who sits third to the left of U.

Here 2 conditions will generate:

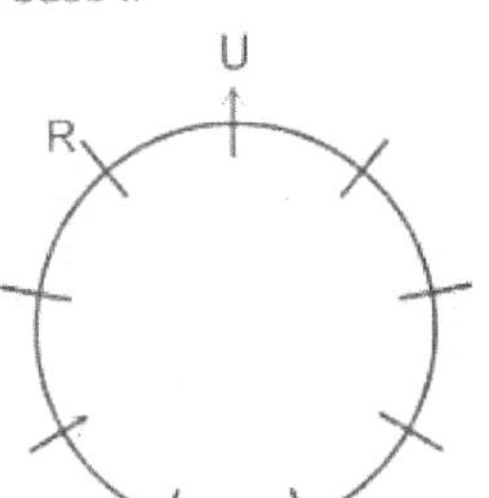
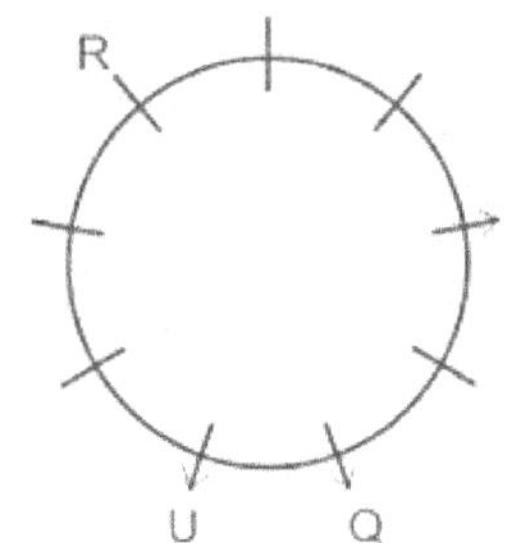

Only three persons are sitting between T and S.

And S is second to the right of U.

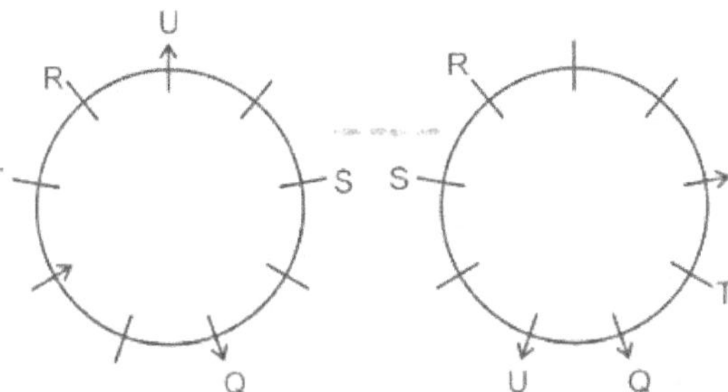

Here 2 more conditions will generate as 3 persons are sitting between T and S.

Case III is generated by Case I

And Case IV is generated by Case II.

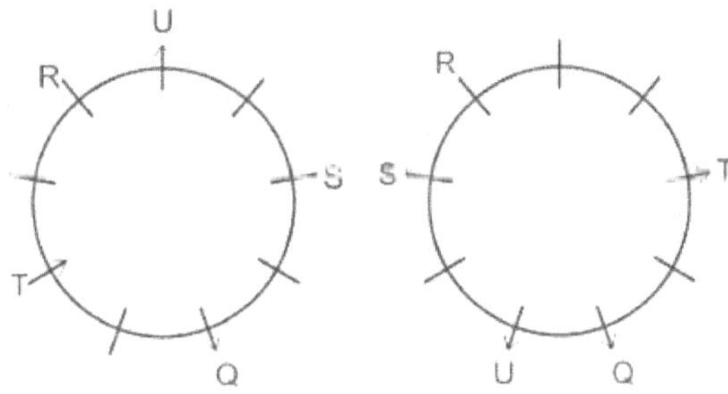

V is second to the left of X and faces opposite direction of Q.

Q is in the middle of X and V.

Here we have to eliminate Case II and Case IV, as they does not follow this above condition.

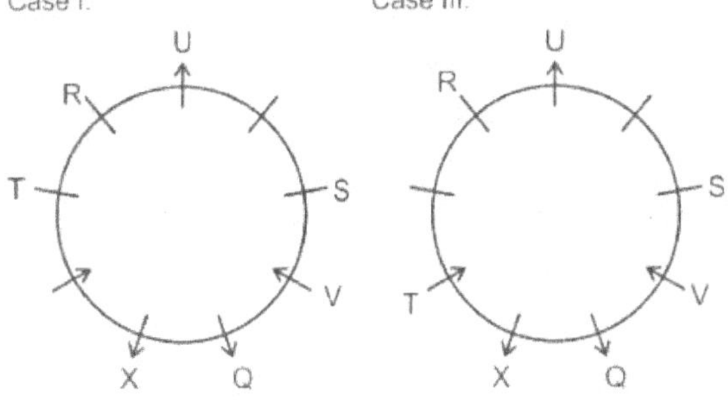

W is not an immediate neighbour of U and sits third to the right of P.

Here Case I will eliminate.

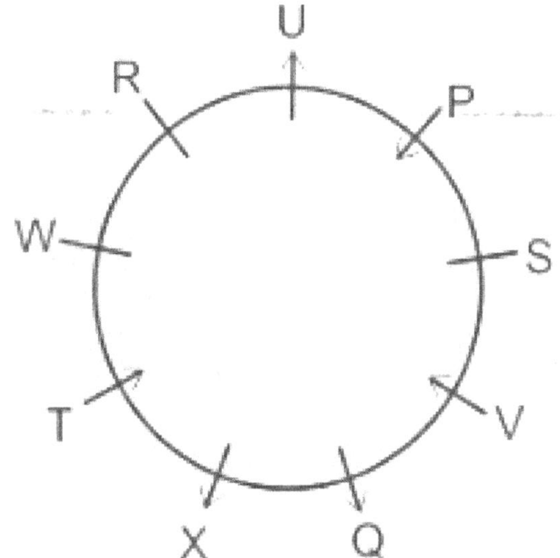

W and P are facing same direction but opposite to R, S and X.

So, R and S will face outside. And W and P will face inside.

So, the final diagram of the given condition is:

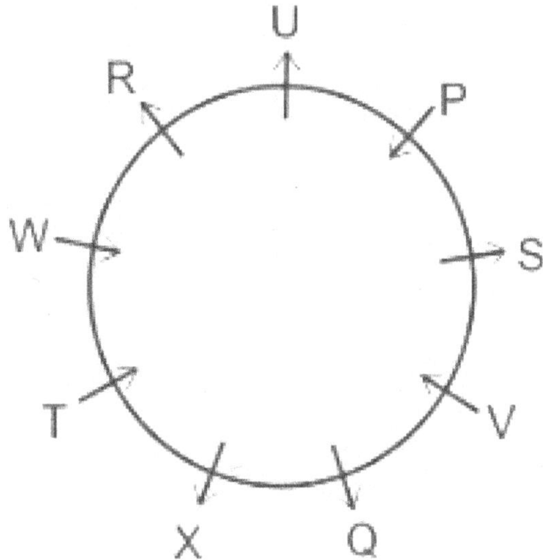

76. So, immediate right of X is T.

Hence, the correct option is (C).

77. Thus, the position of W is both, fourth to the left of V and fifth to the right of V.

So, Both (A) & (B).

Hence, the correct option is (E).

78. So, 5 persons are facing outside the table - R, U, S, Q and X.

Hence, the correct option is (D).

79. As we can see that:

R is immediate left of W → True

R is second to the right of P → True

R is fifth to the left of V → True

R is immediate left of U → True

All the statements are true.

So, All are correct.

Hence, the correct option is (E).

80. If all the persons are arranged in English Alphabet series in anti-clock wise direction starting towards the right of P.

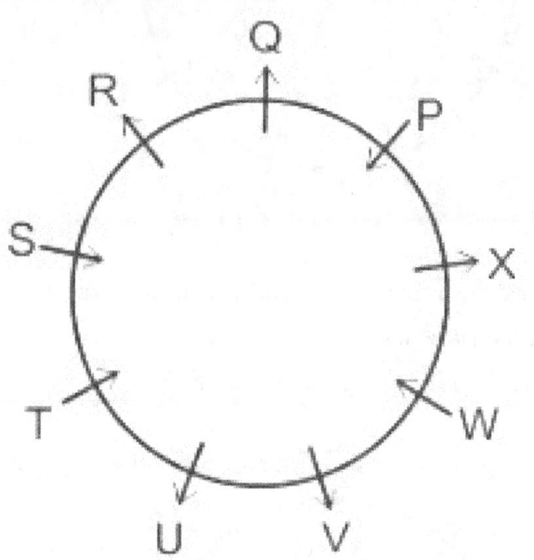

Thus, we can see that R and T will not change their places.

So, only two persons will not change their places.

Hence, the correct option is (B).

81. Given Statement :

Y	W	@	1	&	C	N	3	P	L	B	9	↑	=	D	◊	E	2	£	M	V	$	7	#	4	F	G	5

Condition: Symbols which are not immediately preceded by a number and also not immediately followed by a letter

Y	W	@	1	&	C	N	3	P	L	B	9	↑	=	D	◊	E	2	£	M	V	$	7	#	4	F	G	5

So, two is correct.

Hence, the correct option is (C).

82. Given Statement :

Y	W	@	1	&	C	N	3	P	L	B	9	↑	=	D	◊	E	2	£	M	V	$	7	#

In each pair, the corresponding elements of both the terms occupy the same position from the beginning and end of the given sequence.

So, $ F 2 D is correct.

Hence, the correct option is (E).

83. Such numbers may be shown in the sequence as follows:

Y	W	@	1	&	C	N	3	P	L	B	9	↑	=	D	◊	E	2	£	M	V	$	7	#

Therefore, required sum = 2 * (1 + 9 + 2 + 7) = 2 * 19 = 38

So, 38 is correct.

Hence, the correct option is (D).

84. In all other groups, the first element moves five steps forward to give the second element, the second element moves three steps backward to give the third element; the third element moves two steps forward to give the fourth element.

So, L D B = does not belong to the group.

Hence, the correct option is (C).

85. The new arrangement is :

1	@	W	Y	3	N	C	&	9	B	L	P	◊	D	=	↑	M	£	2	E	#	7	$	V

There are 13 elements between 9 & $.

So, the middle one will be 7th element to the right of 9, which is ↑

Hence, the correct option is (A).

Ques (86-90): 1) Gaurav sits at one of the extreme ends of the row.

2) Only two boys sit between Gaurav and Akash.

3) The one who faces Akash sits to the immediate left of Deepa.

4) The one who faces Chaitrali sits to the immediate left of Chetan. (This eliminates case 3).

Case 1:

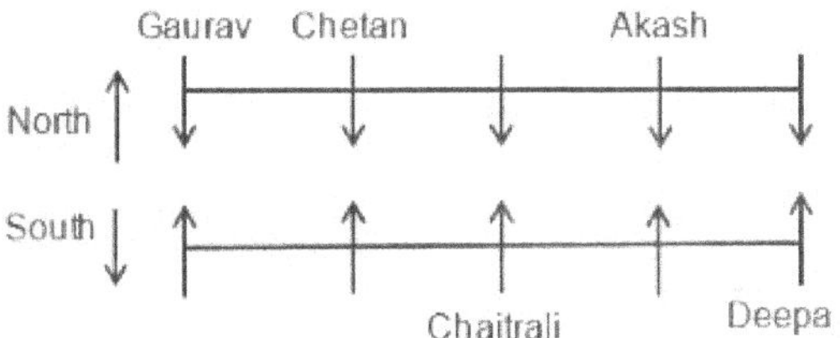

Case 2:

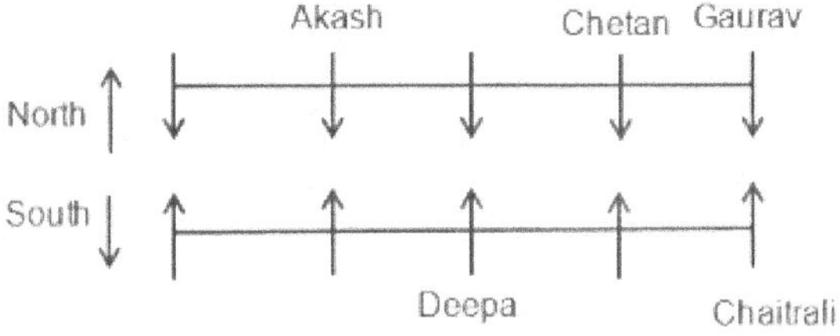

Case 3:

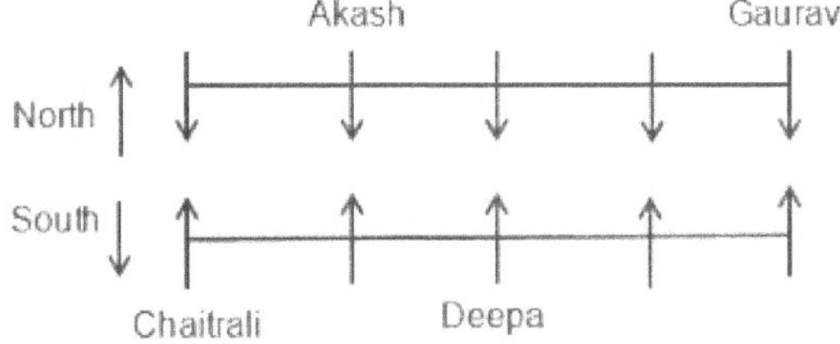

5) Esha sits second to the right of Aditi.

6) Neither Chaitrali nor Deepa faces Monu. (This eliminates case 1).

Case 1:

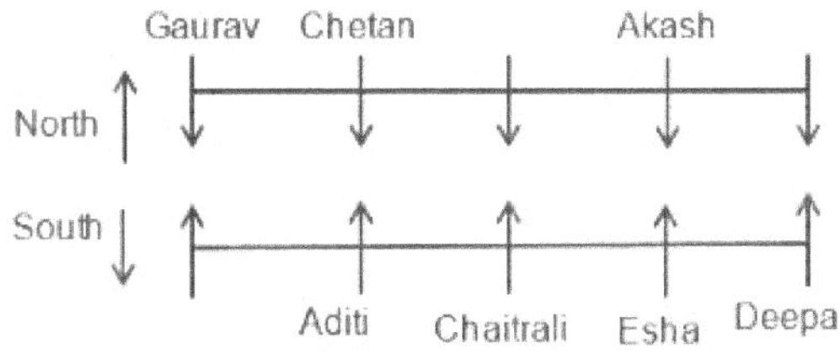

Case 2:

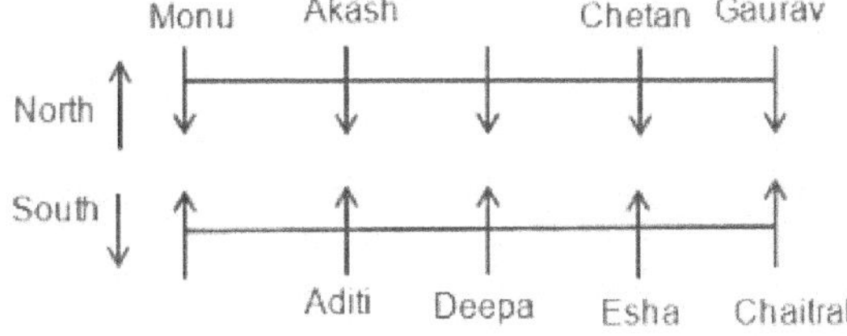

Final arrangement:

Case 2:

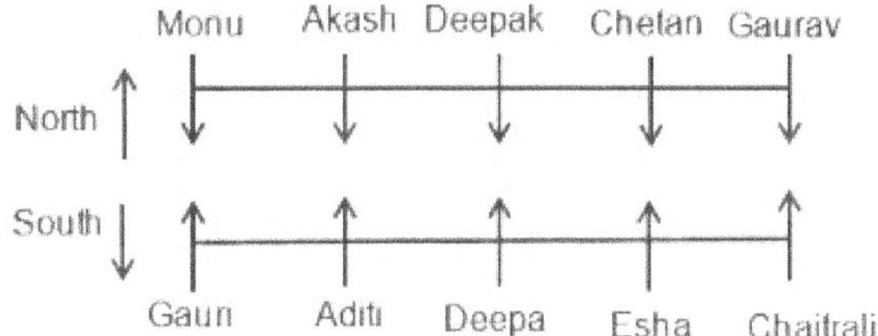

86. So, Deepak faces Deepa.

Hence, the correct option is (C).

87. So, no one sits between Deepak and Chetan.

Hence, the correct option is (A).

88. So, Monu and Chaitrali sit at extreme ends.

Hence, the correct option is (D).

89. So, Deepak sits in the middle of the row is only true about Deepak.

Hence, the correct option is (B).

90. In all the given pairs the boy faces opposite to the girl except Deepak – Chaitrali.

So, 'Deepak - Chaitrali' does not belong to the group.

Hence, the correct option is (E).

91. The least possible diagram for the given statements is as follows,

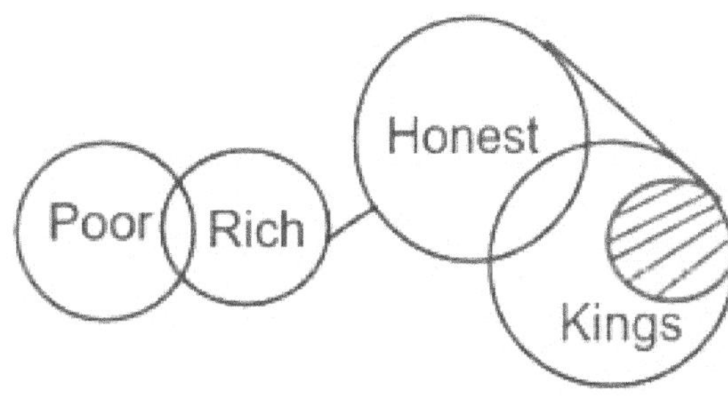

Conclusions:

I. All kings can be honest. → Fales (Only a few kings are honest → some kings are honest and some kings are not honest).

II. Some honest is not rich. → True (No honest is rich → some honest is not rich).

III. All poor is king. → Fales (it is definitely false).

So, only conclusion II follow.

Hence, the correct option is (B).

92. The least possible diagram for the given statements is as follows,

Conclusions:

I. Some Facebook is Insta. → False (it is possible but not definite).

II. Some App is WhatsApp. → False (it is definitely false).

III. Some Insta are WhatsApp. → False (it is possible but not definite).

So, none follow.

Hence, the correct option is (E).

93. The least possible diagram for the given statements is as follows,

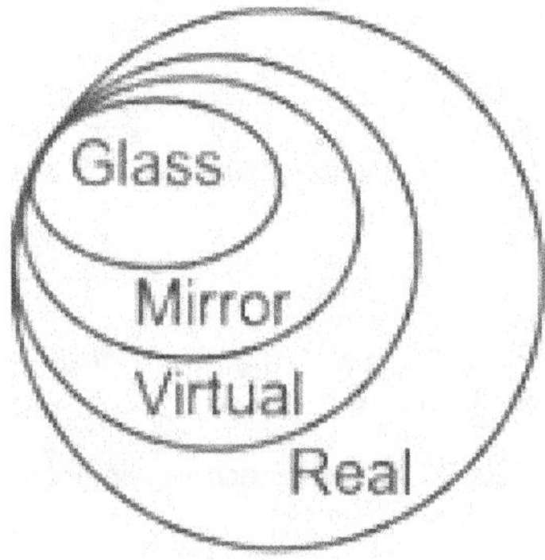

Conclusions:

I. All good can be roads. → True (Possibility is given so it is true).

II. All kings can be royal. → True (Possibility is given so it is true).

III. Some good is roads. → True (it is definitely true).

So, all conclusion are follows.

Hence, the correct option is (D).

94. The least possible diagram for the given statements is as follows,

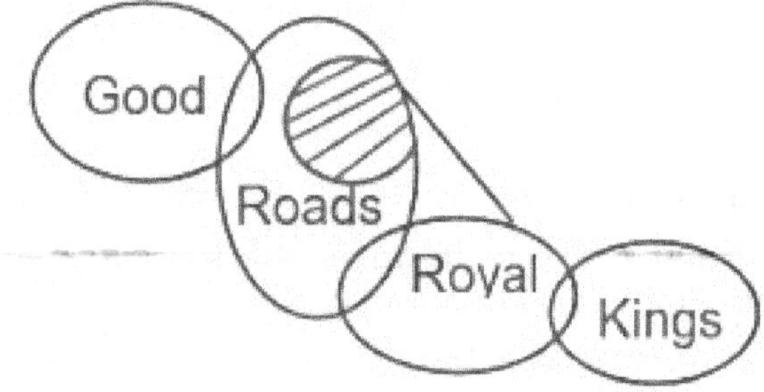

Conclusions:

I. Some real is glass. → True (it is definitely true).

II. All virtual is glass → False (It is possible but not definite).

III. All real is mirror → False (It is possible but not definite).

So, only conclusion I follow.

Hence, the correct option is (A).

95. The least possible diagram for the given statements is as follows,

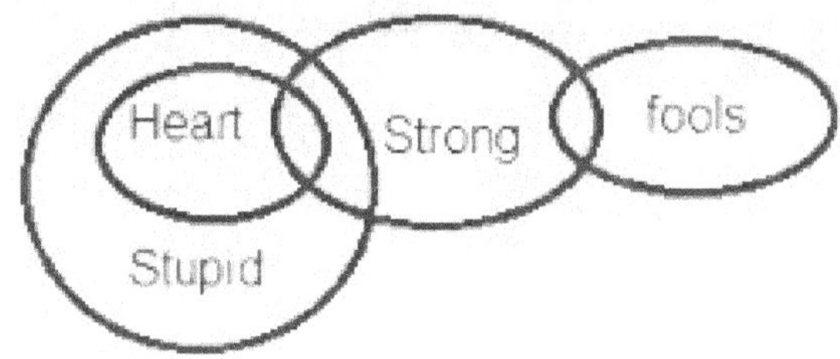

Conclusions:

I. All Strong is stupid. → False (it is possible but not definite).

II. Few fools are stupid. → False (it is possible but not definite).

III. All fools are stupid. → False (it is possible but not definite).

So, None conclusion follows

Hence, the correct option is (E).

Ques (96-100):Person = Priya, Shreya, Julie, Neha, Pallavi, Asha, and Rekha

Brands = Samsung, Nokia, Oppo, Vivo, Apple, Realme, and Redmi

Networks = Airtel, Jio, and Idea

1) Julie is registered on Airtel.

2) Asha uses either Nokia or Vivo.

Person	Brand	Network
Priya		
Shreya		
Julie		Airtel
Neha		
Pallavi		
Asha	Nokia/Vivo	
Rekha		

3) Pallavi is registered on one of the networks only with the person who uses Nokia.

4) Asha is registered on the same network as the Redmi user.

5) Either Priya or Rekha uses Redmi.

(The above three statements imply that Pallavi and Asha are not on the same network. This also means that Asha does not use Nokia. She uses Vivo).

Person	Brand	Network
Priya		
Shreya		
Julie		Airtel
Neha		
Pallavi		
Asha	Vivo	
Rekha		

6) Priya and Julie are registered on the same network along with the Oppo user.

(Implies, Priya, Julie and the Oppo user are registered on Airtel. Also, as not more than three people can be on the same network, implies, Priya does not use Redmi otherwise there would be four people using the same network. Hence, Rekha uses Redmi phone).

7) Shreya is registered on Jio.

(Implies, Shreya does not use Oppo as she is not registered on Airtel. This leaves us with only option i.e. Neha because Pallavi shares the network with only one person. Hence, Neha uses Oppo. Also, now it is clear that Shreya uses Nokia because she is the only person who could form a team with Pallavi. Thus, Pallavi and Shreya use Jio and Asha and Rekha uses Idea because it is the only possibility left).

Person	Brand	Network
Priya		Airtel
Shreya	Nokia	Jio
Julie		Airtel
Neha	Oppo	Airtel
Pallavi		Jio
Asha	Vivo	Idea
Rekha	Redmi	Idea

8) The Apple user is not registered on Airtel.

(Implies, Pallavi must be the Apple user as she is not using Airtel.)

9) Priya does not use Samsung.

(Implies, Priya use Realme and Julie use Samsung as it is the only possibility left).

Person	Brand	Network
Priya	Realme	Airtel
Shreya	Nokia	Jio
Julie	Samsung	Airtel
Neha	Oppo	Airtel
Pallavi	Apple	Jio
Asha	Vivo	Idea
Rekha	Redmi	Idea

96. Clearly, Julie uses Samsung.

Hence, the correct option is (C).

97. Clearly, Neha is registered on Airtel.

Hence, the correct option is (D).

98. Clearly, Asha and Rekha are registered on Idea network.

Hence, the correct option is (D).

99. Clearly, Pallavi uses Apple phone.

Hence, the correct option is (A).

100. Clearly, Neha uses Oppo.

Hence, the correct option is (B).

English Language

Ques (1-5):Direction: Read the passage and answer the questions that follow.

Technically recession is when an economy suffers two consecutive quarters of negative economic performance. It refers to shrinking economic output, sometimes also known as negative economic growth or economic decline.

In short, it implies that the economic activity of a country is declining. This is never a good thing. In South Africa's case, it's particularly serious because the country needs strong economic growth to make inroads into unemployment, which currently stands at more than 27%.

South Africa desperately needs a strong economy for other reasons too. The first is that the living standards of its citizens can't improve without economic growth. The second is that the economy needs to grow for the government to be able to increase revenue to meet its growing social welfare budget.

There are other ways to describe a recession, although the technical definition is one that's generally accepted. Other definitions include "an economy performing below potential" or "an increase in the output gap". As an aside, it's interesting to note that there's a technical definition for a recession, but no agreed definition for a depression.

South Africa's economy showed marginal positive growth for 2016, although it then contracted in the fourth quarter of the year. With a similar contraction in the first quarter of 2017, the country entered a technical recession.

If the economy shows positive growth for the remaining three quarters of this year, South Africa will avert a recession for the calendar year 2017. Economic activity contracted over a wide range of sectors, including construction, manufacturing and transport. Only mining and agriculture made a positive contribution to output growth. All other sectors contracted. This reflects subdued demand throughout the South African economy.

Q.1 In South Africa, the economic activity of which of these sectors declined?

A. Construction   **B.** Agriculture
C. Mining   **D.** All of these
E. Both (B) and (C)

Q.2 Which of these is similar in meaning to 'avert'?

A. Signify   **B.** Focus
C. Distract   **D.** Resemble
E. Prevent

Q.3 Which of these can avoid recession in 2017?

A. Positive growth in the rest of 2017
B. Positive growth in 2016

C. Maximum economic output in 2017
D. Steep decline in unemployment
E. None of these

Q.4 In which year did South Africa enter into recession?

A. 2017   **B.** 2016
C. 2018   **D.** 2020
E. None of these

Q.5 Recession can also be described as-

A. An increase in output gap
B. A country undergoing depression
C. An economy performing less than required
D. All of these
E. Both (A) and (C)

Q.6 Direction: Select the most appropriate word to fill in the blanks.

The distance seems _______ than we thought it would be.
A. Further   **B.** Farther   **C.** Nearest   **D.** Farthest
E. Farer

Ques (7-11):Direction: In the passage given below there are 5 blanks, each followed by a word given in bold. Each blank has four alternative words given in options (A), (B), (C) and (D). You have to tell which word will best suit the respective blank. Mark (E) as your answer if the word given in bold after the blank is your answer i.e No change required.

Introduce a prosecution guided investigation, as is the ___(A) [tradition]across the world. Prosecutors cannot stay ___(B) [abreast]from investigations and only give judgments on the proposed charge sheet. It is often too late to make any changes at all. The prosecution's guidance is necessary in collecting, ___(C) [absolution], sifting, sequencing the evidence and seeking warrant and other legal advice. Separating the prosecution from the police has not helped. The prosecution is unaccountable, and hardly makes any impression on the judiciary. When a case fails, it is routine to criticise the police for every ___(D)[rejoice]and forget the case.

Reviving the nearly___(E)[abysmal]women helpline, women help desk in all police stations, and regular monitoring of all the calls/complaints received and the police's response must be made a criterion for performance evaluation.

Q.7 Which of the following fits in the blank labelled (A)?

A. Liturgy   **B.** Ritual
C. Norm   **D.** Rite
E. No improvement

Q.8 Which of the following fits in the blank labelled (B)?

A. Aloof   **B.** Stray
C. Erratic   **D.** Steady
E. No improvement

Q.9 Which of the following fits in the blank labelled (C)?

A. Conforming   **B.** Collating
C. Persisting   **D.** Acclimating
E. No improvement

Q.10 Which of the following fits in the blank labelled (D)?
A. Alteration   **B.** Lapse
C. Progresssion   **D.** Accustom
E. No improvement

Q.11 Which of the following fits in the blank labelled (E)?
A. Defunct   **B.** Dreary
C. Dismal   **D.** Somber
E. No improvement

Ques (12-13):Direction: In the following sentence, a part of the sentence is underlined. There are some alternatives to the underlined part which may improve the sentence. Choose the correct alternative. In case no improvement is needed to choose option 'No improvement' as your answer.

Q.12 The teachers are the builders of your future.
A. Their   **B.** There   **C.** Her   **D.** Our
E. No error

Q.13 We received the money, that's so kind of you to help us.
A) so kind in
B) so kind by
C) so kind for
A. Only A
B. Only B
C. Only C
D. Both A and B
E. No improvement needed

Ques (14-18):Directions: In the following question, some part of the sentence may have errors. Find out which part of the sentence has an error and select the appropriate option. If a sentence is free from error, select 'No Error'.

Q.14 Once appointed by the President, (A)/the council of ministers (B)/as responsible (C)/to the house. (D)/No error (E)
A. Once appointed by the President
B. The council of ministers
C. As responsible
D. To the house
E. No error

Q.15 The time has come for policy makers (A) / in India to understand the damage (B) / which is caused as a result of (C) / a vast gap in perception and reality. (D)/No error (E)
A. The time has come for policy makers
B. In India to understand the damage
C. Which is caused as a result of
D. A vast gap in perception and reality
E. No error

Q.16 Since two days, (A)/I have not taken (B)/the breakfast (C)/but dinner. (D)/No error (E)
A. Since two days   **B.** I have not taken
C. But dinner   **D.** No error

E. None of these

Q.17 Any coalition (A)/which contains Miss Jayalalitha as a major ally (B)/and Ms. Mamta as a minor partner (C)/do not need outside support. (D)/No error (E)
A. Any coalition
B. Which contains Miss Jayalalitha as a major ally
C. And Ms. Mamta as a minor partner
D. Do not need outside support
E. No error

Q.18 The perception of security (A)/held by the power elites (B)/tend to ignore the basic reality that (C)/contradictions of civil society have grown since nuclear explosion. (D)/No error (E)
A. The perception of security
B. Held by the power elites
C. Tend to ignore the basic reality that
D. Contradictions of civil society have grown since nuclear explosion
E. No error

Ques (19-23):Directions: Given below are four sentences, three of which are jumbled. Pick the option that gives the correct order.

Q.19 A. Organization of American States, NATO, and other international organizations.
B. The United States is a representative democracy with three separate branches of government.
C. It is also a permanent member of the United Nations Security Council.
D. It is a founding member of the United Nations, World Bank, International Monetary Fund.
A. CDBA   **B.** BDAC   **C.** BACD   **D.** BDCA
E. BADA

Q.20 A. Before the 12th century, It is to be identified as Carnatic classical music.
B. And has been evolving since the 12th century.
C. It is a tradition that originated in Vedic ritual chants.
D. Shastriya Sangeet is the classical music of North India.
A. DCBA   **B.** DCAB   **C.** ABCD   **D.** ABDC
E. DCBD

Q.21 A: They work in their fields.
B: Most of the people in India live in villages.
C: A farmer grows crops in his fields.
D: People in villages are mostly farmers.
A. BDAC   **B.** DBCA   **C.** ADCB   **D.** CADB
E. CABD

Q.22 A: They cannot synthesise food.
B: How do they survive and from where do they derive nutrition?
C: There are some plants that do not have chlorophyll.
D: Like humans and animals such plants depend on the food produced by other plants.
A. CABD   **B.** ABCD

C. DBCA   **D.** BCAD
E. None of these

Q.23 A: It is high time for us to put a check on it.
B: It is true.
C: A small family is a happy family.
D: Our country's population has been increasing at a rapid pace.
A. ADCB   **B.** DCBA   **C.** BDCA   **D.** CBDA
E. DACA

Ques (24-28): Fill in the blank with the correct option.

Q.24 Now he _______ about new car as his old one is not working and rates of new modern cars are running down.
A. is thinking   **B.** was thinking
C. thought   **D.** has thinking
E. had thinking

Q.25 I _______ going anywhere for a few days as my exam is there next week and I have to score good marks in it.
A. will not be   **B.** will not been
C. had not   **D.** has not
E. has not been

Q.26 The children were lined up _______ a queue for some food.

[SBI Apprentice, 2021]

A. for   **B.** on   **C.** in   **D.** since
E. because

Q.27 The number of incomplete projects as compared to the completed ones ________ from 10% in 2014 to 18% in 2018.

[SBI Apprentice, 2021]

A. has increased   **B.** have increased
C. increased   **D.** has been increasing
E. had increased

Q.28 It was the poetry that came from the heart of the old man _______ was the master of poetry.
A. who   **B.** whom
C. them   **D.** whose
E. none of these

Ques (29-30):Direction: In the following question, out of the four alternatives, select the alternative which will improve the underlined part of the sentence. In case no improvement is needed, select "No improvement".

Q.29 Some people think acoustic recordings are **superior then** digital ones.
A. Superior than
B. Superior to
C. Superior than that of
D. No Improvement
E. None of these

Q.30 Many a **students was** killed in a drowning accident during a picnic.
A. Student was   **B.** Students were

C. Students have been   **D.** No Improvement
E. None of these

Numerical Ability

Q.31 What should come in place of the question mark '?' in the following number series?
68, 71, 65, 74, 62, ?
A. 72   **B.** 82   **C.** 79   **D.** 83
E. 77

Q.32 What should come in place of the question mark '?' in the following number series?
63, 80, 99, ?, 143, 168
A. 121   **B.** 122   **C.** 124   **D.** 126
E. 120

Q.33 What should come in place of the question mark '?' in the following number series?
12, 15, 24, 39, 60, ?
A. 77   **B.** 81   **C.** 83   **D.** 87
E. 91

Q.34 What should come in place of the question mark '?' in the following number series?
7, 8, 17, 52, ?, 1046
A. 209   **B.** 316   **C.** 329   **D.** 263
E. 291

Q.35 What should come in place of the question mark '?' in the following number series?
16, 160, 281, 381, ?, 526
A. 432   **B.** 442   **C.** 462   **D.** 452
E. 472

Q.36 The speed of a boat along with the current and against the current is 16 km/hr and 12 km/hr respectively. What is the speed of the boat (in km/hr) in still water?
A. 2 km/hr   **B.** 7 km/hr   **C.** 14 km/hr   **D.** 12 km/hr
E. 16 km/hr

Q.37 Four friends rented a house. Kamal used the house for 3 months, Vibhor used it for 5 months, Hari for 8 months, and Kishor for 2 months. Find the rent of the house if Kamal's share of rent is Rs. 3,000.
A. Rs. 13,000   **B.** Rs. 14,000
C. Rs. 15,000   **D.** Rs. 17,000
E. Rs. 18,000

Q.38 A man can travel 50 km in 2.5 hours and 200 km in 4 hours. Find his average speed.
A. 38 km/hr   **B.** 37.5 km/hr
C. 36.4 km/hr   **D.** 38.46 km/hr
E. 34 km/hr

Q.39 The average of 12 numbers is 35. The average of the first nine numbers is 40. The average of the last two numbers is 25. Find the tenth number.
A. 20   **B.** 10   **C.** 12   **D.** 15
E. 8

Q.40 If the difference between C.I. and S.I. for 2 years is Rs. 16 and the rate of interest is 10%, then find the time if the simple interest on the same principal amounts to Rs. 640?

A. 5 years   **B.** 2 years   **C.** 1 years   **D.** 4 years
E. 3 years

Q.41 A mixture of 20 litres of alcohol and water contains 15% of alcohol. How much alcohol should be added to the mixture so that the mixture contains 20% of alcohol.

A. 2.25 litres   **B.** 1.50 litres
C. 1.25 litres   **D.** 2.50 litres
E. 3.50 litres

Q.42 Three years ago, Anuj's age was 3 times the age of Raman and the sum of their ages were 96 years. Find the present age of Raman.

A. 24 years   **B.** 27 years   **C.** 28 years   **D.** 25 years
E. 29 years

Q.43 Mr. Y works as four times as fast as Mr. Z and takes 12 days less than to do a piece of work than Mr. Z. Find out in how many days Mr. Z can complete a work.

A. 12 days   **B.** 14 days   **C.** 16 days   **D.** 17 days
E. 18 days

Q.44 Tap A can fill a tank in 5 hours and Tap B can empty a tank in 8 hours. Both the taps are open together. In how much time tank is filled?

A. $\frac{20}{3}$ hours   **B.** $\frac{1}{3}$ hours   **C.** $\frac{30}{7}$ hours   **D.** $\frac{40}{3}$ hours
E. $\frac{50}{7}$ hours

Q.45 A dice is rolled once. Find the probability of getting a prime even number on a dice.

A. $\frac{1}{3}$ **B.** $\frac{1}{2}$ **C.** $\frac{1}{5}$ **D.** $\frac{1}{6}$
E. $\frac{2}{5}$

Ques (46-50):Direction: In the given question, two equations numbered I and II are given. Solve both the equations and mark the appropriate answer.

Q.46 I. $x^2 - 13x + 30 = 0$
II. $y^2 + 5y + 4 = 0$
A. x > y
B. x < y
C. x ≥ y
D. x ≤ y
E. x = y or relationship between x and y cannot be established

Q.47 I. $x^2 + 17x + 72 = 0$
II. $y^2 + 11y + 30 = 0$
A. x > y
B. x < y
C. x ≥ y
D. x ≤ y
E. x = y or relationship between x and y cannot be established

Q.48 I. $2x^2 - 39x + 189 = 0$

II. $y^2 - 16y + 63 = 0$
A. x > y
B. x < y
C. x ≥ y
D. x ≤ y
E. x = y or relationship between x and y cannot be established

Q.49 I. $x^2 - 27x + 180 = 0$
II. $y^2 - 31y + 240 = 0$
A. x > y
B. x < y
C. x ≥ y
D. x ≤ y
E. x = y or relationship between x and y cannot be established

Q.50 I. $5x^2 + 29x - 42 = 0$
II. $20y^2 - 9y - 18 = 0$
A. x > y
B. x < y
C. x ≥ y
D. x ≤ y
E. x = y or relationship between x and y cannot be established

Ques (51-55):Direction: Study the following table to answer the question that follows.

The table given below shows the marks obtained by five students in five different subjects.

Maximum marks: 100

Name of the students	SUBJECTS				
	Hindi (100)	English (100)	Math (100)	Social Science (100)	Drawings (100)
Kunal	92	91	93	94	95
Shivam	81	82	86	87	76
Pulkit	90	85	85	66	79
Puneet	43	42	69	75	86
Kiran	71	86	71	56	78

Q.51 What are the total marks obtained by Shivam?
A. 314   **B.** 412   **C.** 514   **D.** 654
E. 456

Q.52 What are the average marks obtained by Kunal and Shivam in Hindi?
A. 76.5   **B.** 86.5   **C.** 66.5   **D.** 46.5
E. 56.5

Q.53 What is the overall percentage of Kiran?
A. 42.4%   **B.** 82.4%   **C.** 72.4%   **D.** 62.4%
E. 52.4%

Q.54 How many students have scored the maximum marks in two or more subjects?
A. 1   **B.** 2   **C.** 3   **D.** 4
E. 5

Q.55 Marks obtained by Kunal in Drawings is what percent marks obtained by Puneet in the same subject?
A. 124.56%   **B.** 110.46%   **C.** 117.78%   **D.** 145.67%
E. 189.45%

Q.56 Find the area of the circle whose radius is equal to the radius of a cylinder having height 21 cm and volume 12936 cm³.
A. 566 cm²   **B.** 415 cm²   **C.** 814 cm²   **D.** 616 cm²
E. 516 cm²

Ques (57-65):Direction: What approximate value should come in the place of the question mark '?' in the following question?

Q.57
$$(345.97 + 129.88 - 45.03) + (34.87 \div 6.96 \times 2.99) =? - \sqrt{1521}$$

[SBI Clerk, 2021]

A. 503   **B.** 485
C. 602   **D.** 354
E. None of these

Q.58 $(17.76)^2 + (20.99)^2 = (2)^7 +?$
A. 581   **B.** 650   **C.** 532   **D.** 648
E. 637

Q.59 $(23.42 + 17.43) \div 2 \times 4 - 48.25 + 643.86 =?$
A. 521   **B.** 634   **C.** 598   **D.** 676
E. 741

Q.60 $? \%$ of $599.97 + 16.03 \times 18.98 = (20.99)^2 - 5.03$
A. 21   **B.** 22   **C.** 23   **D.** 24
E. 25

Q.61 12.5% of $799 + 25\%$ of $399 - 149.89 =?$
A. 60   **B.** 50
C. 70   **D.** 80
E. None of these

Q.62 45% of $300 - (?)^2 = 56\%$ of $75 - 10\%$ of 510
A. 18   **B.** 14   **C.** 16   **D.** 12
E. 19

Q.63 19.99% of $1224.98 - \sqrt{(1295.93)} \times 3.99 - 87.69 =?$
A. 12   **B.** 13   **C.** 15   **D.** 23
E. 33

Q.64 $32.99 \times 3.98 + (5.01)^2 - 75.02 \div 14.99 +? = 159.99$
A. 2   **B.** 3   **C.** 4   **D.** 6
E. 8

Q.65 $15 \times 252 \div 60 + 170 =? +63$
A. 438   **B.** 170   **C.** 300   **D.** 414

E. 180

Reasoning Ability

Ques (66-68):Direction: These questions are based on the following information.

There are seven family members – P, Q, R, S, T, U, and V. R is the maternal grandmother of V. Q is the husband of R. S is the brother-in-law of Q. P is the nephew of S. T is the mother of V. U is the son-in-law of Q. There are four males in the family.

Q.66 How is V related to P?
A. Daughter
B. Nephew
C. Niece
D. Son
E. Cannot be determined

Q.67 How is P related to Q?
A. Daughter   **B.** Son
C. Nephew   **D.** Son-in-law
E. None of these

Q.68 Which of the following T's father?
A. S   **B.** R   **C.** Q   **D.** P
E. U

Ques (69-72):Direction: Read the following information carefully and answer the questions that follow:

Pratyush, Zeenat, Rakesh, Esha, Lalit and Girish are six actors. Zeenat have done films less than only Rakesh. Girish have done five films more than Pratyush. Pratyush have done two films less than Esha. Lalit have done films more than Girish.The least films done by these actors is 50 films.

Q.69 How many actors have done films more than Girish?
A. Two   **B.** Four   **C.** One   **D.** Three
E. Five

Q.70 Who have done third highest number of films?
A. Lalit   **B.** Zeenat   **C.** Rakesh   **D.** Esha
E. Pratyush

Q.71 What may be the number of films done by Lalit?
A. 55   **B.** 52   **C.** 50   **D.** 58
E. 49

Q.72 Who have done the second least number of films?
A. Girish   **B.** Esha   **C.** Pratyush   **D.** Lalit
E. Zeenat

Ques (73-76):Direction: In the following question assuming the given statements to be True, find which of the conclusion among the given conclusion(s) is/are definitely True and then give your answers accordingly.

Q.73 Statements: M ≥ T; M < P; S > T
Conclusions:
I. S = M
II. T < P
III. P > S

A. Only I is true   **B.** I, II and III are True
C. Only II is True   **D.** II and III are True
E. None is true

Q.74 Statements:

X > C ≥ V > Y; U = V < T ≤ H; T < B

Conclusions:

I. Y < X

II. X ≥ B

III. V < B

A. None
B. Only conclusion I follows
C. None of these
D. Both conclusion I and III follow
E. Only conclusion III follows

Q.75 Statements:

P ≤ Q > R = S; S < T; T = P > U; V < U

Conclusions:

I. Q = P

II. Q > P

III. P < V

A. Only III is True
B. Both I and II are True
C. Only II is True
D. Only I is True
E. Either I or II is True

Q.76 Statements: A > P ≥ K; Q > M > T; P > T

Conclusions:

I. T < K

II. K > A

III. A > K

A. Only I is true
B. Only II is true
C. Only I and II are true
D. Only II and III are true
E. Only III is true

Q.77 The distance between N and P is 50 m and that between Q and R is 40 m. Q is to the west of R, which is to the east of N at a distance of 70 m. P is to the west or northwest or north of Q.

If Q is to the south of P, what is the distance between P and Q?

A. 10m   **B.** 50m   **C.** 15m   **D.** 30m
E. 40m

Ques (78-82):Direction: Read the information given below and answer the question that follows.

Seven persons Abrahim, Akshay, Amish, Anush, Arob, Arak and Atul live on different floors of 7-storey building. Each of them bought T-shirts of different brands viz J&J, Lee Cooper, Levis, Polo, Roadster, UCB and Wrogn. The lowermost is numbered as 1 and the topmost as 7.

Neither Abrahim nor Arob bought UCB t-shirt. One person lives between Amish and Atul. Atul bought Levis T-shirt and lives just below the one, who bought Wrogn T-shirt. Abrahim lives two floors above Amish's floor and both live on prime numbered floor. Three persons live between the persons, who bought J&J and Polo T-shirt. Anush bought Roadster T-shirt. Arob lives just above Arak.

Q.78 How many persons live above Amish's floor?
A. Four   **B.** Two   **C.** Three   **D.** Five
E. Six

Q.79 Which of the following combination is definitely true?
A.   3 – UCB – Amish
B.   7 – J&J – Arob
C.   5 – Roadster – Anush
D.   2 – Wrogn – Akshay
E.   6 – Abrahim – Polo

Q.80 How many persons live between Arob and the one, who bought Levis T-shirt?
A. Five   **B.** Three   **C.** Four   **D.** Two
E. One

Q.81 ______ lives just above the one, who bought Roadster T-Shirt.
A. Arak   **B.** Akshay   **C.** Anush   **D.** Abrahim
E. Atul

Q.82 Who lives on the topmost floor?
A. Arak   **B.** Arob   **C.** Amish   **D.** Anush
E. Abrahim

Q.83 How many such pairs of letters are there in the word "HURRICANE" that has as many letters between them in the word as in the alphabet?
A. Two   **B.** Three   **C.** One   **D.** Six
E. Four

Ques (84-86):Direction: Study the following information carefully and answer the given questions.

In a certain language 'aa bb ca' means 'she is poem', 'bb aa ti ki' means 'poem is an engineer', 'si bb za pi' means 'her hobby is dancing', 'ca bb za ui' means 'she is still dancing'.

Q.84 Code 'ti' is for which word in the given language?
A. An   **B.** Engineer
C. Either (A) or (B)   **D.** Is
E. Her

Q.85 In a certain language 'my hobby is singing' is coded as 'pp si bb uz', then what would be the code for 'hobby'?
A. uz
B. pi
C. bb
D. si
E. Can not be determined

Q.86 Which of the following means 'poem' in that language?
A. bb   **B.** ca   **C.** aa   **D.** za
E. ui

Ques (87-91):Direction: Read the following information carefully and answer the questions that follow:

Nine persons are sitting in a row. Some of them are facing north while some are facing south. P sits at the 2nd position from one of the ends. R sits 3rd to the right of P. Only 2 persons sit between R and S. U sits 2ndto the right of S. Immediate neighbours of S are facing the opposite direction to that of S. Immediate neighbours of U faces the opposite direction. T sits second to the right of U. W and T faces the opposite direction. The ones sitting at the ends of row faces the opposite direction. Q is not a neighbour of U and P. W sits at one of the extreme ends. V sits adjacent to T. X does not face south.

Q.87 Who is sitting at the left end of the row?

[IDBI Bank Assistant Manager, 2021]

A. X **B.** P
C. Q **D.** W
E. None of these

Q.88 How many persons are sitting between P and U?

[IDBI Bank Assistant Manager, 2021]

A. 3 **B.** 2
C. 4 **D.** 1
E. None of these

Q.89 Who is sitting second to the right of V?

[IDBI Bank Assistant Manager, 2021]

A. W
B. T
C. R
D. None of these
E. Cannot be determined

Q.90 Who is sitting in the middle of the row?

[IDBI Bank Assistant Manager, 2021]

A. T **B.** R **C.** U **D.** V
E. P

Q.91 Four of the following five belong to a group following a certain pattern. Who does not belong to the group?

[IDBI Bank Assistant Manager, 2021]

A. PT **B.** TU **C.** UT **D.** US
E. RV

Ques (92-95):Direction: In the question below are given two statements followed by two conclusions numbered I and II. You have to take the given statements to be true even if they seem to be at variance with commonly known facts. Read all the conclusions and then decide which of the given conclusions logically follows from the given statements disregarding commonly known facts.

Q.92 Statements:
I. No car is bus.
II. No bus is truck.

Conclusions:
I. Some bus is car.
II. No truck is car.
A. Only I follow
B. Only II follow
C. Both I and II follows
D. Either I or II follow
E. None follow

Q.93 Statement:
Some Table is Chair.
All Chair are Furniture.
Conclusion:
I. Some Table is Furniture.
II. All furniture is Table.
A. Only I follow
B. Only II follow
C. Both I and II follow
D. Either I or II follow
E. Neither I nor II follow

Q.94 Statements:
I. Some caps are hat.
II. No hat is a shirt.
Conclusions:
I. Some shirts are not cap.
II. All shirts being cap is a possibility.
A. Only I follow
B. Only II follow
C. Both I and II follows
D. Either I or II follow
E. None follow

Q.95 Statements:
Maximum roses are gmail.
Minimum biology are roses.
Conclusions:
I. 20% of biology are gmail.
II. No gmail is biology.
A. Either I or II follows
B. Only II follows
C. None follows
D. Both I and II follows
E. Only I follows

Ques (96-100):Direction: Study the following information carefully to answer the given questions:

Arpita, Amit, Ankit, Amita, Amitesh, Aman, Amina and Ankita are eight students in a class. They are sitting together around a circular table facing towards the centre in the class. Amina sits third to the right of Aman. Ankita sits second to the left of Arpita. Amina and Aman are not neighbours of Ankita. Amit sits third to the right of Ankit. Amina is not an immediate neighbour of Ankita. Ankita and Ankit are not immediate neighbours of Amita.

Q.96 Who is sitting between Aman and Amita?
A. Amitesh **B.** Amit **C.** Ankita **D.** Ankit

E. Arpita

Q.97 Who is sit third to the left of Arpita?

A. Amitesh　　　**B.** Amit　　　**C.** Amita　　　**D.** Ankit

E. Amina

Q.98 How many persons are sitting between Ankit and Amina starting from Ankit in an anticlockwise direction?

A. One　　　　　　　**B.** Two

C. Three　　　　　　**D.** Four

E. More than four

Q.99 What is the position of Ankit with respect to Amita?

A. Immediate right　　　**B.** Immediate left

C. Second to the left　　**D.** Third to the right

E. Fourth to the left

Q.100 Four of the following five are alike in a certain way based on their sitting positions in the given arrangement and so form a group. Which does not belong to that group?

A. Ankit - Amit　　　　**B.** Amina - Ankit

C. Arpita - Amita　　　**D.** Ankita - Amina

E. Aman - Amina

// Smart Answer Sheet //

Correct Percentage of students who answered correctly.   **Skipped** Percentage of students who skipped.

Q.	Ans.	Correct / Skipped	Q.	Ans.	Correct / Skipped	Q.	Ans.	Correct / Skipped	Q.	Ans.	Correct / Skipped	Q.	Ans.	Correct / Skipped
1	A	7.39 % / 83.62 %	17	D	0.64 % / 98.5 %	33	D	9.74 % / 88.44 %	49	D	4.18 % / 88.97 %	65	B	0.54 % / 99.25 %
2	E	4.6 % / 85.12 %	18	C	0.43 % / 98.5 %	34	A	6.85 % / 88.65 %	50	E	3.32 % / 89.08 %	66	C	3.32 % / 89.19 %
3	A	6.75 % / 85.22 %	19	B	0.32 % / 98.5 %	35	C	4.93 % / 88.75 %	51	B	8.03 % / 89.08 %	67	B	4.28 % / 89.3 %
4	A	10.17 % / 85.23 %	20	A	0.64 % / 98.5 %	36	C	4.5 % / 88.43 %	52	B	7.82 % / 89.72 %	68	C	5.57 % / 89.18 %
5	E	4.5 % / 85.22 %	21	A	1.28 % / 98.51 %	37	E	6.32 % / 88.54 %	53	C	6.32 % / 89.83 %	69	D	4.18 % / 89.29 %
6	B	4.93 % / 85.33 %	22	A	1.07 % / 98.5 %	38	D	3.21 % / 88.55 %	54	A	3.43 % / 89.93 %	70	A	4.39 % / 89.61 %
7	C	4.5 % / 85.33 %	23	D	0.32 % / 98.5 %	39	B	6.1 % / 88.55 %	55	B	3.75 % / 90.25 %	71	D	3.64 % / 89.4 %
8	A	3.85 % / 85.44 %	24	A	1.28 % / 98.51 %	40	D	2.36 % / 88.54 %	56	D	1.07 % / 93.04 %	72	B	4.18 % / 89.29 %
9	B	1.93 % / 85.44 %	25	A	0.96 % / 98.5 %	41	C	3.0 % / 88.43 %	57	B	0.75 % / 98.82 %	73	C	7.92 % / 89.3 %
10	B	4.07 % / 85.44 %	26	C	1.5 % / 98.5 %	42	B	3.64 % / 88.54 %	58	E	0.86 % / 98.82 %	74	D	7.17 % / 89.3 %
11	A	2.78 % / 85.55 %	27	C	0.11 % / 98.5 %	43	C	2.89 % / 88.54 %	59	D	0.75 % / 98.82 %	75	E	5.35 % / 89.4 %
12	D	8.99 % / 85.76 %	28	A	1.39 % / 98.5 %	44	D	4.07 % / 88.44 %	60	B	0.64 % / 98.82 %	76	E	7.49 % / 89.3 %
13	E	6.53 % / 85.87 %	29	B	0.21 % / 98.51 %	45	D	2.78 % / 88.44 %	61	B	0.86 % / 98.93 %	77	E	1.61 % / 89.29 %
14	C	1.28 % / 98.51 %	30	A	0 % / 100 %	46	A	6.85 % / 88.44 %	62	D	0.86 % / 98.93 %	78	A	1.18 % / 89.4 %
15	C	0.43 % / 98.5 %	31	E	10.71 % / 88.43 %	47	B	6.85 % / 88.65 %	63	B	0.64 % / 98.93 %	79	D	1.07 % / 89.94 %
16	C	0.96 % / 98.5 %	32	E	8.78 % / 88.33 %	48	C	2.68 % / 88.75 %	64	E	0.64 % / 99.25 %	80	A	1.18 % / 90.25 %

Q.	Ans.	Correct		Q.	Ans.	Correct		Q.	Ans.	Correct		Q.	Ans.	Correct		Q.	Ans.	Correct
		Skipped				Skipped				Skipped				Skipped				Skipped
81	D	1.5 %		85	D	3.21 %		89	E	0.96 %		93	A	6.0 %		97	A	1.71 %
		89.83 %				90.47 %				91.76 %				91.22 %				93.79 %
82	B	1.82 %		86	C	5.25 %		90	B	1.39 %		94	B	2.78 %		98	D	1.18 %
		89.83 %				90.47 %				91.65 %				91.44 %				94.11 %
83	B	2.68 %		87	D	1.18 %		91	D	0.32 %		95	A	2.46 %		99	E	1.82 %
		89.72 %				90.36 %				91.33 %				91.97 %				94.43 %
84	C	6.1 %		88	A	1.5 %		92	E	3.64 %		96	B	2.03 %		100	D	1.18 %
		89.83 %				91.22 %				91.11 %				92.19 %				94.54 %

//Hints and Solutions//

1. The explanation of the given question is:

The following is stated in the passage: "Economic activity contracted over a wide range of sectors, including construction, manufacturing, and transport. Only mining and agriculture made a positive contribution to output growth."

Hence, the correct option is (A).

2. The explanation of the given question is:

Avert means prevent or ward off (an undesirable occurrence).

Let's look at the meanings of the given options-

Signify means be an indication of.

Focus means the center of interest or activity.

Distract means prevent (someone) from concentrating on something.

Resemble means have a similar appearance to or qualities in common with (someone or something); look or seem like.

Prevent means keep (something) from happening.

Clearly, 'prevent' is the correct word.

Hence, the correct option is (E).

3. The explanation of the given question is:

The following is stated in the passage: "If the economy shows positive growth for the remaining three quarters of this year, South Africa will avert a recession for the calendar year 2017".

Clearly, option (A) is the most appropriate.

Hence, the correct option is (A).

4. The explanation of the given question is:

The following is stated in the passage: "South Africa's economy showed marginal positive growth for 2016, although it then contracted in the fourth quarter of the year. With similar contraction in the first quarter of 2017, the country entered a technical recession".

Clearly, in 2017 the country entered into recession.

Hence, the correct option is (A).

5. The explanation of the given question is:

The following is stated in the passage: "There are other ways to describe a recession, although the technical definition is one that's generally accepted. Other definitions include "an economy performing below potential" or "an increase in the output gap".

Both options (B) and (C) can be described as a recession.

Hence, the correct option is (E).

6. In this sentence, a comparison is made between actual distance and the estimated distance, that's why the comparative degree is used.

Both 'further' and 'farther' are comparative adjectives but American English speakers favour 'farther' for physical distances (Eg - Let's go to the park that is farther away) and 'further' for figurative distances (Eg - What you're saying couldn't be further away from the truth).

So, 'Farther' is the correct answer.

Other options are rejected because :

'Nearest' and 'farthest' cannot be used because they are in the superlative degree.

'Farer' is a person/passenger who pays to travel i.e. traveler.

Hence, the correct option is (B).

7. The sentence conveys the rule followed around the world. So, the required word must mean the same as standard or rule.

Liturgy means a form according to which public religious worship, especially Christian worship, is conducted. There is no mention of form.

Ritual means a religious or other solemn ceremony or act. There is no indication of any religious act.

Norm means something that is usual, typical, or standard. This is correct as it fulfils the requirement.

Rite means relating to or done as a religious or solemn rite. It is inappropriate with respect to the context.

Tradition means the transmission of customs or beliefs from generation to generation or the fact of being passed on in this way. It is unsuitable for the passage.

Hence, the correct option is (C).

8. The sentence wants to convey that it is not possible for the prosecutors to stay away from the investigation. So, the required word must mean the same as uninvolved.

Aloof means conspicuously uninvolved. This is correct as it fulfils the requirement.

Stray means move away aimlessly from a group or from the right course or place. Prosecutors do not move away in groups.

Erratic means not even or regular in pattern or movement; unpredictable. Prosecutors cannot be irregular.

Steady means firmly fixed, supported, or balanced. Prosecutors are not firmly fixed.

Abreast means alongside or level with something. This is inappropriate with respect to the context.

Hence, the correct option is (A).

9. The required word must mean combining..

Conforming means to comply with rules, standards, or laws. The sentence talks about the events in which the prosecution's guidance is necessary. So, this word is inappropriate.

Collating means to collect and combine (texts, information, or data). This is correct as it fulfils the requirement.

Persisting means continue in an opinion or course of action in spite of difficulty or opposition. The prosecution cannot persist.

Acclimating means adjusting. There is no need for adjusting by the prosecution.

Absolution means formal release from guilt, obligation, or punishment. This word is unsuitable.

Hence, the correct option is (B).

10. The sentence conveys how the police are criticized for every failure in the case. So, the required word must mean the same as failure.

Alteration means the process of changing. The police cannot change the case.

Lapse means a brief or temporary failure of concentration, memory, or judgement. This is correct as it fulfils the requirement.

Progression means the process of developing or moving gradually towards a more advanced state. This is the opposite of our requirement.

Accustom means customary; usual. This is inappropriate with respect to the context.

Rejoice means feel or show great joy or delight. There is no joy in the case.

Hence, the correct option is (B).

11. The presence of the word reviving indicates that the required word must mean the same as not functioning.

Defunct means no longer existing or functioning. This is correct as it fulfils the requirement.

Dreary means depressingly dull and bleak or repetitive. This is inappropriate with respect to the context.

Dismal means causing a mood of gloom or depression. The helpline cannot be gloomy.

Sombre means having or conveying a feeling of deep seriousness and sadness. The helpline cannot convey deep sadness.

Abysmal means extremely bad; appalling. The helpline cannot be bad.

Hence, the correct option is (A).

12. 'your' is the wrong solution because it's not about one person's future. Our future also so 'our' is the correct solution. 'their', 'her' and 'there' all are wrong.

So, the correct solution is, The teachers are the builders of our future.

Hence, the correct option is (D).

13. No improvement needed is correct.

The phrase 'that's so kind of you' is appreciating the person for something he/she has done. Prepositions 'in', 'by' and 'for' do not fit in with the object 'you' Thus, are incorrect.

Hence, the correct option is (E).

14. Change 'are' to 'is' because the subject 'council of ministers' is considered as one unit.

Hence, the correct option is (C).

15. Change 'is' to 'has been' to correct the error of tense to indicate that the damage has been done in present perfect.

Hence, the correct option is (C).

16. Delete 'the' before breakfast. Because before 'meal' article is not used except for a particular purpose.

Hence, the correct option is (C).

17. Change 'do not' to 'does not' to correct the error in subject-verb agreement. Because the subject is 'Any coalition' (singular).

Hence, the correct option is (D).

18. Change 'tend' to 'tends' to correct the error of subject verb agreement. Because the subject 'the perception of security' is expressing one or singular idea.

Hence, the correct option is (C).

19. The sentence 'B' is independent of any other sentence as it is giving general information about the noun 'The United States'. Hence the sentence 'A' is the first part.

The pronoun 'It' mentioned in the sentence 'C' and 'D' refers back to the noun 'The United States, both 'C' and 'D' could be the second part, but the adverb 'also' indicates that something is mentioned before the sentence 'C'. so 'D' is the second part.

The sentence 'A' completes the sentence 'D'. Hence, 'A' follows 'D'.

The sentence 'C' is the concluding paragraph. Hence, 'C' is the last part.

Hence, the correct option is (B).

20. The paragraph is about 'North Indian classical Music'.

The sentence 'D' is independent of any other sentence as it is giving general information about the noun "Shastriya Sangeet". Hence, the sentence 'D' is the first part.

The pronoun 'It' mentioned in the sentence 'C' refers back to the noun 'Shastriya Sangeet' mentioned in the sentence 'D'. Hence, D follows C.

The sentence 'B' haven't any subject, The pronoun 'It' mentioned in the sentence 'C' act as the subject for the sentence 'B'. Hence, B is the third part.

The sentence 'A' is the concluding sentence. Hence, it is the last part.

Hence, the correct option is (A).

21. Sentence B comes first as it states a general fact and is independent of any other statement.

Sentence D follows B as it tells about the occupation of people living in villages.

Sentence A follows D as it begins with the pronoun 'they' that refers to 'farmers' mentioned in D.

Sentence C follows A as it tells what a farmer does in his fields.

Thus, the sequence becomes:

- B: Most of the people in India live in villages.
- D: People in villages are mostly farmers.
- A: They work in their fields.
- C: A farmer grows crops in his fields.

Hence, the correct option is (A).

22. Sentence C comes first as it introduces the main concern of the paragraph, i.e., plants that don't have chlorophyll.

Sentence A follows C as it tells that the plants that don't have chlorophyll can't synthesise food.

Sentence B follows A as it asks that how and from where these plants get their nutrition.

Sentence D follows B as it answers the question asked in B.

Thus, the sequence becomes:

- C: There are some plants that do not have chlorophyll.
- A: They cannot synthesise food.
- B: How do they survive, and from where do they derive nutrition?
- D: Like humans and animals, such plants depend on the food produced by other plants.

Hence, the correct option is (A).

23. Sentence C comes first as it is independent of any other sentence and states a famous saying.

Sentence B follows C as it tells that the quote mentioned in C is true.

Sentence D follows B as it states that the population of our country is increasing at a fast pace.

Sentence A follows D as it mentions that we need to put a check on our ever-increasing population.

Thus, the sequence becomes:

- C: A small family is a happy family.
- B: It is true.
- D: Our country's population has been increasing at a rapid pace.
- A: It is high time for us to put a check on it.

Hence, the correct option is (D).

24. The keyword 'Now' indicates that "an activity in progress at the present time--probably started in the past and will continue".

It indicates that the sentence is in present continuous tense.

The sentence structure should be: subject + is/are/am+ v+ing+ object.

Therefore, 'is thinking' is the most appropriate option for the given blank.

Hence, the correct option is (A).

25. The future is continuous tense to say that an action is going on at some time in the future.

Example: At five o'clock, I will be meeting with the management about my raise.

The general structure of future continuous tense is- will/shall + be + V1+ ing.

In the above sentence, the subject 'I' will not attend the function in the future.

Since the sentence is in a negative sense, we will put 'not' after 'will'.

Hence, the correct option is (A).

26. In the given blank, we need to use 'in'

'line up' is a noun phrase that means 'a series of things that have been gathered together to be part of a particular event.' After this ask a question where they line up hence, you need to reply with an adverbial phrase.

Hence, to make an adverbial phrase you need to use a preposition so 'since and because' are incorrect. According to the context, the preposition 'in' is correct.

Hence, the correct option is (C).

27. In the given blank, we need to use 'increased' to complete the sentence.

In the given sentence, the time reference is given in the past i.e. 'in 2014 and in 2018' hence we need to use the past indefinite tense instead of any perfect tense.

Let's see an example:

He was very popular in high school.

Hence, the correct option is (C).

28. Here we have to use subjective case of pronoun, expect 'who' all others are possessive and objective case of pronouns.

Pronoun - a pronoun is a word that can take the place of a noun.

Example - he, she, it, they, etc.

From the given meaning we can conclude that the correct answer is who.

Hence, the correct option is (A).

29. The use of 'then' is wrong in the given sentence.

Usually 'than' is used in the comparative degree, but with words like superior, inferior, senior, junior, prior, anterior, posterior and prefer 'to' is used.

Examples,

- He is a junior to me.
- Modern music is often considered inferior to that of the past.
- According to the rule and examples that are given above, 'superior to' will be used in the underlined part of the sentence.

Hence, the correct option is (B).

30. The use of a plural subject 'students' is wrong in the given sentence.

'Many a' is always followed by a singular subject and a singular verb.

- **Examples,**
- Many a man has fallen victim to this deadly virus.
- Many a student has passed this exam.
- According to the rule and examples that are given above, 'student was' will be used in the underlined part of the sentence.

Hence, the correct option is (A).

31. The series follows the following pattern:

68 + 3 = 71

71 - 6 = 65

65 + 9 = 74

74 - 12 = 62

62 + 15 = 77

Hence, the correct option is (E).

32. The series follows the following pattern:

$8^2 - 1 = 63$

$9^2 - 1 = 80$

$10^2 - 1 = 99$

$11^2 - 1 = 120$

$12^2 - 1 = 143$

$13^2 - 1 = 168$

Hence, the correct option is (E).

33. The series follows the following pattern:

12 + 3 = 15

15 + 9 = 24

24 + 15 = 39

39 + 21 = 60

60 + 27 = 87

Hence, the correct option is (D).

34. The series follows the following pattern:

7 × 1 + 1 = 8

8 × 2 + 1 = 17

17 × 3 + 1 = 52

52 × 4 + 1 = 209

209 × 5 + 1 = 1046

Hence, the correct option is (A).

35. The series follows the following pattern:

16 + 144 = 160

160 + 121 = 281

281 + 100 = 381

381 + 81 = 462

462 + 64 = 526

Hence, the correct option is (C).

36. Let the speed of the boat in still water be u and the speed of current be v.

Speed of boat along the stream = u + v = 16 km/hr

Speed of boat against the stream = u - v = 12 km/hr

Speed of boat in still water = $\frac{1}{2} \times [(u + v) + (u - v)] = \frac{1}{2} \times 28$

∴ Speed of boat in still water = 14 km/hr

Hence, the correct option is (C).

37. Given:

Kamal used a house for 3 months.

Vibhor used a house for 5 months.

Hari and Kishor used a house for 2 months.

Share of Kamal's rent = Rs. 3,000

Ratio of share of Kamal, Vibhor, Hari and Kishor = 3 : 5 : 8 : 2

Let the rent of the house is Rs. x.

According to question:

$\Rightarrow \frac{3x}{18} = 3000$

$\Rightarrow x = \frac{(3000 \times 18)}{3}$

$\Rightarrow x = 18,000$

∴ Rent is Rs.18,000.

Hence, the correct option is (E).

38. Given: Time taken to travel 50 km = 2.5 hours

Time taken to travel 200 km = 4 hours

Average speed = $\frac{Total\ distance}{total\ time} = \frac{250}{6.5}$ km/hr

Average speed = 38.46 km/hr

∴ The average speed is 38.46 km/hr.

Hence, the correct option is (D).

39. Given:

Average of 12 numbers = 35

Average of first nine numbers = 40

Average of last two numbers = 25

Formula: Average = $\dfrac{sum\ of\ all\ item}{number\ of\ item}$

Sum of 12 numbers = (35 × 12) = 420

⇒ Sum of 9 numbers = (40 × 9) = 360

⇒ Sum of last two numbers = (25 × 2) = 50

∴ Value of 10th number = 420 − 360 − 50 = 10

Hence, the correct option is (B).

40. Let the principle is P.

For 2 years, S.I. - C.I. = Rs. 16

Rate of Interest = 10%

Simple interest = $\dfrac{(P \times R \times T)}{100}$

Difference between the compound interest and simple interest

on a certain sum for 2 years = P × $\left(\dfrac{R}{100}\right)^2$

⇒ P × $\dfrac{10^2}{100^2}$ = 16

⇒ P = Rs. 1600

Simple interest = $\dfrac{(P \times R \times T)}{100}$

⇒ 640 = $\dfrac{(1600 \times 10 \times T)}{100}$

⇒ T = 4 years

Hence, the correct option is (D).

41. Given:

Quantity of mixture = 20 litres

Quantity of alcohol in mixture = 15%

Let x litres of alcohol is added to mixture.

Quantity of alcohol in 20 litres = 15% of 20

$= 20 \times \dfrac{15}{100} = 3$ litres

As per question,

⇒ $\dfrac{(3+x)}{(20+x)} = \dfrac{20}{100}$

⇒ 5(3 + x) = 20 + x

⇒ 4x = 5

⇒ x = 1.25 litres

∴ 1.25 litres of alcohol is added in the mixture to make 20% alcohol in mixture.

Hence, the correct option is (C).

42. Given:

Anuj's age = 3(Raman's age)

Anuj's age + Raman age = 96

Let the Raman's age three years ago was x years.

Anuj's age = 3x

⇒ 3x + x = 96

⇒ x = 24

∴ Present age of Raman = 24 + 3 = 27 years

Hence, the correct option is (B).

43. Given:

Mr. Y efficiency = 4(Mr. Z efficiency)

Let the Mr. Z completes a work in x days.

Then, Y completes in $\left(\dfrac{x}{4}\right)$ days

According to question:

⇒ x − $\left(\dfrac{x}{4}\right)$ = 12

⇒ $\dfrac{3x}{4}$ = 12

⇒ x = 16 days

∴ Z completes a work in 16 days.

Hence, the correct option is (C).

44. Given:

Tap A filled tank = 5 hours

Tap B empty a tank = 8 hours

Tap A filled a tank in 1 hour = $\left(\dfrac{1}{5}\right)$

Tap B empty a tank in 1 hour = $\left(\dfrac{1}{8}\right)$

Time required to filled a tank = $\left(\dfrac{1}{5}\right) - \left(\dfrac{1}{8}\right)$

$= \dfrac{3}{40} = \dfrac{40}{3}$ hours

∴ Time required to fill a tank is $\dfrac{40}{3}$ hours.

Hence, the correct option is (D).

45. Given:

A dice is rolled once

Probability = $\dfrac{(Number\ of\ favorable\ outcomes)}{(Total\ number\ of\ outcomes)}$

Total number of outcomes = 1, 2, 3, 4, 5 and 6.

The only prime and even number is 2.

∴, Required Probability = $\dfrac{1}{6}$

Hence, the correct option is (D).

46. I. $x^2 - 13x + 30 = 0$

$\Rightarrow x^2 - 3x - 10x + 30 = 0$

$\Rightarrow (x - 3)(x - 10) = 0$

$\Rightarrow x = 3, 10$

II. $y^2 + 5y + 4 = 0$

$\Rightarrow y^2 + y + 4y + 4 = 0$

$\Rightarrow (y + 4)(y + 1) = 0$

$\Rightarrow y = -4, -1$

Value of x	Value of y	Relation
3	−4	x > y
3	−1	x > y
10	−4	x > y
10	−1	x > y

So, x > y

Hence, the correct option is (A).

47. I. $x^2 + 17x + 72 = 0$

$\Rightarrow x^2 + 9x + 8x + 72 = 0$

$\Rightarrow (x + 8)(x + 9) = 0$

$\Rightarrow x = -8, -9$

II. $y^2 + 11y + 30 = 0$

$\Rightarrow y^2 + 5y + 6y + 30 = 0$

$\Rightarrow (y + 5)(y + 6) = 0$

$\Rightarrow y = -5, -6$

Value of x	Value of y	Relation
−8	−5	x < y
−8	−6	x < y
−9	−5	x < y
−9	−6	x < y

So x < y

Hence, the correct option is (B).

48. I. $2x^2 - 39x + 189 = 0$

$\Rightarrow 2x^2 - 18x - 21x + 189 = 0$

$\Rightarrow 2x(x - 9) - 21(x - 9) = 0$

$\Rightarrow (x - 9)(2x - 21) = 0$

$\Rightarrow x = 9, \dfrac{21}{2}$

II. $y^2 - 16y + 63 = 0$

$\Rightarrow y^2 - 7y - 9y + 63 = 0$

$\Rightarrow y(y - 7) - 9(y - 7) = 0$

$\Rightarrow (y - 7)(y - 9) = 0$

$\Rightarrow y = 7, 9$

Value of x	Value of y	Relation
9	7	x > y
9	9	x = y
$\dfrac{21}{2}$	7	x > y
$\dfrac{21}{2}$	9	x > y

$\therefore x \geq y$

Hence, the correct option is (C).

49. I. $x^2 - 27x + 180 = 0$

$\Rightarrow x^2 - 12x - 15x + 180 = 0$

$\Rightarrow (x - 12)(x - 15) = 0$

$\Rightarrow x = 12, 15$

II. $y^2 - 31y + 240 = 0$

$\Rightarrow y^2 - 15y - 16y + 240 = 0$

$\Rightarrow (y - 15)(y - 16) = 0$

$\Rightarrow y = 15, 16$

Value of x	Value of y	Relation
12	15	x < y
12	16	x < y
15	15	x = y
15	16	x < y

So, x ≤ y

Hence, the correct option is (D).

50. I. $5x^2 + 29x - 42 = 0$

$\Rightarrow 5x^2 + 35x - 6x - 42 = 0$

$\Rightarrow 5x(x + 7) - 6(x + 7) = 0$

$\Rightarrow (x + 7)(5x - 6) = 0$

$\Rightarrow x = -7, \dfrac{6}{5}$

II. $20y^2 - 9y - 18 = 0$

$\Rightarrow 20y^2 + 15y - 24y - 18 = 0$

$\Rightarrow (5y - 6)(4y + 3) = 0$

$\Rightarrow y = \dfrac{-3}{4}, \dfrac{6}{5}$

Comparison between x and y (via Tabulation):

Value of x	Value of y	Relation
-7	$\dfrac{-3}{4}$	x < y
-7	$\dfrac{6}{5}$	x < y
$\dfrac{6}{5}$	$\dfrac{-3}{4}$	x > y
$\dfrac{6}{5}$	$\dfrac{6}{5}$	x = y

So, relationship between x and y cannot be established.

Hence, the correct option is (E).

51. From the given table,

Marks obtained by Shivam in different subjects are 81, 82, 86, 87 and 76.

Therefore, total marks obtained by Shivam = 81 + 82 + 86 + 87 + 76 = 412

Hence, the correct option is (B).

52. Given:

Marks obtained by Kunal and Shivam in Hindi are 92 and 81.

Average marks obtained by Kunal and Shivam in Hindi $= \dfrac{92+81}{2} = 86.5$

Hence, the correct option is (B).

53. Given:

Marks obtained by Kiran in different subjects = = 71+ 86 + 71 + 56 + 78 = 362

Total marks = 500

Required percentage: $\left(\dfrac{362}{500}\right) \times 100 = 72.4\%$

Hence, the correct option is (C).

54.

Highest marks scored in particular subject	Name of the students
Hindi	Kunal
English	Kunal
Math	Kunal
Social Science	Kunal
Drawings	Kunal

Only one student got the maximum marks in 2 or more subjects.

Hence, the correct option is (A).

55. Given:

Marks obtained by Kunal in Drawings: 95

Marks obtained by Puneet in drawings: 86

Required percentage: $\left(\dfrac{95}{86}\right) \times 100 = 110.46\%$

Hence, the correct option is (B).

56. Volume of cylinder $= \pi r^2 h = 12936$

$\Rightarrow \dfrac{22}{7} \times r^2 \times 21 = 12936$

$\Rightarrow r^2 = \dfrac{12936 \times 7}{22 \times 21}$

$\Rightarrow r^2 = 196$

$\Rightarrow r = \sqrt{196}$

$\Rightarrow r = 14 \; cm$

Radius of the cylinder = radius of the circle $= 14 \; cm$

Area of the circle $= \pi r^2 = \dfrac{22}{7} \times 14 \times 14 = 616 \; cm^2$

Hence, the correct option is (D).

57. Calculation:

$(345.97 + 129.88 - 45.03) + (34.87 \div 6.96 \times 2.99)$
$= ? - \sqrt{1521}$

$\Rightarrow (346 + 130 - 45) + (35 \div 7 \times 3) = ? - \sqrt{1521}$

$\Rightarrow (476 - 45) + (35 \div 7 \times 3) = ? - \sqrt{1521}$

$\Rightarrow 431 + (5 \times 3) = ? - \sqrt{1521}$

$\Rightarrow 431 + 15 = ? - 39$

$\Rightarrow 446 = ? - 39$

$\Rightarrow ? = 39 + 446$

$\Rightarrow ? = 485$

$\therefore$ Required value of ? is 485

Hence, the correct option is (B).

58. Given:

$(17.76)^2 + (20.99)^2 = (2)^7 + ?$

Calculation:

$(17.76)^2 + (20.99)^2 = (2)^7 + ?$

$\Rightarrow (18)^2 + (21)^2 = (2)^7 + ?$

$\Rightarrow 324 + 441 = 128 + ?$

$\Rightarrow ? = 765 - 128$

$\Rightarrow ? = 637$

$\therefore$ The value of (?) is 637.

Hence, the correct option is (E).

59. Given:

$(23.42 + 17.43) \div 2 \times 4 - 48.25 + 643.86 = ?$

Calculation:

$(23.42 + 17.43) \div 2 \times 4 - 48.25 + 643.86 = ?$

$\Rightarrow (23 + 17) \div 2 \times 4 - 48 + 644 = ?$

$\Rightarrow 40 \div 2 \times 4 + 596 = ?$

$\Rightarrow 20 \times 4 + 596 = ?$

$\Rightarrow ? = 676$

$\therefore$ The value of (?) is 676.

Hence, the correct option is (D).

60. Given:

$?\%$ of $599.97 + 16.03 \times 18.98 = (20.99)^2 - 5.03$

Calculation:

$?\%$ of $599.97 + 16.03 \times 18.98 = (20.99)^2 - 5.03$

$\Rightarrow ?\%$ of $600 + 16 \times 19 = 21^2 - 5$

$\Rightarrow 6 \times ? + 304 = 441 - 5$

$\Rightarrow 6 \times ? = 436 - 304$

$\Rightarrow 6 \times ? = 132$

$\Rightarrow ? = 22$

∴ 22 should come in place of the question mark (?).

Hence, the correct option is (B).

61. Given:

12.5% of $799 + 25\%$ of $399 - 149.89 = ?$

Calculation:

Since, we need to find out the approximate value, we can write these values to their nearest integers.

12.5% of $799 + 25\%$ of $399 - 149.89 = ?$

$\Rightarrow 12.5\%$ of $800 + 25\%$ of $400 - 150 = ?$

$\Rightarrow (1/8) \times 800 + (1/4) \times 400 - 150 = ?$

$\Rightarrow 100 + 100 - 150 = ?$

$\Rightarrow ? = 50$

∴ The value of '?' is 50.

Hence, the correct option is (B).

62. Given:

45% of $300 - (?)^2 = 56\%$ of $75 - 10\%$ of 510

Calculation:

45% of $300 - (?)^2 = 56\%$ of $75 - 10\%$ of 510

$\Rightarrow 45 \times 3 - (?)^2 = 14 \times 3 - 51$

$\Rightarrow ?^2 = (45 \times 3) + 51 - (14 \times 3)$

$\Rightarrow ? = \sqrt{144}$

$\Rightarrow ? = 12$

∴ The value of (?) is 12.

Hence, the correct option is (D).

63. Given:

19.99% of $1224.98 - \sqrt{(1295.93)} \times 3.99 - 87.69 = ?$

Calculation:

19.99% of $1224.98 - \sqrt{(1295.93)} \times 3.99 - 87.69 = ?$

$\Rightarrow 20\%$ of $1225 - \sqrt{1296} \times 4 - 88 = ?$

$\Rightarrow (20/100) \times 1225 - 36 \times 4 - 88 = ?$

$\Rightarrow (1225/5) - 144 - 88 = ?$

$\Rightarrow 245 - 232 = ?$

$\Rightarrow ? = 13$

∴ 13 will come in place of the question mark ('?').

Hence, the correct option is (B).

64. Given:

$32.99 \times 3.98 + (5.01)^2 - 75.02 \div 14.99 + ? = 159.99$

Calculation:

$32.99 \times 3.98 + (5.01)^2 - 75.02 \div 14.99 + ? = 159.99$

$\Rightarrow 33 \times 4 + 5^2 - 75 \div 15 + ? = 160$

$\Rightarrow 132 + 25 - 5 + ? = 160$

$\Rightarrow 152 + ? = 160$

$\Rightarrow ? = 160 - 152$

$\Rightarrow ? = 8$

∴ 8 should come in place of the question mark (?).

Hence, the correct option is (E).

65. Given:

$15 \times 252 \div 60 + 170 = ? + 63$

Calculation:

$15 \times 252 \div 60 + 170 = ? + 63$

$\Rightarrow 63 + 170 = ? + 63$

$\Rightarrow ? = 170$

∴ The value of ? is 170.

Hence, the correct option is (B).

Ques (66-68): From the given information,

(i) T is the mother of V. R is the grandmother of V.

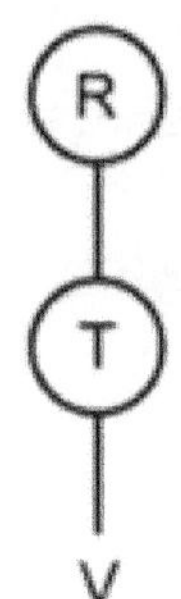

(ii) Q is the husband of R. S is the brother-in-law of Q.

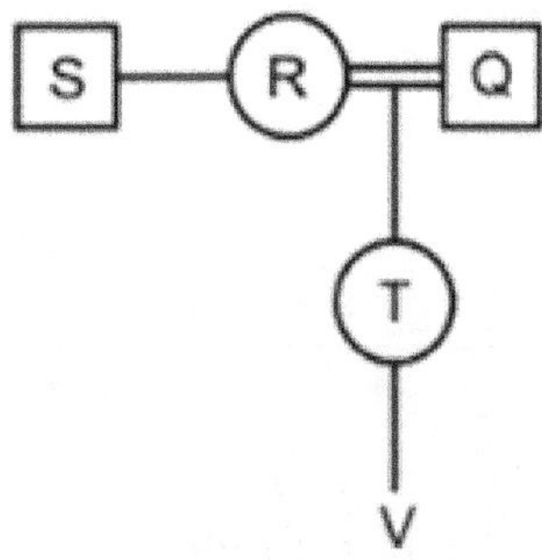

(iii) U is the son-in-law of Q. P is the nephew of S.

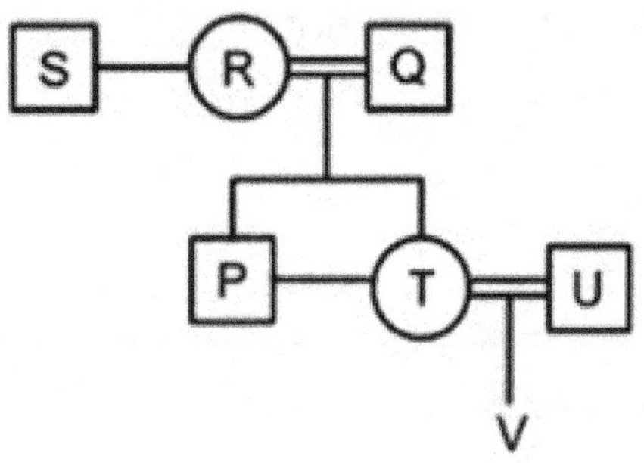

(iv) There are 4 males in the family. It means V is female.

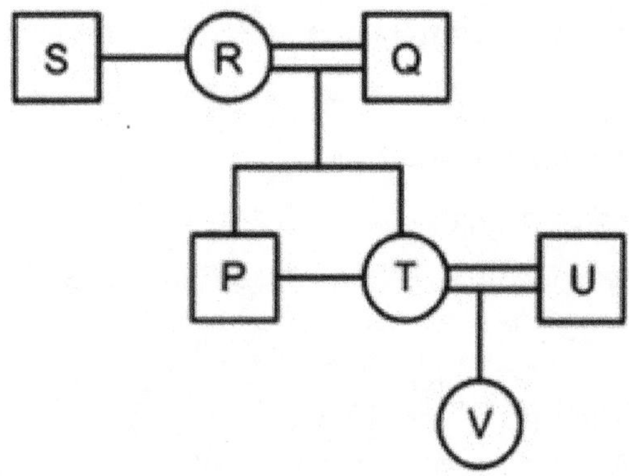

66. So, V is the niece of P.

Hence, the correct option is (C).

67. So, P is the son of Q.

Hence, the correct option is (B).

68. So, Q is the father of T.

Hence, the correct option is (C).

Ques (69-72):Persons: Pratyush, Zeenat, Rakesh, Esha, Lalit and Girish

i) Zeenat have done films less than only Rakesh.

Rakesh > Zeenat > __ > __ > __ > __

ii) Girish have done five films more than Pratyush.

Girish (x + 5) > Pratyush (x)

iii) Pratyush have done two films less than Esha.

Girish (x + 5) > Esha (x + 2))> Pratyush (x)

iv) Lalit have done films more than Girish.

Lalit > Girish (x + 5) > Esha (x + 2))> Pratyush (x)

v) The least films done by these actors is 50 films.

Rakesh > Zeenat > Lalit > Girish (55) > Esha (52)) > Pratyush (50)

69. So, three persons have done films more than Girish.

Hence, the correct option is (D).

70. So, Lalit have done third highest number of films.

Hence, the correct option is (A).

71. So, 58

Hence, the correct option is (D).

72. So, Esha have done the second least number of films.

Hence, the correct option is (B).

73. Given statements: M ≥ T; M < P; S > T

On combining: P > M ≥ T < S

Conclusions:

I. S = M → False (as P > M ≥ T < S → thus clear relation between S and M cannot be determined)

II. T < P → True (as P > M ≥ T → P > T)

III. P > S → False (as P > M ≥ T < S → thus clear relation between P and S cannot be determined)

So, only conclusion II is true.

Hence, the correct option is (C).

74. Given Statements:

X > C ≥ V > Y; U = V < T ≤ H; T < B

On Combining:

X > C ≥ V > Y, X > C ≥ U = V < T ≤ H, B > T ≤ H

Conclusions:

I. Y < X → True (as X > C ≥ V > Y → X > Y)

II. X ≥ B → False (as X > C ≥ U = V < T < B → thus clear relation between X and B cannot be determined)

III. V < B → True (as U = V < T < B → V < B)

So, only conclusion I and III follow.

Hence, the correct option is (D).

75. Given statements: P ≤ Q > R = S; S < T; T = P > U; V < U

On combining: Q ≥ P = T > S = R; T = P > U > V

Conclusions:

I. Q = P → False (as R = S < T → R < T and T = P > U → U < T → thus clear relation between R and U cannot be determined)

II. Q > P → False (as Q ≥ P > U > V → Q > V)

III. P < V → False (as V < U < P = T → V < P)

Note: conclusion I and II forms complementary pair.

So, either I or II follows.

Hence, the correct option is (E).

76. Given statements: A > P ≥ K; Q > M > T; P > T

On combining: A > P > T < M < Q; P ≥ K

Conclusions:

I. T < K → False (as P > T; P ≥ K; relation between T and K cannot be determined)

II. K > A → False (as A > P; P ≥ K; A > P ≥ K; A > K)

III. A > K → True (as A > P; P ≥ K; A > P ≥ K; A > K)

So, only III is true.

Hence, the correct option is (E).

77. From the given data:

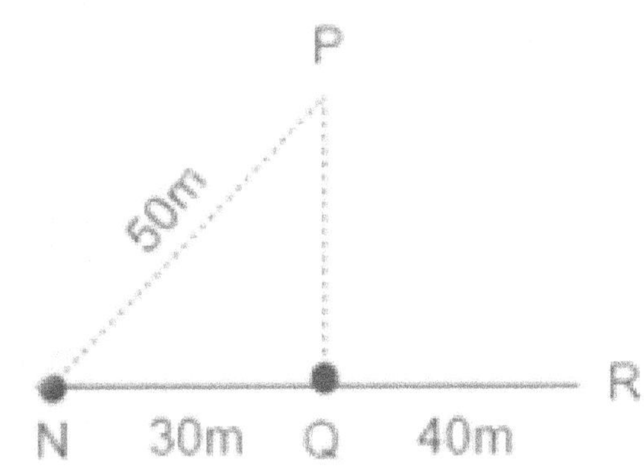

From Formula:

$NP^2 = NQ^2 + PQ^2$

∴ $NP = \sqrt{NP^2 - NQ^2}$

= $\sqrt{(50)^2 - (30)^2}$

= $\sqrt{2500 - 900}$

= $\sqrt{1600} = 40m$

Hence, the correct option is (E).

Ques (78-82):Persons: Abrahim, Akshay, Amish, Anush, Arob, Arak and Atul.

Brands: J&J, Lee Cooper, Levis, Polo, Roadster, UCB and Wrogn.

1) Abrahim lives two floors above Amish's floor and both live on prime numbered floor.

Floor	Case 1 Person	T-shirt Brand	Case 2 Person	T-shirt Brand
7	Abrahim			
6				
5	Amish		Abrahim	
4				
3			Amish	
2				
1				

2) Atul bought Levis T-shirt and lives just below the one, who bought Wrogn T-shirt.

3) One person lives between Amish and Atul.

Floor	Case 1 Person	T-shirt Brand	Case 2 Person	T-shirt Brand
7	Abrahim			
6				
5	Amish		Abrahim	
4		Wrogn		
3	Atul	Levis	Amish	
2				Wrogn
1			Atul	Levis

4) Arob lives just above Arak.

5) Anush bought Roadster T-shirt.

6) Three persons live between the persons, who bought J&J and Polo T-shirt.

Floor	Case 1 Person	T-shirt Brand	Case 2 Person	T-shirt Brand
7	Abrahim		Arob	J&J / Polo
6	Anush	Roadster	Arak	
5	Amish	J&J / Polo	Abrahim	
4	Akshay	Wrogn	Anush	Roadster
3	Atul	Levis	Amish	Polo / J&J
2	Arob		Akshay	Wrogn
1	Arak	Polo / J&J	Atul	Levis

7) Neither Abrahim nor Arob bought UCB t-shirt. So, case 1 would be invalid.

Floor	Person	T-shirt Brand
7	Arob	J&J / Polo
6	Arak	UCB
5	Abrahim	Lee Cooper
4	Anush	Roadster
3	Amish	Polo / J&J
2	Akshay	Wrogn
1	Atul	Levis

78. So, four persons live above Amish's floor.

Hence, the correct option is (A).

79. So, '2 – Wrogn – Akshay' is the correct answer.

Hence, the correct option is (D).

80. So, five persons live between Arob and the one, who bought Levis T-shirt.

Hence, the correct option is (A).

81. So, Abrahim lives just above the one, who bought Roadster T-Shirt.

Hence, the correct option is (D).

82. So, Arob lives on the topmost floor.

Hence, the correct option is (B).

83. The given word can be represented as follows,

Letters	H	U	R	R	I	C	A	N	E
Position	8	21	18	18	9	3	1	14	5

So. We get 3 such pairs "IH", "EI" and NR".

Hence, the correct option is (B).

Ques (84-86): From the given data,

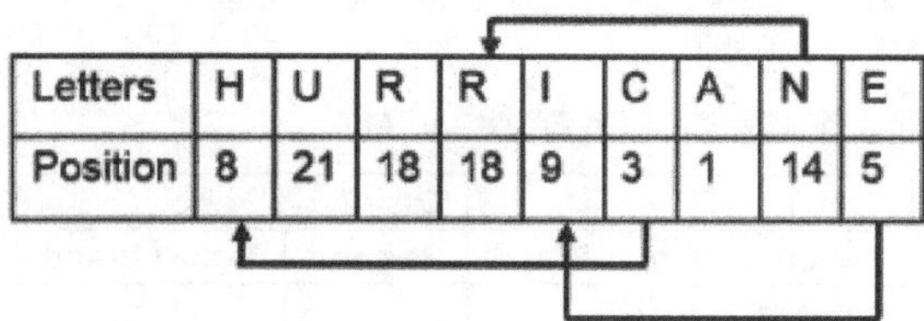

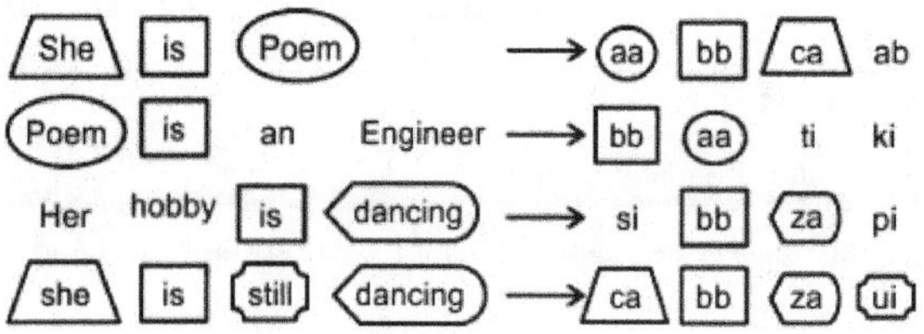

84. So, 'ti' is code for either 'an' or 'engineer'.

Hence, the correct option is (C).

85. Code for 'is' is 'bb'

Code for 'my singing' is 'uz pp',

So, possible code for 'hobby' is 'si'.

Hence, the correct option is (D).

86. So, the possible code for 'poem' is 'aa'.

Hence, the correct option is (C).

Ques (87-91): 1) P sits at the 2nd position from one of the ends.

2) R sits 3rd to the right of P.

3) Only 2 persons sit between R and S.

4) U sits 2nd to the right of S.

Case 1

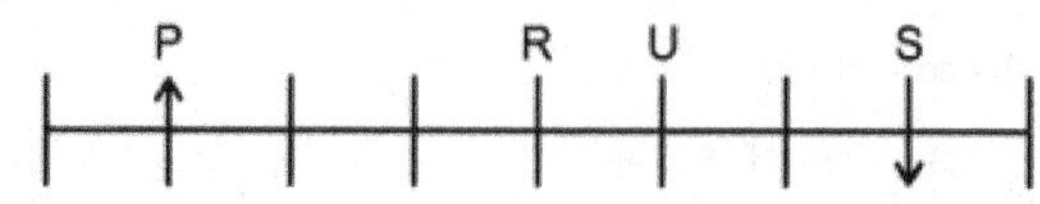

Case 2

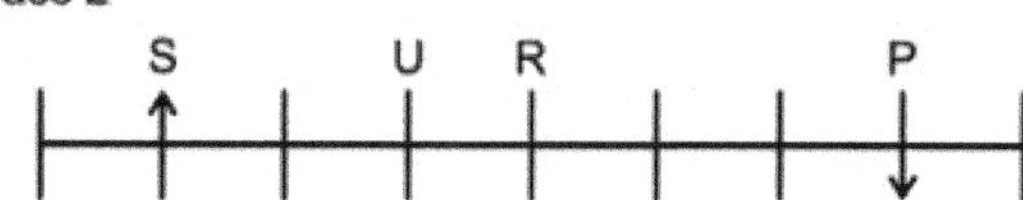

5) Immediate neighbors of S are facing the opposite direction to that of S.

6) Immediate neighbors of U faces the opposite direction.

7) T sits second to the right of U.

8) The ones sitting at the ends of row faces the opposite direction.

Case 1

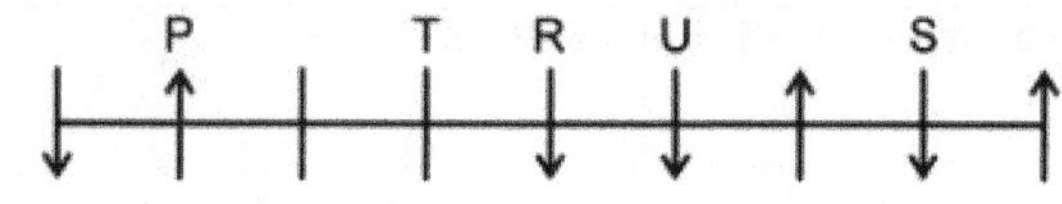

Case 2

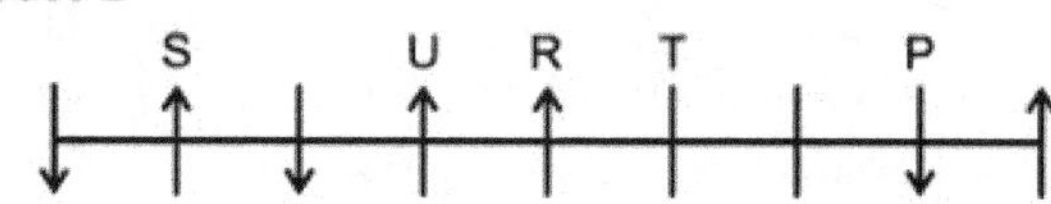

9) Q is not a neighbor of U and P.

10) W sits at one of the extreme ends.

11) V sits adjacent to T.

12) W and T face the opposite direction.

Case 1

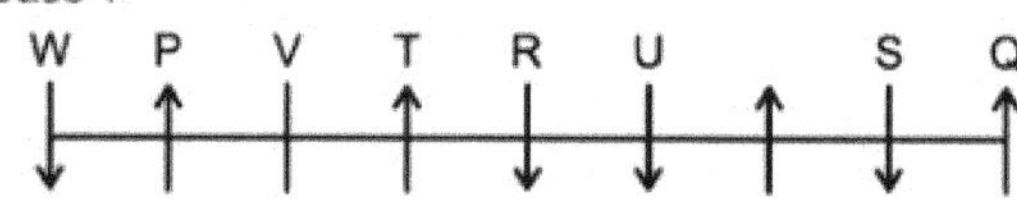

Case 2

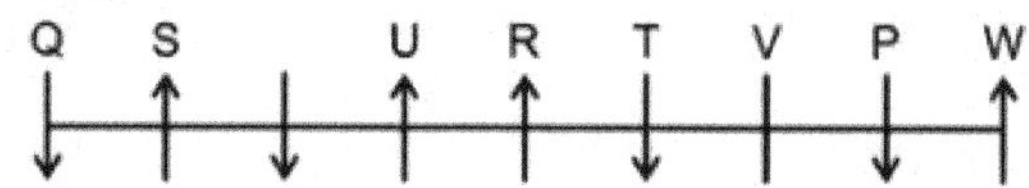

13) X does not face south.

Therefore Case 2 gets eliminated.

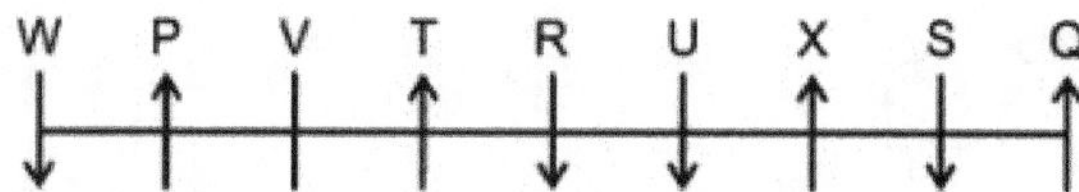

87. So, W is sitting at the left end of the row.

Hence, the correct option is (D).

88. So, 3 persons sit between P and U.

Hence, the correct option is (A).

89. So, We cannot determine the person sitting to the right of V, as we do not know in which direction V is facing.

Hence, the correct option is (E).

90. So, The correct answer is R.

Hence, the correct option is (B).

91. In all the given pairs except US, the second person is sitting second to the right of the first person.

So, US is the correct answer.

Hence, the correct option is (D).

92. The least possible Venn diagram for the given statements is as follows:

Conclusions:

I. Some bus are car → False (No car is a bus is a negative statement so, the positive conclusion doesn't follow)

II. No truck are car → False (there is no definite relation between truck and car)

So, Neither conclusion I nor II follows.

Hence, the correct option is (E).

93. The least possible diagram for the given statements is as follow:

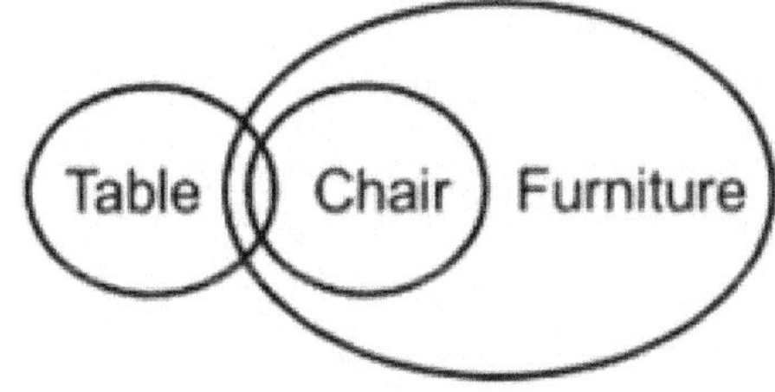

Conclusion:

I. Some Table is Furniture → True (As All Chair is Furniture and some part of Table is also Chair. So, some part of Table is also Furniture.)

II. All Furniture is Table → False (All chair is Furniture but some part of Table is Chair. That's why all Furniture is Table is not possible.)

So, Only I follow.

Hence, the correct option is (A).

94. The least possible Venn diagram for the given statements is as follows:

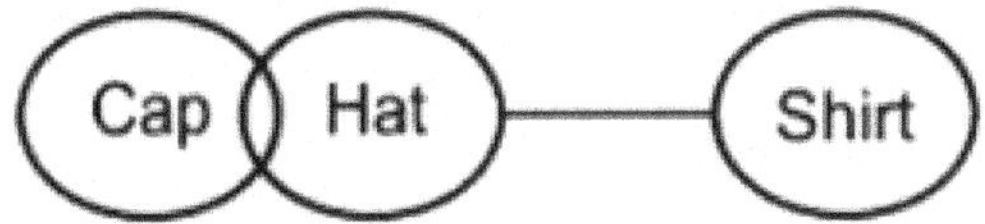

Conclusions:

I. Some shirts are not cap → False (There is no definite relation between cap and shirt)

II. All shirts being cap is a possibility → True (Possibility is true shown in the diagram below)

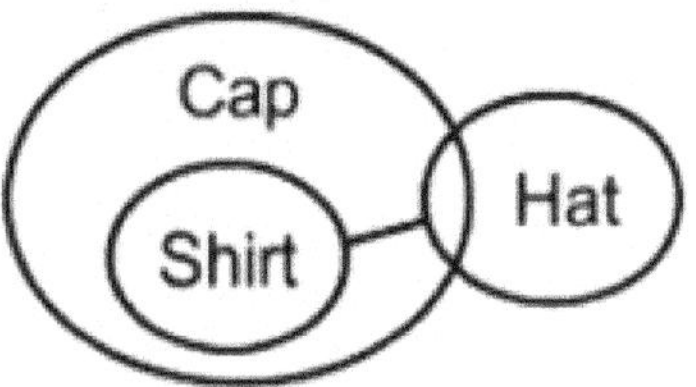

So, only conclusion II follows.

Hence, the correct option is (B).

95. The least possible Venn diagram for the given statements is as follows:

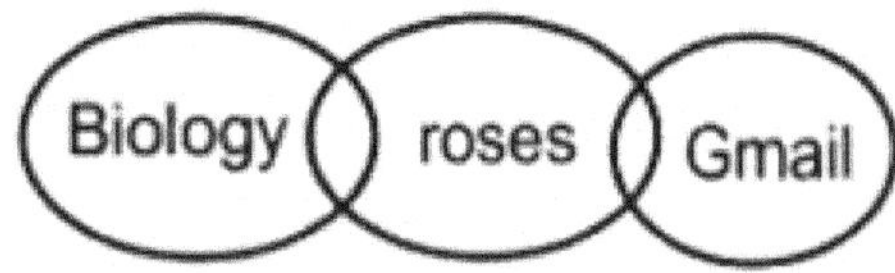

Conclusions:

I. 20% of biology are gmail → False (Here 20% is taken as some, so unknown relations between elements will be false, but possibility can be true).

II. No gmail is biology → False (so unknown relations between elements will be false, but possibility can be true).

So, when two elements are same in the 2 conclusions and one conclusion is positive and second one is negative, then the condition either-or will follow.

So, either I or II follows.

Hence, the correct option is (A).

Ques (96-100):Eight students: Arpita, Amit, Ankit, Amita, Amitesh, Aman, Amina, and Ankita.

1) Amina sits third to the right of Aman.

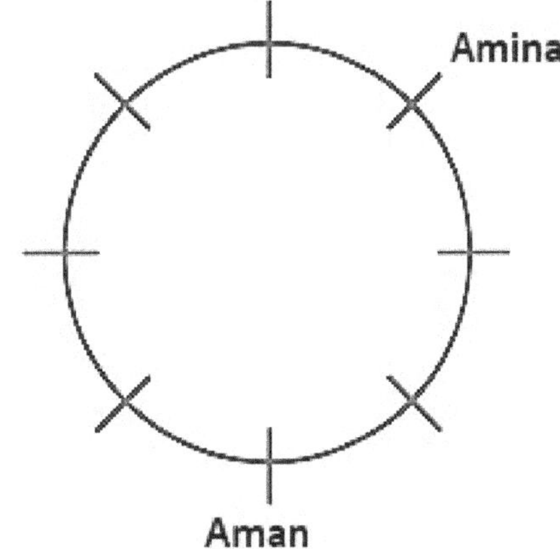

2) Ankita sits second to the left of Arpita.

3) Amina and Aman are not immediate neighbours of Ankita.

So, only one possibility to sit Ankita second to the left of Arpita.

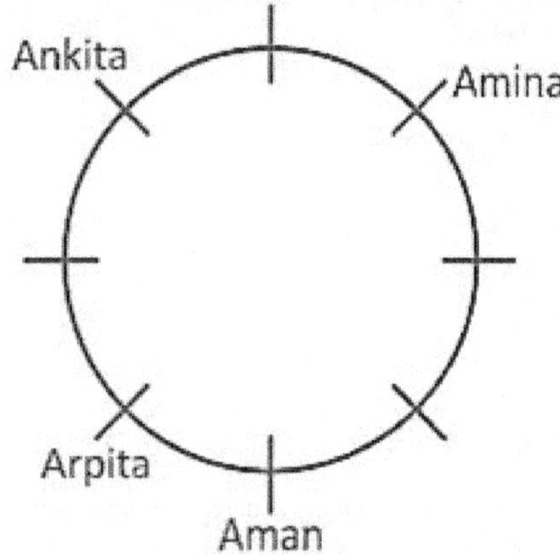

4) Amit sits third to the right of Ankit.

5) Amina is not an immediate neighbour of Ankita.

So, there are two possibilities to sit Amit third to the right of Ankit.

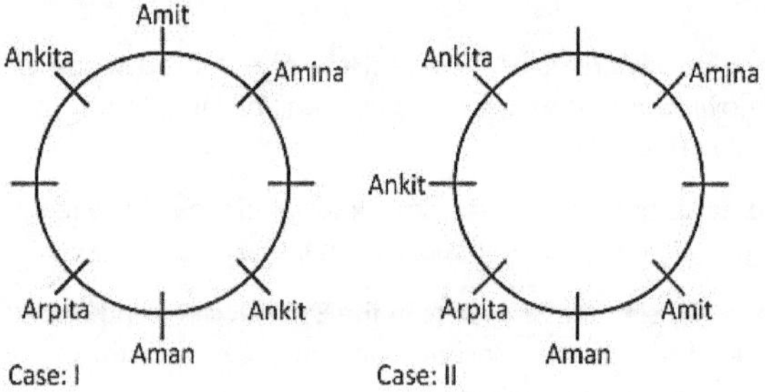

6) Ankita and Ankit are not immediate neighbours of Amita.

So, the first case is not satisfied and taking the second case.

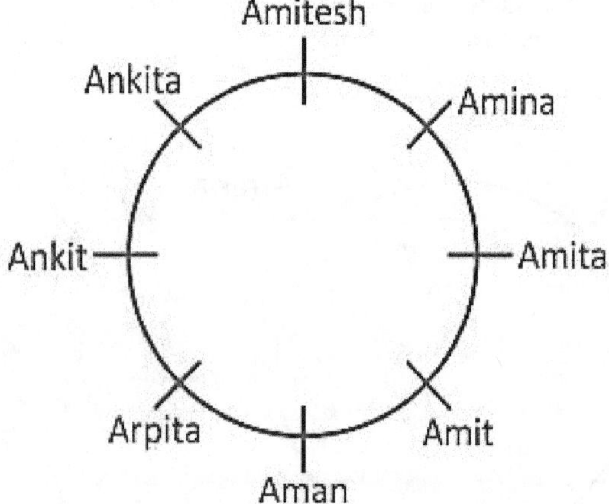

96. So, Amit sitting between Aman and Amita.

Hence, the correct option is (B).

97. So, Amitesh sits third to the lest of Arpita.

Hence, the correct option is (A).

98. So, there are four persons sitting between Ankit and Amina starting anticlockwise from Ankit.

Hence, the correct option is (D).

99. So, Ankit sits fourth to the left of Amita.

Hence, the correct option is (E).

100. First person sits third to the left of the second person. Ankita sits second to the right of Amina.

So, Ankita - Amina is the right answer.

Hence, the correct option is (D).

English Language

Ques (1-7):Direction: Read the following passage and answer the questions given below it. Certain words/phrases are given in bold to help you locate them while answering the questions:

If you look at a Map of the World, you will see, in the left-hand upper corner of the Eastern Hemisphere, two Islands lying in the sea. They are England and Scotland, and Ireland. England and Scotland form the greater part of these Islands. Ireland is the next in size. The little neighboring islands, which are so small upon the Map as to be mere dots, are chiefly little bits of Scotland, broken off, I dare say, in the course of a great length of time, by the power of the restless water.

It is supposed that the Phœnicians, who were an ancient people, famous for carrying on a trade, came in ships to these Islands, and found that they produced tin and lead; both very useful things, as you know, and both produced to this very hour upon the sea-coast. The Phœnicians traded with the Islanders for these metals and gave the Islanders some other useful things in exchange. The Islanders were, at first, poor **savages**, going almost naked, or only dressed in the rough skins of beasts, and staining their bodies, as other savages do, with colored earth and the juices of plants. But the Phœnicians, sailing over to the opposite coasts of France and Belgium, and saying to the people there, 'We have been to those white cliffs across the water, which you can see in fine weather, and from that country, which is called BRITAIN, we bring this tin and lead,' tempted some of the French and Belgians to come over also. These people settled themselves on the south coast of England, which is now called Kent; and, although they were a rough people too, they taught the savage Britons some useful arts, and improved that part of the Islands. It is probable that other people came over from Spain to Ireland, and settled there.

Thus, by little and little, strangers became mixed with the Islanders, and the savage Britons grew into a wild, bold people; almost savage, still, especially in the interior of the country away from the sea where the foreign settlers **seldom** went; but hardy, brave, and strong.

The Britons had a strange and terrible religion, called the Religion of the Druids. It seems to have been brought over, in very early times indeed, from the opposite country of France, anciently called Gaul, and to have mixed up the worship of the Serpent, and of the Sun and Moon, with the worship of some of the Heathen Gods and Goddesses. Most of its ceremonies were kept secret by the priests, the Druids, who pretended to be enchanters, and who carried magicians' wands, and wore, each of them, about his neck, what he told the ignorant people was a Serpent's egg in a golden case. But it is certain that the Druidical ceremonies included the sacrifice of human victims, the torture of some suspected criminals, and, on particular occasions, even the burning alive, in immense wicker cages, of a number of men and animals together. The Druid Priests had

some kind of **veneration** for the Oak, and for the mistletoe— the same plant that we hang up in houses at Christmas Time now—when its white berries grew upon the Oak. They met together in dark woods, which they called Sacred Groves; and there they instructed, in their **mysterious** arts, young men who came to them as pupils, and who sometimes stayed with them as long as twenty years.

Q.1 What tempted the Belgians to travel and settle in England ?
A. The good hospitality of the native people of England.
B. The abundant wealth of the England.
C. The useful metals found in the islands.
D. The poor economic conditions in Belgium at that time.
E. None of these

Q.2 Which of the following statements are true regarding the Religion of the Druids?
I. The priests of the religion are called Druids.
II. The religion originated in France.
III. It is practiced even today
A. I   **B.** II
C. I and II   **D.** I and III
E. I,II and III

Q.3 According to the passage the people from which all countries settled in Kent?
I. France
II. Ireland
III. Belgium
IV. Spain
A. I and II   **B.** I, II and IV
C. I and III   **D.** I, II and III
E. I, II, III and IV

Q.4 Which of the following is not true about the Phoenicians ?
A. They reached Britain for the first time via sea route.
B. They were very good traders.
C. They informed the people of France and Belgium about the useful metals found in Britain.
D. They gifted the Islanders precious metals in exchange for tin and lead.
E. None of these

Q.5 What is the author's feeling towards the Religion of Druids ?
A. He does not seem to express any emotion towards the religion.
B. He finds the religion very odd.
C. He is deeply attached towards the religion.
D. His emotions towards the religion is varying.
E. None of these

Q.6 Choose the word that is most similar in meaning to the word printed in bold as used in the passage.

SELDOM

A. Frequently   **B.** Rarely
C. Awaitedly   **D.** Unapologetically
E. None of these

Q.7 Choose the word which is most similar in meaning to the word printed in bold as used in the passage.

VENERATION

A. Fear   **B.** Worship
C. Respect   **D.** Disrespect
E. None of these

Ques (8-12):Direction: A part of the sentence is under lined in each of the following questions. Choose the option which best replaces the underlined part. If the given sentence is correct in its given form then choose option E as the answer.

Q.8 He missed an important meeting because his flight <u>was late</u>.

A. Is late   **B.** Would be late
C. Been late   **D.** Being late
E. No change required

Q.9 The supreme court <u>acquitted</u> the criminal due to the lack of evidence.

A. Did acquitted   **B.** Have acquitted
C. Has been acquit   **D.** Would have acquit
E. No change required

Q.10 Amid the tensions at the border, the air force chief has asked his troops t<u>o be prepare</u> for the war.

A. To preparing
B. To being prepared
C. To be prepared
D. To have been prepared
E. No change required

Q.11 Ravi did not get calls from any of the top colleges <u>despite score well</u> in the examination.

A. Despite scoring well
B. Despite score having been
C. In spite scoring well
D. Despite the score being
E. No change required

Q.12 Had I not wasted time on a particular question, I <u>have scored</u> the 100 percentile.

A. Had scored   **B.** Would have scored
C. Could have score   **D.** Will have score
E. No change required

Ques (13-17):Direction: Below are given some sentences out of which the sentence numbered 4 has been correctly placed. The rest of the sentences A, B, C, D, E, and F need to be arranged correctly in order to form a logical order.

A. Large machines known as turbines are turned very quickly with the help of heat, wind, or moving water.

B. The moving magnets within the copper wire coils cause electrons to move within the wire – this is electricity.

C. Electricity is not a primary but a secondary energy source.

4. Power stations are places where electricity is generated for power purposes.

D. The moving turbines cause large magnets to turn within copper wire coils.

E. These energy sources are known as primary sources.

F. We get it from the conversion of other sources of energy such as coal, water, oil, nuclear power, and other natural sources.

Q.13 Which of the following is the SEVENTH statement?
A. C   **B.** B   **C.** D   **D.** F
E. E

Q.14 Which of the following is the SIXTH statement?
A. C   **B.** B   **C.** D   **D.** F
E. E

Q.15 Which of the following is the THIRD statement?
[LIC AAO (Generalist), 2021]
A. A   **B.** B   **C.** D   **D.** F
E. E

Q.16 Which of the following is the SECOND statement?
A. A   **B.** B   **C.** D   **D.** F
E. E

Q.17 Which of the following is the FIRST statement?
A. A   **B.** B   **C.** C   **D.** D
E. E

Ques (18-20):Direction: In the following question, out of the following alternatives, select the alternative which best describes the given idioms/phrases.

Q.18 Being French, I felt like **a fish out of water** in the group of Japanese.

A. Feel superior
B. Be in a comfortable position
C. Felt like an enemy
D. Feeling uncomfortable in unfamiliar surroundings
E. Feeling of joy

Q.19 The increase in customs duty by the government has **upset the apple cart** of those car companies who were importing most of their car parts.

A. Do something that causes a plan to go wrong
B. Upset someone
C. Revealing secrets
D. Great support
E. Ruin everything

Q.20 He has taken more responsibilities as he couldn't say 'no' to his boss. I think he has **bitten more than he can chew**, and he'll struggle to handle them all.

A. Agreeing for everything
B. Giving up
C. To try to do something that is too difficult for you

D. Failing to do something
E. Enthusiastic about everything

Ques (21-25): Select the most appropriate word to fill in the blank.

Q.21 We appeal to their reasoning and responsible decision-making to ______ them from purchasing dangerous foods.
A. Cascade   **B.** Upgrade   **C.** Crusade   **D.** Degrade
E. Dissuade

Q.22 Some have likened the leaked document as being the equivalent of the Pentagon Papers that ______ during the Nixon era.
A. Disgraced   **B.** Ceased
C. Surfaced   **D.** Interceded
E. Superseded

Q.23 There is no magic wand to ensure economic reforms and ______ a crisis-like scenario.
A. Alert   **B.** Insert   **C.** Convert   **D.** Expert
E. Avert

Q.24 Prime Minister Narendra Modi will be traveling to Germany and Denmark on a ______ visit in the first week of May.
A. Bilateral   **B.** Collateral
C. Unilateral   **D.** Quadrilateral
E. Ipsilateral

Q.25 India's strategic future is also ______ linked with Russia.
A. Revocable   **B.** Imperfect
C. Unfavorably   **D.** Deadly
E. Inextricably

Ques (26-30): Direction: In the given question, some part of the sentence may have errors. Find out which part of the sentence has an error and select the appropriate option. If a sentence is free from error, select 'No Error'.

Q.26 He has been (A) / toiling hardly (B) / to be able to (C) / provide for his family. (D)
A. (A)   **B.** (B)   **C.** (C)   **D.** (D)
E. No error

Q.27 The brother-in-laws (A) / were very helpful (B) / and supportive of (C) / their choices. (D)
A. (A)   **B.** (B)   **C.** (C)   **D.** (D)
E. No error

Q.28 All pieces (A)/ of informations (B) / given by her (C) / were accurate. (D)
A. (A)   **B.** (B)   **C.** (C)   **D.** (D)
E. No error

Q.29 Three jawans of District (A)/ Reserve Guard were killed (B)/ while ten others were injured (C)/ in an IED blast on Tuesday. (D)
A. (A)   **B.** (B)   **C.** (C)   **D.** (D)
E. No error

Q.30 Despite having lost (A)/ the match, the team was receive (B)/ at the airport with (C)/ a lot of enthusiasm. (D)
A. (A)   **B.** (B)   **C.** (C)   **D.** (D)
E. No error

Numerical Ability

Q.31 Ram drives at an average speed of 78 km/hr and reaches Jodhpur in 40 minutes. If his average speed was 65 km/hr, in how many minutes would he reach Jodhpur, approximately?
A. 36 mins   **B.** 40 mins   **C.** 42 mins   **D.** 45 mins
E. 48 mins

Q.32 Arjun invested Rs. 70000 in a business at the starting of the year. After a few months, Aryan joined him with an investment of Rs 60000. At the end of the year, they shared their profits in the ratio $2:1$. After how many months did Aryan join Arjun.
A. 5   **B.** 6   **C.** 7   **D.** 10
E. 2

Q.33 A pipe A can fill a tank in 5 hours, B in 8 hours and C can empty in 15 hours. If all pipes are opened together, how much time would it take to fill the tank?
A. 4 hours   **B.** 3 hours 20 mins
C. 3 hours 15 mins   **D.** 4 hours 15 mins
E. None of these

Q.34 Arjun bought 7 pens and 13 erasers from a stationery shop for Rs. 121. Riya bought 5 pens and 4 erasers for Rs. 60 from the same shop. Find the cost of 11 pens and 5 erasers.
A. 111   **B.** 127   **C.** 67   **D.** 113
E. 180

Q.35 A sum of money is invested under a simple interest scheme for 4 years at 18.2 per annum. At what rate should the sum be invested under a compound interest scheme for 3 years to receive same amount of interest?
A. 20   **B.** 22.5   **C.** 25   **D.** 17.5
E. 15

Q.36 Devaki invested an amount of Rs. 75,000 to start a hardware business. After eight months Saroj joined her with an amount of Rs. 80,000. At the end of 4 years they earned a profit of Rs. 1,70,000. What is Devaki's share in the profit?
A. Rs. 1,00,000   **B.** Rs. 90,000
C. Rs. 80,000   **D.** Rs. 70,000
E. None of these

Q.37 Direction: Choose the option which best replaces the question mark.
13, 41, 85, 145 ?
A. 221   **B.** 193   **C.** 214   **D.** 237
E. 229

Q.38 Direction: What approximate value should come in place of the question mark (?) in the following questions?

$$\sqrt[3]{\left(\sqrt[3]{511}\right)^2} = ?$$

A. 3   **B.** 4   **C.** 5   **D.** 6
E. 8

Q.39 Direction: Simply the question, and mark what will replace the question mark.

$$1\frac{2}{7} + 2\frac{2}{5} + 3\frac{2}{9} = ?$$

A. $6\frac{286}{315}$ **B.** $6\frac{276}{315}$

C. $6\frac{266}{315}$ **D.** $6\frac{256}{315}$

E. None of the above

Ques (40-43):Direction: Find the approximate values of each of the following expressions.

Q.40 $19.1 \times 9.9 + 22.2 \div 11.1 - 7.4 = ?$

A. 195   **B.** 200   **C.** 175   **D.** 185
E. 170

Q.41 19.99% of $1224.98 - \sqrt{(1295.93)} \times 3.99 - 87.69 = ?$

A. 12   **B.** 13   **C.** 15   **D.** 23
E. 33

Q.42 $323.27 \div 16.96 \times 18.99 = ?$

A. 341   **B.** 351   **C.** 361   **D.** 461

Q.43 25% of 397 + 20% of 502 + 25% of 601 = ?

A. 300   **B.** 350   **C.** 270   **D.** 400
E. 450

Ques (44-48):Direction: The graph below shows the number of seats won by three parties in elections conducted from 1984 - 2014. Study the graph carefully and answer the questions that follow:

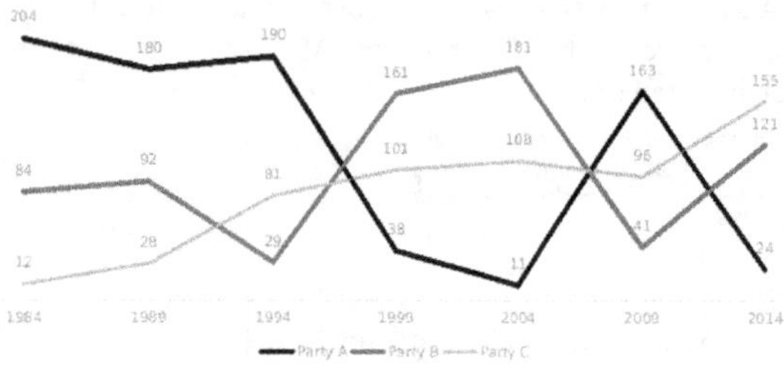

Q.44 What is the percentage increase in the seats of Party C from 1994 to 2014?

A. 152.37%   **B.** 74.58%   **C.** 84.35%   **D.** 91.35%
E. 68.71%

Q.45 What is the average number of seats (approximated to nearest interger) won by Party B across all the years?

A. 120   **B.** 101   **C.** 131   **D.** 108
E. 95

Q.46 The total seats won by Party C for all the years is what percentage of the total seats won by Party A for all the years?

A. 91.98%   **B.** 76.78%   **C.** 62.45%   **D.** 67.81%
E. 71.72%

Q.47 In which year did Party C gain the maximum number of seats as compared to the previous year?

A. 2004   **B.** 2009   **C.** 2014   **D.** 1999
E. 1994

Q.48 In which year was the difference between the highest party and the lowest party (in terms of seats won) the least?

A. 2009   **B.** 2014   **C.** 2004   **D.** 1999
E. 1989

Ques (49-52):Direction: In each of the following number series, the wrong number is given, find out that number.

Q.49 216, 225, 222, 233, 228, 239, 234

A. 234   **B.** 239   **C.** 228   **D.** 233
E. 225

Q.50 100, 96, 105, 89, 113, 78, 127

A. 100   **B.** 105   **C.** 89   **D.** 113
E. 127

Q.51 10, 11, 23, 70, 281, 1403, 8437

A. 23   **B.** 70   **C.** 281   **D.** 1403
E. 8437

Q.52 4, 12, 24, 96, 480, 2880, 20160

A. 12   **B.** 96   **C.** 480   **D.** 2880
E. 20160

Ques (53-57):Direction: In the given question, two equations numbered I and II are given. Solve both the equations and mark the appropriate answer.

Q.53 I. $2x^2 + 4x - 6 = 0$
II. $y^2 + 6y + 9 = 0$
A. $x > y$
B. $x \geq y$
C. $x < y$
D. $x \leq y$
E. $x = y$ or the relationship cannot be established.

Q.54 I. $4x^2 + 56x - 60 = 0$
II. $2y^2 + 28y - 240 = 0$
A. $x > y$
B. $x \geq y$
C. $x < y$
D. $x \leq y$
E. $x = y$ or the relationship cannot be established.

Q.55 I. $x^2 + 13x = 0$
II. $y^2 = 169$
A. $x > y$
B. $x \geq y$
C. $x < y$
D. $x \leq y$
E. $x = y$ or the relationship cannot be established.

Q.56 I. $x^2 = 64$
II. $y^3 = 512$
A. $x > y$

B. $x \geq y$

C. $x < y$

D. $x \leq y$

E. x = y or the relationship cannot be established.

Q.57 I. $x^2 - 58x + 841 = 0$

II. $2y^2 + 58y = 0$

A. $x > y$

B. $x \geq y$

C. $x < y$

D. $x \leq y$

E. x = y or the relationship cannot be established.

Q.58 A sum is to be paid back in 2 equal annual installments. The interest is compounded annually at 6% per annum. If each installment be Rs. 35000 then what is the sum?

A. Rs. 25,600

B. Rs. 72,500

C. Rs. 64,400

D. Rs. 71,764

E. Rs. 71,764

Q.59 The average marks in Mathematics of a class of 35 students is 72. If the marks of two students were misread as 48 and 66 of the actual marks 84 and 65 respectively, then what would be the correct average?

A. 75

B. 72.5

C. 73

D. 70

E. 71.50

Q.60 There are 8 boys and 4 girls are giving an interview for a job. If three of them are selected, then what is the probability that one of the three is a girl and the other two are the boys?

A. $\frac{37}{45}$

B. $\frac{27}{65}$

C. $\frac{28}{55}$

D. $\frac{32}{45}$

E. $\frac{11}{15}$

Q.61 The length of a rectangle is twice that of its breadth. The perimeter of a given rectangle is 90 cm. If length decreased by 5 cm and breadth increased by 5 cm, then the area of the rectangle increased by how much (In cm square)?

A. 55

B. 60

C. 50

D. 70

E. 65

Ques (62-65): What approximate value should come in the place of question mark (?) in the following question?

Q.62 $(46.98 \times 3.94 \div 46.99 \times 4.98^2) \div 4.98 \times 3.98 = 18.99 \times 4.98 \div ?$

A. 19

B. 23

C. $\frac{16}{19}$

D. 15

E. $\frac{19}{16}$

Q.63

$$(\sqrt{256.089} \div \sqrt[3]{64.004} \times 5) + (\sqrt{361.023} + \sqrt{121.05}) = ? + 23$$

A. 35

B. 40

C. 15

D. 27

Q.64

$$\sqrt{4760.99} \times \sqrt{3968.89} + \sqrt{2703.99} + 1.01 = ? \times 5 + \sqrt{24.87} \times \sqrt{3480.88}$$

A. 821

B. 1024

C. 560

D. 8000

E. 1687

Q.65

$$74.99 - 2.99 \times \left[(5.99^2 \div 6.06) \div 3.03\right] \div \left(\tfrac{1}{2.99}\right) + 12.99 = ?$$

A. 70

B. 60

C. 80

D. 90

E. 110

Reasoning Ability

Ques (66-69):Direction: In each of the following question assuming the given statements to be true, find which of the conclusion among given conclusions is/ are definitely true and then give your answers accordingly.

Q.66 Statements: $Q \leq A < D < K \leq M = J = F > Z$

Conclusions:

I. $K > Q$

II. $F \geq K$

[IBPS RRB Scale I, 2020]

A. Only II is True

B. Only I is True

C. Both I and II are True

D. Either I or II is True

E. None is true

Q.67 Statements: $J < G \geq L > N < K \leq F < T = H$

Conclusions:

I. $F > L$

II. $K < H$

A. Only II follows

B. Only I follows

C. Both I and II follow

D. Either I or II follow

E. None follows

Q.68 Statements: $X \leq Y < Z; O < R \leq Q = X$

Conclusions:

I. $Q < Z$

II. $R \leq Y$

A. Only II follows

B. Only I follows

C. Both I and II follow

D. Either I or II follow

E. None follows

Q.69 Statements: $8 \geq 7 < 6 < 5; 2 > 3 > 9 = 8$

Conclusions:

I. $8 \geq 5$

II. $8 < 5$

A. Only II follows

B. Only I follow

C. Both I and II follow

D. Either I or II follows

E. Neither I nor II follows

Ques (70-74):Direction: Read the following information carefully and answer the questions that follow:

In a shop, there are 7 boxes A, B, C, D, E, F, and G kept one above another but not necessarily in the same order. The box at topmost position is numbered 1 and the box at the bottommost position is numbered 7.There are 3 boxes between D and E. Box E is kept above box D. There are 2 boxes between box G and box F. Box B is kept above the box G. Box C is kept just above box E. Box A is kept in an odd number place.

Q.70 What is the position of box C?

A. first   **B.** second   **C.** third   **D.** fourth
E. fifth

Q.71 How many box kept above the box A?

A. 2   **B.** 4   **C.** 5   **D.** 6
E. 1

Q.72 How many boxes are there between box C and box G?

A. 2   **B.** 3   **C.** 4   **D.** 5
E. 6

Q.73 How many boxes are kept below the box F?

A. One   **B.** Two   **C.** Three   **D.** Four
E. Zero

Q.74 Choose the odd one out?

A. F   **B.** A   **C.** G   **D.** B
E. C

Ques (75-78):Direction: A family has seven members namely A, B, C, D, E, F, and G. they are related to each other in the following manner.

F is the only son of A who has three children. C is married to A. E is the maternal aunt of B who is married to D. A and G were of the same gender. Either both or none of the parents are alive.

Q.75 How is G related to E?

A. niece   **B.** nephew
C. sister   **D.** brother-in-law
E. brother

Q.76 How is D related to A?

A. Daughter   **B.** Son
C. Son-in-law   **D.** Daughter-in-law
E. Brother-in-law

Q.77 How is F related to D?

A. Sister-in-law   **B.** Brother-in-law
C. Nephew   **D.** Son
E. None of these

Q.78 Find the odd one out.

[LIC AAO (Generalist), 2021]

A. E   **B.** A   **C.** G   **D.** B
E. D

Q.79 Direction: In the question below, there are two statements followed by two conclusions numbered I and II. You have to take the given statements to be true even if they seem to be at variance with commonly known facts. Read all the conclusions and then decide which of the given conclusions logically follows from the given statements disregarding the commonly known facts.

Statements:
Each four is five.

No five is six.

Conclusions:

I. No four is six.

II. Some five are four.

A. Only conclusion I follows
B. Only conclusion II follows
C. Both I and II follow
D. Neither I nor II follows
E. Either I or II follows

Ques (80-84):Direction: Study the information carefully and answer the given questions below.

Seven Students viz. Ganga, Arnav, Swati, Anup, Samita, Prakash, Parul are sitting around a circle to form a circle facing inside. Anup is sitting second to the left of Arnav. Only two students will sit between Samita and Ganga. Parul is not sitting next to Swati and Samita. Arnav is sitting second to the left of Parul. Ganga is not a neighbour of Anup and Swati.

Q.80 Who is sitting to the immediate right of Parul?

A. Ganga   **B.** Arnav
C. Prakash   **D.** No one
E. None of these

Q.81 If they are made to sit in linear arrangement starting from Arnav at the extreme left followed by Ganga, then who will be sitting third from extreme right end.

A. Parul   **B.** Swati   **C.** Samita   **D.** Ganga
E. Prakash

Q.82 Who is sitting between Swati and Samita?

A. Parul   **B.** Anup   **C.** Arnav   **D.** No one
E. Prakash

Q.83 Who is sitting second to left of the one who is immediate right of Anup?

A. Samita   **B.** Swati
C. Parul   **D.** Prakash
E. None of these

Q.84 How many persons are sitting between Prakash and Parul taking clockwise from Parul?

A. One   **B.** Four   **C.** Three   **D.** Five
E. No one

Ques (85-89):Direction: Following questions are based on five three digit numbers given below.

435 287 941 358 763

Q.85 Which of the following is a common factor of all the given numbers?

A. 13   **B.** 17
C. 23   **D.** 12
E. None of these

Q.86 If we add all three digits of each of the given numbers then, what will be the smallest number we get ?

A. 12   **B.** 13   **C.** 14   **D.** 15
E. 16

Q.87 Find the double of the reverse of the smallest number.

A. 1784   **B.** 1654
C. 1564   **D.** 1348
E. None of these

Q.88 Which of the following is the sum of the reverses of the smallest and the greatest numbers?

A. 929   **B.** 931
C. 934   **D.** 955
E. None of these

Q.89 Find the average of all the given numbers?

A. 556.2   **B.** 556.4   **C.** 556   **D.** 556.8
E. 556.6

Ques (90-93):Direction: Study the following information carefully and answer the given questions.

In a certain code language,

'Shagun knitted mat.' is written as 'Xa Zc Yb',

'Children sat on mat' is written as 'Ax Zc By Dw and

'Shagun taught children 'is written as 'Cx Xa Ax'.

Q.90 What is the code for 'children' in the given code language?

A. By   **B.** Zc   **C.** Ax   **D.** Yb
E. Dw

Q.91 If 'children on mat' is coded as 'Zc Ax Dw', then what does 'By' mean in the given code language?

A. sat   **B.** on   **C.** taught   **D.** mat
E. knitted

Q.92 Which of the following is the code for 'taught' in the given code language?

A. By   **B.** Zc   **C.** Ax   **D.** Cx
E. Dw

Q.93 What is the possible code for 'children knitted Shawl' In the given code language?

A. Ax Yb Cx   **B.** Ax Yb Sh
C. Zc Yb Cx   **D.** Zc Xa Cx
E. Dw By Cx

Q.94 How many such pairs of letters are there in the word 'COMPONENT', each of which has as many letters between them in the word (both forward and backward direction) as they have between them in the English Alphabet?

A. Two   **B.** Four   **C.** Five   **D.** Three
E. One

Q.95 Each of the vowels in the word "WINDOWS" is replaced by the number "5" and each consonant is replaced by a number which is the serial number of that consonant in the word i.e., W by 1, N by 3, and so on. What is the total of all the numbers once the replacement is completed?

A. 20   **B.** 35   **C.** 33   **D.** 31
E. 34

Ques (96-99):Direction: Study the following information to answer the given question.

Eight students P, Q, R, S, T, U, V and W are sitting in a horizontal row. All face in north direction. V sits third to the left of S. Q sits immediate left of R. Four students sit between R and T. W sits to the left of U, who is not adjacent to V. At least three students sit to the left of V. P does not sit at extreme end. T neither sits at the extreme left nor at the second extreme left position.

Q.96 Who sits at extreme left end?

A. Q   **B.** R   **C.** W   **D.** U
E. S

Q.97 How many persons sit to the right of P?

A. Three   **B.** Four   **C.** Five   **D.** Two
E. One

Q.98 Which of the following statement is correct?

A. T sits immediate right of U
B. One person sits between Q and U
C. Q sits second to the left of V
D. S sits third to the right of R
E. All are correct

Q.99 How many students sit between Q and U?

A. Two   **B.** One   **C.** Four   **D.** Three
E. Five

Q.100 Direction: Study the following information carefully and answer the question given below.

Eight persons, A, B, C, D, E F, G, and H are sitting in a row. Four of them are facing south and four are facing north. No three consecutive persons are facing the same direction.

A is not an immediate neighbour of D. E, an immediate neighbour of B, is facing north. H is sitting fourth to the right of B. Both the immediate neighbours of D are facing opposite directions. H is sitting second to the left of C and they are facing the same direction. Both H and B are facing the same direction. Both the immediate neighbours of B are facing the same direction. D is sitting fourth to the right of F. E is sitting at the right end of the row.

Who is sitting second to the left of D?

A. B   **B.** H   **C.** F   **D.** A
E. C

// Smart Answer Sheet //

| Correct | Percentage of students who answered correctly. | Skipped | Percentage of students who skipped. |

Q.	Ans.	Correct / Skipped	Q.	Ans.	Correct / Skipped	Q.	Ans.	Correct / Skipped	Q.	Ans.	Correct / Skipped	Q.	Ans.	Correct / Skipped
1	C	28.18 % / 47.27 %	17	C	6.36 % / 82.28 %	33	E	9.09 % / 61.82 %	49	E	4.09 % / 85.46 %	65	A	0 % / 100 %
2	C	14.55 % / 53.63 %	18	D	14.55 % / 82.72 %	34	D	10.0 % / 66.82 %	50	D	5.0 % / 85.91 %	66	C	10.45 % / 85.0 %
3	C	26.36 % / 51.82 %	19	A	8.18 % / 83.18 %	35	A	0.91 % / 70.91 %	51	D	6.36 % / 85.91 %	67	A	10.45 % / 85.91 %
4	D	14.09 % / 55.91 %	20	C	10.0 % / 84.09 %	36	B	9.55 % / 66.81 %	52	A	5.45 % / 86.37 %	68	C	8.64 % / 85.91 %
5	B	12.27 % / 56.37 %	21	E	0.91 % / 95.45 %	37	A	22.27 % / 63.18 %	53	B	5.45 % / 86.82 %	69	D	6.82 % / 85.45 %
6	B	26.36 % / 52.28 %	22	C	1.36 % / 95.46 %	38	B	22.27 % / 62.28 %	54	E	4.55 % / 86.81 %	70	A	10.45 % / 85.46 %
7	C	13.64 % / 53.63 %	23	E	1.36 % / 95.46 %	39	A	17.27 % / 61.82 %	55	E	3.18 % / 87.73 %	71	B	6.82 % / 85.45 %
8	E	21.82 % / 52.27 %	24	A	2.27 % / 95.46 %	40	D	17.73 % / 69.54 %	56	D	5.45 % / 87.73 %	72	A	7.27 % / 85.46 %
9	E	10.91 % / 54.09 %	25	E	0 % / 100 %	41	B	14.09 % / 73.18 %	57	A	2.27 % / 88.18 %	73	E	6.82 % / 85.45 %
10	C	30.0 % / 55.0 %	26	B	2.73 % / 95.45 %	42	C	13.64 % / 76.81 %	58	C	1.36 % / 88.64 %	74	C	6.82 % / 85.45 %
11	A	25.91 % / 56.36 %	27	A	0.91 % / 95.45 %	43	B	14.09 % / 73.64 %	59	C	3.64 % / 89.54 %	75	A	6.82 % / 85.45 %
12	B	20.0 % / 56.36 %	28	B	1.82 % / 95.45 %	44	D	5.91 % / 78.64 %	60	C	0 % / 100 %	76	C	5.45 % / 85.91 %
13	B	3.64 % / 82.27 %	29	E	1.36 % / 95.46 %	45	B	9.55 % / 77.72 %	61	C	1.82 % / 90.91 %	77	B	5.91 % / 85.45 %
14	C	5.0 % / 82.27 %	30	B	3.18 % / 95.91 %	46	E	3.18 % / 79.55 %	62	E	0.45 % / 97.73 %	78	E	6.36 % / 85.46 %
15	E	4.55 % / 82.72 %	31	E	15.91 % / 62.27 %	47	C	5.91 % / 77.27 %	63	D	0.45 % / 98.19 %	79	C	8.18 % / 85.46 %
16	D	4.55 % / 82.72 %	32	A	8.64 % / 62.72 %	48	A	2.73 % / 80.0 %	64	A	0.45 % / 98.64 %	80	C	9.09 % / 85.46 %

Q.	Ans.	Correct		Q.	Ans.	Correct		Q.	Ans.	Correct		Q.	Ans.	Correct		Q.	Ans.	Correct
		Skipped				Skipped				Skipped				Skipped				Skipped
81	C	4.55 %		85	E	5.0 %		89	D	8.18 %		93	B	9.09 %		97	A	0.45 %
		85.45 %				85.45 %				86.82 %				87.73 %				97.73 %
82	B	10.0 %		86	A	10.45 %		90	C	10.91 %		94	B	5.0 %		98	C	0.45 %
		85.45 %				86.82 %				87.27 %				88.18 %				98.19 %
83	A	7.73 %		87	C	7.73 %		91	A	9.09 %		95	D	2.73 %		99	D	0.45 %
		85.45 %				86.82 %				87.27 %				93.63 %				98.64 %
84	D	5.91 %		88	B	8.64 %		92	D	10.45 %		96	C	0.45 %		100	D	0 %
		85.45 %				87.27 %				88.19 %				97.28 %				100 %

//Hints and Solutions//

1. Towards the end of the second passage, it is given that the Phoenicians informed the people of France and Belgium about the useful metals tin and lead found in England. On hearing this, many from France and Belgium decided to travel to England, and some settled there.

Thus, 'The useful metals found in the islands' is the correct answer.

Hence, the correct option is (C).

2. Statement I is stated in the third line of the last paragraph ie., 'The Britons had a strange and terrible religion, called the Religion of the Druids'.

Statement II in the second line of the last paragraph i.e., 'It seems to have been brought over, in very early times indeed, from the opposite country of France, anciently called Gaul, and to have mixed up the worship of the Serpent, and of the Sun and Moon, with the worship of some of the Heathen Gods and Goddesses'.

Thus, statements I and II are correct.

Statement III cannot be inferred from anywhere in the passage. Thus, III is incorrect.

Hence, the correct option is (C).

3. Towards the end of the second paragraph it is given that on hearing about the tin and lead present in England, some people from France and Belgium traveled to the south coast of England and settled there. This place is now called Kent. Thus, we can say I and III can be observed from the paragraph.

Hence, the correct option is (C).

4. In the second paragraph, it is only given that Phoenicians exchanged other useful things for lead and tin. We do not know the nature of goods the Phoenicians have used for exchange. Thus, D is not true according to the passage.

Hence, the correct option is (D).

5. In the first sentence of the last paragraph the author calls the religion of Druids as strange and terrible. From this we can infer that the author finds the religion peculiar. This is only suggested in option (B).

Hence, the correct option is (B).

6. From the context, we can see that the meaning of the word seldom is "something that is uncommon".

Rarely means not often; seldom.

Thus, option (B) also reflects the same and is the right choice.

Hence, the correct option is (B).

7. From the context we can infer the meaning of the word "veneration" means respect or reverence.

Respect means a feeling of deep admiration for someone or something elicited by their abilities, qualities, or achievements.

Thus, Respect is the word that is most similar in meaning to the word Veneration.

Hence, the correct option is (C).

8. The given sentence is grammatically correct and thus no change is required.

Hence, the correct option is (E).

9. The given sentence is correct in its given form.

Some verbs line 'acquit' don't require any preposition to succeed them.

Thus no change is required.

Hence, the correct option is (E).

10. 'To be' cannot be followed by the first form of the word. Therefore, 'prepare' is incorrect in the given context.

'to preparing' is also incorrect as it should be 'to be prepared'.

The sentence is in the simple present tense, thus the usage of have/have been is also incorrect.

Correct sentence: Amid the tensions at the border, the air force chief has asked his troops to be prepared for the war.

Hence, the correct option is (C).

11. The sentence talks about Ravi not getting calls from top colleges despite having good scores.

The correct usage should be 'despite scoring well'. The usage of 'score' is incorrect in the context.

Correct sentence: Ravi did not get calls from any of the top colleges despite scoring well in the examination.

Hence, the correct option is (A).

12. This is a sentence of conditional type of sentences, where the first action depends on the situation of the second action or vice versa.

The first part of the sentence is in the past tense.

The second part is in present. Thus there is inconsistency in the given sentence.

In order for the sentence to be correct, it should be 'I would have scored the 100 percentile'. This shows that there would have been a possibility then.

Correct sentence: Had I not wasted time on a particular question, I would have scored the 100 percentile.

Hence, the correct option is (B).

13. The paragraph is clearly about electricity and the way it is generated. Therefore, the introductory sentence will be C. F follows C by mentioning the primary sources from where electricity is derived. E follows F by naming these natural sources as primary sources. After sentence 4, there is a clear link with ADB – which gives the process of electricity generation. A – with large moving turbines – is the first sentence among these three sentences. A is followed by D with the role of moving turbines causing magnets to move as well and B concludes the paragraph by stating the last process of generating electricity – moving magnets release electrons within the copper wires.

The correct order is CFE4ADB.

The ordered paragraph is: Electricity is not a primary but a secondary energy source. We get it from the conversion of other sources of energy such as coal, water, oil, nuclear power, and other natural sources. These energy sources are known as primary sources. Power stations are places where electricity is generated for power purposes. Large machines known as turbines are turned very quickly with the help of heat, wind, or moving water. The moving turbines cause large magnets to turn within copper wire coils. The moving magnets within the copper wire coils cause electrons to move within the wire – this is electricity.

Thus, The SEVENTH statement is B.

Hence, the correct option is (B).

14. The paragraph is clearly about electricity and the way it is generated. Therefore, the introductory sentence will be C. F follows C by mentioning the primary sources from where electricity is derived. E follows F by naming these natural sources as primary sources. After sentence 4, there is a clear link with ADB – which gives the process of electricity generation. A – with large moving turbines – is the first sentence among these three sentences. A is followed by D with the role of moving turbines causing magnets to move as well and B concludes the paragraph by stating the last process of generating electricity – moving magnets release electrons within the copper wires.

The correct order is CFE4ADB.

The ordered paragraph is: Electricity is not a primary but a secondary energy source. We get it from the conversion of other sources of energy such as coal, water, oil, nuclear power, and other natural sources. These energy sources are known as primary sources. Power stations are places where electricity is generated for power purposes. Large machines known as turbines are turned very quickly with the help of heat, wind, or moving water. The moving turbines cause large magnets to turn within copper wire coils. The moving magnets within the copper wire coils cause electrons to move within the wire – this is electricity.

Thus, The SIXTH statement is D.

Hence, the correct option is (C).

15. The paragraph is clearly about electricity and the way it is generated. Therefore, the introductory sentence will be C. F follows C by mentioning the primary sources from where electricity is derived. E follows F by naming these natural sources as primary sources. After sentence 4, there is a clear link with ADB – which gives the process of electricity generation. A – with large moving turbines – is the first sentence among these three sentences. A is followed by D with the role of moving turbines causing magnets to move as well and B concludes the paragraph by stating the last process of generating electricity – moving magnets release electrons within the copper wires.

The correct order is CFE4ADB.

The ordered paragraph is: Electricity is not a primary but a secondary energy source. We get it from the conversion of other sources of energy such as coal, water, oil, nuclear power, and

other natural sources. These energy sources are known as primary sources. Power stations are places where electricity is generated for power purposes. Large machines known as turbines are turned very quickly with the help of heat, wind, or moving water. The moving turbines cause large magnets to turn within copper wire coils. The moving magnets within the copper wire coils cause electrons to move within the wire – this is electricity.

Thus, The THIRD statement is E.

Hence, the correct option is (E).

16. The paragraph is clearly about electricity and the way it is generated. Therefore, the introductory sentence will be C. F follows C by mentioning the primary sources from where electricity is derived. E follows F by naming these natural sources as primary sources. After sentence 4, there is a clear link with ADB – which gives the process of electricity generation. A – with large moving turbines – is the first sentence among these three sentences. A is followed by D with the role of moving turbines causing magnets to move as well and B concludes the paragraph by stating the last process of generating electricity – moving magnets release electrons within the copper wires.

The correct order is CFE4ADB.

The ordered paragraph is: Electricity is not a primary but a secondary energy source. We get it from the conversion of other sources of energy such as coal, water, oil, nuclear power, and other natural sources. These energy sources are known as primary sources. Power stations are places where electricity is generated for power purposes. Large machines known as turbines are turned very quickly with the help of heat, wind, or moving water. The moving turbines cause large magnets to turn within copper wire coils. The moving magnets within the copper wire coils cause electrons to move within the wire – this is electricity.

Thus, The SECOND statement is F.

Hence, the correct option is (D).

17. The paragraph is clearly about electricity and the way it is generated. Therefore, the introductory sentence will be C. F follows C by mentioning the primary sources from where electricity is derived. E follows F by naming these natural sources as primary sources. After sentence 4, there is a clear link with ADB – which gives the process of electricity generation. A – with large moving turbines – is the first sentence among these three sentences. A is followed by D with the role of moving turbines causing magnets to move as well and B concludes the paragraph by stating the last process of generating electricity – moving magnets release electrons within the copper wires.

The correct order is CFE4ADB.

The ordered paragraph is: Electricity is not a primary but a secondary energy source. We get it from the conversion of other sources of energy such as coal, water, oil, nuclear power, and other natural sources. These energy sources are known as primary sources. Power stations are places where electricity is generated for power purposes. Large machines known as turbines are turned very quickly with the help of heat, wind, or moving water. The moving turbines cause large magnets to turn within copper wire coils. The moving magnets within the copper wire coils cause electrons to move within the wire – this is electricity.

Thus, The FIRST statement is C.

Hence, the correct option is (C).

18. Fish out of the water means feeling uncomfortable in unfamiliar surroundings.

For example:

When Carla transferred to a new school, she felt like a fish out of water because she didn't know anyone there.

Hence, the correct option is (D).

19. Upset someone's applecart means to do something that causes a plan to go wrong.

For example:

Reema told Harish not to upset the apple cart by revealing where they are going.

Hence, the correct option is (A).

20. Bite off more than you can chew means to try to do something that is too difficult for you

For example:

It feels like I bit off more than I could chew when I promised to complete this worksheet in one day.

Hence, the correct option is (C).

21. The given sentence is talking about appealing not to purchase dangerous food.

Therefore, the most appropriate word to be filled in the blank is 'Dissuade'.

Also, the use of the word "dangerous" in the sentence indicates the use of the word 'dissuade' in the blank.

The word 'Dissuade' means To persuade someone not to take a particular course of action.

Example: Doctors had tried to dissuade patients from smoking.

Hence, the correct option is (E).

22. The given sentence is talking about the leaked document equivalent to Pentagon Papers that became apparent or came to people's attention during the Nixon era.

Therefore, the most appropriate word to be filled in the blank is 'Surfaced'.

Also, the use of the word "equivalent" in the sentence indicates the use of the word 'surfaced' in the blank.

The word 'Surfaced' means To come to people's attention; become apparent.

Example: A rumor has surfaced that the company is about to go out of business.

Hence, the correct option is (C).

23. The given sentence is talking about preventing a crisis-like scenario.

Therefore, the most appropriate word to be filled in the blank is 'Avert'.

Also, the use of the word "crisis" in the sentence indicates the use of the word 'avert' in the blank.

The word 'Avert' means To prevent or warding off an undesirable occurrence.

Example: He managed to avert the closure of the factory.

Hence, the correct option is (E).

24. The given sentence is saying that Prime Minister Narendra Modi will be on a visit involving Germany and Denmark.

Therefore, the most appropriate word to be filled in the blank is 'Bilateral'.

Also, the use of the word "visit" in the sentence indicates the use of the word 'bilateral' in the blank.

The word 'Bilateral' means Involving two groups of people or two countries.

Example: France and Germany have signed a bilateral agreement to help prevent drug smuggling.

Hence, the correct option is (A).

25. The given sentence is saying that India's strategic future is linked with Russia in a way that is impossible to separate.

Therefore, the most appropriate word to be filled in the blank is 'Inextricably'.

Also, the use of the word "linked" in the sentence indicates the use of the word 'inextricably' in the blank.

The word 'Inextricably' means In a way that is impossible to disentangle or separate.

Example: Physical health is inextricably linked to mental health.

Hence, the correct option is (E).

26. In the given sentence, the error in the part is the inappropriate use of the adverb.

Adverbs are words that are used to modify nouns, pronouns, verbs, adjectives, other adverbs, etc.

In the given statement, the word 'hardly' is being used to qualify a statement by saying that it is true to an insignificant degree.

For eg.- The little house in which he lived was hardly bigger than a hut.

Whereas from the sentence we can gather that he works hard to be able to provide for his family.

Therefore, we will replace 'hardly' with 'hard' to make the sentence grammatically correct.

The correct sentence will be: 'He has been toiling hard to be able to provide for his family.'

Hence, the correct option is (B).

27. In the given sentence, the error in the part is the inappropriate use of the noun number.

Nouns are words used to name person, place, animal, thing, emotion, or state.

In the given statement, the incorrect plural form of 'brother-in-law' is being used.

Compound nouns are made plural by adding 's' to the main word.

For eg.- Commander-in-chief - Commanders-in-chief, brother-in-law - brothers-in-law etc.

Therefore, we will replace 'brother-in-laws' with 'brothers-in-law' to make the sentence grammatically correct.

The correct sentence will be: 'The brothers-in-law were very helpful and supportive to their choices.'

Hence, the correct option is (A).

28. In the given sentence, the error in the part is the inappropriate use of the noun number.

Nouns are words used to name person, place, animal, thing, emotion, or state.

In the given statement, the incorrect plural form of 'information' is being used.

Nouns such as jewelry, evidence, information, work, etc are uncountable nouns and can't be made plural by adding 's/es' within a sentence.

Phrases like 'all pieces of', 'many kinds of', 'slices of' etc. are added before uncountable nouns to make them plural.

For eg.- Many kinds of furniture are available in that shop.

Therefore, we will replace 'informations' with 'information' to make the sentence grammatically correct.

The correct sentence will be: 'All pieces of information given by her were accurate.'

Hence, the correct option is (B).

29. The given sentence is in the past tense as can be seen by the use of the verbs 'killed' and 'injured' in the past tense.

There are no errors in the sentence.

Thus, the correct sentence is: 'Three jawans of District Reserve Guard were killed while ten others were injured in an IED blast on Tuesday.'

Hence, the correct option is (E).

30. The sentence is in the past tense as the event is already over, the match has been lost and the team has already arrived at the airport.

This can be seen by the usage of the verb 'lost' and 'was' in the past tense.

This means that the other verbs in the sentence should also be in agreement with this tense of the sentence.

Hence, 'receive' needs to be replaced with 'received' in order to make the sentence grammatically correct.

Thus, the correct sentence is: 'Despite having lost the match, the team was received at the airport with a lot of enthusiasm.'

Hence, the correct option is (B).

31. We know that,

$$\text{Speed} = \frac{distance}{time}$$

The distance to Jodhpur = 78 km/hr × 40 min

$$= 78 \times \frac{40}{60}$$

= 52 km

If the speed is 65 km/hr,

Time taken = $\dfrac{52}{65}$ = 0.8 hr × 60 = 48 mins

Hence, the correct option is (E).

32. We know that,

Investment-months = amount invested × number of months

Arjun invested 70000 for 12 months

So Arjun's investment-months $= 12 \times 70000$

Let the number of months Aryan invested be x.

Aryan's investment-months $= 60000x$

Ratio of profits $=$ Ratio of investment-months

Ratio of their profits $= \dfrac{12 \times 70000}{60000x}$

Given, $\dfrac{12 \times 70000}{60000x} = \dfrac{2}{1}$

$\Rightarrow \dfrac{14}{x}$

$\Rightarrow x = 7$ months.

Therefore, Aryan joined after $12 - 7 = 5$ months.

Hence, the correct option is (A).

33. The rates of filling per hour for the pipes are $\dfrac{1}{5}, \dfrac{1}{8}$ and - $\dfrac{1}{15}$.

So, total time taken = $\dfrac{1}{5} + \dfrac{1}{8} - \dfrac{1}{15}$

$= \dfrac{(24+15-8)}{120}$

$= \dfrac{31}{120}$

$= \dfrac{31}{120} \times 60$

= 15.2 hours

Hence, the correct option is (E).

34. Let the cost of one pen be x and the cost of one eraser be y.

Given,

7x + 13y = 121 .... (i)

5x + 4y = 60 .... (ii)

Multiplying equation (i) by 5 and equation (ii) by 7 and subtracting both we get,

37y = 185

y = 5

Substituting y in equation (ii),

x = 8

So, the cost of 11 pens and 5 erasers = 88 + 25 = 113

Hence, the correct option is (D).

35. Let the sum invested be x

$$\text{Simple interest} = \frac{Principal \times rate \times time}{100}$$

$$\Rightarrow \text{Simple interest} = \frac{x \times 18.2 \times 4}{100}$$

$$\Rightarrow \frac{x \times 182 \times 4}{1000}$$

$$\Rightarrow \frac{91x}{125}$$

We know that,

$$\text{Compound interest} = x\left(1 + \frac{r}{100}\right)^3 - x$$

$$\Rightarrow \frac{91x}{125} = x\left(1 + \frac{r}{100}\right)^3 - x$$

$$\Rightarrow \frac{91}{125} + 1 = \left(1 + \frac{r}{100}\right)^3$$

$$\Rightarrow 1.728 = \left(1 + \frac{r}{100}\right)^3$$

$$\Rightarrow 1.2 = \left(1 + \frac{r}{100}\right)$$

$$\Rightarrow r = 20$$

Therefore, the sum for compound interest has to be invested at 20% per annum.

Hence, the correct option is (A).

36. Total profit at the end of 4 years, $P = \text{Rs. } 1,70,000$

Time period for which Devaki invested money, $t_1 = 4$ years $= 12 \times 4 = 48$ months

Time period for which Saroj invested money, $t_2 = 48 - 8 = 40$ months

Amount invested by Devaki, $I_1 = \text{Rs. } 75,000$

Amount invested by Saroj, $I_2 = \text{Rs. } 80,000$

$$\text{Share of profit of Devaki} = \frac{(I_1 \times t_1 \times P)}{(I_1 \times t_1 + I_2 \times t_2)}$$

$$\Rightarrow \text{Share of profit of Devaki} = \frac{7500 \times 48 \times 170000}{75000 \times 48 + 80000 \times 40} = \text{Rs. } 90,000$$

$\therefore$ Share of profit of Devaki $= \text{Rs. } 90,000$

Hence, the correct option is (B).

37. The pattern followed here is:

$13 = 2^2 + 3^2$

$41 = 4^2 + 5^2$

$85 = 6^2 + 7^2$

$145 = 8^2 + 9^2$

$? = 10^2 + 11^2 = 221$

Hence, the correct option is (A).

38. Value can be approximate then,

$$\sqrt[3]{\left(\sqrt[3]{511}\right)^2} \approx \sqrt[3]{\left(\sqrt[3]{512}\right)^2}$$

$$= \sqrt[3]{8^2}$$

$$= \sqrt[3]{64}$$

$$= 4$$

Hence, the correct option is (B).

39. Given that,

$$1\frac{2}{7} + 2\frac{2}{5} + 3\frac{2}{9}$$

$$= \frac{9 \times 5 \times 9 + 12 \times 7 \times 9 + 29 \times 5 \times 7}{315}$$

$$= \frac{2176}{315}$$

$$= 6\frac{286}{315}$$

Hence, the correct option is (A).

40. Given that,

$$19.1 \times 9.9 + 22.2 \div 11.1 - 7.4$$

Taking approximate values,

$$\approx 19 \times 10 + 2 - 7.4$$

$$= 190 - 5.4$$

$$= 184.6 \approx 185$$

Hence, the correct option is (D).

41. Given,

$$19.99\% \text{ of } 1224.98 - \sqrt{(1295.93)} \times 3.99 - 87.69 = ?$$

$\Rightarrow 20\%$ of $1225 - \sqrt{1296} \times 4 - 88 =?$

$\Rightarrow (20/100) \times 1225 - 36 \times 4 - 88 =?$

$\Rightarrow (1225/5) - 144 - 88 =?$

$\Rightarrow 245 - 232 =?$

$\Rightarrow ? = 13$

$\therefore 13$ will come in place of the question mark ('?').

Hence, the correct option is (B).

42. Given,

$$323.27 \div 16.96 \times 18.99 =?$$

Approximating the value to the nearest integer, we get

$$323 \div 17 \times 19 =?$$

$\Rightarrow 323 \div 17 \times 19 =?$

$\Rightarrow 19 \times 19 =?$

$\therefore ? = 361$

Hence, the correct option is (C).

43. Given that,

25% of 397 + 20% of 502 + 25% of 601

Taking approximate values,

$\approx$ 25% of 400 + 20% of 500 + 25% of 600

$\dfrac{25}{100} \times 400 + \dfrac{20}{100} \times 500 + \dfrac{25}{100} \times 600$

= 100 + 100 + 150

= 350

Hence, the correct option is (B).

44. The number of seats won by Party C in 1994 = 81

The number of seats won by Party C in 2014 = 155

So, the percentage incease is $\dfrac{(155-81)}{81} = \dfrac{74}{81} = 91.35\%$

Hence, the correct option is (D).

45. The number of seats won by Party B in 1984 = 84

The number of seats won by Party B in 1989 = 92

The number of seats won by Party B in 1994 = 29

The number of seats won by Party B in 1999 = 161

The number of seats won by Party B in 2004 = 181

The number of seats won by Party B in 2009 = 41

The number of seats won by Party B in 2014 = 121

So, the total number of seats won by Party B is 709

And the average is $\dfrac{709}{7} = 101.28 \sim 101$

Hence, the correct option is (B).

46. The number of seats won by Party C in 1984 = 12

The number of seats won by Party C in 1989 = 28

The number of seats won by Party C in 1994 = 81

The number of seats won by Party C in 1999 = 101

The number of seats won by Party C in 2004 = 108

The number of seats won by Party C in 2009 = 96

The number of seats won by Party C in 2014 = 155

So, the total number of seats won by Party C is 581.

The number of seats won by Party A in 1984 = 204

The number of seats won by Party A in 1989 = 180

The number of seats won by Party A in 1994 = 190

The number of seats won by Party A in 1999 = 38

The number of seats won by Party A in 2004 = 11

The number of seats won by Party A in 2009 = 163

The number of seats won by Party A in 2014 = 24

So, the total number of seats won by Party A is 810.

So, the required percentage is $\left(\dfrac{581}{810}\right) \times 100 = 71.72\%$

Hence, the correct option is (E).

47. The increase in the number of seats won by Party C in 1989 = 28 - 12 = 16

The increase in the number of seats won by Party C in 1994 = 81 - 28 = 53

The increase in the number of seats won by Party C in 1999 = 101 - 81 = 20

The increase in the number of seats won by Party C in 2004 = 108 - 101 = 7

The increase in the number of seats won by Party C in 2009 = 96 - 108 = -12

The increase in the number of seats won by Party C in 2014 = 155 - 96 = 59

Thus, in 2014 Party C gain the maximum number of seats as compared to the previous year.

Hence, the correct option is (C).

48. The difference between highest and lowest seats in 1984 = 204 - 12 = 192

The difference between highest and lowest seats in 1989 = 180 - 28 = 152

The difference between highest and lowest seats in 1994 = 190 - 29 = 161

The difference between highest and lowest seats in 1999 = 161 - 38 = 123

The difference between highest and lowest seats in 2004 = 181 - 11 = 170

The difference between highest and lowest seats in 2009 = 163 - 41 = 122

The difference between highest and lowest seats in 2014 = 155 - 24 = 131

So, the difference is least in 2009 and equals 122.

Hence, the correct option is (A).

49. Considering the given series,

216, 225, 222, 233, 228, 239, 234

The logic of above series can be explained as,

$225 - 216 = 9 \neq 11$

$222 - 225 = -3 \neq -5$

$233 - 222 = 11$

$228 - 233 = -5$

$239 - 228 = 11$

$234 - 239 = -5$

∴ Wrong number is 225 and correct number is 227.

Hence, the correct option is (E).

50. Considering the given series,

100, 96, 105, 89, 113, 78, 127

The logic of above series can be explained as,

$100 - 96 = 4 = 2^2$

$96 - 105 = -9 = -3^2$

$105 - 89 = 16 = 4^2$

$89 - 113 = -24 \neq -5^2$

$113 - 78 = 35 \neq 6^2$

$78 - 127 = -49 = -7^2$

∴ Wrong number is 113 and correct number is 114.

Hence, the correct option is (D).

51. Considering the given series,

10, 11, 23, 70, 281, 1403, 8437

The logic of above series can be explained as,

$10 \times 1 + 1 = 11$

$11 \times 2 + 1 = 23$

$23 \times 3 + 1 = 70$

$70 \times 4 + 1 = 281$

$281 \times 5 + 1 \neq 1403$ (should be 1406)

$1406 \times 6 + 1 = 8437$

∴ Wrong number is 1403

Hence, the correct option is (D).

52. Considering the given series,

4, 12, 24, 96, 480, 2880, 20160

The logic of above series can be explained as,

$4 \times 2 \neq 12$ (should be 8)

$8 \times 3 = 24$

$24 \times 4 = 96$

$96 \times 5 = 480$

$480 \times 6 = 2880$

$2880 \times 7 = 20160$

∴ Wrong number is 12

Hence, the correct option is (A).

53. First Equation:

$2x^2 + 4x - 6 = 0$

$\Rightarrow 2x^2 + 6x - 2x - 6 = 0$

$\Rightarrow 2x(x + 3) - 2(x + 3) = 0$

$\Rightarrow (x + 3)(2x - 2) = 0$

$\Rightarrow x = -3 \text{ or } x = 1$

Second Equation:

$y^2 + 6y + 9 = 0$

$\Rightarrow y^2 + 3y + 3y + 9 = 0$

$\Rightarrow y(y + 3) + 3(y + 3) = 0$

$\Rightarrow (y + 3)(y + 3) = 0$

$\Rightarrow y = -3$

Value of x	Value of y	Relation
-3	-3	x = y
1	-3	x > y

∴ $x \geq y$

Hence, the correct option is (B).

54. First Equation:

$4x^2 + 56x - 60 = 0$

$\Rightarrow 4x^2 + 60x - 4x - 60 = 0$

$\Rightarrow 4x(x + 15) - 4(x + 15) = 0$

$\Rightarrow (x + 15)(4x - 4) = 0$

$\Rightarrow x = -15 \text{ or } x = 1$

Second Equation:

$2y^2 + 28y - 240 = 0$

$\Rightarrow 2y^2 + 40y - 12y - 240 = 0$

$\Rightarrow 2y(y + 20) - 12(y + 20) = 0$

$\Rightarrow (y + 20)(2y - 12) = 0$

$\Rightarrow$ y = -20 or y = 6

Value of x	Value of y	Relation
-15	-20	x > y
-15	6	x < y
1	-20	x > y
1	6	x < y

$\therefore$ We can observe that no clear relationship cannot be determined between x and y.

Hence, the correct option is (E).

55. First Equation:

$x^2 + 13x = 0$

$\Rightarrow$ x(x + 13) = 0

$\Rightarrow$ x = 0 or x = -13

Second Equation:

$y^2 = 169$

$\Rightarrow y^2 = 13^2$

$\Rightarrow$ y = 13 or y = -13

Value of x	Value of y	Relation
0	13	x < y
0	-13	x > y
-13	13	x < y
-13	-13	x = y

$\therefore$ We can observe that no clear relationship cannot be determined between x and y.

Hence, the correct option is (E).

56. First Equation:

$x^2 = 64$

$\Rightarrow x^2 = 8^2$

$\Rightarrow$ x = -8 or x = 8

Second Equation:

$y^3 = 512$

$\Rightarrow y^3 = 8^3$

$\Rightarrow$ y = 8

Value of x	Value of y	Relation
-8	8	x < y
8	8	x = y

$\therefore x \leq y$

Hence, the correct option is (D).

57. First Equation:

$x^2 - 58x + 841 = 0$

$\Rightarrow x^2 - 29x - 29x + 841 = 0$

$\Rightarrow$ x(x - 29) - 29(x - 29) = 0

$\Rightarrow$ (x - 29) (x - 29) = 0

$\Rightarrow$ x = 29

Second Equation:

$2y^2 + 58y = 0$

$\Rightarrow$ 2y(y + 29) = 0

$\Rightarrow$ y = 0 or y = -29

Value of x	Value of y	Relation
29	0	x > y
29	-29	x > y

$\therefore$ x > y

Hence, the correct option is (A).

58. Given that value of each installment = Rs. 35000

Rate R = 6%

Number of investments = 2

$\Rightarrow$ Value of each installment = $\dfrac{P}{\left(\frac{100}{100+R}\right)+\left(\frac{100}{100+R}\right)^2} =$

$\dfrac{P}{\left(\frac{100}{100+6}\right)+\left(\frac{100}{100+6}\right)^2} = \dfrac{P}{(1.84)}$

$\Rightarrow$ 35,000 × 1.84 = Principal

$\Rightarrow$ Principal = Rs. 64,400

Hence, the correct option is (C).

59. According to the given information,

The average marks of 35 students is 72.

Further, the marks of two students were misread as 48 and 66 of the actual marks 84 and 65 respectively.

= 35 × 72 – 48 – 66 + 84 + 65

= 2520 + 35 = 2555 kg.

$\therefore$ Required correct average marks = $\dfrac{2555}{35}$ = 73

So, the correct average marks would be 73.

Hence, the correct option is (C).

60. Given

Total Number of candidates = 12

Let 'S' be the Sample Space

Then, n(S) = number of ways of three candidates who got selected.

n(S) = $^{12}C_3$ = 220

Let 'E' be the event of 1 girl and 2 boys selected

Therefore, n(E) = number of possibilities of 1 girl out of 4 and 2 boys out of 8

n(E) = $^4C_1 \times {}^8C_2$ = 4 × 28 = 112

Now the required Probability = $\dfrac{112}{220} = \dfrac{28}{55}$

Q.74 Who is the fourth shortest person?

A. Sainoor   **B.** Manya   **C.** Kianshi   **D.** Piyu

E. Simar

Ques (75-79):Direction: Read the following passage carefully and answer the question given below it.

Seven persons Ram, Ronak, Rishu, Gaurav, Shyam, Lokesh and Rinku teach in seven different schools viz- A, B, C, D, E, F and G, but not necessarily in the same order. Each of them has a mobile of a different companies viz- LG, Intex, HTC, Redmi, Sony, Samsung and Lenovo, but not necessarily in the same order. Rinku teaches in school C and he uses neither Intex nor Redmi. Ronak uses Samsung and he teaches in school E. Rishu and Gaurav do not teach in school G and they do not use Redmi. Shyam teaches in school A and he uses LG. The one who teaches in school F and he uses Lenovo. Lokesh teaches in school D and he uses HTC. Rishu does not teach in school B.

Q.75 Ram teaches in which of the following school?

A. G   **B.** F

C. B   **D.** F or B

E. None of these

Q.76 Rishu uses which of the following mobile?

A. Redmi   **B.** Lenovo

C. Intex   **D.** Sony

E. None of these

Q.77 Gaurav teaches in which of the following school?

A. G   **B.** F

C. B   **D.** G or F

E. None of these

Q.78 Which of the following combinations of Person, School and Mobile is correct?

A. Ram – F – Lenovo

B. Gaurav – B – Redmi

C. Ram – G – Redmi

D. Rishu – G – Redmi

E. Ronak – E – Redmi

Q.79 Gaurav uses which of the following mobile?

A. Redmi   **B.** Lenovo   **C.** Sony   **D.** Intex

E. Samsung

Ques (80-83):Direction: Study the information given below carefully and answer the questions that follow.

There are 7 members in the family. There are 2 married couples. R is son of H. S is mother of A. H is son of S. Y and H are married couples. A is aunt of I who is the daughter of Y. I is sister-in-law of J.

Q.80 What is relationship between A and R?

A. Aunt– Nephew   **B.** Father – Son

C. Mother – daughter   **D.** Aunt – Niece

E. Brother – Sister

Q.81 How is Y related to J?

A. Daughter – in – law   **B.** Uncle

C. Daughter   **D.** Mother– in – law

E. Son

Q.82 Who is daughter of H?

A. S   **B.** A   **C.** J   **D.** R

E. I

Q.83 How is S related to I?

A. Grandmother   **B.** Aunt

C. Sister   **D.** Grandfather

E. Brother

Q.84 If in the word "AMERICAN" every vowel changes to the next vowel then rearrange the alphabetic order, how many letters are unchanged?

A. One   **B.** Two

C. Three   **D.** Four

E. None of the above

Ques (85-89):Direction: Read the information given below and answer the question that follows:

Seven classmates Diya, Siya, Tiya, Niya, Pawan, Suresh, and Ankit are standing in a straight line facing north, but not necessarily in the same order.

Suresh stands second from the left end of the line. Only two persons stand between Suresh and Pawan. Only one person stands between Diya and Tiya. Ankit stands third to the left of Tiya. Neither Tiya nor Suresh is the immediate neighbour of Niya.

Q.85 Which of the following pairs at the extreme ends of the line?

A. Siya and Diya   **B.** Ankit and Diya

C. Siya and Niya   **D.** Siya and Pawan

E. Ankit and Niya

Q.86 Which of the following statements is true regarding Siya?

A. Tiya stand to the left of Siya

B. One person stand between Siya and Pawan

C. Ankit stand second right of Siya

D. Niya is the neighbour of Siya

E. Siya stand at one of the extreme end

Q.87 What is the position of Ankit with respect to Suresh?

A. Second to the left   **B.** Immediate left

C. Third to the right   **D.** Immediate right

E. Second to right

Q.88 How many persons sits between Tiya and Niya?

A. One   **B.** Two   **C.** Three   **D.** Four

E. Five

Q.89 What is the position of Tiya from left end of the line?

A. Fourth   **B.** Sixth   **C.** Second   **D.** Fifth

E. First

Q.90 How many such pairs of letters are there in the word DEMOGRAPHY each of which has as many letters between them in the word (in the forward or backward direction) as they have between them in the English alphabetical order?

A. One   **B.** Two

Hence, the correct option is (C).

61. Let 'l' be the length of a given rectangle and 'b' be its breadth.

Here, l = 2b (given)

Perimeter of rectangle = 2(l + b)

$\Rightarrow$ 2 (2b + b) = 90

$\Rightarrow$ 3b = 45

$\Rightarrow$ b = 15 cm

$\Rightarrow$ length l = 2b = 30 cm

Now, when length decreased by 5 cm and breadth increased by 5 cm,

Then, increase in the area of rectangle = (new area) – (old area)

= (30 – 5) × (15 + 5) – (30 × 15)

= 500 – 450

= 50 cm square

So, increase in the area of rectangle is 50 cm square

Hence, the correct option is (C).

62. Given,

(46.98 × 3.94 ÷ 46.99 × 4.98^2) ÷ 4.98 × 3.98 = 18.99 × 4.98 ÷ ?

$\Rightarrow$ (47 × 4 ÷ 47 × 5^2) ÷ 5 × 4 = 19 × 5 ÷ ?

$\Rightarrow$ (188 ÷ 47 × 25) ÷ 5 × 4 = 95 ÷ ?

$\Rightarrow$ (4 × 25) ÷ 5 × 4 = 95 ÷ ?

$\Rightarrow$ 20 × 4 = 95 ÷ ?

$\Rightarrow$ 80 = 95 ÷ ?

$\Rightarrow ? \approx \dfrac{19}{16}$

Hence, the correct option is (E).

63. Given,

$$\left(\sqrt{256.089} \div \sqrt[3]{64.004} \times 5\right) + \left(\sqrt{361.023} + \sqrt{121.05}\right) = ? + 23$$

Acording to the BODMAS Rule,

$$\Rightarrow \left(\sqrt{256} \div \sqrt[3]{64} \times 5\right) + \left(\sqrt{361} + \sqrt{121}\right) = ? + 23$$

$\Rightarrow$ (16 ÷ 4 × 5) + (19 + 11) = ? + 23

$\Rightarrow$ (4 × 5) + (19 + 11) = ? + 23 ($\because$ First division than multiplication)

$\Rightarrow$ 20 + 30 = ? + 23

$\Rightarrow$ 50 - 23 = ?

$\therefore$? = 27

Hence, the correct option is (D).

64. Given,

$$\sqrt{4761} \times \sqrt{3969} + \sqrt{2704} + 1 = ? \times 5 + \sqrt{25} \times \sqrt{3481}$$

$\Rightarrow$ 69 × 63 + 52 + 1 = ? × 5 + 5 × 59

$\Rightarrow$ 4347 + 53 = (? + 59) × 5

$\Rightarrow$ 4400 = (? + 59) × 5

$\Rightarrow$ 880 = (? + 59)

$\Rightarrow$ 821 = ?

$\Rightarrow$? = 821

Hence, the correct option is (A).

65. Given,

$$? = 74.99 - 2.99 \times \left[\left(5.99^2 \div 6.06\right) \div 3.03\right] \div \left(\tfrac{1}{2.99}\right) + 12.99$$

$$= 75 - 3 \times \left[\left(6^2 \div 6\right) \div 3\right] \div \left(\tfrac{1}{3}\right) + 13$$

$$= 75 - 3 \times \left[\left(\tfrac{36}{6} \div 3\right] \div \left(\tfrac{1}{3}\right) + 13$$

$$= 75 - 3 \times \left[\left(\tfrac{6}{3}\right] \times 3 + 13$$

$$= 75 - 3 \times 2 \times 3 + 13$$

$$= 75 - 18 + 13$$

$$= 70$$

Hence, the correct option is (A).

66. Given statements: Q ≤ A < D < K ≤ M = J = F > Z

Conclusions:

I. K > Q → True (as **Q ≤ A < D < K** ≤ M = J = F > Z → K > Q)

II. F ≥ K → True (as Q ≤ A < D < **K ≤ M = J = F** > Z → F ≥ K)

Therefore, both I and II are true.

Hence, the correct option is (C).

67. Given statement: J < G ≥ L > N < K ≤ F < T = H

Conclusion:

I. F > L → False (as L > N < K ≤ F) thus clear relation between F and L cannot be determined as symbols are in reverse order.

II. K < H → True (as K ≤ F → F < T → T = H → So, K < H)

Therefore, only conclusion II follows.

Hence, the correct option is (A).

68. Given statement: X ≤ Y < Z; O < R ≤ Q = X

On combining: O < R ≤ Q = X ≤ Y < Z

Conclusion:

I. Q < Z → True (as Q = X → X ≤ Y → Y < Z → So, Q < Z)

II. R ≤ Y → True (as R ≤ Q → Q = X → X ≤ Y → So, R ≤ Y)

Therefore, both conclusions I and II follow.

Hence, the correct option is (C).

69. Given statement: 8 ≥ 7 < 6 < 5; 2 > 3 > 9 = 8

On combining: 2 > 3 > 9 = 8 ≥ 7 < 6 < 5

Conclusion:

I. 8 ≥ 5 → False (as 8 ≥ 7 < 6 < 5) thus clear relation between 8 and 5 cannot be determined as the symbols are in reverse order.

II. 8 < 5 → False (as 8 ≥ 7 < 6 < 5) thus clear relation between 8 and 5 cannot be determined as the symbols are in reverse order.

Thus, conclusions I and II forms complementary pair

Therefore, either conclusion I or conclusion II follows.

Hence, the correct option is (D).

Ques (70-74): Boxes: A, B, C, D, E, F, and G.

1) There are 3 boxes between D and E.

2) Box E is kept above box D.

3) Box C is kept just above the box E.

S.N	Case 1	Case 2
1	C	
2	E	C
3		E
4		
5		
6	D	
7		D

4) There are 2 boxes between box G and box F.

S.N	Case 1	Case 2
1	C	G/F
2	E	C
3		E
4	G/F	F/G
5		
6	D	
7	F/G	D

5) Box A is kept in an odd number place.

6) Box B is kept above the box G.

Now case 2 did not follow the above-mentioned information, so terminated, as B can't be placed above G as no space left for B to be placed.

Box B will be place at 3rd position as It is given Box B is placed one box above the box G, which means Box B will be placed immediately above box G, which is possible only when Box B is placed at 3rd position.

Now only position is left that is 5th position so Box A will be placed on 5th position and also 5 is a odd number so this condition is also satisfied here.

S.N	Boxes

1	C
2	E
3	B
4	G
5	A
6	D
7	F

70. So, box C is kept in the first position.

Hence, the correct option is (A).

71. So, 4 boxes kept above box A.

Hence, the correct option is (B).

72. So, 2 boxes are present between box C and G.

Hence, the correct option is (A).

73. So, the Zero box kept below box F.

Hence, the correct option is (E).

74. Four of the following are placed in odd places so they form a group but box G is kept in an even place.

So, box G is an odd one.

Hence, the correct option is (C).

Symbol in Diagram	Meaning
◯	Female
▢	Male
——— -------	Married Couple
———	Siblings
|	Difference of A Generation

Ques (75-78):

1. F is the only son of A who has three children. Hence other two children are daughters of A.

2. C is married to A.

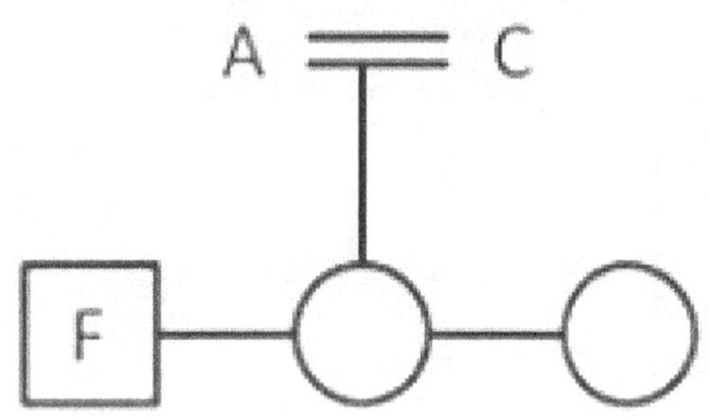

3. E is the maternal aunt of B who is married to D.

Three cases arise here,

Case I: Here, E is assumed to be one of the daughters of A

Since both parents have to be alive, so after making all arrangements we see that 8 members are arising which goes against the information provided.

Since there are 7 members in this family, this case will be eliminated.

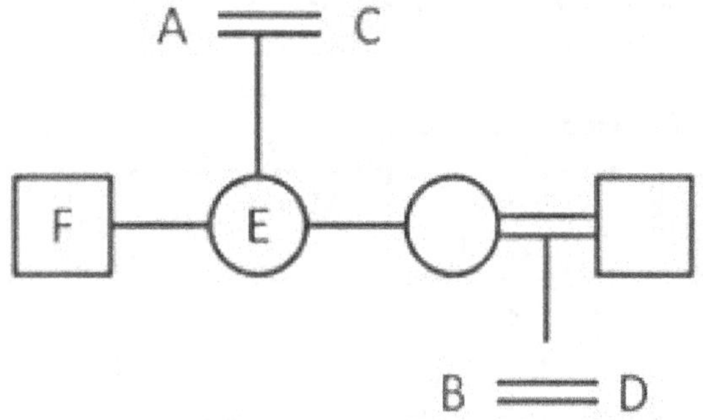

Case II: Here we consider that C is the mother of B and E is the sister of C

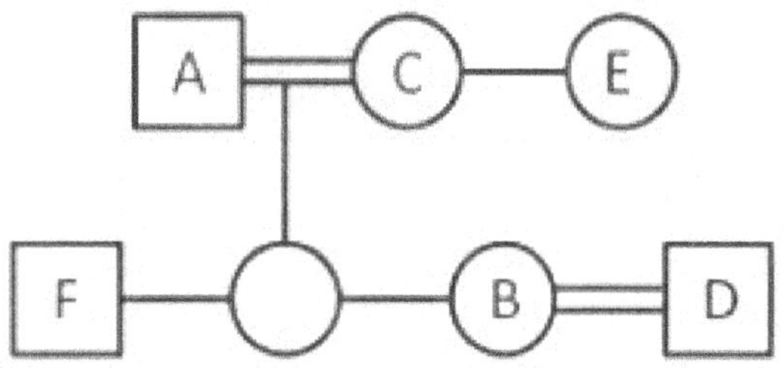

Case III: Here we consider that A is the mother of B and E is the sister of A

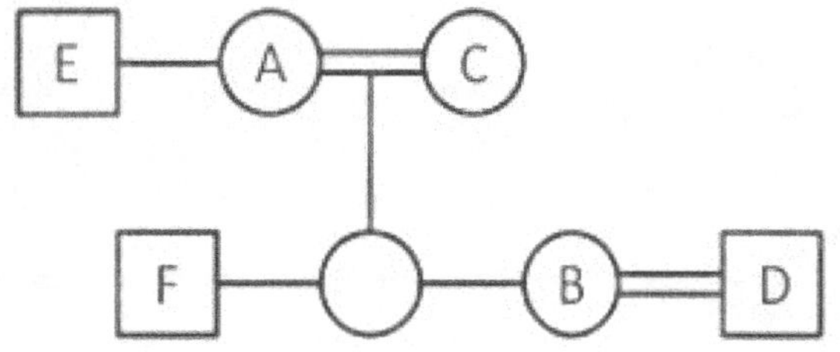

4. A and G were of the same gender.

So, in both cases 2 and 3 only one place is left for the daughter of A and C which will be filled by G

So, G is female and A will also be female according to the given information, Case II is also eliminated in this case.

Case III becomes our final solution here.

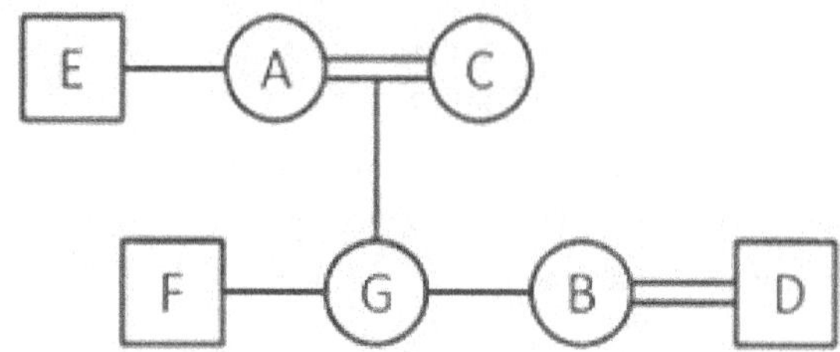

75. So, G is the niece of E.

Hence, the correct option is (A).

76. D being the husband of B who is the daughter of A will be the son-in-law of A.

Hence, the correct option is (C).

77. We can see that F is the brother-in-law of D.

Hence, the correct option is (B).

78. Among all the given options, D is the only male person while all others are female.

Hence, the correct option is (E).

79. The least possible Venn diagram for the given statements is as follows,

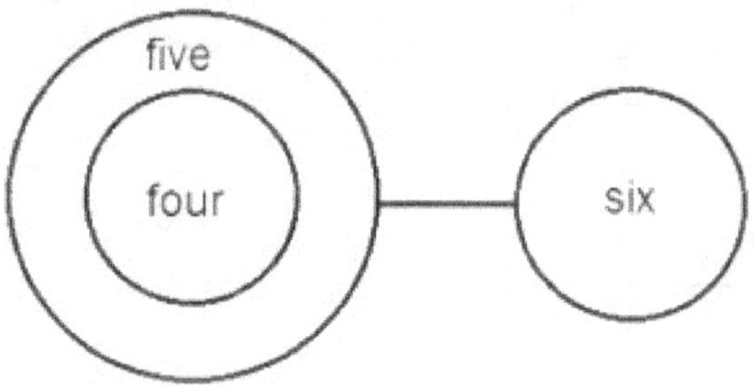

Conclusion:

I. No four is six → True (as all four are five and no five is six)

II. Some five are four → True (as all four are five)

So, both I and II follow is the correct answer.

Hence, the correct option is (C).

Ques (80-84):1) Anup is sitting second to the left of Arnav.

2) Arnav is sitting second to the left of Parul.

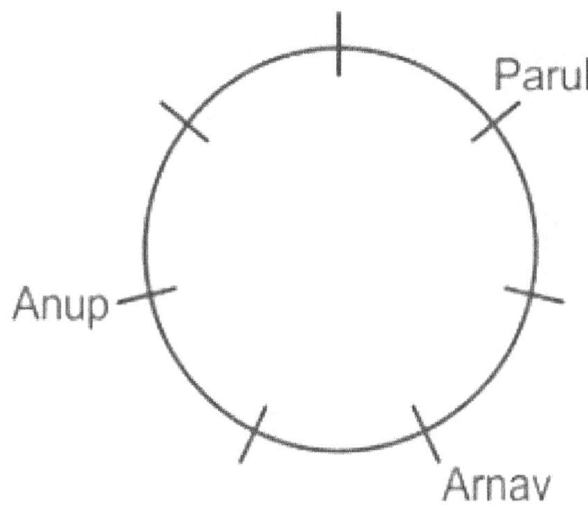

3) Parul is not sitting next to Swati and Samita.

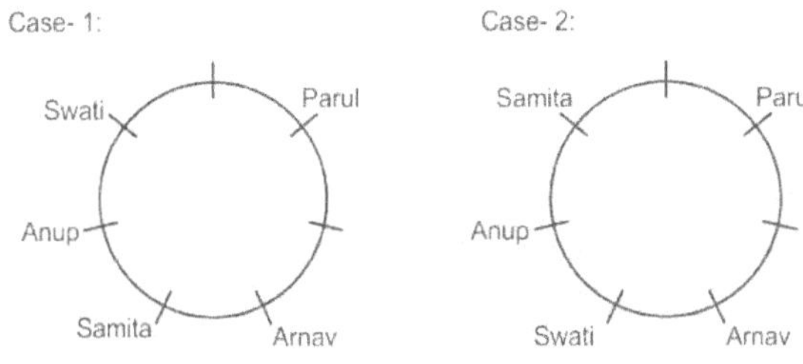

4) Ganga is not a neighbour of Anup and Swati.

5) Only two students will sit between Samita and Ganga.

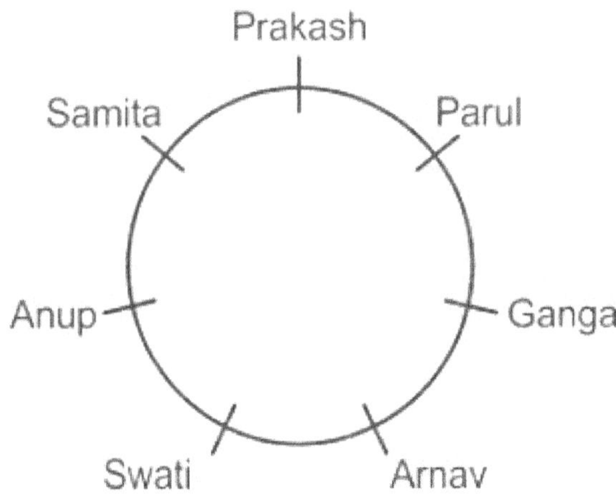

80. So, Prakash is sitting to the immediate right of Parul.

Hence, the correct option is (C).

81. If they are seated in a linear arrangement starting with Arnav at the left end.

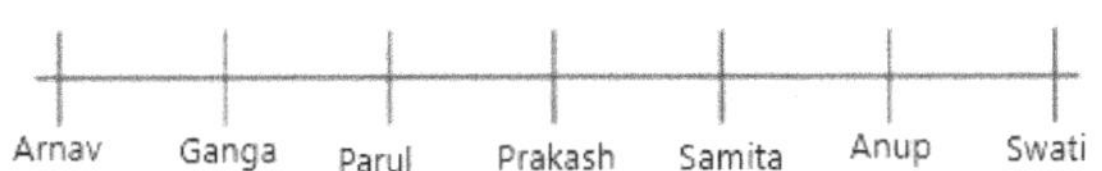

So, Samita is sitting in the third position from the right end.

Hence, the correct option is (C).

82. So, Anup is sitting between Swati and Samita.

Hence, the correct option is (B).

83. Samita is sitting second to the left of the one who is the immediate right of Anup.

Hence, the correct option is (A).

84. Five people are sitting between Prakash and Parul taking clockwise from Parul.

Hence, the correct option is (D).

85. Given numbers are:

435 287 941 358 763

So, no number is a common factor of all the given numbers.

Hence, the correct option is (E).

86. Given numbers are:

435 287 941 358 763

After adding all three digits of these numbers, we get

435 (4 + 3 + 5) = 12

287 (2 + 8 + 7) = 17

941 (9 + 4 + 1) = 14

358 (3 + 5 + 8) = 16

763 (7 + 6 + 3) = 16

So, the smallest number we get = 12

Hence, the correct option is (A).

87. Given numbers are:

435 287 941 358 763

The smallest number = 287

The reverse of smallest number = 782

So, double of the reverse of the smallest number = 1564

Hence, the correct option is (C).

88. Given numbers are:

435 287 941 358 763

Greatest number = 941 and its reverse will be 149

Smallest number = 287 and its reverse will be 782

So, the sum of the reverses of the smallest and the greatest numbers = 149 + 782 = 931

Hence, the correct option is (B).

89. Given numbers are

435 287 941 358 763

Average of the given numbers

$$= \frac{(435 + 287 + 941 + 358 + 763)}{5} = 556.8$$

So, the average of all the given numbers is 556.8

Hence, the correct option is (D).

Ques (90-93): First, let us decode the words,

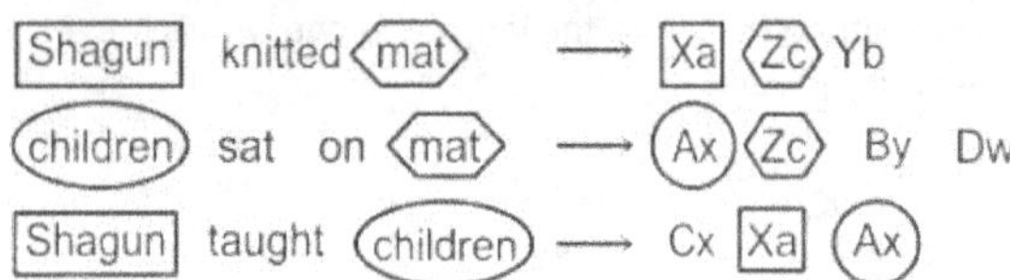

90. So, the code for 'children' in the given code language is Ax.

Hence, the correct option is (C).

91. So, if 'children on mat' is coded as 'Zc Ax Dw', then 'By' mean 'sat' in the given code language.

Hence, the correct option is (A).

92. So, the code for 'taught' in the given code language is Cx.

Hence, the correct option is (D).

93. So, the possible code for 'children knitted Shawl' in the given code language is Ax Yb Sh.

Hence, the correct option is (B).

94. Given letter: COMPONENT

The word can be represented as follows:

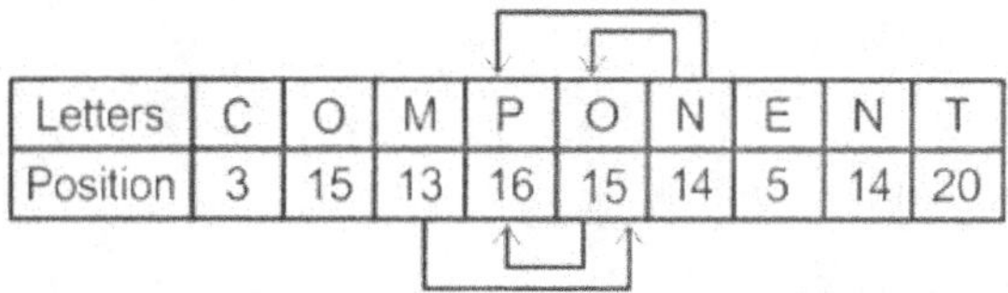

Letters	C	O	M	P	O	N	E	N	T
Position	3	15	13	16	15	14	5	14	20

Thus, there are four pairs.

Backward: NO, NP, OP

Forward: MO

TRICKS: How to remember the position of alphabets.

I. CFILORUX

C	F	I	L	O	R	U	X
3	6	9	12	15	18	21	24

II. EJOTY

E	J	O	T	Y
5	10	15	20	25

Thus, there are four pairs.

Backward: NO, NP, OP

Forward: MO

So, there are four pairs.

Hence, the correct option is (B).

95. We have:

Letter	W	I	N	D	O	W	S
Numerical Value	1	5	3	4	5	6	7

Therefore, required value = 1 + 5 + 3 + 4 + 5 + 6 + 7 = 31.

Hence, the correct option is (D).

Ques (96-99):Students: P, Q, R, S, T, U, V and W.

1) V sits third to the left of S.

2) At least three students sit to the left of V.

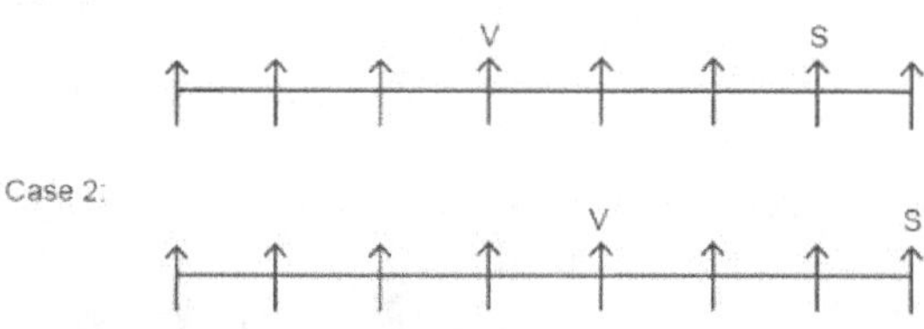

3) Four students sit between R and T.

4) Q sits immediate left of R.

5) T neither sits at the extreme left nor at the second extreme left position.

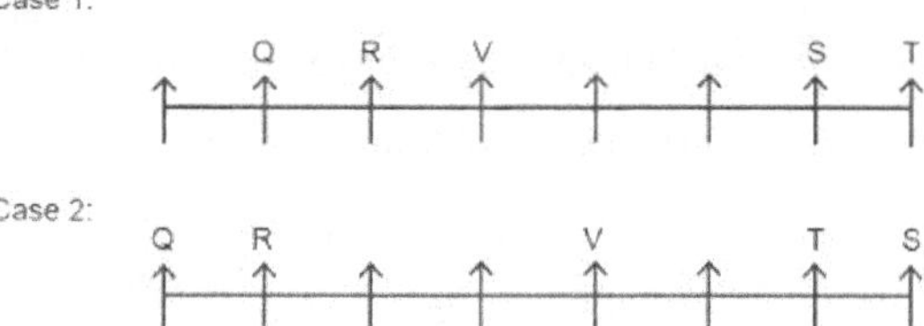

5) W sits to the left of U, who is not adjacent to V. So, case 2 would be invalid as V cannot sit adjacent to U.

6) P does not sit at extreme end. So, W must sit at extreme left end.

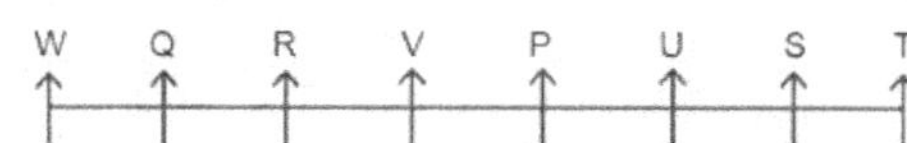

96. W sits at extreme left end.

Hence, the correct option is (C).

97. Three persons sit to the right of P.

Hence, the correct option is (A).

98. Statement (C) is correct.

Hence, the correct option is (C).

99. Three students sit between Q and U.

Hence, the correct option is (D).

100. 1) H is sitting fourth to the right of B.

2) Both H and B are facing the same direction.

3) E, an immediate neighbour of B, is facing north. E is sitting at the right end of the row.

4) Both the immediate neighbours of B are facing the same direction.

(As the immediate neighbours of B are facing the same direction, and E is facing north, implies, B must be facing south as no three consecutive people are facing the same direction).

5) H is sitting second to the left of C and they are facing the same direction.

(As B, H, and C are facing the same direction (acc. to statement 2 and 4), implies, H and C are facing the south direction. Also, B is not sitting on an extreme end because it has two immediate neighbours. Hence, C must be sitting on the west end and B must be sitting on the second seat from the East end).

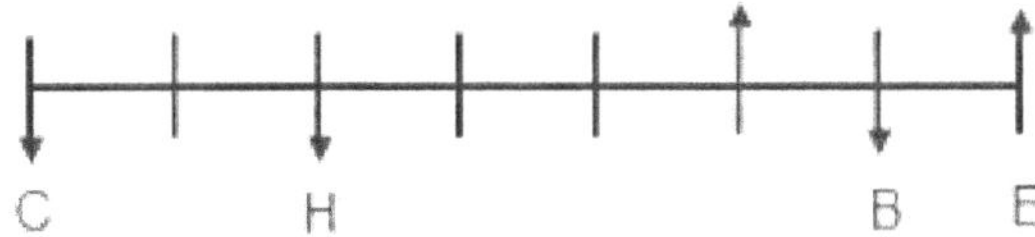

6) D is sitting fourth to the right of F.

(The person sitting between C and H must be facing north as no three consecutive persons are facing the same direction. Hence, it is only possible if F is sitting between C and H and D is sitting to the immediate right of B).

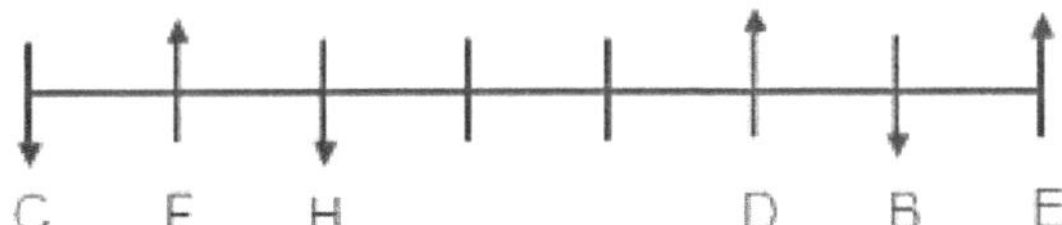

7) Both the immediate neighbours of D are facing opposite directions.

(B, an immediate neighbour of D is facing south, implies, the other immediate neighbour must be facing north. Also, now that we know the four people who are facing north, implies, the person sitting to the immediate left of H must be facing south).

8) A is not an immediate neighbour of D.

(Implies, A must be an immediate neighbour of H and G must be an immediate neighbour of D).

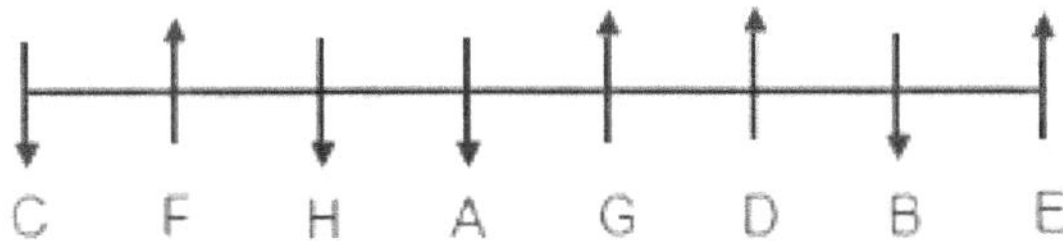

A is sitting second to the left of D.

Hence, the correct option is (D).

English Language

Ques (1-3):Direction: In the following sentence a part of the sentence is underlined. There are some alternatives to the underlined part which may improve the sentence. Choose the correct alternative. In case no improvement is needed choose option E 'No improvement' as your answer.

Q.1 Jane is one of my best friends, I can always tell when she is <u>quixotic</u> and thinking about her troubled childhood.

A. Sentimental   **B.** Grandiose

C. Meticulous   **D.** Eccentric

E. No improvement

Q.2 Moving through the crowd, Daisy used her <u>brusque</u> to bring enthusiasm to the crowd.

A. Opulent   **B.** Vivacity

C. Ramshackle   **D.** Stupidity

E. No improvement

Q.3 Aisha's <u>zestful</u> energy allows her to do well in a high-paced sales environment.

A. Lucrative   **B.** Unfazed

C. Scathing   **D.** Scarring

E. No improvement

Ques (4-11):Direction: Read the passage and answer the questions that follow.

We've all seen reports of studies demonstrating women's inequality at work. It is well established that women are disproportionately under-represented in higher-paid positions and industries, and that there is a gender pay gap of 17.5% between men and women. Lack of pay equity and equal opportunities are the elephants in the room for every woman in the Australian workforce.

Although the causes are complex, research suggests they are based on deep cultural expectations and stereotypes that do not have to do with the efforts of individual women at work. Australia's legislation requiring employers to provide equal opportunity programs for women at work (the Equal Employment for Women at Work Act 1986) has now been amended and renamed the Workplace Gender Equality Act. It now aims to ensure equality at work for both women and men, with a focus on sex discrimination and the treatment of workers with caring responsibilities.

The act applies to the same employers as the previous law: all higher education institutions and non-government employers of more than 100 employees are covered. The exclusion of small businesses appears to be an acknowledgment that smaller organizations may not have the human resources capacity to comply with the requirements. Public employment is also excluded.

It is clear that deep cultural change will be needed to move away from stereotypical expectations about the incompatibility of femininity and leadership; women's inherent responsibility for childcare; and the "normal" worker being a full-time worker free of caring responsibilities according to the historical male model.

Q.4 Women are not equally represented in-

A. Higher paid positions

B. Industries

C. Public spaces

D. All of these

E. Both (A) and (B)

Q.5 Which of these problems are faced by working women in Australia?

A. Unequal pay

B. Unequal opportunities

C. Unequal laws

D. All of these

E. Both (A) and (B)

Q.6 What are the reasons of unequal opportunities for women?

A. Women are not highly educated

B. Women do not put in much efforts

C. There are cultural stereotypes in the society

D. Men are offered a higher pay

E. All of these

Q.7 Workplace Gender Equality Act ensures-

A. Equal opportunities for women at work

B. Equality for both men and women

C. Good jobs for women

D. All of these

E. Both (A) and (B)

Q.8 The Workplace Gender Equality Act is applicable for-

A. Small businesses

B. All higher education institutes of more than 100 employees

C. All government offices with high employers

D. All of these

E. Both (A) and (B)

Q.9 Why are certain places excluded from the Workplace Gender Equality Act?

A. They do not have the human resources to meet its requirements

B. They are small enough to be neglected

C. They offer equal opportunities

D. Both (A) and (B)

E. Both (B) and (C)

Q.10 Which of these is true according to the historical male model?

A. Women can only do household work

B. Only men can become efficient and responsible leaders

C. Only women have caring responsibilities

D. A normal worker has to work full time without any caring responsibilities

E. All of these

Q.11 Which of these is similar in meaning to 'amended'?

A. Altered   **B.** Solved

C. Retreated   **D.** Advised

E. Regained

Ques (12-17):Direction: Read the passage carefully and select the correct answer for the given blank out of the given alternatives.

Business ethics (also known as Corporate ethics) is a form of applied ethics or professional ethics that examines ___(1)__ principles and moral or ethical problems that arise in a ___(2)__environment. It applies to all aspects of business conduct and is relevant to the conduct of individuals and business organisations as a whole. (Wikipedia) Most people agree that high ethical standards ___(3)__both businesses and individuals to conform to sound moral___(4)__. However, some special aspects must be considered when applying ethics to business. To survive, businesses must make a___(5)__. If profits are realised by misconduct then the life of the business may be short-lived. The business must balance their desires for profits against the needs and desires of society. Maintaining this balance can be difficult. To help with this, society has developed rules – both legal and implicit – to guide the business in their efforts to earn ___(6)__in ways that will not harm individuals or society as a whole. (Ferrell, Fraedrich, Ferrell, 2002.)

Q.12 Pick the appropriate word to be filled in blank 1.

A. practical   **B.** ethical

C. social   **D.** analytical

E. political

Q.13 Pick the appropriate word to be filled in blank 2.

A. cheerful   **B.** sad   **C.** bad   **D.** business

E. good

Q.14 Pick the appropriate word to be filled in blank 3.

A. business   **B.** contains   **C.** include   **D.** produce

E. require

Q.15 Pick the appropriate word to be filled in blank 4.

A. principles   **B.** standards

C. ethics   **D.** value

E. education

Q.16 Pick the appropriate word to be filled in blank 5.

A. loss   **B.** head start

C. campaigning   **D.** stand

E. profit

Q.17 Pick the appropriate word to be filled in blank 6.

A. losses   **B.** customers

C. profits   **D.** people

E. leaders

Ques (18-21):Direction: Select the most appropriate word to fill in the blanks.

Q.18 The project believes that there may be a premium market for items that ________ using plastic reclaimed from the ocean.

A. Made   **B.** Was made

C. Have been made   **D.** Is made

E. Has been made

Q.19 I missed the bus ______ I was late.

A. Yet   **B.** Although

C. Though   **D.** However

E. Because

Q.20 I have a friend ______ father is a famous actor.

A. Whose   **B.** Who   **C.** Whos'   **D.** Whom

E. Who's

Q.21 Science has helped power the world through its ______.

A. Status   **B.** Economy

C. Development   **D.** Liberty

E. Poverty

Ques (22-26):Direction: In the question given below, four words are given in bold. These four words may or may not be in their correct positions. The sentence is then followed by options with the correct combination of words that should replace each other in order to make the sentence grammatically and contextually correct. Find the correct combination of words that replace each other. If the sentence is correct as it is, select 'E' as your option.

Q.22 The **leader (A)** of the **brainwash (B)** was very sure that he could **cult (C)** the people into **committing (D)** crimes that he wanted.

A. A-B   **B.** B-C

C. C-D   **D.** D-A

E. No Rearrangement

Q.23 There was a **afterward(A)** going on for a long time for **marriage(B)** between one of the king's sons, first Henry, and **negotiation(C)** Charles, and a **princess(D)** of Spain

A. A-B   **B.** B-C

C. C-D   **D.** A-C

E. No rearrangement

Q.24 Kate was the **rags (A)** of the **family, (B)** and she had single handedly **brought (C)** her family from **matriarch (D)** to riches.

A. D-C   **B.** A-B

C. D-A   **D.** B-C

E. No Rearrangement

Q.25 On Earth, sunlight is scattered and **obvious (A)** through Earth's atmosphere, and is **filtered (B)** as daylight when the Sun is above the **horizon(C).**

A. BAC

B. BCA

C. CAB

D. ACB

E. No rearrangement required

Q.26 Half-way(A) between the **island(B)** of the river(C) and the **bank(D),** a large rock rose out of the water.

A. B-C
B. A-B
C. A-C
D. B-D
E. No rearrangement

Ques (27-28):Direction : Given below are some idioms/phrases followed by four alterative meanings to each. Choose the most appropriate answer from among the options (A), (B), (C) and (D).

Q.27 The icing on the cake:

A. Baked food that is delicate and delicious with a topping
B. Extra benefit over and above an already good deal
C. Getting what you asked for
D. More than what is needed
E. None of the above

Q.28 Counting your chickens:

A. Confident of success
B. Greedily accumulating wealth
C. Being careful about spending money
D. Getting scared because of danger
E. None of the above

Ques (29-30):Direction: In the following question, out of the four alternatives, select the alternative which will improve the underlined part of the sentence. In case no improvement is needed, select 'No improvement'.

Q.29 Sneha agrees that **her older brother is much clever than** her.

A. Her older brother is much clever to her
B. Her elder brother is much clever to
C. Her elder brother is much clever than
D. Her elder brother is much clever for
E. No improvement

Q.30 They put the glass **besides the book at** the table.

A. Beside the book at
B. Beside the book on
C. Besides the book on
D. Beside the book of
E. No improvement

Numerical Ability

Q.31 A train 270 m long is running at a speed of 90 km/hr. How many seconds will it take to cross a 200 m long train running in the opposite direction at a speed of 60 km/hr?

A. $\frac{36}{5}$
B. 60
C. 12
D. 20
E. $\frac{282}{25}$

Q.32 A dealer sold goods at 21% less on cost price but uses false weight, which is 25% less than its original weight. What is his percentage profit or loss?

A. $\frac{16}{3}$%
B. $\frac{22}{3}$%
C. $\frac{14}{5}$%
D. $\frac{17}{5}$%
E. $\frac{12}{5}$%

Q.33 Find the time duration at which principal amount of 10,000 doubles at rate of interest of 10% p.a.

A. 6 years
B. 10 years
C. 8 years
D. 5 years
E. 12 years

Q.34 Find the area of a rhombus having side 10cm and one of its diagonal as 12cm.

A. 96 cm²
B. $48\sqrt{3}$ cm²
C. 112 cm²
D. 144 cm²
E. None of these

Ques (35-39):Direction: In the given question, two equations numbered I and II are given. Solve both the equations and mark the appropriate answer.

Q.35 I. $11x^2 - 27x + 10 = 0$
II. $y^2 - 10y - 24 = 0$

A. x > y
B. x < y
C. x ≥ y
D. x ≤ y
E. x = y or relationship between x and y cannot be established

Q.36 I. $x^2 - 26x + 165 = 0$
II. $y^2 - 38y + 357 = 0$

A. x > y
B. x < y
C. x ≥ y
D. x ≤ y
E. x = y or relationship between x and y cannot be established

Q.37 I. $x^2 + 40x + 231 = 0$
II. $y^2 + 45y + 374 = 0$

A. x > y
B. x < y
C. x ≥ y
D. x ≤ y
E. x = y or relationship between x and y cannot be established

Q.38 I. $x^2 + 20x + 91 = 0$
II. $y^2 - 26y + 105 = 0$

A. x > y
B. x < y
C. x ≥ y
D. x ≤ y
E. x = y or relationship between x and y cannot be established

Q.39 I. $x^2 - 7x - 120 = 0$
II. $y^2 + 43y + 432 = 0$

A. x > y
B. x < y
C. x ≥ y
D. x ≤ y

E. x = y or relationship between x and y cannot be established

Q.40 Four years ago, Anil's age was 4 times the age of Rahul and the sum of their ages were 100 years. Find the present age of Rahul.

A. 24 years   **B.** 27 years   **C.** 28 years   **D.** 25 year
E. 29 years

Q.41 Ratul invested 20% more than Rakesh and Rakesh invested 50% more than Rudra. If the total amount of their investment is Rs. 3,225, how much amount did Ratul invest?

[SBI Apprentice, 2019]

A. Rs. 1,450   **B.** Rs. 1,500
C. Rs. 1,050   **D.** Rs. 1,350
E. Rs. 1,400

Q.42 A person divides a distance into three equal parts. He travels the three parts at the speed of 28 km/h, 56 km/h and 112 km/h respectively. What was his average speed for the entire journey?
A. 96 km/h   **B.** 50 km/h   **C.** 48 km/h   **D.** 24 km/h
E. 40 km/h

Q.43 Raktim can complete $\frac{7}{16}$ part of a work in 21 days, then he complete the remaining with the help of Puja in 18 days. How many days will be needed to complete the total work by Raktim and Puja together?
A. 70 days   **B.** 32 days   **C.** 24 days   **D.** 48 days
E. 16 days

Q.44 A solution of syrup has 15% water. Another solution has 35% water. How many litres of the first solution must be added to the 40L of second solution to make a solution of 23% water?
A. 30   **B.** 40   **C.** 60   **D.** 55
E. 50

Ques (45-54):Direction: What approximate will come in the place of the question mark '?' in the following question?

Q.45 $16.95 \times 2.98 + 8 \div 1.96 - 6.1 = (?)^2$
A. 15.2   **B.** 21.1
C. 7   **D.** 11
E. None of these

Q.46 $9.02 - (? - 10.07) + (20.92)^2 = 461$
A. 0   **B.** 1   **C.** -1   **D.** 2
E. -2

Q.47 $24.97 \times \sqrt{15.99} + 400.04 = \sqrt{?} + 475$
A. 2.5   **B.** 625   **C.** 25   **D.** 15
E. 5

Q.48 9.87% of $[(299.96)^2 + (20.24)^2] = 999.99\%$ of $4 + ?$
A. 8990   **B.** 9899
C. 9000   **D.** 9989
E. None of these

Q.49 $(1 \div 11.91) - (1 \div 4.07) + (1 \div ?) = 0$
A. 6.0   **B.** 6.5   **C.** 7.0   **D.** 7.5
E. 5.5

Q.50 55% of $99.999 + ?^2 = 56\%$ of $850 - 20\%$ of 150
A. 10   **B.** 20   **C.** 45   **D.** 62
E. 36

Q.51 $3.76 \times (5.23 - 1.68) + (50\%$ of $16.05) = ?$
A. 16   **B.** 20   **C.** 24   **D.** 28
E. 78

Q.52 $\sqrt{3.98} + \sqrt{((2.22)^2 + 4.85)} \times 5.69 = 24.71\%$ of?
A. 60   **B.** 70   **C.** 80   **D.** 90
E. 23

Q.53 $\sqrt{289.15} + 3.99 \times (45.01\%$ of $199.99) - ? = 0$
A. 377   **B.** 343   **C.** 363   **D.** 347
E. 309

Q.54 $\dfrac{\left(\left(\frac{2.56}{10.89}\right)+\left(\frac{2.36}{4.58}\right)-\left(\frac{0.99}{4.79}\right)\right)}{[7.05+74.88\% \text{ of } 11.88]}$
A. $\frac{1}{55}$ **B.** $\frac{13}{440}$ **C.** $\frac{3}{55}$ **D.** $\frac{4}{55}$
E. $\frac{6}{55}$

Ques (55-59):Direction: Study the following data and answer the following questions.

Two friends Ram and Sham have a different number of balloons and pins. The difference between the number of balloons Sham and Ram have is 40. The total number of Pins Ram and Sham has 100. The number of Balloons and pins Ram have is 20 less than the number of balloons and pins Sham have. The Pins Ram have is 25% less than the balloons Ram have.

Q.55 Find the average number of balloons both have.
A. 90   **B.** 100   **C.** 85   **D.** 80
E. 70

Q.56 The number of pins Ram have is approx. what percent of the total number of Balloons and pins Ram have?
A. 40%   **B.** 50%   **C.** 43%   **D.** 41%
E. 48%

Q.57 Find the difference between the number of Balloons and pins Sham have.
A. 70   **B.** 50   **C.** 75   **D.** 85
E. 80

Q.58 Find the ratio between the number of balloons and pins both have.
A. 3 : 1   **B.** 2 : 5   **C.** 1 : 3   **D.** 2 : 1
E. 3 : 8

Q.59 The number of pins Sham have is approx. what percent less than the number of pins Ram have?

A. 33% **B.** 30% **C.** 38% **D.** 40%
E. 36%

Ques (60-64):Direction: What should come in place of the question mark '?' in the following number series?

Q.60 25, 27, 30, 35, 42, ?
A. 50 **B.** 49 **C.** 55 **D.** 47
E. 53

Q.61 80, 40, 60, 150, ?, 2362.5
A. 715 **B.** 525 **C.** 625 **D.** 445
E. 475

Q.62 5, 6, 13, ?, 161, 806
A. 58 **B.** 32 **C.** 56 **D.** 40
E. 70

Q.63 151, 153, 156, 161, 168, 179, 192, ?
A. 207 **B.** 205 **C.** 209 **D.** 201
E. 206

Q.64 97, 84, 110, 71, 123, 58, 136, ?
A. 35 **B.** 45 **C.** 55 **D.** 65
E. 75

Q.65 The sum of two numbers is 2490. 6.5% of the first number is equal to 8.5% of the second number. Find the greater number.
A. 1876 **B.** 1600
C. 1411 **D.** 1380
E. None of the above

Reasoning Ability

Ques (66-70):Direction: In the following question assuming the given statement to be true. Find which of the following conclusion(s) among the given conclusions is/are definitely true and then give your answer accordingly.

Q.66 Statement:

F < D ≤ G, K > M > L ≥ G

Conclusion:

I. M > D

II. M = D

A. Only I is true
B. Only II is true
C. Both I and II are true
D. None is true
E. Either I or II is true

Q.67 Statement:

S > M ≥ O, O ≥ P ≥ N > K

Conclusion:

I. O > N

II. N ≤ M

A. None is true
B. Only II is true
C. Both I and II are true

D. Only I is true
E. Either I or II is true

Q.68 Statement: X > Y ≥ Z ≥ W, W > V ≥ U

Conclusion:

I. W < U

II. Y > W

A. Only I is true
B. Only II is true
C. Both I and II are true
D. None is true
E. Either I or II is true

Q.69 Statement: 1 < 2 ≤ 4, 3 > 5 ≥ 6 > 4

Conclusion:

I. 1 = 6

II. 6 > 1

A. Only I is true
B. Only II is true
C. Both I and II are true
D. None is true
E. Either I or II is true

Q.70 Statement: P > M > Q ≥ R, S < N ≤ O ≤ T = R

Conclusion:

I. M > N

II. Q ≤ T

A. None is true
B. Only II is true
C. Both I and II are true
D. Only I is true
E. Either I or II is true

Q.71 If in a certain code language, ELEPHANT is written as FKFOIZOS, which word would be written as FUBKVZUHPM?
A. EAVLUATOIN **B.** EVALAUTOIN
C. EAVLUTIAON **D.** EVALUATION
E. EVALAUITON

Ques (72-74):Direction: Read the instructions carefully and answer the following.

7 friends Navya, Sainoor, Manya, Piyu, Gauri, Kianshi, Simar have different height and they all are arranged in ascending order in a seperate vertical column. Sainoor is taller than Piyu but shorter than Navya. Kianshi is taller than only two persons. Gauri is the seventh tallest person. Simar is neither the tallest nor the shortest. Navya is shorter than only one person. Equal number of people are taller and shorter than Piyu. Sainoor is not the tallest.

Q.72 Who among the following is the tallest?
A. Sainoor **B.** Manya **C.** Piyu **D.** Kianshi
E. Navya

Q.73 How many persons are taller and shorter than Sainoor respectively?
A. 3,3 **B.** 2,4 **C.** 3,2 **D.** 1,3
E. 4,2

C. Three   **D.** Four
E. More than four

Ques (91-95):Direction: Study the following arrangement carefully and answer the questions given below:

L K 1 C D 9 Z Y ^ P 2 N © K S 3 ↑ 5 M T ®

Q.91 How many such digits are there in the series, each of which is immediately preceded as well as immediately followed by letters?
A. Two   **B.** Four
C. Three   **D.** Five
E. None of these

Q.92 Which of the following elements is exactly in the middle of 9 and 3?
A. 2   **B.** Y
C. P   **D.** Z
E. None of these

Q.93 Which of the following elements is tenth to the left of the fifth element from the right end?
A. L   **B.** K   **C.** P   **D.** Y
E. Z

Q.94 If each symbol of the series is replaced with different digits between 1 and 9 which are not present in the given series in ascending order from left to right, then what is the sum of all the digits in the new series?
A. 45   **B.** 37
C. 42   **D.** 32
E. None of these

Q.95 Complete the series:
LKC, 9Z^, 2NK, ?
A. S3K   **B.** 3SN
C. 3↑M   **D.** MTS
E. None of these

Ques (96-100):Direction: Read the information carefully and answer the following questions.

Eight friends S, T, U, V, W, X, Y, Z are sitting on a square table such that two people are sitting on each side but not necessarily in the same order. Five are facing outside the table and remaining are facing inside the table.

S and X are sitting together but facing in the opposite direction. Only two persons are sitting between T and Y who is facing inside. T is sitting immediate left of U who is not sitting near W.Z is sitting between Y and X but not sitting opposite to U.Y is sitting second to the right of X and both are facing in the same direction. V who is facing the same direction as S, is sitting second to the left of both T and Z.

Q.96 Which of the following pair is sitting on the same side of the table?
A. V, Y   **B.** U, Z   **C.** T, W   **D.** V, W
E. W, Z

Q.97 If all the names are arranged according to alphabetical order starting from the position of X in the anti-clockwise direction, then how many letters will remain unchanged?
A. One   **B.** Two   **C.** Three   **D.** None
E. Five

Q.98 Who is sitting second to the right of W?
A. V   **B.** U   **C.** X   **D.** S
E. Y

Q.99 What is the position of X with respect to Z?
A. Third to the left of Z
B. Immediate left
C. Third to right
D. Immediate right
E. Second to left

Q.100 If Z is related to Y, S is related to X, in the same way, which of the following is related to V?
A. W   **B.** V   **C.** U   **D.** Z
E. S

// Smart Answer Sheet //

Correct Percentage of students who answered correctly. **Skipped** Percentage of students who skipped.

Q.	Ans.	Correct / Skipped	Q.	Ans.	Correct / Skipped	Q.	Ans.	Correct / Skipped	Q.	Ans.	Correct / Skipped	Q.	Ans.	Correct / Skipped
1	A	8.43 % / 78.32 %	17	C	15.06 % / 80.12 %	33	B	9.64 % / 79.52 %	49	A	11.45 % / 80.12 %	65	C	0 % / 100 %
2	B	3.01 % / 80.12 %	18	C	5.42 % / 80.12 %	34	A	1.81 % / 79.52 %	50	B	10.24 % / 80.12 %	66	A	11.45 % / 80.72 %
3	E	2.41 % / 80.72 %	19	E	14.46 % / 80.12 %	35	E	9.04 % / 79.51 %	51	B	12.05 % / 80.12 %	67	B	12.05 % / 80.72 %
4	E	16.87 % / 80.12 %	20	A	13.86 % / 80.12 %	36	B	9.64 % / 79.52 %	52	C	6.63 % / 80.12 %	68	D	10.84 % / 81.33 %
5	E	15.06 % / 80.12 %	21	C	13.86 % / 80.72 %	37	E	6.02 % / 79.52 %	53	A	9.64 % / 80.12 %	69	B	12.65 % / 81.33 %
6	C	16.27 % / 80.12 %	22	B	6.63 % / 92.77 %	38	B	11.45 % / 79.51 %	54	B	0.6 % / 81.33 %	70	D	12.65 % / 81.33 %
7	E	8.43 % / 80.12 %	23	D	4.82 % / 92.77 %	39	A	7.23 % / 79.52 %	55	B	1.2 % / 81.33 %	71	D	11.45 % / 81.32 %
8	C	0.6 % / 80.12 %	24	C	4.82 % / 93.37 %	40	A	8.43 % / 79.52 %	56	C	1.81 % / 83.73 %	72	B	8.43 % / 81.33 %
9	A	12.05 % / 80.12 %	25	A	5.42 % / 93.38 %	41	D	4.22 % / 79.51 %	57	E	1.2 % / 84.34 %	73	B	9.64 % / 81.93 %
10	D	7.83 % / 80.12 %	26	D	3.61 % / 93.98 %	42	C	3.01 % / 79.52 %	58	D	0.6 % / 84.94 %	74	D	11.45 % / 82.53 %
11	A	7.83 % / 80.12 %	27	B	3.01 % / 93.98 %	43	B	1.81 % / 79.52 %	59	A	1.2 % / 84.34 %	75	A	6.02 % / 82.53 %
12	B	10.84 % / 80.12 %	28	A	0 % / 100 %	44	C	1.2 % / 79.52 %	60	E	12.65 % / 83.74 %	76	B	7.23 % / 81.93 %
13	D	12.05 % / 80.12 %	29	C	4.82 % / 93.98 %	45	C	15.06 % / 79.52 %	61	B	5.42 % / 83.74 %	77	C	7.83 % / 81.93 %
14	E	6.02 % / 80.12 %	30	B	4.22 % / 93.97 %	46	C	9.64 % / 79.52 %	62	D	9.04 % / 84.94 %	78	C	7.23 % / 81.32 %
15	A	4.82 % / 80.12 %	31	E	4.22 % / 77.11 %	47	B	7.83 % / 79.52 %	63	C	6.63 % / 86.14 %	79	D	7.83 % / 81.33 %
16	E	9.64 % / 80.12 %	32	A	4.22 % / 79.51 %	48	C	6.02 % / 80.12 %	64	B	5.42 % / 87.35 %	80	A	13.25 % / 81.33 %

Q.	Ans.	Correct	Skipped
81	D	11.45 %	81.32 %
82	E	12.65 %	81.93 %
83	A	13.25 %	81.93 %
84	A	2.41 %	81.93 %

Q.	Ans.	Correct	Skipped
85	E	10.84 %	81.93 %
86	B	10.24 %	82.53 %
87	B	11.45 %	82.53 %
88	B	11.45 %	82.53 %

Q.	Ans.	Correct	Skipped
89	A	11.45 %	82.53 %
90	B	9.64 %	82.53 %
91	C	13.25 %	82.53 %
92	A	13.86 %	82.53 %

Q.	Ans.	Correct	Skipped
93	E	11.45 %	83.13 %
94	A	5.42 %	83.74 %
95	C	12.65 %	83.13 %
96	C	2.41 %	83.73 %

Q.	Ans.	Correct	Skipped
97	A	1.2 %	89.76 %
98	B	2.41 %	90.36 %
99	D	1.81 %	90.36 %
100	C	1.81 %	90.36 %

//Hints and Solutions//

1. The word 'quixotic' means 'foolish' and is not suitable here.

Sentimental: prompted by feelings of tenderness, sadness or nostalgia.

Grandiose: magnificent

Meticulous: careful

Eccentric: unconventional and slightly strange (behaviour).

Option (A) is thus correct as the sentence talks about a person's troubled childhood.

Hence, the correct option is (A).

2. The word 'brusque' means 'short;rude' and does not fit here.

Opulent: wealthy

Vivacity: enthusiasm

Ramshackle: poorly constructed

Option (B) is thus correct as the sentence talks about a person's enthusiasm.

Hence, the correct option is (B).

3. The word 'zestful' which means 'enthusiastic' fits here correctly and conveys a proper meaning. It does not need any improvement.

Lucrative: profitable

Unfazed: not perturbed

Scathing: harshly critical

Scarring: that which leaves a scar

Hence, the correct option is (E).

4. The following is stated in the passage: "It is well established that women are disproportionately under-represented in higher-paid positions and industries".

Hence, the correct option is (E).

5. The following is stated in the passage: "Lack of pay equity and equal opportunities are the elephants in the room for every woman in the Australian workforce."

The phrase 'the elephant in the room' means 'a major problem or controversial issue which is obviously present but is avoided as a subject for discussion'.

There is no mention of unequal laws.

Hence, the correct option is (E).

6. The following question is stated in the 1st and 2nd paragraphs of the passage as it tells us the reason why women lack opportunities in the society "Lack of pay equity and equal opportunities are the elephants in the room for every woman in the Australian workforce. Although the causes are complex, research suggests they are based on deep cultural expectations and stereotypes that do not have to do with the efforts of individual women at work. Australia's legislation requiring

employers to provide equal opportunity programs for women at work (the Equal Employment for Women at Work Act 1986) has now been amended and renamed the Workplace Gender Equality Act. It now aims to ensure equality at work for both women and men, with a focus on sex discrimination and treatment of workers with caring responsibilities."

Hence, the correct option is (C).

7. The following is stated in the passage: "Australia's legislation requiring employers to provide equal opportunity programs for women at work (the Equal Employment for Women at Work Act 1986) has now been amended and renamed the Workplace Gender Equality Act. It now aims to ensure equality at work for both women and men, with a focus on sex discrimination and treatment of workers with caring responsibilities."

Hence, the correct option is (E).

8. The following is stated in the passage: "The act applies to the same employers as the previous law: all higher education institutions and non-government employers of more than 100 employees are covered."

Hence, the correct option is (C).

9. The following is stated in the passage: "The exclusion of small businesses appears to be an acknowledgment that smaller organizations may not have the human resources capacity to comply with the requirements."

Hence, the correct option is (A).

10. The following is stated in the passage: "It is clear that deep cultural change will be needed to move away from stereotypical expectations about the incompatibility of femininity and leadership; women's inherent responsibility for childcare; and the "normal" worker being a full-time worker free of caring responsibilities according to the historical male model."

Hence, the correct option is (D).

11. Amended means made minor changes to (a text, piece of legislation, etc.) in order to make it fairer or more accurate, or to reflect changing circumstances.

The meanings of the given words-

Altered means changed in character or composition, typically in a comparatively small but significant way.

Solved means found an answer to, explanation for, or means of effectively dealing with (a problem or mystery).

Retreated means withdrew from enemy forces as a result of their superior power or after a defeat.

Advised means offered suggestions about the best course of action to someone.

Regained means obtained possession or use of (something, typically a quality or ability) again after losing it.

Hence, the correct option is (A).

12. 'Ethical' is the most appropriate word because ethical means moral principles. 'practical' is wrong because there cannot be practical principles same goes for 'social'. 'analytical' means logical reasoning which is also wrong. 'political' is also wrong because it does not fit the context.

Hence, the correct option is (B).

13. 'Business' is the most appropriate word because of the previous line talked about the ethical and moral principles that one must have in a business background. 'cheerful' is wrong because business backgrounds are not cheerful. 'sad' and 'bad' are also wrong and same goes for 'good'.

Hence, the correct option is (D).

14. 'Require' is the most appropriate word because ethical standards will be followed by individuals and business organisations. 'business' does not fit the context of the text. 'include' is wrong because ethical standards cannot include something. 'produce' is wrong because ethical standards cannot produce individuals and business organisation.

Hence, the correct option is (E).

15. 'Principles' is the most appropriate word because it is the moral principles that individuals and business organisation must conform. 'standards' is also wrong because its already mentioned and it would be grammatically incorrect and same goes for 'ethics'. 'value' and 'education' are both wrong because they don't fit the context of the text.

Hence, the correct option is (A).

16. 'Profit' is the most appropriate word because it is mentioned in the following sentence and also it is important for a business to make profit. 'loss' is wrong because it will be opposite to what we have mentioned in the above sentence. 'head start' is also wrong. 'stand' and 'campaigning' both do not follow the context of the text.

Hence, the correct option is (E).

17. 'Profits' is the most appropriate word because a business must get profits. 'losses' is wrong because a business is a not a business if it's in loss. 'customers' is also wrong because efforts in business gets profits and same goes for 'people' and 'leader'.

Hence, the correct option is (C).

18. The project believes that there may be a premium market for items that have been made using plastic reclaimed from the ocean.

- Option (C) -Have been made- "Has been made" is the present perfect passive tense. The present perfect tense (has made) to use describe an action that happened at an unspecified time in the past. For example, She has made a cake. If you have to change this into a passive sentence, it would be written as, A cake has been made by her.

- Option (A) -Made- cannot be chosen because the action that is mentioned in this sentence may have taken place in the past but it has some present consequences.

- Therefore option (B) -Was- made cannot be chosen.

- Option (D) -Is made- which is in the present is clearly not the answer.

- Option (E) -Has been made- cannot be chosen because the subject is plural.

Hence, the correct option is (C).

19. I missed the bus because I was late.

The correct conjunction to be used in the blank is 'because' as it means 'for the reason that; since'. Here, the speaker was late, and that is why he/she missed the bus.

Other options are rejected because:

- 'Yet' is used as a conjunction which means 'but at the same time'.

- 'Although' and 'though' mean 'in spite of the fact that; even though'.

- 'However' means 'in whatever way; regardless of how'.

Hence, the correct option is (E).

20. I have a friend whose father is a famous actor.

'Whose' means belonging to or associated with which person. Eg - Whose bag is this? Here in the sentence, the father is associated with the speaker's friend i.e., it is his/her friend's father.

Other options are rejected because:

- 'Whom' is used instead of 'who' as the object of a verb or preposition. Eg - Whom did he marry?

- 'Who' is used to introduce a clause giving further information about a person or people previously mentioned.

- 'Who's' is a contraction of 'who is' or 'who has' which is wrong.

- 'Whos'' is grammatically incorrect.

Hence, the correct option is (A).

21. Science has helped power the world through its development.

'Development' is a specified state of growth or advancement.

Our world is always developing and science has fuelled its pace i.e. powered the world so that there is an increase in development.

Other options are rejected because:

- 'Status' means a relative social or professional position; standing.

- 'Economy' means the state of a country or region in terms of the production and consumption of goods and services and the supply of money.

- 'Liberty' means a state of being free within society from oppressive restrictions imposed by authority.

- 'Poverty' means the state of being extremely poor.

Hence, the correct option is (C).

22. The correct sentence is: The leader of the cult was very sure that he could brainwash the people into committing crimes that he wanted.

- Part B talks about 'the brainwash' that the leader was carrying out.

- 'Brainwash' is a verb - an action - and thus cannot be preceded by the article 'the' - used exclusively for specific, countable nouns - unless there is a noun immediately after the verb.

- Thus, 'brainwash' needs to be replaced with a specific, countable noun.

- Part C talks about how the leader could 'cult' the people into doing something.

- 'the cult' and 'he could brainwash' are contextually and grammatically correct.

- Therefore, B will replace C and vice versa.

Hence, the correct option is (B).

23. The correct sentence is: There was a negotiation going on for a long time for marriage between one of the king's sons, first Henry, and afterward Charles, and a princess of Spain.

- Afterward: at a later or future time, it is an adverb and incorrectly used in Blank A. Because before blank A there is the use of an article a.

- Afterward starts with vowel therefore it should be followed by article an

- Negotiation: a discussion aimed at reaching an agreement.

- 'Negotiation Charles' this phrase is grammatically and contextually incorrect here

- Therefore A and C should be interchanged

- Marriage: the legally or formally recognized union of two people as partners in a personal relationship

- Princess: a female member of a royal family especially.

Hence, the correct option is (D).

24. The correct sentence is: Kate was the matriarch of the family, and she had single-handedly brought her family from rags to riches.

- Part A talks about 'the rags of the family'.

- This is incorrect as the article 'the' is used for specific, countable, singular nouns and 'rags' is plural.

- Thus, 'rags' needs to be replaced with a singular noun.

- Part D talks about 'from matriarch to riches'

- This is incorrect as the sentence is talking of a specific family and their matriarch, so the noun should be preceded by the article 'the'.

- Also, 'matriarch' is a label that is given to someone, it is not a tangible entity that can be brought 'from' one place to another.

- Thus, 'matriarch' needs to be replaced too.

- 'Was the matriarch of the family' and 'rags to riches' are grammatically and contextually correct.

- Therefore, D will replace A and vice versa.

Hence, the correct option is (C).

25. The correct sentence is: On Earth, sunlight is scattered and filtered through Earth's atmosphere, and is obvious as daylight when the Sun is above the horizon.

- The word 'filtered' is appropriate for the first blank because sunlight passes through the Earth's atmosphere. Therefore, the correct choice is "filtered".

- The word 'obvious' is appropriate for the second blank because the sunlight is visible when we see the sun in the sky. Hence, the correct choice is 'obvious'.

- The word 'horizon' is appropriate for the last blank because when the sun is visible in the horizon we can clearly see the daylight. Hence, the word 'horizon' is the correct choice.

Hence, the correct option is (A).

26. The correct sentence is: Half-way between the bank of the river and the island, a large rock rose out of the water.

- Island: a tract of land surrounded by water and smaller than a continent

- 'Island of the river' is a wrong phrase, river is itself an independent water body.

- Instead, 'bank of the river' is grammatically and conceptually correct

- Bank of the river means the land along the edge of a river

- Therefore, B and D should be interchanged

- Half-way: at or to a point midway between two others.

- River: a large natural stream of water flowing in a channel to the sea, a lake, or another river

Hence, the correct option is (D).

27. The icing on the cake: something that makes a good situation even better.

Example: I love my job and getting public recognition is merely the icing on the cake.

Hence, the correct option is (B).

28. Counting your chickens: usually used in negative statements to mean that someone should not depend on something hoped for until he or she knows for certain that it will happen.

Example: Don't count your chickens (before they hatch) you don't know yet if she will accept your offer.

Hence, the correct option is (A).

29. The correct sentence is: Sneha agrees that **her elder brother is much clever than** her.

- 'Elder' and 'eldest' mean the same as 'older' and 'oldest'.

- We only use the adjectives elder and eldest before a noun (as attributive adjectives), and usually when talking about relationships within a family.

- **Example:** Let me introduce Siga. She's my elder sister.

Hence, the correct option is (C).

30. The correct sentence is: They put the glass **beside the book on** the table.

- Beside means at the side of or next to.
- Example: She sat beside her friend on the bus.
- Besides means in addition to or apart from.
- Example: She's capable of doing the work and a lot more besides.

Hence, the correct option is (B).

31. The relative speed of both the trains running in opposite direction = (90 + 60) km/hr = 150 km/hr

Relative speed $= 150 \times \dfrac{5}{18} = \dfrac{125}{3}$ m/s

Distance covered by both trains = (length of one train + length of another)

Distance = 270 + 200 = 470 m

Time taken to cross each other $= 470 \times \dfrac{3}{125}$ sec $= \dfrac{282}{25}$ sec

Hence, the correct option is (E).

32. Given:

Selling price is 21% less than cost price.

Let Cost price of 1000 gram = Rs. 1000

Selling price of 1000 gram = Rs. 790

But he used false weight.

Cost price of 750 gram = Rs. 750

∴ Selling price of 750 gram = Rs. 790

Profit = Rs. 790 - Rs. 750 = Rs. 40

Profit% $= \dfrac{40}{750} \times 100$

$= \dfrac{16}{3}\%$

Hence, the correct option is (A).

33. Given:

Principal amount = Rs. 10,000

Interest rates = 10% p.a.

Interest = Principal amount = 10,000

$\text{SI} = \dfrac{(P \times T \times R)}{100}$

$10{,}000 = \dfrac{10{,}000 \times 10 \times T}{100}$

$\Rightarrow T = 10{,}000 \times \dfrac{100}{10{,}000} \times 10 = 10$ years

$\Rightarrow$ Time required = 10 years

Hence, the correct option is (B).

34. Given:

the area of a rhombus having side 10cm and one of its diagonal as 12cm.

Side of a rhombus, a = 10cm

One diagonal of rhombus, d_1 = 12cm

Other diagonal of rhombus = d_2

$4a^2 = d_1^2 + d_2^2$

$\Rightarrow 4 \times 10^2 = 12^2 + d_2^2$

$\Rightarrow 256 = d_2^2$

$\Rightarrow d_2 = 16$

Area of Rhombus $= \dfrac{1}{2}(d_2 \times d_1)$

$\Rightarrow \dfrac{1}{2} \times 12 \times 16$

= 96 cm²

∴ The area of a rhombus having side 10cm and one of its diagonal as 12cm is 96 cm².

Hence, the correct option is (A).

35. I. $11x^2 - 27x + 10 = 0$

$\Rightarrow 11x^2 - 22x - 5x + 10 = 0$

$\Rightarrow 11x(x - 2) - 5(x - 2) = 0$

$\Rightarrow (11x - 5)(x - 2) = 0$

$\Rightarrow x = 2, \dfrac{5}{11}$

II. $y^2 - 10y - 24 = 0$

$\Rightarrow y^2 - 12y + 2y - 24 = 0$

$\Rightarrow y(y - 12) + 2(y - 12) = 0$

$\Rightarrow (y + 2)(y - 12) = 0$

$\Rightarrow y = -2, 12$

Value of x	Value y	Relation
2	−2	$x > y$
2	12	$x < y$
$\dfrac{5}{11}$	12	$x < y$
$\dfrac{5}{11}$	−2	$x > y$

∴ x = y or relationship between x and y cannot be established.

Hence, the correct option is (E).

36. I. $x^2 - 26x + 165 = 0$

$\Rightarrow x^2 - 11x - 15x + 165 = 0$

$\Rightarrow x(x - 11) - 15(x - 11) = 0$

$\Rightarrow (x - 11)(x - 15) = 0$

$\Rightarrow x = 11,15$

II. $y^2 - 38y + 357 = 0$

$\Rightarrow y^2 - 17y - 21y + 357 = 0$

$\Rightarrow y(y - 17) - 21(y - 17) = 0$

$\Rightarrow (y - 21)(y - 17) = 0$

$\Rightarrow y = 21,17$

Value of x	Value of y	Relation
11	21	$y > x$
11	17	$y > x$
15	21	$y > x$
15	17	$y > x$

$\therefore x < y$

Hence, the correct option is (B).

37. I. $x^2 + 40x + 231 = 0$

$\Rightarrow x^2 + 33x + 7x + 231 = 0$

$\Rightarrow x(x + 33) + 7(x + 33) = 0$

$\Rightarrow (x + 7)(x + 33) = 0$

$\Rightarrow x = -7, -33$

II. $y^2 + 45y + 374 = 0$

$\Rightarrow y^2 + 34y + 11y + 374 = 0$

$\Rightarrow y(y + 34) + 11(y + 34) = 0$

$\Rightarrow (y + 34)(y + 11) = 0$

$\Rightarrow y = -34, -11$

Value of x	Value of y	Relation
-7	-34	$y > x$
-7	-11	$y > x$
-33	-34	$x > y$
-33	-11	$y > x$

$\therefore x = y$ or relationship between x and y cannot be established.

Hence, the correct option is (E).

38. I. $x^2 + 20x + 91 = 0$

$\Rightarrow x^2 + 7x + 13x + 91 = 0$

$\Rightarrow x(x + 7) + 13(x + 7) = 0$

$\Rightarrow (x + 13)(x + 7) = 0$

$\Rightarrow x = -13, -7$

II. $y^2 - 26y + 105 = 0$

$\Rightarrow y^2 - 21y - 5y + 105 = 0$

$\Rightarrow y(y - 21) - 5(y - 21) = 0$

$\Rightarrow (y - 21)(y - 5) = 0$

$\Rightarrow y = 21,5$

Value of x	Value of y	Relation
-7	21	$y > x$
-7	5	$y > x$
-13	21	$y > x$
-13	5	$y > x$

$\therefore x < y$

Hence, the correct option is (B).

39. I. $x^2 - 7x - 120 = 0$

$\Rightarrow x^2 - 15x + 8x - 120 = 0$

$\Rightarrow x(x - 15) + 8(x - 15) = 0$

$\Rightarrow (x + 8)(x - 15) = 0$

$\Rightarrow x = -8,15$

II. $y^2 + 43y + 432 = 0$

$\Rightarrow y^2 + 27y + 16y + 432 = 0$

$\Rightarrow y(y + 27) + 16(y + 27) = 0$

$\Rightarrow (y + 27)(y + 16) = 0$

$\Rightarrow y = -27, -16$

Value of x	Value of y	Relation
-8	-27	$x > y$
-8	-16	$x > y$
-15	-27	$x > y$
-15	-16	$x > y$

$\therefore x > y$

Hence, the correct option is (A).

40. Given:

Anil's age = 4(Rahul's age)

Anil's age + Rahul age = 100

Let Rahul's age four years ago was x years.

Anil's age = 4x

$\Rightarrow$ 4x + x = 100

$\Rightarrow$ x = 20

$\therefore$ Present age of Rahul = 20 + 4

$\Rightarrow$24 years

Hence, the correct option is (A).

41. Given:

Ratul invested 20% more than Rakesh

Rakesh invested 50% more than Rudra

Total investment amount = Rs. 3225

Let, Rudra invested Rs. 100x.

Amount invested by Rakesh = 150x

Amount invested by Ratul = 150x + (150x × 20%) = 150x + 30x = 180x

Ratio of their investment = 100x : 150x : 180x = 10 : 15 : 18

Investment amount of Ratul = Rs. 3,225 × $\dfrac{18}{43}$ = Rs. 1,350

∴ Investment of Ratul is Rs. 1,350.

Hence, the correct option is (D).

42. Given:

A person travels the three parts at the speed of 28 km/h, 56 km/h and 112 km/h respectively.

Let, total distance covered $= 3x$ km

Time taken to cover first x km $= \dfrac{x}{28}$ hr

Time taken to cover next x km $= \dfrac{x}{56}$ hr

Time taken to cover last x km $= \dfrac{x}{112}$ hr

Total time taken $= \left(\dfrac{x}{28}\right) + \left(\dfrac{x}{56}\right) + \left(\dfrac{x}{112}\right) = \dfrac{7x}{112} = \dfrac{x}{16}$ hr

Average speed $= 3x \div \left(\dfrac{x}{16}\right) = 48$ km/hr

∴ Average speed for the entire journey is 48 km/hr.

Hence, the correct option is (C).

43. Given:

Raktim can complete $\dfrac{7}{16}$ part of a work in = 21 days

Raktim and Puja can complete the remaining work together in = 18 days

Let Raktim and Puja together can complete the total work in X days.

Remaining work $= \left(1 - \dfrac{7}{16}\right) = \dfrac{9}{16}$

Raktim and Puja can do the remaining work together in 18 days.

Raktim and Puja 1 day's work $= \dfrac{9}{(16 \times 18)} = \dfrac{1}{32}$

Raktim and Puja can complete the total work together in = 32 days

∴ Time needed to complete the remaining work is 32 days.

Hence, the correct option is (B).

44. Given:

In first solution of syrup quantity of water = 15%

In second solution syrup quantity of water = 35%

Let, x litres of first solution must be added.

According to the question,

Total litres of first solution × 15% water + Total litres of second solution × 35% water = (Total litres of first solution + Total litres of second solution) × 23% water

$\Rightarrow x \times \left(\dfrac{15}{100}\right) + 40 \times \left(\dfrac{35}{100}\right) = (x + 40) \times \left(\dfrac{23}{100}\right)$

$\Rightarrow 0.15x + 14 = 0.23x + 9.2$

$\Rightarrow 0.08x = 4.8$

$\Rightarrow 8x = 480$

$\Rightarrow x = 60$

∴ 60 litres of first solution must be added.

Hence, the correct option is (C).

45. Given:

$16.95 \times 2.98 + 8 \div 1.96 - 6.1 = (?)^2$

Taking approximate value, we get

$\Rightarrow 17 \times 3 + 8 \div 2 - 6 = (?)^2$

$\Rightarrow 17 \times 3 + 4 - 6 = (?)^2$

$\Rightarrow 51 + 4 - 6 = (?)^2$

$\Rightarrow 55 - 6 = (?)^2$

$\Rightarrow 49 = (?)^2$

$\therefore ? = 7$

Hence, the correct option is (C).

46. Given:

$9.02 - (? - 10.07) + (20.92)^2 = 461$

Since, we need to find out the approximate value, we can write these values to their nearest integers.

Taking approximate value, we get

$9 - (? - 10) + (21)^2 = 461$

$\Rightarrow 9 - ? + 10 + 441 = 461$

$\Rightarrow 9 - ? + 10 + 441 = 461$

$\Rightarrow 460 - ? = 461$

$\Rightarrow -? = 461 - 460$

$\Rightarrow -? = 1$

$\therefore ? = -1$

$\therefore$ the approximate value of question mark (?) in the following question is -1.

Hence, the correct option is (C).

47. Given:

$$24.97 \times \sqrt{15.99} + 400.04 = \sqrt{?} + 475$$

Since, we need to find out the approximate value, we can write these values to their nearest integers.

Taking approximate value, we get

$$25 \times \sqrt{16} + 400 = \sqrt{?} + 475$$

$$\Rightarrow 25 \times 4 + 400 = \sqrt{?} + 475$$

$$\Rightarrow 100 + 400 = \sqrt{?} + 475$$

$$\Rightarrow \sqrt{?} = 500 - 475$$

$$\Rightarrow \sqrt{?} = 25$$

$$\Rightarrow ? = 625$$

$\therefore$ The approximate value of question mark (?) in the following question is 625.

Hence, the correct option is (B).

48. Given:

$$9.87\% \text{ of } [(299.96)^2 + (20.24)^2] = 999.99\% \text{ of } 4 + ?$$

Since, we need to find out the approximate value, we can write these values to their nearest integers.

Taking approximate value, we get

$$10\% \text{ of } [(300)^2 + (20)^2] = 1000\% \text{ of } 4 + ?$$

$$\Rightarrow (10 \div 100) \times (90000 + 400) = (1000 \div 100) \times 4 + ?$$

$$\Rightarrow (1 \div 10) \times (90400) = 10 \times 4 + ?$$

$$\Rightarrow 9040 = 40 + ?$$

$$\Rightarrow 9040 - 40 = ?$$

$$\therefore ? = 9000$$

$\therefore$ The approximate value of question mark (?) in the following question is 9000.

Hence, the correct option is (C).

49. Given:

$(1 \div 11.91) - (1 \div 4.07) + (1 \div ?) = 0$

Since, we need to find out the approximate value, we can write these values to their nearest integers.

Taking approximate value, we get

$$(1 \div 12) - (1 \div 4.) + (1 \div ?) = 0$$

$$\Rightarrow (1 \div ?) = (1 \div 4) - (1 \div 12)$$

Take L.C.M

$$\Rightarrow (1 \div ?) = [(12 - 4) \div 48]$$

$$\Rightarrow (1 \div ?) = 8 \div 48$$

$$\Rightarrow (1 \div ?) = 1 \div 6$$

$$\Rightarrow ? = 6$$

$\therefore$ the approximate value of question mark (?) in the following question is 6.

Hence, the correct option is (A).

50. Given:

$$55\% \text{ of } 99.999 + ?^2 = 56\% \text{ of } 850 - 20\% \text{ of } 150$$

Taking approximate value, we get

$$55\% \text{ of } 100 + ?^2 = 56\% \text{ of } 850 - 20\% \text{ of } 150$$

$$\Rightarrow (55 \div 100 \times 100) + ?^2 = (56 \div 100 \times 850) - (20 \div 100 \times 150)$$

$$\Rightarrow 55 + ?^2 = 476 - 30$$

$$\Rightarrow 55 + ?^2 = 446$$

$$\Rightarrow ?^2 = 446 - 55$$

$$\Rightarrow ?^2 = 391$$

$$\therefore ? \approx 20$$

Hence, the correct option is (B).

51. Given:

$3.76 \times (5.23 - 1.68) + (50\% \text{ of } 16.05) = ?$

Taking approximate value, we get

$4 \times (5 - 2) + (50\% \text{ of } 16) = ?$

$\Rightarrow 4 \times 3 + (50\% \text{ of } 16) = ?$

$\Rightarrow 12 + 8 = ?$

$\therefore ? = 20$

Hence, the correct option is (B).

52. Given:

$$\sqrt{3.98} + \sqrt{((2.22)^2 + 4.85)} \times 5.69 = 24.71\% \text{ of } ?$$

Taking approximate value, we get

$$\sqrt{4} + \sqrt{(2^2 + 5)} \times 6 = 25\% \text{ of } ?$$

$$\Rightarrow \sqrt{4} + \sqrt{(4 + 5)} \times 6 = 25\% \text{ of } ?$$

$$\Rightarrow \sqrt{4} + (\sqrt{9}) \times 6 = 25\% \text{ of } ?$$

$\Rightarrow 2 + 18 = 25\%$ of ?

$\Rightarrow 2 + 18 = 25\%$ of ? $(\because 1.73 \approx 2)$

$\Rightarrow 20 = \left(\frac{25}{100}\right) \times ?$

$\Rightarrow 20 \times \frac{100}{25} = ?$

$? = 80$

Hence, the correct option is (C).

53. Given:

$\sqrt{289.15} + 3.99 \times (45.01\% \text{ of } 199.99) - ? = 0$

Taking approximate value, we get

$\sqrt{289} + 4 \times (45\% \text{ of } 200) - ? = 0$

$\Rightarrow \sqrt{289} + 4 \times (45\% \text{ of } 200) - ? = 0$

$\Rightarrow 17 + 4 \times 90 = ?$

$\Rightarrow 17 + 4 \times 90 = ?$

$\Rightarrow ? = 17 + 360$

$? = 377$

Hence, the correct option is (A).

54. Given:

$$\frac{\left(\left(\frac{2.56}{10.89}\right) + \left(\frac{2.36}{4.58}\right) - \left(\frac{0.99}{4.79}\right)\right)}{[7.05 + 74.88\% \text{ of } 11.88]}$$

Taking approximate value, we get

$$\frac{\left(\left(\frac{3}{11}\right) + \left(\frac{2}{5}\right) - \left(\frac{1}{5}\right)\right)}{[7 + 75\% \text{ of } 12]}$$

$$\Rightarrow \frac{\frac{(15+22-11)}{55}}{(7+9)}$$

$$\Rightarrow \left(\frac{26}{55}\right) \div 16$$

$$\Rightarrow \frac{26}{(55 \times 16)}$$

$$\Rightarrow \frac{13}{440}$$

Hence, the correct option is (B).

55. Let number of balloons and pins Ram have be a and b respectively while number of balloons and pins Sham have be m and n respectively.

$\Rightarrow m - a = 40$

$\Rightarrow n + b = 100$

$\Rightarrow (a + b) = (m + n) - 20$

$\Rightarrow b - n = m - a - 20$

$\Rightarrow b - n = 20$

Solving,

b = 60 and n = 40

$$\Rightarrow b = \frac{75}{100} \times a = \frac{3a}{4}$$

$$\Rightarrow a = \frac{4}{3} \times 60 = 80$$

$\Rightarrow m = 80 + 40 = 120$

Required average $= \frac{(a+m)}{2} = \frac{(80+120)}{2} = 100$

Hence, the correct option is (B).

56. Let number of balloons and pins Ram have be a and b respectively while number of balloons and pins Sham have be m and n respectively.

$\Rightarrow m - a = 40$

$\Rightarrow n + b = 100$

$\Rightarrow (a + b) = (m + n) - 20$

$\Rightarrow b - n = m - a - 20$

$\Rightarrow b - n = 20$

Solving,

b = 60 and n = 40

$$\Rightarrow b = \frac{75}{100} \times a = \frac{3a}{4}$$

$$\Rightarrow a = \frac{4}{3} \times 60 = 80$$

$\Rightarrow m = 80 + 40 = 120$

Required percentage

$$= \frac{60}{(60+80)} \times 100$$

$= 42.85\%$

Hence, the correct option is (C).

57. Let number of balloons and pins Ram have be a and b respectively while number of balloons and pins Sham have be m and n respectively.

$\Rightarrow m - a = 40$

$\Rightarrow n + b = 100$

$\Rightarrow (a + b) = (m + n) - 20$

$\Rightarrow b - n = m - a - 20$

$\Rightarrow b - n = 20$

Solving,

b = 60 and n = 40

$$\Rightarrow b = \frac{75}{100} \times a = \frac{3a}{4}$$

$$\Rightarrow a = \frac{4}{3} \times 60 = 80$$

⇒ m = 80 + 40 = 120

Required difference = m − n

= 120 − 40 = 80

Hence, the correct option is (E).

58. Let number of balloons and pins Ram have be a and b respectively while number of balloons and pins Sham have be m and n respectively.

⇒ m − a = 40

⇒ n + b = 100

⇒ (a + b) = (m + n) − 20

⇒ b − n = m − a − 20

⇒ b − n = 20

Solving,

b = 60 and n = 40

$$\Rightarrow b = \frac{75}{100} \times a = \frac{3a}{4}$$

$$\Rightarrow a = \frac{4}{3} \times 60 = 80$$

⇒ m = 80 + 40 = 120

Required ratio

= (a + m) : (b + n)

= (80 + 120) : (60 + 40)

= 200 : 100

= 2 : 1

Hence, the correct option is (D).

59. Let number of balloons and pins Ram have be a and b respectively while number of balloons and pins Sham have be m and n respectively.

⇒ m − a = 40

⇒ n + b = 100

⇒ (a + b) = (m + n) − 20

⇒ b − n = m − a − 20

⇒ b − n = 20

Solving,

b = 60 and n = 40

$$\Rightarrow b = \frac{75}{100} \times a = \frac{3a}{4}$$

Required percentage

$$\Rightarrow 40 = 60 - 60 \times \frac{?}{100}$$

⇒ ? = 33.33%

Hence, the correct option is (A).

60. The series follows the following pattern:

25 + 2 = 27

27 + 3 = 30

30 + 5 = 35

35 + 7 = 42

42 + 11 = 53

∴ The required term in the series will be 53.

Hence, the correct option is (E).

61. The series follows the following pattern:

80 × 0.5 = 40

40 × 1.5 = 60

60 × 2.5 = 150

150 × 3.5 = 525

525 × 4.5 = 2362.5

∴ The required term in the series will be 525.

Hence, the correct option is (B).

62. The series follows the following pattern:

5 × 1 + 1 = 6

6 × 2 + 1 = 13

13 × 3 + 1 = 40

40 × 4 + 1 = 161

161 × 5 + 1 = 806

∴ The required term in the series will be 40.

Hence, the correct option is (D).

63. The pattern of the given number series is as following:

151 + 2 = 153

153 + 3 = 156

156 + 5 = 161

161 + 7 = 168

168 + 11 = 179

179 + 13 = 192

192 + 17 = 209

Thus, the value in the place of '?' = 209

Hence, the correct option is (C).

64. The pattern of the given number series is as following:

97 - 13 = 84

84 + 26 = 110

110 - 39 = 71

71 + 52 = 123

123 - 65 = 58

58 + 78 = 136

136 - 91 = 45

∴ the value which will come in place of '?' is 45.

Hence, the correct option is (B).

65. Given-

The sum of two numbers is 2490 .

Let the two numbers are A, B.

$$\Rightarrow A + B = 2490$$

6.5% of the first number is equal to 8.5% of the second number.

$$\Rightarrow 6.5\% \times A = 8.5\% \times B$$

$$\Rightarrow \frac{65}{1000} \times A = \frac{85}{1000} \times B$$

$$\Rightarrow 13 \times A = 17 \times B$$

$$\Rightarrow \frac{A}{B} = \frac{17}{13}$$

Let $A = 17k, B = 13k$

$$\Rightarrow A + B = 2490$$

$$\Rightarrow 17k + 13k = 2490$$

$$\Rightarrow 30k = 2490$$

$$\Rightarrow k = 83$$

First number $= 17k$

$= 17 \times 83$

$= 1411$

Second number $= 13k$

$= 13 \times 83$

=1079

Greater number $= 1411$

Hence, the correct option is (C).

66. Given Statements: F < D ≤ G, K > M > L ≥ G

On combining: F < D ≤ G ≤ L < M < K

Conclusions:

I. M > D → True (as D ≤ G ≤ L < M → D < M)

II. M = D → False (as D ≤ G ≤ L < M → D < M)

Thus, only I is true.

Hence, the correct option is (A).

67. Given Statements: S > M ≥ O, O ≥ P ≥ N > K

On combining: S > M ≥ O ≥ P ≥ N > K

Conclusions:

I. O > N → False (as O ≥ P ≥ N → O ≥ N)

II. N ≤ M → True (as M ≥ O ≥ P ≥ N → M ≥ N)

Thus, only II is true.

Hence, the correct option is (B).

68. Given Statements: X > Y ≥ Z ≥ W, W > V ≥ U

On combining: X > Y ≥ Z ≥ W > V ≥ U

Conclusions:

I. W < U → False (as X > Y ≥ Z ≥ W > V ≥ U → W > U)

II. Y > W → False (as Y ≥ Z ≥ W → Y ≥ W, it is possible but not definite)

Thus, none is true.

Hence, the correct option is (D).

69. Given Statements: 1 < 2 ≤ 4, 3 > 5 ≥ 6 > 4

On combining: 1 < 2 ≤ 4 < 6 ≤ 5 < 3

Conclusions:

I. 1 = 6 → False (as 1 < 2 ≤ 4 < 6 → 1 < 6)

II. 6 > 1 → True (as 1 < 2 ≤ 4 < 6 → 1 < 6)

Thus, only II is true.

Hence, the correct option is (B).

70. Given Statements: P > M > Q ≥ R, S < N ≤ O ≤ T = R

On combining: P > M > Q ≥ R = T ≥ O ≥ N > S

Conclusions:

I. M > N → True (as M > Q ≥ R = T ≥ O ≥ N → M > N)

II. Q ≤ T → False(as Q ≥ R = T → Q ≥ T)

Thus, only I is true.

Hence, the correct option is (D).

71. The pattern for the code is as follows,

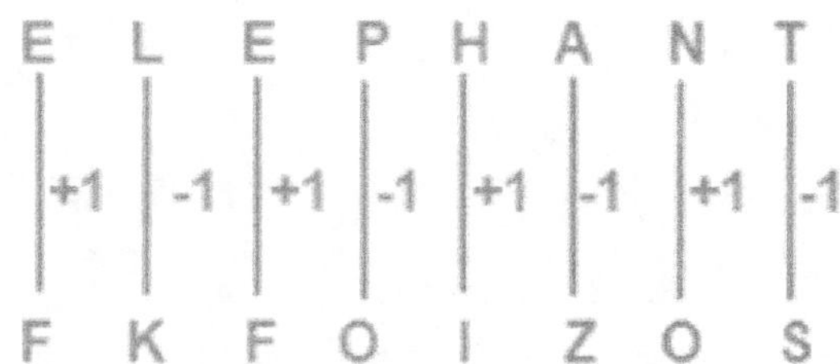

Each letter at odd place in the word is one step behind and each letter at even place in the word is one step ahead of the corresponding letter of the code.

Therefore, EVALUATION is coded as FUBKVZUHPM.

Hence, the correct option is (D).

Ques (72-74):1. Sainoor is taller than Piyu but shortet than Navya.

2. Kianshi is taller than only two persons, which means Kianshi is the 3rd shortest person.

Kianshi

3. Gauri is the seventh tallest person, which means Gauri is the shortest person.

Gauri
Kianshi

4. Navya is shorter than only one person, which means Navya is 2nd tallest person.

Gauri
Kianshi
Navya

5. Equal number of people are taller and shorter than Piyu, which means Piyu is at the 4th position only then equal number of people can be shorter and taller than her.

Gauri
Kianshi
Piyu
Navya

Now we know that, Sainoor is taller than Piyu, but shorter than Navya.

Gauri

Kianshi
Piyu
Sainoor
Navya

As, we know that Simar is neither the tallest nor the shortest, so clearly Simar is second shortest person, Sainoor is not the tallest and Manya is the only person left, so Manya is the tallest.

Gauri
Simar
Kianshi
Piyu
Sainoor
Navya
Manya

72. So, Manya is the tallest.

Hence, the correct option is (B).

73. So, 2 persons are taller and 4 persons are shorter than Sainoor.

Hence, the correct option is (B).

74. So, Piyu is the fourth shortest person.

Hence, the correct option is (D).

Ques (75-79):Seven persons: Ram, Ronak, Rishu, Gaurav, Shyam, Lokesh and Rinku

Schools: A, B, C, D, E, F and G.

Companies: LG, Intex, HTC, Redmi, Sony, Samsung and Lenovo

If we summarize the information given in the question:

1) Ronak uses Samsung and he teaches in school E.

2) Shyam teaches in school A and he uses LG.

3) Lokesh teaches in school D and he uses HTC.

Person	School	Mobile
Ronak	E	Samsung
Shyam	A	LG
Lokesh	D	HTC

4) Rinku teaches in school C and he uses neither Intex nor Redmi.

5) The one who teaches in school F uses Lenovo.

Person	School	Mobile
Ronak	E	Samsung
Shyam	A	LG
Lokesh	D	HTC
Rinku	C	
	F	Lenovo

6) Rishu and Gaurav do not teach in school G and they do not use Redmi. Rishu does not teach in school B.

7) Rinku does not use either Intex or Redmi.

Person	School	Mobile
Ronak	E	Samsung
Shyam	A	LG
Lokesh	D	HTC
Rinku	C	Sony
Rishu	F	Lenovo
	G	
Gaurav	B	

8) Gaurav does not use Redmi. Only Ram is left and one places is left so he will sit there.

Person	School	Mobile
Ronak	E	Samsung
Shyam	A	LG
Lokesh	D	HTC
Rinku	C	Sony
Rishu	F	Lenovo
Ram	G	Redmi
Gaurav	B	Intex

75. Thus, Ram teaches in school G.

Hence, the correct option is (A).

76. Thus, Rishu uses Lenovo.

Hence, the correct option is (B).

77. Thus, Gaurav teaches in school B.

Hence, the correct option is (C).

78. Ram teaches in school G and he uses Redmi.

Thus, Ram – G – Redmi is the correct the combination.

Hence, the correct option is (C).

79. Thus, Gaurav uses Intex.

Hence, the correct option is (D).

Ques (80-83): Number of people: 7

There are two married couples.

Preparing the family tree using the following symbols:

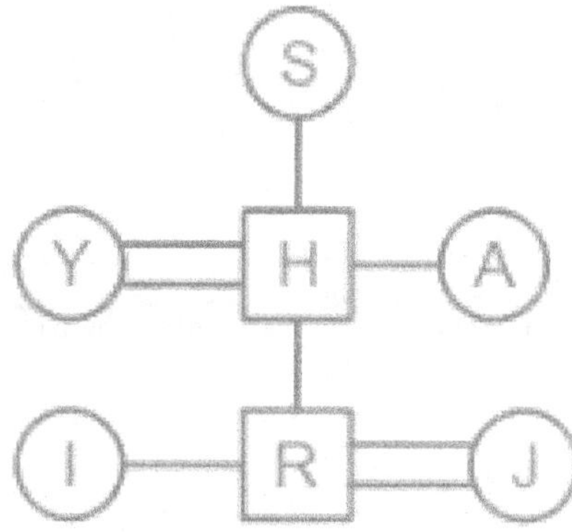

80. Thus, the relationship between A and R is Aunt – Nephew.

Hence, the correct option is (A).

81. Thus, Y is mother – in – law of J.

Hence, the correct option is (D).

82. Thus, I is daughter of H.

Hence, the correct option is (E).

83. Thus, S is grandmother of I.

Hence, the correct option is (A).

84. Given:

Vowel → Next vowel → Alphabetic order

Vowels are A, E, I, O, and U

The word "**AMERICAN**" after changing the vowel to the next vowel is "EMIROCEN"

After alphabetic order rearrangement "EMIROCEN" → "CEEIMNOR"

Letters remained unchanged after rearrangement,

AMERICAN

CEEIMNOR

Thus, E is unchanged

Hence, the correct option is (A).

Ques (85-89):People: Diya, Siya, Tiya, Niya, Pawan, Suresh, and Ankit.

1) Suresh stands second from the left end.

2) Only two persons stand between Suresh and Pawan.

3) Only one person stands between Diya and Tiya.

4) Ankit stands third to the left of Tiya.

So, there are two cases for these conditions:

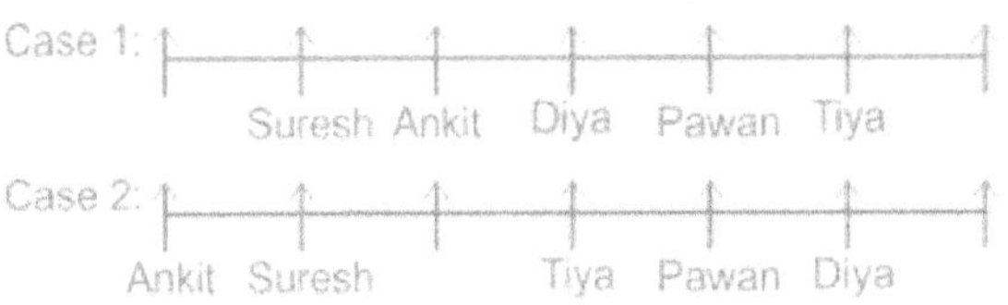

5) Neither Tiya nor Suresh is the immediate neighbour of Niya.

So, Case-1 is not possible and taking case-2.

85. So, Ankit and Niya stand at the extreme ends of the line.

Hence, the correct option is (E).

86. So, One person stands between Siya and Pawan.

Hence, the correct option is (B).

87. So, Ankit is the immediate left of Suresh.

Hence, the correct option is (B).

88. So, Two persons sit between Tiya and Niya.

Hence, the correct option is (B).

89. So, Tiya is Fourth from the left end of the line.

Hence, the correct option is (A).

90.

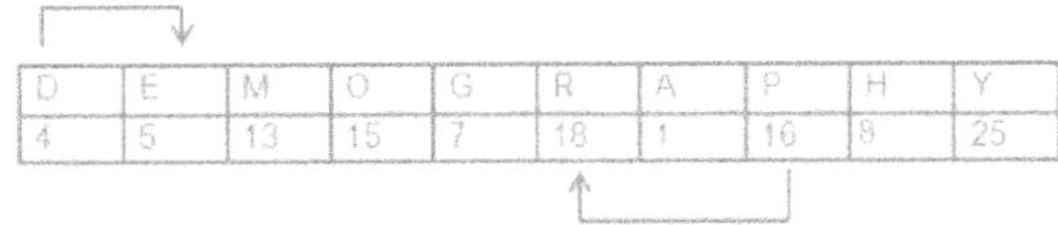

D	E	M	O	G	R	A	P	H	Y
4	5	13	15	7	18	1	16	8	25

Thus, two pairs of letters are there in the word DEMOGRAPHY each of which has as many letters between them in the word (in the forward or backward direction) as they have between them in the English alphabetical order.

Hence, the correct option is (B).

91. Given series: L K 1 C D 9 Z Y ^ P 2 N © K S 3 ↑ 5 M T ®

Digits which are immediately preceded as well as immediately followed by letters are

Left side L K 1 C D 9 Z Y ^ P 2 N © K S 3 ↑ 5 M T ® Right side

So, there are three such digits each of which is immediately followed or preceded by letters.

Hence, the correct option is (C).

92. Given series: L K 1 C D 9 Z Y ^ P 2 N © K S 3 ↑ 5 M T ®

Element exactly between 9 and 3 is 2.

Left side L K 1 C D 9 Z Y ^ P 2 N © K S 3 ↑ 5 M T ® Right side

Hence, the correct option is (A).

93. Left side L K 1 C D 9 Z Y ^ P 2 N © K S 3 ↑ 5 M T ® Right side

Fifth element from the right end = ↑

Tenth to the left of ↑ = Z

Hence, the correct option is (E).

94. Left side L K 1 C D 9 Z Y ^ P 2 N © K S 3 ↑ 5 M T ® Right side

Numbers between 1 and 9 which are not present in the series = 4, 6, 7, 8

Replacing the symbols with these numbers in ascending order from left to right:

L K 1 C D 9 Z Y 4 P 2 N 6 K S 3 7 5 M T 8

1 + 9 + 2 + 3 + 5 + 4 + 6 + 7 + 8 = 45

Hence, the correct option is (A).

95. Left side L K 1 C D 9 Z Y ^ P 2 N © K S 3 ↑ 5 M T ® Right side

L + 1 = K, K + 2 = C

C + 2 = 9,

9 + 1 = Z, Z + 2 = ^

^ + 2 = 2,

2 + 1 = N, N + 2 = K

K + 2 = 3,

3 + 1 = ↑, ↑ + 2 = M

As per the pattern followed the next set of elements is 3↑M.

Hence, the correct option is (C).

Ques (96-100):1. S and X are sitting together but facing in the opposite direction.

2. Y is sitting second to the right of X and both are facing in the same direction.

3. Only two persons are sitting between T and Y who is facing inside.

4. Y and X are facing inside the table from the statement.

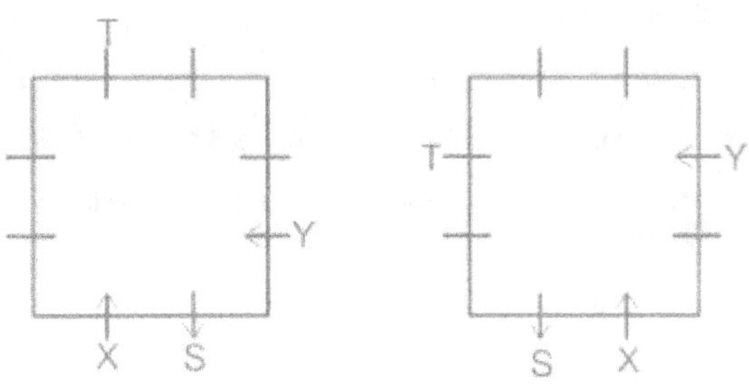

5. T is sitting immediate left of U who is not sitting near W.

6. Z is sitting between Y and X but not sitting opposite to U.

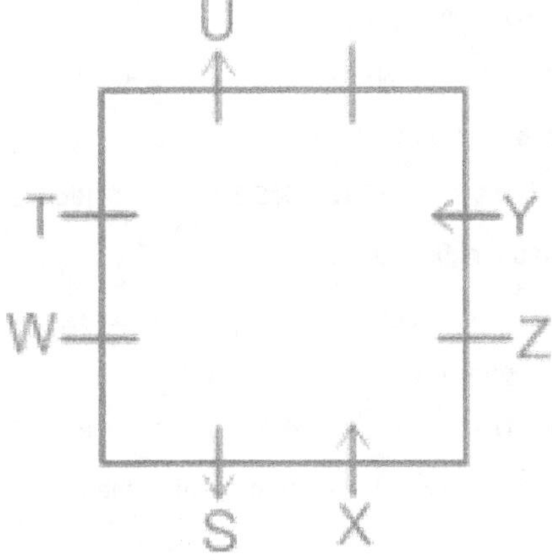

7. V who is facing the same direction as S, is sitting second to the left of both T and Z.

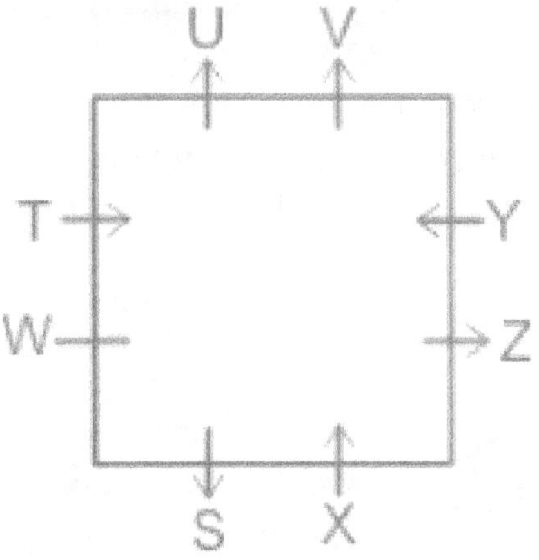

So the final arrangement,

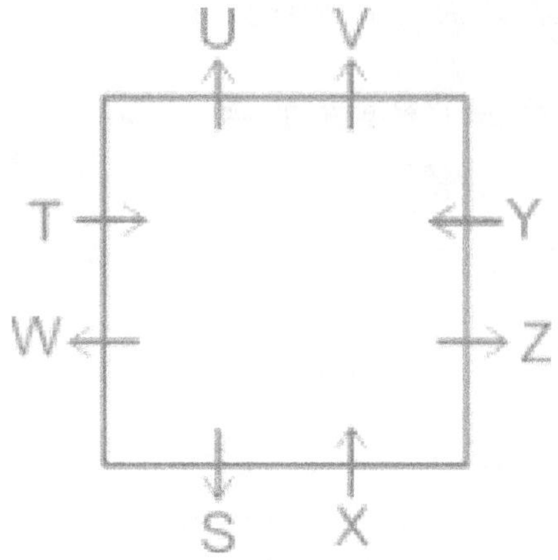

96. Thus, T and W are sitting on the same side of the table.

Hence, the correct option is (C).

97. The position of V remains unchanged.

Thus, If all the names are arranged according to alphabetical order starting from the position of X in the anti-clockwise direction, then one letter will remain unchanged.

Hence, the correct option is (A).

98. Thus, U is sitting second to the right of W.

Hence, the correct option is (B).

99. Thus, X is an immediate right of Z.

Hence, the correct option is (D).

100. Thus, Z is immediate left of Y, S is immediate left of X, in the same way, U is immediate left of V.

Hence, the correct option is (C).

English Language

Ques (1-5):Directions: For the blank in the passage, there are five choices provided. Select the word that makes the most sense when placed in the blank.

Understanding and learning Internet marketing techniques is a must for at-home computer work businesses. Understanding the basics of how to generate free targeted traffic online and the power to sell to them is all one needs. Making money on the net can really be __(1)__ down to these two factors. If you can get targeted traffic and sell to that traffic then the __(2)__ for online business become boundless.

Internet marketing has changed greatly over the years. Once all one had to do was put up a website and optimize the pages with keyword spam. This would get search results and bring in traffic to click on banner ads. Much has changed today, search engines and web surfers are far more refined. They want __(3)__ websites and pages with high-value information. Today Internet __(4)__ for an at-home computer work business requires much more research, skills, and understanding than ever before. Today a website business requires the __(5)__ to come up with a business concept and researching an idea to find a profitable idea.

Q.1 What will come at a place of __(1)__?

A. cracked **B.** shortened
C. broken **D.** boiled
E. lengthened

Q.2 What will come at a place of __(2)__?

A. promise **B.** possibilities
C. talent **D.** impossibilities
E. views

Q.3 What will come at a place of __(3)__?

A. quality **B.** quantity
C. commodity **D.** traction
E. seasoned

Q.4 What will come at a place of __(4)__?

A. business **B.** sustainability
C. production **D.** development
E. marketing

Q.5 What will come at a place of __(5)__?

A. maturity **B.** accountability
C. acceptability **D.** ability
E. skill

Q.6 Direction: Read the sentence to find out whether there is any error in it. The error, if any, will be in one part of the sentence. The number of that part is the answer. If there is no error, the answer is (E). Ignore error of punctuation's if any.

When I went (A) / to the market, I saw (B) / a number of colourful frames was displayed (C) / in the store window. (D) / No error (E)

A. (A) **B.** (B) **C.** (C) **D.** (D)
E. (E)

Q.7 Direction: In the following question, one part of the sentence may have an error. Find out which part of the sentence has an error and click the option corresponding to it. If the sentence is free from error, click the 'No error' option.

If he went out bold to attack (A)/ the oncoming rebels his own troops (B) / might go over to the enemies, or (C) / deliver him into their hands. (D)/ No error

A. (A) **B.** (B) **C.** (C) **D.** (D)
E. No error

Ques (8-10):Directions: Given below is a sentence that may or may not be grammatically viable, choose the most suitable alternative that reflects the grammatically correct sentence.

Q.8 He went through with his plan <u>yet all his friends</u> advised him to abandon it.

A. unless all his friends
B. although all his friends
C. whether all his friends
D. so all his friends
E. if all his friends

Q.9 She advised him to visit <u>Boston as she thought</u> it was the most beautiful city in the world.

A. She advised him to visit Boston, because she thought it was the most beautiful city in the world.

B. She advised him to visit Boston, though she thought it was the most beautiful city in the world

C. She advised him to visit Boston, if she thought it was the most beautiful city in the world.

D. She advised him to visit Boston, yet she thought it was the most beautiful city in the world.

E. She advised him to visit Boston, in order to she thought it was the most beautiful city in the world.

Q.10 The CBI officer <u>look into</u> all the evidence. The case was closed years ago. The jury was hung and could not reach a verdict.

A. Looked into **B.** Look into
C. Looks into **D.** was looked into
E. Looking into

Ques (11-12):Directions: The given question has one blank indicating that something has been omitted. Choose the word for the given options that could fit in the blank correctly.

Q.11 _______ Indians who have migrated to other countries will forget our culture due to overwork.

A. Many **B.** Much
C. Fewer **D.** More

E. None of these

Q.12 If I _________ this match, I would have been the man of the match.

A. Has played   **B.** Have played
C. Had played   **D.** Played
E. None of these

Ques (13-17):Directions: Rearrange the following five sentences A, B, C, D and E in a proper sequence so as to form a meaningful paragraph, and then answer the questions given below.

A. But Galileo began to argue that it was not so.

B. When Galileo was young, people believed that the earth was the center of the Universe.

C. He said that the Earth and the other planets moved around the sun.

D. He was imprisoned for voicing this unorthodox view.

E. This belief was supported by the State and the Church.

Q.13 Which of the following should be the FIRST sentence after rearrangement?

A. A   **B.** B   **C.** C   **D.** D
E. E

Q.14 Which of the following should be the SECOND sentence after rearrangement?

[SBI PO, 2021], [IBPS PO, 2020]

A. A   **B.** B   **C.** C   **D.** D
E. E

Q.15 Which of the following should be the THIRD sentence after rearrangement?

[IBPS PO, 2020]

A. A   **B.** B   **C.** C   **D.** D
E. E

Q.16 Which of the following should be the FOURTH sentence after rearrangement?

[SBI PO, 2021]

A. A   **B.** B   **C.** C   **D.** D
E. E

Q.17 Which of the following should be the FIFTH sentence after rearrangement?
A. A   **B.** B   **C.** C   **D.** D
E. E

Ques (18-19):Directions: Each of the following sentences has a blank space and five words are given below. Click on the word which you consider the most APPROPRIATE to fit the blank.

Q.18 Children sometimes _____ on peanuts.
A. overcome   **B.** obstruct
C. choke   **D.** deprive
E. overpower

Q.19 When he is sad, he _____ to his bedroom.
A. rewinds   **B.** recoils
C. overcome   **D.** scrambled
E. retreats

Q.20 Choose the correct sentence from the following:
A. They care for their children.
B. Mothers is trying to calm their kids.
C. He do not want to work with me.
D. She eat cookies.
E. All of the above is correct

Ques (21-30):Direction: Read the passage and answer the questions that follow. Some words may be highlighted for you. Pay careful attention.

The Directive Principle of State Policy to provide for primary education to all children has failed in its objectives. At present, almost half of India's population is still illiterate. Through the ages, the illiterate masses have been exploited. The present-day politicians have exploited them for their perverted interests. This has resulted in the formation of unstable coalition governments at the Centre. Social evils like drug abuse, consumption of alcohol and child labour are a result of illiteracy among the masses. Kerala has concentrated on mass education and has, thus, **controlled** many social evils. With the nation hovering around the 1 billion marks and around 48 per cent of its population still illiterate, there is hardly a ray of hope for India. In the near future, the rising illiterate population would further impede the growth and development of the nation. The Directive Principles of State Policy **inter alia** provide that the State shall endeavour to provide for free and compulsory education to all children below the age of 14 years, within a period of ten years from the commencement of the Constitution of India. However, because of the lack of resources and foresight among politicians, this dream has never been realized. The **prevalence** of illiteracy among the masses has made them vulnerable to exploitation, as they are unaware of their rights and privileges. The Indian masses have throughout the age remained illiterate and naive because education had been the privilege of only the Brahmins and the upper classes. The **underprivileged** looked up to them, but never **envied** them. On the contrary, the masses resigned themselves to their fate. The Government launched the National Literacy Mission (NLM) with the objective of achieving total adult literacy in 1988. The objective was to achieve total adult literacy among 80 million adults in the age group of 15-35 by the year 1995. Non-Governmental Organization should also take part in the literacy mission to help the government in achieving its targets sooner than proposed. Though total adult literacy is a stupendous task, we must contribute our bit in achieving the desired targets.

Q.21 Why it is said that there is hardly any ray of hope for India?
A. India's population is around 1 billion
B. 48 percent of the population is illiterate
C. It will provide free education to children
D. It has an adult literacy
E. None of the above

Q.22 Why citizens are vulnerable to exploitation?
A. They are literate
B. They are unaware of their rights and privileges.
C. There's mass education
D. Lack of resources
E. None of the above

Q.23 From the options given below, select the most appropriate synonym for the word "**controlled**".
A. Loose
B. Wild
C. Rampant
D. Irrepressible
E. Administer

Q.24 From the options given below, select the most appropriate synonym for the word "**underprivileged**".
A. Deprived
B. Privileged
C. Wealthy
D. Prosperous
E. None of the above

Q.25 Who has failed in its objectives?
A. The government
B. The illiterate citizens
C. The Directive Principle of State Policy
D. The Constitution of India
E. None of the above

Q.26 From the options given below, select the most appropriate antonym for the word "prevalence".
A. Disappearance
B. Ubiquity
C. Universality
D. Regularity
E. Frequency

Q.27 From the options given below, select the most appropriate antonym for the word "envied".
A. Wealthy
B. Despise
C. Irrepressible
D. Regularity
E. Begrudge

Q.28 From the given options, select the most appropriate meaning for the phrase - 'inter alia'.
A. Among other things
B. To commence
C. Ordered
D. Endorse
E. None of the above

Q.29 Why did the government launch National Literacy Mission (NLM)?
A. To be socially strong
B. To gain resources
C. To achieve total literacy
D. To end exploitation
E. To achieve total illiteracy

Q.30 The objective was to achieve total adult literacy among ______________ in the age group of 15-35 by the year 1995.
A. 80 million adults
B. 70 million adults
C. 60 million adults
D. 50 million adults
E. 75 million adults

Numerical Ability

Q.31 7 years ago, the ratio of the ages of Mohit and Rohit was 12:13. 14 years so, the ratio of their ages will be 19:20. Find the sum of the present ages of Mohit and Rohit?
A. 95
B. 87
C. 97
D. 89
E. 79

Ques (32-34):Directions: Solve the given quadratic equations and establish the relation between them.

Q.32 I: $x = \sqrt{1444}$
II: $y^2 = 1444$
A. $x > y$
B. $x = y$, or relation cannot be established
C. $y > x$
D. $x \geq y$
E. $y \geq x$

Q.33 I: $x^2 + 4x - 221 = 0$
II: $y^2 + 52y + 667 = 0$
A. $x \leq y$
B. $y > x$
C. $x \geq y$
D. $x = y$, or relation cannot be established
E. $y < x$

Q.34 I: $3x^2 - 12x + 9 = 0$
II : $4y^2 + 80y + 256 = 0$
A. $x > y$
B. $x < y$
C. $x \geq y$
D. $x \leq y$
E. $x = y$, or relation cannot be established

Q.35 In the given questions, two equations numbered I and II are given. You have to solve both the equations and mark the appropriate answer.
I. $x^2 = 49$
II. $y^2 - 16y + 63 = 0$
A. $x > y$
B. $x \leq y$
C. No relation in x and y or x = y
D. $x \geq y$
E. $x < y$

Ques (36-39): What will come in the place of the question mark '?' in the following question?

Q.36
$$\sqrt{\left[4 \times \sqrt{\left\{4 \times \sqrt{(2 \times 6^2 \div 3^2 \times 2)} \times 64\right\} \times 2}\right]} = ?$$
A. 1032
B. 512
C. 256
D. 16
E. 4

Q.37 $(32 \text{ of } 2 - 64^{0.5} \times 256^{0.25}) \div 2^4 = ?$
A. 3
B. 1
C. 4
D. $\frac{3}{2}$
E. 2

Q.38 120% of 60 + $?^2$ = 70 ÷ 14 × 36 + 13

A. 14   **B.** 11   **C.** 18   **D.** 21
E. 28

Q.39 $\sqrt[2]{25 \times 20 + 5 \times 25} \times \sqrt[2]{25[5(7-2)]} = 5^?$
A. 3   **B.** 4
C. 5   **D.** 6
E. None of the above

Q.40 The present age of Ram and Rohit are in the ratio of 7 : 8 respectively. After 6 years, the respective ratio between the age of Ram and Rohit will be 9 : 10. What is the age of Rohit after 10 years?
A. 30 years   **B.** 34 years   **C.** 40 years   **D.** 42 years
E. 27 years

Q.41 A, B and C can complete a work in 10, 20 and 30 days respectively. If D can destroy the same work in 15 days. Find the time taken by all of them to complete the whole work.
A. $\frac{50}{7}$ days   **B.** $\frac{60}{7}$ days
C. $\frac{20}{3}$ days   **D.** $\frac{40}{7}$ days
E. None of these

Q.42 The ratio of the speed of a boat in still water and the speed of the river is 7 : 3. A person covers 30 km in upstream and 40 km in downstream in 0.5 hours. What is the speed of the boat in still water?
A. 16.1 km/hr   **B.** 161 km/hr
C. 32 km/hr   **D.** 150 km/hr
E. None of these

Q.43 The income of Aman is Rs. 30,000 per month and his expenditure is Rs. 20,000 per month. In the next month, his income increases by Rs. 10,000 per month, and expenditure increases to Rs. 25,000 per month. In the next month, his savings increases by what percent?

[IBPS PO, 2021]

A. 55%   **B.** 25%
C. 100%   **D.** 12.5%
E. None of these

Q.44 A square sheet of paper is converted into a cylinder by rolling it along its length. What is the ratio of the base radius to the side of the square?
A. $\frac{1}{2\pi}$ **B.** $\frac{\sqrt{2}}{\pi}$ **C.** $\frac{1}{\sqrt{2}\pi}$ **D.** $\frac{1}{\pi}$
E. $\frac{1}{3\pi}$

Q.45 A phone is listed at Rs. 2500 and the discount offered is 10%. What additional discount must be given to bring the net selling price to Rs. 2000?
A. $11\frac{1}{9}\%$ **B.** $12\frac{8}{21}\%$ **C.** $13\frac{8}{9}\%$ **D.** $\frac{11}{3}\%$
E. $\frac{12}{3}\%$

Q.46 A and B invest in a business in a ratio 3 : 2. If 30% of total profit goes to charity and A investment 18 months and B investment 15 months. If A profit is Rs. 1800 then find the profit of B.
A. Rs. 1000   **B.** Rs. 1200
C. Rs. 1400   **D.** Rs. 1800

E. None of these

Q.47 Direction: In the given questions, two equations numbered I and II are given. You have to solve both the equations and mark the appropriate answer.
I: $x^2 + 3x - 54 = 0$
II: $y^2 - 21y + 54 = 0$
A. x > y
B. x < y
C. x ≥ y
D. x ≤ y
E. No relation in x and y or x = y

Q.48 What will come in the place of the question mark '?' in the following question?
13 × 25% of 200 - 12 × 66.66% of 50 = ?
A. 200   **B.** 250   **C.** 230   **D.** 290
E. 260

Q.49 Two trains A and B are coming from the same direction, with speeds of 90 km/h and 72 km/h. The length of A and B is 200 m and 160 m respectively. In how much time they can cross each other completely?
A. 80 sec   **B.** 72 sec
C. 60 sec   **D.** 50 sec
E. None of these

Q.50 A vendor marked a product, 20% above the cost price and sold the product for Rs. 7776 by giving two successive discounts of 10% each. Find the cost price of the product and the loss percentage of the vendor.
A. 8000, 2.8%   **B.** 4000, 2.8%
C. 8200, 1.6%   **D.** 8400,1.6%
E. None of the above

Q.51 A mixture of 60 liters of wine and water contains 20% of water. How much water should be added to the mixture so that the water will be 36% in the final mixture?
A. 10 liters   **B.** 15 liters
C. 12 liters   **D.** 20 liters
E. None of these

Ques (52-56):Directions: Study the chart and answer the following questions.

The line graph show number of Jio and Airtel users in 5 different states.

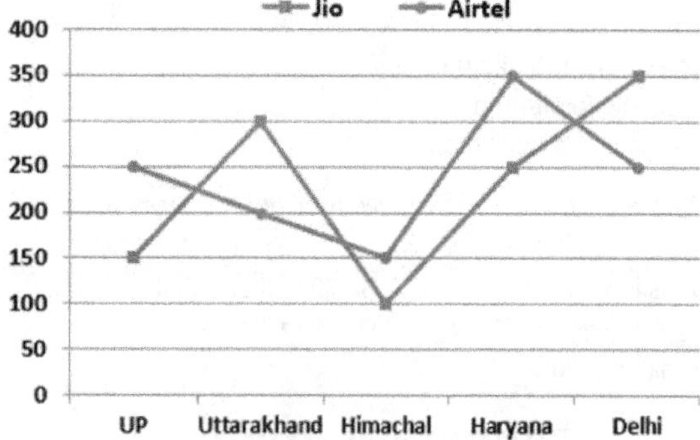

Q.52 Jio users in Uttarakhand are how much percentage more than Airtel users in Himachal?

A. 50%
B. 150%
C. 100%
D. 1%
E. None of these

Q.53 What is the difference of Jio users in Haryana and Airtel users in Delhi?

A. 250
B. 1
C. 0
D. 100
E. 50

Q.54 What is the ratio of Jio users in Delhi to Airtel users in UP?

A. 8 : 5
B. 5 : 8
C. 7 : 5
D. 5 : 7
E. None of these

Q.55 What is the average of Jio users in Delhi, Uttarakhand and Haryana?

A. 900
B. 300
C. 600
D. 200
E. None of these

Q.56 How many total Airtel users are there in all five states together?

A. 1250
B. 1200
C. 1150
D. 1000
E. None of these

Ques (57-61):Direction: Given table shows the data of patients in 4 different hospitals.

Hospital	Total Patients	Active Patients (still in Hospital)	Recovered Patients (discharged)
A	200	150	35
B	150	120	20
C	200	160	30
D	180	130	45

NOTE: Total Patients = Active Patients + Recovered Patients + Patients Died

Q.57 What percent of total patients till date is still in the active stage in hospitals A and C?

A. 82%
B. 77.5%
C. 62.5%
D. 65%
E. 72%

Q.58 What is the difference between the number of deaths in hospital A and of in hospital D?

A. 0
B. 20
C. 5
D. 15
E. 10

Q.59 What is the ratio of the number of recovered patients in hospitals A, B and C to the number of deaths in hospitals B and C?

A. 17 : 4
B. 4 : 17
C. 3 : 1
D. 4 : 1
E. 4 : 7

Q.60 By what percent number of patients recovered in hospitals A and D is more/less than the total number of patients in hospital C till date?

A. 60%
B. 20%
C. 80%
D. 40%
E. 0%

Q.61 What is the average number of death in all hospitals?

A. 12
B. 10
C. 8
D. 14
E. 6

Q.62 What will come in the place of the question mark '?' in the following question?

$$\sqrt[3]{1728} \times \sqrt[3]{4096} \div \sqrt[3]{512} = ?$$

A. 24
B. 36
C. 30
D. 12
E. 16

Q.63 What would be simple interest on the principal amount of Rs. 15,000 with 25% p.a. interest rate annually for 5 years?

A. Rs. 18,750
B. Rs. 9,000
C. Rs. 15,000
D. Rs. 5,000
E. Rs. 1,00,000

Q.64 The ratio of Ram's Salary for May 2020 to his salary for June 2020 was 4 : 3 and the ratio of the salary of June 2020 to October 2020 were 6 : 9. Ram got Rs. 8,000 more salary in October from May 2020, and receives 10% of the salary as Diwali Bonus in October, Find the amount of bonus.

A. Rs.7,000
B. Rs.7,200
C. Rs.7,400
D. Rs.7,240
E. None of these

Q.65 What will come in place of question mark (?) in the following question?

28% of 640 + 34% of 720 = ? × 54

A. 6.82
B. 8.55
C. 4.90
D. 7.85
E. None of these

Reasoning Ability

Ques (66-70):Directions: Read the following and answer the given questions:

Eight family members P, Q, R, S, T, M, N, and K are sitting around a circular table facing inward with equal distance between them but not necessarily in the same order.

R sits opposite of T who sits at the immediate left of M. Two persons are sitting between S and M. Q sits second to the left of N. K and Q are sitting opposite each other.

Q.66 What is the position of T with respect to S?

A. Second to the right
B. Second to the left
C. Opposite
D. Immediately left
E. Immediately right

Q.67 Who is sitting between Q and N when counted from the right of Q?

A. S
B. P
C. K
D. T
E. R

Q.68 Who is sitting at the immediate right of Q?

A. R
B. T
C. P
D. Q
E. N

Q.69 Who is sitting opposite to P?

A. M   **B.** Q   **C.** S   **D.** R
E. N

Q.70 Who was sitting second to the right of N?

A. Q   **B.** K   **C.** S   **D.** P
E. T

Ques (71-74):Directions: Study the following arrangement carefully and answer the questions.

R % Y 9 O @ 8 & V M 1 # L 7 E $ 9 X A £ C 5 N © F 3 I K Ø U 4

Q.71 How many such numbers are there that are immediately followed by a vowel or immediately preceded by a consonant but not both?

A. Three   **B.** One   **C.** Five   **D.** Two
E. Four

Q.72 Which of the following is the fifth to the right of the sixth element from the right end of the above arrangement?

A. 4   **B.** U   **C.** K   **D.** 3
E. I

Q.73 How many such letters are there which are immediately preceded by a symbol and immediately followed by a consonant?

A. Three   **B.** Two   **C.** One   **D.** Four
E. Five

Q.74 What is the sum of all the numbers that are either preceded by or followed by a symbol?

A. 25   **B.** 17   **C.** 22   **D.** 18
E. 21

Ques (75-78):Directions: In the question below are given four statements followed by two conclusions numbered I and II. You have to take the given statements to be true even if they seem to be at variance with commonly known facts. Read all the conclusions and then decide which of the given conclusions logically follows from the given statements disregarding commonly known facts.

Q.75 Statements:

Some C are D.

No C is a E.

All E are F.

Conclusions:

I. No F is a C.

II. At least some D are F.

A. Neither I nor II follows

B. Only I follows

C. Only II follows

D. Either I or II follows

E. Both I and II follow

Q.76 Statement:

No Bad are Good.

All Good are Nice.

Only a few Nice are Sagar.

Conclusions:

I. All Sagar can be Good.

II. Some Nice are not Bad.

A. Only conclusion I follow

B. Only conclusion II follows

C. Either conclusion I or conclusion II follows

D. Neither conclusion I nor conclusion II follows

E. Both conclusion I and conclusion II follows

Q.77 Statement:

No horse is a cat.

Only horse are tiger.

Conclusions:

I. No tiger is cat.

II. Some tiger is cat.

A. Only I follows

B. Only II follows

C. Either I or II follows

D. Neither I nor II follows

E. Both I and II follow

Q.78 Statement:

All belts are leather.

Only a few leather is a bag.

Conclusions:

I. All bags being leather is a possibility.

II. No bag is a belt.

A. Only I follows

B. Only II follows

C. Either I or II follows

D. Neither I nor II follows

E. Both I and II follow

Ques (79-83):Directions: Study the following information carefully and answer the question given below.

Eight persons Geet, Harman, Jyoti, Manisha, Neha, Nikita, Tanisha and Zakir are sitting in two rows at equal distances. Persons sitting in row 1 are facing North and those sitting in row 2 are facing South but not necessarily in the same order. A person sitting in row 1 is facing a person sitting in row 2.

Zakir is sitting at the extreme left of row 1. Tanisha sits second to the right of Zakir. Manisha is sitting opposite Tanisha. One person sits between Jyoti and Neha. Jyoti does not sit at any of the extreme ends. Geet sits to the immediate right of Harman.

Q.79 Which of the following statements are true?

I. Geet sits second to the right of Tanisha.

II. Zakir sits opposite Nikita.

III. Jyoti sits opposite the person sitting immediately right to Manisha.

A. Only statement I is true

B. Only statement II is true

C. Only statement III is true

D. None is true

E. All are true

Q.80 If the persons sitting at the extreme ends in row 1 exchange their position, who sits to the immediate right of Tanisha?

A. Zakir **B.** Geet **C.** Manisha **D.** Neha
E. Jyoti

Q.81 Four of the following are similar in a way and thus form a group. Which of the following does not belong to the group?

A. Nikita **B.** Zakir **C.** Geet **D.** Jyoti
E. Neha

Q.82 Who sits second to the left of the person sitting opposite Nikita?

A. Zakir **B.** Geet **C.** Neha **D.** Jyoti
E. Tanisha

Q.83 Who sits opposite Jyoti?

A. Nikita **B.** Harman **C.** Zakir **D.** Geet
E. Manisha

Ques (84-86):Directions: These questions are based on the following information.

In a family picnic, there are seven members A, B, M, P, R, S and T. B is the son of A. P is the husband of A. B has two children S and T. T is the son of R. M is the sister of B. R has only one girl child.

Q.84 How is the T related to P?

A. Son **B.** Daughter
C. Granddaughter **D.** Grandson
E. None of these

Q.85 How many females in the family?

A. Four **B.** Five
C. Three **D.** Two
E. None of these

Q.86 How is M related to R?

A. Sister
B. Mother
C. Sister-in-law
D. Aunt
E. Cannot be determined

Ques (87-91):Directions: Read the following information carefully and answer the questions that follow:

There are eight boxes - Box 1, Box 2, Box 3, Box 4, Box 5, Box 6, Box 7and Box 8 are kept one above the other from bottom to top in which different types of chocolates - Kit-kat, Munch, Tooty - Frooty, Pulse, Dairymilk, Perk, Barone and Milkybar are kept in it. There are five boxes between Munch and Milkybar. The box of Perk is kept just above Milkybar. The number of boxes between Tooty - Frooty and Kit-kat is one less than the number of boxes is kept between Dairymilk and Barone. The box of Munch is above the box of Milkybar. The box of Dairymilk is kept between Kit-kat and Perk. Pulse is kept at Box 6.

Q.87 Which chocolate box is placed below Pulse?

A. Kit-kat **B.** Dairymilk

C. Tooty -Frooty **D.** Barone
E. Milkybar

Q.88 Munch is related to Kit-kat and Dairymilk is related to Barone. In the same way, Pulse is related to?

A. Munch **B.** Tooty - Frooty
C. None of these **D.** Milkybar
E. Perk

Q.89 Tooty-Frooty is kept at which box number?

A. Box 3 **B.** Box 4 **C.** Box 8 **D.** Box 7
E. Box 5

Q.90 How many boxes are there between Tooty - Frooty and Barone?

A. Four **B.** Five **C.** Three **D.** Two
E. None

Q.91 Which chocolate is kept at Box 8?

A. Dairymilk **B.** Pulse
C. Munch **D.** Kit-kat
E. None of these

Ques (92-96):Directions: Read the following information carefully and answer the questions that follow:

There are eight events - P, Q, R, S, T, U, V and W to be held in a hotel on different dates (3rd or 16th) of four different months (January, February, March and April) of the same year (not necessarily in the same order). Event Q is on an even-numbered date of the month having 31 days. There are three events between event Q and event T. Event S is just before the event U but in different months. Event R is scheduled before event P but not in the month having 31 days. There are more than one events between event T and event R. Event P and event W are scheduled to be held on the same date of different months.

Q.92 Which of the following events are scheduled in February?

A. W, S **B.** Q, W
C. R, S **D.** P, T
E. None of these

Q.93 Which event is scheduled just before event P?

A. R **B.** T **C.** V **D.** W
E. U

Q.94 Which event is scheduled on 3rd January?

A. P **B.** R **C.** T **D.** Q
E. W

Q.95 How many events are scheduled between event T and event R?

A. Four **B.** Five
C. Two **D.** Three
E. None of these

Q.96 When is event V scheduled?

A. 3rd January
B. 3rd March
C. 16th March
D. 16thApril

E.   Cannot be determined

Ques (97-100):Directions: In the following question assuming the given statement to be true, find which of the conclusion(s) among given conclusions is/are definitely true and then give your answers accordingly.

Q.97 Statement: $B < S \leq Q < Y = X > C \geq J$

Conclusion:

I. $S < Y$

II. $X > B$

A.   Only I is true

B.   Either I or II is true

C.   Only II is true

D.   Both I and II are true

E.   None of these

Q.98 Statements: $A < C = D \leq E; B = A > F$

Conclusions:

I. $D > F$

II. $B > E$

A.   Only II is true

B.   Only I is true

C.   Both are true

D.   Neither I nor II is true

E.   Either I or II is true

Q.99 Statement: $D = X \geq C > S = F; D > Y \geq H \geq G$

Conclusion:

I. $G \leq X$

II. $D > F$

A.   Only conclusion I follows

B.   Both conclusion I or II follows

C.   Only conclusion II follows

D.   Either I or II follows

E.   Neither conclusions I nor II follows

Q.100 Statements: $G \geq M = P > C; \ Q < R = B < C$

Conclusions:

I. $M > R$

II. $G \geq B$

A.   Only I follows

B.   Only II follows

C.   Both follows

D.   Either I or II follows

E.   None follows

// Smart Answer Sheet //

Correct — Percentage of students who answered correctly. **Skipped** — Percentage of students who skipped.

Q.	Ans.	Correct / Skipped	Q.	Ans.	Correct / Skipped	Q.	Ans.	Correct / Skipped	Q.	Ans.	Correct / Skipped	Q.	Ans.	Correct / Skipped
1	C	21.74 % / 34.47 %	17	D	5.28 % / 92.24 %	33	E	1.55 % / 92.55 %	49	B	0.62 % / 93.79 %	65	D	1.24 % / 98.14 %
2	B	41.61 % / 37.27 %	18	C	4.66 % / 92.23 %	34	A	4.97 % / 92.86 %	50	A	0.31 % / 93.79 %	66	A	4.66 % / 94.1 %
3	A	38.82 % / 39.75 %	19	E	2.17 % / 92.55 %	35	B	4.04 % / 92.85 %	51	B	0.62 % / 94.1 %	67	E	3.73 % / 94.1 %
4	E	27.33 % / 41.61 %	20	A	1.55 % / 96.59 %	36	D	4.97 % / 92.55 %	52	C	2.8 % / 94.72 %	68	A	4.66 % / 94.41 %
5	D	23.6 % / 44.1 %	21	B	3.11 % / 96.58 %	37	E	1.55 % / 92.55 %	53	C	4.04 % / 95.03 %	69	C	5.28 % / 94.41 %
6	C	4.97 % / 91.92 %	22	B	2.48 % / 96.59 %	38	B	5.28 % / 92.55 %	54	C	3.73 % / 95.34 %	70	B	4.66 % / 94.41 %
7	A	0.31 % / 92.24 %	23	E	2.17 % / 96.59 %	39	B	4.35 % / 92.54 %	55	B	3.73 % / 95.65 %	71	D	1.86 % / 94.41 %
8	B	4.97 % / 92.23 %	24	A	2.17 % / 96.59 %	40	B	2.48 % / 92.55 %	56	B	3.73 % / 95.65 %	72	A	4.66 % / 94.41 %
9	A	6.21 % / 92.24 %	25	C	3.11 % / 96.58 %	41	B	2.17 % / 92.55 %	57	B	1.24 % / 97.21 %	73	C	4.97 % / 94.41 %
10	A	4.97 % / 92.23 %	26	A	0.62 % / 96.58 %	42	B	0.31 % / 92.86 %	58	E	1.55 % / 97.83 %	74	D	4.97 % / 94.41 %
11	A	6.52 % / 92.24 %	27	B	0.31 % / 96.58 %	43	E	0.93 % / 92.86 %	59	A	1.86 % / 97.83 %	75	A	3.73 % / 94.41 %
12	C	3.73 % / 92.23 %	28	A	0.62 % / 96.58 %	44	A	0.62 % / 93.17 %	60	A	0.93 % / 98.14 %	76	E	3.42 % / 94.1 %
13	B	7.45 % / 92.24 %	29	C	3.11 % / 96.89 %	45	A	1.24 % / 93.17 %	61	B	1.24 % / 98.14 %	77	A	3.11 % / 94.09 %
14	E	3.73 % / 92.23 %	30	A	3.11 % / 96.58 %	46	A	0.93 % / 93.17 %	62	A	1.55 % / 98.14 %	78	A	2.8 % / 94.09 %
15	A	3.73 % / 92.23 %	31	D	11.18 % / 74.84 %	47	E	4.35 % / 93.17 %	63	A	1.24 % / 98.14 %	79	C	3.73 % / 94.1 %
16	C	3.42 % / 92.23 %	32	D	2.17 % / 92.55 %	48	B	4.35 % / 93.48 %	64	B	0.31 % / 98.14 %	80	A	3.73 % / 94.1 %

Q.	Ans.	Correct		Q.	Ans.	Correct		Q.	Ans.	Correct		Q.	Ans.	Correct		Q.	Ans.	Correct
		Skipped				Skipped				Skipped				Skipped				Skipped
81	D	3.11 %		85	A	4.66 %		89	D	2.17 %		93	B	1.86 %		97	D	4.66 %
		94.09 %				94.1 %				94.41 %				95.03 %				94.41 %
82	D	3.73 %		86	C	4.35 %		90	B	1.86 %		94	E	1.86 %		98	B	4.66 %
		94.1 %				94.1 %				94.41 %				95.34 %				94.72 %
83	B	3.42 %		87	A	2.17 %		91	C	2.17 %		95	C	1.86 %		99	C	3.42 %
		94.1 %				94.1 %				94.41 %				95.66 %				94.72 %
84	D	4.35 %		88	E	2.17 %		92	C	2.17 %		96	D	1.86 %		100	A	3.42 %
		94.1 %				94.1 %				94.41 %				94.41 %				94.72 %

//Hints and Solutions//

1. The sentence is talking about how making money on the net can be reduced to a couple of factors. In other words, it is talking about how the sentence can be 'broken' down into two factors.

Hence, the correct option is (C).

2. The sentence is talking about how the opportunities or avenues for business become unlimited. In other words, it is talking about how the 'possibilities' become boundless.

Hence, the correct option is (B).

3. The word that fits in the blank should be a synonym of 'standard'. From the options, the only word that is suitable in the blank is 'quality'.

Hence, the correct option is (A).

4. The only word from the options that make sense in this blank is 'marketing'. The sentence is conveying the idea that marketing through the Internet required more research.

Hence, the correct option is (E).

5. The word that comes in the blank should be a synonym of 'capability'. The only words from the options, which can fit in the blank are 'ability' and 'skill'. However, between the two, the word 'ability' is a better fit.

Hence, the correct option is (D).

6. The sentence is in the past tense, so we need to check whether a subject is singular or plural. We take a singular verb if the subject is singular else we opt for a plural verb. In the second part of the sentence, it is clearly mentioned that there were not one or two but many colourful frames, here the error is in sentence (C). Instead of was we should add were.

The correct answer is: "When I went to the market, I saw a number of colourful frames were displayed in the store window".

Hence, the correct option is (C).

7. The error lies in part (A)

- The sentence uses the adjective form 'bold', which is incorrect here.
- As the word refers to the verb 'went out' and not to a noun, it should be in its adverb form, viz, 'boldly'.

Hence, the correct option is (A).

8. Here, in the given sentence the main subject is 'he' and the subject is carrying out his plan, despite his 'friends' reservation.

Let us explore the given option.

The conjunction 'unless' means except if and is used to introduce the case in which a statement being made is not true or valid.

- Example: Unless you want to die step away from the vehicle.
- Meaning to stay that if <u>you</u> do not step away from the <u>vehicle</u> you will die.

This is not the case with the given sentence. Option (A) is incorrect.

The conjunction 'although' is used for in spite of the fact that; even though.

- Example: He ran although his legs had not recovered.
- This means that despite the subject '<u>he</u>' legs not being okay, he still ran.

In the given sentence we are stating that the subject carried out his plan despite the fact that his friends were against it.

So option (B) is correct.

The conjunction 'whether' is used for expressing a doubt or choice between alternatives.

- Example: Whether he is alive or dead it is unclear.
- The current state of the subject is not known.

As this is not the case in the given sentence, option (C) is incorrect.

The conjunction 'so' means and for this reason; therefore.

- Example: He slept late so that he could finish the movie.
- Here the explanation or reason for sleeping late has been explained by using 'so.'

So option (D) is incorrect as a reason is not being specified in the given question.

The conjunction 'if' is used for introducing a conditional clause on the condition or supposition that; in the event that.

- Example: If you want to say something do it now.
- Here we want the subject 'you' to express his disapproval now.

As this is not the case in the given sentence, option 5 is incorrect.

Correct sentence: He went through with his plan although all his friends advised him to abandon it.

Hence, the correct option is (B).

9. The sentence presents a situation and the reason for the situation.

The subordinating conjunction 'because' is used to give reasons.

Thus, 'because' is the correct answer.

Correct sentence: She advised him to visit Boston because she thought it was the most beautiful city in the world.

Hence, the correct option is (A).

10. The sense of the sentence on a whole is such that it is speaking about an event that has occurred in the past 'years ago.'

Option (A) 'looked' is the correct answer because the given statement is in the past tense and the entire statement must be in the same tense.

Option (B) is incorrect because 'look' is in the simple present tense.

Option (C) is incorrect because 'looks' is in the present perfect tense.

Option (D) is incorrect because the given sentence is in the active voice and 'was looked' cannot be used in the active voice sentence.

Option (E) is incorrect because the 'looking' is in the present continuous.

Correct sentence: The CBI officer came looked into all the evidence. The case was closed years ago. The jury was hung and could not reach a verdict.

Hence, the correct option is (A).

11. Let us discuss the correct answer:

- Here we have to choose a determiner that is suitable for giving a sense of a plural countable, a large number of. So 'many' is the correct option.
- Many - a large number of.
- From the given meaning we can conclude that the correct answer is many.

Thus the correct sentence is: "Many Indians who have migrated to other countries will forget our culture due to overwork."

Hence, the correct option is (A).

12. Let us discuss the correct answer:

This sentence is a type-3 conditional sentence the subordinate clause (connecting with the condition word 'If') must be in the past perfect tense.

Past perfect tense - Subject + had + v^3 + object

- Example: He had worked hard to get this position.

From the given meaning we can conclude that the correct answer is had played.

Thus the correct sentence is: "If I had played this match, I would have been the man of the match."

Hence, the correct option is (C).

13. On looking at the above-given passage, we observe that it is based on Galileo who discovered that earth and other planets revolve around the sun. Since the starter of the passage needs a character, thus it starts with B. Now, a belief has been shown in the starter that earth was the center of the Universe. So, support to this belief should be inserted in the next sentence. Thus, the second sentence is E. Since, an opposition was shown by Galileo, thus, the third sentence is A. Now, in order to support his argument, the next sentence that is the fourth one is C. And, the last one is D. Thus, the correct sequence is BEACD.

Hence, the correct option is (B).

14. On looking at the above-given passage, we observe that it is based on Galileo who discovered that earth and other planets revolve around the sun. Since the starter of the passage needs a character, thus it starts with B. Now, a belief has been shown in the starter that earth was the center of the Universe. So, support to this belief should be inserted in the next sentence. Thus, the second sentence is E. Since, an opposition was shown by Galileo,

thus, the third sentence is A. Now, in order to support his argument, the next sentence that is the fourth one is C. And, the last one is D. Thus, the correct sequence is BEACD.

Hence, the correct option is (E).

15. On looking at the above-given passage, we observe that it is based on Galileo who discovered that earth and other planets revolve around the sun. Since the starter of the passage needs a character, thus it starts with B. Now, a belief has been shown in the starter that earth was the center of the Universe. So, support to this belief should be inserted in the next sentence. Thus, the second sentence is E. Since, an opposition was shown by Galileo, thus, the third sentence is A. Now, in order to support his argument, the next sentence that is the fourth one is C. And, the last one is D. Thus, the correct sequence is BEACD.

Hence, the correct option is (A).

16. On looking at the above-given passage, we observe that it is based on Galileo who discovered that earth and other planets revolve around the sun. Since the starter of the passage needs a character, thus it starts with B. Now, a belief has been shown in the starter that earth was the center of the Universe. So, support to this belief should be inserted in the next sentence. Thus, the second sentence is E. Since, an opposition was shown by Galileo, thus, the third sentence is A. Now, in order to support his argument, the next sentence that is the fourth one is C. And, the last one is D. Thus, the correct sequence is BEACD.

Hence, the correct option is (C).

17. On looking at the above-given passage, we observe that it is based on Galileo who discovered that earth and other planets revolve around the sun. Since the starter of the passage needs a character, thus it starts with B. Now, a belief has been shown in the starter that earth was the center of the Universe. So, support to this belief should be inserted in the next sentence. Thus, the second sentence is E. Since, an opposition was shown by Galileo, thus, the third sentence is A. Now, in order to support his argument, the next sentence that is the fourth one is C. And, the last one is D. Thus, the correct sequence is BEACD.

Hence, the correct option is (D).

18. Let's look at the meanings of the given words:

- Choke means have severe difficulty in breathing because of a constricted or obstructed throat or a lack of air.
- Overcome means succeed in dealing with (a problem or difficulty).
- Obstruct means block (an opening, path, road, etc.); be or get in the way of.
- Deprive means prevent (a person or place) from having or using something.
- Overpower means defeat or overcome with superior strength.

Peanuts can get stuck in the throats of children if they are not careful. The only word that can make the sentence contextually and grammatically correct is 'choke'.

The sentence is: Children sometimes choke on peanuts.

Hence, the correct option is (C).

19. Let's look at the meanings of the given options:

- Retreat means withdraw to a quiet or secluded place.
- Rewind means wind or be wound back to the beginning.
- Recoil means suddenly spring or flinch back in fear, horror, or disgust.
- Overcome means succeed in dealing with (a problem or difficulty).
- Scrambled means make one's way quickly or awkwardly up a steep gradient or over rough ground by using one's hands as well as one's feet.

The only word that can make the sentence contextually and grammatically correct is 'retreats' as the sentence is about what the person does when he gets sad.

The sentence is: When he is sad, he retreats to his bedroom.

Hence, the correct option is (E).

20. The sentences 'Mothers is trying to calm their kids.', 'He do not want to work with me.' and 'She eat cookies.' are incorrect.

Subjects and verbs must AGREE with one another in number (singular or plural).

If a subject is singular, its verb must also be singular.

If a subject is plural, its verb must also be plural.

Example:

- Mothers are trying to calm their kids.
- He does not want to work with me.
- She eats cookies.

Therefore, the correct answer is 'They care for their children'.

Hence, the correct option is (A).

21. The given passage is about Adult Illiteracy.

- Let us refer to the line from the passage, "With the nation hovering around the 1 billion marks and around 48 percent of its population still illiterate, there is hardly a ray of hope for India".
- From the given passage we get to know India's population is around 1 billion and out of this 48 percent of the population is illiterate. This is a very large portion of the population.
- It is very hard to change this situation in a short period of time. So, it is said that there is hardly any ray of hope for India

So, '48 percent of the population is illiterate' is the correct option.

Hence, the correct option is (B).

22. The given passage is about Adult Illiteracy.

- Let us refer to the line from the passage, "The prevalence of illiteracy among the

masses has made them vulnerable to exploitation, as they are unaware of their rights and privileges".
- Here, 'prevalence' means the fact or condition of being prevalent; commonness.
- From the given passage we get to know as the masses are illiterate, they lack knowledge on their rights and privileges. Due to these, they tend to become a target of exploitation.

So, 'They are unaware of their rights and privileges' is the correct option.

Hence, the correct option is (B).

23. The given passage is about Adult Illiteracy.

- The given word controlled means the power to influence or direct people's behaviour or the course of events.
- In option 5, administer means to manage or supervise the execution, use, or conduct.

So, 'administer' is the correct synonym for the word.

Let us see the meanings of the other words:

- loose - set free; release.
- wild - living or growing in the natural environment; not domesticated or cultivated.
- rampant - flourishing or spreading unchecked.
- irrepressible - not able to be controlled or restrained.

Hence, the correct option is (E).

24. The given passage is about Adult Illiteracy.

- The underlined word underprivileged means deprived through the social or economic condition of some of the fundamental rights of all members of a civilized society.
- In option (A), Deprived means suffering a severe and damaging lack of basic material and cultural benefits.

So, 'Deprived' is the correct word.

Let us see the meanings of the other words:

- Privileged - having special rights, advantages, or immunities.
- Wealthy - having a great deal of money, resources, or assets; rich.
- prosperous - successful in material terms; flourishing financially.

Hence, the correct option is (A).

25. The given passage is about Adult Illiteracy.

- Let us refer to the line from the passage, "The Directive Principle of State Policy to provide for primary education to all children has failed in its objectives. At present, almost half of India's population is still illiterate".
- From the given passage we get to know that half of India's population is still illiterate. This situation shows

that the Directive Principle of State Policy has failed to achieve its objective of providing primary education to all children.

So, 'The Directive Principle of State Policy' is the correct option.

Hence, the correct option is (C).

26. The given passage is about Adult Illiteracy.

- The given word prevalence means the fact or condition of being prevalent; commonness.
- In option (A), disappearance means an act or the fact of someone or something going missing.

So, 'disappearance' is the correct antonym for the word.

Let us see the meanings of the other words:

- Ubiquity - the fact of appearing everywhere or of being very common.
- Universality - the quality of involving or being shared by all people or things in the world or in a particular group.
- Regularity - the state or quality of being regular.
- Frequency - the rate at which something occurs over a particular period of time or in a given sample.

Hence, the correct option is (A).

27. The given passage is about Adult Illiteracy.

- The given word envied(past tense of envy) means the desire to have a quality, possession, or other desirable thing belonging to (someone else).
- In option (B), despise means a feel contempt or a deep repugnance for.

So, 'despise' is the correct antonym for the word.

Let us see the meanings of the other words:

- Wealthy - having a great deal of money, resources, or assets; rich.
- Irrepressible - not able to be controlled or restrained.
- Regularity - the state or quality of being regular.
- Begrudge - envy (someone) the possession or enjoyment of (something) and give reluctantly or resentfully.

Hence, the correct option is (B).

28. The given passage is about Adult Illiteracy.

- The given phrase 'inter alia' means among other things.
- Here, in the passage, we can see 'to provide education is one of all objectives of the Directive Principles of State Policy
  - For example, The teacher wore many hats including counselor and nurse, inter alia.

So, 'among other things' is the correct option.

'inter alia' is Latin for "among other things." This phrase is often found in legal pleadings and writings to specify one example out of many possibilities.

Hence, the correct option is (A).

29. The given passage is about Adult Illiteracy.

- Let us refer to the line from the passage, "The Government launched the National Literacy Mission (NLM) with the objective of achieving total adult literacy in 1988. The objective was to achieve total adult literacy among 80 million adults in the age group of 15-35 by the year 1995".
- From the given passage we get to know the National Literacy Mission was launched in 1988 by the Government with an objective to achieve total adult literacy in age groups of 15-30 by1995

So, 'To achieve total literacy.' is the correct option.

Hence, the correct option is (C).

30. The given passage is about Adult Illiteracy.

- Let us refer to the line from the passage, "The objective was to achieve total adult literacy among 80 million adults in the age group of 15-35 by the year 1995".
- From the given passage we get to know as the masses are illiterate, they lack knowledge on their rights and privileges. Due to these, The Government launched the National Literacy Mission (NLM) with the objective of achieving total adult literacy in 1988. The objective was to achieve total adult literacy among 80 million adults in the age group of 15-35 by the year 1995.

So, '80 million adults' is the correct option.

Hence, the correct option is (A).

31. Let the ages Mohit and Rohit 7 years ago be 12x and 13x respectively.

14 years from now, the ratio of their ages will be 12x+21 and 13x+21

We know that,

$$\frac{12x+21}{13x+21} = \frac{19}{20}$$

$\Rightarrow$ 240x + 420 = 247x + 399

$\Rightarrow$ 7x = 21 $\Rightarrow$ x = 3

So the present ages of Mohit and Rohit are 12×3+7 = 43, 13×3+7 = 46,

So, the sum of their ages is 43+46 = 89

Hence, the correct option is (D).

32. I: $x = \sqrt{1444}$

$\Rightarrow x = \sqrt{(38 \times 38)}$

$\Rightarrow$ x = 38

II: $y^2 = 1444$

$\Rightarrow y = \pm\sqrt{1444}$

$\Rightarrow y = \pm\sqrt{(38 \times 38)}$

$\Rightarrow y = 38, (-38)$

Comparing the values of x and y,

Value of x	Relation	Value of y
38	=	38
38	>	- 38

From the table, we can conclude that the value of variable x is greater than or equal to y.

$\therefore$ We can say, $x \geq y$.

Hence, the correct option is (D).

33. I: $x^2 + 4x - 221 = 0$

$\Rightarrow x^2 + 17x - 13x - 221 = 0$

$\Rightarrow x (x + 17) - 13(x + 17) = 0$

$\Rightarrow (x + 17) \times (x - 13) = 0$

$\Rightarrow x = 13, (-17)$

II: $y^2 + 52y + 667 = 0$

$\Rightarrow y^2 + 23y + 29y + 667 = 0$

$\Rightarrow y \times (y + 23) + 29 \times (y + 23) = 0$

$\Rightarrow (y + 23) \times (y + 29) = 0$

$\Rightarrow y = (-23), (-29)$

Comparing the values of x and y,

Value of x	Relation	Value of y
13	>	-23
13	>	-29
-17	>	-23
-17	>	-29

From the table, we can conclude that the values of variable x are always greater than y.

$\therefore$ We can say, $y < x$.

Hence, the correct option is (E).

34. I: $3x^2 - 12x + 9 = 0$

$\Rightarrow 3x^2 - 9x - 3x + 9 = 0$

$\Rightarrow 3x(x - 3) - 3(x - 3) = 0$

$\Rightarrow (x - 3) \times (3x - 3) = 0$

$\Rightarrow x = 3, 1$

II: $4y^2 + 80y + 256 = 0$

$\Rightarrow 4y^2 + 16y + 64y + 256 = 0$

$\Rightarrow 4y \times (y + 4) + 64 \times (y + 4) = 0$

$\Rightarrow (y + 4) \times (4y + 64) = 0$

$\Rightarrow y = (-4), (-16)$

Comparing values of x and y,

Value of x	Relation	Value of y
3	>	-4
3	>	-16
1	>	-4
1	>	-16

From the table, we can conclude that the value of variable x is always greater than y.

$\therefore$ We can say, $x > y$.

Hence, the correct option is (A).

35. From I,

$x^2 = 49$

$\Rightarrow x = -7, 7$

From II,

$y^2 - 16y + 63 = 0$

$\Rightarrow y^2 - 9y - 7y + 63 = 0$

$\Rightarrow y(y - 9) - 7(y - 9) = 0$

$\Rightarrow (y - 9)(y - 7) = 0$

Taking,

$\Rightarrow y - 9 = 0$ or $y - 7 = 0$

$\Rightarrow y = 9$ or $y = 7$

Comparison between x and y (via Tabulation):

x	y	Relation
-7	9	x < y
-7	7	x < y
7	9	x < y
7	7	x = y

$\therefore x \leq y$

Hence, the correct option is (B).

36.

$$\sqrt{\left[4 \times \sqrt{\left\{4 \times \sqrt{(2 \times 6^2 \div 3^2 \times 2)} \times 64\right\}} \times 2\right]} = ?$$

$$\Rightarrow \sqrt{\left[4 \times \sqrt{\left\{4 \times \sqrt{(2 \times 36 \div 9 \times 2)} \times 64\right\}} \times 2\right]} = ?$$

$$\Rightarrow \sqrt{\left[4 \times \sqrt{\left\{4 \times \sqrt{16} \times 64\right\}} \times 2\right]} = ?$$

$$\Rightarrow \sqrt{\left[4 \times \sqrt{\left\{4 \times 4 \times 64\right\}} \times 2\right]} = ?$$

$$\Rightarrow \sqrt{\left[4 \times \sqrt{1024} \times 2\right]} = ?$$

$$\Rightarrow \sqrt{\left[4 \times 32 \times 2\right]} = ?$$

$$\Rightarrow \sqrt{256} = ?$$

$\Rightarrow 16 = ?$

$\therefore$ The value of '?' is 16.

Hence, the correct option is (D).

37. $(32 \text{ of } 2 - 64^{0.5} \times 256^{0.25}) \div 24 = ?$

$\Rightarrow (32 \times 2 - 8 \times 4) \div 24 = ?$

$\Rightarrow (64 - 32) \div 24 = ?$

$\Rightarrow 32 \div 16 = ?$

$\Rightarrow 2 = ?$

$\therefore$ The value of '?' is 2.

Hence, the correct option is (E).

38. The given expression is:

$\Rightarrow 1.2 \times 60 + ?^2 = 5 \times 36 + 13$

$\Rightarrow 72 + ?^2 = 180 + 13$

$\Rightarrow ?^2 = 193 - 72$

$\Rightarrow ?^2 = 121$

$\Rightarrow ? = \sqrt[2]{121}$

$\Rightarrow ? = 11$

Hence, the correct option is (B).

39. Given:

$$\sqrt[2]{25 \times 20 + 5 \times 25} \times \sqrt[2]{25[5(7 - 2)]} = 5^?$$

$$\Rightarrow \sqrt[2]{500 + 125} \times \sqrt[2]{25[5(5)]} = 5^?$$

$$\Rightarrow \sqrt[2]{625} \times \sqrt[2]{625} = 5^?$$

$\Rightarrow 25 \times 25 = 5^?$

$\Rightarrow 5^4 = 5^?$

$\therefore$ The value of '?' is 4.

Hence, the correct option is (B).

40. Given:

The ratio of the present age of Ram and Rohit is 7 : 8.

The ratio of age of Ram and Rohit after 6 years is 9 : 10.

Let the present age of Ram and Rohit is 7x and 8x respectively.

After 6 years, the age of Ram = 7x + 6

After 6 years, the age of Rohit = 8x + 6

The ratio of age of Ram and Rohit after 6 years is 9 : 10.

$$\Rightarrow \frac{(7x+6)}{(8x+6)} = \frac{9}{10}$$

$\Rightarrow 70x + 60 = 72x + 54$

$\Rightarrow 2x = 6$

$\Rightarrow x = 3$

The age of Rohit after 10 years = 8 × 3 + 10 = 24 + 10 = 34 years

$\therefore$ The age of Rohit after 10 years is 34 years.

Hence, the correct option is (B).

41. Given:

A complete a work = 10 days

B complete a work = 20 days

C complete a work = 30 days

D destroy a work = 15 days

We know that,

Total Wok Done = Number of Days × Efficiency

Let the efficiencies (work is done per day) of A, B, C and D are a, b, c, and d be respectively.

Let total work be 1 unit.

Efficiency of A,

$\Rightarrow a \times 10 = 1$

$\Rightarrow a = \dfrac{1}{10}$

Efficiency of B,

$\Rightarrow b \times 20 = 1$

$\Rightarrow b = \dfrac{1}{20}$

Efficiency of C,

$\Rightarrow c \times 30 = 1$

$\Rightarrow c = \dfrac{1}{30}$

Efficiency of D,

$\Rightarrow d \times 15 = 1$

$\Rightarrow d = \dfrac{1}{(-15)}$

Time Taken by all of them to complete the whole work = A + B + C + D

$$\Rightarrow \frac{1}{10} + \frac{1}{20} + \frac{1}{30} + \frac{1}{(-15)}$$

$$\Rightarrow \frac{(11-4)}{60}$$

$$\Rightarrow \frac{7}{60}$$

$$\frac{Work\ done}{Efficiency} = \frac{1}{\left(\frac{7}{60}\right)}$$

$$\Rightarrow \frac{60}{7}$$

∴ A, B, C and D all can complete the whole work in $\frac{60}{7}$ days.

Hence, the correct option is (B).

42. Given:

The ratio of the speed of boat in still water to speed of river = 7 : 3

Distance covered in upstream = 30 km

Distance covered in downstream = 40 km

Time taken for the whole journey = 0.5 hours

Concept used:

Speed of boat in upstream = u – v

Speed of boat in downstream = u + v

Where,

u = speed of the boat in still water

v = speed of river

We know that,

$$Speed = \frac{Distance}{Time}$$

Let the speed of boat in still water and speed of river be 7x and 3x respectively.

Total time = Time taken in upstream + Time taken in downstream

$$\Rightarrow 0.5 = \left\{\frac{30}{(7x-3x)}\right\} + \left\{\frac{40}{(7x+3x)}\right\}$$

$$\Rightarrow 0.5 = \left(\frac{30}{4x}\right) + \left(\frac{40}{10x}\right)$$

$$\Rightarrow 0.5 = \frac{(150+80)}{20x}$$

$$\Rightarrow 0.5 = \frac{230}{20x}$$

$$\Rightarrow x = \frac{230}{10}$$

$$\Rightarrow x = 23$$

Speed of boat in still water = 7x

$$\Rightarrow 7 \times 23$$

$$\Rightarrow 161 \text{ km/hr}$$

∴ Speed of boat in still water is 161 km/hr.

Hence, the correct option is (B).

43. Given:

Previous income of Aman = Rs. 30,000 per month

His previous expenditure = Rs. 20,000 per month

His income increases by Rs. 10,000 per month

His new expenditure = Rs. 25,000 per month

We know that,

Savings = Income - Expenditure

And Percentage = $\left(\dfrac{Favourable\ value}{Base\ value}\right) \times 100$

Previous savings of Aman = His previous income – His previous expenditure

$$\Rightarrow Rs. 30,000 – Rs. 20,000$$

$$\Rightarrow Rs. 10,000$$

His new income = Rs. 30,000 + Rs. 10,000

And His new savings = His new income – His new expenditure

$$\Rightarrow Rs. 40,000 – Rs. 25,000$$

$$\Rightarrow Rs. 15,000$$

Increase in savings = Rs. 15,000 – Rs. 10,000 = Rs. 5,000

Now, percentage increase in savings = $\dfrac{Increase\ in\ savings}{Previous\ savings} \times 100$

$$\Rightarrow \frac{Rs.\ 5,000}{Rs.\ 10,000} \times 100$$

$$\Rightarrow \left(\frac{1}{2}\right) \times 100$$

$$\Rightarrow 50\%$$

∴ In next month, the savings of Aman increases by 50%.

Hence, the correct option is (E).

44. The surface area of the cylinder = Surface area of the square

Here height 'h' of the cylinder – Side of the square since it is rolled along its length

$$\Rightarrow 2\pi ra = a^2$$

$$\Rightarrow \text{Base radius } r = \frac{a}{2\pi}$$

$$\Rightarrow \text{The ratio of base radius to the side of square} = \frac{a}{2\pi} : a = \frac{1}{2\pi}$$

∴ The required ratio is $\frac{1}{2\pi}$.

Hence, the correct option is (A).

45. Given,

Marked price = Rs. 2500

Discount = 10%

∴ Discount on marked price = 0.10 × 2500 = 250

∵ Selling price = Marked price – Discount

∴ Selling price becomes = 2500 – 250 = 2250

Let, 'x%' is additional discount given to bring the net selling price to Rs. 2000

$\therefore 2250 - \left(\dfrac{x}{100}\right) \times 2250 = 2000$

$\Rightarrow 2250\left(\dfrac{1-x}{100}\right) = 2000$

$\Rightarrow \dfrac{1-x}{100} = \dfrac{2000}{2250} = \dfrac{8}{9}$

$\Rightarrow \dfrac{x}{100} = \dfrac{1-8}{9} = \dfrac{1}{9}$

$\Rightarrow x = \dfrac{100}{9}$

$\Rightarrow x = 11\dfrac{1}{9}\%$

Hence, the correct option is (A).

46. Given:

Share's ratio A and B is 3 : 2 for 18 months and 15 months

Profit of A is Rs. 1800

Let total profit be = 100 unit

30% profit is given to charity

100 × 30% = 30 unit

So, remaining is = 70 unit

Then A' and B share = 3 : 2 in 18 months and 15 months

3 × 18 : 2 × 15 = 54 : 30

New ratio of A and B is = 9 : 5

Profit of A's = $\dfrac{9}{14} \times 70 = 45$ unit

So, profit of B is = 70 - 45 = 25 unit

Given Rs. 1800 profit = 45 unit

1 unit = 40

B profit = 40 × 25 = Rs. 1000

Profit of B is Rs. 1000.

Hence, the correct option is (A).

47. I: $x^2 + 3x - 54 = 0$

$\Rightarrow x^2 - 6x + 9x - 54 = 0$

$\Rightarrow x \times (x - 6) + 9 \times (x - 6) = 0$

$\Rightarrow (x - 6) \times (x + 9) = 0$

$\Rightarrow x = -9, 6$

II: $y^2 - 21y + 54 = 0$

$\Rightarrow y^2 - 18y - 3y + 54 = 0$

$\Rightarrow y \times (y - 18) - 3 \times (y - 18) = 0$

$\Rightarrow (y - 18) \times (y - 3) = 0$

$\Rightarrow y = 18, 3$

Comparing the values of x and y,

Value of x	Relation	Value of y
-9	<	18
-9	<	3
7	<	18
7	>	3

$\therefore$ From the table, we can conclude, No relation in x and y or x = y

Hence, the correct option is (E).

48. 66.66% $\rightarrow \dfrac{2}{3}$

25% $\rightarrow \dfrac{1}{4}$

Calculation:

13 × 25% of 200 - 12 × 66.66% of 50 = ?

$\Rightarrow 13 \times \dfrac{1}{4} \times 200 - 12 \times \left(\dfrac{2}{3} \times 50\right) = ?$

$\Rightarrow 650 - 12 \times \dfrac{100}{3} = ?$

$\Rightarrow 650 - 400 = ?$

$\therefore ? = 250$

Hence, the correct option is (B).

49. Given:

The length of train A is 200 m and the speed is 90 km/h

The length of train B is 160 m and the speed is 72 km/h

They are coming from the same direction, so the relative speed of them = (90 - 72) km/h

$\Rightarrow 18$ km/h

$\Rightarrow \left\{18 \times \left(\dfrac{5}{18}\right)\right\}$ m/s

$\Rightarrow 5$ m/s

Total distance covered by A and B = (200 + 160) m = 360 m

So, to cross each other completely the required time = $\dfrac{360}{5}$ sec

= 72 sec

$\therefore$ They can cross each other completely in 72 sec.

Hence, the correct option is (B).

50. The selling price of the product = Rs. 7776

Overall discount percentage

$\Rightarrow 10 + 10 - \dfrac{(10 \times 10)}{100}$

$\Rightarrow 19\%$

Marked price of the product = $\dfrac{7776}{0.81}$

$\Rightarrow 9600$

Cost price of the article = $\dfrac{9600}{1.2}$

⇒ 8000

∴ Required percentage = $\dfrac{(8000-7776)}{8000}$

⇒ 2.8%

The loss percentage is 2.8%.

Hence, the correct option is (A).

51. Given:

The total quantity of the mixture is 60 liters

In the mixture water is 20%

After adding water, it will be 36% in the final mixture.

Concept used:

Here we will use the Alligation method

According to the question,

We will add only water to the final mixture

So, we will consider 100% of the water will be added to the final mixture so that in the final mixture the water will be 36%

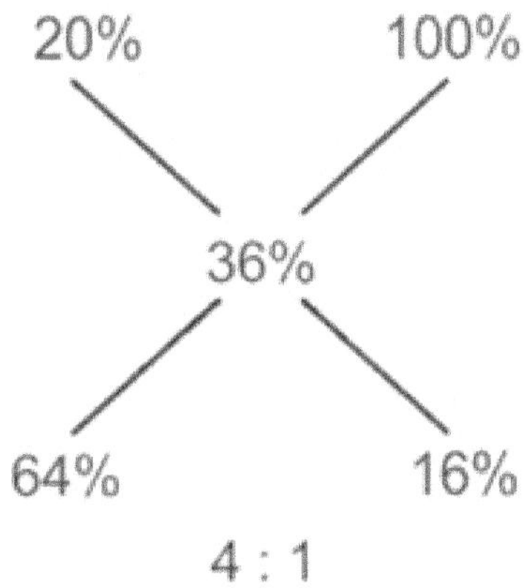

So, the ratio of the initial quantity of the mixture to the quantity of the water added to the mixture will be 4 : 1

Let the initial quantity of the mixture be 4x and the added water be x

So, we can say 4x = 60

⇒ x = $\dfrac{60}{4}$

⇒ x = 15

∴ 15 liters of water should be added to the final mixture.

Hence, the correct option is (B).

52. Given:

Number of Jio users in Uttarakhand = 300

Number of Airtel users in Himachal = 150

Percentage difference = $\left\{\dfrac{(300-150)}{150}\right\} \times 100$

⇒ $\left(\dfrac{150}{150}\right) \times 100$

⇒ 100%

∴ Jio users in Uttarakhand are 100% more than Airtel users in Himachal.

Hence, the correct option is (C).

53. Given:

Number of Jio users in Haryana = 250

Number of Airtel users in Delhi = 250

Difference of Jio users in Haryana and Airtel users in Delhi = 250 − 250

⇒ 0

∴ The difference of Jio users in Haryana and Airtel users in Delhi is 0.

Hence, the correct option is (C).

54. Given:

Number of Jio users in Delhi = 350

Number of Airtel users in UP = 250

The ratio of Jio users in Delhi to Airtel users in UP = 350 : 250

⇒ 7 : 5

∴ The ratio of Jio users in Delhi to Airtel users in UP is 7 : 5.

Hence, the correct option is (C).

55. Given:

Number of Jio users in Delhi = 350

Number of Jio users in Uttarakhand = 300

Number of Jio users in Haryana = 250

We know that,

Average = $\dfrac{Sum\ of\ values}{Number\ of\ values}$

Average of Jio users in Delhi, Uttarakhand and Haryana

= $\dfrac{(350+300+250)}{3}$

⇒ $\dfrac{900}{3}$

⇒ 300

∴ The average of Jio users in Delhi, Uttarakhand and Haryana is 300.

Hence, the correct option is (B).

56. Given:

Number of Airtel users in UP = 250

Number of Airtel users in Uttarakhand = 200

Number of Airtel users in Himachal = 150

Number of Airtel users in Haryana = 350

Number of Airtel users in Delhi = 250

Total Airtel users in all five states together = 250 + 200 + 150 + 350 + 250

= 1200

∴ Total Airtel users in all five states together are 1200.

Hence, the correct option is (B).

57. Total number of patients in A and C = 200 + 200 = 400

Total number of active patients in A and C = 150 + 160 = 310

∴ Required percent $= \frac{310}{400} \times 100 = 77.5\%$

Hence, the correct option is (B).

58. Number of deaths in hospital A = 200 − (150 + 35) = 15

Number of deaths in hospital D = 180 − (130 + 45) = 5

∴ Required difference = 15 − 5 = 10

Hence, the correct option is (E).

59. Number of recovered patients in A, B, and C = 35 + 20 + 30 = 85

Number of deaths in B and C = 150 − (120 + 20) + 200 − (160 + 30) = 20

∴ Required ratio = 85 : 20 = 17 : 4

Hence, the correct option is (A).

60. Number of patients recovered in A and D = 35 + 45 = 80

Total number of patients in C = 200

∴ Required percent $= \frac{200-80}{200} \times 100 = 60$

Hence, the correct option is (A).

61. Number of deaths in hospital A = 200 − (150 + 35) = 15

Number of deaths in B = 150 − (120 + 20) = 10

Number of deaths in C = 200 − (160 + 30) = 10

Number of deaths in hospital D = 180 − (130 + 45) = 5

∴ Required average $= \frac{(15+10+10+5)}{4} = 10$

Hence, the correct option is (B).

62. Given:

$$\sqrt[3]{1728} \times \sqrt[3]{4096} \div \sqrt[3]{512} =?$$

⇒ 12 × 16 ÷ 8 = ?

⇒ 12 × 2 = ?

⇒ 24 = ?

∴ The value of ? is 24.

Hence, the correct option is (A).

63. Given:

Principal amount = Rs. 15,000

Interest rates = 25% p.a.

Time = 5 years

Formula:

$$Sl = \frac{(P \times T \times R)}{100}$$

Where, P = Principal Amount

R = Interest rate

T = Time for which interest is applied on amount

Calculation:

$$SI = \frac{15,000 \times 25 \times 5}{100}$$

⇒ SI = Rs. 18,750

∴ Required SI is Rs. 18,750.

Hence, the correct option is (A).

64. Given:

Ratio of Ram's Salary for May 2020 to his salary for June 2020 = 4 : 3

Ratio of Ram's Salary for June 2020 to October 2020 = 6 : 9

Concept:

If A is x% of B

Than, x% = $\left(\frac{A}{B}\right) \times 100$

Calculation:

Salary in May : Salary in June : Salary in October = 4 × 6 : 6 × 3 : 9 × 3

= 24 : 18 : 27

Or 8x : 6x : 9x

Ram got Rs.8,000 more salary in October from May 2020 = 9x − 8x

⇒ x = 8000

Diwali Bonus amount in October = 10% of (9 × 8000)

= Rs.7,200

∴ Amount of bonus is Rs. 7,200.

Hence, the correct option is (B).

65. Given:

28% of 640 + 34% of 720 = ? × 54

$\Rightarrow \frac{28}{100} \times 640 + \frac{34}{100} \times 720 =? \times 54$

$\Rightarrow 179.2 + 244.8 =? \times 54$

$\Rightarrow 424 = ? \times 54$

$\Rightarrow ? = \dfrac{424}{54}$

$\therefore ? = 7.85$

Hence, the correct option is (D).

Ques (66-70): Eight people : P, Q, R, S, T, M, N, and K.

1) R sits opposite of T who sits at the immediate left of M.

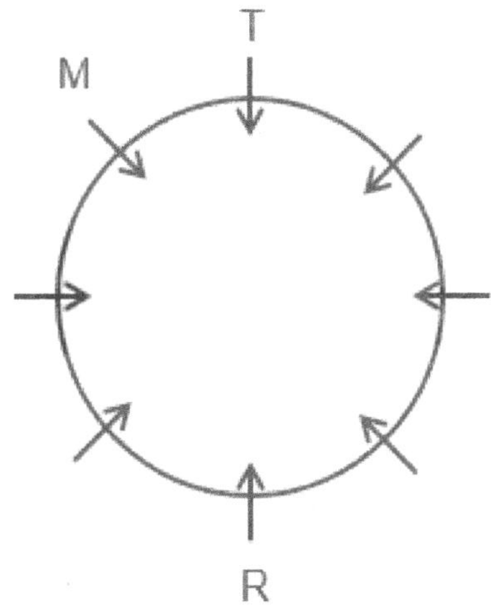

2) Two persons are sitting between S and M.

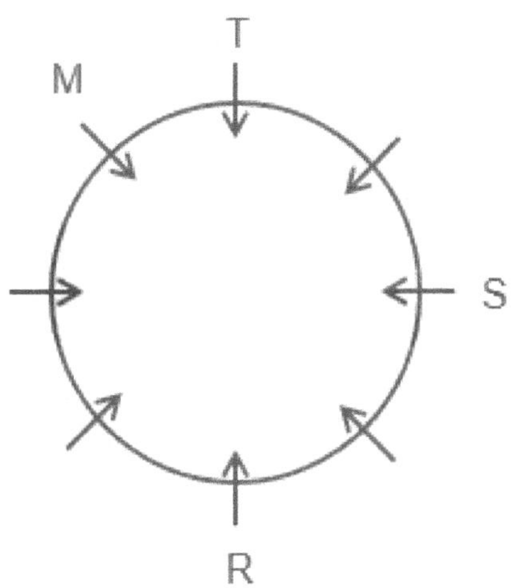

3) K and Q are sitting opposite each other.

4) Q sits second to the left of N.

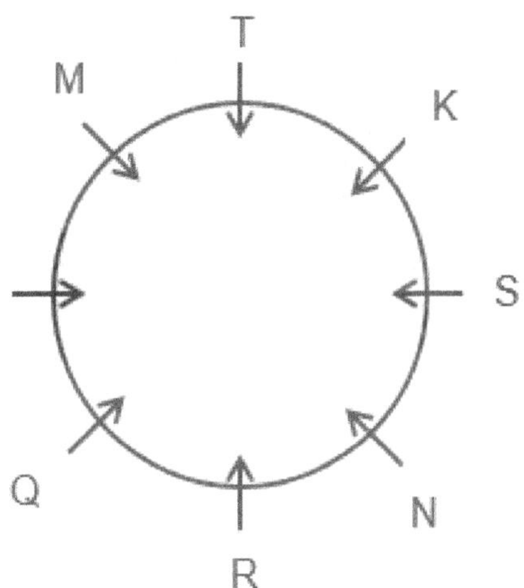

The only person left is P.

Thus, the final arrangement is as follows:

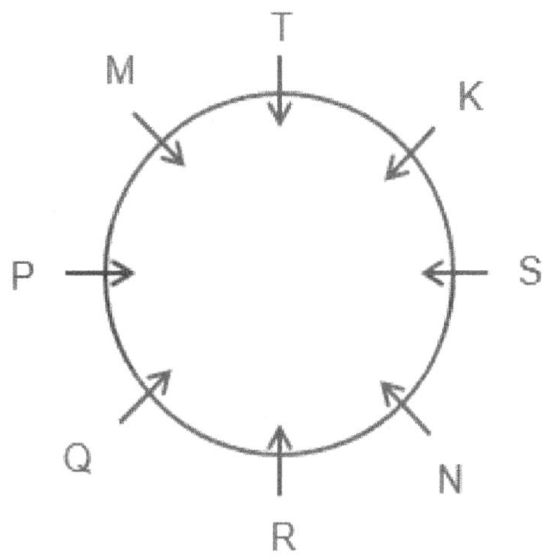

66. So, T is "second to the right" of S.

Hence, the correct option is (A).

67. So, "R" is sitting between Q and N when counted from the right of Q.

Hence, the correct option is (E).

68. So, "R" sits at the immediate right of Q.

Hence, the correct option is (A).

69. So, "S" sits opposite to P.

Hence, the correct option is (C).

70. So, "K" sits second to the right of N.

Hence, the correct option is (B).

71. Given series: R % Y 9 O @ 8 & V M 1 # L 7 E $ 9 X A £ C 5 N © F 3 I K Ø U 4

Numbers that satisfy the given criteria,

R % Y 9 O @ 8 & V M 1 # L 7 E $ 9 X A £ C 5 N © F 3 I K Ø U 4

So, Two is the correct answer.

NOTE: Please read the Instructions Carefully. In this question asked about "or" not "and"

Hence, the correct option is (D).

72. Given series:

Left Side R % Y 9 O @ 8 & V M 1 # L 7 E $ 9 X A £ C 5 N © F 3 I K Ø U 4 Right Side

The sixth element from the right end: 3

Fifth element to the right of 3 : 4

Hence, the correct option is (A).

73. Given series: R % Y 9 O @ 8 & V M 1 # L 7 E $ 9 X A £ C 5 N © F 3 I K Ø U 4

Letters that satisfy the given criteria,

R % Y 9 O @ 8 & V M 1 # L 7 E $ 9 X A £ C 5 N © F 3 I K Ø U 4

So, V is the only letter that is immediately preceded by a symbol and immediately followed by a consonant.

Hence, the correct option is (C).

74. Given series: R % Y 9 O @ 8 & V M 1 # L 7 E $ 9 X A £ C 5 N © F 3 I K Ø U 4

Numbers that satisfy the given criteria,

R % Y 9 O @ 8 & V M 1 # L 7 E $ 9 X A £ C 5 N © F 3 I K Ø U 4

Thus,

8 + 1 + 9 = 18

So, the sum of all the numbers that are either preceded or followed by a symbol is 18.

Hence, the correct option is (D).

75. The least possible Venn diagram for the given statements is as follows:

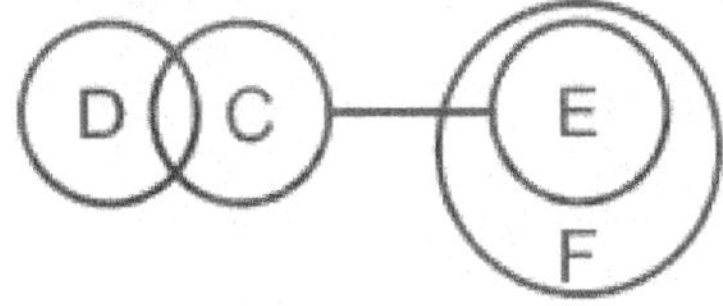

Conclusions:

I. No F is a C → False (It is possible but not definite so its false)

II. At least some D are F → False (It is possible but not definite so its false)

So, Neither I nor II follows.

Hence, the correct option is (A).

76. The least possible diagram is given below:

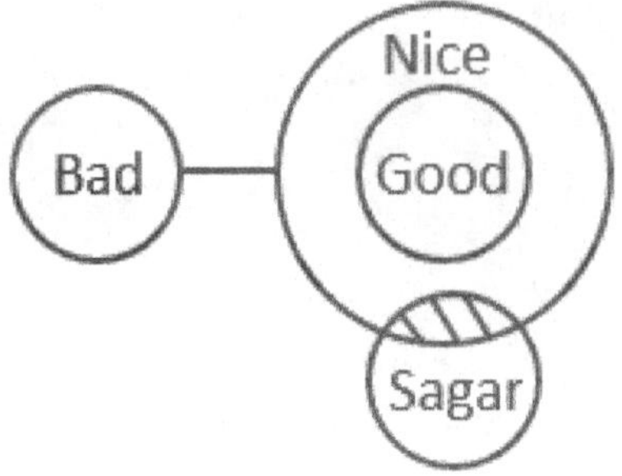

I. All Sagar can be Good → True (In statement it is clearly says Only a few Nice are Sagar and all Good are Nice)

II. Some Nice are not Bad → True (in statement it is clearly says No Bad are Good)

So, Both conclusion I and conclusion II follows.

Hence, the correct option is (E).

77. The least possible diagram for the given statements is as follows:

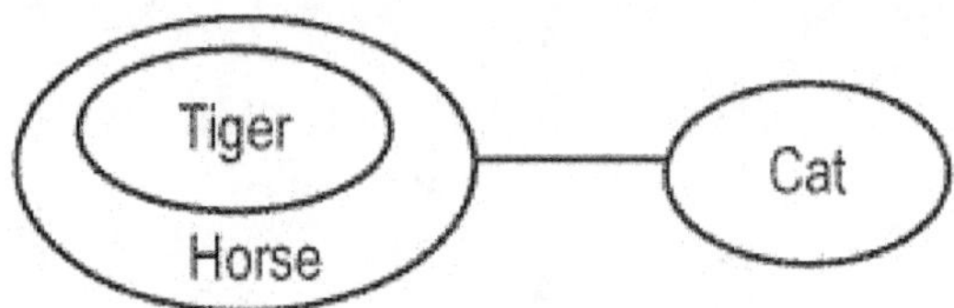

Conclusions:

I. No tiger is cat → True (It is definite)

II. Some tiger is cat → False (It is not possible as no horse is cat and all tiger is horse)

So, only I follow.

Hence, the correct option is (A).

78. The least possible diagram for the given statements is as follows:

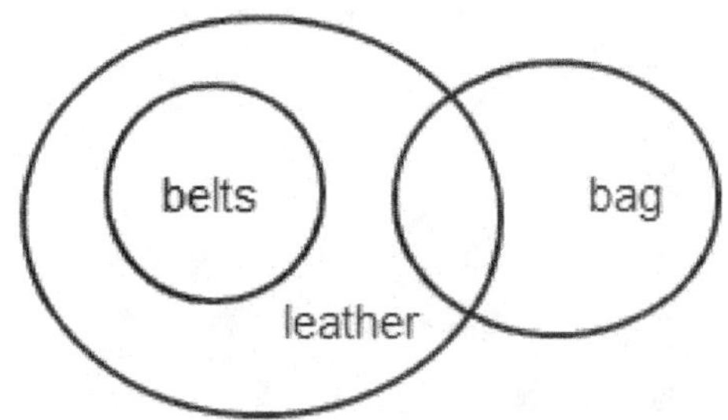

Conclusions:

I. All bags being leather is a possibility. → True (It is possible and in conclusion possibility is given)

II. No bag is a belt → False (It is possible but not definite)

So, only conclusion I follow.

Hence, the correct option is (A).

Ques (79-83): Eight persons: Geet, Harman, Jyoti, Manisha, Neha, Nikita, Tanisha and Zakir

i) Zakir is sitting at the extreme left of row 1.

ii) Tanisha sits second to the right of Zakir.

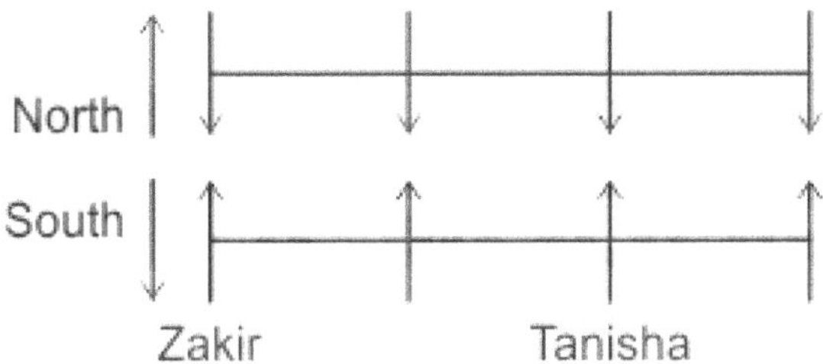

iii) Manisha is sitting opposite Tanisha.

iv) Geet sits to the immediate right of Harman.

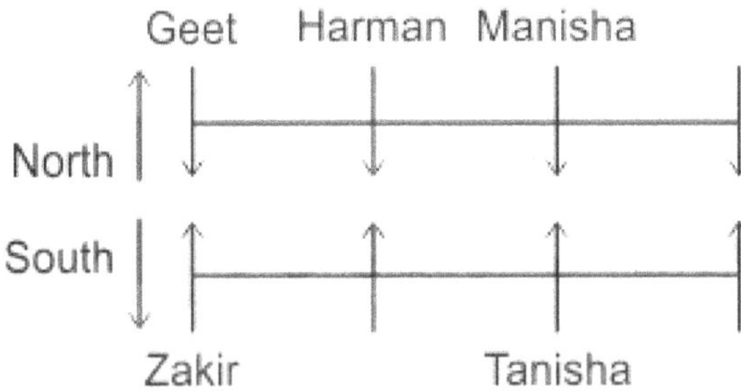

v) One person sits between Jyoti and Neha.

vi) Jyoti does not sits at any of the extreme ends.

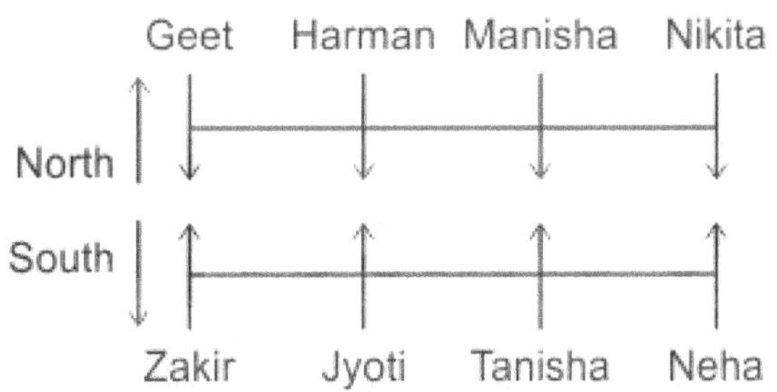

79. I. Geet sits second to the right of Tanisha. → False

II. Zakir sits opposite Nikita. → False

III. Jyoti sits opposite the person sitting immediately right to Manisha. → True

So, only statement III is true.

Hence, the correct option is (C).

80. So, if the persons sitting at the extreme ends in row 1 exchange their position, Zakir sits to the immediate right of Tanisha.

Hence, the correct option is (A).

81. Here Nikita, Zakir. Geet and Neha are sitting at the extreme ends of the row whereas Jyoti is sitting in the middle of the row.

So, Jyoti does not belong to the group.

Hence, the correct option is (D).

82. So, Jyoti sits second to the left of the person sitting opposite Nikita.

Hence, the correct option is (D).

83. So, Harman sits opposite Jyoti.

Hence, the correct option is (B).

Ques (84-86): From the given information:

Symbol in Diagram	Meaning
○	Female
□	Male
═	Married Couple
—	Siblings
│	Difference of A Generation

1) B is the son of A.

2) P is the husband of A. (implying A is the mother of B)

3) B has two children S and T.

4) T is the son of R. (R is the mother of S and T)

5) M is the sister of B.

6) R has one girl child. (S is the daughter of B and R)

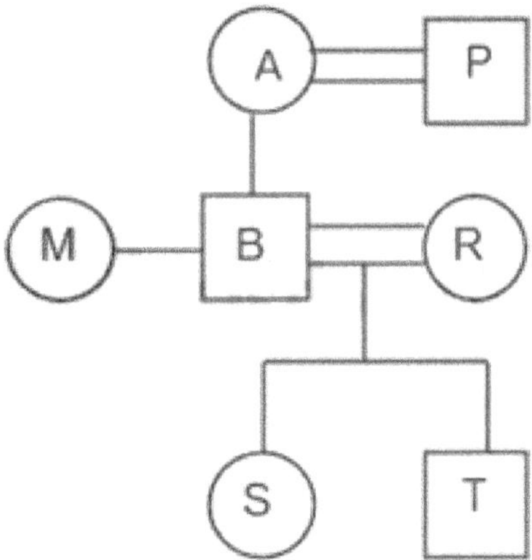

84. So, T is the grandson of P.

Hence, the correct option is (D).

85. So, there are four females in the picnic.

Hence, the correct option is (A).

86. So, M is the sister-in-law of R.

Hence, the correct option is (C).

Ques (87-91): Given that:

8 boxes - Box 1, Box 2, Box 3, Box 4, Box 5, Box 6, Box 7and Box 8 are kept one above the other from bottom to top.

In which different types of chocolates - Kit-kat, Munch, Tooty - Frooty, Pulse, Dairymilk, Perk, Barone and Milkybar are kept in it.

1) There are five boxes between Munch and Milkybar.

2) The box of Munch is above the box of Milkybar.

So, here 2 cases will generate:

BOXES	CHOCOLATES	
	Case I	Case II
Box 8	Munch	
Box 7		Munch
Box 6		
Box 5		
Box 4		
Box 3		
Box 2	Milkybar	
Box 1		Milkybar

3) The box of Perk is kept just above Milkybar.

BOXES	CHOCOLATES	
	Case I	Case II
Box 8	Munch	
Box 7		Munch
Box 6		
Box 5		
Box 4		
Box 3	Perk	
Box 2	Milkybar	Perk
Box 1		Milkybar

4) The box of Dairymilk is kept between Kit-kat and Perk.

BOXES	CHOCOLATES	
	Case I	Case II
Box 8	Munch	
Box 7		Munch
Box 6		
Box 5	Kit-kat	
Box 4	Dairymilk	Kit-kat
Box 3	Perk	Dairymilk
Box 2	Milkybar	Perk
Box 1		Milkybar

5) The number of boxes between Tooty - Frooty and Kit-kat is one less than the number of boxes is kept between Dairymilk and Barone.

So, here the boxes between Dairy milk and Barone is one more than Tooty - Frooty and Kit-kat:

BOXES	CHOCOLATES

	Case I	Case II
Box 8	Munch	Tooty-Frooty
Box 7	Tooty-Frooty	Munch
Box 6	Pulse	Barone
Box 5	Kit-kat	Pulse
Box 4	Dairymilk	Kit-kat
Box 3	Perk	Dairymilk
Box 2	Milkybar	Perk
Box 1	Barone	Milkybar

Here case II will be wrong because:

6) Pulse is kept at Box 6.

So, the correct table is:

BOXES	CHOCOLATES
Box 8	Munch
Box 7	Tooty-Frooty
Box 6	Pulse
Box 5	Kit-kat
Box 4	Dairymilk
Box 3	Perk
Box 2	Milkybar
Box 1	Barone

87. So, Kit-kat is placed just below Pulse.

Hence, the correct option is (A).

88. Munch is related to the Kit-kat → Gap of 2 boxes.

And Dairymilk is related to the Barone → Gap of 2 boxes.

So, Pulse is related to the Perk → Gap of 2 boxes.

Therefore, Pulse is related to Perk.

Hence, the correct option is (E).

89. So, Tooty - Frooty is kept at which box number 7.

Hence, the correct option is (D).

90. So, there are five boxes are there between Tooty - Frooty and Barone.

Hence, the correct option is (B).

91. So, Munch is kept at Box 8.

Hence, the correct option is (C).

Ques (92-96): Events: P, Q, R, S, T, U, V and W

Dates: 3rd or 16th

Months: January, February, March and April

1) Event Q is on an even-numbered date of the month having 31 days.

2) There are three events between event Q and event T.

CASE 1			CASE 2		
DATE → MONTHS ↓	3rd	16th	DATE → MONTHS ↓	3rd	16th
JANUARY		Q	JANUARY		T

FEBRUARY			FEBRUARY		
MARCH		T	MARCH		Q
APRIL			APRIL		

3) Event S is just before the event U but in different months.

CASE 1			CASE 2		
DATE → MONTHS ↓	3rd	16th	DATE → MONTHS ↓	3rd	16th
JANUARY		Q	JANUARY		T
FEBRUARY		S	FEBRUARY		S
MARCH	U	T	MARCH	U	Q
APRIL			APRIL		

4) Event R is scheduled before event P but not in the month having 31 days.

5) There are more than one events between event T and event R.

CASE 1			CASE 2		
DATE → MONTHS ↓	3rd	16th	DATE → MONTHS ↓	3rd	16th
JANUARY		Q	JANUARY		T
FEBRUARY	R	S	FEBRUARY		S
MARCH	U	T	MARCH	U	Q
APRIL			APRIL	R	P

6) Event P and event W are scheduled to be held on the same date of different months.

As event W cannot be scheduled on 16th(same date as P) of any month in case 2, it will be cancelled.

DATE → MONTHS ↓	3rd	16th
JANUARY	W	Q
FEBRUARY	R	S
MARCH	U	T
APRIL	P	V

92. So, event R and event S are scheduled in February.

Hence, the correct option is (C).

93. So, event T is scheduled just before event P.

Hence, the correct option is (B).

94. So, event W is scheduled for 3rd January.

Hence, the correct option is (E).

95. So, two events are scheduled between event T and event R.

Hence, the correct option is (C).

96. So, event V is scheduled on 16th April.

Hence, the correct option is (D).

97. Statement: B < S ≤ Q < Y = X > C ≥ J

I. S < Y ⇒ True (as S ≤ Q < Y ⇒ S < Y)

II. X > B ⇒ True (as B < S ≤ Q < Y = X ⇒ B < X ⇒ X > B)

So, Both I and II are true.

Hence, the correct option is (D).

98. Given statements: A < C = D < E; B = A > F

On combining: F < B = A < C = D < E

I. D > F → True (as F < A < C = D → D > F)

II. B > E → False (as B < C = D < E → B < E)

Thus, the only conclusion I is true.

Hence, the correct option is (B).

99. Given statements: D = X ≥ C > S = F; D > Y ≥ H ≥ G

On combination: G ≤ H ≤ Y < D = X ≥ C > S = F

Conclusions:

I. G ≤ X → False (as G ≤ H ≤ Y < D = X)

II. D > F → True (as D = X ≥ C > S = F)

So, only conclusion II follows.

Hence, the correct option is (C).

100. Given statements: G ≥ M = P > C; Q < R = B < C

On combining above two statements: G ≥ M = P > C > B = R > Q

Conclusions:

I. M > R → True (as M = P > C > B = R)

II. G ≥ B → False (as G ≥ M = P > C > B → G > B)

So, only conclusion I follows.

Hence, the correct option is (A).

English Language

Ques (1-5):Directions: For the blank in the passage, there are five choices provided. Select the word that makes the most sense when placed in the blank.

An objection is often raised against realistic biography because it reveals so much that is important and even sacred about a man's life. The real objection to it will rather be found in the fact that it reveals about a man the precise points which are unimportant. It reveals and asserts and insists on exactly those things in a man's life of which the man himself is wholly unconscious; his exact class in society, the circumstances of his ancestry, the place of his present location. These are things which do not, properly speaking, ever arise before the human ___(1)___. They do not occur to a man's mind; it may be said, with almost equal truth, that they do not occur in a man's life. A man no more thinks about himself as the inhabitant of the third house in a row of Brixton villas than he thinks about himself as a strange animal with two legs. What a man's name was, what his income was, whom he married, where he lived, these are not sanctities; they are ___(2)___.

A very strong case of this is the case of the Brontës. The Brontë is in the position of the mad lady in a country village; her ___(3)___ form an endless source of innocent conversation to that exceedingly mild and bucolic circle, the literary world. The truly glorious gossips of literature, like Mr. Augustine Birrell and Mr. Andrew Lang, never tire of collecting all the glimpses and ___(4)___ and sermons and side-lights and sticks and straws which will go to make a Brontë museum. They are the most personally discussed of all Victorian authors, and the limelight of biography has left few darkened corners in the dark old Yorkshire house. And yet the whole of this biographical investigation, though natural and picturesque, is not wholly suitable to the Brontës. For the Brontë, genius was above all things deputed to ___(5)___ the supreme unimportance of externals. Up to that point, the truth had always been conceived as existing more or less in the novel of manners.

Q.1 What will come at a place of __(1)__?
A. experience
B. remark
C. fathom
D. occurance
E. vision

Q.2 What will come at a place of ___(2)___?
A. sanctimonious
B. heresies
C. irrelevancies
D. ordinary
E. inimical

Q.3 What will come at a place of ___(3)___?
A. eccentricities
B. outgoing
C. events
D. peeves
E. friends

Q.4 What will come at a place of ___(4)___?

A. sightings
B. lives
C. amusements
D. anecdotes
E. passions

Q.5 What will come at a place of __(5)__?
A. remark
B. implement
C. assert
D. define
E. play

Q.6 Direction: In the following question, fill in the blanks in the sentence with the correct option.
The Indian army advanced and the bloody battle ______.
A. Shrank
B. Knocked
C. Commenced
D. Lit
E. None of the above

Ques (7-9):Directions: Fill in the blanks with the most appropriate word from among the given options.

Q.7 The mother's ______ to illness caused her to become sick very easily.
A. Aberration
B. Abjure
C. Susceptibility
D. Temperament
E. Abnegation

Q.8 Ever since the MD has taken the ______of the company, the business has risen dramatically.
A. Accost
B. Accretion
C. Acumen
D. Adamant
E. Helm

Q.9 The overwhelmed baby sitter has no time for ______ and doesn't even try to clean up the mounds of mess while the baby is awake.
A. Rejig
B. Cohort
C. Seamless
D. Orderliness
E. Pester

Ques (10-13):Directions: In the following question, a sentence is given with an idiom or phrase highlighted in bold. Select the option given below that replaces the phrase or idiom in bold and mark that as your answer. Ignore punctuation errors, if any.

Q.10 Their company is trying to revive an income that is **unable to produce successful outcomes**.
A. dead in the water
B. draining the swamp
C. a flash in the pan
D. dead as a dodo
E. a dead ringer

Q.11 Their corporate offices were **being criticized** after their stocks plummeted last week.
A. were under no illusions
B. were thrown under the bus
C. were a goose egg
D. were under a spell
E. were under siege

Q.12 He sold his shares in Nokia and put it into Apple, because he realized they **were ahead of current trends or thinking**.

A. were ahead of the curve
B. were fanning the flames
C. were in the loop
D. were thrown down to the gauntlet
E. were a pipe dream

Q.13 I believe that digital learning is the **only way to succeed**.

A. the bang for the buck
B. only way forward.
C. only a pipe dream
D. a herculean task
E. is ahead of the curve

Ques (14-18):Directions: Read the passage and answer the questions that follow.

India has two national languages for central administrative purposes: Hindi and English. Hindi is the official, and the main link language of India. English is an associate official language. The Indian Constitution also officially approves twenty-two regional languages for official purposes.

Dozens of distinctly different regional languages are spoken in India, which share many characteristics such as grammatical structure and vocabulary. Apart from these languages, Hindi is used for communication in India. The homeland of Hindi is mainly in the north of India, but it is spoken and widely understood in all urban centers of India. In the southern states of India, where people speak many different languages that are not much related to Hindi, there is more resistance to Hindi, which has allowed English to remain a lingua franca to a greater degree.

Since the early 1600s, the English language has had a toehold on the Indian subcontinent, when the East India Company established settlements in Chennai, Kolkata, and Mumbai, formerly Madras, Calcutta, and Bombay respectively. The historical background of India is never far away from the everyday usage of English. India has had a longer exposure to English than any other country which uses it as a second language, its distinctive words, idioms, grammar and rhetoric spreading gradually to affect all places, habits and culture.

In India, English serves two purposes. First, it provides a linguistic tool for the administrative cohesiveness of the country, causing people who speak different languages to become united. Secondly, it serves as a language of wider communication by including a large variety of different people covering a vast area. It overlaps with local languages in certain spheres of influence and in public domains.

Generally, English is used among Indians as a 'link' language and it is the first language for many well-educated Indians. It is also the second language for many who speak more than one language in India.

One can see a Hindi-speaking teacher giving their students instructions during an educational tour about where to meet and when their bus would leave, but all in English. India is, without a doubt, committed to English as a national language. The impact of English is not only continuing but increasing.

Q.14 Which word means the same as 'the refusal to accept or comply with something'?

A. Cohesiveness
B. Distinctive
C. Influence
D. Domains
E. Resistance

Q.15 Which of these is opposite in meaning to 'urban'?

A. Town
B. Rural
C. Household
D. City
E. Suburb

Q.16 The conclusion of the passage is:

A. Speaking English is unavoidable
B. The impact of English can decrease
C. The impact of English will increase
D. People should continue speaking English
E. None of these

Q.17 Hindi speaking teachers:

A. Always speak English
B. Use English to give instructions
C. Never speak English
D. Don't understand English
E. None of these

Q.18 How does English serve as a language of wider communication?

A. By giving importance to regional languages
B. By many adopting it as a first language
C. By serving administrative purposes
D. Both (B) and (C)
E. None of these

Q.19 Directions: Find out which part has an error and mark it as your answer. If there is no error, mark 'No error' as your answer.

None of these (A)/ two officers (B)/ has been looking after (C)/ his department well. (D)

A. (A)
B. (B)
C. (C)
D. (D)
E. No error

Q.20 Directions: Find out which part has an error and mark it as your answer. If there is no error, mark 'No error' as your answer.

The strict boss (A)/ did not give her ascent (B)/ to the employee's (C)/ whimsical request. (D)

A. (A)
B. (B)
C. (C)
D. (D)
E. No error

Q.21 Directions: Find out which part has an error and mark it as your answer. If there is no error, mark 'No error' as your answer.

The Party Chief (A)/ and the Chief Minister (B)/ expressed his views (C)/ on demonetization in India. (D)

A. The Party Chief
B. and the Chief Minister
C. expressed his views
D. on demonetization in India.
E. No error

Q.22 Directions: Find out which part has an error and mark it as your answer. If there is no error, mark 'No error' as your answer.

Unlike Indian laws, US laws provides (A)/ for a contingency fee of lawyering (B)/ where the costs of litigation (C)/ are borne by lawyers. (D)

A. Unlike Indian laws, US laws provides

B. for a contingency fee of lawyering

C. where the costs of litigation

D. are borne by lawyers

E. No error

Q.23 Directions: Find out which part has an error and mark it as your answer. If there is no error, mark 'No error' as your answer.

India's Swachh Bharat Mission is (A)/ receiving globe praise (B)/ for attempting (C)/ to close the sanitation gap. (D)

A. India's Swachh Bharat Mission is

B. receiving globe praise

C. for attempting

D. to close the sanitation gap.

E. No error

Q.24 Direction: In the following question, two statements and five connectors are given. Only one of the connectors from those given can be used to combine the given two statements into one sentence without changing the meaning. Choose that connector as your answer.

I. I live only a few blocks from work

II. I walk to work and enjoy it.

A. Now that   **B.** Rather than

C. Even though   **D.** Only if

E. Just as

Q.25 Direction: In the following question, two statements and five connectors are given. Only one of the connectors from those given can be used to combine the given two statements into one sentence without changing the meaning. Choose that connector as your answer.

I. The floors had been waxed and the furniture got polished by afternoon.

II. The house sparkled but in an empty kind of way.

A. Once   **B.** As

C. When   **D.** Wherever

E. If when

Q.26 Direction: In the following question, two statements and five connectors are given. Only one of the connectors from those given can be used to combine the given two statements into one sentence without changing the meaning. Choose that connector as your answer.

I. The man goes to the park every Sunday

II. He loves watching the ducks in the lake.

A. Until   **B.** Once

C. As   **D.** Although

E. Until

Q.27 Direction: In the following question two statements have been given with connectors given as options. You have to select that option which could connect both the sentences and make them grammatically and contextually correct.

I. China has decided to ban the imports of plastic waste into the country.

II. A lot of countries will have to make new plans for their disposal.

A. Now, Hence   **B.** As, Since

C. Finally, Meanwhile   **D.** Both (A) and (B)

E. Both (A) and (C)

Q.28 Direction: In the following question, two statements and five connectors are given. Only one of the connectors from those given can be used to combine the given two statements into one sentence without changing the meaning. Choose that connector as your answer.

I. I was not in a situation to step out of the house yesterday because of my severe headache.

II. I attended the sales meeting at my office on the instructions of my senior management.

A. Since   **B.** Nevertheless

C. On the other hand   **D.** By comparison

E. Now that

Q.29 Direction: In the following question, two statements and five connectors are given. Only one of the connectors from those given can be used to combine the given two statements into one sentence without changing the meaning. Choose that connector as your answer.

I. I was very tired and exhausted after spending the whole day at the hospital.

II. I went to sleep without having dinner after coming back.

A. So   **B.** In fact

C. Especially   **D.** And

E. As though

Q.30 Direction: In the following question, two statements and five connectors are given. Only one of the connectors from those given can be used to combine the given two statements into one sentence without changing the meaning. Choose that connector as your answer.

I. The minister will definitely come to this locality for election campaigning within the next two days.

II. He may not come here if he is denied the ticket from this constituency by his party.

A. Since   **B.** Unless

C. In addition to   **D.** Of course

E. Except

Numerical Ability

Q.31 A shopkeeper sells 12 pens at a price for which he bought 14 pens. If he has to pay a tax of 10% on the profit obtained, what is his net profit on the overall transaction?

A. 15.33%

B. 16%

C. 16.67%

D. 15%

E. Cannot be determined

Q.32 Ajay can do a particular job in 10 days. Vijay can do the same job in 12 days. Ajay and Vijay start together, but Vijay leaves after 4 days. In how many days(from the beginning) will the work be completed?

A. $8\frac{2}{5}$ **B.** $9\frac{1}{3}$ **C.** $9\frac{1}{5}$ **D.** $7\frac{3}{5}$

E. $6\frac{2}{3}$

Ques (33-37):Directions: What will come in the place of the question mark (?) in the following series?

Q.33 13, 74, ?, 604, 1265, 2358, 4039

A. 361 **B.** 279 **C.** 243 **D.** 225

E. 215

Q.34 23, 46, ?, 86, 83, 166

A. 45 **B.** 89 **C.** 83 **D.** 49

E. 43

Q.35 99, 98, 96, 95, 91, 90, 82, ?

A. 80 **B.** 73 **C.** 74 **D.** 81

E. 66

Q.36 4913, 6859, 12167, 24389, ?

A. 42875 **B.** 35937 **C.** 29791 **D.** 27991

E. 29537

Q.37 15, 17, ?, 29, 45

A. 25 **B.** 19 **C.** 23 **D.** 21

E. 22

Ques (38-42):Directions: Read the information given below carefully and answer the questions which follow.

The following table gives the data of the number of candidates appearing for the BAT Exam every year. On the basis of the data given in the table, answer the question.

Year	Number of Candidates Appeared	Percentage of appeared candidates who qualified	The ratio of Male to Female Qualified Candidates
2010			5 : 4
2011	87500		8 : 7
2012	75000	28%	
2013		65%	5 : 8
2014	120000	40%	

Q.38 The number of candidates appearing in the examination in 2015 increased by 8% from 2011 to 2015. If only 25% of the candidates were able to qualify for the examination, find the number of candidates who qualified for the examination in 2015?

A. 23650 **B.** 29650 **C.** 23750 **D.** 24125

E. 23625

Q.39 If the number of male candidates who qualified in 2012 was 6500, find the ratio of the number of qualified female candidates to the number of qualified male candidates?

A. 29 : 13 **B.** 27 : 15 **C.** 30 : 17 **D.** 29 : 17

E. 19 : 8

Q.40 If the average number of qualified candidates in 2011 and 2014 is 37125. Find the percentage of candidates qualified in 2011?

A. 22.5% **B.** 25% **C.** 35% **D.** 30%

E. 40%

Q.41 If the difference between the qualified male candidates and the qualified female candidates in 2013 was 13650. Find the number of appeared candidates in 2013?

A. 90750 **B.** 91000 **C.** 87500 **D.** 86740

E. 85450

Q.42 If during 2010, the ratio of the candidates who appeared to the candidates who qualified for the exam was 5 : 2. What percent of qualified female candidates constitute the appeared candidates?

A. 30% **B.** 20% **C.** 17.77% **D.** 25%

E. 10%

Ques (43-44):Directions: What will come in place of the question mark '?' in the following question?

Q.43 $47^{.9856} \times 47^{.0144} - 47 = ?$

A. 0 **B.** .137

C. 47 **D.** 900

E. Can't be determined

Q.44 $2\frac{3}{5}$ of $3\frac{1}{13} + 1\frac{2}{3} \times 4\frac{1}{5}$

A. $14\frac{1}{3}$ **B.** $13\frac{1}{13}$

C. $15\frac{1}{13}$ **D.** $16\frac{1}{13}$

E. None of the above

Q.45 A invests Rs.400, B invests Rs.600 into a partnership. After 5 months, B adds Rs.100 and C joined them with Rs.800. After 10 months, A adds Rs.300 to his investment. Their total profit is Rs. 2079 after 1 year. Find the difference between the profit shares of C and A

A. Rs. 30 **B.** Rs. 22 **C.** Rs. 18 **D.** Rs. 40

E. Rs. 36

Q.46 A goods train of length 400 m moving at a speed of 90 kmph crosses a platform of a certain length in 22 seconds. Another train of length 350 m crosses the same platform in 25 seconds. Find the relative speed of both trains if they both travel in the same direction.

A. 13 kmph **B.** 20 kmph **C.** 22 kmph **D.** 15 kmph

E. 18 kmph

Q.47 Pipe P alone can fill the tank in 18 hours and pipe Q alone can fill the tank in 12 hours. Both pipes opened for 7 hours. The fraction of the tank that remained after 7 hours is equal to the fraction of the tank filled by pipe R in one hour. At what time the tank gets filled when all three pipes are opened simultaneously?

A. 7 hours **B.** 4 hours **C.** 3 hours **D.** 9 hours

E. 6 hours

Q.48 3 dice are rolled thrice having numbers from 1 to 6. Find the probability of getting 1 in any of the dice.

A. $\frac{97}{216}$ **B.** $\frac{95}{216}$ **C.** $\frac{93}{216}$ **D.** $\frac{99}{216}$

E. $\frac{91}{216}$

Q.49 If the compound interest on a certain sum at 10% per annum for 3 years and 4 years differ by Rs. 266.2. Find the sum.

A. Rs. 12000   **B.** Rs. 1300

C. Rs. 2000   **D.** Rs. 1800

E. Rs. 1700

Q.50 If an item is sold at a 10% discount to Rohit and a 30% discount to Abhishek and difference between their selling price is Rs. 240. Find the marked price of the article.

A. Rs. 1200   **B.** Rs. 1100   **C.** Rs. 1000   **D.** Rs. 1500

Ques (51-56):Directions: Determine the approximate value of '?' in the following question. (You are not expected to calculate the exact value)

Q.51 $\left(\frac{1.987}{4.914}\right) + \left(\frac{4.895}{6.958}\right) - \left(\frac{0.999}{9.989}\right) = ?$

A. $\frac{11}{10}$ **B.** $\frac{21}{20}$ **C.** $\frac{36}{35}$ **D.** $\frac{51}{50}$

E. $\frac{71}{70}$

Q.52 (75.5% of 5.23) + 7.77 = ?

A. 5   **B.** 12   **C.** 19   **D.** 26

E. 29

Q.53 725.34 + 887.12 – (2 × ?) = 999.88

A. 165   **B.** 306

C. 152   **D.** 290

E. None of these

Q.54 $\frac{(23.01)^2 - (12.92)^2}{(33.92)^2 - (15.98)^2} = ?$

A. 1   **B.** 2   **C.** 0.4   **D.** 0.9

E. 100

Q.55 $\left(\frac{75.12 \times 124.95}{374.85}\right)^2 = ?$

A. 500   **B.** 300   **C.** 256   **D.** 625

E. 100

Q.56 ($\sqrt{64.09}$ × 23.95 - 31) ÷ 6.89 = ?

A. 14   **B.** 35   **C.** 27   **D.** 48

E. 23

Ques (57-61):Directions: The line chart given below represent the salary and expenditure (in Rs.) of Rakesh for the given period.

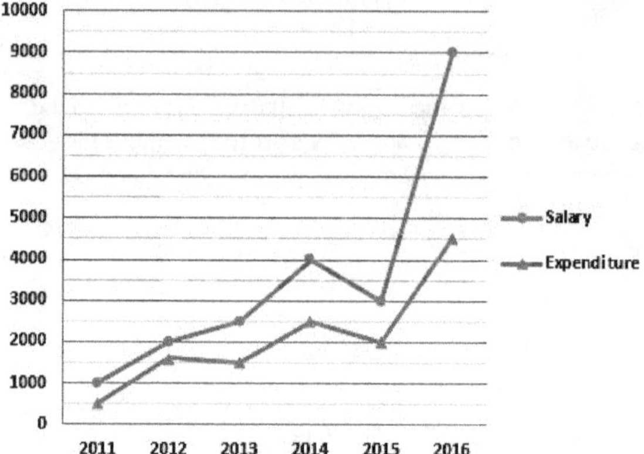

Q.57 In the year 2015, Rakesh invested 50% of his saving in the stock market, where he earned a profit of 300%. What was the profit?

A. 500   **B.** 3000   **C.** 1500   **D.** 780

E. 2000

Q.58 According to a non-government company if a person save at least 27% of his salary in a year that year can be called as "a year of investment". How many years are "a year of investment" during the given period?

A. 5   **B.** 3   **C.** 1   **D.** 7

E. 2

Q.59 Find in which year the percentage increase in the salary of Rakesh was maximum.

A. 2012   **B.** 2013   **C.** 2014   **D.** 2015

E. 2016

Q.60 Find by what percent the salary of Rakesh was increased in 2016 over 2012.

A. 35%   **B.** 230%   **C.** 450%   **D.** 350%

E. 92%

Q.61 Find the compound annual growth rate (CAGR) of the salary of Rakesh during 2011-16. (Given: $9^{\frac{1}{5}} = 1.55$)

A. 55%   **B.** 23%   **C.** 45%   **D.** 88%

E. 92%

Q.62 Directions: In the given question, two equations numbered I and II are given. You have to solve both the equations and mark the appropriate answer.

I. $x^2 = 841$

II. $y^2 - 15y - 76 = 0$

A. x > y

B. x < y

C. x ≥ y

D. x ≤ y

E. x = y or relationship between x and y cannot be established

Q.63 Directions: In the given question, two equations numbered I and II are given. You have to solve both the equations and mark the appropriate answer.

I. $x^2 - 5x - 84 = 0$

II. $y^2 - 3y - 88 = 0$

A. x > y

B. x < y

C. x ≥ y

D. x ≤ y

E. Either x = y or the relationship between x and y cannot be established.

Q.64 Directions: In this question, two equations numbered I and II are given. You have to solve both the equations and find out the correct option.

I. $6x^2 - 49x + 99 = 0$

II. $5y^2 + 17y + 14 = 0$

A. If x ≥ y

B. If x ≤ y

C. If x > y

D. If x < y

E. If the relationship between x and y cannot be established or x = y.

Q.65 Directions: In the given questions, two equations numbered I and II are given. You have to solve both the equations and mark the appropriate answer.

I. $x^2 = 361$

II. $y = \sqrt{361}$

A. x > y

B. x ≥ y

C. x < y

D. x ≤ y

E. x = y or the relationship cannot be established

Reasoning Ability

Ques (66-70):Directions: In the question, three statements are given, followed by three conclusions. You have to consider the statements to be true even if they seem to be at variance from commonly known facts. You have to decide which of the given conclusions, if any, follows from the given statements and select the appropriate option.

Q.66 Statements:

1. Some P are D.

2. All C are A.

3. No P is A.

Conclusions:

I. No C is P.

II. No C is D.

III. Some A are definitely D.

A. Only I follows

B. Only I, II, III follows

C. Only II, III follows

D. Only I, III follows

E. No conclusion follows

Q.67 Statements:

1. All C are X.

2. All X are P.

3. No Q is C.

Conclusions:

I. Some X are not Q.

II. Some Q may be both X and P.

III. Some P are not Q.

A. Only I follows

B. Only I, II, III follows

C. Only II, III follows

D. Only I, III follows

E. No conclusion follows

Q.68 Statements:

1. No F is E.

2. No E is C.

3. No Y is E.

Conclusions:

I. Some F are C.

II. Some Y are F.

III. Some C are Y.

A. Only I, II follows

B. Only I, II, III follows

C. Only II, III follows

D. Only III follows

E. No conclusion follows

Q.69 Statements:

1. All P are T.

2. Some T are J.

3. Some X are J.

Conclusions:

I. Some X may be P.

II. No J is p.

III. Some X may be both J and T.

A. Only I, III follows

B. Only I, II, III follows

C. Only II, III follows

D. Only I, II follows

E. No conclusion follows

Q.70 Statements:

1. All H are E.

2. All E are D.

3. All D are M.

Conclusions:

I. Some M are not H.

II. Some D are not H.

III. Some E are not M.

A. Only I, II follows

B. Only III follows

C. Only I, II, III follows

D. Only II, III follows

E. No conclusion follows

Ques (71-75):Directions: Study the following information and answer the questions given below:

8 persons Amar, Bikram, Charan, Deepak, Edward, Flint, Gautham and Hari are sitting in 2 parallel rows. Both the rows are facing the north and 4 persons are sitting in each of the rows. The rows are arranged such that exactly one person from the second row sits behind a person from the first row. Each one of them likes a different colour among yellow, blue, orange, red, green, white, black and cyan. Further, the following information is known about them.

Amar sits behind the person who likes yellow. The person who likes blue is sitting to the left of Bikram and he is the only neighbour of Bikram. Amar and Bikram are not sitting in the same row. The person who likes yellow is sitting adjacent to the person who likes blue. Amar is sitting adjacent to the person who likes green. The person who likes green is not sitting behind the person who likes blue. Charan is sitting behind the person who likes cyan. Charan does not like green. The persons who like red and orange are sitting adjacent to each other. None of them is a neighbour of the person who likes green. Charan does not like red. Deepak likes white. Flint is sitting adjacent to the person who likes blue. Edward does not like red but he is a neighbour of Amar. Gautham does not like blue.

Q.71 Who likes red?

A. Amar   **B.** Harish   **C.** Gautham   **D.** Bikram
E. Charan

Q.72 Who is sitting behind Flint?

A. Edward   **B.** Amar   **C.** Gautham   **D.** Charan
E. Deepak

Q.73 What colour does the person sitting behind the person who likes white like?

A. Red   **B.** Orange   **C.** Black   **D.** White
E. Green

Q.74 Who likes cyan?

A. Bikram   **B.** Harish   **C.** Gautham   **D.** Amar
E. Edward

Q.75 What colour does Amar like?

A. Green   **B.** Red   **C.** Black   **D.** Orange
E. Cyan

Ques (76-78):Directions: Study the following information and answer the questions given below:

Eight persons – Sheetal, Sam, Soni, Shiva, Sunny, Seema, Saurav and Sita are sitting in a row and all are facing north. Sam, an immediate neighbour of Seema, sits fourth from one of the end. Soni sits immediate right of Seema. Sheetal is second to the left of Saurav. More than three persons sit between Shiva and Sita but none of them sits extreme ends. Shiva is not a neighbour of Sunny. Soni sits third from one of the end.

Q.76 What is the position of Sheetal?

A. Second from the left
B. Third from the right
C. Extreme left
D. Third from the left
E. Extreme right

Q.77 How many persons sit between Soni and Shiva?

A. None   **B.** One   **C.** Two   **D.** Three
E. Four

Q.78 Who sits fourth to the left of Sunny?

A. Sam   **B.** Soni   **C.** Saurav   **D.** Seema
E. Sheetal

Ques (79-81):Directions: Study the information carefully and answer the questions given below:

Among the six persons P, Q, R, S, T and U each have different weight. U is heavier than 3 persons, T is lighter than P. Q is lighter than only R. T is not the lightest. The second heaviest is of 65 kg and the second lightest person is of 33 kg.

Q.79 After arranging the person in ascending order of their weight find the person who comes immediately after T?

A. A   **B.** U
C. Q   **D.** P
E. None of these

Q.80 After arranging the person in ascending order of their weight find the person in the fourth position?

A. U   **B.** T
C. P   **D.** Q
E. None of these

Q.81 After arranging the person in ascending order of their weight from left to right, Persons whose weight is 65 kg is at which position with respect to T?

A. Third to the right   **B.** Fourth to the right
C. Second to the left   **D.** Immediate left
E. Immediate right

Ques (82-85):Directions: The following questions are based on the three-digit numbers given below.

287   894   769   923   456

Q.82 If '1' is added to the last digit of each number, how many numbers thus formed are divisible by 4?

A. None   **B.** One   **C.** Two   **D.** Three
E. Four

Q.83 If in each number the positions of the first and second digits are interchanged then, what will be the sum of the digits of the second-highest number in the new arrangement?

A. 21   **B.** 17   **C.** 22   **D.** 23
E. 15

Q.84 If all digits in each number are arranged in ascending order within the number, which of the following will form the third-highest number in the new arrangement?

A. 456   **B.** 287   **C.** 894   **D.** 769
E. 923

Q.85 What will be the result if the second digit of the highest number is multiplied by the first digit of the lowest number?

A. 18   **B.** 16   **C.** 3   **D.** 4
E. 8

Ques (86-89):Directions: These questions are based on the following information.

P's mother is the sister of R who is Q's daughter. R's brother-in-law has only one son whose grandparents are Q and S, and they have only two daughters. A's husband B is Q's son-in-law.

Q.86 Who is R's sister?

A. P

B. Q

C. S

D. A

E. Cannot be determined

Q.87 Who is B's mother-in-law?

A. P

B. Q

C. S

D. B

E. Cannot be determined

Q.88 What is the relation between Q and A?

A. Father-in law and son-in-law

B. Father and daughter

C. Father/Mother and daughter

D. Mother and daughter

E. Cannot be determined

Q.89 How many grandsons do Q and S have?

A. 1

B. 2

C. 3

D. Either 1 or 2

E. Cannot be determined

Ques (90-94):Directions: Study the following information carefully to answer the given questions.

There are five persons viz. Anil, Diksha, Kishore, Peter and Zuber. They all live in different cities viz Surat, Lucknow, Pune, Nagpur and Udaipur. All of them have different occupations. Kishore lives in Surat but is not an Engineer. The one who is from Pune is a Writer. Zuber is a Lawyer. The engineer is not from Lucknow. Peter is neither a Doctor not a Writer. Anil who is a Manager lives in Nagpur.

Q.90 What is the occupation of the person who is from Udaipur?

A. Lawyer

B. Doctor

C. Writer

D. Manager

E. None of the above

Q.91 What is the occupation of Kishore?

A. Manager

B. Writer

C. Doctor

D. Engineer

E. None of the above

Q.92 Diksha lives in which city?

A. Surat

B. Nagpur

C. Udaipur

D. Lucknow

E. Pune

Q.93 Zuber lives in which city?

A. Surat

B. Lucknow

C. Udaipur

D. Nagpur

E. None of the above

Q.94 Which of the following combination is correct?

A. Lawyer - Udaipur

B. Engineer - Surat

C. Doctor - Nagpur

D. Engineer - Lucknow

E. Doctor - Surat

Q.95 Direction: In a certain code language, 'REGIONAL' is coded as 'RANOIGEL'. How is 'UNIVERSE' written in that language?

A. USREINVE

B. USEVEINE

C. USREVINE

D. UIVSRENE

E. USRNIVEE

Ques (96-100):Directions: In this question, the relationship between different elements is shown in the statements. These statements are followed by two conclusions.

Q.96 Statement: C ≥ M > F < A = B > S

Conclusions:

I. C > B

II. F < S

A. Only conclusion I follow

B. Only conclusion II follows

C. Either conclusion I or II follows

D. Neither conclusion I nor II follows

E. Both conclusions I and II follow

Q.97 Statements: H = M ≤ W; C ≥ W < S

Conclusions:

I. C = M

II. C > M

A. Only conclusion I is true

B. Only conclusion II is true

C. Either conclusion I or II is true

D. Neither conclusion I nor II is true

E. Both conclusions I and II are true

Q.98 Statement: H < Y, Y ≥ R, R > W

Conclusions:

I. W < Y

II. R ≤ Y

A. Only conclusion I is true

B. Only conclusion II is true

C. Either conclusion I or II is true

D. Neither conclusion I nor II is true

E. Both conclusion I and II are true

Q.99 Statement: A ≤ P > B; C > P; F ≤ B

Conclusions:

I. C > A

II. F < P

A. Only conclusions I is true

B. Only conclusions II is true

C. Either conclusions I or II is true

D. Neither conclusions I nor II is true

E. Both conclusions I and II are true

Q.100 Statements: $A \leq B < C$; $A \geq E$; $C \leq F$

Conclusions:

I. $E < C$

II. $F \geq E$

A. Only conclusion I is true

B. Only conclusion II is true

C. Only conclusion I or II is true

D. Neither conclusion I nor II is true

E. Both conclusions I and II are true

// Smart Answer Sheet //

Correct — Percentage of students who answered correctly. **Skipped** — Percentage of students who skipped.

Q.	Ans.	Correct	Skipped	Q.	Ans.	Correct	Skipped	Q.	Ans.	Correct	Skipped	Q.	Ans.	Correct	Skipped	Q.	Ans.	Correct	Skipped
1	E	7.29 %	51.04 %	17	B	7.29 %	92.71 %	33	C	4.17 %	63.54 %	49	C	4.17 %	86.45 %	65	D	8.33 %	89.59 %
2	C	9.38 %	57.29 %	18	D	5.21 %	92.71 %	34	E	28.12 %	58.34 %	50	A	5.21 %	86.46 %	66	A	27.08 %	54.17 %
3	A	21.88 %	56.24 %	19	A	2.08 %	92.71 %	35	D	40.62 %	55.21 %	51	E	8.33 %	86.46 %	67	B	19.79 %	56.25 %
4	D	7.29 %	60.42 %	20	B	1.04 %	92.71 %	36	C	1.04 %	66.67 %	52	B	8.33 %	86.46 %	68	E	31.25 %	56.25 %
5	C	3.12 %	60.42 %	21	C	5.21 %	92.71 %	37	D	30.21 %	58.33 %	53	B	11.46 %	86.46 %	69	A	30.21 %	57.29 %
6	C	8.33 %	86.46 %	22	A	4.17 %	92.71 %	38	E	5.21 %	68.75 %	54	C	10.42 %	86.46 %	70	E	18.75 %	58.33 %
7	C	8.33 %	87.5 %	23	B	2.08 %	92.71 %	39	A	12.5 %	67.71 %	55	D	10.42 %	86.46 %	71	C	7.29 %	67.71 %
8	E	3.12 %	87.5 %	24	A	2.08 %	92.71 %	40	D	5.21 %	69.79 %	56	E	11.46 %	86.46 %	72	B	6.25 %	69.79 %
9	D	1.04 %	86.46 %	25	A	2.08 %	92.71 %	41	B	2.08 %	68.75 %	57	C	4.17 %	86.45 %	73	E	10.42 %	69.79 %
10	A	5.21 %	87.5 %	26	C	6.25 %	92.71 %	42	C	3.12 %	71.88 %	58	A	2.08 %	88.54 %	74	A	9.38 %	70.83 %
11	E	2.08 %	87.5 %	27	D	2.08 %	92.71 %	43	A	14.58 %	61.46 %	59	E	6.25 %	88.54 %	75	C	8.33 %	69.79 %
12	A	5.21 %	87.5 %	28	B	3.12 %	92.71 %	44	E	18.75 %	70.83 %	60	D	5.21 %	88.54 %	76	C	9.38 %	86.45 %
13	B	8.33 %	89.59 %	29	A	6.25 %	92.71 %	45	B	2.08 %	86.46 %	61	A	1.04 %	87.5 %	77	D	11.46 %	86.46 %
14	E	2.08 %	92.71 %	30	B	4.17 %	92.71 %	46	E	4.17 %	86.45 %	62	E	7.29 %	88.54 %	78	A	11.46 %	86.46 %
15	B	7.29 %	92.71 %	31	D	7.29 %	66.67 %	47	E	3.12 %	86.46 %	63	E	8.33 %	88.55 %	79	D	9.38 %	86.45 %
16	C	5.21 %	92.71 %	32	E	16.67 %	62.5 %	48	E	0 %	100 %	64	C	6.25 %	89.58 %	80	A	9.38 %	86.45 %

Q.	Ans.	Correct		Q.	Ans.	Correct		Q.	Ans.	Correct		Q.	Ans.	Correct		Q.	Ans.	Correct
		Skipped				Skipped				Skipped				Skipped				Skipped
81	A	7.29 % 86.46 %		85	D	8.33 % 86.46 %		89	A	8.33 % 86.46 %		93	B	9.38 % 87.5 %		97	C	6.25 % 89.58 %
82	C	9.38 % 86.45 %		86	D	8.33 % 86.46 %		90	E	7.29 % 86.46 %		94	E	9.38 % 87.5 %		98	E	4.17 % 89.58 %
83	B	9.38 % 86.45 %		87	E	6.25 % 86.46 %		91	C	10.42 % 87.5 %		95	C	7.29 % 87.5 %		99	E	5.21 % 89.58 %
84	A	9.38 % 86.45 %		88	C	8.33 % 86.46 %		92	E	9.38 % 87.5 %		96	D	7.29 % 88.54 %		100	A	6.25 % 88.54 %

//Hints and Solutions//

1. An objection is often raised against realistic biography because it reveals so much that is important and even sacred about a man's life. The real objection to it will rather be found in the fact that it reveals about a man the precise points which are unimportant. It reveals and asserts and insists on exactly those things in a man's life of which the man himself is wholly unconscious; his exact class in society, the circumstances of his ancestry, the place of his present location. These are things which do not, properly speaking, ever arise before the human (1)vision.

From the context, we can infer that the missing word is a noun. So, we can eliminate verbs in options (B) and (C). From the paragraph, we can infer that the word means sight or vision. Only something that does not appear in our vision can be considered to be unconscious. So, option (E).

Hence, the correct option is (E).

2. A man no more thinks about himself as the inhabitant of the third house in a row of Brixton villas than he thinks about himself as a strange animal with two legs. What a man's name was, what his income was, whom he married, where he lived, these are not sanctities; they are (2)irrelevancies.

Given the parallel structure of the sentence, the missing word should be a noun. So, we can eliminate options (D) and (E). In the paragraph, the author is trying to say that these details should not really matter while describing a person. So, the word "irrelevancies" is the most appropriate word for the blank.

Hence, the correct option is (C).

3. A very strong case of this is the case of the Brontës. The Brontë is in the position of the mad lady in a country village; her (3)eccentricities form an endless source of innocent conversation to that exceedingly mild and bucolic circle, the literary world.

From the paragraph, we can infer that the Brontes are heavily gossiped about. So, we can eliminate options (B) and (E) as they do not suit the content of the paragraph. It Is given in the paragraph that the gossips collect all sorts of trivia about the Brontes. So, the appropriate word for the blank would be eccentricities.

Hence, the correct option is (A).

4. The truly glorious gossips of literature, like Mr. Augustine Birrell and Mr. Andrew Lang, never tire of collecting all the glimpses and (4)anecdotes and sermons and side-lights and sticks and straws which will go to make a Brontë museum.

The missing word is part of the list - glimpses, sermons, sidelights. The author says that all these would be personal details that could go into a museum on the Brontes. We can eliminate option (A) as it would be a repeat of the word glimpses. Lives and amusements do not fit in the list. Between anecdotes and passions, observers are more likely to note anecdotes and preserve them while writing biographies of people.

Hence, the correct option is (D).

5. For the Brontë, genius was above all things deputed to (5)assert the supreme unimportance of externals. The author says that Charlotte Bronte, through her work, showed that the exterior was irrelevant. Hence, through her work, she made the assertion about the unimportance of externals. So, the missing word should be asserted.

Hence, the correct option is (C).

6. Let us look at the meanings of the words before we decide on the contextually appropriate one.

'Shrank' is the past form of the word 'shrink' and means 'to become smaller in size'.

'Knocked' is 'to make a noise'.

'Commenced' means 'started'.

'Lit' is the past tense and the past participle of the word 'light'.

Given the context, a battle cannot 'shrink', 'knock', or 'light' if an army advances. Therefore, the correct word to use in this context is 'commenced'.

Hence, the correct option is (C).

7. The only correct option is 'susceptibility' that makes the mother prone to sickness.

Aberration ⇒ a state or condition markedly different from the norm

Abjure ⇒ formally reject or disavow a formerly held belief

Temperament ⇒ a person's or animal's nature, especially as it permanently affects their behaviour.

Abnegation ⇒ the denial and rejection of a doctrine or belief

Hence, the correct option is (C).

8. The correct option is helm as it means 'a position of leadership or control' which fits well in the given context.

Accost ⇒ approach and speak to someone aggressively or insistently

Adamant ⇒ impervious to pleas, persuasion, requests, reason

Acumen ⇒ shrewdness shown by keen insight

Accretion ⇒ an increase by natural growth or addition

Hence, the correct option is (E).

9. The correct option is 'orderliness' which means 'being well-arranged and organized'.

Rejig ⇒ organize (something) differently; rearrange.

Cohort ⇒ a group of people with a shared characteristic.

Seamless ⇒ Smooth.

Pester ⇒ trouble or annoy (someone) with frequent or persistent requests or interruptions.

Hence, the correct option is (D).

10. The meaning of the given idioms:

(A) Dead in the water: means 'Unable to function effectively.'

(B) Draining the swamp: is a metaphor which means 'to root out corruption.'

(C) A flash in the pan: means 'a thing or the person whose sudden but brief success is not repeated or repeatable.'

(D) Dead as a dodo: means 'Completely dead or extinct.'

(E) A dead ringer: means 'A person or thing that looks very similar.'

Hence, the correct option is (A).

11. The meaning of the given words in the options.

- Under no illusions: be completely conscious of the real status of the situation.
- Thrown under the bus: to betray a partner, colleague or close friend for self-benefits.
- A goose egg: literally refers to zero or nothing.
- Under a spell: bewitched, held by the power of the magical spell.
- Under siege: to be under attack or face severe criticism.

Therefore, the sentence is: Their corporate offices were **under siege** after their stocks plummeted last week.

Hence, the correct option is (E).

12. The meaning of the given words in the options.

- Ahead of the curve: better than others.
- Fan the flames: to make a bad situation even worse.
- Pipe dream: refers to an impossibility.
- In the loop: to be aware of the information.
- Thrown down to the gauntlet: to accept a challenge.

Therefore, the sentence is: He sold his shares in Nokia and put it into Apple because he realized they were ahead of the curve.

Hence, the correct option is (A).

13. The meaning of the given words in the options.

- Bang for the buck: value for money.
- The way forward: the only way to succeed.
- Pipe dream: refers to an impossibility.
- Herculean task: a task requiring huge amounts of physical strength.
- Ahead of the curve: better than others.

Therefore, the sentence is: I believe that digital learning is the only way forward.

Hence, the correct option is (B).

14. Resistance means the refusal to accept or comply with something.

- Cohesiveness means the quality of forming a united whole.
- Distinctive means characteristic of one person or thing, and so serving to distinguish it from others.

- Influence means the capacity to have an effect on the character, development, or behaviour of someone or something, or the effect itself.
- Domains means specified spheres of activity or knowledge.

Clearly, 'resistance' is correct.

Hence, the correct option is (E).

15. Urban means in, relating to, or characteristic of a town or city.

Let's look at the meaning of the given words-

- Rural means in, relating to, or characteristic of the countryside rather than the town.
- Town means a built-up area with a name, defined boundaries, and local government, that is larger than a village and generally smaller than a city.
- Household means a house and its occupants regarded as a unit.
- City means a large town.
- Suburb means an outlying district of a city, especially a residential one.

Clearly, 'rural' is correct.

Hence, the correct option is (B).

16. It is mentioned that "India is, without a doubt, committed to English as a national language. The impact of English is not only continuing but increasing."

Hence, the correct option is (C).

17. It is mentioned that "One can see a Hindi-speaking teacher giving their students instructions during an educational tour about where to meet and when their bus would leave, but all in English."

Hence, the correct option is (B).

18. Upon reading the passage, we can find that options (B) and (C) together will be the answer.

Hence, the correct option is (D).

19. 'Neither' should be there in place of 'none'.

A pronoun is a word that is used instead of a noun or noun phrase. Pronouns refer to either a noun that has already been mentioned or to a noun that does not need to be named specifically.

'None of the' is used for more than two persons or objects, 'neither of the' is used for two objects.

- E.g. None of the three flowers is red.
- Neither of the two teachers is competent.

The correct sentence should be: Neither of these two officers has been looking after his department well.

Hence, the correct option is (A).

20. 'assent' should be there in place of 'ascent'.

Singular nouns are followed by singular verbs and plural nouns are followed by plural verbs.

"Ascent" means 'a climb or walk to the summit of a mountain or hill' which does not make any sense in the given context.

The correct word in place of 'ascent' would be 'assent' which means 'the expression of approval or agreement'.

- For E.g. The ascent of Fuji presents no difficulties.
- Prince Bagration bowed his head in sign of assent.

The correct sentence is: The strict boss did not give her assent to the employee's whimsical request.

Hence, the correct option is (B).

21. 'their' should be there in place of 'his'.

A pronoun is a word that is used instead of a noun or noun phrase. Pronouns refer to either a noun that has already been mentioned or to a noun that does not need to be named specifically.

When two singular nouns are joined by 'and' refer to two different persons the pronoun used for them should be 'plural'.

- E.g.: Ashwin and Hardik are brothers. They play cricket.

The correct sentence should be: The Party Chief and the Chief Minister expressed their views on demonetization in India.

Hence, the correct option is (C).

22. 'provide' should be there in place of 'provides'

Singular nouns are followed by singular verbs and plural nouns are followed by plural verbs.

A singular noun names one person. place. thing. or idea. while a plural noun names more than one person. place. thing, or idea.

The usage of the verb singular 'provides' is erroneous and needs to be replaced with the plural form of the verb 'provide' to make the sentence grammatically and contextually correct.

According to the subject-verb agreement, if the subject is singular then it is followed by a singular verb and if the subject is plural it is followed by a plural verb. Here the subject is 'US laws' which is plural and hence is followed by a plural verb.

- E.g. The dog chases the cat.
- The dogs chase the cat.

The correct sentence is: Unlike Indian laws, US laws provide for a contingency fee of lawyering, where the costs of litigation are borne by lawyers

Hence, the correct option is (A).

23. 'global' should be there in place of 'globe'

The usage of the noun 'globe' is erroneous and needs to be replaced with the adjective 'global' to make the sentence grammatically and contextually correct. This is because we need an adjective to modify the noun 'praise'. 'Globe' is a noun.

- E.g. This sacrifice was the least he could do for his friend.

- It was as if he'd tossed out a sacrificial lamb to a flock of vultures.

The correct sentence is: India's Swachh Bharat Mission is receiving global praise for attempting to close the sanitation gap.

Hence, the correct option is (B).

24. If we read the two sentences, we can observe that they are related by cause and effect relationship. And among the choices available, only 'now that' can be used in this context as we use it to give an explanation of a new situation.

The connected statement would be:

"Now that" I live only a few blocks from work, I walk to work and enjoy it.

Hence, the correct option is (A).

25. The sentences given suggest that the house sparkled in an empty kind of way after it was waxed and the furniture got polished.

We use once as a conjunction meaning 'as soon as' or 'after'.

The connected statement would be:

"Once" the floors had been waxed and the furniture got polished by afternoon, the house sparkled but in an empty kind of way.

Hence, the correct option is (A).

26. The given sentences suggest that the man goes to a park and the second sentence gives the reason behind his action.

We use as to state the purpose of an object or action.

The connected statement would be:

The man goes to the park every Sunday **"As"** he loves watching the ducks in the lake.

Hence, the correct option is (C).

27. Option (C) is incorrect as neither of the connectors fit in meaningfully. Option (A) and (B) both are correct.

The connected statements would be:

I. China has decided to ban the imports of plastic waste into the country and "Now" a lot of countries will have to make new plans for their disposal.

II. China has decided to ban the imports of plastic waste into the country and "Hence" a lot of countries will have to make new plans for their disposal.

I. A lot of countries will have to make new plans for their disposal "As" China has decided to ban the imports of plastic waste into the country.

II. A lot of countries will have to make new plans for their disposal "Since" China has decided to ban the imports of plastic waste into the country.

Hence, the correct option is (D).

28. The first statement is regarding the issue faced by the person whereas the second statement is regarding the activity on the part of the person despite the problems faced by him or her.

Among the given connectors, only (B) can connect these two statements since it implies 'in spite of something'.

Since is mainly used to indicate the cause-effect relationship whereas on the other hand is used in order to imply something contrasting to what has been said already.

The complete statement would be:

I was not in a situation to step out of the house yesterday because of my severe headache, **"Nevertheless"**, I attended the sales meeting at my office on the instructions of my senior management.

Hence, the correct option is (B).

29. These two statements share a relationship of cause and effect since we are talking about the reason of going to sleep without having dinner also. The reason is that I was very tired for spending the whole day at the hospital.

Among the given options, so can only be used in the given context to imply the cause and effect relationship.

The complete sentence would be:

I was very tired and exhausted after spending the whole day at the hospital, **"So"**, I went to sleep without having dinner after coming back.

Hence, the correct option is (A).

30. Here, the first statement is regarding the certainty of the minister coming to this locality in order to do election campaigning but the second statement gives a condition in which there is a possibility that the minister may not come here for the purpose of election campaigning.

Among the given options, unless may be used to connect the two statements since it can give the condition imposed on something taking place. Since is used to imply the cause-effect relationship whereas in addition to is used to imply that something more may have to be said.

The complete sentence would be:

The minister will definitely come to this locality for election campaigning within the next two days **"Unless"** he is denied the ticket from this constituency by his party.

Hence, the correct option is (B).

31. According to the question,

Selling price of 12 pens = Cost price of 14 pens

$12 \times SP = 14 \times CP$

$\Rightarrow SP = \left(\dfrac{7}{6}\right) \times CP$

Profit = $\dfrac{(SP - CP)}{CP} \times 100\% = 16.67\%$

So, if the cost price is 100, the profit is 16.67

Tax = 10% = $\left(\dfrac{10}{100}\right) \times 16.67 = 1.67$

So, net profit = 16.67 - 1.67 = 15

So, the shopkeeper is making a net profit of 15 when the cost price is 100.

$\Rightarrow$ Net profit percentage = 15%

Hence, the correct option is (D).

32. Let the total amount of work be done by 60 units. (LCM of 10 and 12)

So, Ajay does 6 units of work in 1 day and Vijay does 5 units of work in one day.

So, when they are working together, they can finish 11 units of work in 1 day.

In 4 days, they will complete 44 units of work.

The remaining 16 units of work can be completed by Ajay in $\dfrac{16}{6} = 2\dfrac{2}{3}$ days.

Therefore, total time taken = 4 + $2\dfrac{2}{3} = 6\dfrac{2}{3}$

Hence, the correct option is (E).

33. The series follows the pattern given below:

$13 = 2^4 - 2^2 + 2 - 1$

$74 = 3^4 - 3^2 + 3 - 1$

$243 = 4^4 - 4^2 + 4 - 1$

$604 = 5^4 - 5^2 + 5 - 1$

$1265 = 6^4 - 6^2 + 6 - 1$

$2358 = 7^4 - 7^2 + 7 - 1$

$4039 = 8^4 - 8^2 + 8 - 1$

So, the missing number is 243.

Hence, the correct option is (C).

34. The given series follows the below pattern.

Multiplication by two and subtraction by three.

$46 = 23 \times 2$

$43 = 46 - 3$

$86 = 43 \times 2$

$83 = 86 - 3$

$166 = 83 \times 2$

So, the required number is 43.

Hence, the correct option is (E).

35. The given series follow this pattern is,

$99 - 1^1 = 98$

$98 - 2^1 = 96$

$96 - 1^2 = 95$

$95 - 2^2 = 91$

$91 - 1^3 = 90$

$90 - 2^3 = 82$

So, the number that follows is $82 - 1^4 = 81$

Hence, the correct option is (D).

36. Each of the numbers given in the series is perfect cube of prime numbers.

$4913 = 17^3$

$6859 = 19^3$

$12167 = 23^3$

$24389 = 29^3$

So, $31^3 = 29791$

Hence, the correct option is (C).

37. The difference between consecutive numbers of the series is getting multiplied by 2.

$17 - 15 = 2$

$21 - 17 = 4$

$29 - 21 = 8$

$45 - 29 = 16$

So, the correct answer to replace the question marks is 21.

Hence, the correct option is (D).

38. According to the given data,

Increased number of candidates from 2011 = 8% of 87500 = 7000

Number of candidates appeared in 2015 = 87500 + 7000 = 94500

Number of candidates qualified in 2015 = 25% of 94500 = 23625

Hence, the correct option is (E).

39. According to the given data,

Number of qualified candidates $\Rightarrow$ 28% of 75000 = 21000

Number of qualified female candidates $\Rightarrow$ 21000 - 6500 = 14500

The ratio of Female to Male qualified candidates $\Rightarrow$ 14500 : 6500 $\Rightarrow$ 29 : 13

Hence, the correct option is (A).

40. Number of qualified candidates in 2014

$\Rightarrow$ 40% of 120000 = 48000

Let the number of qualified candidates in 2011 be 'x'.

$\Rightarrow x + 48000 = (2 \times 37125)$

$\Rightarrow x = 26250$

Percentage of qualified candidates,

$\Rightarrow \dfrac{26250}{87500} \times 100 = 30\%$

Hence, the correct option is (D).

41. According to the given data,

Let number of qualified candidates be 13k

Male qualified = 5k and Female qualified = 8k

$\Rightarrow 3k = 13650$

$\Rightarrow k = 4550$

$\Rightarrow 13k = 59150$

Let the number of appeared candidates be 'y'.

$\Rightarrow$ 65% of y = 59150

$\Rightarrow y = 91000$

Hence, the correct option is (B).

42. According to the given data,

Let the number of candidates appeared be '5k'.

The number of candidates qualified will be '2k'.

Number of qualified female candidates

$\Rightarrow \dfrac{4}{9}$ of 2k $= \dfrac{8k}{9}$

Percentage of qualified female candidates

$\Rightarrow \dfrac{\frac{8k}{9}}{5k} \times 100 = 17.77\%$

Hence, the correct option is (C).

43. The formula used is $x^a \times x^b = x^{a+b}$

$47^{.9856} \times 47^{.0144} - 47 = ?$

$\Rightarrow 47^{.9856+.0144} - 47 = ?$

$\Rightarrow 47^1 - 47 = ?$

$\Rightarrow ? = 0$

Hence, the correct option is (A).

44. The given equation is:

$$2\dfrac{3}{5} \text{ of } 3\dfrac{1}{13} + 1\dfrac{2}{3} \times 4\dfrac{1}{5}$$

On simplifying, we get,

$$= \dfrac{13}{5} \times \dfrac{40}{13} + \dfrac{5}{3} \times \dfrac{21}{5}$$

$$= \dfrac{40}{5} + \dfrac{21}{3} = 8 + 7 = 15$$

Hence, the correct option is (E).

45. Given:

Total profit = Rs. 2079

We know that,

Profit ratio = Investment × Time period

Total investment of A = 400 × 10 + 700 × 2 = Rs. 5400

Total investment of B = 600 × 5 + 700 × 7 = Rs. 7900

Total investment of C = 800 × 7 = Rs. 5600

Ratio between their profit shares = 5400 : 7900 : 5600

= 54 : 79 : 56

∴ Required difference = $\dfrac{56}{189} \times 2079 - \dfrac{54}{189} \times 2079$

= Rs. 22

Hence, the correct option is (B).

46. Given:

Length of goods train = 400 m

Speed of Goods train = 90 kmph = $90 \times \dfrac{5}{18}$ = 25 m/s

Length of another train = 350 m

Formula:

Relative speed when trains are moving in the same direction = Speed of one train – Speed of another train

Let the length of the platform be A m.

⇒ $\dfrac{(400+A)}{25}$ = 22

⇒ A = 150 m

Let the speed of other train be B m/s.

⇒ $\dfrac{(350+150)}{25}$ = B

⇒ B = 20 m/s

∴ The relative speed of both trains when they are moving in the same direction = 25 – 20

= 5 m/s = $5 \times \dfrac{18}{5}$ = 18 kmph

Hence, the correct option is (E).

47. Given:

Pipe P's 1 hour's work = $\dfrac{1}{18}$

Pipe Q's 1 hour's work = $\dfrac{1}{12}$

Pipe (P + Q)'s 1 hour's work = $\dfrac{1}{18} + \dfrac{1}{12} = \dfrac{5}{36}$

Pipe (P + Q)'s 7 hours work = $7 \times \dfrac{5}{36} = \dfrac{35}{36}$

⇒ Remaining work = $1 - \dfrac{35}{36} = \dfrac{1}{36}$

Then,

⇒ $\dfrac{1}{36} \times R = 1$

⇒ R = 36

Pipe R's 1 hour's work = $\dfrac{1}{36}$

⇒ Pipe (P + Q + R)'s 1 hour's work = $\dfrac{1}{18} + \dfrac{1}{12} + \dfrac{1}{36} = \dfrac{1}{6}$

∴ It will take 6 hours to fill the tank when all three pipes are opened simultaneously.

Hence, the correct option is (E).

48. Given:

An unbiased dice having 6 faces with numbers from 1 to 6 written in it.

We know that,

Probability = $\dfrac{Total\ favourable\ events}{Total\ events}$

We can get one, two and three.

Probability of getting exactly one = $\left(\dfrac{1}{6}\right) \times \left(\dfrac{5}{6}\right) \times \left(\dfrac{5}{6}\right) \times 3 = \dfrac{75}{216}$

Probability of getting exactly two = $\left(\dfrac{1}{6}\right) \times \left(\dfrac{1}{6}\right) \times \left(\dfrac{5}{6}\right) \times 3 = \dfrac{15}{216}$

Probability of getting exactly three = $\left(\dfrac{1}{6}\right) \times \left(\dfrac{1}{6}\right) \times \left(\dfrac{1}{6}\right) = \dfrac{1}{216}$

All 3 are mutually exclusive.

Whole Probability = Adding all 3 = $\dfrac{(75+15+1)}{216} = \dfrac{91}{216}$

Hence, the correct option is (E).

49. Given:

Time = 3 years, Rate = 10 % per annum, C.I. difference = Rs. 266.2

Formula used:

C.I. difference = $P\left[\left(1 + \dfrac{r}{100}\right)^{t}\right]\left(\dfrac{r}{100}\right)$

Calculation:

$266.2 = P\left[\left(1 + \dfrac{10}{100}\right)^{3}\right]\left(\dfrac{10}{100}\right)$

⇒ $266.2 = P\left(\dfrac{11}{10}\right)^{3}\left(\dfrac{1}{10}\right)$

⇒ P = $\dfrac{(266.2 \times 10 \times 10 \times 10 \times 10)}{(11 \times 11 \times 11)}$

⇒ P = Rs. 2000

Hence, the correct option is (C).

50. Given:

Difference between selling price when the discount rate is 10% and 30% = Rs. 240

Formula used:

Selling price = $\dfrac{(100-Discount\%)}{100}$ × Marked price

Let the marked price be 'x'.

Rohit buy the article at = $\dfrac{90}{100}$ × x

Abhishek buy the article = $\dfrac{70}{100}$ × x

Difference between selling price = 240

$\Rightarrow \dfrac{20}{100}$ × x = 240

$\Rightarrow$ x = 1200

∴ Marked price = Rs. 1200

Hence, the correct option is (A).

51. $\left(\dfrac{1.987}{4.914}\right) + \left(\dfrac{4.895}{6.958}\right) - \left(\dfrac{0.999}{9.989}\right) =?$

Taking approximate values,

$\Rightarrow \left(\dfrac{2}{5}\right) + \left(\dfrac{5}{7}\right) - \left(\dfrac{1}{10}\right) =?$

$\Rightarrow \dfrac{39}{35} - \dfrac{1}{10} =?$

$\therefore ? = \dfrac{71}{70}$

Hence, the correct option is (E).

52. The given expression,

? = (75.5% of 5.23) + 7.77

We can write the given values as,

75.5 ≈ 75, 5.23 ≈ 5 and 7.77 ≈ 8

$\Rightarrow$? = (75% of 5) + 8

$\Rightarrow$? = $\left(\dfrac{75}{100} \times 5\right) + 8$

$\Rightarrow$? = 3.75 + 8

$\Rightarrow$? = 11.75 ≈ 12

∴ ? = 12

Hence, the correct option is (B).

53. Follow BODMAS rules to solve the equation,

$\Rightarrow$ 725.34 + 887.12 − (2 × ?) = 999.88

$\Rightarrow$ 725.34 + 887.12 − 999.88 = 2 × ?

$\Rightarrow$ 1612.46 − 999.88 = 2 × ?

$\Rightarrow$ 612.58 = 2 × ?

∴ ? = 306.29

Hence, the correct option is (B).

54. $\dfrac{(23.01)^2-(12.92)^2}{(33.92)^2-(15.98)^2} =?$

Take approximate values,

$\Rightarrow$ 23.01 ≈ 23

$\Rightarrow$ 12.92 ≈ 13

$\Rightarrow$ 33.92 ≈ 34

$\Rightarrow$ 15.98 ≈ 16

Putting approximated values in the equation,

$\Rightarrow \dfrac{(23)^2-(13)^2}{(34)^2-(16)^2} =?$

Using $a^2 - b^2 = (a + b)(a - b)$, we get

$\Rightarrow \dfrac{(23+13)\times(23-13)}{(34-16)\times(34+16)} =?$

$\Rightarrow \dfrac{36\times10}{18\times50} = 0.4$

∴ ? = 0.4

Hence, the correct option is (C).

55. $\left(\dfrac{75.12\times124.95}{374.85}\right)^2 =?$

Take approximate values,

$\Rightarrow$ 75.12 ≈ 75

$\Rightarrow$ 124.95 ≈ 125

$\Rightarrow$ 374.85 ≈ 375

Putting approximated values in the equation,

$\Rightarrow \left(\dfrac{75\times125}{375}\right)^2 = (25)^2 = 625$

∴ ? = 625

Hence, the correct option is (D).

56. ($\sqrt{64.09}$ × 23.95   31) ÷ 6.89 − ?

Approximating the values to the nearest integer:

$\Rightarrow$ (8 × 24 - 31) ÷ 7 = ?

$\Rightarrow$ (192 - 31) ÷ 7 = ?

$\Rightarrow$? = $\dfrac{161}{7}$

$\Rightarrow$? = 23

Hence, the correct option is (E).

57. Salary in 2015 = Rs. 3000

Expenditure in 2015 = Rs. 2000

Saving = 3000 − 2000 = Rs. 1000

Investment in stock market = $\dfrac{1000}{2}$ = Rs. 500

Profit = 300% of 500 = Rs. 1500

Hence, the correct option is (C).

58. Saving rate = $\dfrac{(Salary - Expenditure)}{Salary} \times 100$

Saving rate for 2011 = $\dfrac{(1000-500)}{1000} \times 100 = 50\%$

Saving rate for 2012 = $\dfrac{(2000-1500)}{2000} \times 100 = 25\%$

Saving rate for 2013 = $\dfrac{(2500-1500)}{2500} \times 100 = 40\%$

Saving rate for 2014 = $\dfrac{(4000-2500)}{4000} \times 100 = 37.5\%$

Saving rate for 2015 = $\dfrac{(3000-2000)}{3000} \times 100 = 33.33\%$

Saving rate for 2016 = $\dfrac{(9000-4500)}{9000} \times 100 = 50\%$

∴ 5 years are a year of investment.

Hence, the correct option is (A).

59. Percentage increase in 2012 = $\dfrac{(2000-1000)}{1000} \times 100 = 100\%$

Percentage increase in 2013 = $\dfrac{(2500-2000)}{2000} \times 100 = 25\%$

Percentage increase in 2014 = $\dfrac{(4000-2500)}{2500} \times 100 = 60\%$

Percentage increase in 2015 = $\dfrac{(3000-4000)}{4000} \times 100 = -25\%$

Percentage increase in 2016 = $\dfrac{(9000-3000)}{3000} \times 100 = 200\%$

∴ In 2016 the percentage increase in the salary of Mohan was maximum.

Hence, the correct option is (E).

60. Salary in 2012 = Rs. 2000

Salary in 2016 = Rs. 9000

∴ Required increase = $\dfrac{(9000-2000)}{2000} \times 100 = 350\%$

Hence, the correct option is (D).

61. Salary in 2011 = Rs. 1000

Salary in 2016 = Rs. 9000

Time period = 5 years

CAGR for period 2011-16 = $\left(\dfrac{Ending\ Salary}{Beginning\ Salary}\right)^{\frac{1}{n}} - 1$

$\Rightarrow \left[\left(\dfrac{9000}{1000}\right)^{\frac{1}{5}} - 1\right] \times 100 = 55\%$

Hence, the correct option is (A).

62. I. $x^2 = 841$

$\Rightarrow x = +29, -29$

II. $y^2 - 15y - 76 = 0$

$\Rightarrow y^2 + 4y - 19y - 76 = 0$

$\Rightarrow (y - 19)(y + 4)$

So, y = 19, y = -4

Value of x	Value of y	Relation
29	19	x > y
29	-4	x > y
-29	19	x < y
-29	-4	x < y

So, the relationship between x and y cannot be established.

Hence, the correct option is (E).

63. I. $x^2 - 5x - 84 = 0$

$x^2 - 12x + 7x - 84 = 0$

$x(x - 12) + 7(x - 12) = 0$

$(x + 7)(x - 12) = 0$

x = -7, x = 12

II. $y^2 - 3y - 88 = 0$

$y^2 - 11y + 8y - 88 = 0$

$y(y - 11) + 8(y - 11) = 0$

$(y + 8)(y - 11) = 0$

y = -8, y = 11

Value of x	Value of y	Result
-7	-8	x > y
-7	11	x < y
12	-8	x > y
12	11	x > y

So, the relationship between x and y cannot be established.

Hence, the correct option is (E).

64. I. $6x^2 - 49x + 99 = 0$

$\Rightarrow (3x - 11)\,(2x - 9) = 0$

$\Rightarrow x = \dfrac{11}{3}, \dfrac{9}{2}$

II. $5y^2 + 17y + 14 = 0$

$\Rightarrow (5y + 7)\,(y + 2) = 0$

$\Rightarrow y = \dfrac{-7}{5}, -2$

So, x > y

Hence, the correct option is (C).

65. Given:

I. $x^2 = 361$

II. y = $\sqrt{361}$

Calculation:

I. $x^2 = 361$

$\Rightarrow x = 19$ or $x = -19$

II. $y = \sqrt{361}$

$\Rightarrow y = 19$

Comparison between x and y (via Tabulation):

Value of x	Relation	Value of y
19	x = y	19
19	x = y	19
-19	x < y	19
-19	x < y	19

∴ We can clearly see that x ≤ y.

Hence, the correct option is (D).

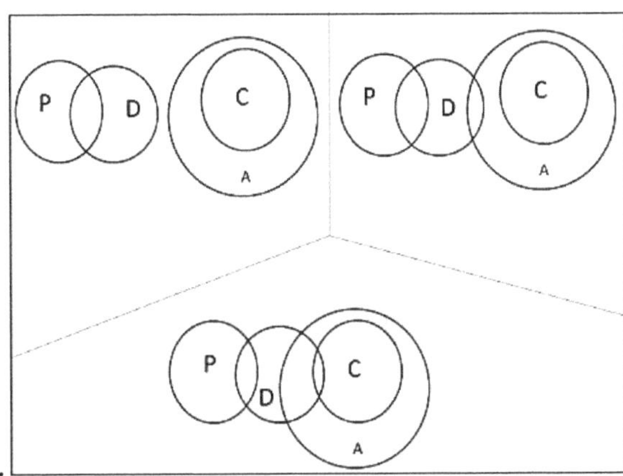

66.

From all the diagrams we can see that all C are A and No P is A so no C is P.

From all the diagrams we can see that Some C maybe D.

From all the diagrams we can see that Some A may/may not D.

So, we can say that only I conclusion follow.

Hence, the correct option is (A).

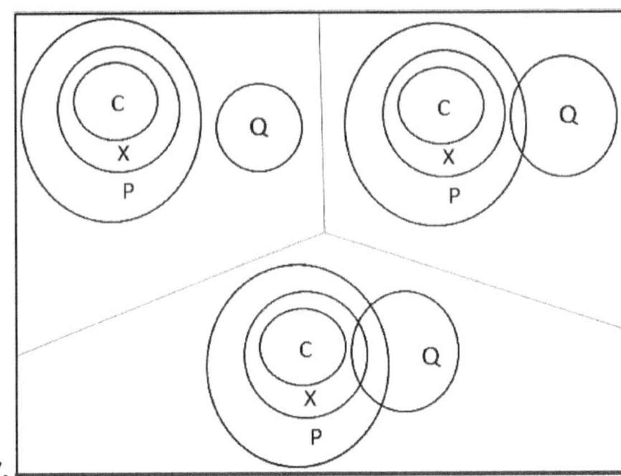

67.

From all the diagrams we can see that all C those are part of X and P can't be Q so conclusions I, III follows.

From all the diagrams we can see that Some Q may be both X and P.

So, we can say that only all I, II, III conclusion follows.

Hence, the correct option is (B).

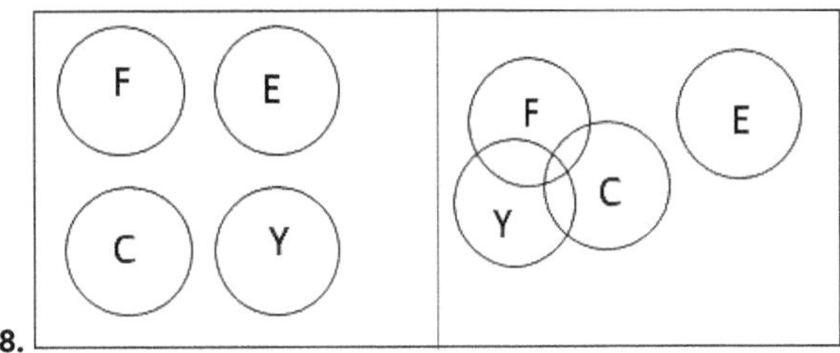

68.

From both the diagrams, we can see that Some F may/may not be C.

From both the diagrams, we can see that Some Y may/may not be F.

From both the diagrams, we can see that Some C may/may not be Y.

So, we can say that no conclusion follows.

Hence, the correct option is (E).

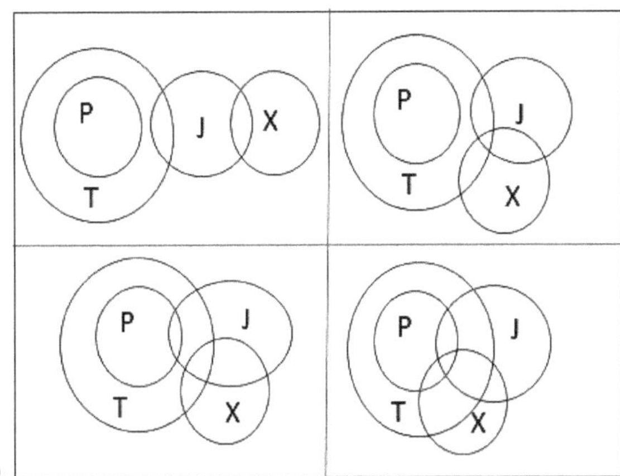

69.

From all the diagrams we can see that Some X may be P.

From all the diagrams we can see that Some J may be P.

From all the diagrams we can see that Some X may be both J and T.

So, we can say that only I, III conclusion follows.

Hence, the correct option is (A).

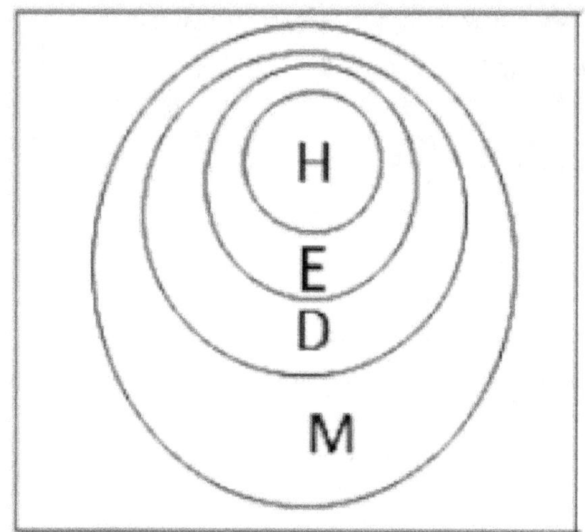

70.

We can see from the diagram that when all H, E, D, M congruent then no conclusion follows.

Hence, the correct option is (E).

Ques (71-75): The person who likes blue is the only neighbour of Bikram and he is sitting to the left of Bikram. Therefore, Bikram must be sitting at the right corner. Bikram and Amar are not sitting in the same row. Therefore, Amar must be sitting in row 2. Amar sits behind the person who likes yellow. The person who likes yellow is sitting adjacent to the person who likes blue.

Yellow	Blue		
			Bikram
		Amar	

Amar is sitting adjacent to the person who likes green. The person who likes green is not sitting behind the person who likes blue. Therefore, the person who likes green must be sitting at the left corner of row 2. Charan is sitting behind the person who likes cyan. Charan does not like green. Therefore, Charan must be sitting behind B and B must be liking cyan.

Yellow	Blue	Cyan	
			Bikram
	Amar		Charan
Green			

The persons who like red and orange are sitting adjacent to each other. None of them is a neighbour of the person who likes green. Therefore, Charan and his neighbour must be liking red and orange. Charan does not like red. Therefore, Charan must be liking orange and his neighbour must be liking red. Deepak likes white. Therefore, Deepak must be sitting at the left corner of row 1. Amar must be liking black.

White	Yellow	Blue	Cyan
Deepak			Bikram
	Amar		Charan
Green	Black	Red	Orange

Flint is sitting adjacent to the person who likes blue. Therefore, Flint must be liking yellow. Edward does not like red but he is a neighbour of A. Therefore, Edward must be liking green. Gautham does not like blue. Therefore, Gautham must be liking red and Harish must be liking blue. The final arrangement is as follows:

White	Yellow	Blue	Cyan
Deepak	Flint	Hari	Bikram
Edward	Amar	Gautham	Charan
Green	Black	Red	Orange

71. Gautham likes red.

Hence, the correct option is (C).

72. Amar is sitting behind Flint.

Hence, the correct option is (B).

73. Edward is the person sitting behind the person who likes white. Edward likes green.

Hence, the correct option is (E).

74. Bikram likes cyan.

Hence, the correct option is (A).

75. Amar likes black.

Hence, the correct option is (C).

Ques (76-78): Persons - Sheetal, Sam, Soni, Shiva, Sunny, Seema, Saurav and Sita

1. Sam, an immediate neighbour of Seema, sits fourth from one of the end.

2. Soni sits immediate right of Seema.

3. Soni sits third from one of the end.

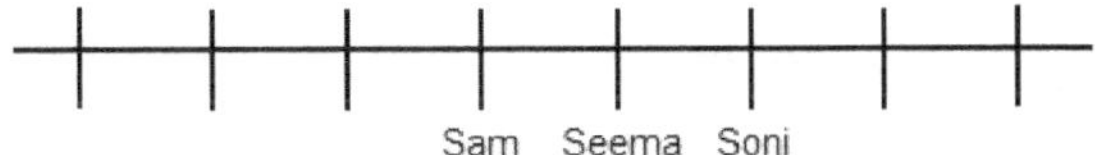

4. Sheetal is second to the left of Saurav.

5. More than three persons sit between Shiva and Sita but none of them sits extreme ends.

6. Shiva is not a neighbour of Sunny.

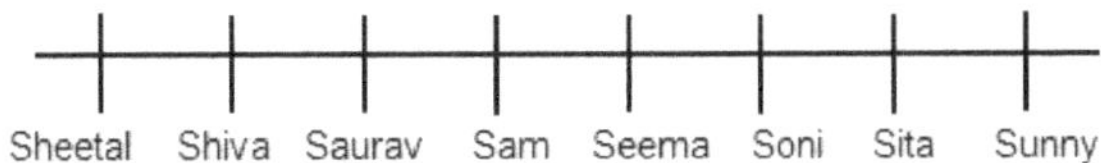

76. So, Sheetal sits extreme left end of the row.

Hence, the correct option is (C).

77. So, three persons sit between Soni and Shiva.

Hence, the correct option is (D).

78. So, Sam sits fourth to the left of Sunny.

Hence, the correct option is (A).

Ques (79-81):(i) T is lighter than P → P > T

(ii) Q is lighter than only R → R > Q

(iii) T is not the lightest, U is heavier than 3 persons.

According to the given data, the order of persons from heaviest to lightest is:

R > Q > U > P > T > Sand Weight of Q = 65 kg, Weight of T = 33 kg

If the people are arranged in ascending of their weight, then the order becomes:

S, T, P, U, Q, R

79. Clearly, P comes immediately after T.

Hence, the correct option is (D).

80. Clearly, U is in the fourth position after arrangement.

Hence, the correct option is (A).

81. So, Q is third to the right of T.

Hence, the correct option is (A).

82. Given series: 287   894   769   923   456

1) If '1' is added to the last digit of each number.

Actual Numbers: 287   894   769   923   456

Corresponding results: **288**   895   770   **924**   457

So, two such numbers are formed which is divisible by 4.

Hence, the correct option is (C).

83. Given series: 287   894   769   923   456

1) If in each number the positions of the first and second digits are interchanged.

Actual Numbers: 287   894   769   923   456

Corresponding results: **827**   984   679   293   546

The second highest number formed = 827

Sum = 8 + 2 + 7 = 17

Hence, the correct option is (B).

84. Given series: 287   894   769   923   456

1) If all digits in each number are arranged in ascending order within the number.

Actual series: 287   894   769   923   456

Numbers arranged in ascending order: 278   489   679   239   **456**

So, '456' will be the third-highest number after the new arrangement.

Hence, the correct option is (A).

85. Given series: 287   894   769   923   456

Highest number: 923

Lowest number: 287

The second digit of the highest number = 2

The first digit of the lowest number = 2

Result if the second digit of the highest number is multiplied by the first digit of the lowest number = 2 × 2 = 4

So, the result will be '4' if the second digit of the highest number is multiplied by the first digit of the lowest number.

Hence, the correct option is (D).

Ques (86-89): From the given information,

Symbol in Diagram	Meaning
◯	Female
▢	Male
═══	Married Couple
———	Siblings
│	Difference of A Generation

1) P's mother is R's sister.

2) R is Q's daughter.

3) R's brother-in-law has only one son whose grandparents are Q and S who have only two daughters.

4) A's husband is B.

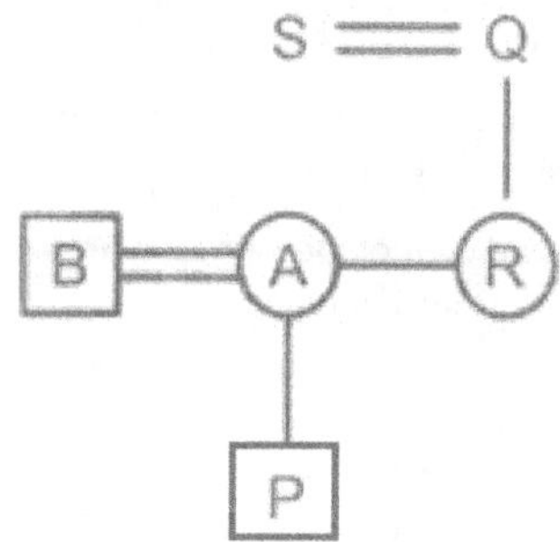

86. So, R's sister is A.

Hence, the correct option is (D).

87. As the gender of Q and S is not specified here, we cannot determine B's mother-in-law.

Hence, the correct option is (E).

88. Here, the gender of Q is not specified,

So, Q can be the mother or the father of A.

Therefore, the relation between Q and A will be 'Father/Mother and daughter.

Hence, the correct option is (C).

89. So, S and Q have only one Grandson.

Hence, the correct option is (A).

Ques (90-94): Five persons:- Anil, Diksha, Kishore, Peter and Zuber

Cities:- Surat, Lucknow, Pune, Nagpur and Udaipur

1) Kishore lives in Surat but is not an Engineer.

2) Anil who is a Manager lives in Nagpur.

3) Zuber is a Lawyer.

Person	City	Occupation	
Diksha			
Anil	Nagpur	Manager	
Kishore	Surat		Engineer
Zuber		Lawyer	
Peter			

4) Peter is neither a Doctor not a Writer.

5) The one who is from Pune is a Writer.

This implies that Diksha is from Pune and is a Writer

6) Engineer is not from Lucknow.

Person	City	Occupation
Diksha	Pune	Writer
Anil	Nagpur	Manager
Kishore	Surat	Doctor
Zuber	Lucknow	Lawyer
Peter	Udaipur	Engineer

90. The occupation of the person who is from Udaipur is Engineer.

So, none of the above is the correct answer.

Hence, the correct option is (E).

91. So, the occupation of Kishore is "Doctor".

Hence, the correct option is (C).

92. So, Diksha lives in Pune.

Hence, the correct option is (E).

93. So, Zuber lives in Lucknow.

Hence, the correct option is (B).

94. So, the correct combination among the given options is "Doctor – Surat".

Hence, the correct option is (E).

95. The pattern for the code is as follows,

Similarly,

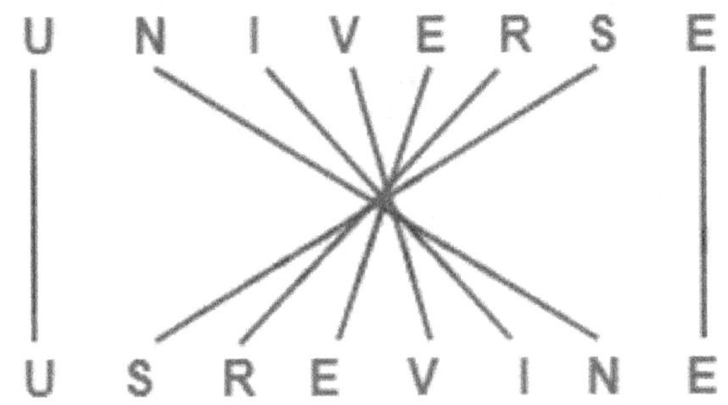

So, 'UNIVERSE' will become 'USREVINE'.

Hence, the correct option is (C).

96. Statement: C ≥ M > F < A = B > S

Conclusions:

I. C > B ⇒ It's not true as C > F and B > F so no direct relationship between C and B can be established.

II. F < S ⇒ It's not true as A > S and A > F so no direct relationship between S and F can be established.

So, neither conclusion I nor II follows.

Hence, the correct option is (D).

97. Given statements are: H = M ≤ W; C ≥ W < S

On rearranging: H = M ≤ W ≤ C; W < S

Conclusions:

I. C = M (False as C ≥ M)

II. C > M (False as C ≥ M)

But both the conclusions form a complementary pair; so either I or II follows.

Hence, the correct option is (C).

98. Given statements are: H < Y, Y ≥ R, R > W

On combining: H < Y ≥ R > W

Conclusions:

I. W < Y (True)

II. R ≤ Y (True)

So, both the conclusion follows.

Hence, the correct option is (E).

99. Statements: A ≤ P > B; C > P; F ≤ B

⇒ A ≤ P > B ≥ F; C > P

Conclusions:

I. C > A ⇒ true as C > P and A ≤ P ⇒ C > P ≥ A ⇒ C > A

II. F < P ⇒ true as P > B ≥ F ⇒ P > F

So, both conclusions I and II are true.

Hence, the correct option is (E).

100. Statements: A ≤ B < C; A ≥ E; C ≤ F

On combining: E ≤ A ≤ B < C ≤ F

Conclusions:

I. E < C ⇒ true as C > B and B ≥ E so C > E

II. F ≥ E ⇒ false as F > B and B ≥ E so F > E

So, only conclusion I is true.

Hence, the correct option is (A).

English Language

Ques (1-4):Directions: The given sentence has been broken up into four different parts. The error, if any, will be in any one part of the sentence. Select the option which contains the part of the sentence which has an error (spelling, grammatical or contextual). If there is no error, choose option E.

Q.1 His speech was very thought-provoking and (A)/well appreciated by them who attended (B)/the World Economic Forum held in (C)/the capital of Japan. (D)/No Error (E)

A. (A) **B.** (B) **C.** (C) **D.** (D)
E. (E)

Q.2 The Supreme Court's judgment on Friday (A)/in the matter of Essar Steel's bankruptcy are a (B)/landmark in the short history of (C)/insolvency and bankruptcy resolution in India. (D)/No error (E)

A. (A) **B.** (B) **C.** (C) **D.** (D)
E. (E)

Q.3 Multiple survey has demonstrated that (A)/social evils such as dowry and female infanticide (B)/are still widely prevalent (C)/in our country. (D)/No error (E)

A. (A) **B.** (B) **C.** (C) **D.** (D)
E. (E)

Q.4 It was indeed distressing (A)/that so many people (B)/are living in poverty (C)/in a land blessed with such abundant human and natural resources. (D)/No error (E)

A. (A) **B.** (B) **C.** (C) **D.** (D)
E. (E)

Ques (5-9):Direction: In the following questions, a sentence is given with five words marked as (A), (B), (C), (D) & (E), These words may or may not be placed in their places. Four options with different arrangements of these words are given. Mark the option with the correct arrangement as the answer. If there is no change required, mark 'No rearrangement required' as your answer.

Q.5 Spain **imposed** (A)/one of the **toughest** (B)/lockdowns **early** (C)/on in the pandemic and then **relaxed** (D)/curbs over the **summer**. (E)

A. DCBAC
B. CAEBD
C. ABCED
D. EDCBA
E. No Rearrangement Required

Q.6 The **icons** (A)/and college students **symbols** (B)/young adult pop culture **school** (C)/and **used** (D)/from the 'Harry Potter' and 'The Hunger Games' **books**. (E)

A. EDABC
B. DACBE
C. CDABE

D. BACDE
E. No Rearrangement Required

Q.7 Mobile **amount** (A)/in India have mostly **forgotten** (B)/to keep a check on the **users** (C)/of data they **cheap** (D)/and they have **consume** (E), data packs to thank for this.

A. ECABD
B. DECBA
C. CBAED
D. ACBDE
E. No Rearrangement Required

Q.8 A US ballot (A)/cast her astronaut (B)/from the International Space Station on Thursday, making her Earth (C)/heard in the presidential election (D)/despite being 408km above the voice. (E)

A. EACDB
B. ABDCE
C. BAEDC
D. DABCE
E. No Rearrangement Required

Q.9 The Goods and Services Tax (GST) **October** (A)/which is **health** (B)/to be a measurement of economic **considered** (C)/is **expected** (D)/to cross the Rs.1 lakh crore mark in the **collection**. (E)

A. ECBDA
B. BACDE
C. EDCBA
D. DEACB
E. No Rearrangement Required

Ques (10-15):Direction: Read the passage and answer the following questions.

Many different factors affect how well we learn. While we can't control all of these factors, there are many that we can. For example, fuel for our brain comes from calories in the food we eat. In fact, 20% of the calories we eat are used by our brain. Although not all calories help the brain, research suggests that some foods, such as egg yolk, whole grains, nuts, fish, dark leafy green vegetables, beans, strawberries, and blueberries might be especially good for concentration and memory.

Drinking enough water is also important. The brain is more than 70% water. If we don't drink enough water, it affects our concentration. We need around six to eight glasses of non-sugary, non-alcoholic fluid each day. Moreover, studies suggest that the brain does not do well with sudden rushes of sugar, so sweet, fizzy drinks do not help the brain either. Remember also the importance of oxygen, which is carried to the brain by your blood. When you move your body, your blood flow increases and your brain gets more oxygen. Going for a walk, running, or riding a bike really help get oxygen to the brain, as do stretching and breathing deeply.

Besides exercise, rest is important. Getting enough rest boosts our mood and helps us concentrate. What's more, when we are asleep, the brain practices what we did during the day. We actually learn in our sleep. If you have a hard time falling asleep, try listening to gentle music, thinking positive thoughts, or reading something funny to relax. Avoid video games and exciting TV shows in the hour before bedtime. Stress can also stop the brain from working at its best. Some people fight stress by imagining a beautiful box. When it's time to concentrate on something, they imagine filling that box with all the things that give them stress. Then they imagine putting that box away until they have time to deal with whatever is inside.

Yet another way to boost your brainpower is to create an environment where you work well. Many people, for instance, work better in light from a window. Temperature can also make a difference. A room that is too warm might make you feel sleepy. Lots of people find it easier to concentrate in rooms that are tidy. Some people find it helpful to listen to music when they study while others prefer silence. Get rid of any distractions, whatever they may be. For example, turn off your cell phone and let people in your home know that you need to be left alone.

Q.10 What does the author suggest when one cannot fall asleep?

1. Eat nuts, fish, or beans

2. Listen to gentle music

3. Think positive thoughts

A. Only 1   **B.** Only 2

C. Only 3   **D.** All except 1

E. All except 3

Q.11 When does the brain get more oxygen?

A. While riding a bicycle

B. While playing an exciting video game

C. While sleeping

D. While staying awake for long hours

E. While eating sugary foods

Q.12 Which of the following is bad for the brain?

A. Taking a rest.

B. Eating strawberries or blueberries.

C. Drinking six to eight glasses of a fizzy drink.

D. Listening to music.

E. Riding a bicycle.

Q.13 Which of the following statements is TRUE about stress?

A. Stress makes you feel excited.

B. Stress boosts our mood and helps us to concentrate.

C. Stress helps in more oxygen supply.

D. Stress stops the brain from working at its best.

E. Stress can help sleep better.

Q.14 According to the passage, the word 'concentration' refers to:

A. extreme agitation of the mind.

B. the action of interfering.

C. the interruption of a settled and peaceful condition.

D. the action or power of focusing all of one's attention.

E. the relative amount of a particular substance contained within a solution or mixture.

Q.15 According to the passage, the word 'boosts' refers to:

A. helps or encourages (something) to increase or improve.

B. makes or becomes smaller or fewer in size, amount, intensity, or degree.

C. sinks to or towards the ground.

D. allows or enables to escape from confinement.

E. steals (something).

Ques (16-20):Direction: Fill in the Blank with an appropriate word.

Q.16 Some economists believe that the indicators of economic growth should be _______ housing, education and health services rather than mere increases in a country's Gross Domestic product.

A. Redeemable   **B.** Expensive

C. Affordable   **D.** Pretentious

E. Munificent

Q.17 The digital _______ of societies has resulted in sharply reduced demand for products such as paper and steel.

A. Cohesion   **B.** Destruction

C. Transformation   **D.** Divide

E. Ingenuity

Q.18 While the Chinese people may resent America for the current trade war, they have also for long looked at America with _______.

A. Anxiety   **B.** Admiration

C. Inspiration   **D.** Trepidation

E. Apprehension

Q.19 The _______ rise in interest rates for loans coupled with higher taxes will lead to the country's economy slowing down considerably.

A. Insignificant   **B.** Infinitesimal

C. Vacuous   **D.** Substantial

E. Prodigal

Q.20 The country is highly _______ to periodic spells of famine and starvation due to the backwardness of its farming technology.

A. Dependent   **B.** Vulnerable

C. Adaptable   **D.** Chaotic

E. Impervious

Ques (21-25):Direction: In the question given below, the sentence/part of the sentence is in bold. Five alternatives are given for the bold words. Choose the correct alternative that will improve the sentence or mark the option corresponding to it. Choose option (E) if no improvement is required.

Q.21 I **wish you were** the secretary of our union.

A. wish you are

B. wish you will be

C. wish you shall

D. wish you will have to be

E. No improvement is required

Q.22 It's high time I **had bought a new pair** of scissors.
- **A.** buy a new pair
- **B.** have bought a new pair
- **C.** bought a new pair
- **D.** am buying a new pair
- **E.** No improvement is required

Q.23 My car **broke off** on the way back home today and we could not even find a service center.
- **A.** broke in
- **B.** broke down
- **C.** broke away
- **D.** broke up
- **E.** No improvement is required

Q.24 Public spats are rare in the asset-management industry, where companies **typically resolved disputes** behind closed doors.
- **A.** Typically resolved dispute
- **B.** Typical resolving disputes
- **C.** Typically resolve disputes
- **D.** Typical resolve dispute
- **E.** No improvement is required

Q.25 His appetite was **not sate by** any means, but he knew the danger of overloading his stomach, so he stopped.
- **A.** Not sated with
- **B.** Not sates by
- **C.** Not sating by
- **D.** Not sated by
- **E.** No improvement is required

Ques (26-29):Direction: Read the passage carefully and select the correct answer for the given blank out of the given alternatives.

Reserve Bank of India (RBI) will now be given ___(1)___to take over as the regulator of Housing Finance Firms (HFFs) instead of NHB (National Housing Bank) as announced on July 5, 2019, by ___(2)___Minister Nirmala Sitharaman. The ___(3)___will also provide a one-time six-month partial guarantee to state-run banks for the acquisition of up to 1 trillion rupees ($14.6 billion) of highly-rated ___(4)___from NBFCs (Non-Banking Financial Company).

Q.26 Pick the appropriate word to be filled in blank (1).
- **A.** stage
- **B.** position
- **C.** gifts
- **D.** power
- **E.** acceptance

Q.27 Pick the appropriate word to be filled in blank (2).
- **A.** general
- **B.** finance
- **C.** chief
- **D.** prime
- **E.** temporary

Q.28 Pick the appropriate word to be filled in blank (3).
- **A.** minister
- **B.** army
- **C.** foreign
- **D.** people
- **E.** government

Q.29 Pick the appropriate word to be filled in blank (4).

- **A.** assets
- **B.** money
- **C.** business
- **D.** property
- **E.** lives

Q.30 Directions: The given sentence has been broken up into four different parts. The error, if any, will be in any one part of the sentence. Select the option which contains the part of the sentence which has an error (spelling, grammatical or contextual). If there is no error, choose option E.

To an insurance company(A)/the law relating to(B)/the principles of subrogation and(C)/contribution are of great importance.(D)/No Error (E)
- **A.** To an insurance company
- **B.** The law relating to
- **C.** The principles of subrogation and
- **D.** Contribution are of great importation
- **E.** No Error

Numerical Ability

Q.31 Product of the age of Tania and Ronita is 12 years. If Tania is 4 years younger than Ronita, what will be the age of Ronita after 5 years?
- **A.** 12 years
- **B.** 13 years
- **C.** 11 years
- **D.** 10 years
- **E.** 16 years

Q.32 Prashant has a bag, which contains 5 Orange, 4 Yellow, and 3 Brown balls. Three balls are drawn at random. What is the probability that all are of a different colour?
- **A.** $\frac{40}{41}$
- **B.** $\frac{3}{11}$
- **C.** $\frac{3}{44}$
- **D.** $\frac{2}{11}$
- **E.** None of these

Q.33 The ratio of Solution "A" and Solution "B" in the bottle is 3:2 when 10 L of the mixture is taken out and is replaced by Solution "B", the ratio becomes 2:3. The total quantity of the mixture in the bottle is?
- **A.** 32 L
- **B.** 38 L
- **C.** 30 L
- **D.** 29 L
- **E.** 26 L

Q.34 If the difference between Compound interest and simple interest on a certain sum of money at 4% per annum for 2 years is Rs. 20. Find the sum of money.
- **A.** Rs. 12000
- **B.** Rs. 12500
- **C.** Rs. 13000
- **D.** Rs. 14000
- **E.** Rs. 15000

Ques (35-38):Direction: In each of the following number series, the wrong number is given, find out that number.

Q.35 -4, -6, -10, -18, -34, -68, -130
- **A.** -10
- **B.** -18
- **C.** -34
- **D.** -68
- **E.** -120

Q.36 11, 31, 69, 131, 223, 352, 521
- **A.** 69
- **B.** 131
- **C.** 223
- **D.** 352
- **E.** 521

Q.37 2, 9, 30, 93, 283, 849
- **A.** 9
- **B.** 30
- **C.** 93
- **D.** 283
- **E.** 849

Q.38 6, 7, 16, 51, 208, 1058, 6276
A. 51 **B.** 208 **C.** 1058 **D.** 6276
E. 7

Ques (39-43):Direction: In the given question, two equations numbered I and II are given. Solve both the equations and mark the appropriate answer.

Q.39 I. $x^3 = 8$
II. $y^2 = 4$
A. $x > y$
B. $x < y$
C. $x \geq y$
D. $x \leq y$
E. $x = y$ or the relationship between x and y cannot be established.

Q.40 I. $x^2 - 3x + 2 = 0$
II. $y^2 = 1$
A. $x > y$
B. $x < y$
C. $x \geq y$
D. $x \leq y$
E. $x = y$ or the relationship between x and y cannot be established.

Q.41 I. $x^{\frac{5}{2}} = \sqrt{243}$
II. $2y^{\frac{3}{2}} = \sqrt{256}$
A. $x > y$
B. $x < y$
C. $x \geq y$
D. $x \leq y$
E. $x = y$ or relationship between x and y cannot be established.

Q.42 I: $x^2 - 2x - 35 = 0$
II: $2y^2 + 72y + 70 = 0$
A. $x > y$
B. $x \geq y$
C. $x < y$
D. $x \leq y$
E. $x = y$ or the relationship between x and y cannot be established.

Q.43 I. $3x^2 - 47x + 160 = 0$
II. $6y^2 - 59y + 119 = 0$
A. $x > y$
B. $x < y$
C. $x \geq y$
D. $x \leq y$
E. $x = y$ or relationship between x and y cannot be established.

Ques (44-48):Direction: Go through the statements given below and answer the question based on it.

1. Ram plans a trip with his family. Ram divides the total budget into category of Travel, Stay and food and for shopping. The budget of stay and food and shopping is 50% and 25% more than the budget of travel.

2. 75% of total budget of travel is spend on air tickets and rest on taxi and cabs. 30% of total budget of stay and food is spend on food and rest on stay.

3. 85% money is spending on shopping and Rs. 2700 is saved from the total budget of shopping.

Q.44 What is total budget of trip?
A. Rs. 54000 **B.** Rs. 52000
C. Rs. 56000 **D.** Rs. 58000
E. Rs. 57000

Q.45 What is the difference of amount spend on air tickets and taxi?
A. Rs. 7200 **B.** Rs. 6500
C. Rs. 7500 **D.** Rs. 6000
E. None of these

Q.46 How much money did Ram spend on food?
A. Rs. 6020 **B.** Rs. 6280
C. Rs. 6400 **D.** Rs. 6480
E. None of these

Q.47 Money spend on stay is how much percentage less / more than the budget for shopping?
A. 10% **B.** 12% **C.** 14% **D.** 16%
E. 18%

Q.48 What is the average of amount of money spend on Taxi, Food and saving?
A. Rs. 4260 **B.** Rs. 4350 **C.** Rs. 4450 **D.** Rs. 4520
E. Rs. 4320

Q.49 The average age of 10 students is 20 years. If the age of teacher is also included, the average age is increased by 10%. Find the age of a teacher.
A. 12 years **B.** 36 years **C.** 45 years **D.** 41 years
E. 42 years

Q.50 A dealer marks the price of an item at Rs. 4200. If he offers two successive discounts of 7% each. Then, what will be the selling price?
A. Rs. 1035.75 **B.** Rs. 1260.96
C. Rs. 1300.56 **D.** Rs. 1405.75
E. Rs. 3632.58

Q.51 A Rectangular shape garden whose length 15 cm is surrounded by a path that is wide a 4cm. If the area of the garden is 120 cm² and the graveling cost of that garden is Rs 5 per cm², then what is the total cost of graveling the path?
A. Rs. 1000 **B.** Rs. 1200 **C.** Rs. 150 **D.** Rs. 1240
E. None

Ques (52-53):Direction: The following question is accompanied by two statements (I) and (II). You have to determine which statements(s) is/are sufficient/necessary to answer the questions.

Q.52 Chintu, Pintu, and Bittu start a business. Find the total profit earn by them.

I. Chintu, Pintu, and Bittu invested the amounts in the ratio of 3 : 2 : 6 and the ratio of investment's time is 4 : 3 : 5.

II. If the difference between the investment of Pintu and Bittu is Rs. 8,400.

A. The statement I alone is sufficient to answer the question, but the statement II alone is not sufficient.

B. The statement II alone is sufficient to answer the question, but the statement I alone is not sufficient.

C. Both the statements I and II together are needed to answer the question.

D. Either statement I alone or statement II alone is sufficient to answer the question.

E. Neither statement I nor statement II is sufficient to answer the question.

Q.53 Find the ratio of time for which Lucky, Arpit, and Ankush contributed their capitals.

I. In the investment, Arpit invests 50% more than Lucky and 25% less than Ankush.

II. In the profit, Ankush earns 20% more than Lucky and 25% less than Arpit.

A. The statement I alone is sufficient to answer the question, but the statement II alone is not sufficient.

B. The statement II alone is sufficient to answer the question, but the statement I alone is not sufficient.

C. Both the statements I and II together are needed to answer the question.

D. Either statement I alone or statement II alone is sufficient to answer the question.

E. Neither statement I nor statement II is sufficient to answer the question.

Ques (54-62):Direction: What will come in the place of the question mark '?' in the following question?

Q.54 $\sqrt{(\sqrt{8100} + \sqrt{6241})} = ?$

A. 14   **B.** 16
C. 19   **D.** 13
E. None of these

Q.55 $[(140 \div 20) \times 25 \div 7 \times 250] \div 50 \times 5 = ?$
A. 525   **B.** 725
C. 755   **D.** 625
E. None of these

Q.56 $(4575 - 1740 - 2250) = ? - 39 + \sqrt{9025}$
A. 729   **B.** 629
C. 625   **D.** 529
E. None of these

Q.57 $(45\% \text{ of } 60 - \sqrt{121}) \times ? = 1488$
A. 94   **B.** 93
C. 95   **D.** 96
E. None of these

Q.58 $\frac{2}{3}$ of 48 + [7 + (-16) + 24 - 7] = ?
A. 42   **B.** 40

C. 38   **D.** 36
E. None of these

Q.59 $11 \times 66 - 21 \times 22 + 91 \times 19 = ?$
A. 1993   **B.** 1994
C. 1995   **D.** 1996
E. None of these

Q.60 $65 \times 5 - 60 \times 75\% + 80 - 10^2 = ?$
A. 430   **B.** 260
C. 334   **D.** 330
E. None of these

Q.61 $\left\{\left(\frac{2970}{66}\right) \times \left(\frac{3960}{88}\right)\right\}^{\left(\frac{1}{2}\right)} + 200\% \text{ of } 6.5 + 6 = x^3$
A. 64   **B.** 44
C. 16   **D.** 4
E. None of these

Q.62 $\left\{(18) \times \left(\frac{1650}{25}\right) \div (36)\right\} + \left\{\left(\frac{391}{17}\right) + \left(\frac{624}{26}\right)\right\} = ?$
A. 63   **B.** 73
C. 85   **D.** 80
E. None of these

Q.63 What will come in the place of the question mark '?' in the following question?
$78 + 85 - (13 \times 8) + (81 \div 3) = ?$
A. 84   **B.** 86
C. 92   **D.** 96
E. None of these

Q.64 A and B has equal working efficiency. A farmer hires both of them for 20 days. But A catches cold and hence remain on leave for 3 days. So B's efficiency increases by 40% then find extra days he will take to complete the work?
A. $\frac{30}{7}$ **B.** $\frac{32}{9}$ **C.** $\frac{31}{3}$ **D.** $\frac{34}{5}$
E. $\frac{39}{5}$

Q.65 Direction: In each of the following number series, the wrong number is given, find out that number.

1, 5, 20, 57, 121, 221, 365
A. 57   **B.** 20   **C.** 121   **D.** 5
E. 365

Reasoning Ability

Ques (66-68):Direction: In the question below are given three statements followed by two conclusions numbered I and II. You have to take the given statements to be true even if they seem to be at variance with commonly known facts. Read all the conclusions and then decide which of the given conclusions logically follows from the given statements disregarding commonly known facts.

Q.66 Statements:
Some cube are square.

Some square are triangle.

All triangle are circle.

Conclusions:

I. Atleast some circle are cube.

II. No circle is a cube.

A. Only II follows

B. Only I follows

C. Either I or II follow

D. Neither I nor II follow

E. Both I and II follow

Q.67 Statements:

All engineers are dentist.

No dentist is a nurse.

All nurses are manager.

Conclusions:

I. No engineer is a manager.

II. All dentist being manager is a possibility.

A. Only I follow

B. Only II follow

C. Neither I nor II follow

D. Either I or II follow

E. Both I and II follow

Q.68 Statements:

Some houses are igloo.

No igloo is a hut.

No hut is a bunglow.

Conclusions:

I. All house being hut is a possibility.

II. Maximum igloo are bunglow.

A. Either I or II follow

B. Only II follow

C. Neither I nor II follow

D. Both I and II follow

E. Only I follow

Ques (69-71):Direction: Study the following information carefully and answer the given questions.

In a certain language

'ab ja pa' means 'seeta is intelligent',

'pt pa ja', means 'seeta is smart',

'ja ta na' means 'she is playing',

'ka na la' means 'she likes ice-cream'.

Q.69 Which of the following means 'seeta' in that code langauge?

A. ta

B. pa

C. na

D. ka

E. Either (A) or (B)

Q.70 What would be the code for 'seeta likes ice-cream'?

A. ab ja pa

B. pa ka la

C. ta la ja

D. ka ta na

E. Either (A) or (C)

Q.71 Code for 'na ja pt' is for which of the following sentence in the given language?

A. She is smart

B. Seeta is smart

C. She likes playing

D. Seeta is intelligent

E. Can not be determined

Ques (72-76):Direction: Study the following information carefully and answer the questions given below.

Six persons K, O, G, S, A, and L are sitting around a hexagon table such that all the persons are sitting on the middle of the sides of the table but not necessarily in the same order. All of them are facing inside. No person is sitting on the corner of the table.

L is second to the right of G. A and O are immediate neighbours. There are only 2 persons sitting between L and K. O and S are not immediate neighbours of K.

Q.72 How many persons sit between A and G when counted from the right of G?

A. Three

B. Two

C. One

D. Four

E. More than four

Q.73 Who sits exactly opposite to G?

A. A

B. L

C. K

D. O

E. S

Q.74 What is the position of L with respect to A?

A. Third to the right

B. Second to the left

C. Immediate right

D. Second to the right

E. Immediate left

Q.75 Which of the following is true?

A. A and S are immediate neighbours

B. G is third to the left of K

C. S is immediate left of L

D. O is not immediate neighbour of L

E. K is second to the right of S

Q.76 Who is sitting immediate right of A?

A. O

B. G

C. S

D. L

E. K

Ques (77-79):Directions: Study the information given below carefully and answer the questions that follow:

Sheela started from her office towards the North and covered a distance of 50 m and then turned to her right and walked 20 m to the market. Then she again turned to her right and walked 25 m and finally, she again turned to her right and walked 30 m to reach her home.

Q.77 Total distance covered by sheela from office to reach her home?

A. 100

B. 125

C. 115

D. 90

E. None of these

Q.78 In which direction market is from her office ?

A. North **B.** South
C. East **D.** North-East
E. North-West

Q.79 In which direction is her Home to the Market?

A. South **B.** West
C. South-West **D.** North-West
E. None of the above

Ques (80-84):Direction: Study the following information carefully and answer the questions given below it.

There are seven friends A, B, C, D, E, F and G. Each one goes on a trip on different days from Monday to Sunday but not necessarily in the same order.

C travels on the day after the day B travels. G travels on the day just before the day on which E travels. The number of persons between the one who travels on Wednesday and B is the same as the number of persons between D and G. F travels on Wednesday. E travels on the day which is 4 days after the day on which D travels. D doesn't travel on the day after the day on which F travels.

Q.80 Who goes on Sunday?

A. B **B.** A
C. G **D.** C
E. None of these

Q.81 On which day D travels?

A. Tuesday **B.** Friday
C. Sunday **D.** Monday
E. None of these

Q.82 How many persons go after G?

A. One **B.** Two
C. Three **D.** Four
E. More than four

Q.83 Who does go on Tuesday?

A. G **B.** B
C. C **D.** D
E. None of these

Q.84 How many persons goes between C and the one who goes on Thursday?

A. Three **B.** One
C. Two **D.** Four
E. More than four

Ques (85-87):Directions: Study the following information carefully and answer the questions based on it:

In a family, there are eight members. A is mother of B, who is brother of C. C and Q are siblings. Y is daughter of P. Z is brother in law of B, who is son of D. A has only one son. There are only two married couples in the family. P is married to B.

Q.85 How is P related with Z?

A. Brother **B.** Sister
C. Nephew **D.** Niece

E. None of these

Q.86 How is C related with Y?

A. Aunt **B.** Daughter
C. Uncle **D.** Granddaughter
E. None of these

Q.87 How many male members are there in the family?

[IBPS SO HR Officer, 2020], [IBPS RRB Office Assistant, 2020], [IBPS Agriculture field Officer (AFO), 2020]

A. Four **B.** Three
C. Five **D.** Two
E. None of these

Ques (88-92):Direction: Study the following information carefully and answer the question given below.

Eight persons A, B, C, D, W, X, Y and Z are sitting in two rows with equal members in each row. Members of row numbered 1 are facing North and those in row 2 are facing South. Each member in one row is sitting exactly opposite a member in the other row.

A sits in the row facing South facing W. W sits third to the left of D. Y who sits second to the right of X. C sits to the immediate left of Z.

Q.88 What is the position of A with respect to B?

A. Second to the right **B.** Third to the right
C. Immediate left **D.** Immediate right
E. Third to the left

Q.89 Who sits opposite C?

A. D **B.** A **C.** Y **D.** Z
E. X

Q.90 Four of the following are similar in a certain way and thus form a group. Which of the following does not form a group?

A. Z **B.** A **C.** X **D.** B
E. Y

Q.91 Which of the following statement is correct?

i) W sits second to the left of Z.

ii) B sits between C and D.

iii) Y sits second to the right of C.

A. Only statement (i) is true.
B. Only statement (ii) is true.
C. Only statement (iii) is true.
D. None is true.
E. All are true.

Q.92 Who sits at the extreme position in row 2?

A. W and X **B.** A and D **C.** A and X **D.** D and X
E. A and W

Ques (93-96):Direction: In the following question assuming the given statements to be true, find which of the conclusion(s) among given conclusions is/are definitely true and then give your answers accordingly.

Q.93 Statements:

$N \geq H \leq T > R = E; E > O < P = I$

Conclusion:

I. N > E

II. T > O

A. Only conclusion I follows

B. Both conclusion I or II follows

C. Only conclusion II follows

D. Either I or II follows

E. Neither conclusions I nor II follow

Q.94 Statements:

A > B < C = D; D < E < F

Conclusions:

I. A < E

II. E > B

A. Only I is True

B. Only II is True

C. Both I and II are True

D. None is True

E. Neither I nor II is True

Q.95 Statements:

H < A > R = D; I ≤ K ≥ P; H < P

Conclusions:

I. K > R

II. D ≤ K

A. Only II is true

B. Only I is true

C. Both I and II are true

D. Either I or II is true

E. None is true

Q.96 Statements:

P = Q ≤ R; T = P; T > S

Conclusions:

I. Q < S

II. R < S

[IBPS RRB Scale I, 2020]

A. Only I is True

B. Only II is True

C. Both I and II are True

D. Either I or II is True

E. None is True

Ques (97-99):Direction: Read the following information carefully and answer the question that follow:

There are seven person Manav, Rohan, Amit, Harsh, Rajat, Mohit and Sumit. Harsh got more marks than Manav and less marks than Rohan. Rohan did not get the highest marks. Amit got more marks than only Sumit & Rajat. Rajat got least marks. Second lowest person got 45 marks.

Q.97 How many marks did Rajat get?

A. 55   B. 58   C. 42   D. 60

E. 53

Q.98 How many persons got the least marks than Mohit?

A. 4   B. 3   C. 6   D. 5

E. 2

Q.99 If the sum of Sumit and Rohan score is 113 and the sum of Manav and Rohan score is 124. What is the score of Manav?

A. 63   B. 56

C. 51   D. 79

E. None of these

Q.100 How many such pairs of letters are there in the word DOLPHIN (in both the forward and backward directions) which have as many letters between them in the words as there are in the English alphabetical order?

A. One   B. Four

C. Two   D. Three

E. None of these

// Smart Answer Sheet //

Correct — Percentage of students who answered correctly. **Skipped** — Percentage of students who skipped.

Q.	Ans.	Correct	Skipped
1	B	5.56 %	46.82 %
2	B	9.52 %	85.72 %
3	A	6.35 %	86.51 %
4	C	3.17 %	87.31 %
5	E	8.73 %	87.3 %
6	C	10.32 %	87.3 %
7	C	8.73 %	87.3 %
8	C	7.14 %	87.3 %
9	A	7.14 %	87.3 %
10	D	9.52 %	87.31 %
11	A	11.11 %	87.3 %
12	C	8.73 %	87.3 %
13	D	10.32 %	87.3 %
14	D	7.94 %	87.3 %
15	A	10.32 %	87.3 %
16	C	6.35 %	87.3 %

Q.	Ans.	Correct	Skipped
17	C	10.32 %	87.3 %
18	B	3.17 %	87.31 %
19	D	5.56 %	87.3 %
20	B	5.56 %	87.3 %
21	E	1.59 %	87.3 %
22	C	3.97 %	87.3 %
23	B	8.73 %	87.3 %
24	C	7.94 %	87.3 %
25	D	4.76 %	87.3 %
26	D	11.11 %	88.1 %
27	B	11.11 %	88.1 %
28	E	11.11 %	88.1 %
29	A	9.52 %	88.1 %
30	D	1.59 %	94.44 %
31	C	4.76 %	89.68 %
32	B	1.59 %	89.68 %

Q.	Ans.	Correct	Skipped
33	C	2.38 %	89.68 %
34	B	2.38 %	89.68 %
35	D	7.14 %	89.69 %
36	D	3.17 %	89.69 %
37	D	3.97 %	89.68 %
38	C	5.56 %	89.68 %
39	C	5.56 %	89.68 %
40	C	4.76 %	89.68 %
41	B	0.79 %	89.69 %
42	E	3.97 %	89.68 %
43	E	2.38 %	89.68 %
44	A	0 %	100 %
45	A	0 %	100 %
46	D	0 %	100 %
47	D	0 %	100 %
48	A	0 %	100 %

Q.	Ans.	Correct	Skipped
49	E	4.76 %	89.68 %
50	E	4.76 %	89.68 %
51	D	0.79 %	89.69 %
52	C	2.38 %	89.68 %
53	C	0 %	100 %
54	D	7.94 %	89.68 %
55	D	7.14 %	89.69 %
56	D	7.14 %	90.48 %
57	B	8.73 %	90.48 %
58	B	7.94 %	90.47 %
59	A	5.56 %	90.47 %
60	B	7.14 %	91.27 %
61	D	1.59 %	91.27 %
62	D	3.17 %	91.27 %
63	B	2.38 %	95.24 %
64	A	0 %	100 %

Q.	Ans.	Correct	Skipped
65	B	1.59 %	96.82 %
66	C	7.94 %	89.68 %
67	B	4.76 %	89.68 %
68	C	7.14 %	89.69 %
69	B	8.73 %	89.68 %
70	B	8.73 %	89.68 %
71	A	7.94 %	89.68 %
72	A	9.52 %	89.69 %
73	D	9.52 %	89.69 %
74	B	9.52 %	89.69 %
75	C	9.52 %	89.69 %
76	E	9.52 %	89.69 %
77	B	8.73 %	89.68 %
78	D	9.52 %	89.69 %
79	C	7.94 %	89.68 %
80	D	3.97 %	89.68 %

Q.	Ans.	Correct		Q.	Ans.	Correct		Q.	Ans.	Correct		Q.	Ans.	Correct		Q.	Ans.	Correct
		Skipped				Skipped				Skipped				Skipped				Skipped
81	D	5.56 %		85	B	3.97 %		89	C	7.14 %		93	C	9.52 %		97	C	9.52 %
		90.47 %				89.68 %				89.69 %				89.69 %				89.69 %
82	C	5.56 %		86	A	7.94 %		90	A	6.35 %		94	B	9.52 %		98	C	7.94 %
		90.47 %				89.68 %				89.68 %				89.69 %				89.68 %
83	E	3.97 %		87	B	6.35 %		91	A	7.14 %		95	E	7.14 %		99	B	7.94 %
		90.47 %				89.68 %				89.69 %				89.69 %				90.47 %
84	C	3.97 %		88	A	7.14 %		92	C	7.14 %		96	E	7.94 %		100	B	0.79 %
		89.68 %				89.69 %				89.69 %				89.68 %				94.45 %

//Hints and Solutions//

1. We need to replace THEM with THOSE for making the sentence grammatically and contextually correct.

Because WHO is a subjective case used for the antecedent before it. If it is a subjective case, the antecedent should also be a subjective case.

As we know THEM is objective and the subjective case of it is THOSE.

Correct sentence: His speech was very thought-provoking and well appreciated by those who attended the World Economic Forum held in the capital of Japan.

Hence, the correct option is (B).

2. In Part (B) the error lies in the wrong usage of the subject-verb agreement. The subject 'judgement' is singular so it should follow the singular verb 'is' instead of 'are'.

Correct sentence: The Supreme Court's judgment on Friday in the matter of Essar Steel's bankruptcy is a landmark in the short history of insolvency and bankruptcy resolution in India.

Hence, the correct option is (B).

3. The error is that survey should be replaced by the word surveys and the verb has should be replaced by the word have

Because the words such as Some, Few, Many, Several, Various, Different, Certain, Other, Numerous, Multiple, etc are always followed by Plural Countable Noun and Plural Verb

Correct sentence: Multiple surveys have demonstrated that social evils such as dowry and female infanticide are still widely prevalent in our country.

Hence, the correct option is (A).

4. The sentence has tense inconsistency.

Part (A) has the First and Third-person singular past tense of the be a verb, 'was' while part (C) has the verb 'are' which is present indicative plural, and second-person singular of the be a verb.

Thus, the correct verb usage in part (C) should be 'were' which is the plural past indicative since the sentence denotes an observation made in the past.

Correct sentence: It was indeed distressing that so many people were living in poverty in a land blessed with such abundant human and natural resources.

Hence, the correct option is (C).

5. The given sentence is contextually and grammatically correct and thus requires no rearrangement.

Hence, the correct option is (E).

6. Let us consider (A), (B), (C), (D), and (E) to be five blanks, with (A), being the first (B), the second, and so on.

- The first blank requires a noun in the singular form as it is preceded by the article 'the' and is followed by the noun 'students' in the plural form. Thus, the correct answer is 'school'.

- The second blank requires a verb in the past tense in order to describe the action that 'school and college students' took in terms of the 'young pop culture icons and symbols'. Thus, the correct answer is 'used'.

- The third blank requires a noun that can be ascribed to the label 'young pop culture' and this is not a title usually associated with 'school'. Thus the correct answer is 'icons'.

- The fourth blank requires a noun that too can be ascribed to the label 'young pop culture' and since there is no option that allows 'books' in the fourth blank the answer is 'symbols'.

- The fifth blank requires a noun in the plural form that has had products with the names 'Happy Potter' and 'The Hunger Games'. Thus, the answer is 'books'.

Arranged sentence: The school and college students used young adult pop culture icons and symbols from the 'Harry Potter' and 'The Hunger Games' books.

Hence, the correct option is (C).

7. Let us consider (A), (B), (C), (D), and E to be five blanks, with (A) being the first, (B) the second, and so on.

- The first blank requires a living noun, as the word in the blank carries out the act of 'forgetting' something, which is only something humans can do. While 'amount' is not a living noun, 'users' is and thus the correct answer is 'users'.

- The second blank requires a past participle and thus the correct answer is 'forgotten'.

- The third blank requires a non-living quantitative noun that can be used to refer to 'data', thus the correct answer is 'amount'.

- The fourth blank requires a verb as it is preceded by a possessive pronoun, which cannot be succeeded by an adjective like 'cheap'. Thus, the correct answer is 'consume'.

- The last blank requires an adjective that describes the data packs which Indian users have been consuming a lot of, thus the correct answer is 'cheap'.

Arranged sentence: Mobile users in India have mostly forgotten to keep a check on the amount of data they consume and they have cheap data packs to thank for this.

Hence, the correct option is (C).

8. Let us consider (A), (B), (C), (D), and (E) to be five blanks, with (A) being the first, (B) the second, and so on.

- The first blank requires a noun that refers to a living thing as it makes the action of 'casting' something, which can only be done by living things and a 'ballot' is a non-living thing. Thus the correct answer is 'astronaut'.

- The second blank requires a non-living noun as only a non-living thing can be 'cast', thus the correct answer is 'ballot'.

- The third blank requires a non-proper noun as there is only one 'Earth' (that we know of) and so it does not belong to any particular person, so it cannot be preceded by a possessive pronoun like 'her'. Thus, the correct answer is 'voice'.

- The fourth blank is preceded by the adjective 'presidential' which refers to something related to the president, and of the available options, 'election' is the most appropriate answer.

- The fifth blank requires a proper noun as it is preceded by the article 'the' which is used to refer to proper nouns, thus the correct answer is 'Earth'.

Arranged sentence: A US astronaut cast her ballot from the International Space Station on Thursday, making her voice heard in the presidential election despite being 408km above the Earth.

Hence, the correct option is (C).

9. Let us consider (A), (B), (C), (D), and (E) to be five blanks, with (A) being the first, (B) the second, and so on.

- In the first blank, a noun is required that represents an act, a tax like GST cannot be a type of time period - a month like October, thus the correct answer is 'collection'.

- The second blank requires a verb in the past tense, 'health' is a noun and thus is not something that a tax like 'GST' can be, thus the correct answer is 'considered'.

- The third blank requires a noun, like 'health' because an adjective like 'economic' cannot be used to describe a verb like 'considered'.

- The fourth blank requires a verb in the past tense. The verb 'expected' is in the correct position.

- The fifth blank requires a noun, something that represents a time frame during which something can or has been achieved, thus 'October' is the correct answer.

Arranged sentence: The Goods and Services Tax (GST) collection, which is considered to be a measurement of economic health is expected to cross the Rs.1 lakh crore mark in October.

Hence, the correct option is (A).

10. The passage is about the factors that affect learning.

The following is stated in the passage: "If you have a hard time falling asleep, try listening to gentle music, thinking positive thoughts, or reading something funny to relax. Avoid video games and exciting TV shows in the hour before bedtime."

The above sentence is exhaustive in its recommendations for falling asleep. It includes only points 2 and 3.

Hence, the correct option is (D).

11. The passage is about the factors that affect learning.

The following is stated in the passage: "...riding a bike really helps get oxygen to the brain."

Hence, the correct option is (A).

12. The passage is about the factors that affect learning.

The following is stated in the passage: "..studies suggest that the brain does not do well with sudden rushes of sugar, so sweet, fizzy drinks do not help the brain either."

Clearly, one shouldn't drink fizzy drinks as they are harmful to the brain.

Hence, the correct option is (C).

13. The passage is about the factors that affect learning.

The following is stated in the passage: "Stress can also stop the brain from working at its best."

Hence, the correct option is (D).

14. The passage is about the factors that affect learning.

The sentence that contains the word 'concentration' is as follows: "The brain is more than 70% water. If we don't drink enough water, it affects our concentration."

In this case, it is clear that not drinking enough water would negatively affect one's attention and focus.

Hence, the correct option is (D).

15. The passage is about the factors that affect learning.

The sentence that contains the word 'boosts' is as follows: "Getting enough rest boosts our mood and helps us concentrate."

This sentence means that resting enough would help improve our mood and help us concentrate.

Hence, the correct option is (A).

16. Meaning of the given words:

- Redeemable means to get or win back.

- Expensive means costly.

- Affordable means having a cost that is not too high.

- Pretentious means making unjustified or excessive claims.

- Munificent means to be very liberal in giving or bestowing.

It is clear from the statement that the word 'affordable' is more suitable than the other options.

Complete sentence: Some economists believe that the indicators of economic growth should be affordable housing, education, and health services rather than mere increases in a country's Gross Domestic Product.

Hence, the correct option is (C).

17. Meaning of the given words:

- Cohesion means the act or state of sticking together tightly.

- Destruction means to ruin.

- Transformation means to change in composition or structure.

- Divide means to separate into two or more parts, areas, or groups.
- Ingenuity means cleverness or inventiveness.

It is clear from the statement that the word 'transformation' is more suitable than the other options.

Complete sentence: The digital transformation of societies has resulted in sharply reduced demand for products such as paper and steel.

Hence, the correct option is (C).

18. Meaning of the given words:

- Anxiety means apprehensive uneasiness or nervousness; mentally distressing concern.
- Admiration means to feel respect and approval for.
- Inspiration means the act of influencing, moving or guiding.
- Trepidation means to have a nervous or fearful feeling.
- Apprehension means suspicion or fear especially of future evil.

It is clear from the statement that the word 'admiration' is more suitable than the other options.

Complete sentence: While the Chinese people may resent America for the current trade war, they have also for long looked at America with admiration.

Hence, the correct option is (B).

19. Meaning of the given words:

- Insignificant means small in size, quantity or number.
- Infinitesimal means immeasurably or incalculably small.
- Vacuous means to be emptied of or lacking content.
- Substantial means considerable in quantity or significantly great.
- Prodigal means characterized by profuse or wasteful expenditure.

It is clear from the statement that the word 'substantial' is more suitable than the other options.

Complete sentence: The substantial rise in interest rates for loans coupled with higher taxes will lead to the country's economy slowing down considerably.

Hence, the correct option is (D).

20. Meaning of the given words:

- Dependent means relying on another for support.
- Vulnerable means to be open to attack or damage.
- Adaptable means to be suited by nature, character or design for a particular purpose or situation.
- Chaotic means to be in a state of utter confusion.
- Impervious means not capable of being damaged or harmed.

It is clear from the statement that the word 'vulnerable' is more suitable than the other options.

Complete sentence: The country is highly vulnerable to periodic spells of famine and starvation due to the backwardness of its farming technology.

Hence, the correct option is (B).

21. The given sentence expresses a hypothetical situation and, therefore, should have past subjunctive 'were'. Past subjunctive possesses grammatically the same form as that of the past simple tense and is used to refer to present or future time of action (especially wish).

So we have the statement 'I wish you were the secretary of our union' is correct both grammatically and meaningfully.

Hence, the correct option is (E).

22. Often when we mean to express something that should be done (by this time) and which is already a bit late to be in action, grammatically we can use 'It's high time' followed by the past subjunctive.

Here the past subjunctive is 'bought'. Therefore the past perfect subjunctive 'had bought' is incorrect here.

Correct sentence: It's high time I bought a new pair of scissors.

Hence, the correct option is (C).

23. The sentence uses the form broke off, which is incorrect and needs improvement.

The correct phrasal verb to be used here is 'broke down' because if a machine or a vehicle 'breaks down' it means that it has stopped working.

Correct sentence: My car broke down on the way back home today and we could not even find a service center.

Hence, the correct option is (B).

24. By observing the above-mentioned sentence we can conclude that it is in the present tense. The phrase 'typically resolved disputes' is in the past tense and therefore does not fit into the sentence grammatically.

Option (A) is rejected because it is in the past tense.

Option (B) and (D) are rejected because they do not fit into the sentence structurally or meaningfully.

This leaves us with option (C), i.e., typically resolve disputes, to be the only correct answer.

Correct sentence: Public spats are rare in the asset-management industry, where companies typically resolve disputes behind closed doors.

Hence, the correct option is (C).

25. The word 'sate' means 'to satisfy'. By observing the above-mentioned sentence we can conclude that it is in the past tense. The phrase 'not sate by' does not match with the tense of the rest of the sentence and therefore needs to be corrected.

The preposition 'with' means 'accompanied by'. The phrase 'not sated with' does not make any sense and therefore option (A) is rejected.

Option (B) and (C) are rejected because they are in the present tense.

This leaves us with option (D), i.e., not sated by, to be the only correct answer.

Correct sentence: His appetite was not sated by any means, but he knew the danger of overloading his stomach, so he stopped.

Hence, the correct option is (D).

26. 'power' is the correct solution because RBI needs power to control everything.

'position' alone cannot do anything.

'gifts', 'acceptance' and 'stage' all are wrong.

Hence, the correct option is (D).

27. 'finance' is the correct solution because these are money, bank, and finance-related matters which are handled by Finance minister.

a 'general' minister cannot handle money-related matters.

'chief' minister handles the state and 'prime' minister manages the country.

'temporary' is also wrong.

Hence, the correct option is (B).

28. 'government' is the correct solution because it is the government that manages everything.

'minister' alone cannot decide on anything.

'army', 'foreign' and 'people' all are wrong because they don't have the authority to make decisions for the country.

Hence, the correct option is (E).

29. 'assets' is the correct solution because according to the passage the government is giving assets to the people.

'money' and 'property' both are wrong because they can be included in assets.

'business' and 'lives' both are wrong because the government cannot give these things.

Hence, the correct option is (A).

30. The fragment D of the sentence is erroneous.

Reason:

The subject of the sentence is 'the law', NOT 'the principles of subrogation and contribution'. Hence, the usage of the verb 'are' in fragment D is erroneous. The correct verb in place of 'are' should have been 'is'.

Correct Sentence:

To an insurance company, the law relating to the principles of subrogation and contribution is of great importance.

Hence, the correct option is (D).

31. Given:

Product of the age of Tania and Ronita = 12 years

Let the age of Tania be x years

Age of Ronita = (x + 4) years

According to the question,

$\Rightarrow (x) \times (x + 4) = 12$

$\Rightarrow x^2 + 4x = 12$

$\Rightarrow x^2 + 4x - 12 = 0$

$\Rightarrow x^2 + (6 - 2) x - 12 = 0$

$\Rightarrow x^2 + 6x - 2x - 12 = 0$

$\Rightarrow x(x + 6) - 2(x + 6) = 0$

$\Rightarrow (x + 6) (x - 2) = 0$

$\Rightarrow x = -6, 2$

Present age of Ronita = (2 + 4) = 6 years

Age of Ronita after 5 years = (6 + 5) = 11 years

∴ The age of Ronita after 5 years is 11 years.

Hence, the correct option is (C).

32. n(S) = number of ways of drawing 3 balls out of 12

$$= {}^{12}C_3 = \frac{(12 \times 11 \times 10)}{(3 \times 2 \times 1)} = 220$$

n(E) = Number of ways of drawing 3 balls of diffrent colour (1 balls out of 5) or (1 balls out of 4) or (1 balls out of 3)

n(E) = ${}^5C_1 \times {}^4C_1 \times {}^3C_1$ = (5 × 4 × 3) = 60

$$P(E) = \frac{n(E)}{n(S)} = \frac{60}{220} = \frac{3}{11}$$

∴ Required Probability = $\dfrac{3}{11}$

Hence, the correct option is (B).

33. Given:

Initially A : B = 3 : 2

Finally A : B = 2 : 3

Using Replacement Concept of Mixture and Allegation.

$$\left(\frac{Quantity\ remaining}{Initial\ quantity} \right) = \left(1 - \left(\frac{Quantity\ replaced}{Total\ quantity} \right) \right)$$

For solution A,

$$\Rightarrow \frac{2}{3} = \left(1 - \left(\frac{10}{X} \right) \right)$$

$\Rightarrow X = 30$

∴ The total quantity of the mixture in the bottle = 30 L

Hence, the correct option is (C).

34. Given that,

Compound Interest (C.I.) – Simple Interest (S.I.) = Rs. 20

Rate = 4% per annum

Time = 2 years

We know that,

C.I. – S.I. = Principal $\left(\dfrac{Rate}{100}\right)^2$

So,

$20 = $ principal $\left(\dfrac{4}{100}\right)^2$

Principal = $\dfrac{(20 \times 100 \times 100)}{(4 \times 4)}$

Principal = Rs. 12500

Hence, the correct option is (B).

35. Given:

-4, -6, -10, -18, -34, -68, -130

The following model has been followed:

-4		-6		-10		-18		-34		-66		-130
	-2		-4		-8		-16		-32		-64	
		×2		×2		×2		×2		×2		

∴ The wrong number in the given series is -68.

Hence, the correct option is (D).

36. Given:

11, 31, 69, 131, 223, 352, 521

The logic behind the given pattern is as follows.

$\Rightarrow 2^3 + 3 = 11$

$\Rightarrow 3^3 + 4 = 31$

$\Rightarrow 4^3 + 5 = 69$

$\Rightarrow 5^3 + 6 = 131$

$\Rightarrow 6^3 + 7 = 223$

$\Rightarrow 7^3 + 8 = 351$

$\Rightarrow 8^3 + 9 = 521$

∴ The wrong number in the given series is 352.

Hence, the correct option is (D).

37. Given:

2, 9, 30, 93, 283, 849

The logic behind the given pattern is as follows.

$\Rightarrow 2 \times 3 + 3 = 9$

$\Rightarrow 9 \times 3 + 3 = 30$

$\Rightarrow 30 \times 3 + 3 = 93$

$\Rightarrow 93 \times 3 + 3 = 282$

$\Rightarrow 282 \times 3 + 3 = 849$

∴ The wrong number in the given series is 283.

Hence, the correct option is (D).

38. Given:

6, 7, 16, 51, 208, 1058, 6276

The logic behind the given pattern is as follows.

$\Rightarrow 6 \times 1 + 1 = 7$

$\Rightarrow 7 \times 2 + 2 = 16$

$\Rightarrow 16 \times 3 + 3 = 51$

$\Rightarrow 51 \times 4 + 4 = 208$

$\Rightarrow 208 \times 5 + 5 = 1045$

$\Rightarrow 1045 \times 6 + 6 = 6276$

∴ The wrong number in the given series is 1058.

Hence, the correct option is (C).

39. Given

I. $x^3 = 8$

$\Rightarrow x^3 = 2^3$

$\Rightarrow x = 2$

II. $y^2 = 4$

$\Rightarrow y^2 - 4 = 0$

$\Rightarrow (y + 2)(y - 2) = 0$

$\Rightarrow y = 2, -2$

Comparison between x and y (via Tabulation):

value of x	value of y	Relation
2	2	x = y
2	-2	x > y

∴ $x \geq y$

Hence, the correct option is (C).

40. Given

I. $x^2 - 3x + 2 = 0$

$\Rightarrow x^2 - 2x - 1x + 2 = 0$

$\Rightarrow x(x - 2) - 1(x - 2) = 0$

$\Rightarrow (x - 1)(x - 2) = 0$

$\Rightarrow x = 1, 2$

II. $y^2 = 1$

$\Rightarrow y^2 - 1 = 0$

$\Rightarrow (y + 1)(y - 1) = 0$

$\Rightarrow y = 1, -1$

Comparison between x and y (via Tabulation):

Value of x	Value of y	Relation
1	1	x = y
1	-1	x > y
2	1	x > y
2	-1	x > y

$\therefore x \geq y$

Hence, the correct option is (C).

41. Given

I. $x^{\frac{5}{2}} = \sqrt{243}$

$\Rightarrow x^{\frac{5}{2}} = (243)^{\frac{1}{2}}$

$\Rightarrow x^{\frac{5}{2}} = (3^5)^{\frac{1}{2}}$

$\Rightarrow x^{\frac{5}{2}} = 3^{\frac{5}{2}}$

$\Rightarrow x = 3$

II. $2y^{\frac{3}{2}} = \sqrt{256}$

$\Rightarrow y^{\frac{3}{2}} = \left(\frac{1}{2}\right) \times \sqrt{256}$

$\Rightarrow y^{\frac{3}{2}} = \sqrt{\left(\frac{256}{4}\right)}$

$\Rightarrow y^{\frac{3}{2}} = \sqrt{64}$

$\Rightarrow y^{\frac{3}{2}} = 4^{\frac{3}{2}}$

$\Rightarrow y = 4$

$\therefore x < y$

Hence, the correct option is (B).

42. Given

I: $x^2 - 2x - 35 = 0$

$\Rightarrow x^2 - 7x + 5x - 35 = 0$

$\Rightarrow x \times (x - 7) + 5 \times (x - 7) = 0$

$\Rightarrow (x - 7) \times (x + 5) = 0$

$\Rightarrow x = 7, -5$

II: $2y^2 + 72y + 70 = 0$

$\Rightarrow 2y^2 + 2y + 70y + 70 = 0$

$\Rightarrow 2y \times (y + 1) + 70 \times (y + 1) = 0$

$\Rightarrow (y + 1) \times (2y + 70) = 0$

$\Rightarrow y = 1, \dfrac{70}{2}$

$\Rightarrow y = (-1), (-35)$

Comparison between x and y (via Tabulation):

Value of x	Relation	Value of y

7	>	-1
7	>	-35
-5	<	-1
-5	>	-35

$\therefore$ Relationship between x and y cannot be established.

Hence, the correct option is (E).

43. Given

I. $3x^2 - 47x + 160 = 0$

$\Rightarrow 3x^2 - 32x - 15x + 160 = 0$

$\Rightarrow x (3x - 32) - 5 (3x - 32) = 0$

$\Rightarrow (x - 5) (3x - 32) = 0$

$\Rightarrow x = 5, \dfrac{32}{3}$

II. $6y^2 - 59y + 119 = 0$

$\Rightarrow 6y^2 - 17y - 42y + 119 = 0$

$\Rightarrow y (6y - 17) - 7 (6y - 17) = 0$

$\Rightarrow (6y - 17) (y - 7) = 0$

$\Rightarrow y = \dfrac{17}{6}, 7$

Comparison between x and y (via Tabulation):

Value of x	Value of y	Relation
5	$\dfrac{17}{6}$	x > y
5	7	x < y
$\dfrac{32}{3}$	$\dfrac{17}{6}$	x > y
$\dfrac{32}{3}$	7	x > y

$\therefore$ Relationship between x and y cannot be established

Hence, the correct option is (E).

44. According to the statements given above.

The budget of stay and food and shopping is 50% and 25% more than the budget of travel.

Let the budget for travel is 100% and then for stay and food is 150% and for shopping is 125%

$\therefore$ Travel : Stay and food : Shopping = 100 : 150 : 125 = 4 : 6 : 5

Now, 15% of 5X = 2700

$\Rightarrow$ X = Rs. 3600

By the information given in the three statements above the following table can be formed

Travel		Stay and food		Shopping	
4X		6X		5X	
Air tickets	Taxi	Stay	Food	Spending	Saving
75%	25%	70%	30%	85%	15%
Total saving from shopping budget = Rs. 2700					

From the table given above value of x is Rs. 3600

Total budget of trip = 4X + 6X + 5X = 15X = 15 × 3600 = Rs. 54000

So, the total budget of trip is Rs. 54000

Hence, the correct option is (A).

45. According to the statements given above.

The budget of stay and food and shopping is 50% and 25% more than the budget of travel.

Let the budget for travel is 100% and then for stay and food is 150% and for shopping is 125%

∴ Travel : Stay and food : Shopping = 100 : 150 : 125 = 4 : 6 : 5

Now, 15% of 5X = 2700

⇒ X = Rs. 3600

By the information given in the three statements above the following table can be formed

Travel		Stay and food		Shopping	
4X		6X		5X	
Air tickets	Taxi	Stay	Food	Spending	Saving
75%	25%	70%	30%	85%	15%
Total saving from shopping budget = Rs. 2700					

From the table given above

Total budget for Travel = 4X

Amount spend on air tickets = 75% of 4X = 3X

And Amount spend on taxi = 25% of 4X = X

∴ Required difference = 3X − X = 2X

Now, the value of X is Rs. 3600

∴ Difference = 2X = 2 × 3600 = Rs. 7200

So, the required difference is Rs. 7200

Hence, the correct option is (A).

46. According to the statements given above.

The budget of stay and food and shopping is 50% and 25% more than the budget of travel.

Let the budget for travel is 100% and then for stay and food is 150% and for shopping is 125%

∴ Travel : Stay and food : Shopping = 100 : 150 : 125 = 4 : 6 : 5

Now, 15% of 5X = 2700

⇒ X = Rs. 3600

By the information given in the three statements above the following table can be formed

Travel		Stay and food		Shopping	
4X		6X		5X	
Air tickets	Taxi	Stay	Food	Spending	Saving
75%	25%	70%	30%	85%	15%
Total saving from shopping budget = Rs. 2700					

From the table given above

Amount of money spend on food = 30% of 6X = 1.8X

Now, value of X is Rs. 3600

∴ Money spend on food = 1.8 × 3600 = Rs. 6480

So, the money spend on food is Rs. 6480

Hence, the correct option is (D).

47. According to the statements given above.

The budget of stay and food and shopping is 50% and 25% more than the budget of travel.

Let the budget for travel is 100% and then for stay and food is 150% and for shopping is 125%

∴ Travel : Stay and food : Shopping = 100 : 150 : 125 = 4 : 6 : 5

Now, 15% of 5X = 2700

⇒ X = Rs. 3600

By the information given in the three statements above the following table can be formed

Travel		Stay and food		Shopping	
4X		6X		5X	
Air tickets	Taxi	Stay	Food	Spending	Saving
75%	25%	70%	30%	85%	15%
Total saving from shopping budget = Rs. 2700					

We know that

$$\text{Required percentage} = \left(\frac{First\ quantity}{Second\ quantity}\right) \times 100$$

From the table given above

Money spend on Stay = 70% of 6X = 4.2X

And budget for shopping = 5X

∴ Required percentage = $\left(\frac{(5X - 4.2X)}{5X}\right) \times 100 = 16\%$

So, required percentage is 16%

Hence, the correct option is (D).

48. According to the statements given above.

The budget of stay and food and shopping is 50% and 25% more than the budget of travel.

Let the budget for travel is 100% and then for stay and food is 150% and for shopping is 125%

∴ Travel : Stay and food : Shopping = 100 : 150 : 125 = 4 : 6 : 5

Now, 15% of 5X = 2700

⇒ X = Rs. 3600

By the information given in the three statements above the following table can be formed

Travel		Stay and food		Shopping	
4X		6X		5X	
Air tickets	Taxi	Stay	Food	Spending	Saving
75%	25%	70%	30%	85%	15%

Total saving from shopping budget = Rs. 2700

We know that

Average = $\dfrac{(Sum\ of\ all\ terms)}{Total\ number\ of\ terms}$

From the table given above

Amount of money spend on Taxi = 25% of 4X = X

Amount of money spend on Food = 30% of 6X = 1.8X

Amount of money spend on Taxi = 15% of 5X = 0.75X

∴ Average = $\dfrac{(X + 1.8X + 0.75X)}{3} = \dfrac{3.55X}{3} = \dfrac{(3.55 \times 3600)}{3} =$ Rs. 4260

So, the average of amount of money spend on Taxi, Food and saving is Rs. 4260

Hence, the correct option is (A).

49. Given:

The average age of 10 students = 20 years

Average age is increased by 10%, when teacher age is included.

We know that,

Average = $\dfrac{sum\ of\ all\ observation}{total\ number\ of\ observations}$

Sum of the ages of 10 students = 200 years

⇒ 10% increased in average age = 10% of 20 = 2

⇒ New average age = 22 years

⇒ Sum of the ages of 10 students and teacher = 22 × (11) = 242 years

⇒ Age of teacher = 242 – 200 = 42 years

Hence, the correct option is (E).

50. Given:

MP is Rs. 4200, two successive discounts are 7% each.

We know that

SP = MP – discount

MP = Rs 4200; first discount = 4200 × $\left(\dfrac{7}{100}\right)$ ⇒ Rs. 294

Price after first discount = 4200 – 294 ⇒ Rs. 3906

Second discount = 3906 × $\left(\dfrac{7}{100}\right)$ ⇒ Rs. 273. 42

Price after second discount = 3906 – 273.42

⇒ Rs. 3632.58

Hence, the correct option is (E).

51. We know that,

Area of rectangular garden = length × breadth

⇒ 120 = 15 × breadth

⇒ breadth = $\dfrac{120}{15}$

⇒ breadth = 8 cm

Now,

Length of rectangular garden including path = 15 + 4 + 4

⇒ 23 cm

Breadth of rectangular garden including path = 8 + 4 + 4

⇒ 16 cm

Now,

Area of rectangular garden including path = 23 × 16

⇒ 368 cm²

Now,

Area of path = Area of rectangular garden including path – Area of rectangular shape garden

⇒ 368 – 120

⇒ 248 cm²

Now,

Total cost gravelling the path = Area of path × gravelling cost

⇒ 248 × 5

⇒ Rs. 1240

∴ The Total cost of graveling path = Rs. 1240

Hence, the correct option is (D).

52. Statement (I)

Ratio of amount = Chintu : Pintu : Bittu

⇒ 3 : 2 : 6

Ratio of time – 4 : 3 : 5

Total investment = 3 × 4 : 2 × 3 : 6 × 5

⇒ 12 : 6 : 30

⇒ 6 : 3 : 15

Statement (II)

If the difference of Pintu and Bittu is Rs. 8,400

From statement I and II

When Pintu = 3, then Bittu = 10

Difference = 10 – 3 = 7

Total = 6 + 3 + 10 = 19

⇒ 7 = 8,400

⇒ 19 = ?

Total profit = $\left(\dfrac{8,400}{7}\right)$ × 19 = 22,800

∴ Total profit of Pintu, Chintu and Bittu = Rs. 22,800

So, both the statements I and II together are needed to answer the question.

Hence, the correct option is (C).

53. Let the investment of Lucky be 100

Arpit invests 50% more than Lucky

So, Investment of Arpit = $100 \times \dfrac{150}{100} = 150$

Arpit invests 25% less than Ankush

So, Investment of Ankush = $150 \times \dfrac{100}{75} = 200$

The ratio of investment = Arpit : Lucky : Ankush

$\Rightarrow 150 : 100 : 200$

$\Rightarrow 3 : 2 : 4$

Statement (II)

Let the profit of Lucky be 100

Ankush earns 20% more than Lucky

So, profit of Ankush = $100 \times \dfrac{120}{100} = 120$

Ankush earns 25% less than Arpit

So, profit earns by Arpit = $120 \times \dfrac{100}{75} = 160$

The ratio of profit = Arpit : Lucky : Ankush

$\Rightarrow 160 : 100 : 120$

$\Rightarrow 8 : 5 : 6$

Let the time of Arpit be T_1

Let the time of Lucky be T_2

Let the time of Ankush be T_3

Time of Arpit = $T_1 = \dfrac{Profit}{Capital\ investment}$

$\Rightarrow \dfrac{8}{3}$

Time of Lucky = $T_2 = \dfrac{5}{2}$

Time of Ankush = $T_3 = \dfrac{6}{4} = \dfrac{3}{2}$

The ratio of time = $T_1 : T_2 : T_3$

$\Rightarrow \dfrac{8}{3} : \dfrac{5}{2} : \dfrac{3}{2}$

$\Rightarrow \left(\dfrac{8}{3}\right) \times 6 : \left(\dfrac{5}{2}\right) \times 6 : \left(\dfrac{3}{2}\right) \times 6$

$\Rightarrow 16 : 15 : 9$

$\therefore$ Ratio of time = $16 : 15 : 9$

So, both statements I and II together are needed to answer the question.

Hence, the correct option is (C).

54. Considering the following given question

$\Rightarrow \sqrt{\left(\sqrt{8100} + \sqrt{6241}\right)} = ?$

$\Rightarrow \sqrt{(90 + 79)} = ?$

$\Rightarrow \sqrt{169} = ?$

$\therefore ? = 13$

Hence, the correct option is (D).

55. Considering the following given question

$[(140 \div 20) \times 25 \div 7 \times 250] \div 50 \times 5 = ?$

$\Rightarrow [(140 \div 20) \times 25 \div 7 \times 250] \div 50 \times 5 = ?$

$\Rightarrow [7 \times 25 \div 7 \times 250] \div 50 \times 5 = ?$

$\Rightarrow [25 \times 250] \div 50 \times 5 = ?$

$\Rightarrow 6250 \div 50 \times 5 = ?$

$\Rightarrow 125 \times 5 = ?$

$\therefore ? = 625$

Hence, the correct option is (D).

56. Considering the following given question

$(4575 - 1740 - 2250) = ? - 39 + \sqrt{9025}$

$\Rightarrow (4575 - 1740 - 2250) = ? - 39 + \sqrt{9025}$

$\Rightarrow (4575 - 3990) = ? - 39 + \sqrt{9025}$

$\Rightarrow 585 = ? - 39 + \sqrt{9025}$

$\Rightarrow 585 = ? - 39 + 95$

$\Rightarrow 585 + 39 = ? + 95$

$\Rightarrow 624 = ? + 95$

$\Rightarrow 624 - 95 = ?$

$\Rightarrow 529 = ?$

$\therefore ? = 529$

Hence, the correct option is (D).

57. Given that,

$(45\% \text{ of } 60 - \sqrt{121}) \times ? = 1488$

$\Rightarrow (45\% \times 60 - 11) \times ? = 1488$

$\Rightarrow \left(\dfrac{45}{100} \times 60 - 11\right) \times ? = 1488$

$\Rightarrow (27 - 11) \times ? = 1488$

$\Rightarrow 16 \times ? = 1488$

$\Rightarrow ? = \dfrac{1488}{16}$

⇒ ? = 93

Hence, the correct option is (B).

58. Given that,

$$\frac{2}{3} \text{ of } 48 + [7 + (-16) + 24 - 7] = ?$$

⇒ 2 × 16 + {7 - 16 + 24 - 7} =?

⇒ 32 + 8 = ?

⇒ ? = 40

Hence, the correct option is (B).

59. Given that,

11 × 66 – 21 × 22 + 91 × 19

⇒ 726 – 462 + 1729 = ?

⇒ ? = 1993

Hence, the correct option is (A).

60. Given that,

$65 × 5 – 60 × 75\% + 80 – 10^2 = ?$

⇒ 325 – 45 + 80 – 100 = ?

⇒ 325 – 65 = ?

⇒ 260

∴ ? = 260

Hence, the correct option is (B).

61. Considering the given equation

$$\left\{\left(\frac{2970}{66}\right) \times \left(\frac{3960}{88}\right)\right\}^{\left(\frac{1}{2}\right)} + 200\% \text{ of } 6.5 + 6 = x^3$$

$$\Rightarrow \{45 \times 45\}^{\left(\frac{1}{2}\right)} + 200\% \text{ of } 6.5 + 6 = x^3$$

⇒ 45 + 13 + 6 = x^3

⇒ 64 = x^3

⇒ x = 4

Hence, the correct option is (D).

62. Considering the given equation

$$\left\{(18) \times \left(\frac{1650}{25}\right) \div (36)\right\} + \left\{\left(\frac{391}{17}\right) + \left(\frac{624}{26}\right)\right\} = ?$$

⇒ {18 × 66 ÷ 36} + {23 + 24} = ?

⇒ 33 + 47 = ?

⇒ ? = 80

Hence, the correct option is (D).

63. Given:

78 + 85 – (13 × 8) + (81 ÷ 3) = ?

Calculation:

78 + 85 – (13 × 8) + (81 ÷ 3) = ?

⇒ 163 - 104 + 27 = ?

⇒ ? = 190 - 104

? = 86

∴ The value of ? is 86

78 + 85 – (13 × 8) + (81 ÷ 3) = ?

⇒ 163 - 104 + 27 = ?

⇒ ? = 190 - 104

? = 86

∴ The value of ? is 86

Hence, the correct option is (B).

64. Let each of them individually takes d days to complete a work 'x'.

Both of them working simultaneously take 20 days to complete work.

So, Time taken = $\dfrac{totalwork}{W_A + W_B}$

$20 = \dfrac{x}{[\left(\frac{x}{d}\right) + \left(\frac{x}{d}\right)]}$

d = 40

Work done in 17 days = $17\left(\dfrac{2x}{d}\right)$

Work done in 17 days = $\dfrac{34x}{40} = \dfrac{17x}{20}$

Work left = x - $\dfrac{17x}{20}$

Work left = $\dfrac{3x}{20}$

Increase in efficiency = $\dfrac{W_{B,N} - W_{B,O}}{W_{B,O} \times 100}$

$\dfrac{140}{100} = \dfrac{W_{B,N}}{W_{B,O}}$

$$W_{B,N} = 7 \times \dfrac{\left(\frac{x}{40}\right)}{5} = \left(\dfrac{7x}{200}\right)$$

∴ Time taken = $\dfrac{\left(\frac{3x}{20}\right)}{\left(\frac{7x}{200}\right)} = \dfrac{30}{7}$ days

Hence, the correct option is (A).

65. Given:

The given number series is:

1, 5, 20, 57, 121, 221, 365

Calculation:

The given number series follows the relation:

$$1 + 2^2 = 5$$

$5 + 4^2 = 21$

$21 + 6^2 = 57$

$57 + 8^2 = 121$

$121 + 10^2 = 221$

$221 + 12^2 = 365$

$\therefore$ The wrong number in the given series is 20

Hence, the correct option is (B).

66. The least possible Venn diagram for the given statements is as follows:

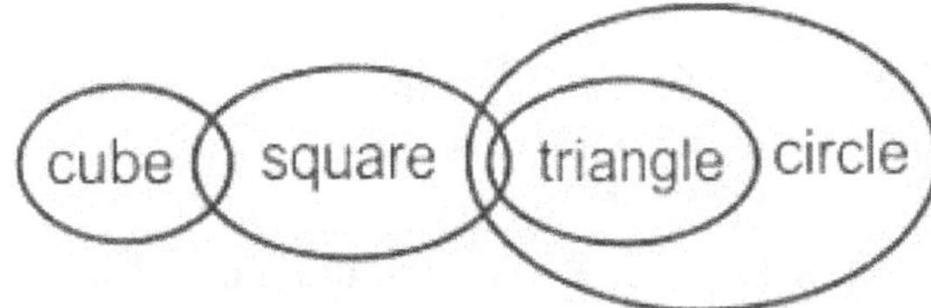

Conclusions:

I. Atleast some circle are cube → False (As there is no given relation between the cube and the circle, so we cannot give a definite conclusion).

II. No circle is a cube → False (As there is no given relation between the cube and the circle, so we cannot give a definite conclusion).

And here both I and II make a complementary pair.

(When two entities are same in two conclusions and both are false, so they form a complementary pair, hence either - or condition will generate).

So, either I or II follow.

Hence, the correct option is (C).

67. The least possible Venn diagram for the given statements is as follows:

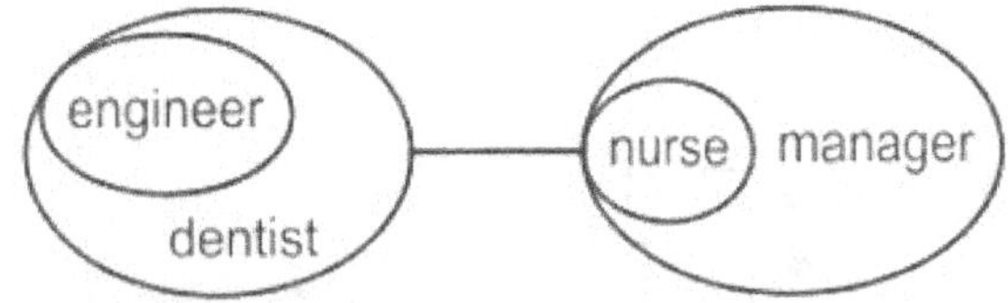

Conclusions:

I. No engineer is a manager → False (As there is no given relation between the cube and the circle, so we cannot give a definite conclusion). There is a possibility diagram :

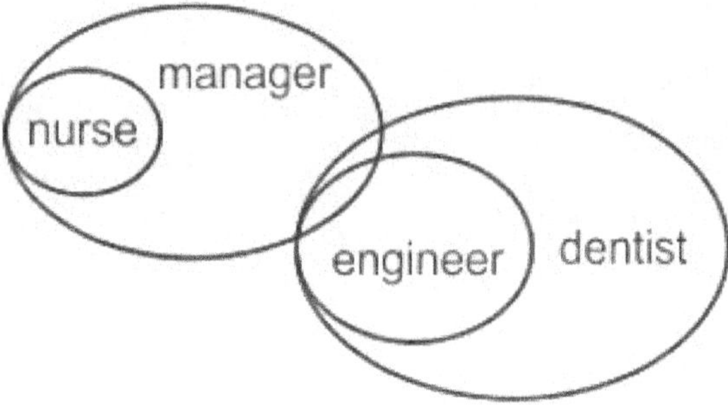

So, we can say there is a possibility for some engineers are managers, but not definitely.

II. All dentist being manager is a possibility.→ True, As there is also a possibility diagram:

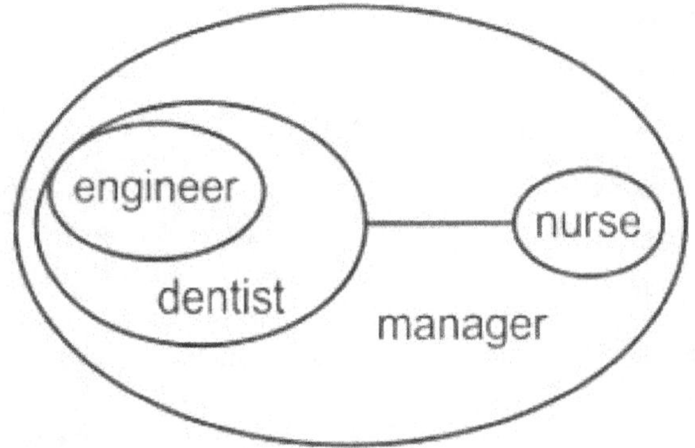

So, we can see from the above figure that all dentist being manager is a possibility is true.

So, Only II follows.

Hence, the correct option is (B).

68. The least possible Venn diagram for the given statements is as follows:

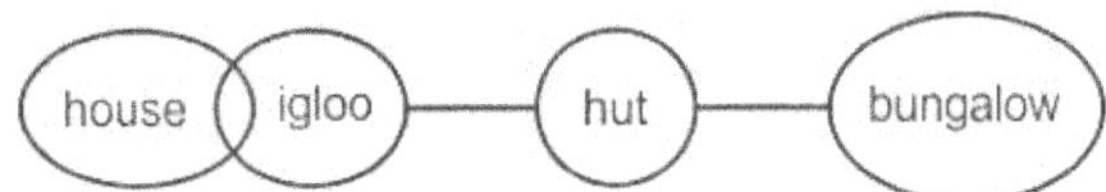

Conclusions:

I. All houses being hut is a possibility. → False (As some part of house is in igloo, which can never be hut, so all house can never be hut).

II. Maximum igloo are bunglow. → False (As there is no certain statement or relation given between igloo and bunglow, so we can not say a definife conclusion). (As Maximum is considered as "some").

So, Neither I nor II follow.

Hence, the correct option is (C).

Ques (69-71):

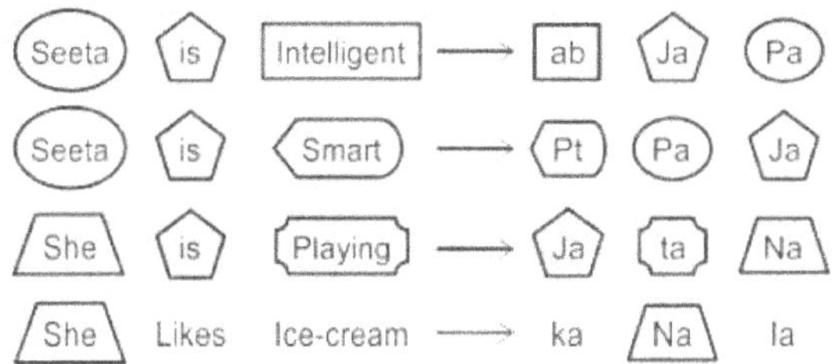

69. So, seeta is coded as 'pa'.

Hence, the correct option is (B).

70. Code for 'seeta' is 'pa',

Code for 'likes' is either 'ka' or 'la',

Code for 'ice-cream' is either 'ka' or 'la'.

So, the possible code for 'seeta likes ice-cream' is 'pa ka la'.

Hence, the correct option is (B).

71. Code 'na' corresponds to 'she',

Code 'ja' corresponds to 'is',

Code 'pt' corresponds to 'smart'

So, code 'na ja pa' is for 'she is smart'.

Hence, the correct option is (A).

Ques (72-76): Persons: K, O, G, S, A, and L

1. L is second to the right of G.

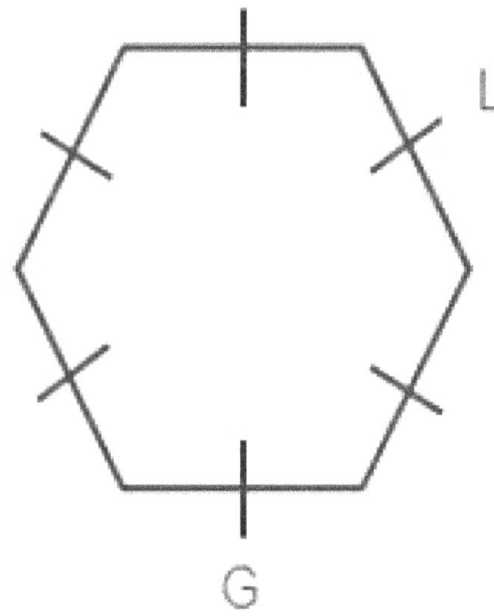

2. There are only 2 persons sitting between L and K.

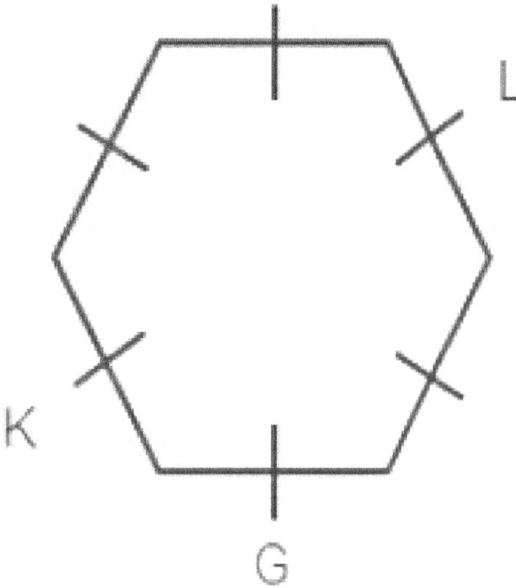

3. O and S are not immediate neighbour of K.

So, A is immediate neighbour of K.

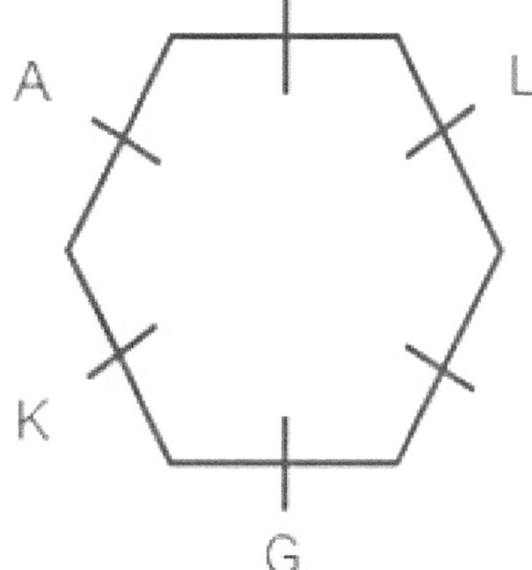

4. A and O are immediate neighbours.

Now only S is left, who will sit on immediate right of G.

The final arrangement is shown below:

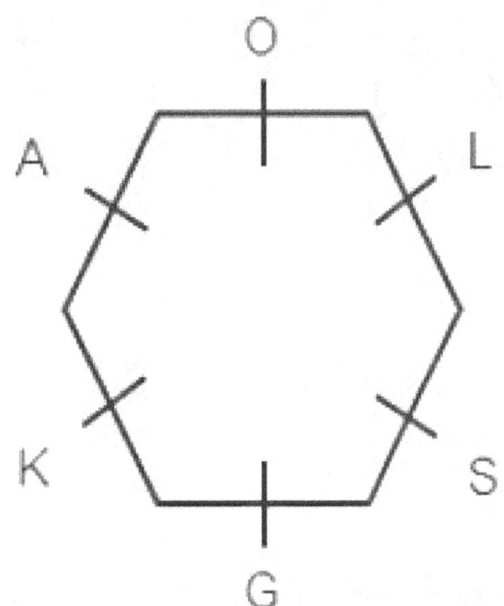

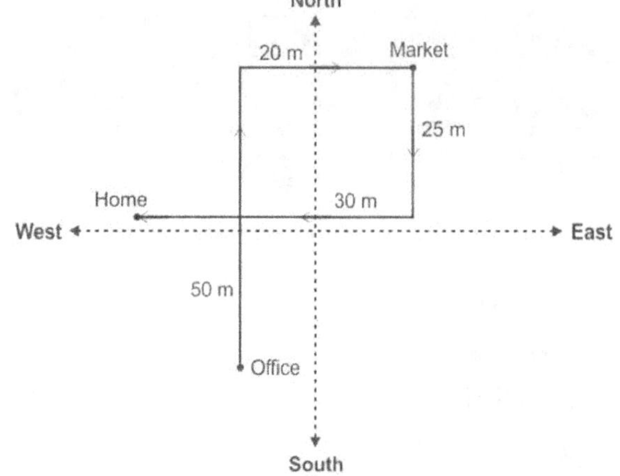

72. So, three persons sits between A and G when counted from right of G.

Hence, the correct option is (A).

73. So, O sits exactly opposite to G.

Hence, the correct option is (D).

74. So, L sits second to the left from A.

Hence, the correct option is (B).

75. 1. A and S are immediate neighbours → False (A and S are sitting opposite to each other)

2. G is third to the left of K → False (G is immediate right of K)

3. S is immediate left of L → True

4. O is not immediate neighbour of L → False (O is immediate neighbour of L)

5. K is second to the right of S → False (K is second to the left of S)

So, 'S is immediate left of L' is the correct statement.

Hence, the correct option is (C).

76. So, K is sitting immediate right of A.

Hence, the correct option is (E).

Ques (77-79): We have drawn the figure according to the information given in the question,

77. From the figure total distance covered by Sheela is (50 + 20 + 25 + 30) = 125 m.

So, Sheela covered a 125 m distance to reach her home.

Hence, the correct option is (B).

78. So, From the figure, it is clear that the market is in the North-East direction from her office.

Hence, the correct option is (D).

79. So, from the figure, it is clear that the Home of Sheela is in South-West direction to the Market.

Hence, the correct option is (C).

Ques (80-84): Seven people: A, B, C, D, E, F and G

1) F travels on Wednesday.

2) D doesn't travel on the day after the day on which F travels.

Case 1:

Day	Person
Monday	D
Tuesday	
Wednesday	F
Thursday	
Friday	
Saturday	
Sunday	

Case 2:

Day	Person
Monday	
Tuesday	D
Wednesday	F
Thursday	
Friday	
Saturday	
Sunday	

3) E travels on the day which is 4 days after the day on which D travels.

4) The number of persons between the one who travels on Wednesday and B is the same as the number of persons between D and G.

5) G travels on the day just before the day on which E travels.

Case 1:

Day	Person
Monday	D
Tuesday	
Wednesday	F
Thursday	G
Friday	E
Saturday	B
Sunday	

Case 2:

Day	Person
Monday	
Tuesday	D
Wednesday	F
Thursday	
Friday	G
Saturday	E
Sunday	

C goes on Sunday.

So, the correct answer is C.

Using statement 5, Case 2 will be eliminated as there is a gap of 2 days between D and G. F travels on Wednesday. So, B will travel on Saturday. But E travels on Saturday.

6) C travels on the day after the day B travels.

Case 1:

Day	Person
Monday	D
Tuesday	A
Wednesday	F
Thursday	G
Friday	E
Saturday	B
Sunday	C

This is the final arrangement.

80. So, 'C' goes on Sunday.

Hence, the correct option is (D).

81. So, D travels on Monday.

Hence, the correct option is (D).

82. So, three people go after G.

Hence, the correct option is (C).

83. A goes on Tuesday. A is not given in options.

So, 'None of these' is the correct answer.

Hence, the correct option is (E).

84. G goes on Thursday.

Two persons go between C and the one who goes on G.

So, 'Two' is the correct answer.

Hence, the correct option is (C).

Symbol in Diagram	Meaning
◯	Female
▢	Male
═══	Married Couple
───	Siblings
│	Difference of A Generation

Ques (85-87):

In a family there are eight members.

1) A is mother of B, who is brother of C. C and Q are siblings.

2) Y is daughter of P. Z is brother in law of B, who is son of D.

3) A has only one son. There are only two married couples in the family. P is married to B.

The family tree is as follows:

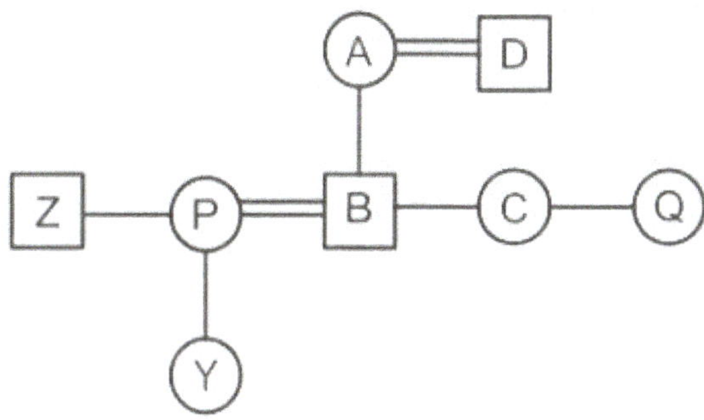

85. So, we can see that P is the sister of Z.

Hence, the correct option is (B).

86. So, we can see that C is the Aunt of Y.

Hence, the correct option is (A).

87. So, we can see that there are three male members.

Hence, the correct option is (B).

Ques (88-92):Eight persons: A, B, C, D, W, X, Y and Z

i) A sits in the row facing South facing W.

ii) W sits third to the left of D.

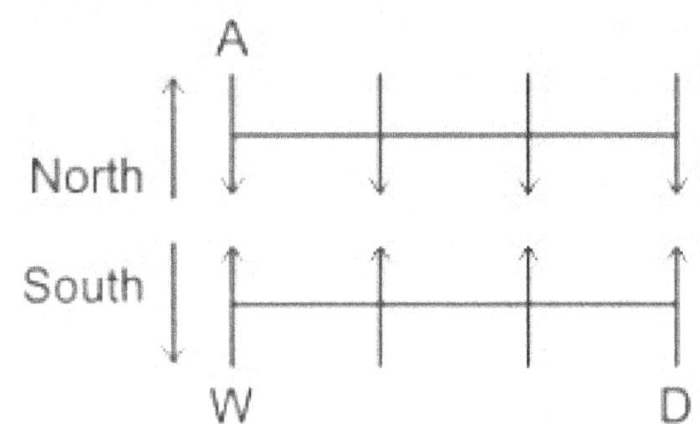

iii) Y who sits second to the right of X.

iv) C sits to the immediate left of Z.

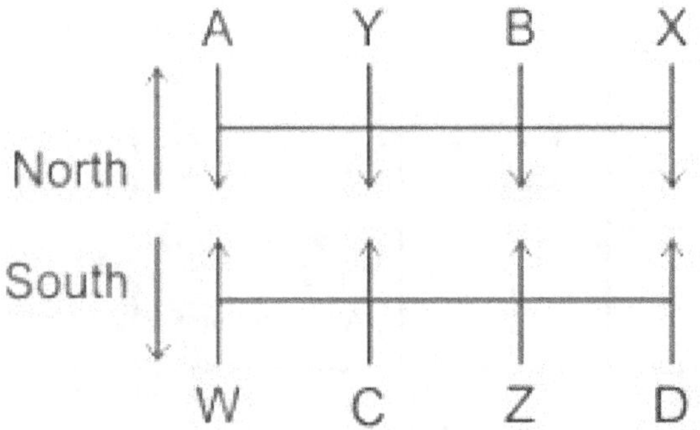

88. So, A sits second to the right of B.

Hence, the correct option is (A).

89. So, Y sits opposite C.

Hence, the correct option is (C).

90. Here, A, Y, B and X are facing South whereas Z is facing North.

So, Z does not belong to the group.

Hence, the correct option is (A).

91. i) W sits second to the left of Z. → True

ii) B sits between C and D. → False

iii) Y sits second to the right of C.→ False

So, only statement (i) is correct.

Hence, the correct option is (A).

92. So, A and X sits at extreme positions in row 2.

Hence, the correct option is (C).

93. Given statements: N ≥ H ≤ T > R = E; E > O < P = I

On combination: N ≥ H ≤ T > R = E > O < P = I

Conclusion

I. N > E → False (as N ≥ H ≤ T > R = E)

II. T > O → True (as T > R = E > O)

So, only conclusion II follows.

Hence, the correct option is (C).

94. Given statements: A > B < C = D; D < E < F

On combining: A > B < C = D < E < F

Conclusions:

I. A < E → False (as A > B < C = D < E < F → A > B < C = D < E → thus clear relation between A and E cannot be determined)

II. E > B → True (as A > B < C = D < E < F → B < C = D < E → E > D = C > B → E > B)

Therefore, conclusion II is True.

Hence, the correct option is (B).

95. Given Statements: H < A > R = D; I ≤ K ≥ P; H < P

On Combining: I ≤ K ≥ P > H < A > R = D

Conclusions:

I. K > R → False (As, K ≥ P > H < A > R → Clear relation between K and R cannot be determined)

II. D ≤ K → False (As, K ≥ P > H < A > R = D→ Clear relation between D and K cannot be determined)

So, none of the conclusion is true

Hence, the correct option is (E).

96. Given statements: P = Q ≤ R; T = P; T > S

On combining: S < P = Q = T ≤ R

I. Q < S → False (as S < P = Q)

II. R < S → False (as S < T ≤ R)

Therefore none follows.

Hence, the correct option is (E).

Ques (97-99): Seven person Manav, Rohan, Amit, Harsh, Rajat, Mohit and Sumit.

1) Amit got more marks than only Sumit & Rajat and Rajat got least marks.

—— > —— > —— > —— > Amit > Sumit > Rajat

2) Harsh got more marks than Manav and less marks than Rohan and Rohan did not get the highest marks.

Mohit > Rohan > Harsh > Manav > Amit > Sumit > Rajat

3) Second lowest person got 45 marks.

Mohit > Rohan > Harsh > Manav > Amit > Sumit > Rajat
                                                45

97. 42 is the possible score which Rajat scored.

Hence, the correct option is (C).

98. So, the answer is 6.

Hence, the correct option is (C).

99. 4) Sum of Sumit and Rohan score = 113, score of Sumit is 45 then score of Rohan is 68.

5) Sum of Manav and Rohan score = 124, score of Rohan is 68 then score of Manav is 56.

So, the score of Manav is 56.

Hence, the correct option is (B).

100. Given word: DOLPHIN

The alphabets are positioned in the following order:

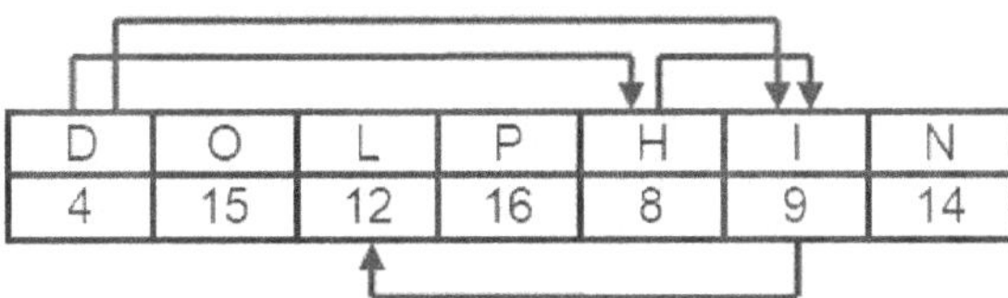

Alphabets	A	B	C	D	E	F	G	H	I	J	K	L	M
Positional value	1	2	3	4	5	6	7	8	9	10	11	12	13
Positional value	26	25	24	23	22	21	20	19	18	17	16	15	14
Alphabets	Z	Y	X	W	V	U	T	S	R	Q	P	O	N

The given word can be represented as follows:

D	O	L	P	H	I	N
4	15	12	16	8	9	14

In forward direction: DH, DI, HI

In backward direction: IL

Thus, here are four pairs of such letters.

Hence, the correct option is (B).

English Language

Ques (1-2):Directions: In the following question, the sentence given with a blank to be filled in with an appropriate word. Select the correct alternative out of the four and indicate it by selecting the appropriate option.

Q.1 The __________ of global awareness in today's youth has never been more important than it is today.

A. Tolerance
B. Relevance
C. Remembrance
D. Deliverance
E. None of these

Q.2 Amanda realized that it was no longer necessary to _______ Sam everywhere he went.

A. Accord
B. Accommodate
C. Accompany
D. Accentuate
E. Emulate

Q.3 Fill in the blanks with the suitable option.

The vast cleaning system _______ to not only collect discarded fishing nets and large visible plastic objects, but also microplastics.

A. Are designed
B. Is designing
C. Were
D. Was designing
E. Is designed

Ques (4-5):Directions: Select the most appropriate meaning of the underlined idiom.

Q.4 Prince George is said to be **a chip off the old block**, very well mannered.

A. Similar in behaviour to the parents
B. Chipping a log of wood
C. Cutting a block of old stone
D. Bringing in firewood
E. Unlike the parents

Q.5 People with a suspicious nature like **to keep everyone at an arm's length**.

A. Stay at a physical distance.
B. Hold someone by the arm.
C. Punch someone's arm.
D. Become over-friendly.
E. Avoid becoming friendly with someone.

Ques (6-7):Directions: Select the most appropriate word to fill in the blank.

Q.6 To prevent violence, it is _____ that global governance becomes genuinely democratic.

A. Essential
B. Credential
C. Prudential
D. Evidential
E. Sequential

Q.7 Last year the company looked _______ but in recent weeks it has begun to have problems.

A. Incomprehensible
B. Invincible
C. Incorrigible
D. Impressive
E. Impossible

Ques (8-10):Directions: Select the most appropriate meaning of the given idiom.

Q.8 To play with fire

A. To fight fires like a fireman
B. To pour oil on a burning fire
C. To act in a dangerous and risky way
D. To hold revenge against someone
E. To put someone on fire

Q.9 To ring one's own bell

A. To think properly
B. To indulge in self-praise
C. To commit a theft
D. To be one's publicity agent
E. None of the above

Q.10 Catch the tartar

A. A concocted story
B. To catch a dangerous person
C. To fulfill the purpose
D. Bitter relation
E. To turn out

Ques (11-15):Directions: A sentence/a part of the sentence is underlined. Five alternatives are given to the underlined part, which will improve the meaning of the sentence. Choose the correct alternative. In case no improvement is needed, click the option corresponding to 'No improvement'.

Q.11 After an <u>impressed performance</u> at the Syed Mushtaq Ali T20 Trophy, there was an intense bidding war over Khan between Punjab Kings and Royal Challengers Bangalore.

A. impressive pro forma
B. impressed pro forma
C. impression performance
D. impressive performance
E. No improvement

Q.12 Diabetes is a severe metabolic disorder that <u>caused high blood</u> glucose.

A. causing high blood
B. causes high blood
C. cause highly blood
D. highest blood
E. No improvement

Q.13 The environment provides us with life-sustaining resources, and it is <u>essential preserve</u> and protect it.

A. essential to preserve
B. essential preserving

C. essential preserved

D. essential will be preserved

E. No improvement

Q.14 Social media is now <u>filled by people</u> claiming the Earth is flat, climate change isn't real, and it is not a surprise.

A. fill by people

B. filled with people

C. filled across people

D. filled towards people

E. No improvement

Q.15 <u>Having been passed</u> my driving test, I was able to buy my first car.

A. Having passed

B. Having being passed

C. I passed

D. I have been passed

E. No improvement

Ques (16-25):Direction: Read the passage and answer the following questions.

Ever since the first gleaming towers sprang out of the desert, Dubai has gotten used to rapid change. It's no stranger to **boom-and-bust.** What's happening now is different: a slow bleed. The city's iconic builders are ploughing ahead. Cranes are everywhere. But no one is sure who'll occupy all that new retail and office space. Already, Dubai's malls are noticeably less full of stores and restaurants than they once were. Expatriates, the lifeblood of the economy, have started to pack up and go home -- or at least talk about it, as the cost of living and doing business surges. Corporate mainstays, from Emirates airline to developer Emaar Properties, just reported disappointing third-quarter profits. The stock market is having its worst year since 2008. Business unease was already apparent in April when Sheikh Mohammed bin Rashid Al Maktoum convened a meeting with more than 100 executives in his palace overlooking the Persian Gulf. The bosses raised issues including hefty government fees –- which are eroding the comparative advantage of tax-free Dubai –- to strict visa rules that push foreigners out when they lose their jobs. The conclave was followed by a flurry of decisions, still working their way through the system. But a fix for what's **ailing** Dubai may be beyond the powers of its ruler. Sheikh Mohammed and his predecessors built a fishing village into a hub for finance, trade and tourism in the region –- but now that region is changing, perhaps for good.

The oil slump since 2014 hit big spenders from neighbouring Gulf states who used to flock to Dubai (tourists from China and India are filling the gap, but they're more price-conscious). Saudis, in particular, are feeling the pinch, as their own government imposes fiscal **austerity** and confiscates private wealth. The city's role as a trading post is being undermined by a global tariff war –- and in particular by the U.S. drive to shut down commerce with nearby Iran. Now that the state of Dubai is part of the UAE, has become an active player in those conflicts, fighting in civil wars from Libya to Yemen and joining the Saudi-led boycott of Qatar.

Dubai also faces consequences of its own success. Lacking energy resources of its own, the city had little choice but to build a non-oil economy. The 2014 crash jolted other Gulf countries into following suit. They're all planning for a post-crude era and trying to emulate their thriving neighbour by marketing their own capitals as regional hubs. Dubai remains preeminent in that role. But it's an increasingly high-cost base. In 2013, it ranked as the 90th most expensive place for ex-pats to live, according to New York-based consultant Mercer. It's now vaulted to 26th on the list.

Government, builders and businesses alike are all looking to one event on the horizon that may come to the rescue. Dubai will host the World Expo fair in 2020. Meant to **showcase** the city's future prospects, it's become almost an end in itself, a reason to keep the cranes at work. "The biggest saving grace,'' Haque calls it.

Q.16 What is the main context of the passage?

A. Lack of natural resources in Dubai

B. Dependence of Dubai on other countries

C. Dubai's stagnant position and its efforts to regain its sheen

D. Commercial problems in Dubai increase conflicts in the region

E. The problems in Dubai caused by the USA

Q.17 Which of the following can be inferred about the present state of Dubai?

I. People are moving out of the country thereby leading to lesser business.

II. Businesses present in Dubai are suffering from losses and are not being able to earn profits like before.

III. Excessive number of shopping malls filled with stores are present but not bringing much profit.

A. Only II **B.** Both I and II

C. Both II and III **D.** Only I

E. All of the above

Q.18 Which of the following was the scenario in Dubai earlier?

A. The government made business easy in Dubai and laws were not stringent

B. Dubai was a place of growth and a hub of business

C. The government was strict with the laws earlier which had made profits for Dubai

D. Business thrived there but in different forms, especially related to oil and malls were lesser in number

E. Both (A) and (B)

Q.19 Which of the following is not a reason for declining business in Dubai?

I. Consequential involvement of Dubai in regional conflicts.

II. Strict visa rules that push foreigners out when they lose their jobs.

III. Too much of people rushing into the place to do business but not knowing the appropriate sector.

IV.Stringent laws by the government and confiscation of private property.

A. Only III **B.** Only II

C. Both II and III **D.** Both I and IV

E. All of the above

Q.20 Which of the following is/are true according to the passage?

I. Lower cost of living in Dubai can attract more people to do business here.

II. Indians and Chinese are price-conscious tourists.

III. The Gulf countries are trying to walk on the same path as that Dubai and are creating similar businesses.

A. Only II   **B.** Both I and II
C. Both II and III   **D.** Only I
E. All of the above

Q.21 Which of the following is the purpose of holding the World Expo fair in 2020?

A. To remove the obstacles it has faced in business for some years

B. To shift the idea of an oil-dependent economy to a non-oil one

C. To make up for the scarcity of resources it has

D. To end regional conflicts

E. To show the world the ability that Dubai has in the field of business

Q.22 What do you mean by boom and bust?

A. Glamour and power of money
B. Achieving prosperity all of a sudden
C. Sudden prosperity followed by an abrupt decline
D. Celebration after a long time
E. Respite from poverty

Q.23 Which of the following is OPPOSITE in meaning to the word 'ailing'?

A. Prosperous   **B.** Frivolous
C. Smart   **D.** Healthy
E. None of these

Q.24 Which of the following is SIMILAR in meaning to the word 'austerity'?

A. Sternness   **B.** Growth
C. Rudeness   **D.** Greed
E. Wisdom

Q.25 Which of the following is SIMILAR in meaning to the word 'showcase'?

A. Initiate   **B.** Strengthen
C. Justify   **D.** Focus
E. Display

Ques (26-30):Direction: In the following question, one part of the sentence may have an error. Find out which part of the sentence has an error and click the option corresponding to it. If the sentence is free from error, click the 'No error' option.

Q.26 None of these (A)/ two officers (B)/ has been looking after (C)/ his department well. (D)/

A. (A)/   **B.** (B)/   **C.** (C)/   **D.** (D)/
E. No error

Q.27 The strict boss (A)/ did not give her ascent (B)/ to the employee's (C)/ whimsical request. (D)/

A. (A)/   **B.** (B)/   **C.** (C)/   **D.** (D)/
E. No error

Q.28 The Party Chief (A)/ and the Chief Minister (B)/ expressed his views (C)/ on demonetization in India. (D)/

A. (A)/   **B.** (B)/   **C.** (C)/   **D.** (D)/
E. No error

Q.29 Unlike Indian laws, US laws provides (A)/ for a contingency fee of lawyering (B)/ where the costs of litigation (C)/ are borne by lawyers. (D)/

A. (A)/   **B.** (B)/   **C.** (C)/   **D.** (D)/
E. No error

Q.30 India's Swachh Bharat Mission is (A)/ receiving globe praise (B)/ for attempting (C)/ to close the sanitation gap. (D)/

A. (A)/   **B.** (B)/   **C.** (C)/   **D.** (D)/
E. No error

Numerical Ability

Q.31 The savings of Radha is 80% less than the salary of Radha. 30% of expenditure spends on Rent, 45% of expenditure on shopping and remaining Rs. 2000 on Food. The amount spends on Rent is what percent of the total salary of Radha?

A. 20%   **B.** 24%   **C.** 30%   **D.** 50%
E. 28%

Q.32 If $A : B : C = 2 : 4 : 3$ and $C : D : E = 6 : 2 : 5$, then $A : B : C : D : E = ?$

A. 2 : 4 : 6 : 2 : 5   **B.** 4 : 8 : 6 : 4 : 5
C. 4 : 8 : 6 : 2 : 5   **D.** 2 : 4 : 3 : 2 : 5
E. None of these

Q.33 The ratios of alcohol and water in 3 mixtures are 3 : 2, 2 : 3, and 4 : 1. Respectively. All the mixtures are mixed. Now, find the ratio of alcohol and water in the new mixture.

A. 1 : 2   **B.** 1 : 5   **C.** 1 : 3   **D.** 2 : 3
E. 3 : 2

Q.34 A lent out Rs. 5000 and Rs. 'A' on compound interest for 3 years and 4 years respectively at the rate of interest of 10%. The difference between compound interest is Rs. 2986. Find the value of A.

A. Rs. 10000   **B.** Rs. 9000
C. Rs. 8000   **D.** Rs. 15000
E. Rs. 5000

Q.35 A boat whose speed in still water is 25kmph goes 70km downstream and 45km upstream in 5 hours. Find the ratio between the downstream speed and upstream speed.

A. 7 : 3   **B.** 3 : 8   **C.** 3 : 5   **D.** 4 : 3
E. 1 : 8

Ques (36-40):Directions: Read the given line graph carefully and answer the following questions.

The line-Graph shows the number of people who visited the park in four days of a week (Saturday, Sunday, Monday, and Wednesday)

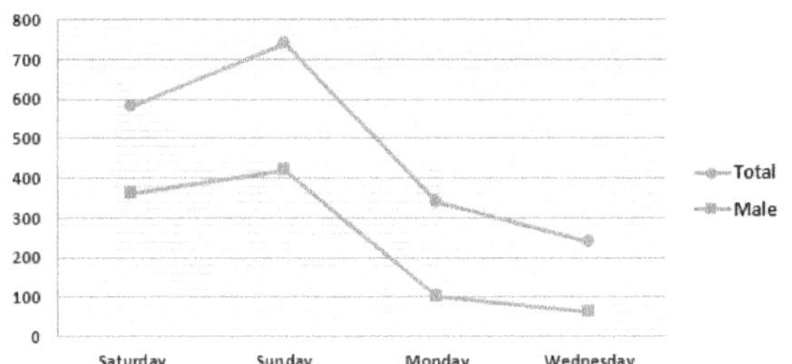

Q.36 Find the total males visited on all days of the week, if people visited in the park on Tuesday and Friday are 25% of females visited on Monday and Wednesday respectively and the ratio of males to females on Tuesday and Friday is same as 1 : 2 and only 10 couples visited on Thursday.

A. 780 **B.** 1000 **C.** 858 **D.** 985
E. 758

Q.37 The average number of males visited on Saturday and Wednesday are what percent more or less than the total number of females on the remaining two days?

A. 65% **B.** 62.5% **C.** 58.8% **D.** 56.4%
E. 66%

Q.38 What is the ratio of the number of males visited on Wednesday to the total number of people visited on that day?

A. 13 : 58 **B.** 3 : 10 **C.** 5 : 6 **D.** 1 : 4
E. 12 : 5

Q.39 The number of males visited on Saturday and Monday together is how much more/less than the average number of females visited on Sunday and Wednesday?

A. 456 **B.** 224 **C.** 212 **D.** 180
E. 210

Q.40 The number of males visited on Sunday and Monday together is what percent more or less than the number of females on Sunday?

A. 56% **B.** 57.32% **C.** 64% **D.** 59.86%
E. 62.5%

Ques (41-42): What approximate value should come in place of the question mark (?) in the following question?

Q.41 $(10)^{7.3} \div (100)^{4.15} \times (1000)^2 + 99999 = ? \times 10^5$

A. 10 **B.** 25 **C.** 33 **D.** 9
E. 2

Q.42 $\dfrac{599.1375 \times 0.0793 \times 3.976}{0.0773 \times 72.581 \times 69.749} = ?$

A. 0.12 **B.** 0.47 **C.** 0.64 **D.** 0.76
E. 0.93

Q.43 What approximate value (to nearest whole number) should come in place of question mark (?) in the following question?

$$? = (5280)^{\frac{1}{4}}$$

A. 8 **B.** 6 **C.** 2.45 **D.** 2.52
E. 7.25

Ques (44-48):Directions: In the given question, two equations numbered I and II are given. Solve both the equations and mark the appropriate answer.

Q.44 I. $x^2 + x - 156 = 0$

II. $y^2 + y - 182 = 0$

A. x > y
B. x < y
C. x ≥ y
D. x ≤ y
E. x = y or the relationship between x and y cannot be established

Q.45 I. $x^2 - 18x + 77 = 0$

II. $y^2 + 3y - 70 = 0$

A. x > y
B. x ≥ y
C. y > x
D. y ≥ x
E. x = y, Relation doesn't exist

Q.46 I. $3x^2 - 2\sqrt{21}x + 7 = 0$

II. $3y^2 + \sqrt{3}y - 2 = 0$

A. x > y
B. x < y
C. x ≥ y
D. x ≤ y
E. x = y or relationship between x and y cannot be established

Q.47 I. $2x^2 + 5x - 250 = 0$

II. $7y^2 - 22y + 3 = 0$

A. x > y
B. x < y
C. x ≥ y
D. x ≤ y
E. x = y or relationship between x and y cannot be established

Q.48 I. $(169)^{\frac{1}{2}}x + \sqrt{289} = 134$

II. $(361)^{\frac{1}{2}}y^2 - 270 = 1269$

A. x < y
B. x > y
C. x ≥ y
D. x ≤ y
E. x = y or relation cannot be established

Q.49 For shopkeepers, the marked price of an article Rs. 4000. He sells the same article at a discount of 5% to A. A sells the same article to B. B sells the same article at Rs. 7700 without discount and earns 10% of profit percentage. Find the profit percentage earned by A.

A. 82.34% **B.** 88.45% **C.** 80.48% **D.** 81.23%
E. 84.21%

Q.50 A alone can complete the work in 12 days and B alone can complete the work in 16 days. They both work for 5 days then left the work. The remaining work is completed by C in 6.5 days. In what time A, B, and C can complete 3/4th of the work?

A. 7 days   **B.** 2 days   **C.** 4 days   **D.** 8 days
E. 10 days

Q.51 In a test series scores of Sachin are 80, 84, 89, 75, 76, 82, 78, 81. Find the average of his score if he got out in every inning.

A. 80.65   **B.** 77.125   **C.** 82.875   **D.** 80.625
E. 79.075

Q.52 A cube whose side is 6 cm. Cut a maximum volume of cone and find out the ratio of waste material to the volume of the cone.

A. $1:2$ **B.** $33:13$
C. $31:11$ **D.** $24:25$
E. None of these

Ques (53-57):Directions: Study the following information carefully to answer the given questions:

Indore Municipal Corporation (IMC) has started permitting business and shops to open for the general public to the places following health safety measures and rejecting those who fail to meet health standards.

The five business sectors are as following Grocery Stores, Cloth stores, Refreshment joints, Milk parlors, and Automotive showrooms. The bar chart shows the number of business sectors applied for permission and the number of business approval given by IMC.

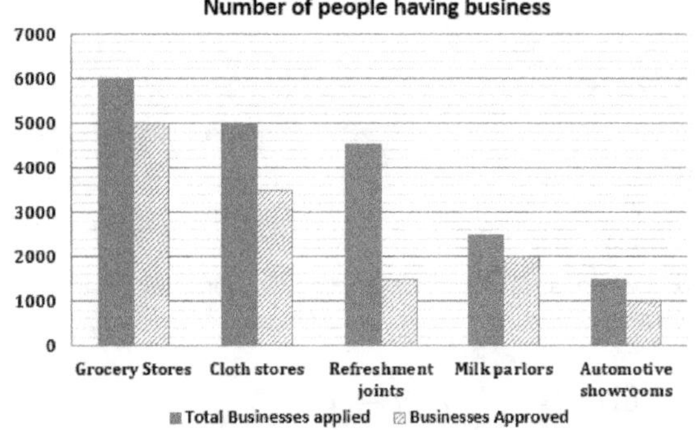

Q.53 Find the difference between the Milk parlors received permission and Refreshment joints denied permission by IMC.

A. 500   **B.** 2000
C. 1000   **D.** 1500
E. None of these

Q.54 Find the ratio between the businesses in five sectors received permission to businesses in five sectors denied permission to start the business.

A. $2:1$ **B.** $3:1$
C. $1:2$ **D.** $1:3$
E. None of these

Q.55 The number of Clothes stores whose permission got rejected by IMC is what percent more than the number of Automotive showrooms whose permission got rejected by IMC.

A. 250%   **B.** 100%

C. 150%   **D.** 50%
E. None of these

Q.56 What is the respective ratio of the number of businesses approved in Grocery Stores and Milk parlor together to of the number of businesses approved in Cloth stores and Automotive showroom together?

A. $14:9$ **B.** $16:7$
C. $12:5$ **D.** $16:9$
E. None of these

Q.57 Find the total number of businesses whose permission got rejected by Indore Municipal Corporation.

A. 6000   **B.** 5500
C. 5000   **D.** 6500
E. None of these

Q.58 Harry and Ron started a business investing Rs. 50000 and Rs. 35000 respectively. Due to incompetent handling, they suffered a loss of Rs. 7480 at the end of one year. They hired Hermione 12 months after starting the business, on a promise to give 12% of the profit as compensation for handling the business. Hermione invested Rs. 25000 in the business. In the 2nd year, they covered all losses and made an additional profit of Rs. 4520. Find Harry's earnings from the business at the end of two years.

A. Rs. 3360   **B.** Rs. 400   **C.** Rs. 4800   **D.** Rs. 2055
E. Rs. 3055

Ques (59-65): What approximate value should come in place of the question mark (?) in the following question?

Q.59 $(27.84 + 31.90) \div 14.84 = 97.79 \div 13.98 - ?$

A. 3   **B.** 10   **C.** 7   **D.** 5
E. 11

Q.60 $(?)^2 + 34.98\%$ of $1998 + 26.98\%$ of $402 = 3208.359$

A. 37   **B.** 41   **C.** 49   **D.** 57
E. 61

Q.61
$$2159.9 \div \sqrt{729} + 37.5\% \, of \, 24.04 + ? = 42.83 \times 12.93$$

A. 370   **B.** 470   **C.** 485   **D.** 415
E. 394

Q.62 $289.89\% \, of \, 399.88 + \left(\sqrt{441} + \sqrt{361}\right) - 1 = ?$

A. 1188   **B.** 1177   **C.** 1155   **D.** 1199
E. 1166

Q.63 $29^2 + 34.12\% \, of \, 700 \div \sqrt[2]{2744.213} = ? + \sqrt[2]{2197}$

A. 945   **B.** 855   **C.** 895   **D.** 845
E. 865

Q.64 $59.99 \div 60.01 + 17.91 \times 3.05 - 10.97 = ?$

A. 44   **B.** 47   **C.** 46   **D.** 42
E. 43

Q.65 (179.8 × 19.91 – 23.99 × 6.03) ÷ (67.95 × 36.03 ÷ 17.95 + 35.97) = ?

A. 20   **B.** 21   **C.** 22   **D.** 23
E. 24

Reasoning Ability

Ques (66-70):Directions: In the next five questions, the relationship between different characters is given in the statements followed by two conclusions. You have to determine which of the conclusion is true based on the statement.

Q.66 Statements: Y ≤ K < M > B = I, A ≥ M > O ≥ K
Conclusions:

1. A ≥ Y
2. B < O

A. Only conclusion 1 is necessarily true
B. Only conclusion 2 is necessarily true
C. Either conclusion 1 or 2 is necessarily true
D. Neither conclusion 1 or 2 is necessarily true
E. Both conclusions are necessarily true

Q.67 Statements: R > P = Q ≤ H ≤ N, H > U < P
Conclusions:

1. U < N
2. N ≥ P

A. Only conclusion 1 is necessarily true
B. Only conclusion 2 is necessarily true
C. Either conclusion 1 or 2 is necessarily true
D. Neither conclusion 1 or 2 is necessarily true
E. Both conclusions are necessarily true

Q.68 Statements: D > S ≥ C < U < A, Y = X ≤ B < U
Conclusions:

1. X ≤ C
2. Y > C

A. Only conclusion 1 is necessarily true
B. Only conclusion 2 is necessarily true
C. Either conclusion 1 or 2 is necessarily true
D. Neither conclusion 1 or 2 is necessarily true
E. Both conclusions are necessarily true

Q.69 Statements: V > P = I ≥ F < L, A ≤ I < C
Conclusions:

1. F ≥ A
2. A < V

A. Only conclusion 1 is necessarily true
B. Only conclusion 2 is necessarily true
C. Either conclusion 1 or 2 is necessarily true
D. Neither conclusion 1 or 2 is necessarily true
E. Both conclusions are necessarily true

Q.70 Statements: C < T ≥ M > N, G < U ≤ A > C
Conclusions:

1. T > N
2. N < G

A. Only conclusion 1 is necessarily true
B. Only conclusion 2 is necessarily true
C. Either conclusion 1 or 2 is necessarily true
D. Neither conclusion 1 or 2 is necessarily true
E. Both conclusions are necessarily true

Ques (71-75):Directions: Study the following information carefully to answer the given questions:

Nine persons A, B, C, D, E, F, G, H and J are sitting around a circular table but not necessarily in the same order. All are facing towards the center. A sits 2nd to the right of B. F sits 4th to the left of A. C sits third to the right of F. G is immediate neighbor of J. G sits 2nd to the right of H. D sits 2nd to the left of E. E is not an immediate neighbor of A.

Q.71 Who among the following person sits 3rd to the right of E?

A. B   **B.** A
C. C   **D.** F
E. None of these

Q.72 How many persons sit between from left of E to F?

A. Two   **B.** One
C. Three   **D.** None
E. More than three

Q.73 Who among the following person sit exactly between E and C?

A. B   **B.** D
C. A   **D.** F
E. None of these

Q.74 Who among the following persons sits immediate right of A?

A. B   **B.** C
C. D   **D.** G
E. None of these

Q.75 Four of the following five are alike in certain way based from a group, find the one which does not belong to that group?

A. E – C   **B.** B – F   **C.** D – J   **D.** A – C
E. C – H

Ques (76-78):Directions: Study the given information carefully and answer the questions given below.

In a certain code language, "break the old rule" is written as "te od ul re", "follow the tough rule" is written as "gu lw te ul", "rule is always tough" is written as "wa mn ul gu".

Q.76 What is the code for 'rule?

A. te   **B.** ul   **C.** gu   **D.** lw
E. re

Q.77 What is the code for 'break'?

A. od   **B.** re
C. te   **D.** Either 'od' or 're'
E. Either 're' or 'te'

Q.78 What is the code for 'always follow'?

A. lw wa
B. mn te
C. mn lw
D. Either (A) or (B)
E. Either (A) or (C)

Ques (79-81):Directions: Read the following information carefully to answer the question that follows:

There are six members P, Q, R, S, T and U in the family of three generations. There is no single parent in the family. U is paternal aunt of T. R is mother-in-law of S's husband. Q has only one child. S and Q are not married to each other.

Q.79 How is U related to S?
A. Daughter
B. Sister-in-law
C. Sister
D. Mother
E. Daughter-in-law

Q.80 Who is the father of S?
A. Can't be determined
B. P
C. Q
D. T
E. None of these

Q.81 How R is related to T?
A. Daughter
B. Father
C. Grandmother
D. Sister
E. None of these

Ques (82-86):Directions: Study the following information carefully to answer the given questions.

There are seven friends Preeti, Dhruv, Ankita, Aarti, Laksh, Aditya and Eshan who goes for a morning walk daily at different time slots 6 a.m., 11 a.m., 2 p.m., 4 p.m., 6 p.m., 9 p.m., and 10 p.m. respectively. Aarti goes for a walk immediately after Ankita. Dhruv goes for a walk after 2 p.m. but he is not the last one. Preeti goes for a walk at 6 p.m. There is a four-hour of the gap between Preeti and Aditya. Laksh goes for a walk immediately after Aditya.

Q.82 When Eshan go for his walk?
A. 10 p.m.
B. 6 p.m.
C. 9 p.m.
D. 11 a.m.
E. 6 a.m.

Q.83 Who was the 1st person goes for the walk?
A. Aarti
B. Aditya
C. Ankita
D. Laksh
E. None of the above

Q.84 How many persons go for a walk between Aarti and Laksh?
A. Two
B. Three
C. Four
D. One
E. Five

Q.85 Who goes for a walk at 9 p.m.?
A. Eshan
B. Preeti
C. Aditya
D. Dhruv
E. None of the above

Q.86 What is the time gap in hours between Preeti and Aditya scheduled walk?
A. 3 hours
B. 2 hours
C. 4 hours
D. 5 hours
E. 1 hour

Ques (87-91):Directions: Study the following arrangement of alphabets and answer the questions given below:

Q W E R T Y U I O P A S D F G H J K L Z X C V B N M

Q.87 Which letter is fifth to the left of the seventh letter to the right of the eighteenth letter from the right end?
A. A
B. W
C. X
D. P
E. G

Q.88 If all the vowels in the series are dropped, which letter would be the tenth to the right of the fifteenth letter from the right end?
A. J
B. C
C. S
D. D
E. None of these

Q.89 If the group of the first 5 letters is interchanged with the group of the last 5 letters such that the order of the letters within the group remain the same, then which letter will be the seventh to the left of the ninth letter from the left end?
A. C
B. W
C. V
D. B
E. Y

Q.90 If the alternate letters are dropped starting from the first letter, which letter will be the fifth to the left of the eight-letter from the right end?
A. M
B. C
C. P
D. W
E. Z

Q.91 Which letter is fifth to the right of the letter which is second to the right of the seventeenth letter from the left end?
A. Q
B. J
C. L
D. O
E. B

Ques (92-94):Directions: In the question below are given two statements followed by two conclusions numbered I and II. You have to take the given statements to be true even if they seem to be at variance with commonly known facts. Read all the conclusions and then decide which of the given conclusions logically follows from the given statements disregarding commonly known facts.

Q.92 Statements:
All colors are rainbows.
All rainbows are rain.
Conclusions:
I. All rain is colors.
II. All colors are rain.
A. Only I follows
B. Only II follows
C. Either I or II follows
D. Neither I nor II follows
E. Both I and II follow

Q.93 Statements:
All dogs are fox.
No fox is a cat.
Conclusions:
I. No dog is a cat.

II. Some dogs are cat.
A. Only I follows
B. Only II follows
C. Either I or II follows
D. Neither I nor II follows
E. Both I and II follow

Q.94 Statements:

All exit polls are political.

Some exit polls are true

Conclusions:

I. Some true is not political.

II. Some political is not exit polls.

A. Only I follows
B. Only II follows
C. Either I or II follows
D. Neither I nor II follows
E. Both I and II follow

Ques (95-99):Directions: Study the given information carefully and answer the following questions below.

Eight persons S, T, U, V, W, X, Y and Z are sitting in a row facing either North or South direction but not necessarily in the same order. Z sits third to the left of X and faces opposite to that of X. Three persons are sitting between V and X. V and X are facing North direction. The immediate neighbours of Z face the same direction but opposite to that of Z. W is sitting 5th to the right of T who is facing north and neither of them is sitting at extreme positions. Y who faces the South direction sits at one of the positions at the left of V. S who is an immediate neighbour of V is sitting 4th to the right of W.

Q.95 Who sits at the extreme end of the row?
A. W   **B.** S   **C.** X   **D.** V
E. T

Q.96 What is the position of X with respect to U?
A. Third to the left
B. Third to the right
C. Second to the left
D. Second to the right
E. Cannot be determined

Q.97 Which of the following statements is correct?
A. S sits fifth to the left of X
B. U is an immediate neighbour of V
C. T sits at one of the extreme ends
D. Three people sit to the right of Z
E. U is neighbour of V and W

Q.98 Four are the same in a certain way thus form a group. Who among the following does not belong to the group?
A. X   **B.** W   **C.** U   **D.** V
E. T

Q.99 How many people sit to the right of S?
A. 4
B. 1

C. 2
D. 3
E. Cannot be determined

Q.100 In a certain code language, '15-78-25-36' is written as '28-154-48-70'. What will be the code for '23-63-42-81' in that code language?

[SSC MTS, 2019]

A. 125-511-152-982   **B.** 46-126-84-164
C. 44-124-82-160   **D.** 65-218-362-542
E. 45-218-362-642

// Smart Answer Sheet //

Correct — Percentage of students who answered correctly. **Skipped** — Percentage of students who skipped.

Q.	Ans.	Correct / Skipped
1	B	2.56 % / 87.18 %
2	C	8.97 % / 87.18 %
3	E	7.69 % / 88.46 %
4	A	7.69 % / 88.46 %
5	E	7.69 % / 88.46 %
6	A	6.41 % / 93.59 %
7	B	1.28 % / 93.59 %
8	C	6.41 % / 93.59 %
9	B	3.85 % / 93.59 %
10	B	0 % / 100 %
11	D	6.41 % / 93.59 %
12	B	6.41 % / 93.59 %
13	A	6.41 % / 93.59 %
14	B	6.41 % / 93.59 %
15	A	3.85 % / 93.59 %
16	C	1.28 % / 93.59 %
17	B	1.28 % / 93.59 %
18	B	2.56 % / 93.59 %
19	A	2.56 % / 93.59 %
20	E	0 % / 100 %
21	E	5.13 % / 93.59 %
22	C	0 % / 100 %
23	D	1.28 % / 93.59 %
24	A	0 % / 100 %
25	E	5.13 % / 93.59 %
26	A	2.56 % / 93.59 %
27	B	2.56 % / 93.59 %
28	C	5.13 % / 93.59 %
29	A	3.85 % / 93.59 %
30	B	3.85 % / 93.59 %
31	B	2.56 % / 84.62 %
32	C	6.41 % / 84.62 %
33	E	3.85 % / 84.61 %
34	A	1.28 % / 84.62 %
35	A	1.28 % / 84.62 %
36	D	0 % / 100 %
37	B	1.28 % / 85.9 %
38	D	5.13 % / 85.9 %
39	E	1.28 % / 85.9 %
40	E	1.28 % / 84.62 %
41	E	2.56 % / 84.62 %
42	B	5.13 % / 84.61 %
43	A	0 % / 100 %
44	E	10.26 % / 84.61 %
45	B	8.97 % / 84.62 %
46	A	2.56 % / 85.9 %
47	E	3.85 % / 85.89 %
48	C	2.56 % / 85.9 %
49	E	1.28 % / 87.18 %
50	C	2.56 % / 88.47 %
51	D	3.85 % / 88.46 %
52	C	0 % / 100 %
53	C	2.56 % / 88.47 %
54	A	2.56 % / 88.47 %
55	E	1.28 % / 89.75 %
56	A	1.28 % / 91.03 %
57	D	1.28 % / 91.03 %
58	B	0 % / 100 %
59	A	3.85 % / 94.87 %
60	C	2.56 % / 94.88 %
61	B	2.56 % / 96.16 %
62	D	2.56 % / 96.16 %
63	D	0 % / 100 %
64	A	1.28 % / 96.16 %
65	A	0 % / 100 %
66	D	24.36 % / 56.41 %
67	E	24.36 % / 56.41 %
68	C	3.85 % / 56.41 %
69	B	26.92 % / 58.98 %
70	A	35.9 % / 58.97 %
71	B	10.26 % / 84.61 %
72	D	8.97 % / 84.62 %
73	A	10.26 % / 84.61 %
74	E	10.26 % / 84.61 %
75	D	10.26 % / 84.61 %
76	B	10.26 % / 84.61 %
77	D	10.26 % / 84.61 %
78	E	7.69 % / 84.62 %
79	B	2.56 % / 84.62 %
80	C	2.56 % / 84.62 %

Q.	Ans.	Correct / Skipped
81	C	3.85 % / 84.61 %
82	A	11.54 % / 84.61 %
83	C	11.54 % / 84.61 %
84	D	10.26 % / 84.61 %

Q.	Ans.	Correct / Skipped
85	D	10.26 % / 84.61 %
86	C	10.26 % / 85.89 %
87	A	5.13 % / 85.9 %
88	B	6.41 % / 87.18 %

Q.	Ans.	Correct / Skipped
89	C	6.41 % / 87.18 %
90	D	6.41 % / 85.9 %
91	E	5.13 % / 87.18 %
92	B	7.69 % / 87.18 %

Q.	Ans.	Correct / Skipped
93	A	8.97 % / 88.47 %
94	D	3.85 % / 88.46 %
95	C	3.85 % / 88.46 %
96	D	3.85 % / 92.3 %

Q.	Ans.	Correct / Skipped
97	A	3.85 % / 92.3 %
98	B	2.56 % / 92.31 %
99	E	1.28 % / 92.31 %
100	C	1.28 % / 96.16 %

//Hints and Solutions//

1. For something to have relevance means for it to be appropriate or be connected to something.

To have 'tolerance' means to have the ability to bear something that one does not wish to bear.

'Remembrance' is the act of remembering something.

'Deliverance' is the act of setting something free.

Hence, the correct option is (B).

2. To accompany someone means to 'go with' or 'give company to' as a companion.

The meanings of other words are:

Accord: give or grant someone (power, status, or recognition)

Accommodate: (of a building or other area) provide lodging or sufficient space for.

Accentuate: make more noticeable or prominent.

Emulate: match or surpass (a person or achievement), typically by imitation.

The complete sentence will be: Amanda realized that it was no longer necessary to accompany Sam everywhere he went.

Hence, the correct option is (C).

3. After going through the sentence it can be said that it is in the passive voice.

So, option (B) -Is designing- and option (D)-Was designing- should be ignored.

Option (A) -Are designed- cannot be chosen because the subject is a singular number.

So, option (E) -Is designed- is the answer.

Hence, the correct option is (E).

4. A chip off the old block means to be similar in behaviour to the parents.

As the sentence explains that Prince George is just like his parents who are very well mannered.

Chipping a log of wood / Cutting a block of old stone / Bringing in firewood / are incorrect as they are talking about cutting something physically, and physically bringing the firewood.

Unlike the parents, means not like the parents.

So, options (B), (C), (D), and (E) are incorrect.

Hence, the correct option is (A).

5. To keep everyone at an arm's length means to avoid becoming friends with someone in order to avoid getting emotionally involved or hurt.

As the sentence explains that people who have a suspicious nature do not like to become friends with anyone. [Avoid becoming friendly with someone].

Stay at a physical distance/ Hold someone by the arm has different meanings-- one is to physically stay away, and the second is to hold someone.

Punch someone's arm means to hurt someone.

Become over-friendly means excessively friendly.

Hence, the correct option is (E).

6. The given sentence is saying it is absolutely necessary that global governance becomes democratic to prevent violence.

- Therefore, the most appropriate word to be filled in the blank is 'Essential'.

- Also, the use of the word "prevent" in the sentence indicates the use of the word 'essential' in the blank.

- The word 'Essential' means Absolutely necessary; extremely important.
    - Example: Mutual understanding is essential to friendship.

Complete Sentence: To prevent violence, it is essential that global governance becomes genuinely democratic.

Let us explore the other options:

- Credential means A qualification, achievement, quality, or aspect of a person's background.

- Prudential means Involving or showing care and forethought.

- Evidential means Of or providing evidence.

- Sequential means Forming or following in a logical order or sequence.

Hence, the correct option is (A).

7. The sentence makes it understood that we need an adjective that qualifies the noun company and it contrasts the meaning of the second clause.

Let's understand the meaning of options:

- Invincible(adj) - Incapable of being overcome or subdued

- Incomprehensible(adj) - Incapable of being explained or accounted for

- Incorrigible(adj) - Impervious to correction by punishment

- Impressive(adj) - Making a strong or vivid impression

- Impossible(adj) - Not capable of occurring or being accomplished or dealt with

The correct sentence is- Last year the company looked invincible but in recent weeks it has begun to have problems.

Hence, the correct option is (B).

8. To play with fire is an idiomatic expression that means doing something dangerous that may result in great harm and cause many problems.

- You're playing with fire if you try to cheat on the test.

This means that option (C) - To act in a dangerous and risky way is the most appropriate meaning of the given idiom.

Hence, the correct option is (C).

9. To ring one's own bell: announce one's own successes; praise oneself

- As he won, the winner rang his bell on and on, till he stopped panting and could laugh and talk properly.

Thus, it can be concluded that the idiom 'To ring one's own bell' means to indulge in self-praise.

Hence, the correct option is (B).

10. The most appropriate meaning of the given idiom 'Catch the tartar' is 'To desire the unattainable'.

Let's look at the meaning and example of the given phrasal verb:

- Catch the tartar- "To encounter or be forced to reckon with someone or something that proves more powerful, troublesome, or formidable than one expected.".
  - E.g. It looks like we caught a Tartar when we tried to muscle their store out of the area.

Thus from the explanation given above, we find that the 2nd option is the correct choice.

Hence, the correct option is (B).

11. The error lies in the usage of the word impressed instead of impressive.

- The usage of the word impressed is wrong here as it is a *verb* it does not grammatically fit the sentence.
- *Performance* is a *noun,* and we need an *adjective* here to modify it.
- Here, we have to use the adjective impressive, which means making or tending to make a marked impression, i.e., having the power to excite attention, awe, or admiration.
- The *adjective* impressive is modifying or giving additional information about the *noun performance* here as *'the performance was impressive'.*

So, the correct sentence is: After an impressive performance at the Syed Mushtaq Ali T20 Trophy, there was an intense bidding war over Khan between Punjab Kings and Royal Challengers Bangalore.

Hence, the correct option is (D).

12. The error is in the usage of 'caused' in the underlined part.

- Here, the sentence talks about diabetes and how it is both reversible as well as chronic.
- The correct word for the underlined part must be 'causes' which means make (something, especially something bad) happen. The sentence is a factual sentence so it is in the present tense. 'Causes' is the correct word because 'metabolic disorder' is singular.

- 'caused' must be replaced with 'causes'.

Thus the correct sentence is: *Diabetes is a severe metabolic disorder that causes high blood glucose. Diabetes can be both reversible as well as chronic.*

Hence, the correct option is (B).

13. The error is in the usage of 'essential preserve' in the underlined part.

- The sentence talks environment and the need to protect it.
- The correct word for the underlined part must be 'essential to preserve' in which 'preserve' means maintain (something) in its original or existing state. The sentence is in simple present tense and the underlined word must have an infinitive form of the verb. So, 'to preserve' is the correct word.
- 'essential preserve' must be replaced with 'essential to preserve'.

Thus the correct sentence is: *The environment provides us with life-sustaining resources, and it is essential to preserve and protect it.*

Hence, the correct option is (A).

14. The error is in the usage of 'by' in the underlined part.

- The sentence talks about how social media is affecting people by spreading fake news.
- The correct preposition for the underlined part is 'with' which means accompanied by (another person or thing). The sentence states that social media now contains people or is full of people spreading fake news.
- 'by' must be replaced with 'with'.

Thus the correct sentence is: *Social media is now filled with people claiming the Earth is flat, climate change isn't real, and it is not a surprise.*

Hence, the correct option is (B).

15. The given phrase is to be replaced with 'Having passed.'

- The given sentence is a participle phrase. *When we want to emphasize that one thing happened before another, we can use a perfect participle for the earlier action.*
- In the given sentence, *we cannot write a participle phrase in a passive voice because in the main clause the subject has already been mentioned which is 'I' so don't write a passive voice in the participle phrase.*
- Let's see an example:
  - Having forgotten to take my keys, I had to borrow a set from my landlord.

So the correct sentence is: *Having passed my driving test, I was able to buy my first car.*

Hence, the correct option is (A).

16. The passage is based on the idea of declining business in Dubai and the place losing its previous shine and glamour. The author has stated the reasons and Dubai's efforts to regain the lost position.

Hence, the correct option is (C).

17. It is mentioned in the passage that the expatriates are moving out of the place due to the high cost of living. This has hampered business like never before. Thus I is correct. It is mentioned that 'Corporate mainstays, from Emirates airline to developer Emaar Properties, just reported disappointing third-quarter profits. The stock market is having its worst year since 2008.' Thus II is correct too. Statement III is incorrect as the passage states that there are malls present but they do not have sufficient stores and most of them are empty.

Hence, the correct option is (B).

18. Option (A) cannot be determined as anywhere in the passage has it been mentioned that the laws are stricter now, or they were lenient earlier. It was a place of fast growth and development was conspicuously present everywhere. Option (A) and (C) are thus ruled out. Option (D) and (E) are also incorrect.

Hence, the correct option is (B).

19. All the options are valid except for statement III. The scenario is totally different than what is mentioned in statement III. People are moving out of the country due to the high cost of living.

Hence, the correct option is (A).

20. All the statements are mentioned in the passage. It is mentioned that the high cost of living drives people out of the country. Thus, a lower cost of living will definitely help people to come and do business in Dubai.

'The oil slump since 2014 hit big spenders from neighbouring Gulf states who used to flock to Dubai (tourists from China and India are filling the gap, but they're more price-conscious). Saudis, in particular, are feeling the pinch, as their own government imposes fiscal austerity and confiscates private wealth.' Thus, statement II can be inferred from the passage.

'Dubai also faces consequences of its own success. Lacking energy resources of its own, the city had little choice but to build a non-oil economy. The 2014 crash jolted other Gulf countries into following suit. They're all planning for a post-crude era and trying to emulate their thriving neighbor by marketing their own capitals as regional hubs.' Thus, statement III is correct.

All the options are therefore correct.

Hence, the correct option is (E).

21. It is mentioned in the passage 'Government, builders and business alike are all looking to one event on the horizon that may come to the rescue. Dubai will host the World Expo fair in 2020. Meant to showcase the city's future prospects.'

Hence, the correct option is (E).

22. The phrase 'boom and bust' means 'a situation in which a period of great prosperity or rapid economic growth is abruptly followed by one of economic decline.'

Hence, the correct option is (C).

23. The word 'ailing' means 'sick; unwell.' The meanings of the words are:

Prosperous: wealthy

Frivolous: not having any serious purpose or value.

Healthy: in a good physical or mental condition; in good health

Hence, the correct option is (D).

24. The word 'austerity' means 'sternness.'

Growth: the process of increasing in size

Rudeness: lack of manners; discourteousness

Greed: an intense and selfish desire for something, especially wealth, power, or food.

Wisdom: the quality of having experience, knowledge, and good judgment; the quality of being wise

Hence, the correct option is (A).

25. The word 'showcase' means 'exhibit; display.'

Initiate: cause (a process or action) to begin

Strengthen: make or become stronger

Justify: show or prove to be right or reasonable

Focus: pay particular attention to

Hence, the correct option is (E).

26. 'Neither' should be there in place of 'none'.

A pronoun is a word that is used instead of a noun or noun phrase. Pronouns refer to either a noun that has already been mentioned or to a noun that does not need to be named specifically.

'None of the' is used for more than two persons or objects, 'neither of the' is used for two objects.

- E.g. None of the three flowers is red.
- Neither of the two teachers is competent.

The correct sentence should be: Neither of these two officers has been looking after his department well.

Hence, the correct option is (A).

27. 'assent' should be there in place of 'ascent'.

Singular nouns are followed by singular verbs and plural nouns are followed by plural verbs.

"Ascent" means 'a climb or walk to the summit of a mountain or hill' which does not make any sense in the given context.

The correct word in place of 'ascent' would be 'assent' which means 'the expression of approval or agreement'.

- For E.g. The ascent of Fuji presents no difficulties.

- Prince Bagration bowed his head in sign of assent.

The correct sentence is: The strict boss did not give her assent to the employee's whimsical request.

Hence, the correct option is (B).

28. 'their' should be there in place of 'his'.

A pronoun is a word that is used instead of a noun or noun phrase. Pronouns refer to either a noun that has already been mentioned or to a noun that does not need to be named specifically.

When two singular nouns are joined by 'and' refer to two different persons the pronoun used for them should be 'plural'.

- E.g.: Ashwin and Hardik are brothers. They play cricket.

The correct sentence should be: The Party Chief and the Chief Minister expressed their views on demonetization in India.

Hence, the correct option is (C).

29. 'provide' should be there in place of 'provides'

Singular nouns are followed by singular verbs and plural nouns are followed by plural verbs.

A singular noun names one person. place. thing. or idea. while a plural noun names more than one person. place. thing, or idea.

The usage of the verb singular 'provides' is erroneous and needs to be replaced with the plural form of the verb 'provide' to make the sentence grammatically and contextually correct.

According to the subject-verb agreement, if the subject is singular then it is followed by a singular verb and if the subject is plural it is followed by a plural verb. Here the subject is 'US laws' which is plural and hence is followed by a plural verb.

- E.g. The dog chases the cat.
- The dogs chase the cat.

The correct sentence is: Unlike Indian laws, US laws provide for a contingency fee of lawyering, where the costs of litigation are borne by lawyers

Hence, the correct option is (A).

30. 'global' should be there in place of 'globe'

The usage of the noun 'globe' is erroneous and needs to be replaced with the adjective 'global' to make the sentence grammatically and contextually correct. This is because we need an adjective to modify the noun 'praise'. 'Globe' is a noun.

- E.g. This sacrifice was the least he could do for his friend.
- It was as if he'd tossed out a sacrificial lamb to a flock of vultures.

The correct sentence is: India's Swachh Bharat Mission is receiving global praise for attempting to close the sanitation gap.

Hence, the correct option is (B).

31. Given:

Savings = 80% less than salary

Formula used:

$$X\% \text{ of } Y = \frac{XY}{100}$$

Let the salary of Radha be Rs. M

Savings of Radha = M $-\ \dfrac{80}{100} \times$ M = Rs. $\dfrac{M}{5}$

Expenditure of Radha = M $-\ \dfrac{M}{5}$ = Rs. $\dfrac{4M}{5}$

According to the question,

$$\frac{25}{100} \times \frac{4M}{5} = 2000$$

$\Rightarrow$ M = 10000

Amount spent on rent = $\dfrac{30}{100} \times \dfrac{4}{5} \times 10000$ = Rs. 2400

$\therefore$ Required percentage = $\dfrac{2400}{10000} \times 100 = 24\%$

Hence, the correct option is (B).

32. Given:

A : B : C = 2 : 4 : 3

C : D : E = 6 : 2 : 5

Calculation:

A : B : C = 2 : 4 : 3 ----(i)

C : D : E = 6 : 2 : 5 ----(ii)

Making ratio Equal, multiply equation (i) by 2, we get

A : B : C = 4 : 8 : 6

On combining,

A : B : C : D : E = 4 : 8 : 6 : 2 : 5

Hence, the correct option is (C).

33. Given:

The ratio of 3 mixtures are 3 : 2; 2 : 3 and 4 : 1

If 3 mixtures having 2 components in the ratio a : b, c : d, and e : f are mixed then the ratio of each component in the final mixture is calculated as

$$= \frac{\left\{ \left[\frac{a}{(a+b)}\right] + \left[\frac{c}{(c+d)}\right] + \left[\frac{e}{(e+f)}\right] \right\}}{\left\{ \left[\frac{b}{(a+b)}\right] + \left[\frac{d}{(c+d)}\right] + \left[\frac{f}{(e+f)}\right] \right\}}$$

Required ratio = $\left[\left(\dfrac{3}{5}\right) + \left(\dfrac{2}{5}\right) + \left(\dfrac{4}{5}\right)\right] : \left[\left(\dfrac{2}{5}\right) + \left(\dfrac{3}{5}\right) + \left(\dfrac{1}{5}\right)\right]$

= $\left(\dfrac{9}{5}\right) : \left(\dfrac{6}{5}\right) = 3 : 2$

Hence, the correct option is (E).

34. Given:

Amount lent for 3 years = Rs. 5000

Let P = principal, R = rate of interest and N = time period

Compound interest = $P\left(1 + \dfrac{R}{100}\right)^n - P$

Compound interest in 3 years = $5000 \times \left(1 + \dfrac{10}{100}\right)^3 - 5000 =$ Rs. 1655

Compound interest in 4 years = 2986 + 1655 = Rs. 4641

$\Rightarrow A\left(1 + \dfrac{10}{100}\right)^4 - A = 4641$

$\Rightarrow A = 10000$

The amount invested for 4 years is Rs. 10000.

Hence, the correct option is (A).

35. Given:

Speed of a boat in still water = 25 kmph

Formula:

Speed downstream = Speed of a boat in still water + Speed of the stream

Speed upstream = Speed of a boat in still water – Speed of the stream

Let the speed of the stream be A kmph.

$\Rightarrow \dfrac{70}{(25+A)} + \dfrac{45}{(25-A)} = 5$

$\Rightarrow 350 - 14A + 225 + 9A = 625 - A^2$

$\Rightarrow A^2 - 5A - 50 = 0$

Solving,

$(A - 10)(A + 5) = 0$

$\Rightarrow A = 10$ or (-5)

Speed of the stream is 10 kmph.

$\Rightarrow$ Downstream speed = 25 + 10 = 35 kmph

$\Rightarrow$ Upstream speed = 25 – 10 = 15 kmph

$\therefore$ Required ratio = 35 : 15

= 7 : 3

Hence, the correct option is (A).

36. Given:

Day	Total People	Male
Saturday	580	360
Sunday	740	420
Monday	340	100
Wednesday	240	60

People visited on Tuesday = 25% of 240 = 60

$\Rightarrow$ Male visited on Tuesday = $\dfrac{1}{3} \times 60 = 20$

People visited on Friday = 25% of 180 = 45

$\Rightarrow$ Male visited on Friday = $\dfrac{1}{3} \times 45 = 15$

Male visited on Thursdays = 10   (∵ 10 couples visited on Thursday which means 10 males and 10 females)

$\therefore$ Total males visited on all days = 100 + 20 + 60 + 10 + 15 + 360 + 420 = 985

Hence, the correct option is (D).

37. Given:

Day	Total People	Male
Saturday	580	360
Sunday	740	420
Monday	340	100
Wednesday	240	60

Average of males on Saturday and Wednesday = $\dfrac{(360+60)}{2} =$ 210

The remaining two days means days other than Saturday and Wednesday and i.e. Sunday and Monday.

Total people (Male + Female) on Sunday and Monday = 740 + 340 = 1080

Total male on Sunday and Monday = 420 + 100 = 520

Total number of females on the remaining two days = 1080 - 520 = 560

$\Rightarrow$ Difference = 560 - 210 = 350

$\therefore$ Required percent = $\left(\dfrac{350}{560}\right) \times 100 = 62.5\%$

Hence, the correct option is (B).

38. Given:

Day	Total People	Male
Saturday	580	360
Sunday	740	420
Monday	340	100
Wednesday	240	60

$\therefore$ Required ratio = 60 : 240 = 1 : 4

Hence, the correct option is (D).

39. Given:

Day	Total People	Male
Saturday	580	360
Sunday	740	420
Monday	340	100
Wednesday	240	60

Number of male visited in Saturday and Monday = 360 + 100 = 460

Average of Females on Sunday and Wednesday = $\dfrac{(320+180)}{2} =$ 250

$\therefore$ Required difference = 460 – 250 = 210

Hence, the correct option is (E).

40. Given:

Day	Total People	Male
Saturday	580	360
Sunday	740	420
Monday	340	100
Wednesday	240	60

Number of male visited on Sunday and Monday = 420 + 100 = 520

Female on Sunday = 320

$\Rightarrow$ Difference = 520 – 320 = 200

$\therefore$ Required percent = $\left(\dfrac{200}{320}\right) \times 100 = 62.5\%$

Hence, the correct option is (E).

41. According to BODMAS first we have to solve 'brackets' followed by 'of' then 'division' then 'multiplication' and later 'addition', 'subtraction'.

$(10)^{7.3} \div (100)^{4.15} \times (1000)^2 + 99999 = ? \times 10^5$

We can write,

$(10)^{7.3} \div (10)^{8.3} \times (10)^6 + 99999 = ? \times 10^5$

$(10)^5 + 99999 = ? \times 10^5$

$\dfrac{((10)^5 + 99999)}{10^5} = ?$

$1 + 0.99999 = ?$

? = 2 approx.

Hence, the correct option is (E).

42. $? = \dfrac{599.1375 \times 0.0793 \times 3.976}{0.0773 \times 72.581 \times 69.749} \approx \dfrac{600 \times 0.07 \times 4}{0.07 \times 73 \times 70}$

$\Rightarrow ? = \dfrac{168}{357.7}$

$\Rightarrow ? = \dfrac{1680}{3577}$

$\Rightarrow ? = 0.469 \approx 0.47$

Hence, the correct option is (B).

43. $(5325)^{\frac{1}{4}}$

Let us factorize the number given:

$5280 = 2 \times 2 \times 2 \times 2 \times 2 \times 3 \times 5 \times 11$

$(5280)^{\frac{1}{4}} = (2^4 \times 330)^{\frac{1}{4}}$

We know that, $4^4 = 256$ and $5^4 = 625$

So, the nearest value to 330 is 256.

So, $(5280)^{\frac{1}{4}} = (24 \times 330)^{\frac{1}{4}} = 2 \times 4 = 8$

? = 8 (nearest whole number value).

Hence, the correct option is (A).

44. Equation I.

$x^2 + x - 156 = 0$

$\Rightarrow x^2 + 13x - 12x - 156 = 0$

$\Rightarrow x(x + 13) - 12(x + 13) = 0$

$\Rightarrow (x + 13)(x - 12) = 0$

$\Rightarrow x + 13 = 0$ or $x - 12 = 0$

$\Rightarrow x = -13$ or $x = 12$

Equation II.

$y^2 + y - 182 = 0$

$\Rightarrow y^2 + 14y - 13y - 182 = 0$

$\Rightarrow y(y + 14) - 13(y + 14) = 0$

$\Rightarrow (y + 14)(y - 13) = 0$

$\Rightarrow y + 14 = 0$ or $y - 13 = 0$

$\Rightarrow y = -14$ or $y = 13$

Value of x	Value of y	Relation
-13	-14	x > y
-13	13	x < y
12	-14	x > y
12	13	x < y

$\therefore$ x > y and x < y the relationship between x and y cannot be established.

Hence, the correct option is (E).

45. According to the given equations:

I. $x^2 - 18x + 77 = 0$

$\Rightarrow x^2 - 11x - 7x + 77 = 0$

$\Rightarrow x(x - 11) - 7(x - 11) = 0$

$\Rightarrow (x - 11)(x - 7) = 0$

$\Rightarrow x = 7, 11$

II. $y^2 + 3y - 70 = 0$

$\Rightarrow y^2 + 10y - 7y - 70 = 0$

$\Rightarrow y(y + 10) - 7(y + 10) = 0$

$\Rightarrow (y + 10)(y - 7) = 0$

$\Rightarrow y = -10, 7$

x	y	Relation
7	-10	x > y
7	7	x = y
11	-10	x > y
11	7	x > y

$\therefore x \geq y$

Hence, the correct option is (B).

46. I. $3x^2 - 2\sqrt{21}x + 7 = 0$

$\Rightarrow 3x^2 - \sqrt{21}x - \sqrt{21}x + 7 = 0$

$\Rightarrow \left(\sqrt{3}x - \sqrt{7}\right)\left(\sqrt{3}x - \sqrt{7}\right) = 0$

$\Rightarrow x = \dfrac{\sqrt{7}}{\sqrt{3}}, \dfrac{\sqrt{7}}{\sqrt{3}}$

II. $3y^2 + \sqrt{3}y - 2 = 0$

$\Rightarrow 3y^2 - \sqrt{3}y + 2\sqrt{3}y - 2 = 0$

$\Rightarrow (\sqrt{3}y - 1)(\sqrt{3}y + 2) = 0$

$\Rightarrow y = \dfrac{1}{\sqrt{3}}, \dfrac{-2}{\sqrt{3}}$

Value of x	Value of y	Relation
$\dfrac{\sqrt{7}}{\sqrt{3}}$	$\dfrac{1}{\sqrt{3}}$	x > y
$\dfrac{\sqrt{7}}{\sqrt{3}}$	$\dfrac{-2}{\sqrt{3}}$	x > y
$\dfrac{\sqrt{7}}{\sqrt{3}}$	$\dfrac{1}{\sqrt{3}}$	x > y
$\dfrac{\sqrt{7}}{\sqrt{3}}$	$\dfrac{-2}{\sqrt{3}}$	x > y

$\therefore$ x > y

Hence, the correct option is (A).

47. I. $2x^2 + 5x - 250 = 0$

$\Rightarrow 2x^2 - 20x + 25x - 250 = 0$

$\Rightarrow 2x(x - 10) + 25(x - 10) = 0$

$\Rightarrow (2x + 25)(x - 10) = 0$

$\Rightarrow x = \dfrac{-25}{2}, 10$

II. $7y^2 - 22y + 3 = 0$

$\Rightarrow 7y^2 - 21y - y + 3 = 0$

$\Rightarrow 7y(y - 3) - 1(y - 3) = 0$

$\Rightarrow (7y - 1)(y - 3) = 0$

$\Rightarrow y = \dfrac{1}{7}, 3$

Value of x	Value of y	Relation
$\dfrac{-25}{2}$	$\dfrac{1}{7}$	x < y
$\dfrac{-25}{2}$	3	x < y
10	$\dfrac{1}{7}$	x > y
10	3	x > y

So, the relationship between x and y cannot be established.

Hence, the correct option is (E).

48. I. $(169)^{\frac{1}{2}}x + \sqrt{289} = 134$

$\Rightarrow 13x + 17 = 134$

$\Rightarrow 13x = 134 - 17$

$\Rightarrow 13x = 117$

$\Rightarrow x = 9$

II. $(361)^{\frac{1}{2}}y^2 - 270 = 1269$

$\Rightarrow 19y^2 - 270 = 1269$

$\Rightarrow 19y^2 = 1269 + 270$

$\Rightarrow 19y^2 = 1539$

$\Rightarrow y^2 = 81$

$\Rightarrow y = \pm 9$

So, when x = +9, x = y for y = +9 and x > y for y = -9

$\therefore$ We can observe that x ≥ y.

Hence, the correct option is (C).

49. Given:

The marked price of an item = Rs. 4000

Discount percentage for B = 5%

The selling price of an item sold by B = Rs. 7700

Formula:

Profit percentage = $\dfrac{(Selling\ price - Cost\ price)}{(Cost\ price)} \times 100$

Calculation:

Cost price of an item for B = $7700 \times \dfrac{100}{110}$ = Rs. 7000

The cost price of an item for B = selling price of an item for A = Rs. 7000

$\Rightarrow$ Cost price of an item for A = $4000 \times \dfrac{95}{100}$ = Rs. 3800

$\therefore$ Profit percentage = $\dfrac{(7000 - 3800)}{3800} \times 100$

$\Rightarrow$ 84.21%

$\therefore$ The required percentage = 84.21%

Hence, the correct option is (E).

50. Given:

A's 1 day's work = $\dfrac{1}{12}$

B's 1 day's work = $\dfrac{1}{16}$

Let C's 1 day's work be $\dfrac{1}{C}$.

(A + B)'s 1 day's work = $\dfrac{1}{12} + \dfrac{1}{16} = \dfrac{7}{48}$

$\Rightarrow$ (A + B)'s 5 days Work = $5 \times \dfrac{7}{48} = \dfrac{35}{48}$

Remaining work = $1 - \dfrac{35}{48} = \dfrac{13}{48}$

$\Rightarrow 6.5 = \dfrac{13}{48} \times C$

$\Rightarrow C = 24$

C's 1 day's work = $\dfrac{1}{24}$

$\Rightarrow$ (A + B + C)'s 1 day's work = $\dfrac{1}{12} + \dfrac{1}{16} + \dfrac{1}{24} = \dfrac{9}{48} = \dfrac{3}{16}$

$\therefore$ Required time = $\dfrac{3}{4} \times \dfrac{16}{3}$ = 4 days

Hence, the correct option is (C).

51. Given:

Scores of Sachin in 8 innings are = 80, 84, 89, 75, 76, 82, 78, 81

Concept:

Average is sum of all element divided by total number of elements.

Sum of Sachin's scores = 80 + 84 + 89 + 75 + 76 + 82 + 78 + 81 = 645

Average = $\dfrac{645}{8}$ = 80.625

$\therefore$ The required average = 80.625

Hence, the correct option is (D).

52. Given:

Side of a cube = 6 cm

The volume of a cube = (Side)^3

The volume of a cone = $\left(\dfrac{1}{3}\right) \times \pi \times r^2 \times h$

Maximum cone which can formed by cube

Height of cone = 6 cm

Radius of cone = 3 cm

The volume of cone = $\left(\dfrac{1}{3}\right) \times \pi \times (3)^2 \times 6$

$\Rightarrow 18\pi$

The volume of a cube = $(6)^3$

$\Rightarrow 216$

Waste part of a cube = Volume of a cube − Volume of a cone

$\Rightarrow 216 - 18\pi$

Ratio of waste part to the cone = $\left[\dfrac{(216-18\pi)}{18\pi}\right]$

$\Rightarrow \dfrac{\left[216-\left(18\times\frac{22}{7}\right)\right]}{\left(18\times\frac{22}{7}\right)}$

$\Rightarrow \dfrac{\left[\frac{(1512-396)}{7}\right]}{\left(18\times\frac{22}{7}\right)}$

$\Rightarrow \dfrac{\left(\frac{1116}{7}\right)}{\left(\frac{396}{7}\right)}$

$\Rightarrow \dfrac{31}{11}$

$\Rightarrow 31 : 11$

Hence, the correct option is (C).

53. The number of Milk parlors approved = 2000

The number of Refreshment joints applied for permission = 4500

The number of Refreshment joints approved = 1500

$\Rightarrow$ The number of Refreshment joints rejected = 4500 − 1500 = 3000

$\therefore$ Required difference = 3000 − 2000 = 1000

Hence, the correct option is (C).

54. The number of business applied for permission = (6000 + 5000 + 4500 + 2500 + 1500)

The number of business applied for permission in five sectors = 19500

The number of business approved = (5000 + 3500 + 1500 + 2000 + 1000)

$\Rightarrow$ The number of business approved in five sectors = 13000

$\Rightarrow$ The number of business rejected in five sectors = 19500 − 13000 = 6500

$\Rightarrow$ The number of business rejected in five sectors is 6500.

$\therefore$ Required ratio = 13000 : 6500 = 2 : 1

Hence, the correct option is (A).

55. The number of Clothes stores applied for permission = 5000

The number of Clothes stores approved = 3500

$\Rightarrow$ The number of Clothes stores rejected = 5000 − 3500 = 1500

The number of Automotive showrooms applied for permission = 1500

$\Rightarrow$ The number of Automotive showrooms approved = 1000

$\Rightarrow$ The number of Automotive showrooms rejected = 1500 − 1000 = 500

So, Difference between businesses rejected = 1500 − 500 = 1000

$\therefore$ Required percentage = $\left(\dfrac{1000}{500}\right) \times 100$ = 200%

Hence, the correct option is (E).

56. The number of business approved in Grocery Stores and Milk parlor = 5000 + 2000 = 7000

The number of business approved in Cloth stores and Automotive showroom = 3500 + 1000 = 4500

$\therefore$ Required Ratio = 7000 : 4500 = 14 : 9

Hence, the correct option is (A).

57. The number of business applied for permission = (6000 + 5000 + 4500 + 2500 + 1500)

⇒ The number of business applied for permission in five sectors = 19500

The number of business approved = (5000 + 3500 + 1500 + 2000 + 1000)

⇒ The number of business approved in five sectors = 13000

⇒ The number of business rejected for permission in five sectors = 19500 – 13000 = 6500

∴ The number of business rejected for permission in five sectors is 6500.

Hence, the correct option is (D).

58. Given:

Ratio of investments of Harry and Ron = 50000 : 35000 = 10 : 7

They suffered a loss of Rs. 7480, which will be divided in the ratio 10 : 7

Therefore,

Loss suffered by Harry = $\dfrac{10}{17}$ × 7480 = Rs. 4400

Loss suffered by Ron = 7480 – 4400 = Rs. 3080

Now, Hermione invested= Rs. 25000

∴ Ratio of investments of Harry, Ron and Hermione = 50000 : 35000 : 25000 = 10 : 7 : 5

In the 2nd year, they covered all losses and made an additional profit = Rs. 4520.

∴ Total profit made in 2nd year = 7480 + 4520 = Rs. 12000

Out of this, 12% is given to Hermione as compensation for handling the business.

∴ Hermione's income for handling business = 12% of 12000 = Rs. 1440

The remaining profit will be divided among the three in the ratio of their investments.

So, Remaining profit = 12000 – 1440 = Rs. 10560

Therefore,

Harry's share in 2nd year's profit = $\dfrac{10}{22}$ × 10560 = Rs. 4800

Harry's earning in 2 years = 2nd year's profit – 1st year's loss = 4800 – 4400 = Rs. 400

Hence, the correct option is (B).

59. Given:

(27.84 + 31.90) ÷ 14.84 = 97.79 ÷ 13.98 – ?

We can write the given values as:

27.84 ≈ 28 and 31.90 ≈ 32

14.84 ≈ 15 and 97.79 ≈ 98 and 13.98 ≈ 14

Then,

⇒ (28 + 32) ÷ 15 = 98 ÷ 14 – ?

⇒ 60 ÷ 15 = 98 ÷ 14 – ?

⇒ 4 = 7 – ?

⇒ ? = 7 – 4

⇒ ? ≈ 3

Hence, the correct option is (A).

60. Given:

(?)² + 34.98% of 1998 + 26.98% of 402 = 3208.359

⇒ (?)² = 3208.3 – (699.3 + 108.54)

⇒ (?)² = 2400.46

⇒ (?)² = (49)²

⇒ ? = 49

Hence, the correct option is (C).

61. Given:

$$2159.9 \div \sqrt{729} + 37.5\% \text{ of } 24.04 + ? = 42.83 \times 12.93$$

$$\Rightarrow 2160 \div 27 + 37.5\% \text{ of } 24 + ? = 559$$

$$\Rightarrow 80 + \frac{3}{8} \times 24 + ? = 559$$

$$\Rightarrow 89 + ? = 559$$

$$\therefore ? = 470$$

Hence, the correct option is (B).

62. Given:

$$289.89\% \text{ of } 399.88 + \left(\sqrt{441} + \sqrt{361}\right) - 1 = ?$$

Taking approximate value, we get:

$$289.89\% \text{ of } 400 + \left(\sqrt{441} + \sqrt{361}\right) - 1 = ?$$

$$\Rightarrow (290 \div 100) \times 400 + (21 + 19) - 1 = ?$$

$$\Rightarrow 1160 + 40 - 1 = ?$$

$$\Rightarrow 1200 - 1 = ?$$

$$\therefore ? = 1199$$

Hence, the correct option is (D).

63. Given:

$$29^2 + 34.12\% \text{ of } 700 \div \sqrt[2]{2744.213} = ? + \sqrt[2]{2197}$$

Taking approximate value, we get

$$29^2 + 34.12\% \text{ of } 700 \div \sqrt[2]{2744} = ? + \sqrt[2]{2197}$$

$$\Rightarrow 841 + (34 \div 100) \times 700 \div 14 = ? + 13$$

$$\Rightarrow 841 + (238 \div 14) = ? + 13$$

$$\Rightarrow 841 + 17 = ? + 13$$

$$\Rightarrow 858 = ? + 13$$

$$\Rightarrow ? = 858 - 13$$

$$\therefore ? = 845$$

Hence, the correct option is (D).

64. Follow the BODMAS rule to solve this question,

$59.99 \div 60.01 + 17.91 \times 3.05 - 10.97 = ?$

$\Rightarrow 60 \div 60 + 18 \times 3 - 11 = ?$

$\Rightarrow 1 + 54 - 11 = ?$

$\Rightarrow 55 - 11 = ?$

$\therefore ? = 44$

Hence, the correct option is (A).

65. Follow the BODMAS rule to solve this question,

$(179.8 \times 19.91 - 23.99 \times 6.03) \div (67.95 \times 36.03 \div 17.95 + 35.97) = ?$

$\Rightarrow (180 \times 20 - 24 \times 6) \div (68 \times 36 \div 18 + 36)$

$\Rightarrow (3600 - 144) \div (68 \times 2 + 36)$

$\Rightarrow 3456 \div (136 + 36)$

$\Rightarrow 3456 \div 172$

$\Rightarrow 20.09 \approx 20$

$\therefore$ The value of ? is 20.

Hence, the correct option is (A).

66. $Y \leq K < M > B = I, A \geq M > O \geq K$

From these statements, we can conclude that $Y \leq K < O < M \leq A$ and $M > B = I$

Conclusion 1 is incorrect as A > Y but they can never be equal.

Conclusion 2 is incorrect as there is no relationship between O and B.

They can be equal, or O can be greater or less than B.

Hence, the correct option is (D).

67. $R > P = Q \leq H \leq N, H > U < P$

From these statements, we can conclude that $U < P = Q \leq H \leq N$ and $P < R$

We can see that both the conclusions follow from the conclusion we have drawn using both statements.

Hence, the correct option is (E).

68. $D > S \geq C < U < A, Y = X \leq B < U$

From these statements, we can conclude that $X = Y \leq B < S < D$ and $A > U > C \leq S$

None of the conclusions definitely follow. But together, they make an exhaustive set i.e. they cover all the possibilities that can be between X(=Y) and C.

Hence, the correct option is (C).

69. $V > P = I \geq F < L, A \leq I < C$

From these statements, we can conclude that $L > F \leq P = I \geq A$ and $C > I = P < V$

We can see that conclusion 1 need not necessarily follow as F can be less than A as well.

Conclusion 2 follows the conclusion that we have drawn based on the given statements.

Hence, the correct option is (B).

70. $C < T \geq M > N, G < U \leq A > C$

From these statements, we can conclude that $C < A \geq U > G$ and $C < T \geq M > NS$

We can see that conclusion 1 follows from the above conclusion. But no relationship can be established between N and G as N can be greater, equal, or less than G.

So, conclusion 2 doesn't follow.

Hence, the correct option is (A).

Ques (71-75): Persons: A, B, C, D, E, F, G, H and J.

(1) A sits 2nd to the right of B.

(2) F sits 4th to the left of A.

(3) C sits third to the right of F.

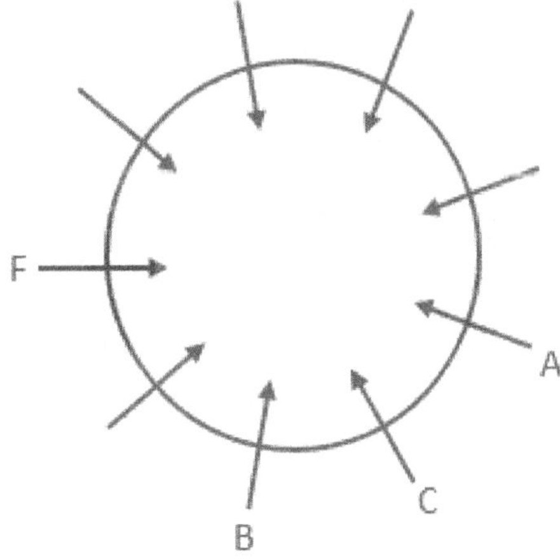

(4) G sits 2nd to the right of H.

(5) G is immediate neighbor of J.

Since G is immediate neighbor of J and sits second to the right of H, two possible cases can be made.

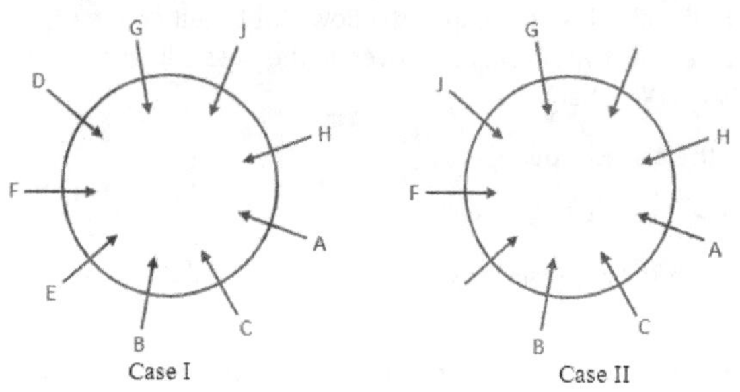

Case I   Case II

Case II can be further categorized as Case II (a) and Case II (b) as per the position of J.

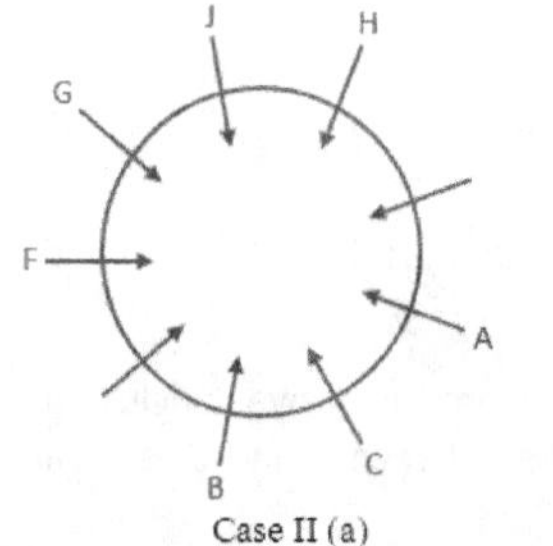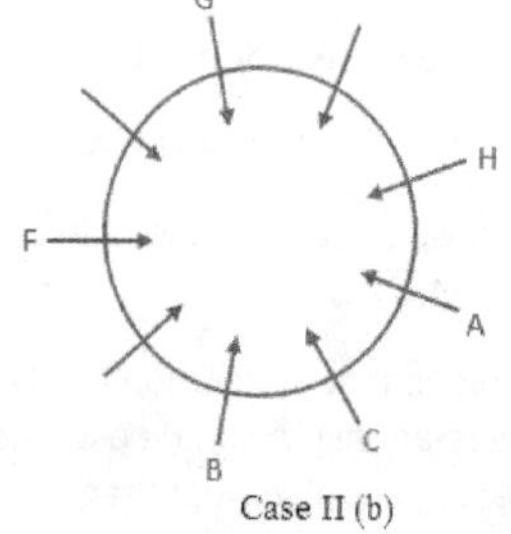

Case II (a)   Case II (b)

(6) D sits 2nd to the left of E.

Case I gets eliminated as no such arrangements can be made.

(7) E is not an immediate neighbor of A.

Case II (b) gets eliminated as no such arrangement is possible.

So, the final arrangement is Case II (a).

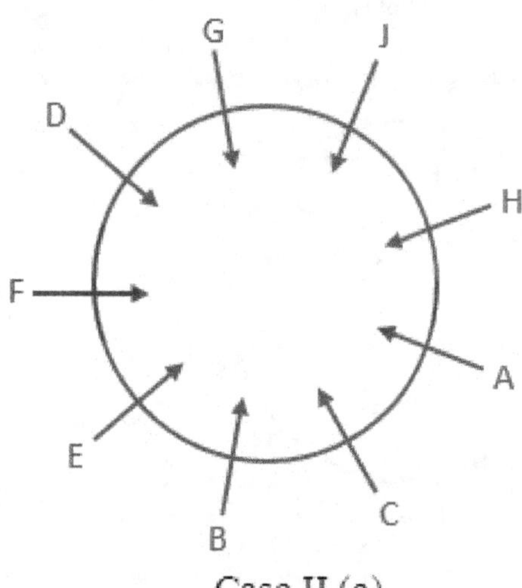

Case II (a)

71. Thus, A sits third to the right of E.

Hence, the correct option is (B).

72. Thus, nobody sits between E and F.

Hence, the correct option is (D).

73. Thus, B sits between E and C.

Hence, the correct option is (A).

74. Thus, H sits immediate right of A.

Hence, the correct option is (E).

75. Persons: A, B, C, D, E, F, G, H and J.

(1) A sits 2nd to the right of B.

(2) F sits 4th to the left of A.

(3) C sits third to the right of F.

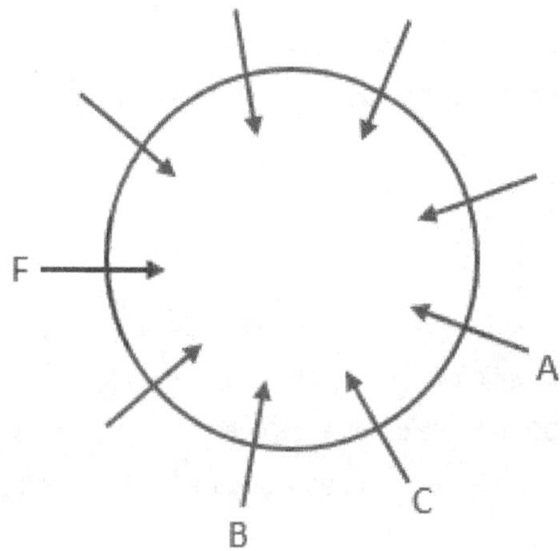

(4) G sits 2nd to the right of H.

(5) G is immediate neighbor of J.

Since G is immediate neighbor of J and sits second to the right of H, two possible cases can be made.

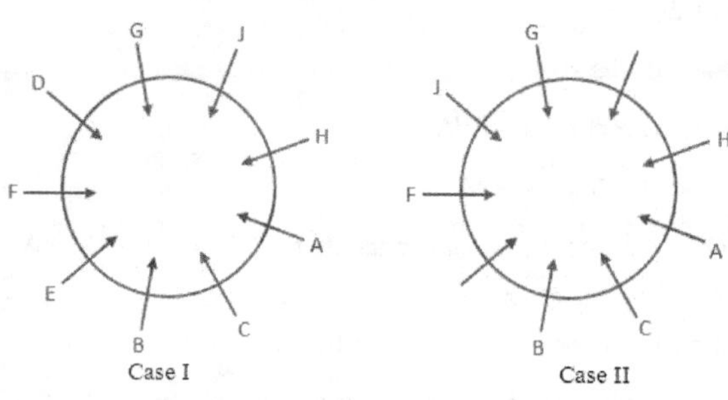

Case I   Case II

Case II can be further categorized as Case II (a) and Case II (b) as per the position of J.

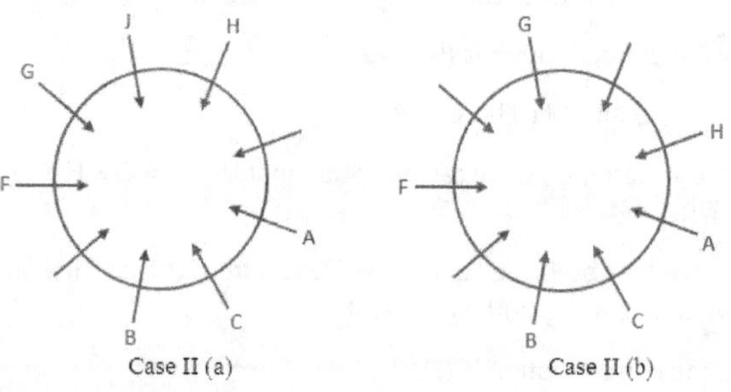

Case II (a)   Case II (b)

(6) D sits 2nd to the left of E.

Case I gets eliminated as no such arrangements can be made.

(7) E is not an immediate neighbor of A.

Case II (b) gets eliminated as no such arrangement is possible.

So, the final arrangement is Case II (a).

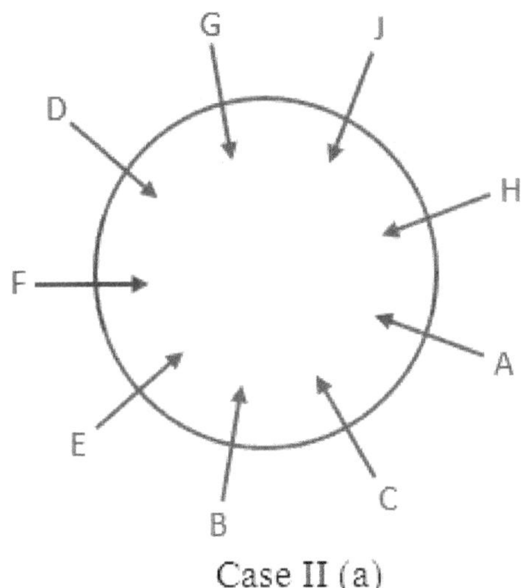

Case II (a)

Symbol in Diagram	Meaning
○	Female
□	Male
══	Married Couple
──	Siblings
│	Difference of A Generation

Thus, A-C is the odd one out as the rest of the pairs are not immediate neighbors of each other.

Hence, the correct option is (D).

Ques (76-78):

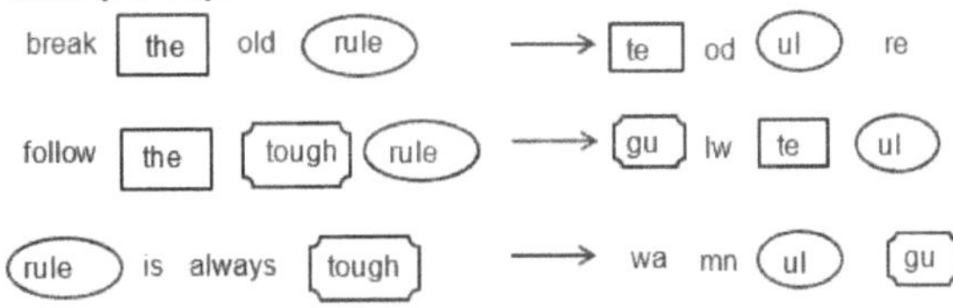

76. So, the code for 'rule is 'ul'.

Hence, the correct option is (B).

77. So, the code for 'break' is either 'od' or 're'.

Hence, the correct option is (C).

78. So, the code for 'always follow' is either 'lw wa' or 'mn lw'.

Hence, the correct option is (E).

Ques (79-81): From the given information,

1. U is the paternal aunt of T. R is the mother-in-law of S's husband.

2. Q has only one child.

3. S and Q are not married to each other.

Based on the given data, we can draw the family tree,

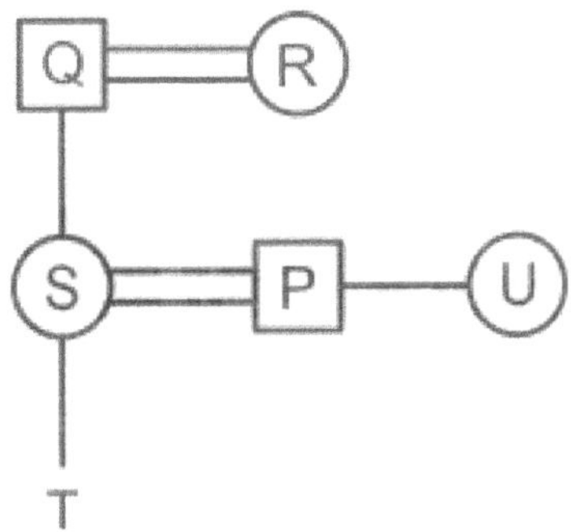

79. So, U is the sister-in-law of S.

Hence, the correct option is (B).

80. So, Q is the father of S.

Hence, the correct option is (C).

81. So, R is the grandmother of T.

Hence, the correct option is (C).

Ques (82-86): Seven friends:- Preeti, Dhruv, Ankita, Aarti, Laksh, Aditya and Eshan

Time slots:- 6 a.m., 11 a.m., 2 p.m., 4 p.m., 6 p.m., 9 p.m., and 10 p.m.

1) Preeti goes for a walk at 6 p.m.

2) There is a four-hour of gap between Preeti and Aditya.

Now Aditya can go walk at either 2:00 pm or 10:00 pm.

3) Laksh goes for a walk immediately after Aditya.

This implies that Aditya goes for walk at 2:00 pm and Laksh goes for walk at 4:00 pm.

Timing	Persons
6 a.m.	
11 a.m.	
2 p.m.	Aditya
4 p.m.	Laksh
6 p.m.	Preeti
9 p.m.	
10 p.m.	

4) Dhruv goes for a walk after 2 p.m. but he is not the last one.

5) Aarti goes for a walk immediately after Ankita.

Timing	Persons
6 a.m.	Ankita
11 a.m.	Aarti
2 p.m.	Aditya
4 p.m.	Laksh
6 p.m.	Preeti
9 p.m.	Dhruv
10 p.m.	Eshan

82. So, Eshan goes for his walk at 10 p.m.

Hence, the correct option is (A).

83. So, Ankita was the 1st person goes for the walk.

Hence, the correct option is (C).

84. So, One person goes for a walk between Aarti and Laksh.

Hence, the correct option is (D).

85. So, "Dhruv" goes for a walk at 9 p.m.

Hence, the correct option is (D).

86. Preeti goes for a walk at 6 p.m.

Aaditya goes for a walk at 2 p.m.

So, the time gap in hours between them:- 6 – 2 = 4 hours.

Hence, the correct option is (C).

87. Eighteenth letter from the right end → O

Seventh letter to the right of O → H

Fifth letter to the left of H → A

Hence, the correct option is (A).

88. After removing all the vowels, the series becomes:

Q W R T Y P S D F G H J K L Z X C V B N M

Now, the fifteenth letter from the right end → S

Tenth letter to the right of S → C

Hence, the correct option is (B).

89. After interchanging,

C V B N M Y U I O P A S D F G H J K L Z X Q W E R T

Now, the ninth letter from the left end → O

Seventh letter to the left of O → V

Hence, the correct option is (C).

90. The series formed after dropping alternate letters starting from the first letter:

W R Y I P S F H K Z C B M

Eighth letter from the right → S

Fifth letter to the left of S → W

Hence, the correct option is (D).

91. Q W E R T Y U I O P A S D F G H J K L Z X C V B N M

Seventeenth letter from the left end → J

The second letter to the right of J → L

Fifth to the right of L → B

Hence, the correct option is (E).

92. The least possible diagram for the given statements is as follows:

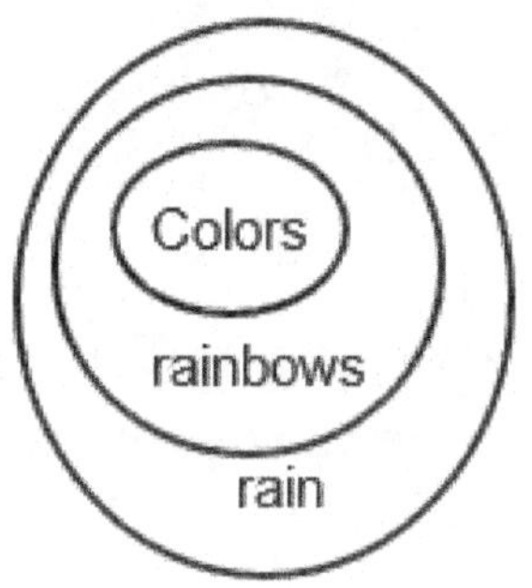

Conclusions:

I. All rain is colors → False (It is possible but not definite)

II. All colors are rain → True (the whole area of color is under are of rain so all colors are definitely rain)

So, only conclusion II follows.

Hence, the correct option is (B).

93. The least possible diagram for the given statements is as follows:

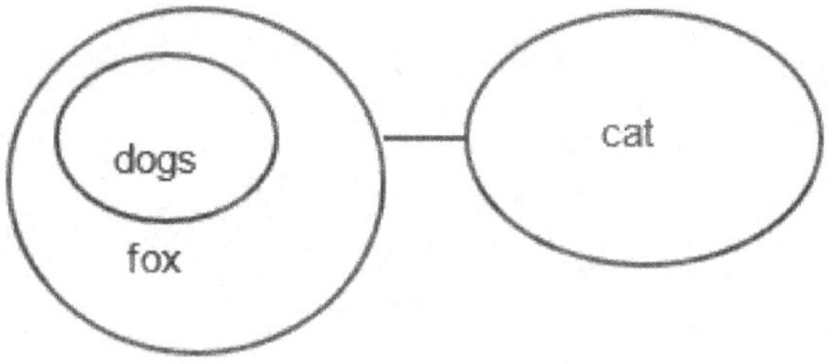

Conclusions:

I. No dog is a cat → True (No fox is a cat so whatever is inside fox is also not cat)

II. Some dog are cat → False (It is not possible as no dog is a cat)

So, only conclusion I follows.

Hence, the correct option is (A).

94. The least possible diagram for the given statements is as follows:

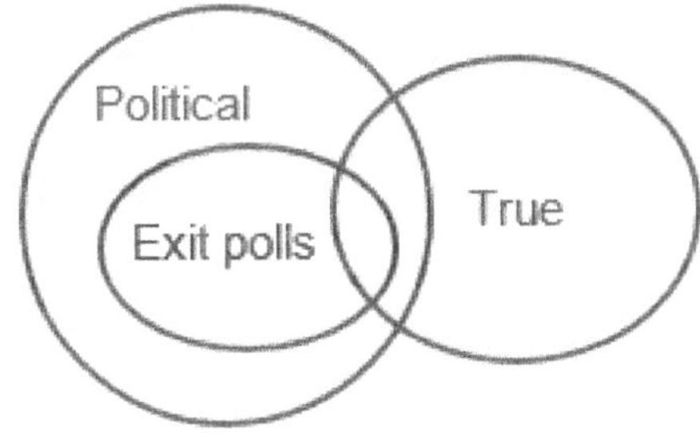

Conclusions:

I. Some true is not political → False (It is possible but not definite)

II. Some political is not exit polls → False (It is possible but not definite)

So, Neither I nor II follows.

Hence, the correct option is (D).

Ques (95-99): Persons: S, T, U, V, W, X, Y and Z

1) W is sitting 5th to the right of T who is facing north and neither of them is sitting at extreme positions.

2) S who is an immediate neighbour of V is sitting 4th to the right of W.

This means W is facing south.

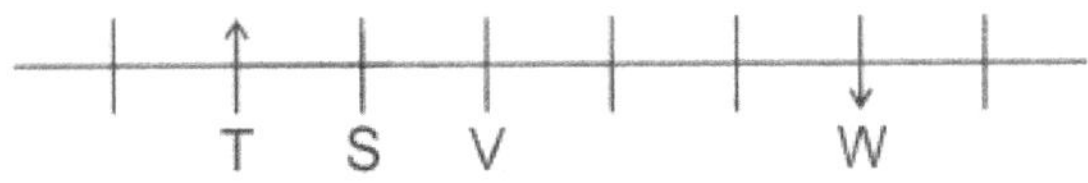

3) Three persons are sitting between V and X. V and X are facing North direction.

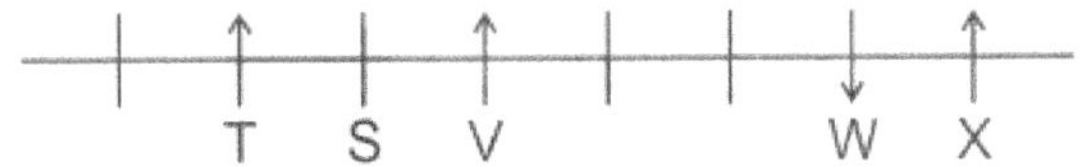

4) Z sits third to the left of X and faces opposite to that of X.

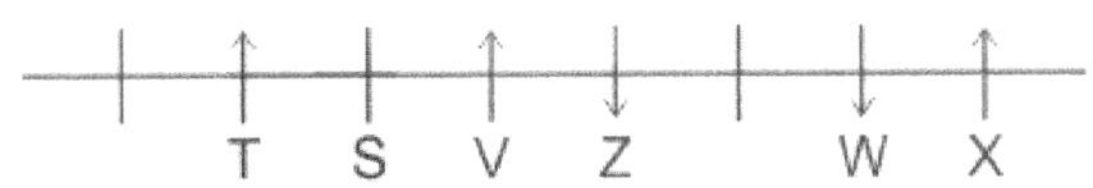

5) Immediate neighbours of Z face the same direction but opposite to that of Z.

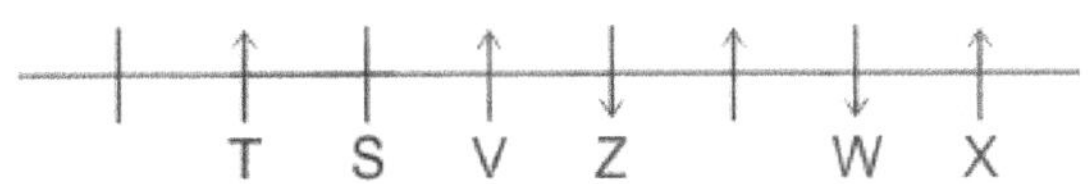

6) Y who faces the South direction sits at one of the positions at the left of V.

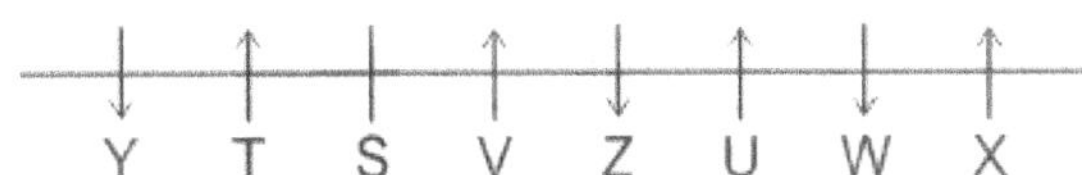

95. So, X sits at the extreme end of the row.

Hence, the correct option is (C).

96. So, X sits second to the right of U.

Hence, the correct option is (D).

97. (A) S sits fifth to the left of X - true

(B) U is an immediate neighbour of V - false (Z sits between U and V)

(C) T sits at one of the extreme ends - false (X and Y sit at the extreme ends)

(D) Three people sit to the right of Z - false (4 people sit to the right of Z)

(E) U is neighbour of V and W - false (U is the neighbour of W and Z)

So, S sits fifth to the left of X.

Hence, the correct option is (A).

98. So, W does not belong to the group as all others are facing North and W is facing South.

Hence, the correct option is (B).

99. As the direction of S cannot be determined, the number of persons sitting to the right of S cannot be determined.

Hence, the correct option is (E).

100. The logic is:

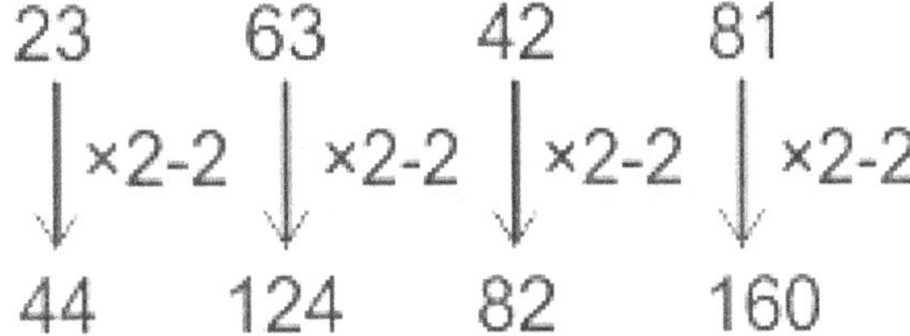

Similarly,

Thus, '44-124-82-160' is the correct answer.

Hence, the correct option is (C).

English Language

Ques (1-4):Direction: Read the sentence given below to find out if it contains any error. The error, if any, will be in one part of the sentence. If the sentence is error-free, select option (E). Ignore error of punctuation if any.

Q.1 Dean wasn't sure if it was her (A)/ natural aversion to anything (B)/ involving law enforcement (C)/ or concern to her boss' future (D)/. No error (E)

A. (A) **B.** (B) **C.** (C) **D.** (D)
E. (E)

Q.2 The secretary(A)/ has diploma(B)/ in both Education(C)/ and Linguistics.(D)/ No error. (E)

A. (A) **B.** (B) **C.** (C) **D.** (D)
E. (E)

Q.3 This was not a mangy (A)/ or vicious creature standing in front of him, (B)/ but a breathtaking beautiful,(C)/ gigantic wolf. (D) No error. (E)

A. (A) **B.** (B) **C.** (C) **D.** (D)
E. (E)

Q.4 Sing and playing(A)/ the guitar was(B)/ her all-time (C)/favorite hobby. (D)/ No error(E)

A. (A) **B.** (B) **C.** (C) **D.** (D)
E. (E)

Ques (5-11):Direction: In the following passage, some of the words have been left out. Read the passage carefully and select the correct answer for the given blanks out of the given alternatives.

Canada, the world's second ____ (1) country by landmass, Is effectively ____ (2) out of land even though the real-estate infrastructure is ____ (3) compared to anywhere else in the world. This is happening due to the worsening imbalance ____ (4) supply and demand. The buyers in the country want large homes however builders can't ____ (5) them due to the unavailability of enough space in and around the major cities where people work. Canadians usually ____ (6) single detached houses and now these may soon be out of ____ (7) in the places where people want to live.

Q.5 Choose the most appropriate word for blank (1):

A. biggest **B.** smaller
C. tiny **D.** larger
E. None of these

Q.6 Choose the most appropriate word for blank (2):

A. drowning **B.** running
C. blooming **D.** sticking
E. None of these

Q.7 Choose the most appropriate word for blank (3):

A. glowing **B.** tiring
C. booming **D.** separating
E. None of these

Q.8 Choose the most appropriate word for blank (4):

A. between **B.** among
C. for **D.** into
E. None of these

Q.9 Choose the most appropriate word for blank (5):

A. give **B.** help
C. leave **D.** provide
E. None of these

Q.10 Choose the most appropriate word for blank (6):

A. reject **B.** prefer
C. option **D.** dismiss
E. None of these

Q.11 Choose the most appropriate word for blank (7):

A. cease **B.** penetrate
C. reach **D.** thrust
E. None of these

Ques (12-19):Direction: Read the passage given below and answer the following questions. Some words may be highlighted for you. Pay careful attention.

The more things change, the more they remain the same, or so goes the adage. But that was before Covid-19 brought the world to its knees. One of the most drastic changes has perhaps been for the Big Fat Indian wedding, in which the virus has shrunk to size zero overnight. A typical Indian wedding, till recently, could last for days with multiple **extravagant** events. There were reasons for it too. In addition to endless singing and dancing, time and space had to be allotted to ritual turmeric baths, Mehendi sessions, sit-down dinners — all of which would climax, after a slow, torturous grind, in the form of a grand traditional wedding ceremony.

Then, last year, the Great Indian Wedding was forced to shed weight. Pandemic-induced restrictions led to a cap on the number of wedding guests. The second wave of the virus is expected to turn the wedding industry even leaner. Over one crore people associated with the industry, directly or indirectly, are estimated to have lost their jobs owing to the pandemic. As the wedding industry clutches on to e-invitations and Zoom meets for survival, allied services and personnel, such as printing establishments and artisans who work in the ateliers of fashion designers, are enduring losses.

In this context, what the virus has done is raise, quite **inadvertently**, questions on a people's relationship with ethics and consumption. Could the pandemic then bring about a decisive transformation in contemporary culture's endorsement of excess, ostentation, and pomp? After all, in this age of the pandemic, Indian couples are increasingly resorting to organize smaller — more intimate — ceremonies. There is a bit of altruism thrown in too: a newly-married couple in Bengal donated the money meant for their wedding feast to feed the poor. But vanity, much like the virus, cannot be eradicated with ease. Reports show that those who are not able to have the destination wedding of their dreams are splurging on a designer trousseau instead; guests who can no longer make it to the wedding are being sent lavish gifts; and the menu, instead of being spartan, is getting even more **elaborate**. The pandemic has changed the way people live, but cultural traditions — weddings and their paraphernalia — appear to be far more resilient. This brings to the fore a worrying possibility. It seems that even disruptions and death of the scale that the world has witnessed in the course of the coronavirus have not been enough for sections of affluent Indians to turn **empathetic** to suffering. The Great Fat Indian Wedding that survives, albeit in a trimmer shape, may well be an embodiment of a shocking insularity.

Q.12 Which wave of the virus is expected to turn the wedding industry leaner?

A. First wave

B. Second wave

C. Third wave

D. Fourth wave

E. None of these

Q.13 Over how many people who are associated with the wedding industry have lost their jobs due to the pandemic?

A. 1 million

B. 1 crore

C. 10 crore

D. 10 million

E. None of these

Q.14 In this age of pandemic, what are the Indian couples resorting to?

A. No people at all in the wedding

B. Less cultural traditions

C. Bigger ceremonies

D. Smaller and more intimate ceremonies

E. None of these

Q.15 In the above passage, in which state, a newly married couple donated money meant for their wedding feast to feed the poor?

A. Assam

B. Punjab

C. Bengal

D. Bihar

E. None of these

Q.16 What is the synonym of the word 'extravagant'?

A. Miser

B. Frugal

C. Thrifty

D. Spendthrift

E. None of these

Q.17 What is the synonym of 'inadvertently'?

A. Deliberately

B. Predetermined

C. Unintentionally

D. Foreseen

E. None of these

Q.18 What is the antonym of 'elaborate'?

A. Simple

B. Complicated

C. Detailed

D. Bewildering

E. None of these

Q.19 What is the antonym of 'empathetic'?

A. Compassionate

B. Merciless

C. Sensitive

D. Sympathetic

E. None of these

Q.20 Direction: In the following question, five words are given, out of which only one word is wrongly spelt. Find the wrongly spelt word and indicate it by selecting the appropriate option.

A. Dissolves

B. Indefinite

C. Absurd

D. Triumph

E. Retreive

Q.21 Direction: In the following question, five words are given, out of which only one word is wrongly spelt. Find the wrongly spelt word and indicate it by selecting the appropriate option.

A. Inviolable

B. Clutered

C. Unfit

D. Adhere

E. Curious

Q.22 Direction: In the following question, five words are given, out of which only one word is wrongly spelt. Find the wrongly spelt word and indicate it by selecting the appropriate option.

A. Guarded

B. Cherished

C. Prevarricate

D. Legitimate

E. Abominate

Q.23 Direction: In the following question, five words are given, out of which only one word is wrongly spelt. Find the wrongly spelt word and indicate it by selecting the appropriate option.

A. Increment

B. Superficial

C. Retreat

D. Sustenence

E. Intensive

Q.24 Direction: In the following question, five words are given, out of which only one word is wrongly spelt. Find the wrongly spelt word and indicate it by selecting the appropriate option.

A. Shettarable

B. Brittle

C. Extraordinary

D. Crisp

E. Shivery

Ques (25-27):Direction: Select the phrase/connector from the given options which can be used to form a single sentence from the two sentences given below, implying the same meaning as expressed in the statement sentence. Pick out the option which when used combines the two sentences as one.

Q.25 The recent food carnival was really happening and there was an array of food stalls. Complimentary drinks were provided to all who visited the carnival.

I. Nevertheless

II. Although

III. Besides

A. Only I

B. Only II

C. Only III

D. Both I and III

E. All of the above

Q.26 India will prevail in a conventional war. It would be a hard-fought battle, but India would tire out the Pakistanis.

I. In contrast to Pakistan,

II. Against Pakistan,

III. Hostile to Pakistan,

A. Only I	**B.** Only II
C. Only III	**D.** Both I and II
E. Both II and III	

Q.27 Many of the arts and sciences make up Western civilization and culture. Philosophy was first defined by the Greeks around the fifth-century B.C.E.

I. As

II. While

III. Since

A. Only I	**B.** Only II
C. Only III	**D.** Both I and III
E. All of the above	

Ques (28-30):Direction: The question below has one blank, which is indicating that something has been omitted. Find out which option can be used to fill up the blank in the sentence in the same sequence to make it meaningfully complete.

Q.28 Buying a home is one of the most ___________ financial decisions we need to take.

A. Important	**B.** Impatient
C. Honest	**D.** Drastic
E. None of the above	

Q.29 Mortgage or home loan ___________ is essentially a life policy that covers the borrower against the non-payment of loan in case of his / her death.

A. Institution	**B.** Function
C. Insurance	**D.** Rate
E. None of the above	

Q.30 To keep tabs on high-value cash withdrawals, the Budget has ___________ banks to levy TDS on withdrawals in excess of Rs. 1 crore.

A. Encouraged	**B.** Empowered
C. Decided	**D.** Demonstrated
E. None of the above	

Numerical Ability

Ques (31-40):Direction: What will come in the place of the question mark '?' in the following question?

Q.31 45% of $4500 + \left(\dfrac{165}{\sqrt{225}}\right) = ?$

A. 2036	**B.** 1036
C. 3036	**D.** 4036
E. None of these	

Q.32 $\sqrt[3]{3375} \times 75\%$ of $400 = \dfrac{?}{2}$

A. 8000	**B.** 7000	**C.** 9000	**D.** 5000
E. 4000			

Q.33 $75.33 + 654.5 + 2.465 = ? + 32.64$

A. 599.64	**B.** 799.64	**C.** 699.64	**D.** 700.64
E. 899.64			

Q.34 $\left[\left\{2 \times \left(\frac{1}{4}\right) + 4\right\} \times 8\right] = ? \times 20$

A. 1.9	**B.** 2.8
C. 3.8	**D.** 1.8
E. None of these	

Q.35 $?\%$ of $400 \times \left(\dfrac{3}{4}\right) + 300 = 66.66\%$ of 900

A. 100	**B.** 260	**C.** 70	**D.** 180
E. 50			

Q.36 $(1836 \div ?) \div 9 = 17$

A. 15	**B.** 13
C. 11	**D.** 12
E. None of these	

Q.37 $(?)^2 \times (15)^2 \div (60)^2 = 16$

A. 36	**B.** 16	**C.** 64	**D.** 4
E. 12			

Q.38 22% of $855 - ? = 20\%$ of 500

A. 88.1	**B.** 89.2	**C.** 87.1	**D.** 85.5
E. 87.9			

Q.39 $\left(\dfrac{50}{7}\right)$ of $294 - 8^3 = 1750 - ?$

A. 185	**B.** 292	**C.** 312	**D.** 182
E. 162			

Q.40

$(\sqrt{1024} + 19 \times 12) \div \sqrt{676} - 4 + 4680 \div ? = 474$

A. 10	**B.** 8	**C.** 16	**D.** 3
E. 11			

Ques (41-45):Direction: In the given question, two equations numbered I and II are given. Solve both the equations and mark the appropriate answer.

Q.41 I. $x^2 - 6x - 40 = 0$

II. $y^2 - 7y + 12 = 0$

A.	$x > y$
B.	$x < y$
C.	$x \geq y$
D.	$x \leq y$
E.	No relation in x and y or x = y

Q.42 I. $x^2 - 5x - 50 = 0$

II. $y^2 + 15y + 50 = 0$

A.	$x > y$
B.	$x < y$
C.	$x \geq y$
D.	$x \leq y$
E.	No relation in x and y or x = y

Q.43 I. $x^2 - 19x + 78 = 0$

II. $y^2 + 14y = 0$

A.	$x > y$
B.	$x < y$
C.	$x \geq y$

D. x ≤ y

E. x = y or relationship between x and y cannot be established

Q.44 I. $x^2 + 7x - 120 = 0$

II. $y^2 - 7y - 120 = 0$

A. x > y

B. x < y

C. x ≥ y

D. x ≤ y

E. x = y or relationship between x and y cannot be established

Q.45 I. $x^2 + x - 12 = 0$

II. $y^2 + 10y - 39 = 0$

A. x < y

B. x > y

C. x ≤ y

D. x ≥ y

E. x = y or the relation between x and y can't be established.

Ques (46-50):Direction: Study the following Pie chart carefully and answer the following questions:

Pie-chart given below shows investment (in terms of percentage) out of total investment of five different persons.

Total Investment = Rs.1,50,000

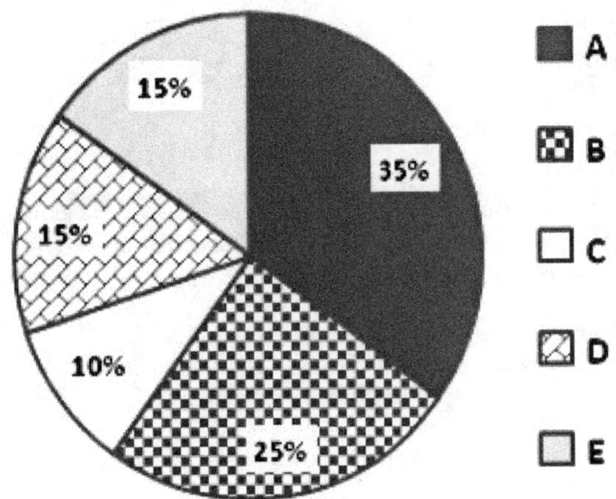

Q.46 What is the ratio of A and C investment together to B and D investment together is?

A. 10 : 11

B. 11 : 10

C. 8 : 9

D. 9 : 8

E. None of these

Q.47 If B invests two times its given investment, then what percent of the D and E investment together is B's investment?

A. $\frac{150}{3}$%

B. $\frac{650}{3}$%

C. $\frac{500}{3}$%

D. $\frac{700}{3}$%

E. None of these

Q.48 A, C and F started a business together. F invested Rs 3000 more than the amount invested by C. F left the business after 8 months of starting of business. After 2 more months C left the business. If the total profit at the end of the year is Rs 15400. The share of F is?

A. Rs 2400

B. Rs 2500

C. Rs 3600

D. Rs 4500

E. None of these

Q.49 By what percent is the average investment of A, B and E together more or less than investment of C and D together?

A. 100%

B. 75%

C. 50%

D. 25%

E. 0%

Q.50 If B and E started a business together. B left the business 9 months after starting of business but E continued for the entire year. Find the difference profits shares of B and E. if total profit at the end of the year is Rs 18000?

A. Rs 1200

B. Rs 1800

C. Rs 1500

D. Rs 2000

E. None of these

Ques (51-55):Direction: Refer to the given line graph below.

The line graph shows the number of students present in a class in all the given days.

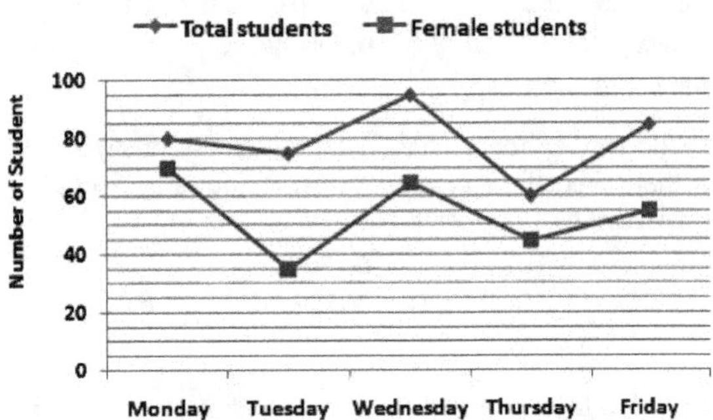

Q.51 Find the difference between the total number of girls present on Thursday and Friday and the total number of boys present on the same day.

A. 50

B. 54

C. 55

D. 59

E. None of these

Q.52 Find the ratio between the total number of boys present in the class on Tuesday and Wednesday and the number of girls present in the class on Thursday.

A. 2 : 3

B. 3 : 4

C. 9 : 14

D. 14 : 9

E. None of these

Q.53 Boys present in the class on Monday and Tuesday is how much percent more than that on Wednesday (in approximate)?

A. 46%

B. 56%

C. 70%

D. 66%

E. None of these

Q.54 If the total number of students present on Saturday is 25% more than the total number of students present on Thursday and the ratio between boys and girls is 2 : 3, find the number of girls who are present in the class on Saturday.

A. 45

B. 40

C. 50   **D.** 60
E. None of these

Q.55 Find the average number of boys present in the class during all given days.
A. 60   **B.** 45
C. 35   **D.** 25
E. None of these

Q.56 A and B can complete a work in 35 and 45 days respectively. If A and C together complete the same work in 25 days. Find the time taken by C alone to complete a work.
A. 55 days   **B.** $\frac{175}{2}$ days
C. 85 days   **D.** $\frac{185}{3}$ days
E. None of these

Q.57 In a school seats for class 9th, 10th and 11th were in the ratio of 8 : 10 : 12. But the management decided to increase the number of seats from next academic year by 30%, 40%, and 50% respectively. Find the ratio of increased seats?
A. 26 : 45 : 35   **B.** 26 : 35 : 45
C. 35 : 26 : 45   **D.** 45 : 35 : 26
E. None of these

Q.58 A bowl contains 16 marbles of three colors, 6 red, 4 blue and rest of purple. Three marbles are drawn one by one and not replaced. What is probability that the marbles drawn are of three different colors and first being red color?
A. $\frac{1}{35}$ **B.** $\frac{1}{7}$ **C.** $\frac{4}{35}$ **D.** $\frac{2}{7}$
E. $\frac{3}{35}$

Q.59 A train running at a speed of 54 km/h crosses a tree in 13 seconds. In how much time will it cross 75 m long platform?
A. 15 sec   **B.** 16 sec   **C.** 17 sec   **D.** 18 sec
E. 19 sec

Q.60 A boat running upstream takes 4 hours 24 minutes to cover a certain distance, while it takes 2 hours to cover the same distance running downstream. What is the ratio between the speed of the boat and speed of the water current?
A. 8 : 3   **B.** 4 : 5
C. 6 : 5   **D.** 7 : 4
E. None of these

Q.61 A is to receive $\frac{1}{8}$th of C's share and B is to receive Rs. 500 more than what A and C together will receive. If Rs. 5000 are to be distributed in this manner then find difference in amount received by B and A.
A. Rs. 2800   **B.** Rs. 2500   **C.** Rs. 7500   **D.** Rs. 5000
E. Rs. 1500

Q.62 What profit percent is made by selling an article at a certain price if by selling at $\frac{4}{5}$ of that price there would have been a loss of 10%.
A. 14.5%   **B.** 18%
C. 12.5%   **D.** 15%
E. None of these

Q.63 A cylinder is melted and formed into a cone that has the radius, half of the cylinder. What will happen to the height?
A. $\frac{3}{4}$th of the cylinder
B. $\frac{1}{12}$th of the cylinder
C. $\frac{4}{3}$th of the cylinder
D. 12 times of the cylinder
E. Same as that of the cylinder

Q.64 The simple interest on a certain sum of money invested at a certain rate for 2 years is Rs 1200 . The compound interest of the same sum of money invested at the same rate of interest for 2 years is Rs 1290 . What was the principal?
A. Rs. 12000   **B.** Rs. 16000
C. Rs. 6000   **D.** Rs. 4000
E. Rs. 5000

Q.65 After striking the floor, a ball rebounds to $\frac{4}{5}^{th}$ of the height from which it has fallen. Find the total distance that it travels before coming to rest if it has been gently dropped from a height of 120 meters.
A. 540 mtrs   **B.** 960 mtrs
C. 1080 mtrs   **D.** 1120 mtrs
E. 1160 mtrs

Reasoning Ability

Ques (66-70):Direction: The following questions are based on five three digit numbers given below:

453   619   574   471   372

Q.66 If in each number, both first and third digits are added and after that second digit is subtracted from that addition then how many numbers are less than 2 after mentioned operation?
A. Three   **B.** Four   **C.** None   **D.** Two
E. One

Q.67 If second digit will be interchanged with third digit in each number, then which number will be the second highest number after rearrangement?
A. 453   **B.** 619
C. 574   **D.** 372
E. None of these

Q.68 If all the digit in each of the numbers are arranged in descending order within the number then, which of the following will be the highest number in the new arrangement of numbers?
A. 453   **B.** 372
C. 574   **D.** 619
E. None of these

Q.69 If in each number, all the odd digit is added by 1 and all the even digit is added by 2 then, which of the following will be the lowest number after mentioned operation?
A. 619   **B.** 574   **C.** 372   **D.** 471
E. 453

Q.70 If in each number, all the three digits are arranged in ascending order within the number, which of the following will be the second lowest number after rearrangement?

A. 453   **B.** 574
C. 471   **D.** 619
E. None of these

Ques (71-75):Direction: Read the instructions carefully and answer the question below.

In one of the buildings in an apartment, there are eight floors. The first residential floor of the building is numbered one, the second is numbered two and so on. Eight persons, P, Q, R, S, T, U, V, and W lives on these eight floors of the building but not necessarily in the same order.

S lives on the floor which is just next to W's floor. Q lives on one of the floors above V's floor. Three people live between the floors on which T and R live. V lives four floors above W. Two persons live between the floors on which U and S live. W lives on an even-numbered floor.

Q.71 V lives on which floor of the building?

A. 5th floor   **B.** 6th floor   **C.** 2nd floor   **D.** 8th floor
E. 4th floor

Q.72 Who lives on the top floor?

A. R   **B.** Q   **C.** T   **D.** V
E. P

Q.73 How many people live above the floor on which U live?

A. Two   **B.** Five   **C.** Three   **D.** Four
E. One

Q.74 R lives on which floor of the building if it is given that he lives on one of the floors below P?

A. 4th floor   **B.** 6th floor   **C.** 3rd floor   **D.** 2nd floor
E. 1st floor

Q.75 Who lives on the 5th floor of the building?

A. P   **B.** Q   **C.** S   **D.** W
E. R

Q.76 Direction: Study the following information carefully and answer the question given below.

How many such pairs of letters are there in the word 'SECOND', each of which has as many letters between them in the word (both forward and backward direction) as they have between them in the English Alphabet?

A. None   **B.** One   **C.** Two   **D.** Three
E. Four

Q.77 Direction: Read the below given information carefully and answer the following questions.

Five people are sitting in a row according to their height. Only T is shorter than R. Q is taller than P and S. Height of P is between Q and S. The shortest person's height is 135 cm and the tallest person's height is 165 cm.

What can be possible height of R?

A. 130 cm   **B.** 165 cm   **C.** 140 cm   **D.** 175 cm
E. 125 cm

Q.78 Direction: Read the following information carefully and answer the given question.

In an auction, the jewelry made of different metals P, Q, R, S, and T are there. They are tested and ranked against expensiveness. Q and S are equally expensive. T was the least expensive brand among them. S was less expensive than R but more expensive than P.

Which of the following is true?

A. R was the most expensive among them
B. P was more expensive than Q
C. S was in the middle.
D. P was the most expensive among them
E. None of these

Ques (79-83):Direction: Study the following information carefully and answer the given questions.

Eight friends K, L, M, N, O, P, Q, and R have to deliver lectures on either the 8th or 15th of four different months among January, April, June, and August but not necessarily in the same order. Not more than 2 persons will give a lecture in a month. Only one person will deliver a lecture each day. K delivers his lecture on the 8th of a month which has only 30 days. Only three lectures were delivered between K and L. O delivers the lecture immediately after L. Number of persons who give the lecture after O is the same as the number of persons who give the lecture before P. Only two persons give lectures between P and M. Q and M give their lectures in the same month. N gives the lecture before R.

Q.79 Who gives the lecture on 8th August?

A. K   **B.** L   **C.** M   **D.** P
E. Q

Q.80 How many lectures were delivered after Q?

A. 5   **B.** 6   **C.** 4   **D.** 7
E. 3

Q.81 Who among the following doesn't deliver the lecture in the month having 30 days?

A. Q   **B.** M   **C.** K   **D.** N
E. L

Q.82 Who delivers the lecture immediately before R?

A. M   **B.** L   **C.** P   **D.** O
E. Q

Q.83 Who gives the lecture on 15th April?

A. L   **B.** O   **C.** Q   **D.** M
E. K

Ques (84-86):Direction: In the question below are given three statements followed by two conclusions numbered I and II You have to take the given statements to be true even if they seem to be at variance with commonly known facts. Read all the conclusions and then decide which of the given conclusions logically follows from the given statements disregarding commonly known facts.

Q.84 Statements:
Only a few Blue is Black.
Some Black is Grey.

All Grey is Red.

Conclusions:

I. All Red is Blue.

II. No Red is Blue.

A. Only I follows

B. Only II follows

C. Both I and II follow

D. Either I or II follows

E. Neither I nor II follows

Q.85 Statements:

All Z is X.

Some W is Z.

No A is W.

Conclusions:

I. All A is X.

II. Some X is not A.

A. Only I follows

B. Only II follows

C. Either I or II follows

D. Neither I nor II follows

E. Both I and II follow

Q.86 Statements:

Some Black is Red.

All Red is Blue.

No Blue is Green.

Conclusions:

I. All Green Can be Black.

II. Some Green is Red.

A. Only I follows

B. Only II follows

C. Both I and II follow

D. Neither I nor II follows

E. Either I or II follows

Ques (87-88):Direction: In the following question assuming the given statements to be true, find which of the conclusion among given conclusions is/are definitely true and then give your answers accordingly.

Q.87 Statements: P < S > T; Q = T > R

Conclusions:

I. Q < S

II. R < T

A. Only I is true

B. Only II is true

C. Neither I nor II is true

D. Both are true

E. Either I or II is true

Q.88 Statements: A = B < C; D < C = E

Conclusions:

I. D > B

II. A < E

A. Only I is true

B. Either I or II is true

C. Both are true

D. Neither I nor II is true

E. Only II is true

Q.89 Direction: Read the instructions carefully and answer the question below.

How many pairs of digits in the number 856214 have as many numbers between them as in the series of natural numbers both in backward and forward directions?

A. Three   B. Four   C. Five   D. Two

E. One

Ques (90-92):Direction: Study the information given below carefully and answer the questions that follow.

Naksh goes 15 km north, and then he turned to his right and went 8 km to reach School. He further turned to his right and went 15 km to reach Library. He now turned left and went 8 km to reach Theatre. He further turned right and went 10 km and reaches Workshop. Finally, he turned right and went 16 km to reach Hostel.

Q.90 What is the shortest distance between Starting point and School?

A. 15 km   B. 17 km   C. 8 km   D. 16 km

E. 19 km

Q.91 Theatre is in which direction with respect to School?

A. South East   B. North

C. South   D. East

E. North West

Q.92 Hostel is in which direction with respect to starting point?

A. North East   B. North

C. South   D. East

E. North West

Ques (93-97):Direction: Read the following information carefully and answer the questions given below.

Eight persons Ds, Fg, Lm, Ms, Nd, Pe, Ps, and Xy are sitting around a circular table but not necessarily in the same order. Some of them are facing away from centre and some of them are facing towards the centre.

Pe is sitting third to the left of Lm who is facing towards the centre. Ms and Fg are immediate neighbour of Pe. Nd is second to the right of Fg. Fg and Ms face the same direction but opposite to Pe. Ds is not an immediate neighbour of Nd. Xy is second to the right of Ds. Both the immediate neighbour of Nd face the same direction as Ms. Lm faces the same direction as the person who is sitting second to his right.

Q.93 How many persons are sitting between Fg and Xy when counting from the left of Xy?

A. Two   B. One   C. Five   D. Three

E. Four

Q.94 How many persons are facing away from centre between Nd and Ds counting from right of Nd?

A. One   B. Three   C. Four   D. Two

E. Zero

Q.95 Who is sitting opposite to Ds?

A. Xy   **B.** Fg   **C.** Pe   **D.** Lm

E. Ps

Q.96 Who sits second to the left of Ps?

A. Pe   **B.** Ms

C. Lm   **D.** Xy

E. None of the above

Q.97 How many persons are facing away from the centre?

A. Five   **B.** Three   **C.** Four   **D.** Two

E. One

Ques (98-100):Direction: Study the information given below carefully and answer the questions that follow.

A, B, C, D, E, F, and G are the seven members in a family. B is the mother of A who is the brother of G. F is the son of C who is the daughter-in-law of E. E is the father of D who is the sister of G. A is not married. B has two sons and a daughter.

Q.98 How many female members are there in the family?

[IBPS RRB Scale I, 2020]

A. One   **B.** Four

C. Two   **D.** Three

E. Can't be determined

Q.99 How is B related to E?

A. Sister-in-law   **B.** Son

C. Wife   **D.** Husband

E. Mother

Q.100 How is E related to F?

A.   Cousin Sister

B.   Cousin Brother

C.   Paternal Grandfather

D.   Paternal Grandmother

E.   Husband

// Smart Answer Sheet //

Correct — Percentage of students who answered correctly. **Skipped** — Percentage of students who skipped.

Q.	Ans.	Correct	Skipped
1	D	0.88 %	45.61 %
2	B	4.39 %	88.59 %
3	C	2.63 %	88.6 %
4	A	9.65 %	88.6 %
5	A	9.65 %	88.6 %
6	B	6.14 %	88.6 %
7	C	7.02 %	88.59 %
8	A	11.4 %	88.6 %
9	D	9.65 %	88.6 %
10	B	9.65 %	88.6 %
11	C	9.65 %	88.6 %
12	B	11.4 %	88.6 %
13	B	9.65 %	88.6 %
14	D	9.65 %	88.6 %
15	C	11.4 %	88.6 %
16	D	5.26 %	88.6 %
17	C	4.39 %	88.59 %
18	A	7.02 %	88.59 %
19	B	1.75 %	88.6 %
20	E	2.63 %	95.62 %
21	B	2.63 %	95.62 %
22	C	2.63 %	95.62 %
23	D	4.39 %	95.61 %
24	A	3.51 %	95.61 %
25	C	1.75 %	95.62 %
26	E	0 %	100 %
27	B	0.88 %	95.61 %
28	A	4.39 %	95.61 %
29	C	4.39 %	95.61 %
30	B	2.63 %	95.62 %
31	A	8.77 %	88.6 %
32	C	9.65 %	88.6 %
33	C	6.14 %	88.6 %
34	D	8.77 %	88.6 %
35	A	7.89 %	88.6 %
36	D	10.53 %	88.59 %
37	B	9.65 %	88.6 %
38	A	7.02 %	88.59 %
39	E	10.53 %	88.59 %
40	A	7.89 %	88.6 %
41	E	7.89 %	88.6 %
42	C	7.02 %	88.59 %
43	A	5.26 %	88.6 %
44	E	9.65 %	88.6 %
45	E	7.89 %	88.6 %
46	D	8.77 %	88.6 %
47	C	1.75 %	88.6 %
48	A	0 %	100 %
49	E	0.88 %	89.47 %
50	D	0 %	100 %
51	C	4.39 %	89.47 %
52	D	4.39 %	89.47 %
53	D	3.51 %	91.23 %
54	A	1.75 %	92.11 %
55	D	2.63 %	92.11 %
56	B	0.88 %	93.86 %
57	B	3.51 %	93.86 %
58	E	0.88 %	93.86 %
59	D	0.88 %	94.73 %
60	A	0 %	100 %
61	B	0 %	100 %
62	C	0 %	100 %
63	D	0 %	100 %
64	D	0 %	100 %
65	C	0 %	100 %
66	D	6.14 %	88.6 %
67	C	10.53 %	88.59 %
68	D	9.65 %	88.6 %
69	C	7.89 %	89.48 %
70	D	7.89 %	88.6 %
71	B	4.39 %	88.59 %
72	B	5.26 %	89.48 %
73	D	3.51 %	89.47 %
74	C	2.63 %	89.48 %
75	A	4.39 %	89.47 %
76	B	7.89 %	88.6 %
77	C	7.02 %	88.59 %
78	A	6.14 %	88.6 %
79	D	7.89 %	88.6 %
80	A	7.89 %	88.6 %

Q.	Ans.	Correct		Q.	Ans.	Correct		Q.	Ans.	Correct		Q.	Ans.	Correct		Q.	Ans.	Correct
		Skipped				Skipped				Skipped				Skipped				Skipped
81	E	7.02 % 88.59 %		85	B	6.14 % 89.47 %		89	B	5.26 % 90.35 %		93	A	3.51 % 90.35 %		97	C	3.51 % 90.35 %
82	C	7.89 % 88.6 %		86	A	7.02 % 89.47 %		90	B	6.14 % 90.35 %		94	B	2.63 % 91.23 %		98	D	3.51 % 90.35 %
83	D	7.89 % 89.48 %		87	D	9.65 % 89.47 %		91	A	8.77 % 90.35 %		95	E	2.63 % 91.23 %		99	C	4.39 % 91.22 %
84	E	0.88 % 89.47 %		88	E	8.77 % 90.35 %		92	C	7.89 % 90.36 %		96	A	2.63 % 91.23 %		100	C	4.39 % 91.22 %

//Hints and Solutions//

1. The error lies in part (D) of the question.

Instead of the preposition 'to', 'for' will be used.

'Concern for her boss' future' - is the correct usage of the preposition 'to'.

Example-

She has a genuine concern for her friends.

The correct sentence- "Dean wasn't sure if it was her natural aversion to anything involving law enforcement or concern for her boss's future."

Hence, the correct option is (D).

2. The error lies in part (B) of the sentence.

The error is in the noun diploma.

In the latter part of the sentence, we see "both education and linguistics", which means there are two nouns, so it should be plural.

Thus, the usage of 'diplomas' is correct instead of 'diploma'.

'Diplomas' is the plural form of diploma.

So, the correct sentence is- "The secretary has diplomas in both education and linguistics."

Hence, the correct option is (B).

3. The error lies in part (C) of the sentence.

'Breathtaking' is an adjective that means extremely surprising, beautiful, etc.

We already have 'beautiful' and 'gigantic' as adjectives, so we need to use an adverb.

'Breathtakingly' is the correct form of adverb to be used here.

An adverb is a word that modifies (describes) a verb (he sings loudly), an adjective (very tall), another adverb (ended too quickly), or even a whole sentence (Fortunately, I had brought an umbrella).

Adverbs can also modify adjectives and other adverbs. Often, the purpose of the adverb is to add a degree of intensity to the adjective.

Examples-

My cat is incredibly happy to have his dinner.

We will be slightly late to the meeting.

Thus, the correct sentence- "This was not a mangy or vicious creature standing in front of him, but a breathtakingly beautiful, gigantic wolf."

Hence, the correct option is (C).

4. The error lies in part (A) of the sentence.

The use of 'sing' is wrong.

According to the sentence, we see that the first part follows parallelism.

Parallelism, also known as parallel structure or parallel construction, is a balance within one or more sentences of similar phrases or clauses that have the same grammatical structure. The application of parallelism affects readability and may make texts easier to process.

Example- Eating and drinking, dancing and singing, dance and sing, ate and ran, etc.

Thus, the correct sentence is- 'Singing and playing the guitar was her all time favorite hobby.'

Hence, the correct option is (A).

5. The most appropriate word for blank (1) is running. We need a superlative degree word for the given blank.

So, the sentence will be "Canada, the world's second biggest country by landmass."

'Biggest' is the superlative adjective of big.

'Smaller' is the comparative adjective of small.

'Tiny' is the form of the adjective.

'Larger' is the comparative adjective of large.

Hence, the correct option is (A).

6. The most appropriate word for blank (2) is running.

The phrase 'run out' means to be used up; to use something completely so that nothing is left.

So, the complete sentence will be: "country by landmass, is effectively running out of the land even"

Example-

- They ran out of food.
- He just ran out of ideas.
- Time is running out.

Hence, the correct option is (B).

7. The most appropriate word for blank (3) is "booming" which means to grow very quickly in size or value.

So, the complete sentence will be:

"the land even though the real-estate infrastructure is booming compared to anywhere else in the world."

Example-

- The economy is booming and small businesses are flourishing.
- Business was booming , and money wasn't a problem.
- Other options 'glowing, tiring, separating' are incorrect.

Hence, the correct option is (C).

8. The most appropriate word for blank (4) is "between" which means in or into the space that separates two places, people, or objects.

So, the complete sentence will be:

This is happening due to the worsening imbalance <u>between</u> supply and demand.

Example-

- The town lies halfway between Rome and Florence.
- Standing between the two adults was a small child.
- The other prepositions will make the answer incorrect.

Hence, the correct option is (A).

9. The most appropriate word for blank (5) is "provide" which means make available for use; supply.

So, the complete sentence will be-

The buyers in the country want large homes however builders can't <u>provide</u> them due to the unavailability of enough space in and around the major cities where people work.

Example:

- We provided the flood victims with food and clothing.
- The company provides health care and life insurance benefits for all of its employees.
- I will accept the work, provided that you help me.

Hence, the correct option is (D).

10. Prefer means to choose something rather than something else; to like something better.

Example-

- She'd prefer not to drive at night.
- She prefers books to magazines.
- Reject means to to refuse to accept somebody/something.
- Option means something that you can choose to do; the freedom to choose.
- Dismiss means cause to leave.

Hence, the correct option is (B).

11. 'Out of reach' is a phrase that means beyond the capacity of someone to attain or achieve something.

Example-

- The ornaments had been put out of reach of the children's prying fingers.
- Cease means to stop or end.
- Penetrate means to go through or into something, especially when this is difficult.
- Thrust means to push somebody/something suddenly or violently; to move quickly and suddenly in a particular direction.

Hence, the correct option is (C).

12. We can see in the second paragraph, the third sentence, it is mentioned: "The second wave of the virus is expected to turn the wedding industry even leaner". Over one crore people associated with the industry, directly or indirectly, are estimated to have lost

their jobs owing to the pandemic. As the wedding industry clutches on to e-invitations and Zoom meets for survival, allied services and personnel, such as printing establishments and artisans who work in the ateliers of fashion designers, are enduring losses.

Hence, the correct option is (B).

13. We see it is mentioned in the second paragraph, fourth sentence, "Over one crore people associated with the industry, directly or indirectly, are estimated to have lost their jobs owing to the pandemic." As the wedding industry clutches on to e-invitations and Zoom meets for survival, allied services and personnel, such as printing establishments and artisans who work in the ateliers of fashion designers, are enduring losses.

Hence, the correct option is (B).

14. We see in the third paragraph, the second sentence, "Could the pandemic then bring about a decisive transformation in contemporary culture's endorsement of excess, ostentation, and pomp? **After all, in this age of the pandemic, Indian couples are increasingly resorting to organize smaller — more intimate — ceremonies.** There is a bit of altruism thrown in too: a newly-married couple in Bengal donated the money meant for their wedding feast to feed the poor. But vanity, much like the virus, cannot be eradicated with ease."

Hence, the correct option is (D).

15. We can see that it is mentioned in the third paragraph, third sentence- " There is a bit of altruism thrown in too: **a newly-married couple in Bengal donated the money meant for their wedding feast to feed the poor.** But vanity, much like the virus, cannot be eradicated with ease. Reports show that those who are not able to have the destination wedding of their dreams are splurging on a designer trousseau instead; guests who can no longer make it to the wedding are being sent lavish gifts; and the menu, instead of being spartan, is getting even more elaborate."

Hence, the correct option is (C).

16. Spendthrift means a person who spends a lot of money carelessly or wastes money.

Miser, frugal and thrifty are all antonyms of spendthrift.

Miser- a person who loves to have a lot of money but hates to spend it.

Frugal- using only as much money or food as is necessary.

Thrifty- careful in the use of one's money or resources.

Hence, the correct option is (D).

17. Inadvertently means in a way that is not intentional.

'Deliberately, predetermined, and foreseen' are all antonyms of 'inadvertently'.

Deliberately- on purpose

Predetermined- established or decided in advance.

Foreseen- to know or guess that something is going to happen in the future.

Hence, the correct option is (C).

18. Simple means easy to understand, do or use; not difficult or complicated.

'Complicated, detailed and bewildering' are synonyms of elaborate.

Complicated means difficult to analyze, understand or explain.

Detailed means marked by abundant detail or by thoroughness in treating small items or parts.

Bewildering means to confuse and surprise.

Thus from the meaning of the word simple, we can conclude that it is the antonym of the word elaborate.

Hence, the correct option is (A).

19. Empathetic means showing an ability to understand and share the feelings of another.

'Compassionate, sensitive and sympathetic' are all synonyms of empathetic.

Compassionate- feeling or showing concern for someone who is sick, hurt, poor, etc.

Sensitive- showing that you are conscious of and able to understand people's feelings, problems, etc.

Sympathetic- showing that you understand other people's feelings, especially their problems.

Hence, the correct option is (B).

20. The wrongly spelt word is Retreive.

The correct spelling of the word is 'retrieve'.

It means get or bring (something) back from somewhere.

Dissolves: (used about a solid) to become or to make something become liquid.

Indefinite: for a period of time that has no fixed end.

Absurd: not at all logical or sensible; ridiculous.

Triumph: a great success or victory; the feeling of happiness that you have because of this.

Hence, the correct option is (E).

21. The wrongly spelt word is Clutered.

The correct spelling of the word is 'cluttered'.

It means cover or fill (something) with an untidy collection of things.

Inviolable: never to be broken, infringed, or dishonoured.

Unfit: not suitable or not good enough for something.

Adhere: to stick firmly to something.

Curious: wanting to know or learn something.

Hence, the correct option is (B).

22. The wrongly spelt word is Prevarricate.

The correct spelling of the word is 'prevaricate'.

It means speak or act in an evasive way.

Guarded: careful; not giving much information or showing what you feel.

Cherished: to love somebody/something and look after him/her/it carefully.

Legitimate: reasonable or acceptable.

Abominate: to feel hatred for somebody/something.

Hence, the correct option is (C).

23. The wrongly spelt word is Sustenence.

The correct spelling of the word is 'sustenance'.

It means food and drink regarded as a source of strength; nourishment.

Increment: a regular increase in the amount of money that somebody is paid for his/her job.

Superficial: not studying or thinking about something in a deep or complete way.

Retreat: to move backwards in order to leave a battle or in order not to become involved in a battle.

Intensive: involving a lot of work or care in a short period of time.

Hence, the correct option is (D).

24. The wrongly spelt word is Shettarable.

The correct spelling of the word is 'shatterable'.

It means capable of being shattered (very upset).

Brittle: hard but easily broken.

Extraordinary: very unusual.

Crisp: pleasantly hard and dry.

Shivery: shaking or trembling as a result of cold, illness, fear, or excitement.

Hence, the correct option is (A).

25. The best option to fit is 'besides' which acts as a connector that gives the essence of 'in addition to that..' like an add on to the prevailing situation or condition. The other connectors are used in case of contradiction or concluding something. Thus option C is the correct answer.

Sentence- "The recent food carnival was really happening and there was an array of food stalls, besides complimentary drinks, which were provided to all who visited the carnival."

Hence, the correct option is (C).

26. We can clearly decipher from the second statement that the war is against Pakistan. Therefore, option II and III are apt.

New statements:

Against Pakistan, India will prevail in a conventional war that would be a hard-fought battle, but India would tire out the Pakistanis.

Hostile to Pakistan, India will prevail in a conventional war that would be a hard-fought battle, but India would tire out the Pakistanis.

Hence, the correct option is (E).

27. 'Since' and 'as' do not help create a grammatically sound sentence. They are used to join sentences which have a cause-and-effect relationship. While is used to connect two contrasting or comparative clauses. It fits the sentences well. Hence, option B is the correct answer.

New statement:

While many of the arts and sciences make up Western civilization and culture, philosophy was first defined by the Greeks around the fifth-century B.C.E.

Hence, the correct option is (B).

28. According to the given context we can see that we are talking about the decision to purchase a home and it is one of the most important and significant decisions in the financial life of a person. Among the given options, we can use the word important to fill the blank and make the sentence meaningful. Other words are irrelevant and can be eliminated from consideration.

This makes Option A the correct choice among the given options.

Hence, the correct option is (A).

29. In the given context we are talking about something that will cover against any default in the home loans in case of untimely death of the borrowers. It is going to be a cover against any kind of unforeseen circumstances during the currency of the loan. Only insurance cover will be able to cover against such issues. Therefore, the correct word would be insurance whereas the rest cannot be used since they do not imply the correct meaning of the given sentence.

This makes Option C the correct choice among the given options.

Hence, the correct option is (C).

30. It is clear from the context of this sentence that the government has put forward in the budget a proposal that will discourage cash transactions in the high value segment. The banks will be able to penalize the customers doing so going forward. The weapon given to the banks is the implementation of TDS on high value cash transactions. Among the given words, we can use the word empowered to indicate that the banks have been enabled to impose tax on cash transactions. Other words are eliminated because they do not imply the intended meaning.

This makes Option B the correct choice among the given options.

Hence, the correct option is (B).

31. Given

$$45\% \text{ of } 4500 + \left(\frac{165}{\sqrt{225}}\right) = ?$$

$$\Rightarrow 45 \times 45 + \left(\frac{165}{15}\right) = ?$$

$$\Rightarrow 2025 + 11 = ?$$

$$\Rightarrow ? = 2036$$

$\therefore$ The value of ? is 2036.

Hence, the correct option is (A).

32. Given

$$\sqrt[3]{3375} \times 75\% \text{ of } 400 = \frac{?}{2}$$

$$\Rightarrow 15 \times \left(\frac{3}{4}\right) \times 400 = \frac{?}{2}$$

$$\Rightarrow 15 \times 300 = \frac{?}{2}$$

$$\Rightarrow ? = 9000$$

$\therefore$ The value of ? is 9000.

Hence, the correct option is (C).

33. Given

$$75.33 + 654.5 + 2.45 = ? + 32.64$$

$$\Rightarrow 732.28 = ? + 32.64$$

$$\Rightarrow ? = 732.28 - 32.64$$

$$? = 699.64$$

$\therefore$ The value of ? is 699.64

Hence, the correct option is (C).

34. Given

$$\left[\left\{2 \times \left(\frac{1}{4}\right) + 4\right\} \times 8\right] = ? \times 20$$

$$\Rightarrow \left[\left\{\left(\frac{1}{2}\right) + 4\right\} \times 8\right] = ? \times 20$$

$$\Rightarrow \left[\left(\frac{9}{2}\right) \times 8\right] = ? \times 20$$

$$\Rightarrow 36 = ? \times 20$$

$$\Rightarrow ? = \frac{36}{20}$$

$$\Rightarrow ? = 1.8$$

$\therefore$ The value of ? is 1.8.

Hence, the correct option is (D).

35. Given

$$?\% \text{ of } 400 \times \left(\frac{3}{4}\right) + 300 = 66.66\% \text{ of } 900$$

$$\Rightarrow ? \times 4 \times \left(\frac{3}{4}\right) + 300 = \left(\frac{2}{3}\right) \times 900$$

$$\Rightarrow ? \times 3 + 300 = 600$$

$$\Rightarrow ? = \frac{300}{3} = 100$$

$\therefore$ The value of ? is 100.

Hence, the correct option is (A).

36. Given

$(1836 \div ?) \div 9 = 17$

$\Rightarrow \left(\dfrac{1836}{?}\right) \times \left(\dfrac{1}{9}\right) = 17$

$\Rightarrow \left(\dfrac{204}{?}\right) = 17$

$\Rightarrow ? = \left(\dfrac{204}{17}\right)$

$\Rightarrow ? = 12$

∴ The value of ? is 12.

Hence, the correct option is (D).

37. Given

$(?)^2 \times (15)^2 \div (60)^2 = 16$

$\Rightarrow (?)^2 \times 15 \times 15 \times \left(\dfrac{1}{60}\right) \times \left(\dfrac{1}{60}\right) = 16$

$\Rightarrow (?)^2 = 16 \times 4 \times 4$

$\Rightarrow ? = \sqrt{256}$

$\Rightarrow ? = 16$

∴ The value of (?) is 16.

Hence, the correct option is (B).

38. Given

22% of 855 - ? = 20% of 500

$\Rightarrow 188.1 - ? = 100$

$\Rightarrow ? = 188.1 - 100$

$\Rightarrow ? = 88.1$

∴ The value of (?) is 88.1.

Hence, the correct option is (A).

39. Given

$\left(\dfrac{50}{7}\right)$ of 294 - 8^3 = 1750 - ?

$\Rightarrow 50 \times 42 - 512 = 1750 - ?$

$\Rightarrow ? = 1750 + 512 - 2100$

$\Rightarrow ? = 162$

∴ The value of (?) is 162.

Hence, the correct option is (E).

40. Given

$(\sqrt{1024} + 19 \times 12) \div \sqrt{676} - 4 + 4680 \div ? = 474$

$\Rightarrow (32 + 228) \div 26 - 4 + 4680 \div ? = 474$

$\Rightarrow 10 - 4 + 4680 \div ? = 474$

$\Rightarrow 4680 \div ? = 468$

$\Rightarrow 4680 \div 468 = ?$

$\Rightarrow ? = 10$

∴ The value of (?) is 10.

Hence, the correct option is (A).

41. Given:

I. $x^2 - 6x - 40 = 0$

II. $y^2 - 7y + 12 = 0$

From I

$x^2 - 6x - 40 = 0$

$\Rightarrow x^2 - 10x + 4x - 40 = 0$

$\Rightarrow x(x - 10) + 4(x - 10) = 0$

$\Rightarrow (x - 10)(x + 4) = 0$

$\Rightarrow x = 10, -4$

From II

$y^2 - 7y + 12 = 0$

$\Rightarrow y^2 - 3y - 4y + 12 = 0$

$\Rightarrow y(y - 3) - 4(y - 3) = 0$

$\Rightarrow (y - 3)(y - 4) = 0$

$\Rightarrow y = 3, 4$

Comparison between x and y (via Tabulation)

Value of x	Value of y	Relation between x & y
10	3	x > y
10	4	x > y
-4	3	x < y
-4	4	x < y

∴ No relation in x and y.

Hence, the correct option is (E).

42. Given:

I. $x^2 - 5x - 50 = 0$

II. $y^2 + 15y + 50 = 0$

From I

$x^2 - 5x - 50 = 0$

$\Rightarrow x^2 - 10x + 5x - 50 = 0$

$\Rightarrow x(x - 10) + 5(x - 10) = 0$

$\Rightarrow (x - 10)(x + 5) = 0$

$\Rightarrow x = 10, -5$

From II

$y^2 + 15y + 50 = 0$

$\Rightarrow y^2 + 10y + 5y + 50 = 0$

$\Rightarrow y(y + 10) + 5(y + 10) = 0$

$\Rightarrow (y + 10)(y + 5) = 0$

$\Rightarrow y = -10, -5$

Comparison between x and y (via Tabulation)

Value of x	Value of y	Relation between x & y
10	-10	x > y
10	-5	x > y
-5	-10	x > y
-5	-5	x = y

$\therefore x \geq y$

Hence, the correct option is (C).

43. Given:

$x^2 - 19x + 78 = 0$

$y^2 + 14y = 0$

Solving equation I we get,

$x^2 - 19x + 78 = 0$

$\Rightarrow x^2 - 13x - 6x + 78 = 0$

$\Rightarrow x(x - 13) - 6(x - 13) = 0$

$\Rightarrow (x - 6)(x - 13) = 0$

$\Rightarrow x = 6, 13$

Solving equation II we get,

$y^2 + 14y = 0$

$\Rightarrow y(y + 14) = 0$

$\Rightarrow y = 0, -14$

Comparison between x and y (via Tabulation):

Value of x	Value of y	Relation
6	0	x > y
6	-14	x > y
13	0	x > y
13	-14	x > y

$\therefore x > y$

Hence, the correct option is (A).

44. Given:

$x^2 + 7x - 120 = 0$

$y^2 - 7y - 120 = 0$

From I,

$x^2 + 7x - 120 = 0$

$\Rightarrow x^2 + 15x - 8x - 120 = 0$

$\Rightarrow x(x + 15) - 8(x + 15) = 0$

$\Rightarrow (x + 15)(x - 8) = 0$

$\Rightarrow x = -15, 8$

From II,

$y^2 - 7y - 120 = 0$

$\Rightarrow y^2 - 15y + 8y - 120 = 0$

$\Rightarrow y(y - 15) + 8(y - 15) = 0$

$\Rightarrow (y + 8)(y - 15) = 0$

$\Rightarrow y = -8, 15$

Comparision between x and y (via Tabulation):

Value of x	Value of y	Relation
-15	-8	x < y
-15	15	x < y
8	-8	x > y
8	15	x < y

$\therefore$ The relationship between x and y cannot be established.

Hence, the correct option is (E).

45. Given:

I. $x^2 + x - 12 = 0$

II. $y^2 + 10y - 39 = 0$

I. $x^2 + x - 12 = 0$

$\Rightarrow x^2 + 4x - 3x - 12 = 0$

$\Rightarrow x(x + 4) - 3(x + 4) = 0$

$\Rightarrow (x + 4)(x - 3) = 0$

$\Rightarrow x = 3, (-4)$

II. $y^2 + 10y - 39 = 0$

$\Rightarrow y^2 - 3y + 13y - 39 = 0$

$\Rightarrow y(y - 3) + 13(y - 3) = 0$

$\Rightarrow (y + 13)(y - 3) = 0$

$\Rightarrow y = (-13), 3$

Value of 'x'	Relation	Value of 'y'
3	>	-13
3	=	3
-4	>	-13
-4	<	3

When we compared the values of X and Y in the table above, we found that there are THREE relations between X and Y i.e., >, = and <. So, a relation cannot be defined.

$\therefore$ After comparison all the values of x and y, the relation is "x = y or the relation between x and y can't be established".

Hence, the correct option is (E).

46. Given:

Investment of A = 35% of 150000 = Rs 52500

Investment of C = 10% of 150000 = Rs 15000

Investment of B = 25% of 150000 = Rs 37500

Investment of D = 15% of 150000 = Rs 22500

Formula:

_____ **(6)** for the overworked doctors, nurses, healthcare professionals, and testing and contact tracing teams.

Q.9 What will come in blank (1)?
A. Wave **B.** Light
C. Peak **D.** Time
E. None of these

Q.10 What will come in blank (2)?
A. Returned **B.** Began
C. Departed **D.** Disappeared
E. None of these

Q.11 What will come in blank (3)?
A. Gained **B.** Lost
C. Vanish **D.** Find
E. None of these

Q.12 What will come in blank (4)?
A. Lessen **B.** Conciliate
C. Mitigate **D.** Aggravating
E. None of these

Q.13 What will come in blank (5)?
A. Agitating **B.** Calm
C. Relaxing **D.** Quieted
E. None of these

Q.14 What will come in blank (6)?
A. Challenges **B.** Acceptance
C. Investigations **D.** Concede
E. None of these

Q.15 Direction: In the sentence given below, one/some parts have errors and others are correct. Find out which part has an error and mark it as your answer. If there is no error mark 'No error' as your answer.
Recently, a group of Assasins was put on a trial by media persons. / (A) One spectator just could not comprehend why everyone was/ (B) shouting at them. Another astute person called it media trail/ (C) and left the discussion./ (D)
A. (A) **B.** (B) **C.** (C) **D.** (D)
E. No error

Q.16 Direction: Read the sentence to find out whether there is any error in it. The error, if any, will be in one part of the sentence. The number of that part is the answer. If there is no error, the answer is (E). Ignore errors of punctuation, if any.
Romanoff was the most ideal and complete spy./(A) Without her, the S.H.I.E.L.D. and Avengers wouldn't be the same./(B) Her sacrifice is enormous and will always be remembered even /(C)if she decides not to continue her journey with us anymore. /(D)
A. (A) **B.** (B) **C.** (C) **D.** (D)
E. No error

Q.17 Direction: Read the sentence to find out whether there is any error in it or not. The error, if any, will be in one part of the sentence. The number of that part is the answer. If there is no error, the answer is (E). Ignore errors of punctuation, if any.

He went to the kitchen, gathered (A)/ the ingredients, switched on (B)/ the gas, and searching for (C)/ the recipe book in the cabinets. (D)/ No error (E)
A. (A) **B.** (B) **C.** (C) **D.** (D)
E. No error

Q.18 Select the wrongly spelt word.
[SSC Sub Inspector (CPO), 2020]
A. Capacity **B.** Ablity
C. Pupil **D.** Teacher
E. Sediment

Q.19 Select the wrongly spelt word.
[SSC Sub Inspector (CPO), 2020]
A. Exprimant **B.** Sediment
C. Occurring **D.** Umbrella
E. Including

Q.20 Select the wrongly spelt word.
[SSC Sub Inspector (CPO), 2020]
A. Presure **B.** Electric
C. Central **D.** Irrigation
E. National

Ques (21-24):Direction: Given below are four sentences in jumbled order. Pick the option that gives their correct order.

Q.21 Select the wrongly spelt word.
A. Minister **B.** Admits
C. Conscioas **D.** Pandemic
E. Returned

Q.22 A. She is the athlete who ran as fast as a bullet in the 400 m race at the World Under-20 Championship in 2018.
B. Kandhulimari village in Dhing has suddenly come into the spotlight of fame.
C. She won a gold medal for the country and the hearts of all Indians.
D. This is the home of Hima Das, nicknamed 'the Dhing Express'
A. DABC **B.** BCAD **C.** BDAC **D.** DBCA
E. ABDC

Q.23 A. He took great care of his subjects and made sure they lived in happiness.
B. Sometimes he himself went amongst the people in disguise to see and learn about their actual state.
C. He sent spies into the kingdom to report to him about the condition of his people.
D. A just and loving king once ruled over a large kingdom.
A. BDAC **B.** DBCA **C.** DACB **D.** CABD
E. ADBC

Q.24 A. In the evening, Tejaswini would sing songs praising the Lord.
B. She would go to the Lord's temple twice a day.
C. Tejaswini was known in the village for her devotion to the Lord.

Required ratio = Sum of Investment of A and C : Sum of Investment of B and D

Sum of Investment of A and C together= 52500 + 15000 = Rs 67500

Sum of Investment of B and D together = 37500 + 22500 = Rs 60000

Required ratio = 67500 : 60000 = 9 : 8

∴ The required answer is 9 : 8.

Hence, the correct option is (D).

47. Given:

Investment of B = 25% of 150000 = Rs 37500

Investment of D = 15% of 150000 = Rs 22500

Investment of E = 15% of 150000 = Rs 22500

Formula:

$$\text{Percentage} = \frac{B\ investment}{(D+E\ investment)}$$

New investment of B = 2 × 37500 = 75000

Sum of Investment of D and E together = 22500 + 22500 = Rs 45000

$$\text{Required \%} = \left(\frac{75000}{45000}\right) \times 100 = \frac{500}{3}\%$$

∴ The required answer is $\frac{500}{3}\%$.

Hence, the correct option is (C).

48. Given:

Investment of A = 35% of 150000 = Rs 52500

Investment of C = 10% of 150000 = Rs 15000

Investment of F = 15000 + 3000 = Rs 18000

Time period of A =12 months

Time period of C = 10 months

Time period of F = 8 months

Formula:

Profit = Investment × time

Investment ratio of A,C and F = 52500 : 15000 : 18000 = 35 : 10 : 12

Time period ratio of A, C and F = 12 : 10 : 8 = 6 : 5 : 4

Profit ratio of A, C and F = 35 × 6 : 10 × 5: 12 × 4 = 105 : 25 : 24

Then 154x = 15400

$$\Rightarrow x = \frac{15400}{154} = 100$$

Then the share of F = 100 × 24 = Rs 2400

∴ The required answer is Rs 2400.

Hence, the correct option is (A).

49. Given:

Investment of A = 35% of 150000 = Rs 52500

Investment of B = 25% of 150000 = Rs 37500

Investment of C = 10% of 150000 = Rs 15000

Investment of D = 15% of 150000 = Rs 22500

Investment of E = 15% of 150000 = Rs 22500

Formula:

$$\text{Average} = \frac{Sum\ of\ observations}{Number\ of\ observations}$$

Sum of investment of A,B and E is = 52500 + 37500 + 22500 = 112500

$$\text{Required Average} = \frac{112500}{3} = 37500$$

Sum of investment of C and D together = 15000 + 22500 = 37500

$$\text{Required percentage} = \frac{(Average\ of\ A,B\ and\ E)}{(Sum\ of\ C\ and\ D)} = \frac{37500}{37500}$$

Required percentage = 0%

∴ The two quantities are same, or we can say, there is 0% increase or decrease in quantities compared.

Hence, the correct option is (E).

50. Given:

Investment of B = 25% of 150000

Investment of E = 15% of 150000

Time period of B = 9 months

Time period of E = 12 months

Formula:

Profit = Investment × time

Investment ratio of B and E is = 25% of 150000 : 15% of 150000 = 5 : 3

Time period ratio of B and E = 9 : 12 = 3 : 4

Profit ratio of B and E = 5 × 3 : 3 × 4 = 5 : 4

Then 9x = 18000

$$\Rightarrow x = \frac{18000}{9} = 2000$$

So, Difference in B and E = 5x - 4x = x = Rs 2000

∴ The required answer is Rs 2000.

Hence, the correct option is (D).

51. Given

Total number of students on Thursday = 60

Number of females students i.e., girls on Thursday = 45

So, Boys present in the class on Thursday = 60-45 = 15

Total number of students on Friday = 80

Number of females students i.e., girls on Friday = 55

So, Boys present in the class on Friday = 80-55 = 35

Formula used

Difference = total number of girls – total number of boys

Total number of boys present on Thursday and Friday = 15 + 30 = 45

Total number of girls present on Thursday and Friday = 45 + 55= 100

Required difference = 100 – 45 = 55

∴ The difference between the total number of girls and boys present on Thursday and Friday is 55.

Hence, the correct option is (C).

52. Given

Boys present in the class on Tuesday = 40

Boys present in the class on Wednesday = 30

Girls present in the class on Thursday = 45

Formula used

Ratio = Boys present on Tuesday and Wednesday: Girls present in the class on Thursday

Total number of boys present on Tuesday and Wednesday = 40 + 30 = 70

Required ratio = Boys present on Tuesday and Wednesday: Girls present in the class on Thursday

$\Rightarrow$ 70: 45 = 14: 9

∴Required ratio of boys and girls present in the class is 14: 9.

Hence, the correct option is (D).

53. Given

Boys present in the class on Monday = 10

Boys present in the class on Tuesday = 40

Boys present in the class on Wednesday = 30

Formula used

$$Percentage = \left(\frac{Value}{Total\ Value}\right) \times 100$$

Total number of boys present in the class on Monday and Tuesday = 10 + 40 = 50

$\Rightarrow$ Required percentage = $\dfrac{(50 - 30)}{30} \times 100 = 66.66\%$

∴ The required approximate percentage is 66%.

Hence, the correct option is (D).

54. Given:

Total number of students present in the class on Saturday = 25% more total student present on Thursday

Ratio between boys and girls = 2: 3

Formula used:

$$Percentage = \left(\frac{Value}{Total\ Value}\right) \times 100$$

Total number of students present in the class on Saturday = 125% of 60 = 75

Girls present in the class on Saturday = $75 \times \dfrac{3}{5} = 45$

∴ The number of girls present in the class on Saturday is 45.

Hence, the correct option is (A).

55. Given

Number of total students present in the class from Monday to Friday respectively = 80, 75, 95, 60, and 85

Number of girls present in the class from Monday to Friday respectively = 70, 35, 65, 45, and 55

Formula used

$$Average = \frac{Sum\ of\ Values}{Number\ of\ values}$$

Boys present in the class on Monday = 80 – 70 = 10

Boys present in the class on Tuesday = 75 – 35 = 40

Boys present in the class on Wednesday = 95 – 65 = 30

Boys present in the class on Thursday = 60 – 45 = 15

Boys present in the class on Friday = 85 – 55 = 30

Average boys present in the class = $\dfrac{(10 + 40 + 30 + 15 + 30)}{5} = 25$

∴ The average boys present in the class from Monday to Friday is 25.

Hence, the correct option is (D).

56. Let the efficiencies (work is done per day) of A, B, and C are a, b and c be respectively.

Let total work be 1 unit.

Then, (a × 35) = 1

$\Rightarrow a = \dfrac{1}{35}$

Then, (b × 45) = 1

$\Rightarrow b = \dfrac{1}{45}$

Then, (a + c) × 25 = 1

$\Rightarrow (a + c) = \dfrac{1}{25}$

Then, c = (a + c) - a

$\Rightarrow c = \dfrac{1}{25} - \dfrac{1}{35}$

$\Rightarrow \dfrac{2}{175}$

Time Taken by C to complete the whole work alone

$\dfrac{Total\ work\ done}{Efficiency} = \dfrac{1}{\frac{2}{175}}$

$\Rightarrow \dfrac{175}{2}$ days

$\therefore$ C can complete the whole work in $\dfrac{175}{2}$ days.

Hence, the correct option is (B).

57. Let the number of seats for class 9th, 10th and 11th respectively = 8x, 10x, 12x

Number of increase seats for class 9th, 10th and 11th respectively,

$\Rightarrow$ (130% of 8x), (140% of 10x) and (150% of 12x)

$\Rightarrow \left(\dfrac{130}{100} \times 8x\right), \left(\dfrac{140}{100} \times 10x\right)$ and $\left(\dfrac{150}{100} \times 12x\right)$

$\Rightarrow \left(\dfrac{52x}{5}\right)$, (14x) and (18x)

Required ratio,

$\Rightarrow \dfrac{52x}{5} : 14x : 18x$

$\Rightarrow 52x : 70x : 90x$

$\Rightarrow 26 : 35 : 45$

$\therefore$ The ratio of increased seats is 26 : 35 : 45.

Hence, the correct option is (B).

58. There are two options in this scenario

➡ Case 1 – Red, Blue, Purple would be drawn out

$\Rightarrow$ Case 2 = Red, Purple, Blue would be drawn out

$\Rightarrow$ Probability in case 1 = $\left(\dfrac{6}{16}\right) \times \left(\dfrac{4}{15}\right) \times \left(\dfrac{6}{14}\right)$

$\Rightarrow$ Probability in case 2 = $\left(\dfrac{6}{16}\right) \times \left(\dfrac{6}{15}\right) \times \left(\dfrac{4}{14}\right)$

$\Rightarrow$ Probability = $\left(\left(\dfrac{6}{16}\right) \times \left(\dfrac{4}{15}\right) \times \left(\dfrac{6}{14}\right)\right) +$ $\left(\left(\dfrac{6}{16}\right) \times \left(\dfrac{4}{15}\right) \times \left(\dfrac{6}{14}\right)\right)$

$\Rightarrow$ Probability = $2 \times \dfrac{(6 \times 4 \times 6)}{(16 \times 15 \times 14)}$

$\Rightarrow$ Probability = $2 \times \dfrac{18}{420}$

$\Rightarrow$ Probability = $\dfrac{3}{35}$

$\therefore$ Probability of drawing out three different marbles of different colors with first being red is $\dfrac{3}{35}$.

Hence, the correct option is (E).

59. Given:

Speed of train = 54 km/h

Time train takes to cross a tree = 13 sec

Length of a platform = 75 m

Formula used:

Speed = $\dfrac{Distance}{Time}$

Speed of the train in m/sec = 54 × $\left(\dfrac{5}{18}\right)$ = 15 m/sec

$\Rightarrow$ Length of the train = 15 × 13 = 195 m

Time taken to cross the platform = $\dfrac{(195 + 75)}{15}$

$\Rightarrow$ Time taken to cross the platform = $\dfrac{270}{15}$ = 18 sec

$\therefore$ The time train will take to cross the platform is 18 sec.

Hence, the correct option is (D).

60. Let the man's rate upstream be x kmph and that downstream be y kmph.

Then, distance covered upstream in 4 hrs 24 min = Distance covered downstream in 2 hrs.

Time in fraction = $4\dfrac{24}{60} = \dfrac{22}{5}\ hrs.$

$\Rightarrow \left(x \times \dfrac{22}{5}\right)$ = (y × 2)

$\Rightarrow \dfrac{22x}{5}$ = 2y

$\Rightarrow y = \dfrac{11x}{5}$

$\Rightarrow$ Required ratio = $\dfrac{(y+x)}{2} : \dfrac{(y-x)}{2}$

$\Rightarrow \dfrac{(y+x)}{2} : \dfrac{(y-x)}{2}$

$\Rightarrow \dfrac{\left(\frac{11x}{5}+x\right)}{2} : \dfrac{\left(\frac{11x}{5}-x\right)}{2}$

$\Rightarrow \dfrac{16x}{5} \times \dfrac{1}{2} : \dfrac{6x}{5} \times \dfrac{1}{2}$

$\Rightarrow \dfrac{16x}{10} : \dfrac{6x}{10}$

$\Rightarrow 8 : 3$

$\therefore$ Ratio between the speed of the boat and speed of the water current is 8 : 3.

Hence, the correct option is (A).

61. Let, c's share be X

$\Rightarrow$ A's share = $\dfrac{X}{8}$

$\Rightarrow$ B's share = $\left(\dfrac{9}{8}\right) \times X + 500$

$\Rightarrow X + \left(\dfrac{X}{8}\right) + \left(\dfrac{9X}{8}\right) + 500 = 5000$

$\Rightarrow 9X + 2000 = 20000$

$\Rightarrow 9X = 18000$

$\Rightarrow X = 2000$

$\Rightarrow B - A = \left(\dfrac{9X}{8}\right) + 500 - \left(\dfrac{X}{8}\right)$

$\Rightarrow B - A = X + 500$

$\Rightarrow B - A = 2500$

$\therefore$ Difference between amount received by B and A is Rs. 2500.

Hence, the correct option is (B).

62. Let certain price be x.

S.P = $\dfrac{4x}{5}$

Loss = 10%

C.P = $\left(\dfrac{4x}{5}\right) \times \left(\dfrac{100}{90}\right) = \dfrac{8x}{9}$

On selling at x,

Profit = x $-$ $\dfrac{8x}{9}$ = $\dfrac{x}{9}$

$\Rightarrow$ Profit% = $\dfrac{\left(\frac{x}{9}\right)}{\left(\frac{8x}{9}\right)} \times 100 = 12.5\%$

$\therefore$ Profit is 12.5%.

Hence, the correct option is (C).

63. Volume of cylinder = $\pi r_1^2 h_1$

Volume of cone = $\left(\dfrac{1}{3}\right) \pi r_2^2 h_2$

$r_2 = \dfrac{r_1}{2}$

$2r_2 = r_1$

$\left(\dfrac{1}{3}\right) \pi r_2^2 h_2 = \pi (2r_2)^2 h_1$

$h_2 = 12\, h_1$

$\therefore$ Height of cone will be 12 times that of cylinder.

Hence, the correct option is (D).

64. Let, the principal $=$ Rs. $100x$ and rate of interest $= r\%$

Simple interest for 2 years $=$ Rs. 1200

$\therefore$ Simple interest for 1 year $=$ Rs. $\dfrac{1200}{2}$ = Rs. 600

$\therefore$ Compound interest for 1st year $=$ Rs. 600

$\therefore$ Compound interest for 2nd year $=$ Rs. $(1290 - 600) =$ Rs. 690

$\therefore$ Difference between compound and simple interest for 2nd year $=$ Rs. $(690 - 600) =$ Rs. 90

According to the question,

$\Rightarrow 600 \times 1 \times \dfrac{r}{100} = 90$

$\Rightarrow 6r = 90$

$\Rightarrow r = 15$

$\therefore$ Rate of interest $= 15\%$

According to the question,

$\Rightarrow 100x \times 2 \times \dfrac{15}{100} = 1200$

$\Rightarrow 30x = 1200$

$\Rightarrow x = 40$

$\therefore$ The principal $=$ Rs. (100×40)

$=$ Rs. 4000

Hence, the correct option is (D).

65. Given:

A ball dropped from a height of $120\, m$.

$S_\infty = \dfrac{a}{1 - \tau}$

After dropping $120\, m$ height the ball bounce $= 120 \times \dfrac{4}{5} = 96\, m$

$\Rightarrow$ First term $(a) = 120 + 96 = 216\, m$

$\Rightarrow$ Common ratio $(r) = \dfrac{4}{5}$

$\therefore$ Total distance that it travels before coming to rest

$= \dfrac{216}{\left(1 - \frac{4}{5}\right)}$

$= \dfrac{216}{\left(\frac{1}{5}\right)} = 216 \times 5$

$= 1080\, m$

Hence, the correct option is (C).

Ques (66-70):Given series:

453   619   574   471   372

66. If in each number, both first and third digits are added and after that second digit is subtracted from that addition then the numbers are:

453 $\to$ 7 - 5 = 2

$619 \rightarrow 15 - 1 = 14$

$574 \rightarrow 9 - 7 = 2$

$471 \rightarrow 5 - 7 = -2$

$372 \rightarrow 5 - 7 = -2$

So, there are two numbers less than 2.

Hence, the correct option is (D).

67. When second digit will be interchanged with third digit in each number, the number formed:

435   691   547   417   327

So, the second highest number after rearrangement is 547.

Hence, the correct option is (C).

68. If all the digits in each of the numbers are arranged in descending order within the number then:

543   916   754   741   732

So, the highest number after new arrangement is 916 (619).

Hence, the correct option is (D).

69. If in each number, all the odd digit is added by 1 and all the even digit is added by 2 then the number formed:

664   830   686   682   484

So, the lowest number is 484 (372).

Hence, the correct option is (C).

70. After arranging in ascending order within the number, the number formed:

345   169   457   147   237

So, the second lowest number is 169.

Hence, the correct option is (D).

Ques (71-75):1) V lives four floors above W.

2) W lives on an even-numbered floor.

(As there are only eight floors here, implies, there are two possibilities i.e., either W lives on the second floor or the fourth floor because only then we can place V four floors above W.)

3) Q lives on one of the floors above V's floor.

(As Q lives above V's floor, implies, V does not live on the 8th floor which further implies W does not live on the 4th floor (in that case V would live on the 8th floor). Thus, W lives on the 2nd floor and V lives on the 6th floor.)

Floor	Person
8th	
7th	
6th	V
5th	
4th	
3rd	
2nd	W

1st	

4) Two persons live between the floors on which U and S live.

5) S lives on the floor which is just next to W's floor.

(If we place S on the 3rd floor (just a floor above W) then U would be on 6th floor which is not possible as V is already there. Implies, S is on the first floor and U is on the 4th floor.)

Floor	Person
8th	
7th	
6th	V
5th	
4th	U
3rd	
2nd	W
1st	S

6) Three people live between the floors on which T and R live.

(It is only possible if we place T and R on the 7th and the 3rd floor but not necessarily in the same order. Also, now that we know that either T or R is on the 7th floor, we can place Q on the 8th floor according to statement 3. Now, that only P is left to be placed in the table, we can safely place him on the 5th floor as it is the only possibility left.)

Floor	Person
8th	Q
7th	T/R
6th	V
5th	P
4th	U
3rd	T/R
2nd	W
1st	S

71. Clearly, V lives on the 6th floor of the building.

Hence, the correct option is (B).

72. Clearly, Q lives on the top floor of the building.

Hence, the correct option is (B).

73. Clearly, four people live above the floor on which U live.

Hence, the correct option is (D).

74. Clearly, in this case, R lives on the 3rd floor of the building.

Hence, the correct option is (C).

75. Clearly, P lives on the 5th floor of the building.

Hence, the correct option is (A).

76.

Letters	S	E	C	O	N	D
Position	19	5	3	15	14	4

So, there is 'one' pair in the word 'SECOND', each of which has as many letters between them in the word (both forward and backward direction) as they have between them in the English Alphabet.

Hence, the correct option is (B).

77. From the given information,

1) Only T is shorter than R. It means that R will be second shortest and T will be shortest among them.

_ > _ > _ > R > T

2) Q is taller than P and S. Here Q will be tallest and possibility between P and S.

Q > P/S > P/S > R > T

3) Height of P is between Q and S. so that here P will be 2nd highest here.

Q > P > S > R > T

4) Height of the person's given as shortest person have height 135cm. and tallest person have height 165cm.

Q (165 cm) > P > S > R > T (135 cm).

As height of R is between Q and T so the value between Q and T's height.

So, Possible height of R will be 140 cm.

Hence, the correct option is (C).

78. 1) Q and S are equally expensive.

Q = S

2) T is the least expensive jewelry.

_ > _ > _ > _ > T

3) S was less expensive than R but more expensive than P.

R > S > P

4) The expensiveness of the R is more than that of Q.

R > Q = S > P > T

Options (A): R was the most expensive among them → True

Option (B): P was more expensive than Q → False

Option (C): S was in the middle. → False (Either Q or S can be at the middle)

Option (D): P was the most expensive among them → False

So, R was the most expensive among them is true.

Hence, the correct option is (A).

Ques (79-83):Person: K, L, M, N, O, P, Q, and R.

Month: January, April, June, and August

Dates: 8th & 15th

1) K delivers his lecture on the 8th of a month which has only 30 days.

2) Only three lectures were delivered between K and L.

3) O delivers the lecture immediately after L.

(Here 2 cases are possible, Case1: K delivers his lecture on the 8th of April, Case2: K delivers his lecture on the 8th of June.

Case 1:

Months	Dates	Person
January (31 days)	8	
	15	
April (30 days)	8	K
	15	
June (30 days)	8	
	15	
August (31 days)	8	L
	15	O

Case 2:

Months	Dates	Person
January (31 days)	8	L
	15	O
April (30 days)	8	
	15	
June (30 days)	8	K
	15	
August (31 days)	8	
	15	

4) Number of persons who give the lecture after O is the same as the number of persons who give the lecture before P.

5) Only two persons give lectures between P and M.

Case 1:

Months	Dates	Person
January (31 days)	8	P
	15	
April (30 days)	8	K
	15	M
June (30 days)	8	
	15	
August (31 days)	8	L
	15	O

Case 2:

Months	Dates	Person
January (31 days)	8	L
	15	O
April (30 days)	8	
	15	M
June (30 days)	8	K
	15	
August (31 days)	8	P
	15	

6) Q and M give their lectures in the same month.

(From here Case 1 is eliminated because no vacant position for Q as according to statement 6 Q and M give their lecture in the same month)

Months	Dates	Person
January (31 days)	8	L
	15	O
April (30 days)	8	Q
	15	M
June (30 days)	8	K
	15	
August (31 days)	8	P
	15	

7) N gives the lecture before R.

The final arrangement will be as follows:

Months	Dates	Person
January (31 days)	8	L
	15	O
April (30 days)	8	Q
	15	M
June (30 days)	8	K
	15	N
August (31 days)	8	P
	15	R

79. So, P gives the lecture on 8th August.

Hence, the correct option is (D).

80. So, 5 lectures were delivered after Q.

Hence, the correct option is (A).

81. So, L doesn't deliver the lecture in the month having 30 days.

Hence, the correct option is (E).

82. So, P delivers the lecture immediately before R.

Hence, the correct option is (C).

83. So, M gives the lecture on 15th April.

Hence, the correct option is (D).

84. The least possible Venn diagram for the given statements is as follows:

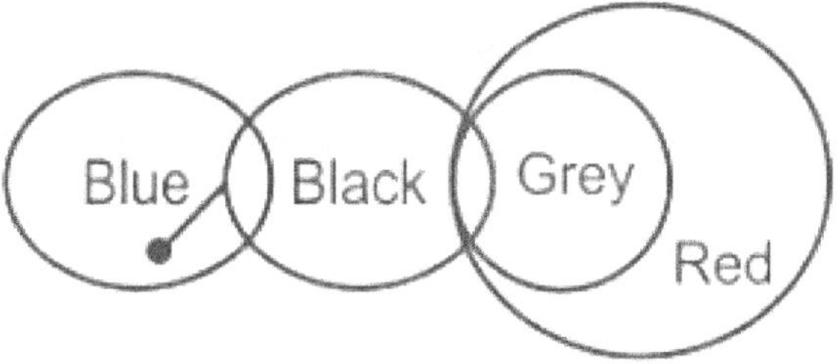

Conclusions:

I. All Red is Blue → False (As there is no direct relation between red and blue, so All Red is Blue is possible but not definite. So, it is false)

II. No Red is Blue → False (As there is no direct relation between red and blue, so All Red is Blue is possible but not definite. So, it is false)

So, Neither I nor II follows.

Hence, the correct option is (E).

85. The least possible Venn diagram for the given statements is as follows:

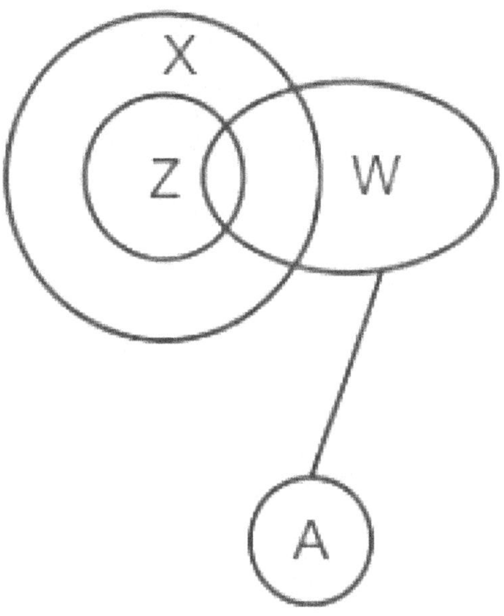

Conclusions:

I. All A is X → False (As there is no direct relation between A and X, All A is X is possible but not definite. So it is false)

II. Some X is not A → True (Some part of X which is common between Z and W will not be A as No A is W. So it is true)

So, Only II follow.

Hence, the correct option is (B).

86. The least possible Venn diagram for the given statements is as follows:

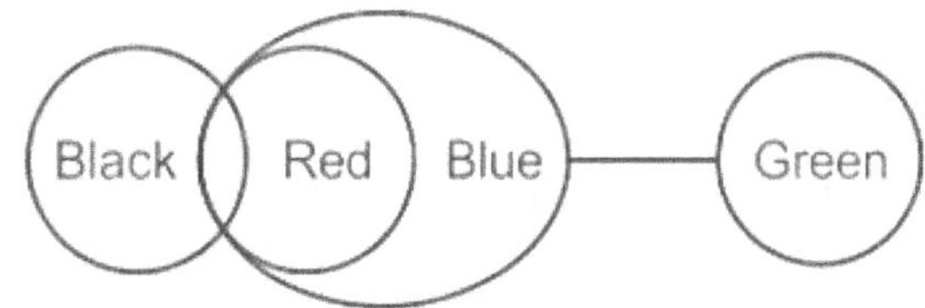

Conclusions:

I. All Green Can be Black → True (As there is no direct relation between green and black so All Green can be Black is possible but not definite. So, it is true)

II. Some Green is Red → False (As All Red is Blue and No Blue is green, Some green is red is not possible. So, it is false)

So, Only I follow.

Hence, the correct option is (A).

87. Given statements: P < S > T; Q = T > R

On combining: P < S > T = Q > R

I. Q < S → True (as S > T = Q → Q < S)

II. R < T → True (as T = Q > R → R < T)

Both conclusions are true, so, both are true.

Hence, the correct option is (D).

88. Given statements: A = B < C; D < C = E

On combining: A = B < C = E > D

I. D > B → False (as B < C = E > D → thus direct relation between D and B can't be determined)

II. A < E → True (as A = B < C = E → A < E)

Thus, only conclusion II is true.

Hence, the correct option is (E).

89. Given number: 856214

Digits	8	5	6	2	1	4
Position	1	2	3	4	5	6

Thus, we get 4 pairs:

Forward: (5, 6), (2, 4)

Backward: (2, 1), (8, 6)

So, the correct answer is four.

Hence, the correct option is (B).

Ques (90-92): The figure according to the information given in the question will be as follows:

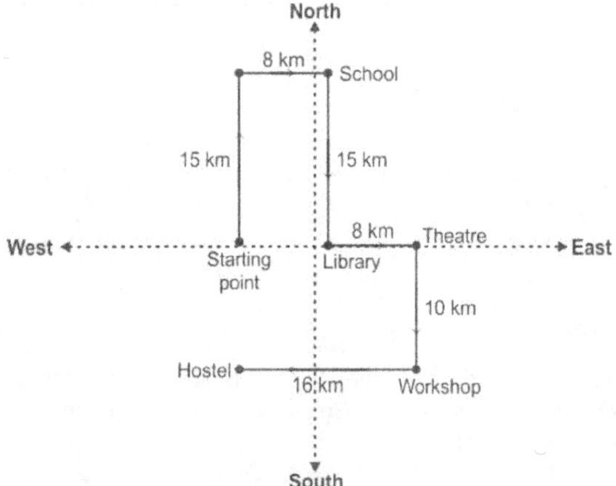

90. Applying Pythagoras Theorem

The shortest distance between starting point and School will be:

$$\sqrt{(15^2 + 8^2)} = \sqrt{(225 + 64)} = \sqrt{289} = 17 \text{ km}$$

So, the shortest distance between Starting point and School is 17 km.

Hence, the correct option is (B).

91. So, Theatre is in Southeast direction with respect to School.

Hence, the correct option is (A).

92. So, Hostel is to the South of Starting Point.

Hence, the correct option is (C).

Ques (93-97):Persons: Ds, Fg, Lm, Ms, Nd, Pe, Ps, and Xy

i) Pe is sitting third to the left of Lm who is facing towards the centre.

ii Ms and Fg are immediate neighbour of Pe.

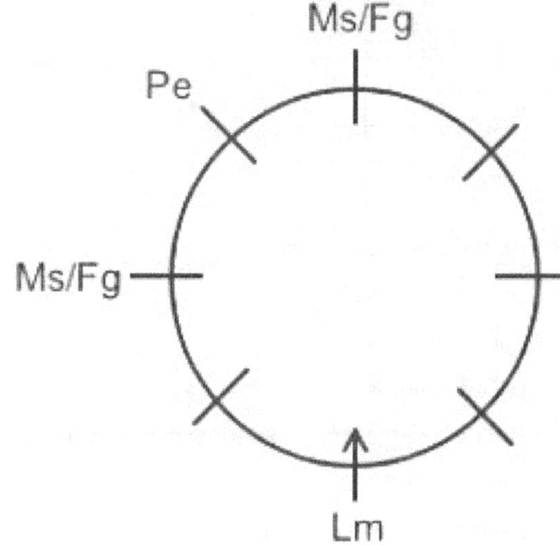

iii) Fg and Ms face the same direction but opposite to Pe.

iv) Nd is second to the right of Fg.

v) Ds is not an immediate neighbour of Nd.

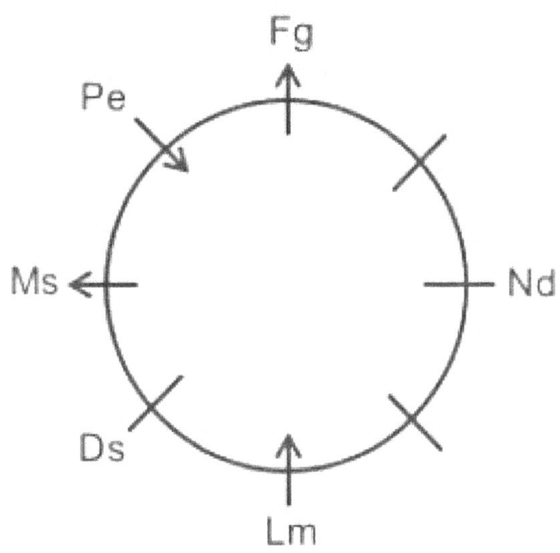

vi) Xy is second to the right of Ds.

vii) Both the immediate neighbour of Nd face the same direction as Ms.

viii) Lm faces the same direction as the person who is sitting second to his right.

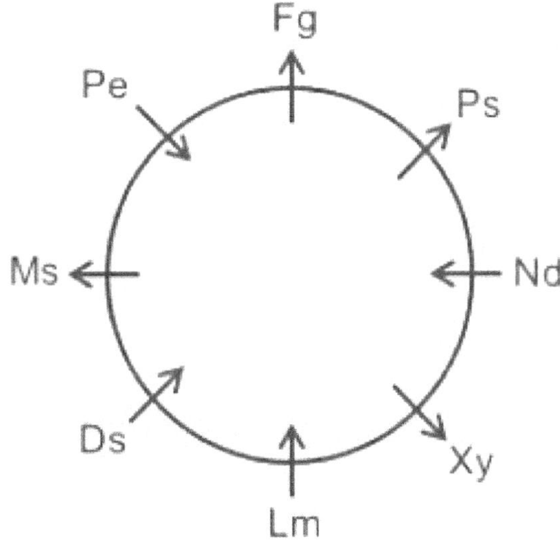

93. So, "Two" persons are sitting between Fg and Xy when counting from the left of Xy.

Hence, the correct option is (A).

94. So, three persons are facing away from centre between Nd and Ds counting from right of Nd.

Hence, the correct option is (B).

95. So, "Ps" is sitting opposite to Ds.

Hence, the correct option is (E).

96. So, "Pe" sits second to the left of Ps.

Hence, the correct option is (A).

97. So, Four persons are facing away from the centre.

Hence, the correct option is (C).

Ques (98-100): The family tree diagram for the given information:

Symbol in Diagram	Meaning
◯	Female
▢	Male
══	Married Couple
───	Siblings
│	Difference of A Generation

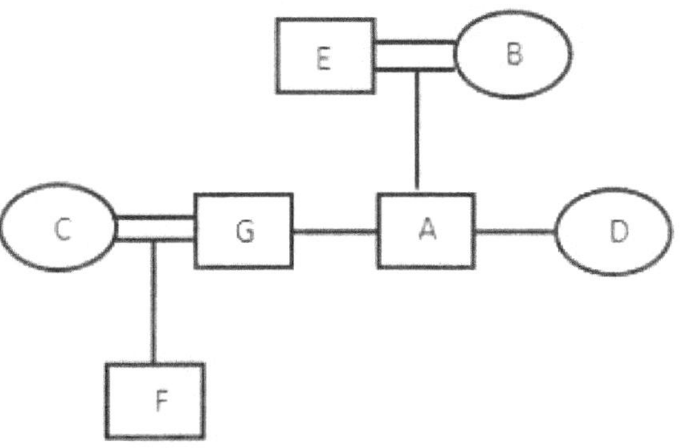

98. Clearly, there are three members of the family.

Hence, the correct option is (D).

99. Clearly, B is the wife of E.

Hence, the correct option is (C).

100. Clearly, E is the paternal grandfather of F.

Hence, the correct option is (C).

English Language

Ques (1-8):Direction: Read the passage given and answer the following question. Some words are given in bold. Pay careful attention.

Scientists from four Canadian universities used Fitbits and spy mics to record over 14,000 hours of sound from the secret lives of Canada lynx, a medium-sized cat-like North American predator. It is usually found across Canada and the north-American US region. Canada lynx are difficult to study for researchers because of their elusive nature. This led researchers to use the latest **miniaturized** technology to gain insights into their lives, a first in remote wildlife research. Researchers attached accelerometers and small audio recorders as collars to the animals, which are one of the top **predators** of the boreal forest of Canada.

On 26 lynx that were the subject of the study, researchers deployed a total of 39 collars with the recording devices that captured over 14,470 hours of data.

"The first time going through the audio files... you just hear the chaos. And then click a little bit further along and you hear what you think is bones cracking," said Emily Studd, the lead researcher and a postdoctoral fellow at the University of Alberta, in an interview to CBS.

In the recorded audio, the animals can be heard bonding, fighting, cleaning themselves, and even whining after losing a meal. Studd and her colleagues spent five years on the study that offers the science community a peek into the animals' lives". I spent three years in the field specifically tracking them, and rarely ever saw them," Studd underscores the challenges of studying the predators' lives. According to her, because predators need to sneak up on their prey, they are naturally **secretive** animals.

The new study, which was published in the British Ecological Society's journal Methods of Ecology and Evolution, opens up a new possibility of using such technologies to study and monitor the hunting behavior of predators. These technologies can make documentation of even the smallest activities of **elusive** animals possible.

Q.1 The passage is talking about which predator?

A. Canadian cat
B. Canadian leopard
C. Canadian lynx
D. Canadian jaguar
E. None of these

Q.2 Researchers deployed a total of how many collars?

A. 40
B. 37
C. 39
D. 38
E. None of these

Q.3 Which of the following statement(s) is/are true according to the passage?

I - Researchers attached small audio recorders as collars to the animals.

II - According to Emily Studd, predators need to sneak up on their prey, they are naturally secretive animals.

III - The predator is usually found across Canada and the South-American US region.

A. Only II and III
B. Only I and III
C. Only I and II
D. Only III
E. None of these

Q.4 Emily Studd, the lead researcher and a postdoctoral fellow, interviewed to CBS at which university?

A. University of Alberta
B. University of Canada
C. University of Britain
D. University of America
E. None of these

Q.5 What is the antonym of 'secretive'?

A. Open
B. Quiet
C. Reticent
D. Uncommunicative
E. None of these

Q.6 Out of the given words in options, which one is the most similar to 'elusive'?

A. Palpable
B. Tangible
C. Problematical
D. Evasive
E. None of these

Q.7 What is the opposite of 'predator'?

A. Destroyer
B. Prey
C. Exploiter
D. Savior
E. None of these

Q.8 What is the synonym of 'miniaturized'?

A. Hefty
B. Grand
C. Minuscule
D. Massive
E. None of these

Ques (9-14):Direction: In the following passage, some of the words have been left out. Read the passage carefully and select the correct answer for the given blanks out of the given alternatives.

The farmers began camping in the outskirts of Delhi when the first wave of the pandemic was past its _____ **(1)**. They upped the ante in the next four months and did not backtrack even after the virus _____ **(2)** with a vengeance. By the Morcha's own admission, some 470 farmers have ___ **(3)** their lives — it is not clear how many of those deaths were due to Covid. Any swelling of the ranks of the protesters now carries the risk of _____ **(4)** the health crisis, especially with the virus mutating into a more infectious variant. The ___ **(5)** farmers risk harming not just themselves but carrying the contagion back to their villages and risking the lives of their family members, friends, neighbors, and co-workers. This could present another set of

D. In the morning, she would take with her a pot of milk and a bunch of flowers as an offering.

A. DCAB   **B.** CBDA   **C.** ACDB   **D.** CADB
E. BADC

Q.25 Direction: Rearrange the following five sentences/group of sentences (A), (B), (C), (D), and (E) in the proper sequence to form a meaningful paragraph; then answer the questions given below them.

A. The first factory for the industrial production of cheese opened in Switzerland in 1815.

B. The mass production of cheese made it readily available to the poorer classes.

C. Earliest proposed dates for the origin of cheese making range from around 8000 BCE, when sheep were first domesticated.

D. Factory-made cheese overtook traditional cheese making in the World War II era.

E. There is no conclusive evidence indicating where cheese making originated, whether in Europe, Central Asia or the Middle East.

Which of the following should be the second sentence after rearrangement?

A. B   **B.** C   **C.** D   **D.** A
E. E

Ques (26-27):Direction: Select the phrase/connector from the given three options which can be used to form a single sentence from the two sentences given below, implying the same meaning as expressed in the statement sentences.

Q.26 Jake teaches the kids who live in the neighborhood. They meet in the evenings after he comes home from work.

i. Jake teaches the kids

ii. After returning home

iii. In the evenings,

A. Both i and ii   **B.** Only iii
C. Only ii   **D.** i, ii and ii
E. None of these

Q.27 The Dandi March was an act of nonviolent civil disobedience. The Dandi March was led by M.K. Gandhi.

I. Led by M.K. Gandhi

II. The Dandi March, which was

III. Being an act of nonviolent

A. Only I   **B.** Only III
C. Only II   **D.** Both I and II
E. None of these

Ques (28-30):Direction: Find out which part of the sentence has an error and select the appropriate option. If a sentence is free from error, select 'No Error'.

Q.28 A lot of (A)/ equipments are (B)/ required to play (C)/ cricket safely.(D) / No error

A. A   **B.** B   **C.** C   **D.** D
E. No error

Q.29 My grandfather is always happy (A)/ and eager to give (B)/ us advices when (C)/ we ask for it. (D)/ No error

A. A   **B.** B   **C.** C   **D.** D
E. No error

Q.30 He watched her climb into /(A) a compartment of the train, and /(B) he chose the same one /(C) so he could watch her more close. /(D) No error /(E)

A. A   **B.** B   **C.** C   **D.** D
E. E

Numerical Ability

Q.31 What will come in the place of the question mark '?' in the following question?

25% of 212 + 5% of 140 = 2 × 11% of 500 + ?

A. -46   **B.** -32   **C.** -50   **D.** -60
E. -25

Q.32 What will come in the place of the question mark '?' in the following question?

$$\left(\frac{3}{13}\right) \text{ of } \left\{\frac{325}{(3)^{-3}}\right\} \times ?^2 = 25 \times 10^4 \times (1.5)^4$$

A. 675   **B.** 75   **C.** 575   **D.** 625
E. 25

Q.33 What should come in the place of the question mark '?' in the following question?

12 × 87 + 12 × 114 + 93 × 12 − 44 × 12 = ?

A. 2000   **B.** 2500
C. 3000   **D.** 3500
E. None of these

Q.34 What should come in the place of the question mark '?' in the following question?

$$\left(\sqrt{0.1024}\right) + \left(\sqrt{0.2401}\right) + \left(\sqrt{0.1225}\right) - \left(\sqrt{0.6400}\right) = (?)^2$$

A. 0.36   **B.** 0.6
C. 0.216   **D.** 0.66
E. None of these

Q.35 What should come in the place of the question mark '?' in the following question?

$$\sqrt[3]{2197} + \sqrt[3]{1728} + \sqrt[3]{3375} = 8 \times ?$$

A. 4   **B.** 6
C. 5   **D.** 7
E. None of these

Q.36 What should come in the place of the question mark ' ?' in the following question ?

$$\frac{150}{25} - \sqrt{625} + \frac{183}{3} + 1.2 \times 5 = ?$$

A. 53   **B.** 48
C. 60   **D.** 56
E. None of these

Q.37 What should come in the place of the question mark '?' in the following question?

$$427 - 112 + (32)^{\frac{2}{5}} + (9)^{\frac{3}{2}} - 35 \times 4 = ?$$

A. 164   **B.** 150
C. 197   **D.** 100
E. None of these

Q.38 What should come in the place of the question mark '?' in the following question?

$$18 + 12 \times 6 - 12 \div 3 + \frac{77}{11} = ?$$

A. 73   **B.** 83
C. 93   **D.** 133
E. None of these

Q.39 What will come in the place of the question mark '?' in the following question?

125% of 120 + 55% of 460 - 21 ÷ 7 = 250% of ?

A. 60   **B.** 100   **C.** 400   **D.** 200
E. 160

Q.40 What should come in place of the question mark (?) in the following question?

$(12)^3 \div 4 + 15 \times 13 - ? + 4 = 21 \times 30$

A. 5   **B.** 4   **C.** 2   **D.** 1
E. 0

Q.41 A milkman, in 50 liters mixture of milk and water keeps the ratio of milk and water in 3 : 2. One day he decided this ratio is to be 2 : 3, then find quantity of water to be further added in the mixture.

A. 25 liters   **B.** 30 liters
C. 40 liters   **D.** 41 liters
E. None of these

Q.42 An amount of Rs. 400 becomes Rs. 424 in 3 years at a certain rate of simple interest, If the rate of interest increases by 8%, then find what amount will Rs. 400 becomes in 2 years?

A. Rs. 450   **B.** Rs. 425
C. Rs. 480   **D.** Data inadequate
E. None of these

Q.43 A train 300 meter long crosses a lamppost in 25 seconds. Calculate the speed of the man running in opposite direction who takes 20 seconds to cross the train.

A. 15 m/s   **B.** 5 m/s   **C.** 10 m/s   **D.** 2 m/s
E. 3 m/s

Ques (44-48):Direction: Study the bar graph and answer the following question.

In Bar Graph, shows the number of students passed in XII class from 6 schools.

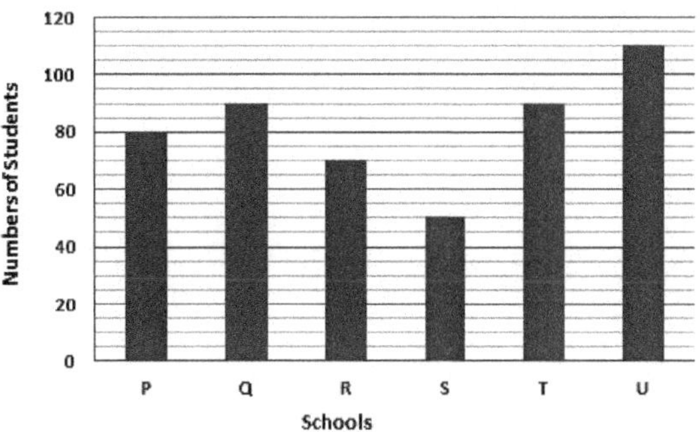

Q.44 If the fail percentage of school P is 60% then, find number of students who failed from school P is what percentage of the number of students passed from school T.

A. 80%   **B.** 133.33%   **C.** 105%   **D.** 110%
E. 90%

Q.45 If ratio between the total number of students who passed to the total number of students who failed from all schools is 7 : 3, then find the total number of failed students from all schools together.

A. 210   **B.** 250
C. 140   **D.** 220
E. None of these

Q.46 Students passed from school P, Q, S and U together is how much more than the average of passed students of school R and T together?

A. 250   **B.** 280   **C.** 380   **D.** 480
E. 550

Q.47 Failed students of school U is 20 more than that of school R. if the ratio between total strength of school U and school R is 5 : 3, then find the total number of failed students from both schools together.

A. 45   **B.** 50
C. 60   **D.** 40
E. None of these

Q.48 Pass percentage of school S is equal to that of school Q. Find the total strength of school Q is what % more than that of school S.

A. 70%   **B.** 80%
C. 75%   **D.** 65%
E. None of these

Q.49 In the given question, two equations numbered I and II are given. Solve both the equations and mark the appropriate answer.

I. $5x^2 - 18x + 9 = 0$

II. $3y^2 + 5y - 2 = 0$

A. x > y
B. x < y
C. x ≥ y
D. x ≤ y
E. x = y or relationship between x and y cannot be established

Q.50 In the given question, two equations numbered I and II are given. Solve both the equations and mark the appropriate answer.

I. $3x^2 - 7x + 2 = 0$

II. $2y^2 - 11y + 15 = 0$

A. x > y

B. x < y

C. x ≥ y

D. x ≤ y

E. x = y or relationship between x and y cannot be established

Q.51 In the given question, two equations numbered I and II are given. Solve both the equations and mark the appropriate answer.

I. $(625)^{\frac{1}{4}}x + \sqrt{1225} = 155$

II. $\sqrt{196}y + 13 = 279$

A. x > y

B. x < y

C. x ≥ y

D. x ≤ y

E. x = y or relationship between x and y cannot be established

Q.52 In the given question, two equations numbered I and II are given. Solve both the equations and mark the appropriate answer.

I. $12x^2 + 11x + 12 = 10x^2 + 22x$

II. $13y^2 - 18y + 3 = 9y^2 - 10y$

A. x > y

B. x < y

C. x ≥ y

D. x ≤ y

E. x = y or relationship between x and y cannot be established

Q.53 In the given question, two equations numbered I and II are given. Solve both the equations and mark the appropriate answer.

I. $x^2 = 81$

II. $y^2 - 18y + 81 = 0$

A. x > y

B. x < y

C. x ≥ y

D. x ≤ y

E. x = y or relationship between x and y cannot be established

Q.54 Veer and Ayush together have purchased a rectangular land of area 648 m². They have decided to split it into two halves with a single straight line and the cost of fencing the common boundary is paid by Veer, then find the minimum possible cost incurred by Veer in fencing his half at the rate of Rs. $\frac{2}{m}$?

A. Rs. 150   B. Rs. 200   C. Rs. 180   D. Rs. 144

E. Rs. 156

Q.55 The average weight of 20 students of a class is 60 kg. A student left the class and new student replaced the old one whose weight is 45 kg. Hence, the average weight of students increased by 1 kg. Find the ratio of old and new student's weight.

A. 9 : 13   B. 13 : 9

C. 8 : 7   D. 7 : 8

E. None of these

Q.56 The ratio of the ages of Tina and Jatin is 23 : p. Tina is 10 years younger to Rahul. After 16 years, Rahul will be 72 years old. If the difference between the ages of Jatin and Tina is equal to the age of Rahul 4 years ago, find the value of p.

A. 45   B. 47   C. 42   D. 49

E. 52

Q.57 P and Q started a business together and after 3 months P added $\frac{1}{3}$ of his original investment and after 3 months to that he added same amount he invested at first. Q invested $\frac{1}{4}$ amount of what she originally invested after 4 months. What would the ratio of profits be after 12 months if initial investment by both of them was in ratio 3 : 4?

A. 8 : 9   B. 5 : 4   C. 9 : 8   D. 4 : 5

E. 6 : 5

Q.58 What will come in place of the question mark (?) in the following number series?

1, 10, 24, 63, 227, ?

A. 916   B. 1016   C. 1116   D. 816

E. 716

Q.59 Find the missing number(?) in the series 180, 80, 60, 80, 240,?

A. 480   B. 960   C. 1920   D. 1760

E. 1480

Q.60 In following number series, the wrong number is given, find out that number.

6.4, 10.8, 15.2, 18.6, 24, 28.4

A. 6.4   B. 10.8   C. 15.2   D. 18.6

E. 12.4

Q.61 What should come in place of the question mark (?) in the following number series?

2, 9, 28, 65, 126, ?

A. 234   B. 217

C. 134   D. 126

E. None of these

Q.62 What should come in place of the question mark (?) in the following number series?

10, 11, 24, 75, ?

A. 304   B. 314

C. 103   D. 369

E. None of these

Q.63 A Bike is sold at profit of Rs. 2000, which is 10% of its cost price. If its C.P is increased by 50% and it is still sold at a profit of 10%, then find the new selling price?

A. 35000 **B.** 36000
C. 33000 **D.** 32000
E. None of the above

Q.64 Saima invested Rs. 1,60,000 in a business. Shifa joined the business after some months with Rs. 48,000. The total profit was divided between them in the ratio of 5 : 1 at the end of the year. The investment time period of Shifa was what % of the investment time period of Saima?

A. $\frac{80}{3}$% **B.** $\frac{200}{3}$% **C.** $\frac{160}{3}$% **D.** $\frac{210}{3}$%
E. $\frac{190}{3}$%

Q.65 If $(a+b):(b+c):(c+a) = 7:6:5$ and $a+b+c = 27$, then what will be the value of $\frac{1}{a}:\frac{1}{b}:\frac{1}{c}$?

A. $4:3:6$ **B.** $3:4:2$ **C.** $3:6:4$ **D.** $3:2:4$
E. $3:5:4$

Reasoning Ability

Q.66 Direction: In the question below are given two statements followed by two conclusions numbered I and II. You have to take the given statements to be true even if they seem to be at variance with commonly known facts. Read all the conclusions and then decide which of the given conclusions logically follows from the given statements disregarding commonly known facts.

Statements:

All Toy is Bottle.

Some Toy are Machine.

Conclusions:

I. No Toy is Bottle.

II. Some Machine are Bottle.

A. Only I follow
B. Only II follow
C. Either I or II follows
D. Neither I nor II follows
E. Both I and II follows

Q.67 Direction: In the question below are given three statements followed by two conclusions numbered I and II You have to take the given statements to be true even if they seem to be at variance with commonly known facts. Read all the conclusions and then decide which of the given conclusions logically follows from the given statements disregarding commonly known facts.

Statements:

Only a few Ice is Cube.

Some Cube is Circle.

Some Circle are Square.

Conclusions:

I. Some Ice is not Cube.

II. Some Cube is Square.

A. Only I follow
B. Only II follow
C. Both I and II follow
D. Either I or II follows
E. Neither I nor II follows

Ques (68-72):Direction: Study the following information carefully and answer the question that follows:

Eight persons Fiona, Liz, Cody, Zack, Ashley, Betty, Derek and Patrick are sitting on a circular table facing away from centre but not necessarily in the same order.

Betty is sitting third to the left of Cody. Patrick is sitting second to the right of Ashley. Derek is sitting second to the left of Cody. Zack is not a neighbour of Ashley or Patrick. Fiona does not sit opposite to Derek. Ashley is sitting opposite to Betty.

Q.68 Which of the following pair is the immediate neighbour of Liz?

A. Patrick and Betty **B.** Ashley and Patrick
C. Derek and Zack **D.** Ashley and Cody
E. Betty and Zack

Q.69 Which of the following statements is/are definitely true?

I. Derek sits opposite to Ashley.

II. Betty sits second to the right of Zack.

III. Fiona sits opposite to Cody.

A. Only statement I is true
B. Only statement II is true
C. Only statement III is true
D. None is true
E. All are true

Q.70 How many persons are sitting between Liz and Zack when counted from right of Liz?

A. 2 **B.** 1 **C.** 3 **D.** 4
E. 5

Q.71 If Betty exchanges her position with Patrick then who is sitting third to the left of Betty?

A. Ashley **B.** Zack **C.** Derek **D.** Cody
E. Liz

Q.72 Who sits opposite to Cody?

A. Derek **B.** Fiona **C.** Liz **D.** Zack
E. Patrick

Ques (73-77):Direction: Study the following arrangement carefully and answer the question.

H % 1 P ! F S ? * X 7 C T 4 $ 9 3 > @ / 6 N Q 5

Q.73 In the given arrangement, how many numbers are there which are immediately followed by a symbol?

A. None **B.** One **C.** Two **D.** Three
E. Four

Q.74 What is the sum of the numbers between the element '*' and '>'?

A. 24 **B.** 17 **C.** 19 **D.** 23
E. 21

Q.75 If all the symbols are dropped from the arrangement then what would be the sixth element from the right end?

A. 9   **B.** T   **C.** 4   **D.** C
E. 7

Q.76 If all the numbers are dropped from the above arrangement, which of the following will be the fifth to the right of fourth from the left end?

A. ?   **B.** S   **C.** *   **D.** X
E. C

Q.77 How many letters are immediately preceded by consonants and immediately followed by a symbol?

A. None   **B.** One   **C.** Two   **D.** Three
E. Four

Ques (78-80):Direction: Study the following information carefully and answer the question given below:

A person starts from point A and goes 3 km north to reach point B and then turns right and goes for 5 km to point C before taking a right turn. Point D is at a distance of 7 km south of point C. After reaching point D he takes a left turn and goes for 2 km to reach point E and then again he takes a left turn and goes for 4 km to reach point F. Point G is 3 km to the east of point F. G started walking in the south for 4 km to reach H.

Q.78 Point H is 4 km to the south of point G, then what is the distance between point H and point D?

A. 5 km   **B.** 6 km   **C.** 7 km   **D.** 8 km
E. 2 km

Q.79 What is the shortest distance between point E and G?

A. 3 km   **B.** 10 km
C. 13 km   **D.** 5 km
E. None of the above

Q.80 A is in which direction and at what distance from point F?

A. 5 km East   **B.** 7 km West
C. 9 km South   **D.** 7 km North
E. 5 km West

Ques (81-85):Direction: Study the given information carefully and answer the following question below.

In a shop, 6 boxes containing books of different subjects are kept. They are – Physics, Chemistry, Biology, mathematics, English, Hindi. Each box has a number written on it from 1 to 6 but not necessarily in that order. The boxes are arranged in a stack in ascending order with the lowest numbered box at the top.

The box containing Physics book is kept at the top. There are three boxes between the box of Physics books and box of Hindi books which is immediately above the box of Biology books. Box of Mathematics books is kept immediately above box of English books and immediately below box of Chemistry books.

Q.81 Which box contains Chemistry books?

A. 1   **B.** 2   **C.** 3   **D.** 4
E. 5

Q.82 Which subject books does the box immediately above the box of Hindi books contain?

A. Physics   **B.** English
C. Mathematics   **D.** Chemistry
E. Biology

Q.83 Which books does box 6 contain?

A. Hindi   **B.** English
C. Biology   **D.** Chemistry
E. Physics

Q.84 Which box is just below the box containing books of Chemistry?

A. 1   **B.** 2   **C.** 3   **D.** 4
E. 5

Q.85 Which box contains Hindi books?

A. 1   **B.** 2   **C.** 3   **D.** 4
E. 5

Ques (86-88):Direction: Study the following information carefully and answer the given question.

In a certain code language 'ma nd ki si dn' means 'Chetan and Aniket is friend', 'ke ma og ot' means 'Chetan go to market', 'ki ot og ho' means 'Aniket go to school', 'ma si ni ot ho' means 'Chetan is going to school'.

Q.86 Code 'nd' is for which word in the given language?

A. friend   **B.** and
C. market   **D.** Either (A) or (B)
E. school

Q.87 What would be the code for 'Chetan go to school'?

A. ki ma ni ot   **B.** og ot ma ho
C. ma nd ot ke   **D.** ki ma ot og
E. si ma ki ot

Q.88 Which of the following means 'Chetan' in that code language?

A. dn   **B.** nd   **C.** ma   **D.** si
E. ki

Ques (89-93):Direction: Study the following information carefully and answer the question given below.

Five friends: A, B, C, D and E met at a party. They live in different cities among – Delhi, Mumbai, Bangalore, Chennai and Hyderabad and work in different companies among – P, Q, R, S and T, not necessarily in the same order.

(i) A lives in Delhi but does not work in company Q.

(ii) C works in company T.

(iii) The person who lives in Bangalore works in company S.

(iv) Neither D nor B lives in Chennai.

(v) B works in company P and E lives in Hyderabad.

Q.89 Annual Entrepreneur Awards were organized by Company T and the person working in Company R was awarded. In which city were the Awards organized and where does the person who was awarded lives?

A. Delhi, Bangalore
B. Chennai, Delhi
C. Hyderabad, Bangalore
D. Mumbai, Hyderabad
E. Either (A) or (B)

Q.90 For which company does the person who lives in Hyderabad works?
A. Q
B. P
C. T
D. R
E. Cannot be determined

Q.91 In which city does the person who works in company P lives?
A. Chennai
B. Delhi
C. Mumbai
D. Either (A) or (B)
E. Either (B) or (C)

Q.92 The Company in which D works acquires the company in which A works. The two friends now work for which company?
A. Q
B. R
C. S
D. P
E. T

Q.93 There was a merger of Company P and T and there was a reshuffle of employees. The persons belonging to both the Companies were relocated. and their places of residences were exchanged. Who lives in Mumbai after reshuffle?
A. B
B. D
C. E
D. C
E. A

Q.94 In the following question, assuming the given statements to be true, find which of the given conclusions is/are definitely true and then choose the right option accordingly.
Statements: X ≤ S < W; P ≥ O > W.
Conclusions:
I. S < P
II. X < O
A. Only I is true
B. Only II is true
C. Both I & II are true
D. Neither I nor II is true
E. Either I or II is true

Q.95 Direction: In the following question assuming the given statements to be True, find which of the conclusion among given conclusions is / are definitely True and then give your answers accordingly.
Statements:
Q = G > P ≥ M; U ≤ I ≤ H = L < Q
Conclusions:
I. H > P
II. M > G
A. Neither I nor II is True
B. Both I and II are True
C. Only II is True
D. Only I is True

E. Either I and II is True

Ques (96-100):Direction: Read the following information carefully and answer the question that follows.

One of the six types of biscuit Coconut, 20-20, Good Day, 50-50, Tiger and Bounce is eaten on each day of the week starting from Monday and end on Saturday.

1) Coconut biscuit must be eaten immediately before Tiger biscuit.

2) Good day is not eaten on Tuesday.

3) 20-20 must be eaten on the day following the day on which Bounce is eating.

4) 50-50 must be eaten on Friday only & should not be immediately preceded by 20-20.

5) Tiger must not eat on the last day.

Q.96 Which biscuit is eaten on the Wednesday?
A. 20-20
B. Good Day
C. Coconut
D. 50-50
E. Bounce

Q.97 Which of the following pair is correct according to the given arrangement ?
A. Tuesday – 20-20
B. Friday – Good day
C. Saturday – Tiger
D. Monday – 50-50
E. None of these

Q.98 Which of the following biscuit is eaten just before the Tiger biscuit?
A. 20-20
B. Bounce
C. Good Day
D. Coconut
E. 50-50

Q.99 Good Day biscuit eaten on which of the following days?
A. Monday
B. Wednesday
C. Thursday
D. Saturday
E. Tuesday

Q.100 How many biscuits are eaten between 20-20 and 50-50?
A. None
B. One
C. Two
D. Three
E. Four

// Smart Answer Sheet //

Correct Percentage of students who answered correctly. **Skipped** Percentage of students who skipped.

Q.	Ans.	Correct / Skipped	Q.	Ans.	Correct / Skipped	Q.	Ans.	Correct / Skipped	Q.	Ans.	Correct / Skipped	Q.	Ans.	Correct / Skipped
1	C	10.09 % / 43.12 %	17	C	3.67 % / 88.07 %	33	C	8.26 % / 88.99 %	49	A	2.75 % / 90.83 %	65	A	0 % / 100 %
2	C	11.01 % / 87.16 %	18	B	5.5 % / 93.58 %	34	B	4.59 % / 88.99 %	50	B	5.5 % / 90.83 %	66	B	7.34 % / 89.91 %
3	C	6.42 % / 88.08 %	19	A	5.5 % / 93.58 %	35	C	6.42 % / 88.99 %	51	A	4.59 % / 90.82 %	67	A	5.5 % / 89.91 %
4	A	10.09 % / 88.08 %	20	A	4.59 % / 93.58 %	36	B	3.67 % / 88.99 %	52	C	1.83 % / 90.83 %	68	B	7.34 % / 89.91 %
5	A	6.42 % / 88.08 %	21	C	3.67 % / 93.58 %	37	C	0.92 % / 88.99 %	53	D	5.5 % / 90.83 %	69	C	9.17 % / 89.91 %
6	D	2.75 % / 88.08 %	22	C	3.67 % / 93.58 %	38	C	10.09 % / 88.99 %	54	D	0.92 % / 90.82 %	70	D	8.26 % / 89.91 %
7	B	1.83 % / 88.08 %	23	C	4.59 % / 93.58 %	39	E	9.17 % / 89.0 %	55	A	0.92 % / 90.82 %	71	D	10.09 % / 89.91 %
8	C	3.67 % / 88.07 %	24	B	5.5 % / 93.58 %	40	D	7.34 % / 88.99 %	56	D	0 % / 100 %	72	B	10.09 % / 89.91 %
9	C	7.34 % / 88.07 %	25	B	1.83 % / 93.58 %	41	A	1.83 % / 89.0 %	57	C	0 % / 100 %	73	C	8.26 % / 89.91 %
10	A	7.34 % / 88.07 %	26	D	0 % / 100 %	42	C	3.67 % / 89.91 %	58	B	0 % / 100 %	74	D	8.26 % / 89.91 %
11	B	10.09 % / 88.08 %	27	D	1.83 % / 95.42 %	43	E	0.92 % / 89.91 %	59	D	0 % / 100 %	75	A	6.42 % / 90.83 %
12	D	6.42 % / 88.08 %	28	B	2.75 % / 95.42 %	44	B	5.5 % / 89.0 %	60	D	0 % / 100 %	76	D	6.42 % / 89.91 %
13	A	8.26 % / 88.07 %	29	C	1.83 % / 95.42 %	45	A	3.67 % / 88.99 %	61	B	2.75 % / 91.75 %	77	B	6.42 % / 90.83 %
14	A	8.26 % / 88.07 %	30	D	0.92 % / 94.49 %	46	A	5.5 % / 89.91 %	62	A	2.75 % / 94.5 %	78	A	5.5 % / 90.83 %
15	A	3.67 % / 88.07 %	31	C	10.09 % / 88.99 %	47	C	0 % / 100 %	63	C	0 % / 100 %	79	D	5.5 % / 89.91 %
16	A	0 % / 100 %	32	E	1.83 % / 89.0 %	48	B	0 % / 100 %	64	B	0 % / 100 %	80	B	5.5 % / 89.91 %

Q.	Ans.	Correct		Q.	Ans.	Correct		Q.	Ans.	Correct		Q.	Ans.	Correct		Q.	Ans.	Correct
		Skipped				Skipped				Skipped				Skipped				Skipped
81	B	6.42 %		85	E	6.42 %		89	B	8.26 %		93	D	7.34 %		97	A	4.59 %
		89.91 %				89.91 %				89.91 %				89.91 %				90.82 %
82	B	8.26 %		86	D	6.42 %		90	A	9.17 %		94	C	8.26 %		98	D	6.42 %
		89.91 %				89.91 %				89.91 %				89.91 %				90.83 %
83	C	7.34 %		87	B	5.5 %		91	C	9.17 %		95	A	5.5 %		99	D	5.5 %
		89.91 %				89.91 %				89.91 %				89.91 %				90.83 %
84	C	5.5 %		88	C	7.34 %		92	C	3.67 %		96	C	5.5 %		100	C	3.67 %
		89.91 %				89.91 %				89.91 %				90.83 %				92.66 %

//Hints and Solutions//

1. It is mentioned in the first paragraph of the first sentence, "Scientists from four Canadian universities used Fitbits and spy mics to record over 14,000 hours of sound from the secret lives of Canada lynx, a medium-sized cat-like North American predator."

Hence, the correct option is (C).

2. It is mentioned in the second paragraph, "On 26 lynx that were the subject of the study, researchers deployed a total of 39 collars with the recording devices that captured over 14,470 hours of data."

Hence, the correct option is (C).

3. In statement I, it is mentioned in the first paragraph's last sentence, "Researchers attached accelerometers and small audio recorders as collars to the animals, which are one of the top predators of the boreal forest of Canada." Thus, this is true.

In statement II, it is mentioned in the fourth paragraph's last sentence, " According to her, because predators need to sneak up on their prey, they are naturally secretive animals." Thus, this is also true according to the passage.

In statement III, it is mentioned in the second sentence of the first paragraph, "The predator is usually found across Canada and the north-American US region." It is found in the north-American US region and not the south-American US region. Thus, this statement is not true.

Hence, the correct option is (C).

4. It is mentioned in the third paragraph, "The first time going through the audio files... you just hear the chaos. And then click a little bit further along and you hear what you think is bones cracking," said Emily Studd, the lead researcher and a postdoctoral fellow at the University of Alberta, in an interview to CBS."

Hence, the correct option is (A).

5. Secretive means liking to keep things secret from other people.

Example: Her secretive manner had made me curious.

Its synonyms are: quiet, reserved, introverted, self-contained, discreet, uncommunicative, unforthcoming, reticent, taciturn, silent.

Its antonyms are: open, communicative, chatty.

Hence, the correct option is (A).

6. Elusive means not easy to catch, find or remember.

Example: The elusive criminal was arrested.

Its synonyms are: Cagey, evasive, slippery, etc

Its antonyms are: palpable, easy, tangible, identifiable, artless, problematic, etc.

Evasive means trying to avoid something; not direct.

Hence, the correct option is (D).

7. Predator means an animal that kills and eats other animals.

Prey means an animal that is hunted or killed by another animal for food

Thus, prey is the correct opposite of predator.

Hence, the correct option is (B).

8. Miniaturized means to make on a smaller scale.

Example - A rainbow of colorful, miniaturized candles can make for thoughtful gifts for friends at the office, teachers at the school and even for neighbors

Its synonyms are - minuscule, minute, micro, tiny, small, etc.

Its antonyms are - grand, great, massive, hefty, big, huge, etc.

Hence, the correct option is (C).

9. The most appropriate answer is peak.

Peak means the point at which something is the highest, best, strongest, etc.

Example-

She's at the peak of her career.

Holiday flights reach a peak during August.

Wave, Light, time are not appropriate answers.

Hence, the correct option is (C).

10. Returned means to come or go back to a place.

Example- I leave on 10 July and return on 6 August.

Returned is the most appropriate answer.

The correct sentence- 'They upped the ante in the next four months and did not backtrack even after the virus returned with a vengeance.'

Began (It is the past tense of begin) means to start doing something.

Departed (past tense of depart) means to leave a place, usually at the beginning of a journey.

Disappeared (past tense of disappear) means to vanish, to become impossible to see or to find, to stop existing.

Hence, the correct option is (A).

11. Lost means unable to find your way; not knowing where you are; that cannot be found or that no longer exists.

The sentence is talking about farmers losing their lives. So , the most appropriate answer is 'lost'.

Gained means to obtain or win something, especially something that you need or want; to gradually get more of something.

Vanish means to get to disappear suddenly or in a way that you cannot explain.

Also, we do not use 'vanish their lives', it'll be incorrect. The proper usage is 'lost their lives'.

Find means to discover something that you want or that you have lost after searching for it.

Hence, the correct option is (B).

12.

- Aggravating means to make a situation worse; to make something worse or more serious; to make somebody angry or annoyed.
- 'Lessen', 'mitigate', 'conciliate' are all antonyms of 'aggravate'.
- Lessen means to become less; to make something less.
- Conciliate- to try to make a group of people less angry, especially in order to end a dispute.
- Mitigate- to make something less serious, painful, unpleasant, etc.

Hence, the correct option is (D).

13. Agitating means to make other people feel very strongly about something so that they want to help you achieve it.

Example-

From the habit of fifty years, all this had a physically agitating effect on the old general.

'Calm', 'relaxing' and 'quieted' are antonyms of 'agitating'.

Hence, the correct option is (A).

14.

- Challenges is the most appropriate word for the given blank.
- Challenges mean something new and difficult that forces you to make a lot of effort
- Example- Are you prepared for the challenges ahead?
- Acceptance means the act of accepting or being accepted.
- Investigations the action of investigating something or someone; formal or systematic examination or research.
- Concede to admit that something is true although you do not want to.

Hence, the correct option is (A).

15. The correct answer is Option (A) i.e., 'error lies in part A of the sentence.'

In part, (A) of the sentence, the usage of 'was' is incorrect Instead, use 'were'

In the given sentence, 'A group of' is acting as a determiner which is used for the noun 'Assasins' and it is in plural form hence, the verb should be written according to the noun given after the determiner.

A determiner is a word that is used at the beginning of a noun group to indicate, for example, which thing you are referring to or whether you are referring to one thing or several. Some common determiners are: A number of, the number of, some of, etc.

So the correct sentence is: 'Recently, a group of Assasins were put on a trial by media persons. One spectator just could not comprehend why everyone was shouting at them. Another astute person called it media trail and left the discussion'.

Hence, the correct option is (A).

16. In part (A) of the sentence, the usage of "most" before "ideal" & 'complete' is wrong as they are already in the superlative form.

Hence, the correct option is (A).

17. Option (C) is incorrect because of the wrong usage of 'searching' in Part C of the sentence.

It is important to remember that when coordinating conjunctions such as 'and', 'but', 'so', 'or', 'yet', etc. are used to join parts of sentences or clauses, parallel structure is followed.

In the given sentence, all the verbs except 'searching' are used in the Past Tense.

The usage of 'searching' instead of 'searched' disrupts the flow of the sentence.

So, 'searching' should be replaced by 'searched' to make the sentence correct.

Correct sentence: "He went to the kitchen, gathered the ingredients, switched on the gas, and searched for the recipe book in the cabinets."

Hence, the correct option is (C).

18. 'Ablity': There is no such word in English or we can say that there is some spelling mistake in this word, correct spelling is 'Ability'.

'Ability' means possession of the means or skill to do something.

Hence, the correct option is (B).

19. 'Exprimant': There is no such word in English or we can say that there is some spelling mistake in this word, correct spelling is 'Experiment'.

'Experiment' means to try out new ideas or methods.

Hence, the correct option is (A).

20. 'Presure': There is no such word in English or we can say that there is some spelling mistake in this word, correct spelling is 'Pressure'.

'Pressure' means continuous physical force exerted on or against an object by something in contact with it.

Hence, the correct option is (A).

21. The correct spelling is 'conscious'.

Conscious means 'able to see, hear, feel, etc. things; awake'.

Example- The injured driver was still conscious when the ambulance arrived.

Hence, the correct option is (C).

22. While arranging the parts of the passage, we should find some grammatical or contextual connections between them:

- Sentence B introduces us to the village 'Kandhulimari'. It is the introductory sentence and will be put in the first place.
- Sentence D tells us about the belongingness of Hima Das with the given village. It will be put in second place.
- Sentence A tells us about how fast the above-mentioned athlete at the World Under-20 Championship in 2018. It will be put in third place.
- The last sentence is C as it mentions the event of the athlete winning a gold medal in the above-mentioned championship.

Thus, the correct order is - BDAC.

Hence, the correct option is (C).

23. While arranging the parts of the passage, we should find some grammatical or contextual connections between them:

- Sentence D introduces us to the subject 'a king'. It is the introductory sentence and will be put in the first place.
- Sentence A tells us about the king's attitude towards his subjects. It will be put in second place.
- Sentence C tells us about the instance of sending spies to get information about the people's condition. It will be put in third place.
- The last sentence is B as it mentions the extent up to which the king could go for the welfare of the people of his kingdom.

Thus, the correct order is: DACB.

Hence, the correct option is (C).

24. The first statement of a sentence jumbled question is usually an independent general statement, a noun, a universal fact, the starting of an incident, or it starts with 'most' or 'once'.

Part C will be the first sentence because it is talking about a past happening. It talks about a girl named 'Tejaswini' who is known in her village for her devotion to the Lord.

Part B will be the second sentence because it is connected with Part B. And further explains 'How many times she visits the temple a day'.

Part D will be used next because it tells us about her visit in the morning to the temple.

And finally, Part A will be used because it tells us about her visit to the temple in the evening.

Correct Sentence: "Tejaswini was known in the village for her devotion to the Lord. She would go to the Lord's temple twice a day. In the morning, she would take with her a pot of milk and a bunch of flowers as an offering. In the evening, Tejaswini would sing songs praising the Lord."

Hence, the correct option is (B).

Q.25 The first sentence is E as it start discussing about the origination of cheese making.

The second sentence is C as it mentions the time when the process of cheese making started.

The third sentence is A as it informs about the first factory of cheese which was opened in Switzerland.

The fourth sentence is D as it mentions the consequence of preparing cheese in the factories.

The fifth sentence is B because it concludes the passage by mentioning that cheese is available to poor classes because of mass production.

Thus the correct sequence is ECADB. The second sentence is C.

Hence, the correct option is (B).

26. All three of the above-mentioned connectors can be used to connect the sentences, without changing the initial meaning of the sentence.

i. Jake teaches the kids who live in the neighborhood in the evenings after he comes home from work.

ii. After returning home from work, Jake teaches the kids who live in the neighborhood in the evenings.

iii. In the evenings, after returning home from work, Jake teaches the kids who live in the neighborhood.

Hence, the correct option is (D).

27. The only ways of beginning the sentence is with I and II.

'Led by M.K. Gandhi, the Dandi March was an act of nonviolent civil disobedience.'

'The Dandi March, which was an act of nonviolent civil disobedience was led by M.K. Gandhi.'

III cannot act as a link.

Hence, the correct option is (D).

28. The error is in part b of the sentence, due to the wrong usage of uncountable noun.

We use the uncountable noun 'equipment' to mean 'the set of things that you need for a particular purpose', such as tools or clothing. Uncountable nouns are always considered to be singular.

Equipment is an uncountable noun and is not used in '-s form'.

The plural of equipment is equipment.

Since uncountable nouns are singular, they also require singular verbs.

Correct sentence: A lot of equipment is required to play cricket safely.

Hence, the correct option is (B).

29. The error is in part C of the sentence, due to the wrong usage of an uncountable noun.

Advice is an uncountable noun and is not used in the -s form.

The plural of advice is advice.

Correct sentence: My grandfather is always happy and eager to give us advice when we ask for it.

Hence, the correct option is (C).

30. In part D of the sentence, the usage of 'close' is incorrect instead of it use 'closely'

In the given sentence, 'watch' is an action verb hence with the action verb we usually use an adverb, not an adjective that's why 'close' is incorrect.

Adverbs always give the reply to 'how? when? where? why?' and the Adjectives always give the reply of 'what kind of? which one?' In the given sentence we are getting the reply of 'How?' hence use an adverb.

Correct sentence: He watched her climb into a compartment of the train, and he chose the same one so he could watch her more closely.

Hence, the correct option is (D).

31. Given:

25% of 212 + 5% of 140 = 2 × 11% of 500 + ?

$$\Rightarrow \left(\frac{1}{4}\right) \times 212 + \left(\frac{1}{20}\right) \times 140 = 2 \times \left(\frac{11}{100}\right) \times 500 + ?$$

⇒ 53 + 7 = 110 + ?

⇒ ? = 60 -110 = -50

∴ The value of (?) is -50

Hence, the correct option is (C).

32. Given:

$$\left(\frac{3}{13}\right) \text{ of } \left\{\frac{325}{(3)^{-3}}\right\} \times ?^2 = 25 \times 10^4 \times (1.5)^4$$

⇒ 3 × 25 × 3³ × ?² = 25 × 10⁴ × (1.5)⁴

$$\rightarrow 3^{(1+3)} \times 25 \times ?^2 = 25 \times 10000 \times \frac{(3)^4}{(2)^4}$$

$$\Rightarrow ?^2 = \frac{10000}{16}$$

⇒ ?² = 625

⇒ ? = 25

∴ The value of (?) is 25

Hence, the correct option is (E).

33. Given:

12 × 87 + 12 × 114 + 93 × 12 − 44 × 12 = ?

⇒ 1044 + 1368 + 1116 − 528 = ?

⇒ 3528 − 528 = ?

⇒ ? = 3000

∴ The value of '?' is 3000.

Hence, the correct option is (C).

34. Given:

$$\left(\sqrt{0.1024}\right) + \left(\sqrt{0.2401}\right) + \left(\sqrt{0.1225}\right) - \left(\sqrt{0.6400}\right) = (?)^2$$

$$\left(\sqrt{\frac{1024}{10000}}\right) + \left(\sqrt{\frac{2401}{10000}}\right) + \left(\sqrt{\frac{1225}{10000}}\right) - \left(\sqrt{\frac{6400}{10000}}\right) = (?)^2$$

$$\Rightarrow \left(\frac{32}{100}\right) + \left(\frac{49}{100}\right) + \left(\frac{35}{100}\right) - \left(\frac{80}{100}\right) = (?)^2$$

$$\Rightarrow \frac{(116 - 80)}{100} = (?)^2$$

$$\Rightarrow \frac{36}{100} = (?)^2$$

$$\Rightarrow ? = \left(\frac{\sqrt{36}}{100}\right)$$

$$\Rightarrow ? = \frac{6}{10}$$

⇒ ? = 0.6

∴ The value of '?' is 0.6.

Hence, the correct option is (B).

35. Given:

$$\sqrt[3]{2197} + \sqrt[3]{1728} + \sqrt[3]{3375} = 8 \times ?$$

⇒ 13 + 12 + 15 = 8 × ?

⇒ 40 = 8 × ?

$$\Rightarrow ? = \frac{40}{8} = 5$$

⇒ ? = 5

∴ The value of '?' is 5.

Hence, the correct option is (C).

36. Given:

$$\frac{150}{25} - \sqrt{625} + \frac{183}{3} + 1.2 \times 5 = ?$$

$$\Rightarrow \frac{150}{25} - 25 + \frac{183}{3} + 1.2 \times 5 = ?$$

$$\Rightarrow 6 - 25 + 61 + 1.2 \times 5 = ?$$

$$\Rightarrow 6 - 25 + 61 + 6 = ?$$

$$\Rightarrow ? = 48$$

∴ The value of ' ?' is 48.

Hence, the correct option is (B).

37. Given:

$$427 - 112 + (32)^{\frac{2}{5}} + (9)^{\frac{3}{2}} - 35 \times 4 = ?$$

⇒ 427 − 121 + 4 + 27 − 140 = ?

⇒ 427 + 31 − 261 = ?

⇒ 458 − 267 = ?

⇒ ? = 197

∴ The value of '?' is 197.

Hence, the correct option is (C).

38. Given:

$18 + 12 \times 6 - 12 \div 3 + \dfrac{77}{11} = ?$

⇒ 18 + 72 - 4 + 7 = ?

⇒ 18 + 68 + 7 = ?

⇒ ? = 93

∴ 93 will come in place of the question mark ('?').

Hence, the correct option is (C).

39. Given:

125% of 120 + 55% of 460 - 21 ÷ 7 = 250% of ?

$\Rightarrow \left(\dfrac{125}{100}\right) \times 120 + \left(\dfrac{55}{100}\right) \times 460 - 3 = \left(\dfrac{250}{100}\right) \times ?$

$\Rightarrow \left(\dfrac{5}{4}\right) \times 120 + \left(\dfrac{11}{20}\right) \times 460 - 3 = \left(\dfrac{5}{2}\right) \times ?$

$\Rightarrow 150 + 253 - 3 = \left(\dfrac{5}{2}\right) \times ?$

$\Rightarrow 400 = \left(\dfrac{5}{2}\right) \times ?$

⇒ ? = 160

∴ 160 should come in place of the question mark (?).

Hence, the correct option is (E).

40. Given:

$(12)^3 \div 4 + 15 \times 13 - ? + 4 = 21 \times 30$

⇒ 1728 ÷ 4 + 195 - ? + 4 = 630

⇒ 432 + 195 + 4 - ? = 630

⇒ ? = 631 - 630

⇒ ? = 1

∴ 1 should come in place of the question mark (?).

Hence, the correct option is (D).

41. Given:

Amount of mixture of milk and water is 50 liters

Actual ratio of milk and water is 3 : 2

Ratio required of milk and water is 2 : 3

In actual ratio:

Quantity of milk in the mixture,

$\Rightarrow \dfrac{(50 \times 3)}{5}$ liters = 30 liters

Quantity of water in the mixture,

⇒ (50 – 30) liters = 20 liters

According to question new ratio = 2:3

Let the quantity of water added in the mixture be x liters,

Then,

Milk : water = 30 : (20 + x)

$\Rightarrow \dfrac{2}{3} = \dfrac{30}{(20 + x)}$

⇒ 90 = 40 + 2x

⇒ 50 = 2x

⇒ x = 25 liters

∴ The quantity of water to be added in the mixture is 25 liters.

Hence, the correct option is (A).

42. Given:

Principle = Rs. 400

Amount = Rs. 424

$R = \dfrac{(S.I. \times 100)}{(P \times T)}$

S.I = A – P

Where,

R → Rate of Interest

S.I. → Simple Interest

P → Principle

T → Time

A → Amount

S.I. = Amount – Principle = 424 – 400 = Rs. 24

$R = \dfrac{(24 \times 100)}{(400 \times 3)} = 2\%$

It is given in the question that new rate is 8% more than previous rate of interest.

New rate = 2% + 8% = 10%

New S.I. = $\dfrac{(400 \times 10 \times 2)}{100}$ = Rs. 80

New Amount = 400 + 80 = Rs. 480

∴ The new amount is Rs. 480.

Hence, the correct option is (C).

43. Given:

Length of train = 300 m

Time taken to cross the lamppost = 25 seconds

Time taken to cross man running in the opposite direction = 20 seconds

Relative speed while going in the opposite direction = sum of the speeds of objects.

Distance covered in crossing post or man is the length of the train.

Speed = $\dfrac{distance}{time}$

Speed of train = $\dfrac{300}{25}$ = 12 m/s

Let the speed of man be x m/s

Time taken to cross the train = 20s = distance of train/relative speed

Relative speed = 12 + x

$20 = \dfrac{300}{(12 + x)}$

12 + x = 15

Speed of man = 15 − 12 = 3 m/s

∴ Speed of the running man is 3 m/s.

Hence, the correct option is (E).

44. Given that:

Fail percentage of school P is 60%. Then, pass percentage of school P is 40%.

Percentage = $\left(\dfrac{Actual}{Total}\right)$ × 100

From the given graph,

Students who passed in school P = 80

40% = 80

1% = 2

60% = 60 × 2 = 120   {Failed students of school P)

Now, the number of students passed from school T = 90

Then, the required percentage = $\left(\dfrac{120}{90}\right)$ × 100 = $\left(\dfrac{4}{3}\right)$ × 100

= 133.33%

∴ The required percentage is 133.33%.

Hence, the correct option is (B).

45. Given:

Ratio between passed and failed students from all schools = 7 : 3

Total number of passed students = 80 + 90 + 70 + 50 + 90 + 110 = 490

⇒ 7 units = 490

⇒ 1 unit = 70

Failed students = 3 units = 70 × 3 = 210

∴ The total number of failed student from all schools is 210.

Hence, the correct option is (A).

46. Given that:

Student passed from school,

P = 80, Q = 90, R = 70, S = 50, T = 90, U = 110

Average = $\left(\dfrac{Sum\ of\ observations}{Number\ of\ observations}\right)$

Students passed from school P, Q, S and U together = 80 + 90 + 50 + 110 = 330

Average of passed students of school R and T = $\dfrac{(70 + 90)}{2}$ = $\dfrac{160}{2}$ = 80

Then, the required difference = 330 – 80 = 250

∴ The required difference is 250.

Hence, the correct option is (A).

47. Given Data:

Ratio between total strength of schools U and R = 5 : 3

Let failed students in school R be y,

So, failed students in school U = y + 20

According to the question,

Ratio of total strength of U and R = 5 : 3

$\dfrac{(110 + y + 20)}{(y + 70)} = \dfrac{5}{3}$

⇒ 330 + 3y + 60 = 5y + 350

⇒ 2y = 40 ⇒ y = 20

So, the failed students in school R = 20 and in school U = 20 + 20 = 40

So, The total number of failed student from both school U and R together = 40 + 20 = 60

∴ The total number of failed student from both school U and R together is 60.

Hence, the correct option is (C).

48. Given that:

Pass percentage of school S = pass percentage of school Q

Students passed in S = 50, students passed in Q = 90

Percentage = $\left(\dfrac{Actual}{Total}\right)$ × 100

Let the pass percentage of students = x %

So, the total strength of school S = $\left(\dfrac{50}{x}\right)$ × 100 = $\dfrac{5000}{x}$

Total strength of school Q = $\left(\dfrac{90}{x}\right)$ × 100 = $\dfrac{9000}{x}$

The total strength of school Q is more than that of school S = $\left(\dfrac{9000}{x}\right) - \left(\dfrac{5000}{x}\right) = \dfrac{4000}{x}$

The required % = $\left[\dfrac{\left(\dfrac{4000}{x}\right)}{\left(\dfrac{5000}{x}\right)}\right] \times 100 = \left(\dfrac{4}{5}\right) \times 100 = 80\%$

∴ Total strength of school Q is 80% more than that of school S.

Hence, the correct option is (B).

49. I. $5x^2 - 18x + 9 = 0$

$\Rightarrow 5x^2 - 15x - 3x + 9 = 0$

$\Rightarrow 5x (x - 3) - 3 (x - 3) = 0$

$\Rightarrow (5x - 3) (x - 3) = 0$

$\Rightarrow x = \dfrac{3}{5}$ or 3

II. $3y^2 + 5y - 2 = 0$

$\Rightarrow 3y^2 + 6y - y - 2 = 0$

$\Rightarrow 3y (y + 2) - 1 (y + 2) = 0$

$\Rightarrow (3y - 1) (y + 2) = 0$

$\Rightarrow y = \dfrac{1}{3}$ or -2

Comparison between x and y (via Tabulation):

Value of x	Value of y	Relation
$\dfrac{3}{5}$	$\dfrac{1}{3}$	x > y
$\dfrac{3}{5}$	-2	x > y
3	$\dfrac{1}{3}$	x > y
3	-2	x > y

∴ Clearly x > y

Hence, the correct option is (A).

50. I. $3x^2 - 7x + 2 = 0$

$\Rightarrow 3x^2 - 6x - x + 2 = 0$

$\Rightarrow 3x (x - 2) - 1 (x - 2) = 0$

$\Rightarrow (x - 2) (3x - 1) = 0$

$\Rightarrow x = 2$ or $\dfrac{1}{3}$

II. $2y^2 - 11y + 15 = 0$

$\Rightarrow 2y^2 - 6y - 5y + 15 = 0$

$\Rightarrow 2y (y - 3) - 5 (y - 3) = 0$

$\Rightarrow (y - 3) (2y - 5) = 0$

$\Rightarrow y = 3$ or $\dfrac{5}{2}$

Comparison between x and y (via Tabulation):

Value of x	Value of y	Relation
2	3	x < y
2	$\dfrac{5}{2}$	x < y
$\dfrac{1}{3}$	3	x < y
$\dfrac{1}{3}$	$\dfrac{5}{2}$	x < y

∴ Clearly x < y

Hence, the correct option is (B).

51. I. $(625)^{\frac{1}{4}}x + \sqrt{1225} = 155$

$\Rightarrow (5^4)^{\frac{1}{4}}x + 35 = 155$

$\Rightarrow 5x = 155 - 35 \Rightarrow 5x = 120$

$\Rightarrow x = \dfrac{120}{5} = 24$

II. $\sqrt{196}y + 13 = 279$

$\Rightarrow 14y = 279 - 13 = 266$

$\Rightarrow y = \dfrac{266}{14} = 19$

Comparison between x and y (via Tabulation):

Value of x	Value of y	Relation
24	19	x > y

∴ Clearly x > y

Hence, the correct option is (A).

52. I. $12x^2 + 11x + 12 = 10x^2 + 22x$

$\Rightarrow 2x^2 - 11x + 12 = 0$

$\Rightarrow 2x^2 - 8x - 3x + 12 = 0$

$\Rightarrow 2x (x - 4) - 3 (x - 4) = 0$

$\Rightarrow (x - 4) (2x - 3) = 0$

$\Rightarrow x = 4$ or $\dfrac{3}{2}$

II. $13y^2 - 18y + 3 = 9y^2 - 10y$

$\Rightarrow 4y^2 - 8y + 3 = 0$

$\Rightarrow 4y^2 - 6y - 2y + 3 = 0$

$\Rightarrow 2y (2y - 3) - 1 (2y - 3) = 0$

$\Rightarrow y = \dfrac{1}{2}$ or $\dfrac{3}{2}$

Comparison between x and y (via Tabulation):

Value of x	Value of y	Relation
4	$\dfrac{1}{2}$	x > y
4	$\dfrac{3}{2}$	x > y
$\dfrac{3}{2}$	$\dfrac{1}{2}$	x > y
$\dfrac{3}{2}$	$\dfrac{3}{2}$	x = y

∴ Clearly x ≥ y

Hence, the correct option is (C).

53. I. $x^2 = 81$

$$\Rightarrow x = \sqrt{81} = \pm 9$$

II. $y^2 - 18y + 81 = 0$

$\Rightarrow (y - 9)^2 = 0$

$\Rightarrow y = 9$

Comparison between x and y (via Tabulation):

Value of x	Value of y	Relation
9	9	x = y
-9	9	x < y

$\therefore$ Clearly $x \leq y$

Hence, the correct option is (D).

54. Given:

Area of the half part of land = 324 m²

Cost of fencing Veer's Land = Rs. $\dfrac{2}{m}$.

Area of Rectangle = L × B

The perimeter of Rectangle = 2(L + B)

Cost of fencing for Veer's Land = Rs. $\dfrac{2}{m}$ × Perimeter of Veer's land.

Let the length and breadth of Veer's part be L m and B m respectively.

$\Rightarrow$ L × B = 324

For a minimum cost of fencing, the perimeter should be minimum, and it will be possible only.

When L = B

$\Rightarrow$ L² = 324

$\Rightarrow$ L = 18 m

The perimeter of Veer's land = 72 m

Cost of fencing for Veer's Land = Rs. $\dfrac{2}{m}$ × Perimeter of Veer's land.

$\Rightarrow$ Rs. 2 × 72

Cost of fencing = Rs. 144

$\therefore$ The Cost of fencing for Veer's Land is Rs. 144.

Hence, the correct option is (D).

55. Given:

Average weight of 20 students of a class = 60 kg

Weight of old student who left = 45 kg

Increase in average weight of students = 1 kg

$$\text{Average} = \dfrac{Sum\ of\ observation}{No.\ of\ observation}$$

Total weight of 20 students = 20 × 60 kg = 1200 kg

New average of weight of the students will be = 60 + 1 = 61

Let the weight of new student = x kg

So According to question,

$\Rightarrow$ New average weight of students = 61

$$\Rightarrow \dfrac{(1200 - 45 + x)}{20} = 61$$

$\Rightarrow$ 1200 – 45 + x = 61 × 20

$\Rightarrow$ x = 1220 - 1200 + 45

$\Rightarrow$ x = 65 kg

Ratio of old and new student's weight = 45 : 65 = 9 : 13.

$\therefore$ The Required ratio is 9 : 13

Hence, the correct option is (A).

56. Given:

Let the ratio between the ages of Tina and Jatin be 23x : px, where x is a common variable.

Present age of Rahul = 72 - 16 = 56 years

Present age of Tina = 56 - 10 = 46 years

By equating the age of Tina with the ratio of the age of Tina and Jatin: 23x = 46 $\Rightarrow$ x = 2

According to the question: 2p - 46 = 56 - 4

2p = 98

$\therefore$ p = 49

Hence, the correct option is (D).

57. Given:

P : Q = 3 : 4

$$\text{At 9 months} = P + \left(P \times \left(\dfrac{1}{3} \right) \right)$$

$$\text{At 6 months} = P + \left(P \times \left(\dfrac{1}{3} \right) \right) + P$$

$$\text{At 8 months} = Q + \left(Q \times \left(\dfrac{1}{3} \right) \right)$$

Let initial investment by P and Q be 3x and 4x,

The total investment by P = 3x × 3 + 4x × 3 + 7x × 6 = 63x

The total investment by Q = 4x × 4 + 5x × 8 = 56x

The ratio of Profit = 63x : 56x = 9 : 8

$\therefore$ Profits of P and Q after 12 months would be in ratio 9 : 8

Hence, the correct option is (C).

58. Given:

1, 10, 24, 63, 227, ?

Considering the above series, the logic can be explained as follows,

10 - 1 = 9

24 - 10 = 14

63 - 24 = 39

227 - 63 = 164

? - 227 = let's say x

Taking the double differences,

14 - 9 = 5

39 - 14 = 25

164 - 39 = 125

By observing the pattern of double difference we can say,

x - 164 = 625

$\Rightarrow$ x = 789

So, ? - 227 = 789

$\Rightarrow$? = 1016

Hence, the correct option is (B).

59. Given:

$\Rightarrow$ 180 x 0.5- 10 = 80

$\Rightarrow$ 80 x 1- 20 = 60

$\Rightarrow$ 60 x 2 - 40 = 80

$\Rightarrow$ 80 x 4 - 80 = 240

$\Rightarrow$ 240 x 8 - 160 = 1760

$\therefore$ The required answer is 1760.

Hence, the correct option is (D).

60. The pattern of given series is:

2 × 2.2 + 2 = 6.4

4 × 2.2 + 2 =10.8

6 × 2.2 + 2 = 15.2

8 × 2.2 + 2 = 19.6 $\neq$ 18.6

10 × 2.2 + 2 = 24

12 × 2.2 + 2 = 28.4

$\therefore$ The wrong answer is 18.6

Hence, the correct option is (D).

61. The logic behind the given series is as follows:

2   9   28   65   126   217

7   19   37   61   91

12   18   24   30

Logic: double difference between the consecutive terms is consecutive multiples of 6.

$\therefore$ The value of '?' is 217.

Hence, the correct option is (B).

62. The logic behind the given series is as follows:

10 × 1 + 1 = 11

11 × 2 + 2 = 24

24 × 3 + 3 = 75

75 × 4 + 4 = 304

$\therefore$ The value of '?' is 304.

Hence, the correct option is (A).

63. Given:

Percent decrease = 10%

Net effect = 5% increase

S.P. = C.P. + Profit

Gain% = $\left(\dfrac{(S.P.-C.P.)}{C.P.}\right) \times 100$

Here, 10% of C.P. = 2000

original price of bike is 20000

Now original price is increased by 50%

20000 + (0.5 × 2000)

20000 + 10000 = 30000

Profit of 10% on C.P. = (10/100) × 30000

Profit = 3000

S.P. = 30000 + 3000

$\therefore$ Price of new bike is Rs. 33000.

Hence, the correct option is (C).

64. Given,

Investment of Saima = Rs. 1,60,000

Investment of Shifa = Rs. 48,000

Ratio of their profits = 5 : 1

Concept used:

The Profit is directly proportional to Amount invested multiplied by Time period

Calculation:

Let the time period for Shifa be x months

Investment of Saima = Rs. 1,60,000

Time period of Saima's investment = 12 months

Total amount invested by Saima in 12 months = Rs. 1,60,000 × 12

= Rs. 19,20,000

Now, investment of Shifa = Rs. 48,000

Time period of Shifa's investment = x months

Total amount invested by Shifa in x months = Rs. 48,000x

Now, as we know that the profit is directly proportional to the amount invested

And the ratio of their profit = 5 : 1

So, $\dfrac{19,20,000}{48000x} = \dfrac{5}{1}$

$5x = 40$

$x = 8$

Shifa's investing time period = 8 months

Now, Percentage of Shifa's time period of Saima's time period

$= \left(\dfrac{8}{12}\right) \times 100\%$

$= \dfrac{200}{3}\%$

$\therefore$ The time period of Shifa is $\dfrac{200}{3}\%$ of Saima's time period.

Hence, the correct option is (B).

65. Given,

$(a + b):(b + c):(c + a) = 7:6:5$

$a + b + c = 27$

$(a + b):(b + c):(c + a) = 7k:6k:5k$

$\Rightarrow a + b + b + c + c + a = 7k + 6k + 5k$

$\Rightarrow 2(a + b + c) = 18k$

$\Rightarrow (a + b + c) = 9k$

$c = 9k - 7k = 2k$

$a = 9k - 6k = 3k$

$b = 9k - 5k = 4k$

$\dfrac{1}{a}:\dfrac{1}{b}:\dfrac{1}{c} = \dfrac{1}{3k}:\dfrac{1}{4k}:\dfrac{1}{2k}$

$\dfrac{1}{a}:\dfrac{1}{b}:\dfrac{1}{c} == \dfrac{12}{3k}:\dfrac{12}{4k}:\dfrac{12}{2k}$

$a:b:c = 4:3:6$

Hence, the correct option is (A).

66. The least possible Venn diagram for the given statements is as follows:

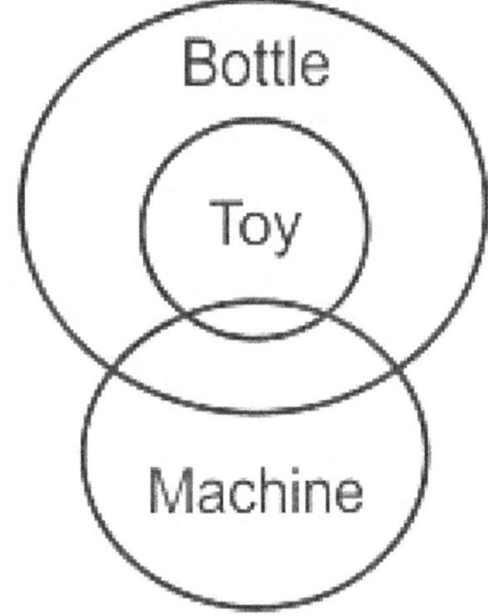

Conclusions:

I. No Toy is Bottle → False (As All Toy is Bottle, No toy is Bottle is not possible. So, it is false).

II. Some Machine are Bottle → True (As All Toy are Bottle and Some Toy are Machine, then some part of toy which is bottle will be machine. So it is true).

So, Only II follow.

Hence, the correct option is (B).

67. The least possible Venn diagram for the given statements is as follows:

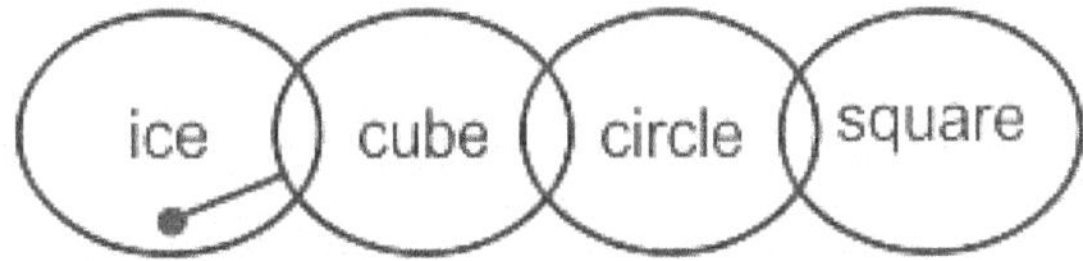

Conclusions:

I. Some Ice is not Cube → True (As Only a few Ice is Cube means some ice is cube and some ice is not cube. So, it is true).

II. Some Cube is Square → False (As there is no direct relation between cube and square so Some Cube is Square is possible but not definite. So, it is false)

So, Only I follow.

Hence, the correct option is (A).

Ques (68-72):8 persons - Fiona, Liz, Chad, Zack, Ashley, Betty, Derek and Patrick.

1) Betty sits third to the left of Cody.

2) Derek is sitting second to the left of Cody.

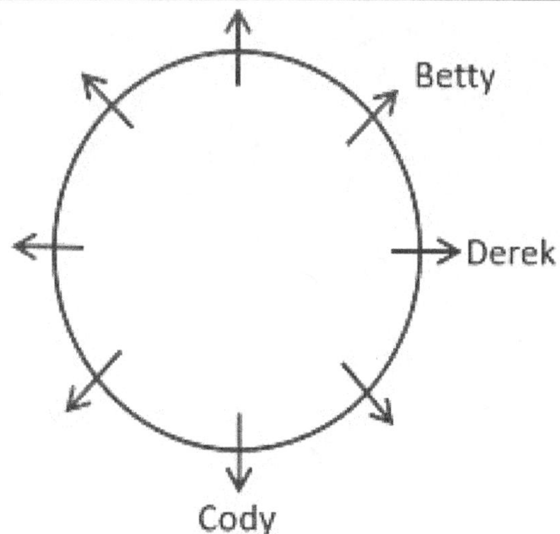

3) Ashley is sitting opposite to Betty.

4) Patrick is sitting second to the right of Ashley.

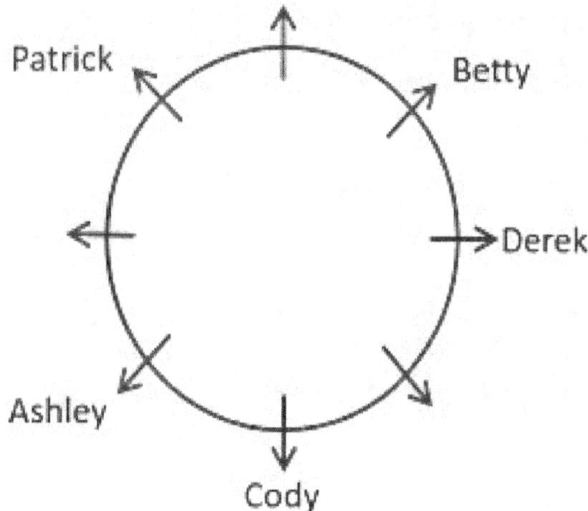

5) Zack is not a neighbour of Ashley or Patrick. Thus, Zack sits between Derek and Cody.

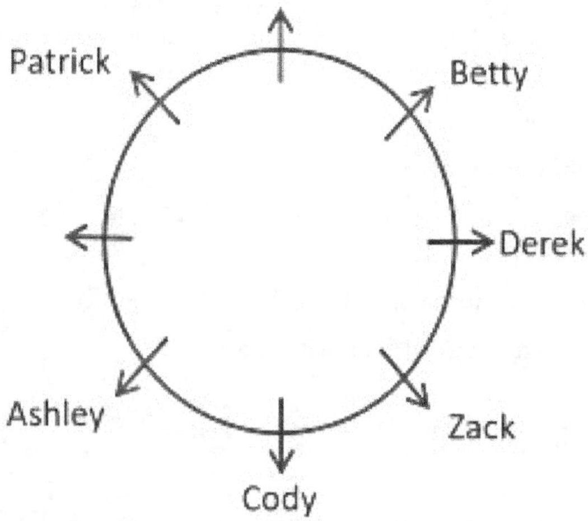

6) Fiona does not sit opposite to Derek. Thus, Fiona sits opposite to Cody. Liz sits opposite to Derek.

The final arrangement will be:

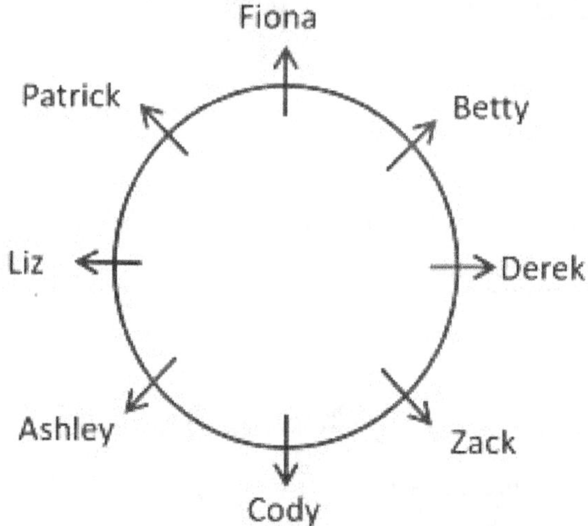

68. So, 'Ashley and Patrick' are immediate neighbors of Liz.

Hence, the correct option is (B).

69. If Betty exchanges her position with Patrick the arrangement will be as follows:

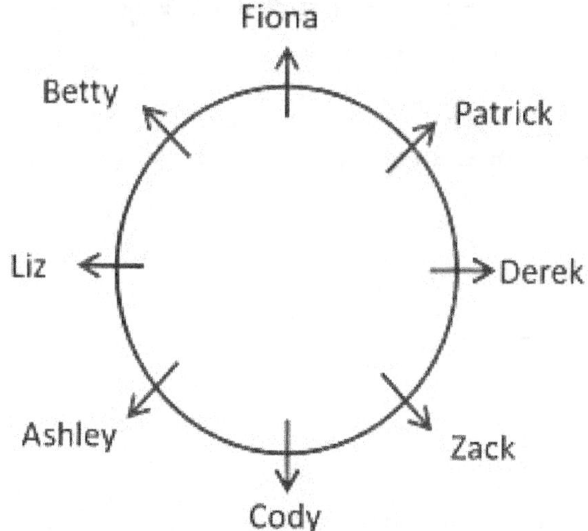

I. Derek sits opposite to Ashley → False.

II. Betty site second to the right of Zack → False.

III. Fiona sits opposite to Cody → True.

So, 'Only statement III is true' is the correct answer.

Hence, the correct option is (C).

70. If Betty exchanges her position with Patrick the arrangement will be as follows:

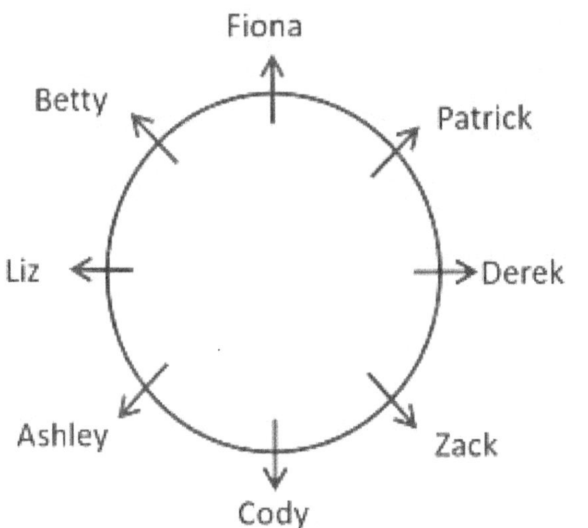

So, '4' persons are sitting between Liz and Zack when counted from right of Liz.

Hence, the correct option is (D).

71. If Betty exchanges her position with Patrick the arrangement will be as follows:

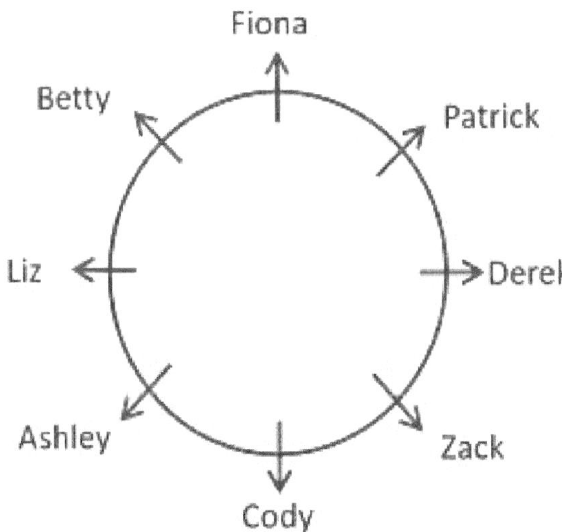

So, 'Cody' is the correct answer.

Hence, the correct option is (D).

72. So, 'Fiona' is the correct answer..

Hence, the correct option is (B).

73. Given Series: H % 1 P ! F S ? * X 7 C T 4 $ 9 3 > @ / 6 N Q 5

1) Numbers which are immediately followed by a symbol.

H % 1 P ! F S ? * X 7 C T 4 **$** 9 3 **>** @ / 6 N Q 5

So, two numbers are there which are immediately followed by a symbol- 4$ and 3>.

Hence, the correct option is (C).

74. Given Series: H % 1 P ! F S ? * X 7 C T 4 $ 9 3 > @ / 6 N Q 5

1) Numbers between '*' and '>'

H % 1 P ! F S ? * X 7 C T 4 $ 9 3> @ / 6 N Q 5

So, the sum of the numbers between '*' and '>' = 7 + 4 + 9 + 3 = 23

Hence, the correct option is (D).

75. Given Series: H % 1 P ! F S ? * X 7 C T 4 $ 9 3 > @ / 6 N Q 5

1) On dropping all the symbols, the arrangement is,

Left Side H 1 P F S X 7 C T 49 3 6 N Q 5 Right Side

2) Element which is sixth from the right end.

Left Side H 1 P F S X 7 C T 4 **9** 3 6 N Q 5 Right Side

So, 9 is sixth from the right end.

Hence, the correct option is (A).

76. Given Series: H % 1 P ! F S ? * X 7 C T 4 $ 9 3 > @ / 6 N Q 5

1) On dropping all the numbers, the arrangement is.

Left Side H % P ! F S ? * X C T $ > @ / N Q Right Side

Right Side + Left Side = Left Side

5th to the Right + 4th to the Left = 9th from the Left

Left Side H % P ! F S ? * X C T $ > @ / N Q Right Side

So, X is fifth to the right of fourth to the left end.

Hence, the correct option is (D).

77. Given series: H % 1 P ! F S ? * X 7 C T 4 $ 9 3 > @ / 6 N Q 5

1) Letters which are immediately preceded by consonants and immediately followed by a symbol.

H % 1 P ! **F S ?** * X 7 C T 4 $ 9 3 > @ / 6 N Q 5

Hence, only one letter is there which is immediately preceded by consonants and immediately followed by a symbol i.e., FS?.

Hence, the correct option is (B).

78. The best possible figure is:

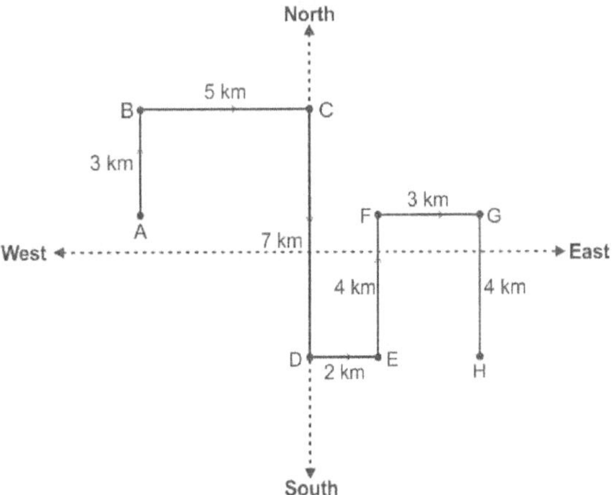

EH = FG = 3 km

DH = DE + EH = 2 + 3 = 5 km

Hence, the correct option is (A).

79. The best possible figure is:

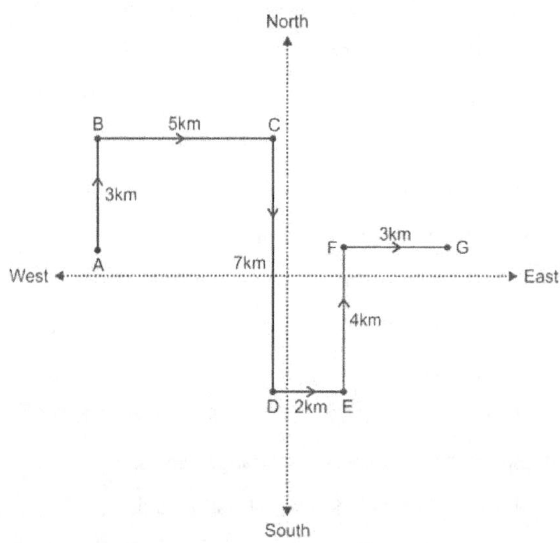

Using the Pythagoras theorem:

$EG^2 = FE^2 + FG^2$

$EG^2 = 16 + 9$

$EG = 5$ km

Hence, the correct option is (D).

80. The best possible figure is:

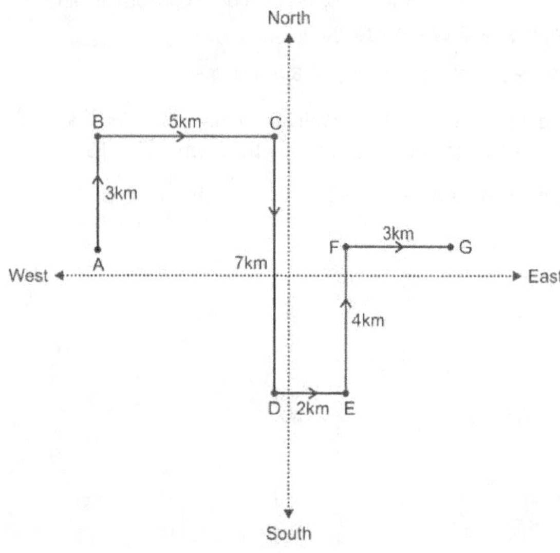

Clearly, A is 7 km to the west of point F.

Hence, the correct option is (B).

Ques (81-85):6 subjects – Physics, Chemistry, Biology, mathematics, English, Hindi.

1) The box containing Physics book is kept at the top.

Box	Subject
1	Physics
2	
3	
4	
5	
6	

2) There are three boxes between the box of Physics books and box of Hindi books which is immediately above the box of Biology books.

Box	Subject
1	Physics
2	
3	
4	
5	Hindi
6	Biology

3) Box of Mathematics books is kept immediately above the box of English books and immediately below box of Chemistry books.

Box	Subject
1	Physics
2	Chemistry
3	Mathematics
4	English
5	Hindi
6	Biology

81. So, box 2 contains Chemistry books.

Hence, the correct option is (B).

82. So, the box above the box of Hindi books contains English books.

Hence, the correct option is (B).

83. So, Box 6 contains Biology books.

Hence, the correct option is (C).

84. So, box 3 is just below the box containing books of Chemistry.

Hence, the correct option is (C).

85. So, box 5 contains Hindi books.

Hence, the correct option is (E).

Ques (86-88):

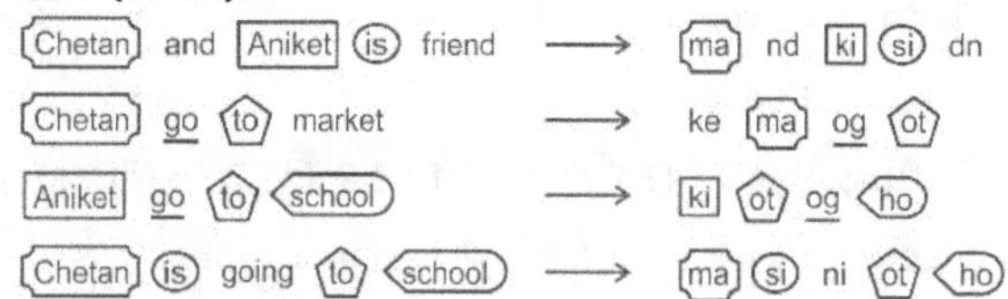

86. So, 'nd' is code for either 'friend' or 'and'.

Hence, the correct option is (D).

87. So, 'Chetan go to school' coded as 'og ot ma ho'.

Hence, the correct option is (B).

88. So, 'Chetan' is coded as 'ma'.

Hence, the correct option is (C).

Ques (89-93):Persons - A, B, C, D and E

City - Delhi, Mumbai, Bangalore, Chennai, Hyderabad

Company - P, Q, R, S and T

1) The person who lives in Bangalore works in company S

2) B works in company P and E lives in Hyderabad.

Persons	City	Company
	Bangalore	S
B		P
E	Hyderabad	

3) A lives in Delhi but does not work in company Q

4) C works in company T.

So, A works in company R and D lives in Bangalore.

Persons	City	Company
D	Bangalore	S
B		P
E	Hyderabad	Q
A	Delhi	R
C		T

5) Neither D nor B lives in Chennai.

So, B lives in Mumbai.

Persons	City	Company
D	Bangalore	S
B	Mumbai	P
E	Hyderabad	Q
A	Delhi	R
C	Chennai	T

89. So, the Awards organized in Chennai and the person who was awarded lives in Delhi.

Hence, the correct option is (B).

90. So, the person who lives in Hyderabad works in company Q.

Hence, the correct option is (A).

91. So, B lives in Mumbai and works in company P.

Hence, the correct option is (C).

92. So, The two friends now work for Company S.

Hence, the correct option is (C).

93. After the merger:

Persons	City	Company
D	Bangalore	S
C	Mumbai	P
E	Hyderabad	Q
A	Delhi	R

B	Chennai	T

So, C lives in Mumbai after reshuffle.

Hence, the correct option is (D).

94. Given statements: X ≤ S < W; P ≥ O > W

On combining: P ≥ O > W > S ≥ X

Conclusions:

I. S < P → True (as P ≥ O > W > S → P > W > S → P > S)

II. X < O → True (as O > W > S ≥ X → O > W > X → O > X)

So, both the conclusions I and II are true.

Hence, the correct option is (C).

95. Given statements: Q = G > P ≥ M; U ≤ I ≤ H = L < Q

On combining: U ≤ I ≤ H = L < Q = G > P ≥ M

Conclusions:

I. H > P → False (as H = L < Q = G > P → thus clear relation between H and P cannot be determined)

II. M > G → False (as G > P ≥ M → M < G)

So, neither I nor II is True.

Hence, the correct option is (A).

Ques (96-100): Biscuits: Coconut, 20-20, Good Day, 50-50, Tiger and Bounce.

Days: Monday, Tuesday, Wednesday, Thursday, Friday and Saturday.

1) 50-50 must be eaten o Friday only & should not be immediately preceded by 20-20.

2) 20-20 must be eaten on the day following the day on which Bounce is eating.

Case 1		Case 2	
Days	Biscuit	Days	Biscuit
Monday		Monday	Bounce
Tuesday	Bounce	Tuesday	20-20
Wednesday	20- 20	Wednesday	
Thursday		Thursday	
Friday	50-50	Friday	50-50
Saturday		Saturday	

3) Coconut biscuit must be eaten immediately before Tiger biscuit. (i.e. Coconut and Tiger must eat on Wednesday and Thursday so case 1 not follow)

4) Tiger must not eat on the last day.

Case-2	
Days	Biscuit
Monday	Bounce
Tuesday	20-20
Wednesday	Coconut
Thursday	Tiger
Friday	50-50

Saturday	Good Day

96. So, Coconut eat on Wednesday.

Hence, the correct option is (C).

97. Thus, the correct pair is Tuesday – 20-20.

Hence, the correct option is (A).

98. Thus, Coconut biscuit eat just before the Tiger biscuit.

Hence, the correct option is (D).

99. Thus, Good Day biscuit eat on Saturday.

Hence, the correct option is (D).

100. Thus, two biscuit products are eaten between 20-20 & 50-50.

Hence, the correct option is (C).

// Notes //

// Notes //